CIVIL WAR ALABAMA

CIVIL WAR ALABAMA

CHRISTOPHER LYLE MCILWAIN SR.

Foreword by G. Ward Hubbs

The University of Alabama Press
Tuscaloosa

The University of Alabama Press
Tuscaloosa, Alabama 35487-0380
uapress.ua.edu

Hardcover edition published 2016.
Paperback edition published 2020.
eBook edition published 2016.

Typeface: Bembo

Cover image: *Battle Flag of the 34th Alabama Infantry*; courtesy of the Alabama Department of Archives and History
Cover design: Todd Lape/Lape Designs

Paperback ISBN: 978-0-8173-6005-4

A previous edition of this book has been catalogued by the Library of Congress.
ISBN: 978-0-8173-1894-9 (cloth)
E-ISBN: 978-0-8173-8924-6

Look not mournfully on the past—it comes not again;
improve the present, for it is thine; go forward with manly
hearts to encounter the mysterious future.

—Henry Wadsworth Longfellow

Contents

Figures

MAPS

Foreword

A century and a half after the shooting stopped, we at last have our first broad narrative account of Alabamians during the Civil War years. Chris McIlwain has merged the latest scholarship with a massive and wide array of contemporary documents into a single whole. The result is a rich account beginning with the fateful road to disunion, through the grief of personal loss, to the humiliation of Confederate surrender.

McIlwain takes his organizational cue from noted Civil War historian James McPherson, who insists that only chronological narratives are able to integrate political, economic, social, and military events in ways that explain the dynamics of a society at war.[1] This is a critical point in the case of Civil War Alabama, because the only other major work on the subject is Walter Lynwood Fleming's 1905 *Civil War and Reconstruction in Alabama*. Fleming, who was a proud neo-Confederate, used a topical approach to highlight and showcase certain incidents of the war era while de-emphasizing, obscuring, or even omitting whatever undermined his belief that Alabama's citizens were overwhelmingly united in supporting the Confederacy. Fleming's influence has been immense and his interpretation largely unchallenged except by a few historians. By contrast, McIlwain's narrative tells the whole story—warts and all—from the beginning through to the end and even beyond.

The result is much more complex than we ever expected. To begin with, McIlwain, himself a lawyer, points to the crucial role of the Alabama legal profession in the decision to secede. He also amasses indisputable evidence regarding the centrality of the institution of slavery in making that decision. Having challenged the conventional wisdom regarding secession, McIlwain moves on to what will probably stir the greatest contention: the extent of Alabamians' commitment to the Confederate government and the war effort.

McIlwain wisely refuses to estimate the exact depth and breadth of Confederate nationalism—or Unionism, for that matter—in Alabama. But he demonstrates that, far more than previously acknowledged, a significant portion of the citizenry opposed those who took over the state government and held power for the four war years. Opposition was not confined to isolated Winston County farmers. Dissenters were to be found throughout the state, from the Shoals to Mobile Bay, from the Tombigbee to the Chattahoochee; they were to be found in every profession, from farmers to judges; and they were to be found in every economic stratum, from poor to wealthy. At times it was as if two civil wars were being fought in Alabama. The campaigns would be led in the newspapers by the "Generals of the Press" as well as on the battlefields by the generals of the armies; the battles would be waged with ballots as well as with bullets.

In discussing the many factors that raised and lowered Alabamians' morale, McIlwain deftly integrates military events, shortages, inflation, and human loss with passages from letters, diaries, and newspapers—many of which have never before been used. (This finished book—which consumed twenty years of painstaking research, writing, and rewriting—contains only a third of his original text and sources.) He shows that pleas for peace were made privately as early as 1861 and became increasingly public as the death toll mounted and Union victories in Alabama's sister states created intense fears of destructive invasions. "The war was very popular," remembered a Methodist minister from west Alabama, "until the coffins began to come back from Richmond."[2] After McIlwain places Alabama's peace movement in its proper context, he explains the movement's failure to extract Alabama from the war. And he identifies the multiple lost opportunities open to Alabama's political leadership that would have averted destruction to the state's industrial base and railroad infrastructure—opportunities that came even after Confederate independence had obviously become a hopeless cause.

As McIlwain demonstrates time and again, the story of Alabamians during the Civil War is a far more tangled tale than the simplistic and romanticized version that we have inherited. It was a time when Alabamians were divided by a strange mixture of politics, exhilaration, and grief. They would emerge from those four short—yet seemingly endless—years no less divided. Such was Civil War Alabama.

G. Ward Hubbs
Birmingham-Southern College

Acknowledgments

I am most grateful to my wonderful wife, Anna, and my children, Elizabeth and Christopher, to whom this book is dedicated. For the most part, they were patient or at least impatiently humored me during the years it took to finish the project.

I am very grateful to Dr. Guy Hubbs, a first-rate historian and friend who helped teach me the craft of writing history, provided timely encouragement, read and reread literally thousands of pages of drafts, and made invaluable suggestions that materially improved the text. Without his assistance, it is likely this book would have never been published in its final form.

The idea of writing *Civil War Alabama* came from Dr. George Rable, who remarked to me several years ago that in researching and writing one of his books, he had noted the absence of a modern, definitive book on this topic. His generous undertaking to read the final manuscript when the prospects of its publication were in doubt and his recommendation that it be published will never be forgotten. He is the epitome of a Christian.

A constellation of other leading historians was also instrumental. Dr. Sarah Wiggins read an early draft of the introduction and provided her typically constructive criticisms. Dr. Michael Fitzgerald, Dr. Alston Fitts III, and Dr. Johanna Shields kindly read and made comments on several early drafts of chapters. Dr. Bertis English and Dr. Ben Severance did the same regarding the full manuscript. I am grateful to Dr. Lonnie Burnett, Dr. Victoria Ott, and others for providing important source materials on which I relied. Craig Remington at the University of Alabama's Cartographic Laboratory provided the excellent maps that appear in the text.

I am also grateful to the many librarians and archivists who provided assistance. Special thanks go to the staffs at the Alabama Department of Archives and History, the Tuscaloosa Public Library, the Birmingham Public Library, the Tutwiler Collection of Southern History, the Huntsville-Madison County Public Library, the Mobile Public Library, the Alabama Supreme

Court Library, the Hoole Special Collections Library, the Bounds Law Library and the Gorgas Library at the University of Alabama, the Auburn University Library of Special Collections and Archives, the Lawrence County Archives, the Dallas County Public Library, the Mervyn H. Sterne Library at the University of Alabama in Birmingham, the David M. Rubenstein Rare Book and Manuscript Collection at Duke University, the Southern Historical Collection at the Wilson Library, University of North Carolina, the National Archives, and the State Historical Society of Pennsylvania. Authors and other lovers of history will certainly benefit from efforts being made by some of these institutions to digitize newspapers and other archival materials from the Civil War era and thereby make them accessible to the general public through the Internet.

A special word of thanks is owed to Dr. Donna Cox Baker of the University of Alabama Press. From the beginning, she recognized the importance of this project and, despite the highs and lows of the peer review process, she was uniformly patient and encouraging.

Last and certainly not least, I am grateful for the loyalty and skills of my legal assistant, Bonnie Sutton, who painstakingly typed and retyped the manuscript through its myriad permutations and revisions. It is fair to say that this book would have never been completed without her.

Christopher Lyle McIlwain Sr.

CIVIL WAR ALABAMA

Introduction

Shortly after receiving news of Confederate General Robert E. Lee's surrender at Appomattox, Virginia, an Ohio newspaper editor predicted that "whatever else may have been sown and reaped in this war, we shall certainly gather from its broad, blood-soaked fields a literary harvest—fiction, personal adventure, history, poetry—so plentiful that it will nourish vast numbers of people for generations."[1] That prophecy has certainly been fulfilled, but only in a limited sense with regard to Alabama. There are several well-researched and well-written books addressing the contributions of Alabamians to the Confederate war effort in the Civil War.[2] The same is true regarding the great battles in which they were involved. But examining the Civil War era merely from the perspective of the officer corps within the warrior class, or other dedicated Confederates in the class of economic elites, yields a very narrow and sometimes inaccurate view of this period.[3] Among other things, it omits analysis of critically important social, political, and economic components of the story in Alabama.

There has been no detailed and broad chronological narrative of Alabama's involvement in secession and civil war.[4] This book is an attempt to fill that important gap while providing a bridge between excellent existing studies of the antebellum period and the Reconstruction era in Alabama.[5] In discussing the momentous course of events during the war, battles and military movements are discussed here to the extent they related to a direct threat to Alabama's internal security and materially influenced public morale and opinion. Those that occurred in states adjoining Alabama are, therefore, stressed over those that occurred in the eastern theater of the war such as in Virginia, and they are integrated with home front events in the narrative.

This book also tries to explain what happened in Alabama during this misunderstood period and to address a multitude of important questions whose answers have long been obscured by deeply engrained myth. How and why was Alabama's secession accomplished? Who were its main proponents and opponents? What was the true role of slavery? Did Alabamians generally support secession and permanent independence? Who started the war and why? Were Alabamians emotionally and economically prepared for war? Who came forward to fight, and who did not? What was the war's effect on Alabama's 964,210 residents—male, female, black, and white? Did the Alabama press keep the public adequately and accurately informed? Was there wartime dissent in Alabama, and was it countenanced? Did the level of support for the war among Alabamians remain consistent? Why did Alabama's involvement in the war last so long? Was the destruction suffered by Alabama in the last stage of the war in towns like Tuscaloosa and Selma avoidable? These questions will be answered as the reader walks through the narrative of events and experiences what one of Alabama's wartime governors called the "carnival of blood."

The war generation did not produce a book of this type, and the reasons may have revolved around postwar politics. To understand this, one must recall that with its vast natural resources, Alabama had held a relatively promising economic position among the Southern states in 1860. As a result of decades of sacrifice, private investment, and hard work, it was positioned to eventually vault into the industrial age. Primarily to facilitate cotton agriculture, roads and bridges had been built in the early antebellum period to supplement available river travel. A few major railroads were later constructed by private entities, including one across north Alabama, as well as others between Selma and Talladega; Montgomery and Pensacola, Florida; and Mobile and east Mississippi.[6] This primitive transportation network had encouraged the development of some industries, including cotton mills, flour mills, and sawmills, as well as a few foundries.[7] Substantial interest had later developed in the valuable mineral resources in northern Alabama, particularly in the region near what is now Birmingham, prompting various groups to initiate plans to penetrate that area with additional railroads from Tuscaloosa, Decatur, Selma, and Montgomery.[8] Despite headwinds working against the flow of outside capital created by periodic sectional conflict, slow progress was being made as the 1850s came to a close.[9] As historian Mills Thornton put it, "The state had clearly reached the industrial takeoff point."[10] More could be expected as long as capital markets in the Northeast and Europe had the necessary confidence in Southern political stability to purchase bonds issued by the railroad corporations to finance the immense cost of construction. Conventional nineteenth-century economic theory held that "capital wants security, protection, and the guarantees of stable institutions" and that it "avoids revolution" and "shuns all uncertainties."[11]

In 1860, the exuberant editor of the *Montgomery Mail* justifiably boasted that "no State in the South now offers the same inducements as Alabama holds out to young men who are thoroughly educated as geologists, mineralogists, civil engineers, and in physical science generally. Look at the railroads that will be built within the next five years! Glance at the vast fields of iron, coal, copper, marble, etc., to be developed within the same time, by these [rail] roads—and then estimate the value and importance to the State of active, well-trained, energetic young men possessing ample knowledge of all the branches of science which must be called into requisition for the working of these immense and varied interests!"[12] Absent the confidence of outside capital markets, however, Alabama railroad entrepreneurs would be forced to look to the state government to provide subsidization.[13] Due to significant opposition among Alabama taxpayers to this sort of public aid, however, that appeared unlikely.[14] This explains, in part, why the class of Alabamians opposed to secession and war included many economic elites who were supporting construction of railroad projects and needed outside credit.

Given the potential for an economic breakthrough, an effort by Alabamians to divide the Union should have been avoided at all costs. In the end it resulted in a tragic, unmitigated disaster for them and their economic future. The sense of loss, depression, betrayal, and outrage among ordinary Alabamians who were the victims of secession and war was profound.[15] They had been told by the politicians that no war would occur following secession, or if it did that little blood would be spilled. But hundreds of thousands of Americans had died before it was all over. As historians William Warren Rogers Sr. and Robert David Ward put it, "If there were Confederates bitter in defeat, the Alabama Unionists were a group bitter in victory—and hopeful of righting the wrongs they had suffered during the fighting."[16] One Talladega County planter placed the blame for the people's resulting social and economic hardships squarely on the Alabama political leaders who had led the state through secession and war. "We are in an awful condition as a people," he wrote, "all to gratify a few wild politicians."[17] A significant level of animosity remained following the Confederate surrender between those who had opposed secession and the war—the Unionists—and those who had promoted secession and prosecuted the war—the Confederates. Violence was common between the two groups. Above all else, Unionists did not want former Confederates to resume political control over them.[18]

When that appeared to be happening under President Andrew Johnson's postwar plan of political restoration and reunion, Unionists from Alabama and elsewhere appealed to Republicans in Congress to provide them relief by way of a different plan. Thus began the period of congressional Reconstruction, the key component of which was the enfranchisement of adult, male, former slaves.[19] The demographics of Alabama at that time are important to understanding the impact of this monumental change in political dynamics. The ratio of white male adults to black male adults was only approximately 52 percent to 48 percent.[20] Thus, if whites were politically divided and blacks were not, a pragmatic—if not principled—coalition of the black voters with white Unionists could control state government. This was the genesis of the Alabama Union Republican Party in 1867.[21] Republicans nominated a white Unionist from Randolph County, William Hugh Smith, in the 1868 governor's race, and with the aid of an election boycott unwisely orchestrated by a coalition of Democrats and former Whigs (called the Democratic and Conservative Party) opposed to Congress's imposition of black suffrage, Smith and other Republicans swept the state offices and a large majority of legislative and congressional seats.[22]

In order to reverse this in the 1870 elections, Democrats placed a premium on eliminating divisions between whites. To some degree they neutralized Unionist animosities by nominating a north Alabama prewar Unionist, Robert Burns Lindsey, as their gubernatorial candidate. This, coupled with racial violence and election fraud, helped them narrowly prevail.[23] But for the 1872 election, Democrats unwisely dumped Lindsey and nominated a south Alabamian who had promoted secession and served as an officer in the Confederate army, Thomas Hord Herndon. Republicans countered with another north Alabama Unionist, David Peter Lewis. This brought white Unionists back to the Republican side and Lewis handily won the election.[24] But it proved to be the last governor's race won by Alabama Republicans until 1986.[25] Alabama Democrats learned from their mistake, and they were greatly assisted by an economic depression that began in 1873 during Lewis's administration.[26] This time Democrats nominated another north Alabama Unionist, George Smith Houston, for governor in the 1874 race. Their strategy worked. Houston prevailed and Democrats captured both houses in the legislature.[27]

As historian William Warren Rogers Sr. notes, "After the Democrats regained permanent control of Alabama in 1874, the overriding concern was for white solidarity. Only by avoiding divisive issues, only by closing the ranks of all voting whites could the excesses, as much imagined as real, of a Radical Republican regime be prevented from recurring."[28] This may have included avoiding reopening old wounds from the Civil War era through publication of accurate, complete histories of the conflict in Alabama.

Politicians and opinion makers recognized the power of history to inspire and motivate—for weal or woe. Several years after the Civil War, a Charleston, South Carolina, lawyer-poet, Paul Hamilton Hayne, addressed a meeting of the Ladies Memorial Association in Montgomery, Alabama, and spoke of efforts then being made by some to write a history of the war.[29] Hayne maintained that it could not be done accurately by that generation because "about us still lingers too densely the smoke of battle, and the bloody haze of slaughter and of sacrifice." He suggested that a "century hence . . . (if we but garner up the great body of our historical facts, and keep them untarnished and unperverted in their splendid integrity) some earnest genius who combines the large sympathetic imagination of the Poet, with the penetrating insight of the Philosopher, will delineate this epoch with the terse vigor of Tacitus, and the picturesque generalization of Thucydides." By then, he continued, "whatever else so consummate an artistic thinker may say, he cannot fail to point out that here in this material 19th century, an age after [Edmund] Burke had declared 'the days of chivalry were passed'—among a people branded by universal Christendom as the upholders of a brutal arrogant Slaveocracy,—a Drama presented itself, which in the course of a solitary *lustrum*, reillustrated act by act, and scene by scene, *all* the rarest virtues of knighthood—the gallantries of an antique Time, with its single-hearted devotion, and uncalculating self-sacrifice—its purity, honor, courage, heroism and majestic patience!"[30]

Former Confederate president Jefferson Davis was of the same mind in terms of focusing any early historical scholarship on the bravery of the military and its members while obscuring the cause of the war and de-emphasizing its results.[31] Davis would have also heartily agreed with one of Hayne's other points: that "conscience" had "commanded" the efforts by Davis and others to create the Confederacy after a "Northern Sectional President had been elected by a Sectional Party, for purely sectional purposes of aggrandisement," and that when conscience had been obeyed, "*Consequences rest with God.*"[32] In other words, neither Davis nor other Southern separatists should be blamed for the horrific results. Davis was obsessed with his historical legacy,[33] as demonstrated by his self-serving memoir. A few years before his death in 1889, Davis wrote that materials then being gathered by the Southern Historical Society were essential to enabling the "future historian . . . to do justice to our cause and conduct" so a "*favorable verdict*" could be "rendered by future generations."[34] By then, Civil War memory would be influenced by sentimental nostalgia and the selectivity of submitting materials to archives.

Meanwhile, as a result of the absence of relatively contemporaneous histories of the war in Alabama, Alabamians who were members of the postwar generations were forced to rely on word-of-mouth parroting of legends and myths passed down from generation to generation. Orator Hayne encouraged this, instructing his Montgomery audience to "teach [your children] that as sons of Confederate sires, they are entitled to a moral heritage grander and higher than ever in Rome's haughtiest day was the heritage of the Caesars. Teach them that a cause for which Robert Lee contended, and Stonewall Jackson died, refuses to slink among the byways of the world's contempt; but dares in the face of earth and heaven to proclaim itself honorable and glorious. Teach them that 'Rebellion,' 'Rebel,' may at times be phrases garmented in the souls 'imperial purple,' whose application no constructive tyranny of language can debase, resting as nobly upon those who own them, as the accolade of knighthood from a monarch's blade. In doing honor to our past, we honor, exalt, spiritualize ourselves."[35] Deflecting blame from Alabama's leaders, the children were also taught that the South's many problems over the subsequent decades were the fault of the North—the "Great Alibi," in Robert Penn Warren's words.[36] These lessons were reinforced in Southern schools where the content of schoolbooks was censored to assure they were consistent with themes of Southern rights, Confederate glory, and unprovoked and unjustified postwar oppression and victimization, or at least did not attempt to counter the prevailing mythology.[37]

The intellectual groundwork for this mode of opinion making was laid before the war. When he advocated the creation of a historical society for Alabama in 1850, then-University of Alabama president Dr. Basil Manly, a noted proslavery Baptist theologian and activist secession Democrat, declared that "the *uses of history* are indispensable," especially for the transfer of "an ingenuous and earnest patriotism" from generation to generation. Indeed, he had continued, "in the absence of verities and authentic narrative, *nations have always resorted to fiction and fable*."[38]

The fiction and fable regarding the war was adopted as the gospel in the first academic history of the Civil War period in Alabama, Walter Lynwood Fleming's flawed *Civil War and Reconstruction in Alabama*, which was published in 1905.[39] Among other things, Fleming downplayed the extent and quality of Unionist sentiment and justified support for secession and war in part by pointing to postwar conditions and incidents. He was not alone in using this spurious logic. An untold number of Unionists had by this time become neo-Confederates as a consequence of the unpopularity of efforts of the federal government to enforce the civil and political rights of blacks.[40] The myths, coupled with omissions of critically important facts, appear to have been mobilized by Fleming—and some of those who followed him in the early historiography—primarily to promote and protect the postwar, white supremacist Democratic Party by portraying the conduct of its members before and during the war in the best possible light.[41] This early scholarship, in turn, became the starting point for those who wrote the textbooks used to teach Alabama history in the early twentieth century, not only in the state's primary and secondary schools but also its post-secondary schools.[42]

Some readers of the present book who have accepted and internalized the myths will find a very different portrait of Civil War Alabama here. This is not a comforting homage to Confederate Alabama. Instead, it is an attempt to objectively analyze the war era and its countless nuances by disregarding the myths and using as many contemporaneous sources as possible. It is written from the perspective of ordinary Alabamians—Confederates and Unionists—who experienced what they repeatedly called this "cruel" and "terrible" war. It was that and much more.[43] And after 150 years, Alabamians deserve a critical analysis.

I
ALABAMA SECEDES

Timeline: October 1859–February 1861

October 16, 1859	John Brown's Raid at Harpers Ferry, Virginia.
November 14, 1859	Alabama legislature convenes.
December 5, 1859	United States Congress convenes.
January 11, 1860	Alabama Democrats convene and adopt the Alabama Platform.
January 23, 1860	Alabama legislature establishes a military department at the University of Alabama.
February 24, 1860	Alabama legislature adopts laws giving financial aid to railroads, as well as the "Do Whatever" resolution.
February 27, 1860	Alabama legislature adjourns.
April 23, 1860	National Democratic Convention opens in Charleston, South Carolina.
April 30, 1860	Alabama delegates walk out of National Democratic Convention.
May 16, 1860	National Republican convention meets in Baltimore.
May 18, 1860	Abraham Lincoln receives the Republican nomination.
June 22, 1860	Stephen Douglas of Illinois receives the nomination for the presidency by one faction of the Democratic Party.
June 23, 1860	John Breckinridge is nominated for the presidency by the other faction of the Democratic Party.
June 28, 1860	Constitutional Union Party nominates John Bell for president.
November 6, 1860	Abraham Lincoln is elected president of the United States.
December 6, 1860	Alabama governor Andrew Barry Moore calls for the election of delegates to a state convention scheduled for January 7 in Montgomery.
December 20, 1860	South Carolina secedes from the Union.
December 24, 1860	Alabamians elect delegates to the state convention.
January 4, 1861	Alabama militia seizes the federal arsenal at Mount Vernon, Alabama.
January 5, 1861	Alabama militia seizes each of the federal forts in Mobile Bay.
January 7, 1861	Alabama convention begins.
January 11, 1861	Alabama secedes from the Union.
February 4, 1861	Provisional Confederate Congress convenes in Montgomery.

February 8, 1861	Confederate Constitution adopted by the Provisional Confederate Congress.
February 9, 1861	Jefferson Davis is elected president of the Confederate States of America by the Provisional Confederate Congress
February 18, 1861	Jefferson Davis is inaugurated president of the Confederate States of America.

1
The "Lawyers' Revolution"

> To think we have been fighting four years to prevent the slaves from being freed [and] now to turn round and free them to enable us to carry on the war. The thing is outrageous.
>
> —Pvt. Grant Taylor, nonslaveholder, Tuscaloosa County, Alabama, January 11, 1865

Secession required three basic ingredients. First, a majority of active voters would have to be convinced that a termination of Alabama's connection to the Union created by their forefathers was necessary. Second, a procedural mechanism would have to be adopted to accomplish that termination. And third, Alabama's ability to defend its decision militarily would have to be beefed up. The groundwork for each of these essential elements was laid in January and February 1860.

The role of convincing the public that secession was necessary was filled by a radicalized faction of Alabama lawyers. Advanced education, practiced skills in public speaking, and professional and financial success led to a unique level of influence for lawyers within Southern communities. Lawyers, indeed, comprised the most powerful and influential profession in the United States for most of the nineteenth century.[1] Without the application by pro-secession lawyers of their powers of persuasion, it is questionable whether secession or civil war would have occurred. In fact, one Alabama historian labeled what was about to take place as a "lawyers' revolution."[2]

Contemporaries and historians have pointed to Montgomery lawyer William Lowndes Yancey as the primary leader of this faction (see figure 1). Born in Georgia in 1814, Yancey was reared in South Carolina until his lawyer father died of malaria in 1817 and his mother moved the family back to her childhood home on a Georgia plantation. In 1821, she married a Northern-born Georgia schoolmaster and Presbyterian minister, whom young Yancey came to despise for his perceived mental and physical cruelty to Yancey's mother and authoritarian control over Yancey and Yancey's brother. Yancey was scarred for life, with bouts of depression that he self-medicated through drug use and poor self-esteem for which he overcompensated with acts of violence and egotism.

After moving to the Alabama Black Belt in the 1830s, Yancey practiced

Figure 1. William Lowndes Yancey (Courtesy of Alabama Department of Archives and History)

law, edited a newspaper, planted cotton, got involved in Democratic Party politics, and was gradually caught up in the increasingly militant proslavery Southern rights movement. In the late 1840s, he became an outspoken critic of the National Democratic Party's failure to adequately ensure the rights of slaveholders in the nation's new western territories and also was an early proponent of secession as the only method to prevent the abolition of slavery.[3] He was initially savaged for this by the press in Alabama. Yancey was, wrote a Mobile newspaper editor in 1848, not motivated by principle, but by "his ruling appetite—a thirst for notoriety" and "that disease of excessive ambition and egotism."[4]

But Yancey persevered and the *Montgomery Advertiser*, one of Yancey's key supporters, would conclude that "he was more, perhaps, than any other person, instrumental in producing the separation of the Southern from the Northern States."[5] A much less admiring John Forsyth, a Georgia-born lawyer and newspaper editor in Mobile whose later influence as a propagandist for the Confederate war effort would be second to none, would observe that "the truth of history . . . requires the observation that posterity must unite with the present generation in pronouncing, in view of Mr. Yancey's instrumentality in precipitating the late war upon an unprepared people, that his pub-

Figure 2. Slave auction in Montgomery (Courtesy of Alabama Department of Archives and History)

lic career as a Southern statesman was an unmixed calamity to the People of the South."[6] But Yancey was actually only the most gifted orator of the secession faction; many other Alabama lawyers were critically important in moving Alabama toward secession—and war.[7]

In 1859, Forsyth accurately described the major hurdle faced by Yancey and the pro-secession faction when he wrote that the Union "will last until the South finds it more intolerable to remain in it than the risks and chances of separation, until some great *vital antagonism* shall come to stir up the deep recesses of the Southern heart, and force it in revolutionary action to sever the political ties that bind it to the [Union]."[8] That "vital antagonism" for slaveholders and nonslaveholders alike was the existence of a direct, immediate threat to the institution of slavery.

In antebellum Alabama, 33,730 slaveholders had a direct, economic stake in keeping the 437,271 slaves working to produce 42 percent of Alabama's 1860 per capita income (see figure 2).[9] In addition, as Montgomery lawyer Milton Saffold would later explain, some nonslaveholders shared this economic tie to slavery: "The 30,000 slaveholders have drawn into dependency upon them—their families—the learned professions, the lawyer, the doctor, preacher, teacher, editor, merchant, mechanic—all professions, trades, and employments, because the slave agricultural interest, the only one developed, paid them incomes; and they gave to the towering monopoly their allegiance."[10] Although some members of these groups may have conceded that slavery in Alabama was not destined to be permanent, all slaveholders had expected to be permitted to diffuse the institution over an extended period of time and without economic loss—either to the West or toward Central and South America—just as the northeastern states had done to the South in the late 1700s and early 1800s while developing their industrial economies.[11]

But still, nonslaveholders with no significant economic stake in slavery actually composed a majority of Alabama's voting population. The fact that many of them fought and died in the Civil War has long been cited as evidence that the war was not over slavery from the South's standpoint. To them, however, freed slaves represented not only economic competitors but potential perpetrators of violence. It cannot be overemphasized that perceptions of white Alabamians of the violent tendencies of blacks had been profoundly shaped by a cataclysmic but now largely forgotten eighteenth-century event, the epicenter of which was the Caribbean island of St. Domingo.[12] Today known as Haiti, it had been the most profitable and, therefore, most important colony of France. Africans had been brought there, enslaved, and exploited to produce cash crops (sugar, coffee, cotton, and indigo) in a plantation system. But a successful, large-scale insurrection by the slaves occurred in the 1790s and, in the end, virtually every white man, woman, and child who did not flee the island was massacred.[13]

Many cultural myths were, for political purposes, produced and perpetuated by the partisan press in Alabama and elsewhere during the later manipulation of the resulting racial paranoia: Blacks were naturally violent and barbaric.[14] Large concentrations of slaves were inherently dangerous. Any talk of emancipation and equality would provoke a slave insurrection, and the actual abolition of slavery would mean the doom of whites.[15] Free blacks desirous of equal rights with whites, in collaboration with white abolitionists, would most likely be the provocateurs of that doom.[16] Once in control, blacks were not capable of governing effectively or attaining economic success, and the result would be misrule and economic ruin. Such stories, rooted in the St. Domingo massacre, were told and retold throughout the nineteenth century.[17]

For many years, William Yancey and other so-called Original Secessionists had been stating their case for secession by playing on this paranoia and citing periodic instances where growing opposition to slavery in the North was becoming evident. But none of those incidents had constituted a direct and immediate threat to the institution of slavery in the South. The leaders of opposition to secession in Alabama had, therefore, been successful in calming public fears. Secession, Unionists had long argued, was a remedy that would "plunge the country into irretrievable ruin" and "would kill the patient instead of relieving his suffering."[18] Most Alabamians, therefore, remained focused on their railroad projects and other commercial interests.

The creation in the 1850s of the Republican Party (what some derisively called the "Black Republican Party"), which was opposed to the spread of slavery into the western territories of the United States, had been worrisome. But the relatively slavery-friendly Democrats had won again in the 1856 presidential election—this time with Pennsylvanian James Buchanan at the head of the ticket and a Kentucky slave owner, John Cabell Breckinridge, as his running mate.[19] Even Yancey had publicly conceded in August 1857 that there was "hope for us in the Union" because the South "has the power to control that great Democratic Party," which had "the controlling power in the Union."[20] But other secessionists remained committed to their goal and impatiently awaited what Yancey called the "next inevitable aggression." In a letter to a Georgian, James Summerfield Slaughter, that was later leaked to the press, Yancey privately predicted that when that occurred, "we shall fire the Southern heart, instruct the Southern mind, give courage to each other, and, at the proper moment, by one organized, concerted action, we can precipitate the cotton states into a revolution."[21]

For Yancey and other Alabama lawyer-secessionists, abolitionist John Brown's ill-fated 1859 paramilitary raid on Harpers Ferry, Virginia, in an effort to spark a slave insurrection finally provided that crucial next aggression.[22] To them it was a gift of God. According to the *Montgomery Mail*, edited by Montgomery lawyer Johnson Jones Hooper, "Providence sent us JOHN BROWN."[23] Heretofore, Southerners could construe Northern intentions as comprising at worst a long-term threat to slavery with little risk in the near term of actual acts of violence to back up that threat, so Southerners were therefore shocked when some Northerners lauded Brown for his bravery in support of freedom. Wrote Hooper, Brown's sudden and unforeseen attack on October 16, 1859, had "radiat[ed] upon the sentiment of the North a light which enabled us to see the very heart-strings of Black Republicanism."[24] Even the pro-Union Tuscaloosa *Independent Monitor* admitted that "Old Brown" was a "God send" to the secessionists, those traitors and "unprincipled political demagogues, of all parties, who prey upon spoils from the public; who, void of patriotism, look not beyond the present times, are reckless of the future, and would care not at all if the temple of our liberties is prostrated by ruthless hands if they can plunder its sanctuary and avoid the ruins."[25]

The first mention in the Alabama press of the attack by Brown's group was in a brief telegraphic report in the *Mobile Daily Register*. A "serious riot" at Harpers Ferry, the entry read, had resulted in the "Arsenal and town" being taken possession of by "the mob, which numbers 600."[26] The next day, the Tuscaloosa *Independent Monitor* dispelled any impression that this was merely a labor dispute like those that had arisen in the North in the wake of the economic Panic of 1857.[27] "From the most reliable accounts it seems that a handful of fanatics—whites and negroes—instigated by some Northern abolitionists, took possession of the government arsenal." Even more ominously, it was reported that maps had been found indicating Brown's planned invasion route was through the plantation regions in the South, including the Alabama Black Belt with its high slave-to-white ratios.[28]

The initial reaction to this news was stunned silence.[29] Not normally at a loss for words, John Forsyth admitted to his readers that "the insurrection a few days ago, at Harper's [*sic*] Ferry, as it was reported to us by the telegraph, was an event so unexpected, so extraordinary and startling that we have reserved comment upon it until we could better understand and realize the nature and merits of the affair."[30] But as the facts were reported, fear quite naturally turned into a desire for revenge against those who were responsible.[31] A north Alabama widow, Sarah Espy of Cherokee County, wrote that the "newspapers are filled with the abolition riot at Harper's Ferry. A great excitement prevails, in some of the Southern states in consequence. May the Northern assassins be put down with their free-negro allies." And, she fearfully concluded, "may the women and children of the South be saved from their Northern murderers."[32]

Growing hysteria led to suspicion that the Northern-born residents of Alabama were among the estimated twenty thousand "abolition emissaries" supposedly sent by Brown and "scattered throughout the Southern States."[33] Following the death of a Northerner in Marengo County, the *Eutaw Whig* claimed that three letters from John Brown had been found in the man's personal effects and that he was "from appearances . . . an active agent or emissary of the men who were at the bottom of the Harper's Ferry plot."[34] A few days later, the *Montgomery Mail* reported the arrest of a man in Prattville "on suspicion of unsoundness" and the discovery of more letters from Brown supposedly in his possession. "We would advise," Montgomery editor Hooper shrieked, "that the citizens of Prattville and the adjacent country immediately organize a Committee of Vigilance, try the case fairly and if the defendant be found to have held correspondence of any sort with the old devil BROWN, *hang him within twenty-four hours*. It is nonsense—nay, it is madness—to talk of law for such offenses. Let our people protect themselves, asserting their inalienable right of self-defence. The law has cracks, crevices, flaws; jails are sometimes unsafe; a strong rope and a stout tree *never* do fail."[35]

So-called vigilance committees had already been formed in Dallas and Lowndes Counties in 1858,[36] and according to the *Selma Reporter*, a peddler suspected of being an "abolition emissary" was almost lynched after a trunk he had left in a Cahaba hotel apparently after leaving town in a hurry was found to contain documents implicating him as "one of the men stationed on this line of old Brown's marked map." After being apprehended in Marion and returned by a deputy sheriff to Cahaba, "an excited crowd surrounded him, and it was feared that he would be punished severely without judge or jury, but the crowd was calmed, and he was lodged in jail." However, the peddler was by no means safe. "He will," it was said, "be allowed ten days . . . to prove himself innocent of any criminal intentions. If he fails to do this, he will doubtless suffer severely, as he certainly should."[37] Law, order, and individual rights were crumbling in this atmosphere of fear and suspicion.

Even moderates were counseling the formation of volunteer militia companies or the augmentation of existing companies.[38] "The recent nefarious attempt at Harper's Ferry, to get up an insurrection among the slaves, though it proved a signal failure—*not one slave, it has been asserted, having joined Brown and his confederates*—should," counseled one newspaper editor who was a Black Belt Union Democrat, "prove a warning to the South to be always prepared to meet such emergencies. And the cheapest and most efficient plan for accomplishing this object, is to organize efficient Volunteer Companies."[39] Of course, the danger in taking such a step was that someone would want to go further and actually use the force for more than defensive purposes, or at least to defend aggressive action that would not otherwise have been taken.

As one Alabama newspaper reported that fall, even the *New York Observer* recognized that the nation was "drifting into a whirlpool from which nothing living is ever drawn . . . unless this spirit of discord, strife and conflict is suppressed, and the era of good feeling is restored."[40] But the lawyer-secessionists, and their allies in the Southern press, were determined to prevent that. The pro-Union Tuscaloosa *Independent Monitor* angrily charged that political demagogues were vigorously striving to "keep alive that dangerous excitement, and constantly add fuel to the flame that is so rapidly consuming the fraternity that should subsist between all parts of the country as between brethren who have and ought to maintain together a common heritage of freedom. . . . The papers teem with threats, and vituperation and warnings; gloomy forebodings are on many tongues; idlers at the street corners gossip brashly of the portentous times; Vigilance Committees are popular, and stray Yankees who happen to be out without a pass are wonderfully in danger of tar and feathers or a trial of strength between their jugulars and a hempen cord!"[41]

It was in this atmosphere of fear and paranoia that the Alabama legislature convened in Montgomery on November 14, 1859. The members of this body had been elected before Brown's act of terror, and so a majority was not necessarily committed and anxious to create a separate government of Southern states. This was demonstrated at the beginning of the session, when William Yancey's supporters attempted to elect him to the seat in the US Senate then held by the much more moderate Benjamin Fitzpatrick. A majority of the legislature opposed Yancey and, as a result, Fitzpatrick, an Elmore County lawyer-planter, succeeded in fending off the challenge.[42]

But all was not lost for the secessionists. They knew, as was the case with several prior legislatures in the 1850s, that some Unionist members were determined to obtain financial aid from the state to complete railroad projects important to them and their constituents. This demand for what was called "State aid" was the Achilles heel of Union opposition to secession measures in the legislature. At this time, Alabama was on its way to creating the railroad infrastructure required for an industrial economy (see map 1). But much more capital was needed to complete this process.

The portion of the Tennessee and Alabama Railroad between Athens and the Tennessee line was nearly finished,[43] but construction had barely begun on the much longer and more expensive stretch between Decatur and Montgomery known as the South and North Railroad (see map 1).[44] Similarly, the North East and South West Railroad, which was projected to run between Meridian, Mississippi, through Tuscaloosa to Chattanooga, Tennessee, had not even completed its roadbed.[45] Although its stockholders had authorized the issuance of $4.3 million dollars in bonds, their marketability was questionable without state endorsement.[46] The Alabama and Tennessee Rivers Railroad had just become operational from Selma to Talladega, but that was not the planned end of the line.[47] Construction had still not commenced on the Selma and Gulf Railroad projected to run from Selma to Pensacola, Florida, and would not as long as stock subscriptions continued to lag while the competing Alabama and Florida Railroad progressed from Montgomery toward Pensacola.[48] The Mobile and Ohio Railroad was not yet completed from Mobile to the Tennessee line, and a loan previously made to it by the state needed to be renewed.[49] With only $631,679 in the state treasury, however, there was obviously not enough to satisfy everyone, thereby creating the perfect conditions for negotiations.[50]

For many reasons, long-standing sentiment against public aid for private

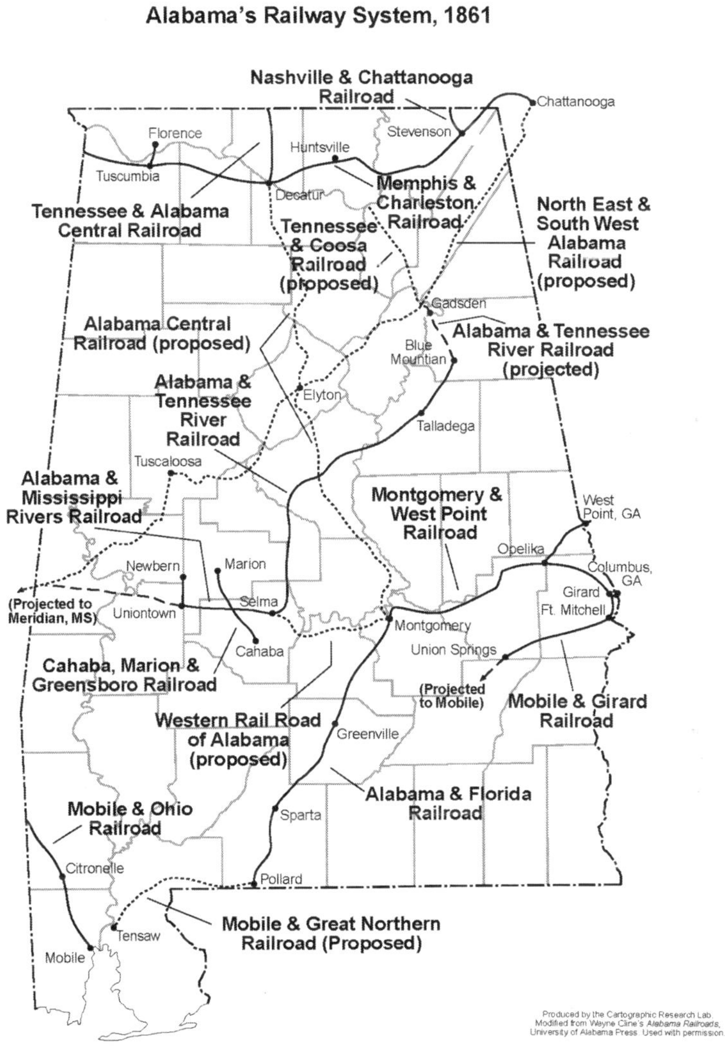

Map 1. Alabama Railroads (From *Alabama Railroads* by Wayne Cline; Courtesy of the University of Alabama Press)

railroads had persisted. Yet this legislature passed several bills of significance that appear to have been a product of logrolling between commercial interests and secessionists.[51] On February 23, 1860, a bill was adopted that replaced a large sum of money ($36,000) taken years earlier from the University of Alabama's endowment, but the same bill required the university, through its president, Landon Cabell Garland, to "establish a military department . . . to place it under military discipline . . . [and] to elect and appoint such military officer or officers, as shall be necessary."[52] On February 18 and 24, the legislature adopted three bills that established a mechanism for loaning an unprecedented amount of money to certain specified railroads, including the North East and South West ($200,000), the Alabama and Tennessee ($225,000), the Selma and Gulf ($140,000), and the Tennessee and Alabama Central ($173,940).[53] Also on February 24, the legislature adopted another bill that appropriated an equally unprecedented sum ($200,000) for the state militia and raised taxes to fund that appropriation.[54]

On the same day the militia bill and two of the railroad aid bills were passed, the legislature adopted a very fateful joint resolution. It required that upon the "election of a President advocating the principles and action of the party in the Northern States calling itself the Republican Party," it was the duty of the governor to issue a proclamation calling upon the qualified voters "to elect delegates to a Convention of the State to consider, determine and *do whatever* in the opinion of said Convention, the rights, interests and honor of the State of Alabama requires to be done for their protection."[55]

A review of available newspapers from this period reveals no cries of alarm from Unionists, even though it was clear that secessionists had just significantly advanced their cause. The expenditures included in this package of measures are particularly striking given that in his annual message to the legislature on November 14, Governor Andrew Barry Moore had addressed the state's woefully underfunded system of public education and almost apologetically concluded that although the appropriation of more money was necessary, "this I deem inexpedient at this time." He held out hope that "after the payment of our bonds, falling due in 1863, the treasury will be in a condition to authorize larger appropriations for this purpose."[56] Since the late 1830s, scrimping and saving until the state's now approximately $3.4 million bonded indebtedness was gone had been the overriding fiscal policy of the state,[57] but now that policy was thrown out the window to secure support for pro-secession measures. With inside knowledge, the *Montgomery Daily Mail* remarked that "this series of measures" had reversed "in a moment, as it were, the whole internal policy of Alabama."[58] Oblivious to the consequences, the Tuscaloosa *Independent Monitor* rejoiced that "the liberal and progressive policy of the present Legislature has inaugurated a new era in the State's legislation. . . . Old-fogyism dazzled by the splendor of [the legislature's] progressive policy has retreated to its den, there to mourn that its days of stay-as-it-were-ism have passed away."[59]

Things were, indeed, changing, but many would not realize how much until it was too late. Dazzled by the amount of financial aid promised to its pet railroad, the North East and South West, the *Independent Monitor* played down the significance of the joint resolution calling for a convention if a Republican were elected president. It pointed out that a few years earlier, Governor Moore had disobeyed a resolution requiring him to call a convention if Congress failed to admit the Kansas Territory to the Union under a proslavery state constitution. The *Independent Monitor*'s editor assured that "we do not believe he will do so should a Black Republican be elected to the Presidency. This event, [a Republican victory] singly and alone, is no breach of any constitutional right of the South."[60] Many Unionist legislators may have come to the same conclusion and rationalized that the reward of railroad aid justified the risk. Only two members had voted against the resolution.[61]

Former governor John Anthony Winston, who had become famous for his staunch opposition to state aid, would later charge that the secessionists had "laid the train for a disunion explosion, by subtle device and cunning deception of an agricultural people, too much immersed in their daily occupation, to watch designing and ambitious political leaders, and too prone to be blindly led by them."[62] But secession was not simply a matter of an absence of political awareness and involvement by yeoman farmers. It was also brought about by their representatives in the legislature who, in their desperation for railroad aid, were willing to risk everything by granting the secessionists broad license, one that could be construed to allow them to take Alabama out of the Union and down the path toward war.

But even though the groundwork for secession had now been laid, secessionists remained concerned that passions would cool and that the election of another Democrat in the 1860 presidential election would foil their plans. The frontrunner for the Democratic nomination was US Senator Stephen Arnold Douglas of Illinois, who was supported by a number of Alabama Unionists focused on Alabama's economic future. The strategy of secessionists was to paint Douglas as a man who was too soft in his support for slavery in this post–John Brown era and to force the National Democratic Party to adopt a proslavery platform so poisonous that it was sure to alienate many Northern Democrats.

Alabama's Douglas Democrats knew this and attempted to counter it at the January 11, 1860, state Democratic Convention in Montgomery where the delegates to the National Democratic Convention at Charleston, South Carolina, would be selected. But at William Yancey's urging, resolutions were adopted by the Alabama convention instructing the Alabama delegation to present what was in essence an ultimatum requiring that the presidential platform contain proslavery provisions. The substance of these resolutions was that territorial legislatures in the West could not enact prohibitory taxes or other "unfriendly legislation" to hinder slavery and that Congress had an affirmative duty to intervene and protect the rights of slave owners to their slaves in the territories. As Yancey would later couch this concept, Southern slave owners were entitled to "equal protection,"[63] a doctrine that would ironically be applied in favor of the slaves rather than their owners in less than a decade. The Alabama delegates were "positively instructed" by another resolution to withdraw from the Charleston Convention if their demands were not met.[64]

The pro-Douglas Huntsville *Southern Advocate* charged that the adoption of what would be called the Alabama Platform was the equivalent of "placing a log across the railroad track and throwing off a loaded train of passengers."[65] Whether or not the National Democratic Convention acceded to the ultimatum, it was widely believed that the Democratic Party would be split, thereby assuring the election of a Republican in November and greatly increasing the possibility of disunion.[66] This would happen if the delegates to the Democratic Convention were unable to agree on the nomination of any candidate with a national following.

But before waiting until April to see who the Democrats might offer up, Southern Whigs unwittingly improved the prospects of the Republicans by launching a third party called the Constitutional Union Party. Its stated purpose, wrote the supportive but skeptical editor of the Tuscaloosa *Independent Monitor*, was to "put down the agitators and ultraists of both sections, and restore peace and concord to our distracted land, lofty goals as hopeless as the new party itself."[67] A state convention of this fledgling party was scheduled to take place on May 23 in Selma, and former Whigs busied themselves in selecting delegates.[68] The upshot of this was that the Southern vote, which was essential for the election of a Democrat, would now be split.[69]

In addition to the legislative arenas, the press, and political parties, the influence of the secessionists was also being felt in other areas, such as the churches. Some historians have assigned ministers of the gospel a primary role in bringing about and sustaining secession.[70] Given the pro-secession activities of divines such as the Tuscaloosa Baptist minister Rev. Basil Manly, that conclusion appears logical on the surface.[71] But members of the churches were the driving force.

Secessionists were able to co-opt other Southern institutions. President Landon Garland's university had received a much-needed increase in funding from the legislature along with a requirement that a military department be created (see figure 3). Contrary to myth, this had little to do with improving discipline. Despite the fact that the military system would not be implemented until September 1860, the discipline among the students was re-

Figure 3. Landon Garland (Courtesy of Alabama Department of Archives and History)

ported in March 1860 to be very good already.[72] Nonetheless, Garland was pushing forward with his plan to make the University of Alabama into what would be called the "West Point of the South."[73]

Even the federal justice system in Alabama was used to promote the secessionists' interests. In April 1860, US district judge William Giles Jones dismissed an indictment against a purchaser of Africans smuggled into the country by slave traders aboard the slave ship *Wanderer*, ruling that purchasers could not constitutionally be prosecuted as "accessories after the fact" under the federal statute criminalizing the African slave trade.[74] This decision, which was in direct conflict with US Supreme Court associate justice John Archibald Campbell's charge to federal grand juries in Alabama the previous year, would later be overruled by Campbell. But for the time being, it gutted several other ongoing prosecutions in Alabama.[75] It also encouraged slave traders to bring more shipments into Mobile Bay, including those 124 souls who arrived aboard the infamous *Clotilde*.[76] With buyers willing to pay gold without fear of prosecution, slave traders would certainly take the risk of providing a steady supply, especially given that about this same time, the pro-secession federal judge in South Carolina ruled that those traders could not be prosecuted either, absent proof that they had actually kidnapped the Africans. As the *New York Times* lamented, "There is no reason why the slave-trade should not be carried on from this moment as vigorously as it has ever been, because no slave-trader can ever have kidnapping proved against him. Others kidnap, and he is but a receiver."[77]

Meanwhile, Alabamians and others across the nation read in their newspapers that the Charleston Convention, which met on April 23, 1860, went according to Yancey's plan. The Alabama delegation and those of six other states walked out of the convention hall when the majority of the delegates refused to adopt a presidential platform that included a provision requiring the federal government to "protect, when necessary, the rights of persons and property . . . in the territories."[78] By the end of the day on Saturday, June 23, three candidates opposed Republican nominee Abraham Lincoln: Tennessean John Bell of the Constitutional Union Party, Democrat Stephen Douglas, and Vice President John Breckinridge, who received the nomination of other Democrats opposed to Douglas at a separate convention in Baltimore.[79] As everyone seems to have recognized, their only chance of defeating Lincoln was either to fuse under one candidate or somehow throw the election into the House of Representatives as had last occurred in 1824.[80]

To the secessionists, that was unlikely, and so the fate of Alabama appeared to be sealed.[81] Lincoln would be elected, Governor Moore would call a convention, and that convention would adopt an ordinance separating the state from the Union. The pro-Douglas *Mobile Daily Register* charged that "not a step have they taken that is not hostile to the unity and harmony of the Democratic Party. Ingenuity could not have devised any plans better calculated to disorganize and destroy the National party than precisely those plans they have devised and executed."[82] The *Register* continued, "They got control of the last Montgomery Democratic Convention, to a destruction of the party, to secession from the Union, and to strengthen the prospects" of the Republican Party.[83] The pro-Douglas Montgomery *Confederation* alleged that Yancey was actually "at the head of this move" to split the Democratic Party "and is now laboring with undiminished activity and energy, to complete and carry out his designs, as were plainly laid down in his letter to Mr. Slaughter of Georgia. He has 'inflamed the Southern mind and fired the Southern heart,' and has now only to 'precipitate the cotton States into a revolution.' God forbid we should ever see this!"[84]

It was probably inevitable that with most of the vocal leaders of the secession movement being lawyers, the legal profession would also receive criticism. Noting that William Yancey's law partner, former Alabama Supreme Court chief justice William Parish Chilton, had introduced in the Alabama Senate a bill bolstering Alabama's militia forces and that Chilton was also at the forefront in his demands for a federal territorial slave code, the Hunts-

Figure 4. Leroy Pope Walker (Courtesy of Alabama Department of Archives and History)

ville *Southern Advocate* probably spoke for many laymen when it charged that "lawyers are, often, bad politicians and dangerous Leaders."[85]

But the faction of Alabama lawyers pushing for secession was undaunted. Catherine Fennell of Marshall County noted that "some of the most eminent lawyers have left their offices and are making stump speeches through the county."[86] Huntsville lawyer Leroy Pope Walker instructed a north Alabama audience that "this whole subject has reached this simple proposition—Shall negroes govern white men, or white men govern negroes?" Remember now, he continued, "that universal emancipation and universal suffrage, go together. When this point is reached, and the ballot is free alike to black and white,—my God! The infamy of such a possibility!" "Submit, then if you dare, for a single day, to the administration of a man who proclaims this doctrine of universal emancipation," he warned, and "all that a freeman holds dear, is soon ended.... The whole social fabric of Southern civilization—the highest best ordered, and most perfect embodiment of human government the world has ever seen will pass away forever"[87] (see figure 4). Similarly, in a speech given at Wetumpka, Talladega lawyer Jabez Lamar Monroe Curry, then a member of Congress, maintained that "as soon as Abe Lincoln takes the Presidential chair, five hundred thousand Wide-awakes [a Republican political club], already drilling for the purpose, will rush over the border, lay waste your fields, emancipate your negroes, and amalgamate the poor man's daughter and the rich man's buck-nigger before your very eyes."[88]

North Alabama had long held the balance of power for the Democratic Party in the state, and according to the Reverend Basil Manly, who was travelling in that region in October 1860 ostensibly on behalf of the Baptist Church, "The political excitement is so high up here, as to absorb every thing."[89] There was good reason for this. As the following entry in the diary of Sarah Espy illustrates, events and hysterical political propaganda had created the belief that this was the most dangerous election in the nation's history, and that the outcome would decide whether there would be peace or war: "The fate of this nation is to be decided by the election of a President. May he who will rule for the general good, be the one chosen, and may peace again bear rule in this glorious land."[90]

Some lawyers of that period might have been bad politicians and dangerous leaders, but the secessionist faction of the bar was undeniably quite effective and well prepared to reach their immediate goals. As Sarah Espy concluded, there "are fearful times in store for us" and "it is the beginning of woe."[91] Similarly, Augustus Benners, a south Alabama planter-lawyer who seems to have always had more prudence and good sense than his Black Belt brethren, wrote that "we are on the eve of great events. How they will terminate God only knows. In war and anarchy I much fear. In god is our trust."[92]

2
"A Leap in the Dark"

Abraham Lincoln's victory in the 1860 presidential election created much consternation and fear in the Deep South. A young lady in Lowndes County, Alabama, Margaret Josephine Miles, noted that "in anticipation of the coming storm, I been practicing shooting, very assiduously."[1] And this time Governor Andrew Barry Moore obeyed the legislature's resolution requiring him to convene a state convention. On December 6, he issued a proclamation scheduling an election of delegates for Christmas Eve, December 24, and calling for a convention to meet on January 7, 1861, in Montgomery, Alabama.[2]

Lawrence County lawyer-Unionist Thomas Peters wrote an impassioned plea for help to the lame-duck president, James Buchanan.[3] In this letter, which was widely published in the North, Peters expressed the position of what will be referred to as Unconditional Unionists—he professed his willingness to support the Union even if it meant the end of slavery. Peters condemned "the unconstitutional usurpations of those who are now plotting in many of the Southern States to destroy the national government, and all those who disagree with them, if they succeed." Perhaps to shame or embarrass Buchanan into stopping the madness, Peters asked Buchanan whether Unionists were "to be protected by the general government, in our lives, our property, and our peace, and our homes, where we are, and where we wish to remain, in quiet comfort."[4] After the war ended, Talladega lawyer-Unionist Lewis Parsons maintained that "a few regiments properly disposed" would have prevented Alabama's secession.[5] But two days before Peters sent his letter, President Buchanan had issued his annual message to Congress in which he had made clear that he constitutionally could not, and would not, use military force to stop states from seceding, even though he believed that secession was unconstitutional.[6] Southern Unionists would, therefore, have to fend for themselves as long as Buchanan was in the White House. Peters was, meanwhile, reportedly hung in effigy and fiercely denounced as disloyal to the South and as an abolitionist.[7]

The militantly Unionist position Peters took would have been truly death-defying in the south Alabama Black Belt, where slave-to-white ratios were extremely high and support for immediate secession very strong. Therefore, Unionists there like Selma lawyer Benjamin Saffold bravely sought election to the convention on what was known as a "cooperationist" platform.[8] Historian Walter Fleming enunciated the traditional view of the Cooperationists in Alabama as being divided into three groups. Some, he wrote, wanted "the cooperation of the southern states within the Union in order to force their rights from the central government." Others, he continued, wanted "the southern states to come to an agreement within the Union and then secede and form a confederacy." The third, he concluded, "wanted a clear understanding among the cotton states before secession." In sum, Fleming thought that two of his three factions favored secession.[9] But he cites no authority for this proposition, and available evidence fails to support it.

To understand the Cooperationists, one must recall the means used by Unionists in South Carolina in the early 1850s to defuse a secession movement that had sprung up in the wake of the so-called Compromise of 1850, which had led to the admission of gold-rich California as a free state. In order to obstruct secession, Unionists successfully argued that it would spark a civil war, and that it was unsafe for South Carolina to secede unless a large number of other slave states seceded with her. Because no other states were then willing to cooperate in this rash and potentially suicidal adventure, South Carolina secessionists were eventually forced to capitulate.[10] Cooperationism was a winning, Union-saving argument then, and 1860-era Unionists in most of the plantation counties in Alabama adopted that strategy after Lincoln's election. As Benjamin Saffold's brother, Milton, later explained, "it was well known [in 1860] that the co-operationists hoped to defeat secession by advocating a co-operation of all the Southern States, which they knew was unattainable."[11] Cooperationism had the added benefit of appearing to Northern Republicans in Congress—who were then reluctantly considering compromise measures regarding the institution of slavery—to be a pro-secession argument, thereby creating bargaining leverage through the illusion that the South was united in favor of secession if a compromise were not reached.[12]

In a letter to the editor of the *Selma Reporter* on December 12, 1860, Benjamin Saffold declared that "I regard a union of at least eight States indispensable to our present and future tranquility, and that this union ought to be made before the secession of any one, because it may be impracticable afterwards." This, he knew, would require a time-consuming convention of the slave states. If Alabama adopted an ordinance of secession without this degree of support from the other Southern states, the issue, according to Saffold, must be "submitted to the people for ratification." Otherwise, he correctly predicted, "there might be difficulty in enforcing the ordinance." The conventional wisdom was that a majority of Alabamians would vote against secession.[13]

According to Cooperationists, Alabama's unilateral secession would endanger slavery, not protect it, ultimately bringing on the horrors of civil war and St. Domingo. Thus, it was a "leap in the dark" (a campaign slogan) that could be avoided only by concerted action simultaneous with a large number of other slave states.[14] But Saffold's minimum requirement of eight states meant that some of the Upper South states would have to make common cause with Alabama. As Saffold certainly recognized, however, the most frequently mentioned must-have states were Virginia, Tennessee, and Kentucky, where there was still only lukewarm support for secession at this point.[15]

Historians may have reached no consensus on whether the Cooperationists of 1860 and 1861 actually favored secession and whether their only difference with the secessionists was of means or timing.[16] But secessionists in Alabama and elsewhere knew cooperationism was actually a strategy of delay and obstruction.[17] As Leroy Pope Walker put it in 1860, "does any Southern man believe that *all* the Southern States are now ready to go out of the Union? Does any man believe that Delaware will ever go? Or that Missouri will ever go? Or that Kentucky will go, as long as the South will permit her to cling in the skirts of the Union? Virginia is not ready to go now, nor is North Carolina, or Tennessee, or Maryland."[18] Similarly, Thomas Hord Herndon, a young Greene County lawyer-secessionist, told an audience that cooperationism was "an insuperable obstacle to the secession of Alabama." As Herndon and other secessionists recognized, "it is not probable, hardly, if at all, possible, that all these States can be brought to act simultaneously in a movement of this kind."[19] Unionists also recognized that the Cooperationist candidates thought like them. David Peter Lewis, a Moulton lawyer-Unionist who ran and handily won on a cooperation platform in north Alabama's Lawrence County, wrote that "nearly fourteen fifteenths" of the voters there were opposed to secession.[20]

Secessionists were adamant that Alabama should secede and join South Carolina, which seceded in mid-December, whether or not any other slave state followed. Opposing this "separate state" secession in a Black Belt county was, therefore, very unpopular and engendered suspicion of one's devotion to the perpetuation of slavery. Thus, when Benjamin Saffold opened his speech at a rally at Summerfield in Dallas County, he made it clear that he was not an abolitionist. In a declaration that would be used against him by his white supremacist political enemies in the postwar period in an effort to undermine his support among black voters, Saffold declared that "there must be no submission to Black Republican rule. We own our slaves by the laws of God," he proclaimed, "and we must defend our property at all hazards, and to the last extremity."[21] For this same reason, the theme of his argument for a convention of the Southern slave states was that it presented the sole method by which the institution of slavery could be saved and a civil war avoided: "I believe that a Southern Convention affords the only possible means by which we shall be enabled out of the thistle of danger to pluck the flower of safety." Saffold also deprecated the secessionists' claims that Alabama's secession was a matter of honor instead of self-destruction: "Gentlemen tell us that the honor of the State forces her to separate State secession. I derive my code of honor from the Bible and I can no where find in that book that suicide is recommended." In addition to predicting (accurately, it would turn out) that secession would be followed by war with the North, heavy taxes, starvation, revolts within the military, a reign of terror, and chaos, Saffold told the audience that "from my inmost heart I believe that the course which the separate State secessionists propose will cause the abolition of slavery, and that it will be attended with scenes of carnage and conflagration which will shock mankind. I am no prophet, but I believe in my every sense that separate State secession will be the precursor of woes to our beloved Alabama, that will make the ears to tingle and the blood to freeze in our veins."[22] But Saffold's risky and unpopular effort was all in vain. Newspaper accounts indicate that after all the speakers had completed their remarks and a resolution favoring a Southern convention was read and presented to the gathering for adoption, an unidentified secessionist leader disrupted the proceedings and the resolution was withdrawn.[23]

Secessionists publicly responded to the claim of Unionists that secession would bring on a civil war between the North and the South in a variety of ways, but mostly with ridicule. In one of his speeches, William Yancey pledged to "undertake to drink all of the blood" that would be shed as a result of secession.[24] Leroy Pope Walker confidently asserted that he would "wipe up with his pocket handkerchief" all the blood that would be shed.[25] This cavalier attitude was in part predicated on the South's virtual monopoly on the production of middling cotton. Cotton was said to be king, and the Northeast, as well as England and Europe, were her subjects. War would cut off the supply to those regions from the South, and as pro-secession newspapers continued to note, efforts to generate alternate supplies in India and elsewhere had failed.[26] Thus, concluded the *Eutaw Observer*, there were "good reasons for believing that secession will not be attended with any bloodshed whatever—necessarily—between the two sections." It asserted there was the "more probability that there will be a war between the Capitalists, the Manufacturers and their operatives—the white slaves of the North. Let them be turned out of employment for the want of cotton, and the factories and residencies of their employers, in less than two months, will be sending their black smoke up to heaven as a witness against them and a testimony of their own wretchedness and folly. But there is no danger of a collision between the two sections of the country."[27]

Secessionists may have seen it as divine intervention that, following the severe drought of the previous summer, Election Day was cold and wet and the turnout low in some areas.[28] Especially in those Black Belt counties like Dallas, where Cooperationists were on the ticket, the turnout helped produce disastrous results for Unionists. Dallas countians had polled a total of 1,792 votes in the presidential election,[29] but on December 24 that number dropped to 1,373, of which Benjamin Saffold received only 358. Two secessionists, including Cahawba lawyer John Tyler Morgan, would instead represent Dallas County.[30]

In north Alabama, where the white population was not as grossly outnumbered by the slave population, the secessionists were handily defeated by a coalition of Unconditional Unionists and Cooperationists. The only exception was in Calhoun County, which was the home of the largest number of South Carolina natives in the state.[31] The turnout was very high in Tuscaloosa County: 2,265 men had voted in the presidential election,[32] but 3,773 went to the polls on December 24. The vast majority voted for Cooperationists: Tuscaloosa attorney William Russell Smith and planter-businessman Robert Jemison Jr.[33] In addition to electing future Republicans David Peter Lewis and James S. Clark in Lawrence County, Cooperationist candidates were successful throughout the Tennessee Valley. In northwest Alabama, attorneys Sidney Cherry Posey and Henry Cox Jones were elected in Lauderdale County over attorneys William Basil Wood and James E. Moore; John Anthony Steele and attorney Richard Sharp Watkins were elected in Franklin County; and apparently without opposition, future Republican Charles Christopher Sheats, a young, little-known schoolteacher, was elected in Winston County, then well-known for its independence.[34]

But the secessionists had captured more counties than the Cooperationists, especially in south Alabama. Secessionists in heavily populated Mobile County had surprised political observers by prevailing despite opposition efforts directed from Washington by US Supreme Court associate justice John Archibald Campbell, a former Alabama lawyer.[35] Secessionists were ecstatic.

Figure 5. Augusta Jane Evans (Courtesy of Alabama Department of Archives and History)

Young Mobile novelist Augusta Jane Evans, a female fire-eater who would become one of the most famous propagandists for the Confederacy during the Civil War, encouraged a Unionist acquaintance to "let us conquer or perish together; delay is ruinous, suicidal;—*the time has come*"[36] (see figure 5).

Opponents of secession had been outlawyered and outfoxed during the last legislative session by trading for state aid to their railroads and other projects, and in exchange giving up control of the state's future to an all-powerful convention. Now the state was poised to take the risky leap in the dark they correctly predicted would entail disastrous legal, social, economic, and political consequences. A worried Limestone County lawyer, Daniel Robinson Hundley, observed that "politically the heavens are dark and portentous, and war, famine and pestilence may all be looked for during the next twelve months."[37] Even to Sarah Espy, who favored secession but only in the absence of a compromise with the North on slavery, the level of confidence in the future was extremely low. She wrote that "the Union will be divided, and the Lord only knows what will come next. May he interpose and save the country."[38] A pro-secession south Alabama woman, Elizabeth Rhodes, also privately expressed worry. Noting "dark clouds overspreading our National Horizon," she was concerned that the result would be "wars and bloodshed on our once prosperous and happy nation." She resolved to "wait and pray God to overrule all things for His glory and the good of mankind."[39]

As a practical matter, the question now became, if secession occurred, would it be permanent or somehow reversed? According to Eufaula lawyer Eli Sims Shorter, the brother of future war governor John Gill Shorter, secession would most certainly be eternal. "The revolution has already begun, and the gates of hell cannot now prevail against it," he bragged.[40] Opponents could only hope that this was only a nightmare from which the state would soon wake. At least two strategies were already being formulated to speed the dawn.

3
"There Will Be a Revulsion"

Opponents of separate state secession had lost in the election for delegates to the convention scheduled to meet on January 7, 1861, but they had not lost hope that the secessionists could somehow be stymied. It is apparent, however, that they were not in agreement on the proper strategy. Some, such as Thomas Peters, believed that at least the threat of federal military intervention was necessary. That had worked in the 1830s, when South Carolina had threatened to "nullify" the enforcement of a federal tariff and President Andrew Jackson had forced the "nullifiers," as they were called, to back down by boldly threatening military action.[1] But as previously discussed, Peters had written President Buchanan in early December to advance this idea, yet Buchanan had once again proven that he was no Andrew Jackson.

Since then, a glimmer of hope for Southern Unionists like Peters appeared when Tennessee senator Andrew Johnson picked up this torch of what the secessionists called "coercion." Johnson had not chosen to work only behind the scenes in an effort to preserve the Union. Instead, he had become the symbolic leader of many anti-secessionists when he took the floor of the US Senate in December 1860 and angrily denied that any state had the right to secede. At the same time, he affirmed that the federal government had the right to use military force to "enforce and execute the law upon individuals within the limits of a State" and to "put down resistance" to those enforcement efforts.[2] For this apostasy, the future US president was vilified by the pro-secession press in Alabama and elsewhere in the South.[3]

In January 1861, Thomas Peters wrote to Senator Johnson an emotional letter of encouragement, one of several Johnson received from Southerners during this period. Peters urged Johnson to maintain the course he had taken and be the "man for the times." According to Peters, strong support for secession was thin and limited to a group of aristocrats resented by nonslaveholders, who would not countenance the custom that, he charged, prevailed in South Carolina, where an elitist legislature elected its governors and "the people have very little to do in politics but choose their own masters." Peters predicted that if the federal government "would execute the laws at all hazards, this would shortly restore peace, although it might be preceded by some bloodshed." Peters concluded that, in any event, "unless [Alabama secessionists] resort to a Military Government, there will be a revulsion" or revolt in favor of the Union.[4]

Many opponents of secession in Alabama were not as outspoken or militant as Johnson or Peters, however, and believed that if the state seceded, they could regain control through the ballot box and reconstruct the Union as long as the federal government did *not* utilize military force and thereby take the focus of disapproval off the secessionists. In other words, they too believed that a "revulsion" could be engineered, but through the state elections in Alabama scheduled for August 1861.[5] This was no pipedream. Alabama's 1860 voting age white population was 113,871, and only 62,012 or 54 percent of that electorate had voted in the December election of delegates.[6] Of those, 35,726 had voted for separate state secession candidates while 26,286 supported cooperation candidates.[7] Thus, only 31 percent of the entire electorate had voted for Alabama to immediately leave the Union regardless of the action of the other slave states. As will be seen, this would equate with the percentage of military age Alabama men who enlisted in the Confederate army before military service became mandatory. Given time the other 69 percent might be convinced to elect new men who would reverse the process. As Huntsville businessman Joseph C. Bradley explained this "Reconstruction" strategy in his own letter to Andrew Johnson, "if we have no immediate Collision with the US—we the Cooperationist[s] of Ala, will start a Candidate for Gov & try & get our state out of the hands of the secessionist—but if difficulties should shortly occur, we will not be able to do so."[8] In addition to avoiding a sectional "collision," these Reconstructionists also feared that Alabama secessionists would seize on some pretext to declare martial law and possibly do away with free elections altogether.

Thus, although Reconstructionists would continue to rouse the electorate utilizing the "leap in the dark" theme in order to undermine public confidence in the pro-secession leaders and their tactics and plans, they had to be careful that nonslaveholders in particular did not become too militant against secession. In essence, like breaking a spirited horse, Reconstructionists would instead appear to jump on board, give the secessionists a semblance of free rein, let them run until they tired, and then rein them back in August. According to a postwar letter from north Alabama lawyer and future Republican governor David Peter Lewis, the Reconstructionists had already selected their candidate for governor: convention delegate and planter-

Figure 6. Robert Jemison Jr. (Courtesy of Alabama Department of Archives and History)

industrialist Robert Jemison Jr. of Tuscaloosa[9] (see figure 6). As would be the case at every stage of the reconstruction process over the next decade, however, Unionists would come very close to managing events, but they would never be able to control all of the key external variables.

Secessionists in Alabama and elsewhere were well aware of the reconstruction plan, and the hotheads among them did everything they could to foil it by provoking a violent reaction by the North they hoped would produce Southern solidarity for permanent separation.[10] This initially involved efforts to spur South Carolina to initiate a military conflict following the clandestine movement of federal troops in Charleston previously stationed at mainland Fort Moultrie to island Fort Sumter on December 26. An unidentified correspondent from Cahawba in Dallas County wrote to South Carolina secessionist Robert Barnwell Rhett on December 28 that "I pray to God that [each of the forts in Charleston] are all in possession of the State. The taking of the forts has been delayed too long, in my judgment. It should have been done the day after secession. Don't flinch an inch from the d___d rotten villainous government of ABE LINCOLN, and his abolition *millions.* Let them come and we will 'welcome them with bloody hands and hospitable graves.'"[11] Despite this plea, the heretofore aggressive South Carolinians somewhat surprisingly responded by merely seizing now empty Fort Moultrie and the other land-based federal installations in Charleston. They did not take the next step of attacking and taking Fort Sumter, even after President Buchanan refused their demand for the federal troops to recede back to Moultrie.

Word from Washington that the federal government intended to tighten its hold on Fort Sumter and other island forts guarding the mouths of key Southern ports presented another opportunity for conflict.[12] On January 3, 1861, Alabama's Governor Moore telegraphed the leader of a pro-secession militia unit in Mobile directing him to seize Forts Morgan and Gaines in Mobile Bay as well as the federal arsenal twenty-eight miles north of Mobile at Mount Vernon. Because Alabama had not yet formally seceded, Moore directed that this be accomplished without bloodshed.[13] Moore's order for the sneak attacks on these lightly defended installations was carried out on January 3 and 4. Fortunately for Reconstructionists, no blood was spilled. Despite outrage in the North, the cautious Buchanan administration did not opt for a military response.[14]

The editor of the *Montgomery Post* nonetheless blasted Moore, charging that he had "either allowed himself to be made the cat's paw of ambitious politicians, or else has acted with an imbecility beneath the dignity of a public functionary of a sovereign State." Moore's order, the editor wrote, intended "as many suppose, to still further inflame the public mind and precipitate the action of the Convention, upon the very eve of its assembling, [was] without any cause whatever—unless it be an imaginary one—and without any authority—unless it be an assumed one." "A dictator on a throne," he concluded, "never assumed more unqualified authority than is being practiced by GOV. MOORE, and yet without either a capacity or will to execute."[15]

Alabama secessionists remained undaunted. When the convention met in the state's house chamber in Montgomery on January 7, 1861, the opening prayer by the Reverend Basil Manly captured the goal of secessionists like him (see figure 7). Manly appealed to the "Lord of all the families of the earth . . . to protect us in the land Thou hast given us, the institution [of slavery] Thou hast established, the rights Thou has bestowed."[16] As expected, the numerical superiority of the secessionists was revealed almost immediately when they narrowly (by eight votes) defeated Robert Jemison Jr.'s bid to preside over the convention. Instead, Perry County lawyer William McLin Brooks, an outspoken separate state secessionist, was selected by a vote of fifty-three to forty-five.[17]

That night following adjournment, opponents of secession conducted a private caucus to discuss their immediate strategy. At this point it was clear the secessionists had the votes to adopt an ordinance of secession. North Alabama delegates were concerned that their constituents would prematurely overreact and trigger a military response by secessionists upon receiving newspaper reports of the debates that would take place in the ensuing days. They agreed that should they "find an unrelenting majority opposing them" in

Figure 7. Rev. Basil Manly (Courtesy of Alabama Department of Archives and History)

the convention they would "exert every effort to prevent any disruption at home."[18] To facilitate this and ultimately control how the proceedings would be portrayed, they also agreed that a resolution would be offered the next day to conduct deliberations in the convention "with closed doors and in secret."[19] Huntsville lawyer Jeremiah Clemens, a Cooperationist, would also be advanced to become the leader of the state militia in order to prevent the secessionists from using that force to impose martial law.[20] As Clemens cryptically explained in a public letter several years later, "I adopted a line of policy which had for its object the restoration of the State to the Union" and "endeavored to assume that position which would enable me to act most effectively in the future. You have here the clue to my whole conduct during the rebellion."[21]

Finally, the opposition agreed to portray the secessionists as antidemocratic and dictatorial in the 1861 election campaign. To lay the groundwork for that, they agreed to propose that any ordinance of secession be submitted to the people in a public referendum before it would become valid. All recognized that the secessionists would never agree to this. In a letter to the *Moulton Democrat* published at about this time, Thomas Peters gave a preview of rhetoric in the upcoming state elections when he denied the right of secession, ridiculed the convention as being without legal authority, and predicted that William Yancey would never allow a referendum on the convention's decisions.[22]

Most histories of the secession movement in Alabama portray the opposition minority in the 1861 convention as being hapless and ineffectual, and the secessionists as being all-powerful. In light of the Reconstructionists' strategy, however, it can be argued that the secessionists actually played into their hands. On January 8, Robert Jemison Jr. began the execution of the plan by offering the resolution for executive sessions, claiming that it was intended to "facilitate the business of the Convention." Tellingly, its adoption spawned intense criticism by the pro-secession press.[23] In addition, a Committee of Thirteen was appointed to make a report on measures to be adopted; it included six Reconstructionists, including Jemison, Jeremiah Clemens, David Peter Lewis, and Richard Sharp Watkins. They were selected to serve with William Yancey, John Tyler Morgan, and five other secessionists, guaranteeing there would be a majority *and* a minority report issued.[24] The next day, Huntsville lawyer-Unionist Nicholas Davis furthered the Reconstructionists' strategy when he offered a resolution calling for the convention to submit any secession ordinance "to the people for their ratification or rejection," in effect daring the secessionists to vote the resolution down. They did, however, and it was lost by a vote of fifty-three to forty-six. Significantly, that vote was by roll call, meaning the identity of those who, according to the Reconstructionists, did not trust the people, could later be made known.[25]

But events outside of Alabama suddenly threatened to undermine Reconstructionist strategy. The inability of Florida's militia to take Fort Pickens in Pensacola's harbor—the southern terminus of the Alabama and Florida Railroad—resulted in Governor Moore ordering several Alabama militia units to hurry to that growing potential hot spot where they joined troops from Florida and Mississippi[26] (see map 2). And when the federal government attempted to reinforce and resupply Fort Sumter on January 9 using a commercial steamship named the *Star of the West*, South Carolina batteries in Charleston Harbor opened fire. The ship was struck several times and chased away, but without either side suffering loss of life.[27] The *Charleston Mercury* happily declared to readers across the South that "War is imminent,"[28] and the following day its headline read "The War Begun."[29] Fortunately for Alabama's Reconstructionists, however, neither of these disconcerting developments prompted a military response from the North.

Alabama secessionists then made a tactical error when a Sumter County delegate introduced a resolution on January 10 that, if adopted, would pledge Alabama to defend South Carolina when that irrationally militant state finally succeeded in provoking a war with the North.[30] Nicholas Davis's motion that this resolution be referred to the Committee of Thirteen, rather than being voted on and passed immediately as secessionists urged, resulted in a priceless and unexpected propaganda bonanza for Reconstructionists. Among those who spoke in favor of this motion was Tuscaloosan William

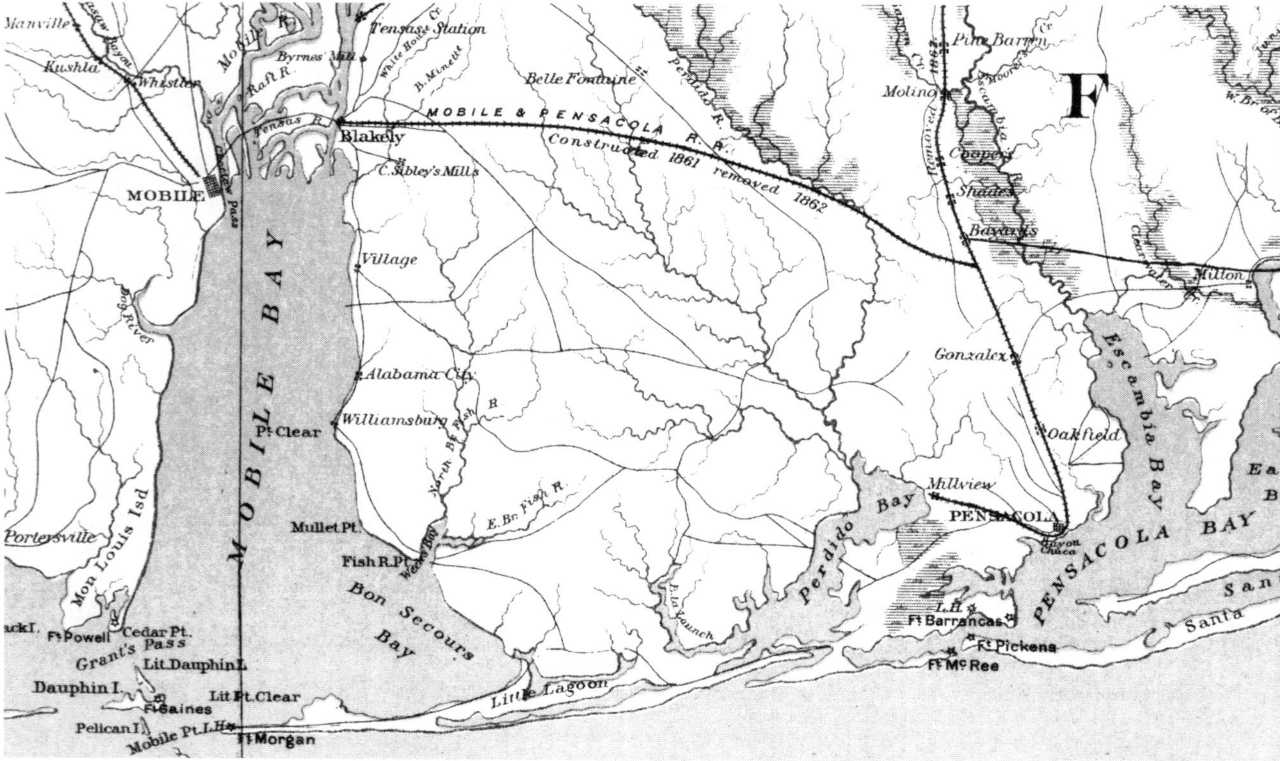

Map 2. Vicinity of Mobile and Pensacola (*Official Military Atlas of the Civil War*)

Figure 8. William Russell Smith (Courtesy of Alabama Department of Archives and History)

Russell Smith, who disingenuously claimed referral would be more likely to result in a consensus on the resolution that would be acceptable to the people (see figure 8). According to Smith's account of the debates, William Yancey lost his temper at this point and, during a half hour of ranting and raving, revealed just how little the peoples' approval actually meant to him on this issue, or even that of secession itself. In the key passage of his harangue, Yancey threatened any dissenters with a "traitor's fate."[31]

Yancey's intemperate remarks shocked even his supporters and elicited an angry response by future gubernatorial candidate Jemison: "Will the gentleman go into those sections of the State and hang all who are opposed to Secession? Will he hang them by families, by neighborhoods, by towns, by counties, by Congressional District? Who, sir, will give the bloody order? Who will be your executioner? Is this the spirit of Southern chivalry? Are those sentiments of the boasted champions of Southern Rights? Are these to be the first fruits of a Southern Republic? Ah! Is this the bloody charity of a party who seeks to deliver our own beloved sunny South from the galling yoke of a fanatical and puritanical abolition majority? What a commentary on the charity of party majorities! The history of the reign of Terror furnishes not a parallel to the bloody picture shadowed forth in the remarks of the gentleman." Nicholas Davis also weighed in with north Alabama's response: "Coming at the head of any force which he can muster, aided and assisted by the Executive of this State, we will meet him at the foot of our mountains, and there with his own selected weapons, hand to hand, and face to face, settle the question of the sovereignty of the people."[32] The convention then adjourned for the day, but this supposedly secret confrontation would quickly become national news.[33]

The next day, the resolution supportive of South Carolina that had sparked the conflict was wisely not brought up for a vote by the secessionists. Instead, after the convention was informed of the secession of Mississippi, the majority and minority reports of the Committee of Thirteen were submitted. The minority report, which called for a pre-secession convention of the slave states and then a public referendum on any secession ordinance, was quickly defeated by a vote of forty-five to fifty-four. When William Yancey then called for a vote on the majority's secession ordinance, a north Alabama delegate, lawyer-Unionist James S. Clark, rose and gave a set speech carefully outlining each of the evils of separate state secession and the benefits of a conference with the other slave states. "If some plan of reconciliation were derived by it which would satisfy the demands of the Southern States, as I confidently believe would be done," he said, "certainly every good patriot would hail it with delight." Clark concluded by imploring in vain that the majority "concede something to the counties of North Alabama."[34]

Finally, on January 11, 1861, the ordinance of secession was brought up for a vote. The reasons for secession, as stated in the ordinance, all involved slavery. "Many and dangerous infractions of the Constitution of the United States" had been committed by "many of the states and people of the northern section"—a reference to John Brown's raid and other slavery-related acts of violence, as well as the enactment of "personal liberty" laws in Northern states intended to foil the enforcement of the federal fugitive slave law. Most recently, according to the ordinance, Lincoln had been elected by "a sectional party hostile to the domestic institutions and to the peace and security of the people of the State of Alabama." As expected, the measure was adopted, but not in the overwhelming manner secessionists had hoped. Sixty-one delegates, including Jeremiah Clemens and six other men elected as Cooperationists, voted for it, but thirty-nine, including Robert Jemison Jr., William Russell Smith, David Peter Lewis, and James S. Clark, voted against.[35]

Alabama secessionists nonetheless professed to be delighted, and Montgomery was the scene of much celebration.[36] But secessionists knew that they had a serious problem on their hands in attempting to reunite the adult populace statewide following almost a year of nonstop political excitement and rising fears of the unknown. South Alabama lawyer-planter Augustus Benners expressed no satisfaction, observing that "it is hard to give any idea of the distressing gloom and sadness that pervades all classes" in his region.[37] The secessionists' task was complicated even more by strong, revengeful feelings by opposition leaders. William Russell Smith, who wrote to his wife on the day before the secession ordinance was adopted, predicted there "will be a day of reckoning for the wicked. . . . There is a calm determination here, to hold our enemies responsible, in the future, before the people whose will has been violated—and whose peace, if not liberty, has been destroyed."[38] Thomas Peters wrote along the same lines to Andrew Johnson on January 15, predicting that "as the Negro is the sole cause of our present troubles, the fury of the non-slaveholders will be turned against him & his Masters and we will have another tragedy of Actaeon and his dogs . . . such as the French tried in their Revolution before Napoleon."[39] During a rally in Huntsville, Unionist Joseph C. Bradley angrily declared that he would "have his neck stretched three feet" and "spend his money to the last dollar" before submitting to disunion, prompting a Huntsville secessionist to worry that "a tempest has been raised that is already beyond control" and that "a successful attempt" would be made "to excite the people of N. Ala. to rebellion versus the State and that we will have civil war in our midst."[40] David Peter Lewis later recalled that "the delegates from North Alabama were apprehensive of a popular outbreak of the people against the action of the convention, embracing the passage of the ordinance, the refusal to submit it to a vote of the people, the sending of troops to Florida, and other similar acts."[41]

Secessionists at the convention sought to smoke out the remaining opponents to their action by setting a date for a public ceremony where all delegates could sign the ordinance of secession. Some Reconstructionists initially stalled, claiming that they would have to first obtain permission from their constituents.[42] The resulting pause allowed Reconstructionist delegates an opportunity to negotiate with the secessionists regarding the terms for their agreement to advise their constituents to at least acquiesce in the decision of the convention. Most immediately, this involved the election by the convention of delegates to what would become known as the Provisional Confederate Congress. Two men were to be selected as at-large delegates and one from each of the seven existing congressional districts. The upshot was that, by agreement, the convention delegates from north Alabama were permitted to elect their representatives. In a move that would be used against him by his postwar political enemies, David Peter Lewis, who had voted against the secession ordinance, signed it after a supplemental county convention back in Moulton instructed him to do so.[43] Lewis was then selected as a Fifth District delegate,[44] but he would not long remain a member of that body because he resigned a few months later. Once the delegates to the Provisional Congress had been selected, and the convention had formally paved the way for Jeremiah Clemens to become the titular commander of the state militia by adopting an ordinance to "provide for the Military Defense of the State of

Alabama,"[45] Alabama's federal congressional delegation was finally recalled from Washington.[46]

But permanent separation was still not assured. Benjamin Fitzpatrick and the other Reconstructionist members of that delegation were returning to their homes, the Alabama delegation to the Provisional Confederate Congress was infiltrated by Reconstructionists, and there were reports of continuing pro-reconstruction activities in north Alabama. Alabama secessionists, therefore, became even more concerned that their plans would ultimately unravel.[47] "I am oppressed," wrote James Lawrence Pugh, a Barbour County lawyer-secessionist and US congressman, "that we are in great danger from the reconstructionists." Pugh's remedy, which he suggested in a letter to a South Carolina secessionist, was to start a war with the North. South Carolina, he wrote, had "the power of putting us beyond the reach of reconstruction by taking Fort Sumter at any cost."[48] But thanks to the efforts of Benjamin Fitzpatrick and others, the situation at both Forts Sumter and Pickens had devolved into an informal truce, at least for the time being.[49] Members of the pro-secession press would, nonetheless, continue to ruminate and obsess over the threat of reconstruction, and the pressure for action would eventually become too great.[50]

II
THE WAR BEGINS

Timeline: February 1861–February 1862

February 8, 1861	Alabama legislature adopts first Stay Law.
February 21, 1861	Huntsville lawyer Leroy Pope Walker is selected as the Confederate secretary of war.
March 5, 1861	Abraham Lincoln's inauguration as president of the United States of America.
March 26, 1861	President Lincoln selects Huntsville lawyer George Washington Lane as Alabama's United States district judge.
April 12, 1861	Fort Sumter is attacked, and Leroy Pope Walker predicts the Confederate flag will soon be flying in Washington, DC.
April 15, 1861	President Lincoln calls for seventy-five thousand volunteers.
April 19, 1861	President Lincoln announces naval blockade of Southern ports.
May 1, 1861	Alabamian John Archibald Campbell resigns from the United States Supreme Court
May 2, 1861	Tennessee secedes from the United States.
May 7, 1861	Alabama and Florida Railroad is completed to Pensacola, Florida.
May 7, 1861	Virginia joins the Confederacy.
May 14, 1861	Provisional Confederate president Jefferson Davis visits Pensacola, Florida.
May 20, 1861	Confederate Provisional Congress votes to move the Confederate capital from Montgomery, Alabama, to Richmond, Virginia.
May 23, 1861	Union army invades Virginia.
May 26, 1861	Union naval blockade of Mobile begins.
June 4, 1861	Robert Jemison Jr. withdraws from the Alabama governor's race
June 27, 1861	Episcopal bishop Leonidas Polk is appointed a Confederate general.
July 4, 1861	Unionist meeting at Looney's Tavern in Winston County.
July 4, 1861	Richard Busteed gives pro-Union speech in Long Island, New York.
July 21, 1861	Battle at Bull Run near Manassas, Virginia.
August 5, 1861	John Gill Shorter elected Alabama's new governor, defeating Thomas Hill Watts.

August 8, 1861	Provisional Confederate Congress adopts the Alien Enemies Act and the Sequestration Act.
September 2, 1861	University of Alabama begins new academic year with 158 cadets.
September 6, 1861	Union Army captures Paducah, Kentucky, at the mouth of the Tennessee River.
September 10, 1861	Leroy Pope Walker resigns as Confederate secretary of war.
September 18, 1861	Leroy Pope Walker is appointed a brigadier general.
October 9, 1861	Battle of Santa Rosa Island near Pensacola, Florida.
October 28, 1861	Alabama legislature convenes in special session.
October 30, 1861	Jeremiah Clemens resigns as major general of the Alabama militia.
November 6, 1861	First popular election for Confederate officials is held, and Jefferson Davis is elected president.
November 8, 1861	Unionists burn railroad bridges in east Tennessee.
November 11, 1861	Mobile and Great Northern Railroad completed.
November 21, 1861	William Yancey of Montgomery and C. C. Clay Jr. of Huntsville are elected by the Alabama legislature to the Confederate Senate.
December 2, 1861	John Gill Shorter is inaugurated governor of Alabama.
December 4, 1861	Prisoners of war begin arriving in Tuscaloosa, Alabama.
December 11, 1861	Alabama legislature adjourns.
December 24, 1861	Secessionist E. C. Bullock dies of typhoid fever in Mobile.
February 3, 1862	William Yancey leaves England for the South.
February 6, 1862	Fort Henry in middle Tennessee is attacked and surrenders to Union forces. February 6, 1862.
February 13, 1862	Battle of Ft. Donelson begins.

4
"Sprinkle Blood in the Face of the People"

Mindful that she faced the prospect of losing her two youngest sons to war if it came, Sarah Espy wrote that "I cannot help feeling dissatisfied for the present, and apprehensive for the future. The fear of my children being reduced to poverty sits heavy upon me."[1] Associate Justice John Archibald Campbell, who had remained in Washington, was making the first of several settlement overtures to future secretary of state William Seward to prevent the Cradle of the Confederacy from becoming the deathbed of the Southern way of life.[2] Campbell was undoubtedly well informed by his Alabama contacts regarding continuing reconstruction activities there, including the first of the newspaper endorsements of Robert Jemison Jr. in the upcoming governor's race.[3] In his communications with Seward and perhaps other Republican leaders, Campbell likely shared his opinion that at least in Alabama, "secession is a cake not turned, and there will not be warmth enough to complete the baking."[4] Campbell's goal was to prevent the collision with the North that Reconstructionists feared—and a growing number of secessionists fervently hoped—would supply that heat. By this time, President Buchanan had refused to surrender Forts Sumter and Pickens, however, and that had painted Republicans into a corner.[5]

The North and the Deep South would continue on a collision course as the new leaders of the two sections made their way by train to their respective capitals, stopping periodically to hint at their possible policies and the prospects for the future. During his trek from Mississippi to Montgomery, Jefferson Davis rode across north Alabama on the Memphis and Charleston Railroad, giving brief speeches in Tuscumbia, Huntsville, and Stevenson in which he attempted to calm growing fears of war[6] (see figure 9). Davis did not reveal—until 1862—his expectation that, "from the beginning," he "looked forward to a long and bloody war."[7] In his inaugural address, which took place on February 18, 1861, at the state capitol after he was sworn in by Alabama Supreme Court chief justice Abram Joseph Walker (see figure 10),

Figure 9. Jefferson Davis (Courtesy of Alabama Department of Archives and History)

Figure 10. Inauguration of Jefferson Davis at Alabama's state capitol (Courtesy of Alabama Department of Archives and History)

Davis alluded to the reconstruction movement, observing that "if I mistake not the judgment and will of the people, a reunion with the States from which we have separated is neither practicable nor desirable."[8]

That was not the universal feeling. Yet for many Unionists who did not wish to be subjected to political and economic repression, silence or subterfuge would soon become the only options, especially when within earshot of known secessionists.[9] Even Lawrence County lawyer-secessionist David Hubbard would be taken in by feigned assurances of acquiescence in north Alabama. He wrote to Governor Moore that the secession movement was not popular in Lawrence County with those whom he classified as "Union Savers," but that the politicos were coming around. The "ambitious who expect to be known throughout the State are not only becoming reconciled but are preparing their followers to be reconciled, and will support the measure as soon as they can do so."[10] But among the newly exposed Reconstructionsts in Lawrence County was David Peter Lewis, who resigned his position in the Provisional Congress in late February when he refused to take an oath of allegiance to the Confederacy.[11]

Leroy Pope Walker was determined that no Reconstructionist would receive the important position of secretary of war in President Davis's new administration. On February 21, after lobbying by former US senator C. C. Clay Jr. and William Yancey, Davis picked Walker.[12] "General" Walker, as he liked to be known, had at one time been the head of the militia in northwest Alabama, but that had been many years ago. Even with that experience, however, he had no qualifications to run a war department. This would soon become evident. But in addition to being a leading north Alabama secessionist, Walker had one attribute that made his selection quite acceptable to secessionists across the Deep South—his financial interest in the Memphis and Charleston Railroad, which had been built in the 1850s from Charleston, South Carolina, through north Alabama to Memphis, Tennessee. Promoters of the road had long envisioned that Charleston Harbor would soon rival New York City as an international port of entry and that economic development along the road would flourish. This potential would be greatly enhanced if Charleston became a duty free port, an impossibility as long as the federal government could use Fort Sumter to provision revenue cutters.[13] This made neutralizing Fort Sumter a priority. As the *Charleston Mercury* had predicted shortly before the selection of Jefferson Davis as president of the Confederacy, "Fort Sumter and Fort Pickens will elect [Davis]."[14] They also aided Walker.

Especially for those who had invested in railroads to Charleston and Pensacola and then pragmatically supported secession as a means of maximizing their profits, the continuing impasse over the federal forts guarding those harbors was becoming increasingly intolerable.[15] The militia units that had hurried to Pensacola were becoming restless and imploring their leaders to permit them to fight or go home.[16] The delay in hostilities had permitted the US Navy to get ships there to resupply and support Fort Pickens, making the taking of that facility difficult without very heavy losses.[17] But with a former soldier and secretary of war (Davis) as president, and Walker—described by the *Charleston Mercury* as a man "with undoubted nerve, spirit, energy and will"—as his secretary of war,[18] some assumed that decisive action would soon be taken.

In his own First Inaugural Address, Abraham Lincoln attempted to avoid war by reaffirming his views on slavery—"that I have no purpose, directly or indirectly, to interfere with the institution of slavery in the States where it exists." But that was not of immediate concern to Confederates at this point. It was his policy toward the seceded states and, in particular, whether he intended to enforce the revenue laws at the ports of entry that was of immediate importance. Lincoln made clear that secession was not constitutionally permitted and that the federal law would be "faithfully executed in all the States." He further declared that the "power confided to me will be used to hold, occupy and possess the property and places belonging to the Government, and to collect the duties [on] imports."[19]

The response by Alabama Confederates was defiant. In Montgomery a Confederate flag was raised shortly after Lincoln's speech,[20] and a couple of days later the *Charleston Mercury* ominously reported that the Tredegar Iron Works in Richmond, Virginia, had received orders from Georgia and Alabama to "cast seventy-five pieces of cannon immediately."[21] This may have been exciting for some Confederate civilians, but not for all. Sarah Espy wrote that "I feel badly, for when the war commences[,] when is it to end and what dire consequences will not fall on us! I fear our happy days are all gone."[22] Reconstructionists certainly agreed. At the Limestone County courthouse in Athens, a Union flag was raised in protest by what were described as the "Union and working men of Athens."[23]

As the secession movement seemingly ground to a halt in Virginia, Maryland, Kentucky, Tennessee, Arkansas, Missouri, and North Carolina, and fewer slave states were out of the Union than in it, continuing signs of strong, affirmative reconstruction sentiment continued to emanate from north Alabama after Lincoln's inauguration.[24] As previously mentioned, Joseph C. Bradley wrote to Tennessee senator Andrew Johnson cautioning against military hostilities lest the reconstruction movement be undermined. On the same day Lincoln confirmed what every Southerner expected were his intentions, a group of residents in Limestone County led by Athens lawyer-Unionist and United States congressman George Smith Houston invaded a rally orchestrated by secessionists at the courthouse in Athens who were attempting to convince a crowd to adopt resolutions creating the illusion that the citizens were ratifying secession and pledging support for the Confederacy.[25] Before those resolutions could be adopted, Houston reportedly addressed the group and urged that they instead adopt a resolution to the effect that "in the event proper guarantees were given by the Northern states the Union should be reconstructed. He spoke disparagingly of a Southern Confederacy and said that it could not sustain itself." After Houston's remarks were "loudly cheered and applauded several times," the organizers of the rally were forced to adjourn without adopting any resolutions. When the meeting was reconvened on March 18, the pro-secession resolutions were rejected and instead, by a vote of 139–69, resolutions were adopted demanding that the Confederate constitution be submitted to the people for their approval or disapproval, and declaring in favor of reconstruction whenever the North gave suitable guarantees for the protection of slavery.[26]

In Franklin County in northwest Alabama, a Union meeting was conducted on March 22 in which those in attendance adopted resolutions deeming secession to be "inexpedient and unnecessary" and declaring that "we are opposed to it in any form." In addition, the attendees resolved that the "refusal to submit the so-called Secession ordinance to the decision of the people, is an outrage upon our rights and liberty, and manifests a spirit of assumption, unfairness and dictatorship."[27] Citizens also met in nearby Winston County and adopted resolutions denouncing Governor Moore for calling the secession convention and the legislature into session; disapproving "our State going out of the Union," as well as those other Southern states that had, "for we think it is uncalled for"; and resolving that those in attendance "do pledge ourselves, our honor and property, to carry out the true principles of our Government."[28]

More newspapers, including the Montgomery *Confederation* and the *Montgomery Weekly Post*, announced their support for Robert Jemison Jr. as the "Peoples' candidate" for governor.[29] The Tuscaloosa *Independent Monitor* began enunciating what were likely the themes for Jemison's campaign in a widely reprinted editorial:

> We hold, first, that the ordinance of secession should have been submitted to the people for their ratification or rejection; secondly, that the ordinances passed by the Convention should have awaited the issue of this decision; thirdly, that the people had the right, and it should have been

> given them, to have chosen the delegates to a Congress which was to have framed for them a government for weal or for woe. And we now demand that the Government formed—its President, Vice President, and officers—should be submitted to the people for their approval or disapproval. If it is not, we shall, come weal or woe, attempt to fire the people's heart, to educate the people's mind to know their rights and to dare maintain them. We are no submissionist, but right is right and wrong is wrong, and we will not betray our trust. We assert that the people have a right to be heard, and, being heard, to be obeyed. And we intend to keep them posted in what we consider to be an infringement of their rights and of their privileges, let the worst come to the worst. If it is treason against the new Confederacy, make the most of it. We know we are right, and, untrammelled and unawed, we will defend the right.[30]

William Russell Smith meanwhile feverishly continued his efforts to complete his book on the proceedings and debates at the Alabama Convention, which he likely intended as a campaign document to demonstrate how antidemocratic and dictatorial the secessionists really were.[31] Any doubt on that question, however, had been dispelled when the majority in the Alabama Convention decided not to permit the people to vote on whether the "permanent" Confederate constitution should be ratified.[32] The editor of the Tuscumbia *North Alabamian* echoed the protest against the manner in which secession was accomplished and Jefferson Davis was selected president of the Confederacy—all without submitting these and other questions to the people. Fearing the imposition of a military despotism, the editor warned that "so long as our people claim the right of self-government, they will watch with zealous vigilance all apparent usurpation of their rights. They will very naturally enquire whether a government formed against their will, is designed for their protection or their subjugation." He expressed particular perturbation that "the separation" of Alabama "from the great body of other States" was "designed to be final; that under no circumstances will they ever consent to a re-union under the stars and stripes [that] have ever been the pride of our friends and the terror of our foes." He praised those delegates, like both from Franklin County, who had refused to sign the ordinance of secession, because it showed "who were in favor of further efforts to restore to the South peace and fraternal relations with the other States."[33] This was hardly a rousing endorsement of what had been wrought in Montgomery.

President Lincoln knew of some of these undercurrents, as well as the March 21 "cornerstone" speech in Savannah, Georgia, by Confederate vice president Alexander H. Stephens intended to quell a reconstruction movement there. Stephens assured anxious Georgians that "our new government is founded upon exactly the opposite idea" from that of the government of the United States in terms of the issue of slavery. The ideological foundations of the Confederacy "are laid," declared Stephens, and "its corner stone rests upon the great truth that the negro is not equal to the white man—that slavery, subordination to the superior race, is his natural condition. (Applause). This, our new government, is the first in the history of the world based upon this great physical, philosophical and moral truth."[34]

Lincoln intended to be particularly careful that his initial political appointees in Alabama and the other Southern states were qualified and respected. He was also savvy enough to know that conciliating proslavery Reconstructionists was essential. Shortly after Lincoln's election, the staunchly Confederate *Montgomery Advertiser and State Gazette* had warned,

> Henceforth, the Government, with all its patronage and power, will be in the hands of the enemies of the Southern States. We will have no voice in the election of President and Vice President—no voice in the appointment of Cabinet officers—no voice in the appointment of foreign ministers and consuls—no voice in the appointment of judges, attorneys, and clerks of the Supreme, Circuit and District Courts of the United States—no voice in the appointment of post-masters and route-agents, who will permeate every nook and corner of the country, and may be abolitionists—no voice in the imposition of tariffs and taxes, which will be laid by Northern avarice to foster Northern industry by filching from the South her hard earned wealth—no voice in the foreign policy of the Government, which will be directed to extend and fortify the Northern States, and to circumscribe, weaken, and finally, to crush the South. Henceforth, the *Abolitionists* will undertake to govern *slaves*. What will be the result? Look at St. Domingo.[35]

From the standpoint of the Alabama legal community, the most important federal position was that of United States district judge, which had become vacant when William Giles Jones of Mobile announced his resignation on the day Alabama seceded.[36] On March 16, Jefferson Davis appointed him to essentially the same post within the newly created Confederate judiciary.[37] On March 26, Lincoln, at the suggestion of Alabama congressmen Williamson R. W. Cobb and George Smith Houston, nominated the venerable George Washington Lane, a former Limestone County circuit judge, old-line Whig, Bell supporter, and (ironically) slaveholder who was the brother-in-law of

Reconstructionist Nicholas Davis,[38] to replace Jones.[39] Lane's nomination was quickly confirmed by the US Senate, and he accepted the nomination with the knowledge that lending his considerable prestige to the Lincoln administration, and in essence becoming its face in Alabama, would generate considerable criticism from secessionists around the state.[40]

They were aghast at these developments. The *Montgomery Mail* reported that "George W. Lane, Lincoln's North Alabama Judge, many think ought to be hanged."[41] A Georgia newspaper editor expressed great concern over what Lane's selection meant. The "policy of the Administration at Washington, as indicative in its appointments of judicial officers for the seceded States," was "more significant of danger to the Confederate States, and inevitable war between the two republics, than any military policy or preparations yet developed." In fact, added the editor, it was "more insidious and heartless than direct forcible coercion, and its design and tendency ought at once to be understood by the people of these States." The Lincoln administration, he accurately declared, hoped that "'a little leaven will leaven the whole lump' thereby ultimately spreading support for Reconstruction."[42]

From the Confederacy's standpoint, Lane's appointment occurred at a bad time. The reality of the cost of financing a new government was setting in, and divisions over economic policy were already developing. The issue of relocating the capital of the Confederacy to another state had been broached in the Confederate Congress, threatening to reverse the promising commercial trends in Montgomery resulting from the economic engine generated by its being the Confederacy's political headquarters.[43] Alabamians who had earlier calculated the value of the old Union might now be considering that of this new, alarmingly outnumbered and underfunded Confederacy. The *Charleston Mercury* had declared that slavery was "the immediate cause of the existence of the Confederacy,"[44] but Lincoln's inauguration on March 4 had not been the signal for more John Brownism as the secessionists had prophesied—and hoped for—during the 1860 campaign. Militia that had been rushed to Pensacola to help take Fort Pickens and often to see their first battle were beginning to pack up and depart, disillusioned because of the lack of action,[45] leaving the *Mobile Mercury* to observe that "the patriotic ardor of the South is ominously cooling down."[46] Even more disturbing, a few public men such as Thomas Peters, George Smith Houston, and George Washington Lane were openly opposing the Confederacy, and nothing could be done about it without risking even more of a backlash by nonslaveholders.

At this juncture, secessionists panicked and chose to go to war in order to cause the collision Reconstructionists had tried to avoid. Several sources indicate that in April 1861, a fanatical Lowndes County delegate to the Alabama Secession Convention, attorney and South Carolina College graduate James Graham Gilchrist, stormed into a meeting at Leroy Pope Walker's office in Montgomery. According to Jeremiah Clemens, who was also present, Gilchrist "censured" Walker "for not having precipitated a war, declaring that the people were already beginning to repent of secession, and would be back in the Union at the end of the year [when the newly elected legislature was scheduled to meet], unless the breach was made wider by an act of war."[47] "You must," implored Gilchrist, "sprinkle blood in the face of the people."[48]

Secret preparations were begun for simultaneous attacks on both Fort Sumter *and* Fort Pickens.[49] This belied Jefferson Davis's later claim in his 1886 speech in Montgomery while laying the cornerstone of the monument to the thousands of Confederate dead that the "carnival of death"—"that war which Christianity alone approved"—was "a holy war of defense."[50] The pretext used to justify attacking Fort Sumter was that the Lincoln administration was attempting to resupply the force at Fort Sumter. But it had been supplying Fort Pickens for several weeks without incident.[51] Thus, the ensuing bloody conflict was a war of choice, not of defense, and a primary reason for the attack was to prevent reconstruction.

Montgomery had direct rail access with Pensacola, so the Confederate War Department could easily issue verbal orders to General Braxton Bragg, the bombastic and temperamental Confederate commander at Pensacola. Charleston, however, was not amenable to such quick communications. It was Leroy Pope Walker who ordered the fateful attack there in a telegram from Montgomery to Confederate General P. G. T. Beauregard, commanding him to "at once demand [Fort Sumter's] evacuation, and if that is refused, proceed in such a manner as you may determine, to reduce it."[52] When the federal commander did not accede to this demand, Beauregard opened fire on the fort two days later. The headlines of the *Charleston Mercury* announced with approval the April 12 bombardment, which enacted what the newspaper said was the "first great scene in the opening drama of what, it is presumed, will be a most momentous military act."[53] But the assault on Fort Pickens in Pensacola harbor had to be aborted when advance word of it was leaked by the local press (the reporter became the first civilian arrested by the Confederate military). The federal commander of the fort then took the precaution of signaling the nearby fleet of warships, which quickly landed reinforcements and ammunition on Santa Rosa Island.[54]

Leroy Pope Walker got carried away while he and President Davis were being serenaded by a happy crowd outside the Exchange Hotel in Montgomery on the night of April 12. Walker rashly predicted that in less than three months, the Confederate flag would be waving from the capitol in

Washington.[55] Thanks to extremist members of the Southern press, Walker's firebell in the night was heard loud and clear throughout the North. A disgusted Montgomery correspondent to a Georgia newspaper wished that the report of Walker's speech had never been circulated because it "naturally raised a storm, which raged through the North and found no Neptune for its master."[56] A Troy, Alabama, newspaper editor was also struck by Walker's imprudence. He later wrote that Walker's declaration "was but the signal for the uprising of the entire North in defense of their capital, and did more to infuse a war spirit into our enemies than anything that had been said or done up to that time, with the exception of the bombardment of Fort Sumter." It "added fuel to the flame which that act had kindled," a flame that would burn intensely for years.[57]

President Lincoln prudently issued a proclamation calling for seventy-five thousand volunteers on April 15.[58] That proclamation gave assurance that collateral damage would be avoided, but seventy-five thousand men motivated by revenge would be very difficult to control. Besides, the pro-Republican *New York Times* had already warned that "the beginning of civil war is the end of slavery."[59]

Despite this, some Alabama Confederates remained deluded that there would be no full-blown war. Young Kate Cumming in Mobile wrote of a military unit leaving there for Virginia: "I thought, like many others, that they were going more on a frolic than anything else, as we could not think it possible that the north really meant to subjugate us." Cumming's later service as a Confederate nurse would graphically demonstrate how wrong she and others had been.[60] Alabama was now in jeopardy, and not all Alabama Confederates were thrilled about this ominous turn of events. Elizabeth Rhodes of Tuskegee lamented that "preparations are going on on both sides for war, war, civil war. What an awful thought."[61] After learning from her military-age son that "the Carolinians have taken Fort Sumpter [*sic*] and that our other volunteer company is ordered to Fort-Pickens," all Sarah Espy could muster was the following: "So I suppose the war is now opened; may the Lord be with us in our weakness, and grant that we may conquer the strong." Espy never became the classic Spartan mother. When her oldest son announced a few days later his determination to enlist, she was not happy: "I do not like it much, but will have to submit."[62] That would not be the last of her many painful sacrifices.

Yet many Alabamians initially believed that upholding the new Confederate government was essential. Pro-Confederacy newspapers like the *Montgomery Mail* did not mince words regarding the "great mission" and "great duty" of the Confederate government now that war had begun. "Compulsory African labor has done, and is doing more to advance and elevate society and to enrich individuals and nations, than any single institution of modern times," and "it will be the great duty of this Confederate government to foster and protect our own peculiar civilization, until African labor redeems all the fertile lands of the South, changes the jungles, and the wilderness, and the solitary places into the well cultivated farms and elegant abodes of enlightened man, and until slavery, as Mr. Hill truly observes, becomes 'its own power in the earth.' "[63] According to the *Mail*, "war has been made upon the Southern people because they have not and will not abolish this institution," and it was "now manifest" that the Lincoln administration would use the government "to destroy—to put into a course of 'ultimate extinction' African Slavery" and to "enforce the political and social equality of the races." The *Mail*'s editor concluded that "this war is waged upon the South to liberate the negroes politically and socially. Then when that is accomplished, amalgamation, as in Massachusetts, is to be brought about."[64]

Alabama slaves were said to have gotten the message too. Two months earlier a Dallas County man had made national news when he reported to the *Cahaba Gazette* "the fact that while he was taking up a subscription to aid in uniforming the Richmond Greys, of Dallas County, John, a slave belonging to Mr. A. W. Coleman, promptly gave ten dollars, remarking that he 'being a slave could not go himself, but that his money, his hogs, his cows and his corn were all at their disposal when needed, without money and without price!' "[65] Given that slaves had no legal right to own property, this report is very dubious. There were actually widespread rumors of slave insurrections. Daniel Hundley noted "Startling news!" of "a most hellish insurrectionary plot among the slaves" in Limestone County. "It seems," he continued, "that the negroes have concluded that Lincoln is going to free them all, and they are everywhere making preparations to aid him when he makes his appearance." Local vigilance committees determined that "Peter Mudd, Andrew Green, and Nicolas Moore, slaves, and one or two free negroes, aided by base white men are the leaders of the proposed servile insurrection." Several were arrested and hung without a courtroom trial.[66]

As secessionists had anticipated, with blood now sprinkled in their faces, and fears rising of an invasion by an army of John Browns, many Unionists in Alabama deferred notions of reconstruction and focused on the defense of their homes. Men who had been the leaders of the Reconstruction vanguard threw up their hands and the movement ground to a halt, at least for the time being. John Archibald Campbell resigned his position on the US Supreme Court, bitter and despondent that he had been unsuccessful in preserving peace so that reconstruction could occur.[67] Benjamin Fitzpatrick had returned to his Alabama plantation following his withdrawal from the US Senate,[68] but like Campbell, he did not change his views on secession. He instead receded from the public eye following the bombardment of Fort Sumter and, until the trends in the war created the possibility of a negotiated peace, avoided public comment. He remained active behind the scenes, however, seeking to undermine secession leaders and planning a return to the Senate.[69]

Robert Jemison Jr. formally withdrew from the governor's race and took a lucrative job in support of the Confederacy.[70] The Confederate Provisional Congress had adopted a bill authorizing President Davis to borrow up to $15 million to support the Confederate government through the sale of ten-year, interest-bearing coupon bonds, with repayment to be made by the imposition of a duty on cotton exported from the Confederate States.[71] The fledgling government would need men of influence in the business community to market the bonds, and those men would deserve compensation for their valuable services. Jemison, along with Tuscaloosans Newton Whitfield and Henry A. Snow, were appointed to serve as commissioners to hawk these questionable investments in Tuscaloosa County.[72] Significantly, once men of means purchased the bonds or accepted Confederate treasury notes in payment for land, goods, or services, they had an important vested interest in an all-out effort to defend and perpetuate the new government. It was that government that was obligated to pay the bonds and notes. In the future, peace without Confederate independence meant bankruptcy for imprudent investors, as Jemison's postwar experience would demonstrate.[73]

Jemison was not the only prominent Unionist to be co-opted by the Confederacy. Florence businessman Robert Miller Patton, a future governor, accepted an appointment as commissioner to sell Confederate bonds under the cotton loan program after the war began, and in that capacity he is said to have raised millions of dollars.[74] Later in the year, Joseph C. Bradley would accept appointment as the Confederate tax collector for Alabama for the "Fifty Million Loan" program, said to be the most lucrative office in Alabama.[75] Henry Cox Jones subsequently received a contract from the Confederate government to manufacture cotton and wool fabrics.[76] Several other moderates, including George Smith Houston (whose son became a Confederate captain), William Russell Smith, David Campbell Humphreys, and Nicholas Davis, sponsored the formation of volunteer military companies to, as Humphreys put it, "drive the invader from our soil." It was likely this move toward militarization by moderates was intended as more of a show of force to ward off invasion than a sudden enthusiasm for an actual battle.[77]

The original reconstruction movement had effectively been decapitated, and men who had been lifelong Unionists were now taking steps that would have significant legal and political consequences for them when Reconstruction finally occurred. Those who refused to take those steps and chose instead to remain loyal to the Union were destined to run a gauntlet of criticism, social and economic ostracism, and violence.

5
"Food for Sad and Gloomy Fits"

One mid-twentieth-century Alabama historian wrote that when Alabama went to war, "all hearts were in the cause."[1] But as later historians have concluded, this myth is not supported by the evidence.[2] John Forsyth, who was intensely pro-Confederacy, lamented more than three years after the attack on Fort Sumter that there were two classes of people in Alabama. One was "a class whose hearts have *never* been in the struggle for independence." The other had, by then, lost heart in that cause.[3] Also contrary to myth, Unionist sentiment did not persist only in north Alabama and southeast Alabama. In several other regions an unknowable number of Unionists below the level of the Reconstructionist leadership continued to smolder with resentment, and some bravely voiced their dissent. In May 1861, William McLin Brooks wrote to Jefferson Davis about the dangerous sentiment among nonslaveholders in Black Belt Perry County. In their minds, "nothing is now in peril in the prevailing war but the title of the master to his slaves." Some "declared that they will 'fight for no rich man's slaves.'"[4] Rumor also had it that there were hundreds of men in Choctaw County, Alabama, willing to "fight against the South & slave owners."[5] Historian Warren Rogers Jr. found a Unionist network even in Montgomery,[6] and Michael Fitzgerald has identified a group of dissenters in Alabama's largest city, Mobile.[7]

Although he was a slave owner, Tuscaloosa lawyer E. W. Peck was another who refused to remain silent—at least initially. According to a postwar, pro-Republican Party Tuscaloosa newspaper, Peck finally made public the outrage he had heretofore kept private: "When secession came, with civil war, and its dreadful proscription of [the] Southern Unionist, E. W. Peck stood like the Roman sentinel on the battlements of Herculaneaum, facing the rolling flood of burning lava, and suffered it to envelop him, rather than desert his post. He denounced secession at the first, he denounced it in the middle, he denounced it in the end. This is the record of E. W. Peck."[8] Word of Peck's nonconformity spread throughout the community. According to another postwar account, "It was with great difficulty an influential citizen prevented [Peck from] being mobbed outright."[9]

Peck later testified that he was "treated with all sorts of contumely." After being burned in effigy, Peck was "informed that efforts were made to hang me in fact" and that "perhaps it would be prudent for me to leave the country." When he did not leave, he was subjected to social ostracism, punishment the professional career of few lawyers can endure.[10] According to another Tuscaloosan, the treatment he received "mortified Judge Peck very exceedingly."[11] Peck testified that he became somewhat of a recluse, with his only public appearances in Tuscaloosa consisting of going to his office and returning home after completing his legal work.[12]

The rough manner in which Peck was handled was eventually common in areas where Confederates held sway. According to prewar Unionist Lewis Parsons, members of the vigilance committee in Montgomery undertook to "stop all intercourse" between citizens of that town and "the Lincoln Government" and to investigate, arrest, and "bring before" that committee "all persons against whom evidence of suspicious actions may be found." In addition, the "police and military companies of the city were empowered and requested to arrest all suspicious persons and bring them before the Committee for trial." Their decision, he concluded, was final.[13] Nicholas Davis later wrote that "men who did not themselves belong to the Confederate Army but who had been foremost in the rebellion, constituted themselves a band of informers and vigilance committees. . . . No man who had not been a secessionist dared to speak a word or do an act [such] as assertion of their rights as defined by Confederate law, for a class held in their hands the civil and military powers."[14] Franklin County lawyer Joshua Burns Moore wrote that the people in his area were "overwhelmed by the tide of secession," and that particularly in communities where Confederate soldiery had control, the people had no safe opportunity to "express their real sentiments."[15] And those identified as disloyal were already being prosecuted for treason in Judge William Giles Jones's Confederate District Court.[16]

But pockets of outspoken opposition remained in areas where Unionists were in the majority. Alabama governor Andrew Barry Moore was well aware of disturbing reports of continuing, openly pro-Union activities in the hill counties of north Alabama about which he began receiving letters in June 1861.[17] Unionists from Lawrence, Walker, Winston, Fayette, and other north Alabama counties met at Looney's Tavern thirteen miles south of Thomas Peters's home in the northern portion of Winston County in order to devise a plan of action. Although there is some disagreement between historians regarding whether this meeting occurred on July 4 in 1861 or 1862,[18] it more likely occurred in 1861, less than a month before the state election. This conclusion is supported by not only the content of resolutions all historians agree were adopted at the meeting but also the fact that the number of letters to Governor Moore warning him of Unionist activities in the area surged shortly thereafter, with several dated July 1861. Moreover, the evidence regarding the 1862 meeting indicates a totally different location and date.[19]

The legend is that Winston County residents at the meeting voted to secede from the state of Alabama and declared that Winston was henceforth a "free state." Actually, however, the resolutions adopted at the meeting were more conservative. One contested the legality of secession and rhetorically argued that if secession were legal, then "a county could cease to be part of the State."[20] But the resolutions did not go so far as to declare Winston to have seceded from Alabama. Rather than immediately banding together to fight for the Union, the Looney's Tavern group resolved *not* to take up arms against the secessionists or for the Union. They instead requested to be left alone, "unmolested, that we may work out our political and financial destiny here in the hills and mountains of northwest Alabama."[21]

The policy officially expressed at the meeting was actually one of neutrality, but there is strong evidence that at an early point, Unionists in this region actually worked to cripple the Confederate war effort.[22] Not only did most refrain from joining any military unit, they actively discouraged others from doing so and later would encourage those who did to desert. As a much-cited letter from a Winston County farmer and veteran of the War of 1812, James Bell, to his pro-secession son made clear, one of the strategies utilized was to encourage class conflict. "I don't see what you nede to care for you, hant got no slaves and all tha want is to git you pupt up and ga to fight for their infurnerl negroes and after you do there fighting you may kiss their hine parts for o tha are."[23] This anti-slaveholder theme had already caused consternation among north Alabama secessionists. The pro-Confederacy Huntsville *Democrat* had previously complained that an "insidious, mean effort has been made to instill the idea into the minds of poor men, that, in the event of war, they would have to do all the fighting, and the rich would be exempt."[24]

Judging from the letters sent to Governor Moore following the Looney's Tavern meeting, area Confederates were clearly worried that some sort of revolt was brewing. A militia officer wrote to Governor Moore that "a very considerable number of the inhabitants of the Counties of Winston, Marion, Fayette, and some of Walker and Morgan" were "actually raising and equipping themselves" to "sustain the old Government of the United States."[25] But no significant action whatsoever was taken against the Looney's Tavern

Unionists by Governor Moore. He did send a letter to a Walker County resident, Josephus Hampton, boldly pledging that "so long as I am Governor of the State the laws against treason and sedition shall be faithfully executed if it takes the whole military power of the State to enforce them." But he was careful to inform Hampton that the letter should not be published.[26] Instead, Moore appears to have relied upon such north Alabama moderates as George Smith Houston to calm the troubled waters. Houston's son had been shipped out in June to north Virginia with Athens lawyer Thomas Hubbard Hobbs and the Ninth Alabama Infantry.[27] Like any parent of a Confederate soldier, Houston would naturally possess a strong hope for the safety of his son's unit. But Houston was averse to coercing anyone to adopt a pro-Confederacy allegiance. Although he knew the extent of treasonous activity in northwest Alabama, he never publicly or privately criticized it. He even misrepresented to Governor Moore that the idea of disloyal activity was fabricated by one political faction to undermine another and that there was no need to take any action, much less send in the troops.[28]

Thought of open dissent temporarily ended for many when news of a great battle at the aptly named stream, Bull Run, near the town of Manassas in north Virginia on Sunday, July 21, slowly began to trickle in. Alabama Confederates justifiably declared and celebrated victory,[29] and Confederate nationalism was probably at its zenith in the state. C. J. Hanks, a young Alabama soldier from Pickens County, wrote to his father about the battle, and the father proudly provided the letter to the Carrollton *West Alabamian* for publication. Hanks bragged that the "Yankees could not stand a *charge bayonets*, and always when our men made a charge, they would take to their heels." Hanks was sure "there is glory enough in this battle for one century."[30] Another from Pickens County wrote home that the battle was "the greatest ever fought on American soil and is one that will stand upon the brightest page of history."[31]

But even great victories in war can be bittersweet. For parents, brothers, sisters, wives, and sweethearts of the combatants, the most important question was—at what cost? In the buildup to what the *Richmond Enquirer* called the "severest battle that was ever fought in this country,"[32] the Alabama press had published information on the casualty rates during the Revolutionary War reflecting that the largest American loss during any single battle was 1,200 men at Germantown in October 1777.[33] In a battle that seemingly involved more running than fighting on both sides, Confederate casualties at Bull Run shockingly exceeded that figure, as did those of the Union army.[34] This was due in part to advancements in military technology. A physician from Mobile, Dr. Josiah Nott, grimly observed after treating many of the wounded on the battlefield that the "*science of war* has been so greatly improved, that we are now enabled to murder our fellow creatures much more successfully than in former times. These *Minnie* [*sic*] balls make such terrible wounds, that almost a half of those placed on the list of wounded will die."[35]

The death toll slowly revealed by the Alabama press reflected losses from every quarter of the state.[36] Particularly hard hit was the Fourth Alabama Infantry, which included the Magnolia Cadets of Selma.[37] Thirty-two men from Selma were either killed or wounded in this battle.[38] According to one correspondent who visited Dallas County in the days after, the "excitement was intense" at Selma and Cahaba, "The 'Governor's Guards' and the 'Magnolia Cadets,' of Selma, were in the thickest of the fight on the Confederate left, and many families of the former place were mourning the loss of brothers, sons and husbands."[39] The families of the wounded were reportedly "enduring all the agony of prolonged suspense" as they awaited word of the seriousness of the injuries. They received little solace when the editor of the *Selma Daily Reporter* reminded that all should "remember that these casualties are the constant attendants of war, and also that wounds like these could not be more honorable—more glorious."[40]

John Henry Cowin, a member of an Alabama regiment, wrote that the Battle of Bull Run was "the bloodiest battle ever fought on the continent."[41] Unionists and Confederates alike pondered how the sobering horrors of war might affect public opinion. Would Confederate nationalism erode as caskets arrived from Virginia? Evidencing what famed South Carolina diarist Mary Boykin Chesnut called a "fool's paradise of conceit," John Forsyth relished the battle's outcome, comparing it to the English defeat of the Spanish Armada. "Its moral effect will be tremendous," he boldly predicted, "and it will immensely strengthen the hands of the peace party" in the North.[42] Forsyth claimed it would "give to our cause the arms of sixty-thousand men in Kentucky, Missouri and Maryland."[43] But when that did not immediately occur, Forsyth began to prod the Confederate military to "press the advantage" to the "further defeat and destruction of the invaders of Virginia."[44]

As Forsyth and others recognized, war is always a gamble. Given the manpower and industrial advantage held by the North, the odds of Confederate independence were much higher in the early going before the North was fully mobilized and the reality of the South's position was brought home to Southerners.[45] When the Confederate army failed to move on to Washington, DC, Forsyth reminded his readers why the South was fighting to begin with, perhaps an indication he sensed disaffection might set in.[46]

Historian Gary Gallagher once questioned whether other members of his profession should be so focused on explaining why the Confederacy did not last any longer than it did. In his opinion, the important question was, in essence, how it lasted so long. According to Gallagher, until that question received adequate attention, "the history of the Confederacy [would] remain imperfectly understood."[47] Some might attribute the Confederacy's longevity to Confederate nationalism. Others might claim that it was a product of hatred of Northerners or fear that a Union victory would lead to the abolition of slavery and an outcome similar to that in St. Domingo.[48] And still others would point to strategic factors. This book is not intended to answer fully the question Gallagher posed. But any comprehensive and objective study must also consider the coercive measures used to squelch dissent in the South and to force dissenters to fight for, or at least financially support, the Confederacy through taxation, acceptance of Confederate money, and other means.

To supplement the work of vigilance committees in Alabama and elsewhere that were actively harassing those suspected of disloyalty,[49] the Provisional Confederate Congress enacted two very important but poorly conceived and vaguely worded laws in August 1861. One of these was known as the Alien Enemies Act. This legislation permitted the initiation of deportation proceedings against all persons over age fourteen who retained their allegiance to the United States.[50] The other law, the Sequestration Act, allowed Confederate authorities to seize property of "alien enemies" in the South.[51] According to one estimate, this property amounted to approximately $300 million in value. Under this law, Confederate district judges were to appoint receivers in each judicial district to take possession of the property using court process. It was made the legal duty of all Southerners, including attorneys, to become informers and disclose to the receivers any information they might have about the whereabouts of that property.[52] The term *alien enemies* would be construed broadly to include anyone who opposed the authority of the Confederate government as well as those who professed allegiance to the United States. Such persons were held not to be entitled to a writ of habeas corpus to challenge their incarceration.[53] These two laws were especially effective against influential property owners in the elimination of vocal dissent. According to historian Walter Fleming, the court of Alabama district judge William Giles Jones, who of course upheld the constitutionality of the Sequestration Act, ultimately became so busy with these types of cases that it "did little else."[54]

It was in this context that the 1861 state elections took place in Alabama. The only gubernatorial candidates were John Gill Shorter and Thomas Hill Watts, neither of whom was promoting peace. The result of the election was, therefore, anticlimactic. As had occurred in every state election since the formation of a two-party system in Alabama, the Democrat, Shorter, prevailed over the Whig, Watts.[55] But a victory by Watts would have changed nothing. Alabama would remain in the war, seemingly for the duration.

President Lincoln's military leaders, meanwhile, prepared to take the war to the heart of the Deep South while forcing the Confederacy to tie down a large portion of its existing military assets in north Virginia and for coastal defense elsewhere.[56] Even the influential prowar *Charleston Mercury* urged its readers not to "deceive themselves with the notion that either the first or second battle of Bull's Run is decisive.... The invading army is neither destroyed nor captured. Our forces are comparatively quite small."[57]

But rather than encouraging the use of the window of opportunity provided by the victory at Bull Run to seek a peace accord, the *Mercury*'s editor called for a rapid escalation of the Confederacy's war effort. He concluded by predicting that a "great and effective victory in the next great fight may end the business, and conclude the troubles of our present position."[58] This song would be sung many times in the coming years. The *Montgomery Advertiser and State Gazette* was highly critical of rumors that the Confederacy was making peace overtures to the North: "Peace propositions must come from the great heart of the enemy to be worth the paper they are written on. Our only proposition should be the sword, until the North is thoroughly whipped and routed from every point of contact with the South, and sues for peace." The *Advertiser* correctly concluded that peace would result "not of one or two victorious battles, but in all probability of a long and bloody war, of which we are now only at the beginning. Let no man be deluded with the idea of a speedy peace."[59]

Some Alabamians who had been assured there would be no war at all were increasingly becoming frustrated, despondent, and weary after only a few months. William Russell Smith wrote home from Tuscumbia reporting that he had "lost *three* companies—who refused to be mustered into service—and actually disbanded and left for home!"[60] In Kentucky with his company recruited in north Alabama, now Captain Daniel Hundley noted that two of his men had already deserted before seeing any action, and that "I weary more and more of the life militaire." As the weather got colder and wet, he rued that "it tires our patriotism to remain in camp in such weather as this." By December, he admitted that "again and again I do pray God end this unholy war!" On New Year's Eve he wrote that the "North has now six hundred thousand men in the field and the South nearly that many, and unless the hand of God should put a stop to the fratricidal strife, it seems that it has just begun."[61] In south Alabama, Augustus Benners wondered why the Confederate army did not simply proceed to Washington and end the war: "The suspense about the movements in the Potomac is awful—it really seems that every day tends to demoralize the army and unless there is some good reason for not advancing, a defeat there would overthrow Davis in the good opinion of his people. Why don't they move, is asked but not exactly answered. The Yankees are threatening the coast & to come down the Miss[issippi] with a great force. When oh when will this ever end?"[62]

Some may have prayed that at least the prediction by secessionists of foreign intervention to end the war would come to pass. As he would throughout the war, John Forsyth certainly held that out as a real possibility in 1861 when he referred to "the pressure of the cotton screw by which we expect to squeeze our recognition out of Great Britain."[63] The power of King Cotton had repeatedly been touted by the pro-secession press,[64] and the ill-equipped William Yancey had been sent to Europe in April to pressure the British king's subjects into joining in a foreign civil war. On a regular basis, several Alabama newspapers had reported on the diminishing cotton inventory in England, confident that as supplies began to run out, the great British navy would be dispatched to defeat the North's increasingly effective naval blockade of Southern ports in order to avoid economically inspired civil unrest among British textile workers.[65] The *Mobile Advertiser and Register* had reported that the available stock of cotton in Liverpool would be used up by the first of December, and that to avoid factory shutdowns at that time, shipments of the 1861 crop would necessarily have to begin in October. "Thus," John Forsyth confidently predicted, "the pressure of the blockade will well begin its work of coercion upon Great Britain within a month from date."[66]

But as Benjamin Saffold had correctly predicted in his Summerfield speech back in December, Britain's public policy opposing slavery would outweigh these economic considerations. "Other nations do not understand our rights as we do," he had argued. "They will regard us as fighting not for liberty but for slavery."[67] Great Britain in particular would not risk a war to protect the South's peculiar institution, choosing instead to develop other sources of supply in India and Egypt.[68] As E. W. Peck later wrote, "King Cotton proved to be a great humbug. The blockade, as it were, successfully shut him up, and imprisoned him, in the midst of his own subjects, and thereby all [the secessionists'] anxious hopes and expectations were disappointed and blasted."[69]

William Yancey had come to the same conclusion following his chilly reception in England as one of the Confederacy's ambassadors. Even after the Confederate victory at Bull Run, the British had continued their policy of nonintervention. Yancey, therefore, submitted his resignation, giving him just enough time to distance himself from the diplomatic failure that would soon become evident.[70] Like Leroy Pope Walker, Yancey had set his sights on a seat in the Confederate Senate, and the fact that, in his absence, dark clouds were forming at home, actually aided Yancey's chances.[71] What he believed Alabamians needed now was a strong advocate in the senate who would force the Confederate government in Richmond to pay more attention to their threatened interests and whip those Yankees before they ever set foot in Alabama rather than continuing with its dangerous policy of what Yancey referred to as "gross neglect."[72] By openly criticizing the government for focusing military efforts in Virginia, however, Yancey risked increasing the level of disaffection.

Some Alabamians still believed that peace ought to be given a chance. This explains why the *Mobile Advertiser* declared in August 1861 that "war is unquestionably less a calamity than peace optimists are prone to argue."[73] Peace sentiment also accounts for the fact that the Huntsville *Democrat* was, at the same time, advising its readers not to write their "relatives or dear friends in the army" what it called "gloomy or discouraging letters." The soldiers, the *Democrat* explained, "have good food for sad and gloomy fits, in their own quiet meditations, without being assisted by despondent missives from home." Instead, it instructed, "write the soldiers cheerful and encouraging letters."[74]

But as time passed with no end in sight, expressions of that sort would prove to be more and more difficult. Pregnant with her sixth child, Emily Beck Moxley of Coffee County wrote to her husband, William, a Confederate major, of her anguish at their separation. "Dear Husband, this paper is wet with your wife's tears. They are shed for you, for one that I love more than heart can tell or words can express. It is the hardest trial I have ever had, by far."[75] After the death of several of their acquaintances, William unsuccessfully attempted to console her, but the war was taking its emotional toll on him as well even before he had ever tasted battle: "How dreadful is war. Such as you have witnessed is [an] every day occurrence some where in consequence of this unholy war, separating the dearest companions on earth, making widows & orphans every day, making the happiest homes desolate, turning joy into mourning."[76]

In a letter from Shelby County to an Alabama soldier, the author wrote that "we have the hardest time here I ever experienced in my life. As for money, there is none to be had; as for coffee, there is not a family, to my knowledge, that has it; they use meal or potatoes, or anything that will turn the water black. As for salt, it is worth $10 per sack. The people are fattening their hogs, but I don't see how they are to get salt to cure the pork, as there is no money, and nothing but money will get salt. I hope this war will soon end, as perhaps it will alter times."[77] (This letter was later found on a Virginia battlefield.) As a result of this sentiment and military setbacks just over the horizon, Unionists would be increasingly successful in encouraging the growth of an organized peace movement in Alabama. As they would learn, however, they too would have a veritable feast of "food for sad and gloomy fits" before it was all over.

6
Evil Times

It is a myth that 1862 was the high water mark of the Confederacy. Part of the problem was that Confederate military strategy was initially based on what is known as a "cordon" or perimeter defense, one focused on guarding all Confederate territory and attempting to repel any and all invasions. As military historian Donald Stoker has noted, this strategy required dispersal—rather than concentration—of forces, leaving the South weak almost everywhere.[1] This fatal defect quickly became evident in terms of the defense of what became known as the western theater, the huge area between the Mississippi River and the Appalachians. The Tennessee and Cumberland Rivers provided ready invasion routes for Union forces. Yet the departmental commander in charge of defending that huge region, Albert Sidney Johnston, was seriously outmanned and outgunned.[2] This critical failure of resource allocation would have very serious consequences for Alabama and the Confederacy.[3] Among other things, it would undermine confidence in Jefferson Davis and the Confederate government to defend the new nation, encourage antiwar sentiment, and lead many of Alabama's political leaders to give priority to Alabama's interests over those of the Confederacy. In other words, the Alabama house would become even further divided against itself.[4]

From late 1861 onward, Alabama was facing threats to its northern and southern borders. While the US Navy and the forces at Fort Pickens kept Confederate troops tied down on the Gulf Coast,[5] Alabama newspapers reported on Union forces based in Illinois and Kentucky who were actively probing southward.[6] Their approach energized Tennessee Unionists. As Alabamians would soon read, Union men in east Tennessee suddenly struck in stunning fashion, burning several railroad bridges that were being used by the Confederate military to transport troops and supplies from the Deep South to Kentucky and Virginia.[7] Confederate forces were sent to east Tennessee to brutally crush their uprising. Those Unionists who were apprehended and not shot or hung, including Andrew Johnson's son-in-law, Tennessee circuit judge David Patterson, would soon experience a frightening odyssey that led to their incarceration in Tuscaloosa.[8]

Prison facilities in the Virginia theater were becoming overcrowded, and so alternate locations further from the front were being identified.[9] In the fall of 1861, Tuscaloosa was chosen as the site of a prison to house not only Union army troops captured during the Battle of Bull Run but also Unionists apprehended in Tennessee.[10] The Confederate government initially planned to house the prisoners primarily in two vacant hotels on Greensboro Avenue, but Robert Jemison Jr. lobbied for the use of an idled paper mill facility owned by a corporation of which he was president.[11] Upon inspection, however, that dilapidated building was determined to be unsuitable.[12] An abandoned cotton factory building was also considered as an alternative. But before any of the prisoners arrived, someone had purchased it to put it back in operation to produce staple goods for civilians and the military.[13] As a result, the Confederacy reverted back to its initial plan of using the hotels to confine the prisoners, although the number of prisoners sent to Tuscaloosa eventually greatly exceeded their capacity while eroding the local food supply.[14]

Some of the five hundred prisoners from the Union army who began arriving in Tuscaloosa on December 4, 1861, described the reception and treatment they received as quite good. In a letter back home that received national attention, one New York soldier wrote that they had been placed in "Washington Hall," an elegant local hotel; another wrote that he and others were staying in the old state capitol building.[15] All reported they were "quite comfortable."[16] In the coming months, members of E. W. Peck's home church, Christ Episcopal, reached out to provide aid to these men.[17] Such fraternization irked some locals. The *Tuscaloosa Observer* complained that the prisoners' relatively comfortable housing was "better than they deserve."[18] Reports of the parole of two Union officers a few weeks after their arrival was too much for the new editor of the *Independent Monitor*: "This must be gratifying intelligence to the *Yankee Sympathizers* in our vicinity, who delight to gallant about the streets and invite to the Oyster Saloons and their private houses to dining, these vandals, whose hands are stained with the blood of our people, who come fighting under banners, inscribed upon which is their motto 'Beauty and Booty.' "[19]

The bridge burners from east Tennessee did not receive such a warm reception. This may have had something to do with the fact that in the wake of their transportation from Montgomery to Tuscaloosa by steamboat, Montgomery and Selma had been beset by arsonists.[20] There were also rumors that Alabama Unionists were organizing with the intention of coming to Tuscaloosa to release the Tennesseans and do God knows what else.[21] Confederate authorities had hoped to house the bridge burners in the new insane asylum, but many Tuscaloosans could not stand the thought of waking up one morning to find that facility burned to the ground. By this time, Leroy Pope Walker had resigned as the Confederacy's secretary of war, so Governor John Gill Shorter telegraphed Walker's successor, Judah Benjamin, telling him that no more prisoners were to be brought to Tuscaloosa.[22] A couple of weeks after their arrival, 123 of the east Tennesseans were herded on a steamboat bound for Mobile.[23] But other Union soldiers would be sent to Tuscaloosa later.

Meanwhile, as outgoing Governor Moore was warning, other Yankees were on the way to Alabama, but not as prisoners.[24] In retrospect, rather than relying on green volunteers from north Alabama to block an invasion, Confederate major general Braxton Bragg and most of his well-drilled sixteen thousand troops at Mobile and Pensacola should have been transferred to Forts Henry and Donelson, the river forts above Alabama on the Tennessee and Cumberland Rivers. This might have forced the Union army to invade Alabama, if at all, by land rather than by river. Confederate general and future University of Alabama president Josiah Gorgas would later write that the failure to do this was the "great mistake of the War." Gorgas blamed President Davis, whom he described as "no military genius,"[25] an assessment with which many Alabama Confederates would come to agree.[26]

Davis might not have been a military genius, but he understood sectional politics quite well. In early December, following appeals for north Alabamians to organize for the defense of their region, newly inaugurated Governor Shorter was receiving warnings from residents there of open support for the United States. A Fayette County man reported that the leader of a Unionist group was "huranghing [*sic*] for Lincoln" and threatening Confederates.[27] In January 1862, a Confederate officer reported to Judah Benjamin from Greene County in the Black Belt that two separate companies consisting of several hundred Union men were in the same region (the Black Belt was predominantly prosecession and prowar, so the fact that a Black Belt county like Greene would produce militant Unionists is surprising).[28] Weakening the defenses of south Alabama in order to bolster the protection afforded less enthusiastic north Alabama was impolitic. And by periodically firing on Confederate targets at Pensacola during the weeks leading up to Union General U. S. Grant's thrust south, Union forces were determined to force Davis and Bragg, as well as south Alabamians like Governor Shorter, to remain wary of an invasion from the coast.[29]

While Bragg assessed the threat level in south Alabama, the Huntsville *Democrat* was reporting that an attack was expected at Fort Henry on the Tennessee River.[30] Two days later, it was reported that General Grant's amphibious forces were landing near that fort.[31] If that fort fell, it would place the virtually undefended Memphis and Charleston Railroad in Alabama in jeopardy. The "vertebrae of the Confederacy," as Leroy Pope Walker called the railroad in a letter to Judah P. Benjamin, had been the primary east-west transportation facility of the Confederate army.[32] Therefore, its capture was a primary military target for Union forces. By taking its rail junction with the Mobile and Ohio Railroad at Corinth, Mississippi, the areas served by those roads could be controlled by Union forces. Union troops could also be transported from Corinth to take Memphis at one end and Chattanooga at the other.[33] Even President Davis signaled that the loss of the Memphis and Charleston Railroad might be a foregone conclusion. On February 3, 1862, he advocated Confederate financing of the completion of another east-west railroad corridor further south between Meridian, Mississippi, and Selma.[34] Coupled with the earlier announcement of a private venture to construct the long-discussed road between Selma and Montgomery,[35] this would permit the transportation of troops and supplies from Mississippi across south Alabama to Atlanta and then to Chattanooga and the Upper South. But construction would take months to accomplish.[36]

On February 6, 1862, Union ironclad gunboats under Flag Officer Andrew Hull Foote, the commander of naval forces in the "Western Waters," began the bombardment of Fort Henry, the fall of which Unionists in Tennessee and Alabama hoped would soon lead to the redemption of their states from the Confederacy. After just two hours, the commander of the fort, whose forces included two companies from Tuscumbia, surrendered unconditionally.[37] The far-reaching implications of this loss to Alabama quickly became crystal clear.[38] Three Union gunboats that had been involved in the bombardment set out in hot pursuit of five Confederate steamers loaded with supplies that reportedly "flew like a deer before a pack of hounds" on the Tennessee River toward north Alabama.[39] Not only were the Union pursuers unmolested in this quest, but according to correspondents of several Northern newspapers, they were actually cheered by onlookers in south Tennessee and north Alabama as they sped onward.[40] Their mission was made much easier when Florence, Alabama, businessmen, less interested in the success of the Confederate war effort than in maintaining the economic benefits associated with continued access to the Memphis and Charleston Railroad south of the Tennessee River, conducted an impromptu stockholders meeting and decided to ignore an order by Confederate General Albert Sidney Johnston to burn the Tennessee River bridge between Florence and Tuscumbia in order to facilitate the escape of the steamers and their cargo. The Confederate steamers were, as a result, unable to pass under the bridge due to unusually high water, and so they had to be destroyed.[41] The Union forces that arrived at Florence at two o'clock that afternoon, February 8, did not molest the railroad or the town. Nor did they take any slaves or cotton. After meeting with a group of citizens who approached with a white flag, the naval commander, Lieutenant Seth Ledyard Phelps of Ohio, gave assurances of "his devotion to the good Florence people, and said he had no intention of interfering with any property or individuals," except Confederate military stores.[42] True to his word, the Union military took only Confederate supplies upon leaving that afternoon.[43]

The fall of Fort Henry, and the ease with which the Union gunboats had penetrated Alabama utilizing its river system, sent shock waves throughout the state. In the ensuing days, Tuscumbia lawyer Joshua Burns Moore wrote that he "never in my life saw a set more completely whipped out at our reverses, than the citizens of Tuscumbia. They are completely panic stricken." He further noted that "some are now doubting our ability to contend with the North—are refusing Confederate money, which of itself implies a doubt of our ultimate success." According to Moore, some of the Franklin County lawyers who had pushed for secession and "were at that time rampant for a fight, wanted the contest to come," and "swore that 1 Southern man could whip 5 Northern ones" were now "fixing to skulk the issue." They were "packing up preparing to run off and leave the poor and moderate men to do the fighting" instead of "shouldering their gun and facing like men the contest they invited." Moore also correctly assessed the impact of this conduct on others in northwest Alabama. "Now do they expect the poor people are fools, not to draw their own conclusion from their action. Do they suppose, the poor men of these counties have forgotten their promises, that there would be 'No war' at the time they were hastening the State into the attitude of rebellion. That when the contest came if in the course of events, it did arrive (which they affirmed it would not), they would be the first to shoulder their guns and fight? My opinion is they are about played out. Let them go." The worst of it, Moore concluded, "is they leave the rest of us in a most deadly contest in pursuing which, we had not the slightest agency—and at a time when retreat and submission, leads us, seems to me, to a certain destruction."[44]

Others would have to fight, a cruel reality with which Sarah Espy in northeast Alabama was now coming to grips. She wrote that one of her sons had "learnt that the rumour of our disasters in Tennessee were but too true," and now two of her sons "both talk of entering the service shortly; Oh! This dreadful war! what miseries are to follow when such lads . . . have to leave their peaceful homes for the unhealthy and disagreeable camp-life." One of her older sons was already in the Confederate military and she did not even know where he was. "God help him, and all the rest of us, for we are sorely troubled. May our enemies be turned backward."[45] Even before the Yankees had reached Alabama, Catherine Fennell, an intensely loyal Confederate young lady from Marshall County, had written that the "cause of the South appears gloomier than it ever has before" due to a lack of foreign recognition and aid. Afterward, she noted that the Yankees' brief visit to Florence had "created great excitement in all this part of the state."[46] But more of this type of unwanted excitement was on the way. Fears of a slave uprising swept the Black Belt, prompting women there to petition Governor Shorter to exempt men from military service to provide security in that region.[47] At Greensboro, Augustus Benners chronicled that "there is considerable gloom in our community on [account] of these things and all sorts of evils are anticipated, among them that their army of feds may march down on Tuscaloosa—another that they may capture Mobile and come up the river. These things," Benners wrote, "are very depressing and the truth is manifest that we have fallen on evil times."[48]

That was an understatement. Just as John Brown's raid had set many Alabamians against the North, Lieutenant Phelps's unexpected act of conciliation was potentially a public relations coup for the federal government. As Unionists had maintained, loyal men were not the target of the Union military. Their rights would be respected, and all that was necessary was that the now seemingly hapless Confederate military in the Deep South capitulate. To facilitate this, many Southerners were already actively assisting the Union war effort by providing critical intelligence of Confederate strengths and weaknesses. According to one newspaper, "the late movements of the enemy disclose the fact that they have received important information from spies in our midst. They would never have ventured to Florence, Ala., with their gunboats, if they had not known that country to be undefended by soldiers. Let a stricter watch be kept upon suspicious persons," it advised, "and let them be summarily dealt with, if detected."[49] The *Tuscumbia Constitution* icily declared that "the Hessians met with one Lincolnite in Florence, who met them at the river and gave them information as to where they could best land,—for which he was paid in Confederate *bacon*."[50] This man, a tailor originally from Vermont, was subsequently arrested, jailed, and charged with stealing that bacon.[51] Given the growing shortages of other items and the prospect of finally being able to sell their cotton crops for real money at the now sky-high prices prevailing in the North, many more would be willing to risk arrest by providing such support.[52]

The Confederate attorney general lamented in his diary that all was lost. "Our people," he continued, "are dispirited and losing confidence."[53] This was certainly the case in Alabama. To hurry the resumption of trade, what the *Montgomery Advertiser and State Gazette* called "faint hearted poltroons" were spreading the word that "everything is lost" and that the South "is virtually conquered."[54] Others, jeered the *Selma Daily Reporter*, "sigh for the restoration of the Union!"[55] The Confederacy's "worst enemies," wrote John Horry Dent, an aristocratic Barbour County planter, "are a set of Unionists and Speculators among us that are numerous and doing vast injury to our cause and our people."[56] His cure for the disease of defeatism was draconian. "A sound discreet policy," he suggested, "would be imprison or hang the Union traitors."[57] Although not necessarily discreet, his advice would soon become accepted practice.

More bad news was on the way. General Grant's forces attacked Fort Donelson on February 13, and after fierce fighting, the Confederate commander surrendered it on the afternoon of February 16.[58] After the now retreating General Albert Sidney Johnston concluded that Nashville was likewise indefensible, Union General Don Carlos Buell's forces entered the panic-stricken city with their brass bands playing "Dixie."[59] The Tennessee legislature, which was then in session, was forced to flee with Tennessee governor Isham Harris through Corinth, Mississippi, to reconvene in Memphis.[60] All now recognized that Alabama was likely next, especially given the retreat of Confederate forces in Tennessee in the direction of northwest Alabama.

Confederates were not happy. Emily Moxley wrote to her husband in Mobile about the news of Nashville's capitulation to the Yankees. "They are gaining the day fast," and "I see no chance for us now, or but very little, at least."[61] Many soldiers in Johnston's army deserted, and many of those that remained were demoralized and full of defeatism.[62] "The people," wrote Catherine Fennell, "are very much dissatisfied with the movement of our army," and the "whole country is in great excitement and prospects are gloomy but we trust in Providence."[63] Sarah Espy wrote that the capitulation of most of Tennessee was "a dreadful stroke on us; it seems that our enemies will overrun us." A few days later she wrote, "This dreadful war! when will it end?"[64] In south Alabama, Augustus Benners was even more blunt: "Every nerve must be strained to sustain ourselves as the Cause is ruined."[65]

The depth and breadth of Confederate defeatism and of Unionism in Alabama in 1862 is now impossible to determine. Despite financial and other incentives provided by a new Confederate law, enlistments to the army were inadequate.[66] And even before the fall of Nashville, the Northern press published accounts about what was called a "Union league" in the South. One newspaper editor claimed that this subversive organization extended "throughout every State in the Southern Confederacy numbering nearly" seven hundred thousand members.[67] Now the *New York Herald* was calling for the Union men of the South to rise in rebellion against Confederate authorities for the purpose of aiding Northern military forces.[68] But like the Southern press in general, the Alabama press belittled these claims as delusive. "The men for whom the advice of the *New York Herald* was intended," claimed the *Montgomery Advertiser*, "are too insignificant to initiate any movement for betraying the South into the hands of its enemies."[69] In light of the uprising that had already occurred in east Tennessee, however, that may have been wishful thinking on the *Advertiser's* part. But open opposition to the Confederacy continued to be very dangerous. In a letter published in the *Mobile Tribune*, a Confederate refugee from Nashville gave Unionists warning: "Let Unionists show their hands and heads now; it is hoped they will. We have friends enough left to watch them; and when the war rolls back, the country will be finally purged of them, for they will have to leave with the Lincoln army."[70]

Alabamians had little protection from acts of retaliation by Confederates for conduct deemed disloyal. A network of lawyers in Alabama and elsewhere had already developed to represent suspects of treason jailed by the Confederate military and to seek writs of habeas corpus from sympathetic civilian judges. Some of those suspects were being released and tried by potentially more sympathetic civilian juries. But Confederates were determined at least to limit that possibility. Jefferson Davis orchestrated the passage on February 27, 1862, by the Confederate Congress, of another coercive law, this one permitting him to suspend the writ of habeas corpus in those areas, including Tennessee and Alabama, threatened by enemy invasion, and to in effect impose martial law.[71] Persons suspected of disloyalty could, therefore, be jailed indefinitely to await a trial by a military court. Martial law would soon be declared in most parts of Alabama, including north Alabama.[72] "So as you see," wrote now Confederate congressman William Russell Smith of Tuscaloosa from Richmond to his wife, "the thing is assuming *French* dimensions," alluding to the horrors of the French Revolution.[73]

The new law was not totally effective. According to a resident of Tuscumbia, the sentiment for peace in the region was growing and becoming increasingly outspoken. "Many of the section talk cooly now about taking the oath of allegiance to Lincoln," he warned Alabama governor John Gill Shorter.[74] Writing Shorter from Huntsville, Alabama Supreme Court associate justice Richard Wilde Walker, a brother of Leroy Pope Walker, confirmed that many north Alabamians were inclined to "make peace on the best terms our oppressors will impose."[75] At about this same time, the *Montgomery Weekly Advertiser* published an excerpt from a private letter stating that "North Alabamians, as I learn, have turned traitors. They are sending off our troops, and say they will have nothing to do with the war, and are selling their cotton to the Yankees at 20 cents [per pound]. The Yankees tell them to send to New York for whatever they want."[76] Reports of another Union meeting in Winston County also surfaced, this time in the southwest portion of the county where it joins Marion County, probably in the vicinity of Natural Bridge. There, according to one worried Confederate civilian, "the people resolved to remain neutral; which simply means that they will join the enemy when they occupy the country."[77]

As the crisis of confidence in the Confederacy among north Alabama Confederates grew, the Confederate military finally decided to transfer General Bragg and the majority of his troops from the coast to the newly forming front along the Memphis and Charleston Railroad in north Alabama and north Mississippi.[78] But this was disconcerting to south Alabamians.[79] Augustus Benners wrote that "our people [are] discouraged by reverses" in Tennessee. As a result of the departure of Bragg, "there is much anxiety felt about Mobile."[80] Bragg's redeployment was nonetheless absolutely essential. A change in strategy from cordon to concentration was to be attempted. On March 1, General Grant had been ordered to take the critically important railroad junction at Corinth,[81] and Confederate military leaders were also anticipating that now snow-covered Huntsville was to be targeted by Union General Don Carlos Buell's forces, who were then occupying Nashville.[82]

Grant's forces, which included those under General William Tecumseh Sherman, were already moving toward their eventual position near Pittsburgh Landing, Tennessee, along the Tennessee River just above the Mississippi state line.[83] Union gunboats were shelling Confederate positions further south.[84] The Tuscumbia *North Alabamian* correctly predicted that "a desperate battle will be fought in that vicinity before many weeks elapse. We do not feel at liberty to say what our Generals are doing to oppose them, but we can say that we need every man that can shoulder a gun to go and meet them."[85] Tension was palpable, but few medications were available to relieve the stress. Alabamians, as a consequence, resorted in record numbers to alcoholic beverages manufactured from corn and other grains, thereby jeopardizing the food supply. Governor Shorter was, therefore, compelled to issue an executive order in March prohibiting the distillation of "Ardent Spirits."[86]

Thanks in part to a company of mounted scouts called the Tishomingo Rangers led by a former Lawrence County, Alabama, sheriff, Captain Philip Dale Roddey, General Albert Sidney Johnston, still the operational commander, knew that Union forces were located around Shiloh Church, three miles southwest of Pittsburgh Landing and eighteen miles northeast of Corinth[87] (see map 3). Johnston also had the element of surprise on his side, as

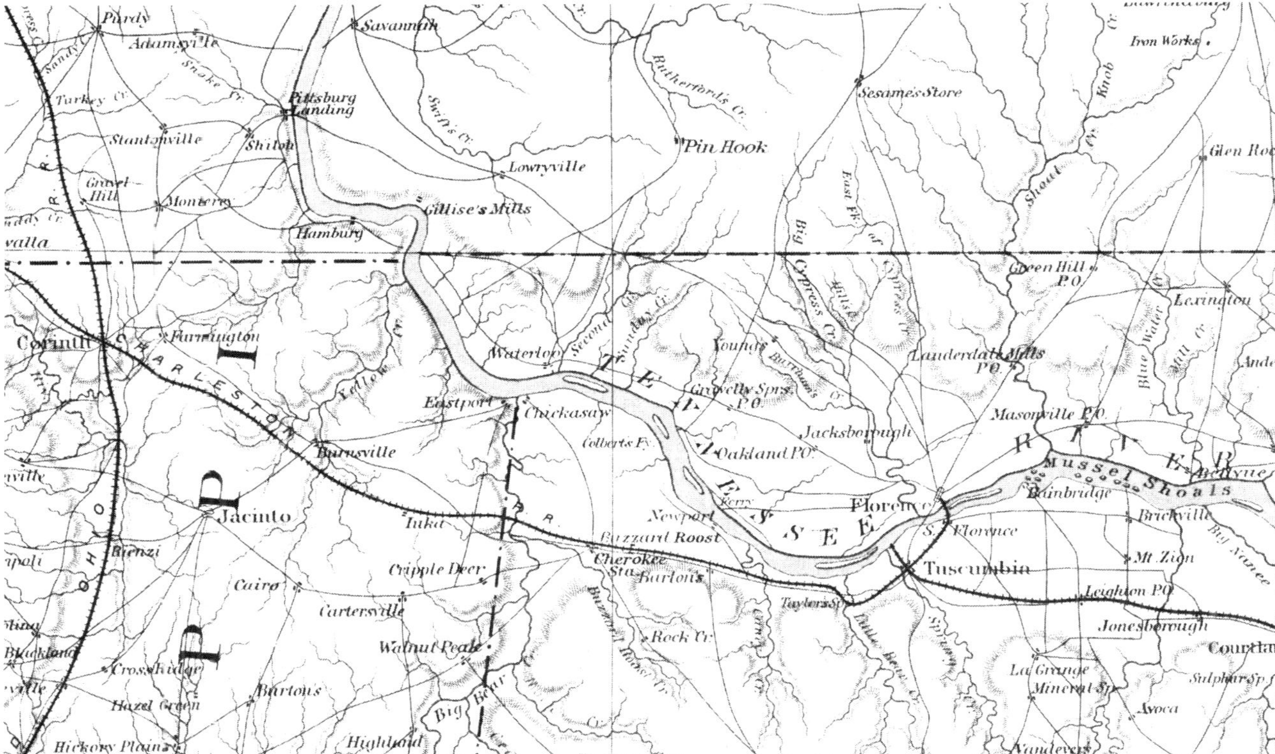

Map 3. Vicinity of Shiloh and northwest Alabama (*Official Military Atlas of the Civil War*)

General Grant did not have a clue that the bulk of the Confederate army at Corinth was on its way to attack him.[88] Despite this, Johnston was killed in action on April 6 (P. G. T. Beauregard replaced him) and his army suffered over ten thousand casualties, including hundreds of Alabamians. The Union army was hit even harder, incurring over thirteen thousand casualties and making the Battle of Shiloh by far the most shockingly bloody battle in the nation's history.[89] Nuns from the Sisters of Charity in Mobile joined numerous other women and men from west Alabama who rushed to the area to nurse the wounded.[90] Although the arrival of Buell's forces on the second and final day of the battle forced the Confederates to retreat back to Corinth, the Alabama press joined the rest of the Southern newspapers in falsely declaring the battle a great Confederate victory. "It is difficult," wrote the always overly optimistic John Forsyth, "to calculate the importance of this victory in a material and moral point of view. Rightly improved and followed up, it should at once restore to us Tennessee."[91]

But there would be no pursuit by either of the exhausted and bloodied armies. And the fact remained that Union forces had come into the Deep South for good, and more were on the way. George Knox Miller, a very committed Confederate soldier from Talladega, wrote to his future wife Celestine describing the conflict and concluding that "such was the great battle of Shiloh fought on the 6th & 7th with no definite result. The enemy's loss was much greater than ours, but altogether it may be considered a drawn battle. We had about 35000 men on the field while the enemy at no time had less than 75000."[92] Miller did not, however, point out that Confederate casualties had reduced the strength of Beauregard's army by a startling 25 percent.[93]

Unionists could only hope that the Union army's presence would open the eyes of those who had followed secessionists down this bloody road. It did, according to historian John Witherspoon DuBose, who lived during that period.[94] E. W. Peck would later write that "a rebellion had been inaugurated and boldly entered upon, without any just appreciation of the dangers and difficulties, to be encountered." Those "who had been mainly instrumental in promoting it, seem to have been ignorant, even to infatuation, of the strength of the [Confederate] government, and character of the people they were setting at defiance, and endeavoring to destroy." They, according to Peck, "had vainly persuaded themselves that no real physical opposition would be interposed to prevent the accomplishment of their unlawful and criminal designs, and if there should be, it was confidently believed it would be feeble in its efforts, and of short duration." "Never had a people beguiled or deceived themselves into a greater error, or a more serious mistake," he continued. "Scarcely, however, had a year elapsed, before their eyes began to be opened to the magnitude of the dangers to which they were soon exposed, and the difficulties in providing the means of carrying on and prosecuting the stupendous war they had so unwisely provoked and brought upon themselves and their country; and which, in the end, was to overwhelm them by defeat and disaster."[95]

Peck's reminiscence accurately captures the shock and dismay among many Alabamians in the weeks following the Battle of Shiloh. Some could point to thousands of Union troops captured there and being transported to Tuscaloosa and other prisons in Selma and Talladega.[96] But thousands of Union soldiers were still near and the naval blockade was slowly placing a stranglehold on Alabama's international commerce, thereby denying the anticipated economic benefits secession had been expected to bring. Confederate diplomatic efforts had failed miserably in their attempts to extort foreign intervention with the aid of King Cotton, while attempts by foreign countries to locate suitable alternative sources of cotton and shorter transportation routes for that staple were moving toward a breakthrough.[97] Things also continued to deteriorate from a military standpoint. Kentucky had been lost, seemingly for the duration, and Tennessee's capital was in Union hands. Although the 1860 Alabama census had revealed 106,000 Alabama men of military age, only approximately 36,000 were in the field.[98] And despite a constant barrage of Confederate propaganda in the Southern press, many soldiers opposed reenlisting and volunteers for military service were very reluctant to come forward.

Therefore, on March 28, 1862, Jefferson Davis had been forced to call for the enactment of another coercive measure, a conscription law (America's first) to compel men between the ages of eighteen and thirty-five to fight. It was a controversial measure that the editor of Greensboro's *Alabama Beacon*, among others, blasted as being "totally inconsistent with the true principles of liberty."[99] Some supportive Confederates feared that the proposed law would not be adopted, and that as a consequence those soldiers who had joined the army for a twelve-month term would come home. The Selma Soldiers' Aid Society "in behalf of the ladies of Selma" issued an emotional appeal intended to pressure the members of units recruited in Dallas County to voluntarily reenlist. "We are surrounded on every side by our enemies. Our country is in more danger now than the day you so gallantly offered your lives for her defence. Your services are more needed [now]." "Come back in glory," they were told, "or come back not again."[100]

Before the conscription law was adopted on April 16, Union forces under a prewar astronomer, General Ormsby Macknight Mitchel, had sped down from Tennessee and captured lightly defended Huntsville, thereby severing the Memphis and Charleston Railroad.[101] Mary Chadick, the wife of a Huntsville minister serving in the Confederate army, noted that there was "a great deal of excitement and consternation among the citizens, as it had not been generally believed the enemy would come here." She also wrote that "there was no opposition" and that "many prominent citizens and refugees made their escape during the day."[102] In other words, Huntsville secessionists did not stand and fight.

North Alabama Unionists like Joshua Burns Moore were not at all surprised that those who had brought on the war were unwilling to fight. When he learned that "the federals have taken Huntsville," he wrote "so much for the revolution" and again ridiculed the secessionists. "Where is the boasted chivalry of North Ala. Alas it is fled to the hills and mountains."[103] By doing so, however, they had not necessarily found sanctuary. There were reports of another Union convention in northwest Alabama, causing concern about the possibility of an uprising of Unionists in north Alabama centered in the hill counties of Winston, Fayette, and Marion.[104] After the Confederate guard at Decatur had raised the drawbridge over the Tennessee River in an attempt to prevent that critical rail junction with the Tennessee and Alabama Railroad from falling into enemy hands, the civilian residents there had lowered it when the Union forces threatened to shell the town. According to the frustrated *Montgomery Advertiser*, "the terrified and unpatriotic citizens [of Decatur] loved their property better than their country's cause."[105]

As Mitchel's men were proceeding west through Lawrence County toward Tuscumbia along the Memphis and Charleston Railroad,[106] reports trickled in of Union naval forces massing and then attacking the outer defenses of New Orleans.[107] On April 29, a Mobile newspaper reported that vital port city's shocking surrender four days earlier.[108] Unreported in Alabama was the mutiny of pro-Union Confederate soldiers at Fort Jackson, which allowed Union troop ships to pass up the Mississippi River to the Crescent City.[109] A British visitor observed that refugees from New Orleans poured into Mobile. There they added to what he described as the "universal feeling of exasperation."[110] Many Alabamians assumed Mobile would be next and that the Union navy would soon be plying the Alabama River.[111] John Cotton, a recent enlistee from Coosa County who was training in a camp of instruction near Montgomery, wrote to his wife, Mariah, that "some of the people [in Montgomery County] are very badly scared and are moveing out there families and they are halling oft the cotton."[112]

Despite this, Unionists were still not free to publicly voice or act on their wishes. They knew that if and when the Confederates reclaimed middle Tennessee or north Alabama, those who had fraternized with the enemy would be forced to leave or possibly face capital charges of treason; in either case, they could lose their property to sequestration. The *Montgomery Advertiser* flatly threatened that "any man at the South who swears to support the Lincoln government by that act expatriates himself and becomes an alien and an enemy of the Confederacy" and would receive the treatment "usually accorded to enemies and traitors."[113] During a public meeting in Montgomery in early May, resolutions were unanimously adopted by a crowd calling for the property of any person who took the oath of allegiance to the United States to "be appropriated to aid in achieving the independence and maintaining the liberty of the country of which they will have proven themselves unworthy."[114]

Even before that occurred, Confederates in occupied areas were attempting to repress Union sentiment.[115] In addition, the Confederate military sent cavalry units from Corinth and Tennessee into north Alabama to make surprise attacks on Union military targets and burn cotton that residents might sell to Northern cotton brokers.[116] These forays were supplemented by raids made by less formal bands of the type earlier encouraged by the south Alabama press. As General Mitchel reported within a month of his arrival in Huntsville, trains were being shot into, his telegraph wires were being cut, and guards at bridges and couriers were being killed.[117] The *Montgomery Advertiser* hoped that, with the aid of these guerrilla tactics, it would not be long before the "astronomical General Mitchel, who is in command of the Yankees in North Alabama, will be made to find that star gazing at the North, is altogether a different affair from conducting military operations in the heart of an enemy's country."[118] The *Mobile Advertiser and Register* predicted that by using "the guerrilla way," the "invading columns of the enemy will soon be hemmed in by a cordon of daring partisans as a wall of fire."[119] Over the next three months, marauding guerrilla bands engaged in a cat-and-mouse game with Union military forces in north Alabama along the Memphis and Charleston and the Tennessee and Alabama Railroads.[120] At the same time, they were harassing and terrorizing Unionist civilians above and below the Tennessee River and making certain that none of the Union meetings that now military governor Andrew Johnson was orchestrating in Tennessee ever occurred again in the Tennessee Valley.

The guerrilla bands were not totally successful in suppressing Union sentiment, however, especially in towns like Huntsville, where there was a constant and significant Union army presence. C. C. Clay Jr. wrote to Governor Shorter from the safety of faraway Macon, Georgia, that his father and other secessionists had been jailed and that planters and businessmen were selling their cotton to the federals in contravention of Confederate law. Clay added that "I feel humiliated that I am not doing something to wrest my home and the land of my birth from the hands of the foe and rescue my relatives and friends from his cowardly prosecutions and oppression." But Clay was not so humiliated that he joined the army.[121] Huntsvillians Jeremiah Clemens, George Washington Lane, William Bibb Figures, David Campbell Humphreys, Nicholas Davis, and many others secretly took the oath of allegiance to the United States during this period, and Davis traveled to Nashville to communicate with Andrew Johnson.[122] Meanwhile, General Mitchel used the Huntsville *Southern Advocate*'s printing press to publish a pro-Union military newspaper, the *Reveille*.[123] He also made use of slaves in the region to provide intelligence regarding northbound Confederate troop movements, writing Secretary of War Edwin Stanton that "I shall soon have watchful guards among the slaves on the plantations bordering the [Tennessee] river from Bridgeport to Florence, and all who communicate to me valuable information I have promised the protection of my Government."[124] Other slaves were used to build military fortifications.[125]

This same basic process was repeated in the town of Athens on the Tennessee and Alabama Railroad. Limestone County had been the site of pro-Union gatherings before the war began, and a pro-Union element continued there that included future Republican Daniel Havens Bingham.[126] Although George Smith Houston would deny it later, he may have taken the oath of allegiance to the federal government. No evidence survives that he later broke that oath.[127] Houston also may have been a member of a group of Athenians who secretly invited Mitchel to send troops to their town, with Mitchel complying with their request. Left to their own devices, the soldiers and the townspeople peacefully coexisted at first, and absent external forces, it was foreseeable that more and more citizens there would take the oath and begin to resume their commercial connections with Nashville and beyond.[128]

Confederates knew from the experience in other occupied areas, however, that the occupation forces could be baited into frustration and summary retaliation against the civilian population. Then the conciliation process prescribed by the Lincoln administration to encourage a resumption of allegiance to the federal government could be thwarted. Under such circumstances, innocents and even friends would be accidentally targeted for punishment, causing harmless fence-sitters and even some Unionists to lose faith. Even before the Yankees had arrived, the *Selma Daily Reporter* advised that in order to "make the situation of the invaders ineffective and exhaustive, wherever they may plant their vile standard, it is only necessary for all our people to *stand aloof from them*, and give them as little aid and comfort as comports with the dictates of patriotism."[129] Those who did not assume such a countenance, and instead treated Union soldiers as human beings, were ridiculed as traitors and scalawags and were marked for unpleasant encounters with guerrillas or disapproving neighbors.[130]

Confederate north Alabamians had gotten the message loud and clear, and so Unionists were forced to avoid public displays of friendship with Union soldiers. As a consequence, the Union army occupiers appear to have drawn what may have been the wrong conclusion about many north Alabamians. In a letter to the *Cincinnati Times*, General Mitchel complained that the "white inhabitants of this part of the country are the most rampant and vicious secessionists I ever met with. They will hardly speak to an officer when they meet him, but look sideways, lest they might inhale his 'Yankee' breath. No matter what the nation, creed or color of a man, if he is for the Union he is a Yankee. The ladies—save the mark—are more vicious, fierce, and rampant than the men."[131]

Three days after Union forces arrived in Athens, a Confederate cavalry unit suddenly attacked the town, routed the surprised Union soldiers, and were cheered by some residents.[132] An exasperated General Mitchel gave orders to his men that were interpreted as permitting retaliation against not only regular military personnel but any civilians who they deemed to be disloyal. On the way to carry out those orders under the command of Russian-born Union brigadier general John Basil Turchin, his men learned to their horror that two wounded Union soldiers had been burned alive during an attack on a train.[133] By the time they entered Athens, the Confederate cavalry unit had already departed, leaving the citizenry to take the brunt of the punishment during what some have called the sack of Athens. The ensuing search for weapons and stolen Union military property led to looting and pillaging of homes and stores and the impressment of horses, fulfilling in part the Confederate prophecy that Union soldiers were motivated solely by a desire for "Beauty and Booty."[134]

Meanwhile, rumors circulated in central and south Alabama in April and May that Union forces would soon strike Tuscaloosa, where 2,300 Union army prisoners, many taken at Shiloh, were imprisoned.[135] If the Yankees had come to Tuscaloosa at this early point, what type of reception would they have received? In addition to the prison, Tuscaloosa had experienced a significant amount of militarization with its designation earlier in the year as the location of a camp of instruction called Camp Jemison to train volunteers and conscripts,[136] and with the University of Alabama's later designation as the location of a second such camp.[137] As the *Tuscaloosa Observer* noted, "this city, at the present time, is beginning to assume quite a war like appearance. Numerous Camps dot our streets in every direction while nearly every day brings new companies of brave hearts and strong arms."[138] Tuscaloosa was also under martial law and controlled by military authorities. For a portion of the spring of 1862, the provost marshal was the soon-to-be infamous Henry Hartmann Wirz, a Swiss-born Louisiana soldier who was then also serving as the commandant of the military prison facilities in Tuscaloosa but would later be placed in charge of a new prison at Andersonville, Georgia.[139] Even then Wirz was derided as a "brutal foreigner" by one of the Tuscaloosa prisoners.[140]

Fear of arrest and sequestration were not the only factors motivating conformity by Tuscaloosa Unionists. Many of them were prominent businessmen, and by now the Confederacy meant business—literally—but on terms favorable only to the government. Under martial law, permits issued by the provost marshal were required to do business, and it is unlikely that men like Sergeant Wirz issued them to anyone whose loyalty to the Cause was suspect.[141] Possibly as a result of a combination of compulsion and economic necessity, the local foundry had contracted with the Confederate government to fabricate cannons and cannonballs,[142] and there was a movement afoot to add a rolling mill to the operation in order to manufacture gunboats.[143] In addition, Charles Foster's tannery produced leather from which a local factory (also owned by Foster) manufactured shoes for the Confederacy; a hat factory manufactured Confederate hats; and the cotton mill manufactured heavy cloth.[144] Dr. Peter Bryce, the superintendent of the insane asylum, permitted the east wing of that facility to be used as a military hospital.[145] Town merchants were also partaking in the war boom, supplying food and other necessaries to military personnel and newly arriving refugees from throughout the South.[146] In the process, these businessmen had attained a vested interest in the status quo, albeit one that would erode as the economy became further devastated by inflation.[147]

The situation was the same further south in Dallas County. The imposition of martial law,[148] coupled with a measure of prosperity brought by contracts with the Confederate government to manufacture ammunition and other war materiel, enhanced Confederate sentiment. The neutralization of the Memphis and Charleston Railroad by Union forces in north Alabama and north Mississippi had ironically been the boon to Selma's economic circumstances for which many Selmans had long prayed. Whereas Selma railroaders had been frustrated during the antebellum period by the failure of the state of Alabama to fund all of their pet projects, military necessity had moved the Confederate Congress to appropriate money to build the new road from Selma to Meridian, Mississippi, in order to provide a replacement connection between eastern states of the Confederacy and the west.[149] Later setbacks in Kentucky and Tennessee would similarly result in Confederate funding to extend the Alabama and Tennessee Railroad from Calhoun County northeast to Rome, Georgia.[150] With a versatile transportation system coming on line, a location in the interior of the state far enough from gradually approaching battle lines, and its close proximity to raw materials such as coal and iron, Selma also quickly became a logical place for the manufacture of badly needed ordnance, naval vessels, and other weapons of war. Former Unionists of Selma were quick to partake in the massive injection of Confederate capital that was to come.[151] As the *Selma Reporter* would later note, "the fact is, some of our people are now prospering as they never prospered before—are fast accumulating wealth."[152]

Even further south, the residents of Mobile remained under martial law and fearful of a naval bombardment following the fall of New Orleans and the recent stunning announcement of the Confederacy's decision to abandon Pensacola.[153] To encourage a capitulation of other port cities, including Mobile, President Lincoln craftily (according to the Alabama press) proclaimed on May 12 that the naval blockade of New Orleans would terminate and that after June 1, commercial intercourse would substantially resume there.[154] In order to partake in that commerce, residents of New Orleans reportedly took the oath of allegiance in great numbers.[155] Would Mobile merchants and cotton brokers, as well as south Alabama cotton planters who were on the verge of bankruptcy, now see peace and reunion as a viable option, especially if slavery could somehow be preserved?

A worried newspaper editor on the Alabama-Georgia line recognized this possibility, observing that the "federal Government, having secured possession of several important Southern ports, intends to try the policy of trading the seceded States back into the Union." As he noted, the *New York Herald* was already predicting that "the establishment of post offices and of courts must soon follow, and the advantages of trade and friendly intercourse being appended, every tendency will then operate upon the feelings of the people in the rebel States to allay hostility and cultivate and restore friendly relations." This "seductive influence of commerce," concluded the editor, "will have to be thwarted by the strong arm of the law or by military authority."[156] President Lincoln knew this might be the case and so was also careful to make clear that the war was still being prosecuted to restore the Union, not to abolish slavery in the Southern states. The same west Georgia newspaper published his controversial proclamation voiding an order issued by one of his generals in South Carolina declaring "forever free" the slaves in Georgia, Florida and South Carolina.[157] For cash-strapped Alabama planters, commerce plus slavery was a potentially powerful magnet for reunion.

In order to steel the resolve of the defenders and remaining residents of Mobile and other Alabama towns in south Alabama, the Alabama press fed the people a steady stream of stories regarding the conduct of occupation forces in New Orleans and, in particular, the controversial means used by the Union commander there, Major General Benjamin Franklin Butler, to suppress pro-Confederate sentiment.[158] Even before that, women along the Gulf Coast were fleeing in droves to towns further inland. According to the Eutaw *Whig*, "our town is filled up with females from Mobile. Every vacant house had been taken and occupied. We hear the same is true of almost every town and village on the rivers in the State."[159] And there is little doubt that Confederate women let the men know their fears of sexual assault and what was expected of them. "Oh! It makes my blood boil to think of it," wrote Catherine Fennell in north Alabama.[160] The *Montgomery Advertiser* declared that if there was now anyone who would not "resolve to use all his energies to secure the final defeat of the barbarous foe . . . such a man has no right to live anywhere, certainly nowhere outside of the North."[161]

This strategy was not uniformly effective. The *Mobile Advertiser and Register* blasted the "grumbling community" for attempting to "demoralize the army, disaffect the people, neutralize the Government, and ruin our cause and the Confederacy if possible." It charged that "a few prominent grumblers in each community, and a few grumbling journals in the country . . . do as much harm as the destruction of a brigade per week."[162] A Dallas County grand jury condemned the "croakers," the "men who are constantly harping upon our inability to succeed in the glorious struggle in which we are engaged; who never have believed that we have gained a victory or ever will gain one, who are always suggesting, in the face of the most brilliant successes of our arms, that the next news will not be so favorable, and slyly hinting at the benefits of reconstruction."[163]

But editors such as those of the *Montgomery Advertiser* grumbled too. In an editorial reprinted in the *New York Times*, it decried President Davis's many failures of leadership and policy and once even praised President Lincoln by comparison. "Their President [Lincoln], although having credit among us for being a clown, had sense enough to know that he did not know everything." Unlike Davis, Lincoln "took counsel, and divided responsibility with those who were versed in their own departments; and when men were found incompetent he had respect enough for an enlightened public opinion to remove those who were obnoxious." The *Advertiser* also hinted that Davis would be deposed if he failed to emulate Lincoln's management style.[164]

The work of these scalawags, croakers, and grumblers, coupled with evil times, was taking its toll. Diarist Margaret Miles in Lowndes County asked, "will the silver lining of this dark dark cloud ever appear[?] nothing but gloom and sorrow hangs around now[.] Oh! Will it ever brighten?"[165] Augustus Benners wrote that "this unnatural & cruel war brings death and mourning to many a hearth stone. How long shall these things be."[166] The answer was much longer than anyone would have believed.

III
THE DECREE OF THE NATION

Timeline: March 1862–January 1863

March 28, 1862	Jefferson Davis calls for the enactment of a conscription law.
April 6, 1862	Battle of Shiloh begins.
April 11, 1862	Huntsville, Alabama, is taken by Union army.
April 16, 1862	Confederate conscription law enacted.
April 25, 1862	Battle of New Orleans begins.
May 2, 1862	Sack of Athens, Alabama, by Union army.
May 29, 1862	Confederates evacuate Corinth, Mississippi.
June 6, 1862	Memphis, Tennessee, falls to Union forces.
June 27, 1862	Stephen F. Hale killed at Gaines Mill, Virginia.
July 5, 1862	Governor Shorter orders Alabama law enforcement officers to apprehend deserters.
July 17, 1862	Braxton Bragg begins movement from Mississippi across Alabama toward Kentucky.
July 29, 1862	Braxton Bragg arrives at Chattanooga.
August 6, 1862	Union General Robert McCook killed by guerrillas in north Alabama.
August 8, 1862	Lumsden's Battery reaches Tuscaloosa but does not leave until August 16.
August 14, 1862	President Lincoln advocates colonization of free blacks to Central America.
August 18, 1862	Confederate Congress convenes.
Late August 1862	Union troops begin leaving north Alabama.
September 1, 1862	The University of Alabama begins academic year.
September 19, 1862	Philip Dale Roddey is authorized to form a brigade in north Alabama.
September 22, 1862	President Lincoln issues Preliminary Emancipation Proclamation.
September 26, 1862	Confederate Congress revises the Conscription law.
October 6, 1862	Governor Shorter issues call for special session of Alabama legislature.
October 8, 1862	Braxton Bragg is defeated at Perrysville, Kentucky, and begins retreat into Tennessee.

October 27, 1962	Alabama legislature meets in special session.
November 17, 1862	C. C. Sheats is expelled from the Alabama legislature.
December 1, 1862	President Lincoln recommends compensated emancipation.
December 13, 1862	Union forces are defeated at the Battle of Fredericksburg, Virginia.
December 17, 1862	Jefferson Davis stops in Montgomery, Alabama.
December 31, 1862	Braxton Bragg is defeated at Stones River, Tennessee.
January 1, 1863	President Lincoln issues the Emancipation Proclamation.

7
"Yankeeizing Southerners"

Some excellent historians point to enlistment figures to demonstrate that the vast majority of Alabamians affirmatively supported the Confederacy and the war effort. Walter Fleming estimated that a total of 89,678 served in the Confederate army during the war, but he admitted the only official records that would provide an accurate figure were somehow lost or destroyed.[1] Even if Fleming's estimate were accurate, however, raw enlistment figures actually provide ambiguous evidence, at best, of what was in the hearts of most white male Alabamians throughout the war. As previously discussed, there is evidence that only 34 percent of Alabama men of military age had joined the Confederate army before the law mandating military service was adopted.[2] Applying the logic of those who equate the level of enlistment with commitment to the quest for Southern independence, what does that say about the 66 percent who did not enlist until legally compelled to do so? The *Selma Reporter* suggested that they were among the disloyal.[3] Historian Kenneth W. Noe concluded that what he classified as older "later-enlisting Confederates" "hated the war above all, hoped for peace, and wanted to go home, preferably the one on earth but, barring that, at least the reconstituted one above."[4]

Such sentiment may have been more widespread in Alabama than we will ever know. The archival record simply does not contain a truly representative sample of information regarding illiterates, conscripts, draft dodgers, women, or even soldiers. And as Noe also observed, this can distort the picture of public opinion.[5] Indeed, what some have assumed to have been broad and deep support in Alabama for the Confederacy and the war has no more solid evidentiary support than the opposite conclusion.

Enlistments did increase after the conscription law went into effect. By June 1862, the *Selma Reporter* was boasting that Alabama had sixty thousand troops in the field.[6] But historian Albert Burton Moore concluded that "the conscription law was the real stimulus to volunteering" at this time.[7] And enlistment figures are also problematic because they tell us nothing of the quality or length of service of the enlistees. Did they serve at the front and kill Yankees, or were they able to obtain bomb-proof positions, safe from the danger of combat? Did they eventually pay substitutes to take their places after "seeing the elephant" (the phrase used by inexperienced soldiers to refer to their first encounter with combat)? Failing that, did they desert? Just as with enlistment figures, no records are available of the total number of Alabamians who used these common battle-avoidance techniques.

Not long after the *Selma Reporter*'s account, news arrived in Alabama that threatened to trigger the increased use of those techniques. Alabamians read shocking reports of Confederate forces abandoning the important rail junction at Corinth on May 29,[8] immediately followed by crushing news of the capitulation of Memphis on June 6 after only a two-hour naval battle.[9] It was at this point that Alabama's future was placed in the hands of General Bragg, who replaced Beauregard.[10] Union forces, meanwhile, solidified their grip on north Alabama.

In late June and early July 1862, north Alabama residents began to join the Union army at an enrolling station in Decatur, Alabama. Most of the credit for inspiring these enlistments has been given to future Alabama Republican Charles Christopher Sheats and his recruiting efforts.[11] But more than Sheats's rhetoric lay behind their decision to leave their families behind and risk capture by Confederate rangers or guerrilla bands attempting to prevent them from reaching Decatur. On June 24, the *Montgomery Advertiser* had announced that the conscription process would soon intensify."[12] North Alabama Unionists, therefore, knew that if they were caught by Confederate officials, they would be forced to fight for a cause in which they did not believe fervently, if at all. On the other hand, joining the Union army placed the welfare of their families at risk. It appears, however, that wealthier Unionists in the region stepped forward to provide support in their absence. According to Union colonel Abel D. Streight, a former New Yorker who had undertaken with elements of his Fifty-First Indiana to protect Unionists on their way to Decatur, the recruits were "mostly poor, though many of them are, or rather were, in comfortable circumstances." Streight reported that they had managed to keep themselves out of the way of marauding gangs by hiding in the "fastnesses of the mountainous wilderness" but had been unable to pay attention to their farms and "consequently many of them are now destitute of food of their own and are living off their more fortunate neighbors."[13]

Some historians have belittled the level of patriotic volunteerism of Alabama Unionists, noting that "only" 2,500–2,600 Alabamians formally joined the Union army during this period.[14] Once again, however, raw enlistment figures are misleading because they do not account for all the variables. For

Unionists, leaving their families to starve or be subjected to retaliation was difficult. In addition, before the process could get fully underway, Confederate cavalry units operating out of Moulton had become aware of the Unionists' efforts to reach Decatur—the only Union army garrison south of the Tennessee River—and were actively attempting to stop them.[15] Union major general George Henry Thomas had ordered three regiments from Courtland to Moulton to "capture or disperse" these Confederates,[16] and this facilitated Streight's successful recruiting mission from Decatur to Days Gap southeast of Danville, which occurred between July 12 and July 16, 1862.[17] Without that level of protection, the number of recruits would have undoubtedly been far less.

Suddenly, a series of events took place that would chill Unionist enlistments, force the Union army to vacate north Alabama (albeit temporarily), and leave to the mercy of the Confederates Thomas Peters and every other north Alabama Unionist who remained. General Braxton Bragg issued orders on July 17 and July 21 splitting his forces in Mississippi into several groups, sending a portion under Brigadier General James Ronald Chalmers to Grand Junction in north Mississippi, a portion into north Alabama, and some to Mobile. He ordered the majority, approximately thirty thousand men along with his headquarters, to Chattanooga with the intention of marching north to middle Tennessee and then into Kentucky.[18] The dramatic move north has received the most historical attention because it represented a break from the cordon defensive strategy and a change to an offensive strategy that would also see the now iconic General Robert E. Lee invading Maryland. But the efforts of all three groups would have significant consequences for Alabama and the South.[19]

It does not take much imagination to discern Bragg's plan regarding north Alabama. Along with harassing Buell's army as it slowly moved across north Alabama toward Confederate-controlled Chattanooga, part of the reason Bragg sent additional forces into the region was to prevent even more Unionists from enlisting at Decatur. As Buell noted following receipt of a report of Confederate forces being sent to Moulton, the "object would be to stop our communication with the Union men of Winston and adjoining counties, who have recently been joining our ranks, to break up our lines along the railroad and throw marauding bodies of cavalry across the river upon my communication."[20] The order issued by Bragg's chief of staff on July 17 directed a cavalry force to "move at once toward the Tennessee River *as near as practicable to Decatur*," communicate with Captain Philip Dale Roddey, and then do "all practicable things to harass the enemy and cut off any detachments or supply trains" and "destroy all cotton within the district of his operations."[21] In accordance with Bragg's order, between 1,500 and 3,000 additional cavalry moved from Mississippi through Russellville and Mount Hope, arriving in Moulton starting on July 24. By August 10, two regiments of infantry and a battery of artillery were also at Moulton.[22] Rather than turning around and annihilating these forces, Buell rushed to protect Nashville should reports of a possible invasion of Kentucky by Confederates in east Tennessee prove to be accurate.[23]

Buell's departure from Huntsville and most of northeast Alabama, which began in late August, left a vacuum that Confederate military and political authorities were quick to fill.[24] C. C. Clay Jr. wrote to Governor Shorter urging that those who had collaborated with the federals during the months of occupation be arrested and prosecuted. "If these traitors escaped 'unwhipped of justice,'" he maintained, "they will continue to exercise a pernicious influence upon the political and moral sentiments of our people."[25] Alabama Unionists in that portion of north Alabama were, therefore, forced to make an agonizing decision between either risking retaliation at home or fleeing for their lives.[26] Many, including US district judge George Washington Lane, chose to leave with Buell's army.[27] So did a number of slaves in the area, but for some their run for freedom would later be cut short in Kentucky where they were caught and returned to slavery.[28] General Grant and his army were still at Corinth,[29] and there was a small Union army presence in northwest Alabama along the Memphis and Charleston Railroad.[30] So Thomas Peters also left, heading west to a plantation he owned in Crittenden County in east Arkansas across the Mississippi River from Union-controlled Memphis. For this, historian Walter Fleming labeled Peters a deserter.[31]

Charles Christopher Sheats, who had somewhat curiously chosen not to seek exile, was arrested by Confederate partisan rangers and jailed.[32] So were some north Alabama businessmen who had traded with the enemy.[33] As William Russell Smith later recalled, "I saw the jails and guardhouses of the country groaning with men against whom nothing could be urged but suspicion of Unionism."[34] Jeremiah Clemens had not left the state and was attacked in downtown Huntsville by a Confederate civilian who had been among those incarcerated during the occupation. According to the *Mobile Advertiser and Register*, a list had been kept of the "Yankeeizing Southerners" like Clemens, who was "beaten within an inch of his life . . . disfiguring him frightfully."[35] Later, according to the *New York Times*, Clemens, George Washington Lane, and Nicholas Davis were hung in effigy in Huntsville.[36]

With Union forces moving through Tennessee toward Kentucky, more of those Alabamians who had merely attempted to remain neutral would now be forced to either support the Confederacy or act openly against it because a new revision to the Conscription Act raised the draft ceiling to age forty-five.[37] Neutrality, according to the *Mobile Tribune*, was treason, just as would be "talk of neutrality in a contest between God and Satan." No choice, it concluded, "is now left to men who live in the South. If they are for us, they are entitled to the protection of our laws and our arms, if they are not for us, they are against us and should be expelled from the land."[38]

Consistent with the sectional split during the antebellum period and the secession crisis, the response in north Alabama did not mirror the sentiments of the south Alabama press. In Huntsville, for example, such Unionists as *Southern Advocate* editor William Bibb Figures openly protested conscription as akin to slavery, a particularly divisive and therefore effective antiwar theme.[39] Robert Stell Heflin and future Alabama Republican governor William Hugh Smith, both of whom were Randolph County lawyers, made speeches at the county courthouse in Wedowee in the fall of 1862 in which they argued that conscription was illegal.[40] Even Sarah Espy in northeast Alabama wrote that the conscript law was "as shameful a one as congress ever passed." She was also incensed that the members of the Confederate Congress had compounded their error when they "passed a law giving themselves $27.00 a year, and the greater part of the time they are at home attending their business." Ominously, she concluded that "I look for a rebellion among ourselves at that rate of going on, for the war taxes the people [pay are] heavy enough."[41]

But then came another turn of events, which occurred a week before Catherine Fennell in north Alabama "pray[ed] Heaven that no evil genius may deter our brave Generals from the immediate invasion of the enemy's country."[42] She was unaware that President Lincoln had announced a stunning change in policy when he released his Preliminary Emancipation Proclamation following the Union army's bloody victory over General Lee at Antietam Creek in Maryland on September 17, 1862.[43] According to historian Bertis English, the news filtered down to Alabama's slaves, some and perhaps all of whom prayed that the proclamation be carried out and began preparing for freedom.[44] Word of the proclamation, meanwhile, sent shockwaves throughout white Alabama and the rest of the South.[45]

Lincoln's year-end deadline for the cessation of hostilities before the proclamation came into effect also placed in a very difficult predicament those Alabama Unionists attempting to bring about peace but also preserve slavery. At least for some period of time, Union army victories at Corinth, Mississippi, on October 3 and 4,[46] and Bragg's embarrassing and demoralizing retreat from Kentucky following the Battle of Perryville on October 8, 1862,[47] might have given them hope that some portions of Alabama would be exempted from Lincoln's proclamation, which would apply only to territory in rebellion. This possibility explains C. C. Clay Jr.'s frantic letter from Huntsville over a month after the proclamation was announced complaining that in north Alabama, "the disloyal stand in open defiance of constitutional authority, and of the few who are brave and patriotic enough to denounce them, and a large portion of those who are true to the Confederate Government, are restrained by fear of the return of the Yankees and menaces of greater outrages than they have yet suffered from free expression of their sentiments and from any organization for their future defense." According to Clay, the "reported retreat of Bragg and the disastrous defeat of [Confederate General Earl] Van Dorn [at Corinth] have caused general dismay." Clay's suggested solution was to beef up the Confederate military presence in the region, especially in Huntsville, and to send in Confederate enrolling officers to force men of military age into the army. No enrolling officers had appeared so far and, according to Clay, "those who ought to be in the Army or to go into it are resorting to every expedient for escaping conscription."[48]

That was the situation throughout the state. As is true in most wars, these "expedients" were most accessible to the wealthy, the prestigious, and the well-connected. Even after several subsequent Confederate victories under General Lee in Virginia, a Huntsville-born Confederate senator from Mississippi, James Phelan Sr., wrote to Jefferson Davis in the fall of 1862 that "it seems as if nine tenths of the youngsters of the land whose relatives are conspicuous in society, wealthy, or influential obtain some safe perch where they can doze with their heads under their wings. Partiality, favoritism, perhaps bribery and corruption, sustain this acknowledged evil."[49] A heartbroken woman in Mobile, whose only son had been conscripted, bitterly complained to Alabama's governor about a "hale hearty young man living in this town named Sidney Douglas," who, she wrote, had "acquired the sobriquet of 'Artful Dodger.'" His parents, she noted, were "well to do," and he had used this to hop from a position as a commissary clerk, to a clerkship in a bank, then membership in a fire brigade, and so on. Douglas, she wrote, had bragged that the "enrolling officers cannot get him" because "he is too smart for them!"[50] Those who were lucky enough to be accepted to the University of Alabama were deemed to be exempt from conscription, resulting in the student body for the fall of 1862 growing to two hundred and many applicants being turned away.[51] Otherwise, wellborn young men might claim exemption under the highly controversial "20 slave" exemption, which generally required as a "police" measure that a white man remain on each plantation that had at least twenty slaves.[52] Or they could hire a substitute to take their place in the army.[53]

Older elites might utilize these latter two techniques or seek appointment or election to exempt government or military positions that would keep them safe and out of the fray. As C. C. Clay Jr. complained to the Confederate secretary of war, "some half dozen are ensconced in the Nitre [*sic*] Bureau office established [in Huntsville]." There were, wrote Clay, even "men here holding office under the Confederate Government [as] receivers under the [sequestration] act, who have been guilty of disloyal acts."[54] Family physicians could also be helpful in avoiding service. Unionist attorney Joshua Burns Moore was exempted from conscription because he was deemed "physically very delicate." But to be on the safe side, he sought appointment as solicitor (district attorney) of his judicial circuit.[55]

For the less affluent, options for avoiding military service were few, and the war was more and more perceived to be a poor man's fight. Some potential conscripts without connections resorted to self-mutilation in order to apply for a medical exemption. Malinda Taylor, the war-weary wife of a Confederate soldier from Tuscaloosa County who was stationed near Mobile, wrote to her husband, Grant, that "Jack Taylor shot off his little finger to keep from going. . . . Waller Stevens shot off 2 of his. Marsh Lee shot off 2 of his."[56] Suicide was also an option.[57]

In northwest Alabama, Unionists of military age who were unable to procure an exemption but wished to remain near their homes to protect their families from the growing number of guerrilla bands and the predicted retaliation of freed slaves had another option by which they could nominally fulfill their military obligation while maintaining law and order in the region. In late August, Captain Roddey had requested permission to increase his command to a full regiment. According to a report by Confederate major general Sterling Price, Roddey expressed optimism that he could "easily raise" that number of men "for the war."[58] General Bragg granted that authority on September 19,[59] and as one of Roddey's officers later wrote, Roddey "found himself in command of twelve or fifteen companies" in a "very few weeks."[60] These would be combined to form the Fifth Alabama Cavalry, and Roddey was elected its colonel.[61]

The military effectiveness of these men was, with some exceptions, poor. When Union forces made a raid on Tuscumbia from Corinth, wrote one resident, "the affair was discreditable to our cavalry. They were not expecting the enemy. A great many scattered off taking care of their individual carcasses. While the fight was going on, a good many came running back to town. I could see them occasionally about a mile south of town scampering off in an opposite direction from the enemy."[62] Another diarist wrote that "it is a standing joke here that Roddey's men spend their whole time hunting their horses or buttermilk. The 'buttermilk cavalry' and 'Life Insurance Concern' are two of their common names."[63] Survival appears to have been Roddey's polestar. For young recruits, such as Thomas Peters's son William and George Smith Houston Jr., Roddey had established what became known as the Bull Pups, a company that served as Roddey's large personal escort.[64] Roddey had personally assured the parents of these young men that if they joined him, he would avoid unnecessary risks and keep their sons safe and close to home. He attempted to keep his word.[65]

Perhaps because Roddey's ranks filled up so quickly or because some could not bring themselves to don Confederate gray, many other north Alabamians and scores of draft dodgers literally headed for the hills and caves of north Alabama, where they attempted to take sanctuary along with thousands of disenchanted and disillusioned Confederate army deserters and parolees seeking to avoid repression while awaiting the end of the war near their homes.[66] Part of the calculus of joiners and deserters alike was the specter of mass slave insurrections on the home front inspired by Lincoln's Emancipation Proclamation. The slave exemption had, according to William Yancey, been one of the Confederate government's safety measures, but it was obvious that one white man was no match for twenty slaves determined to achieve their freedom.[67] Soldiers, therefore, knew their families were potentially in danger.

Governor Shorter had called the Alabama legislature into a special session that convened on October 27, 1862, but if anyone assumed that he did this to promote a peace accord before Lincoln's year-end deadline, they were to be sadly mistaken. On the contrary, a series of measures were adopted in the special session and the general session that followed immediately thereafter to promote the war effort. These included aid to families of Confederate soldiers, the appropriation of $1 million for the defense of the Tennessee Valley and $250,000 for shoes for Alabama soldiers, the authorization of the enrollment of the Creoles (mixed-race residents) of Mobile County in the state militia for the defense of that county, and the appropriation of $500,000 for the defense of Mobile.[68] A resolution was also adopted declaring that Mobile, "the gem of the gulf," should be "defended from street to street, from house to house, and inch by inch, until, if taken, the victor's spoils should be alone a heap of ashes."[69]

But a review of the journals of the Alabama House and Senate reveals evidence of some degree of contrary undercurrents among these salons elected in the immediate aftermath of Bull Run and the bounce in nationalism that Confederate victory engendered. The situation had changed significantly since those heady days, and the mortality of the Confederacy—and the possibility of postwar treason prosecutions—may have been on the minds of some. This was exemplified by the manner in which the Alabama House addressed efforts made to expel jailed Winston County legislator Charles Christopher Sheats. One might have assumed that when a Black Belt legislator offered a resolution on the second day of the special session that Sheats be expelled, it would have been adopted immediately and unanimously. It was instead referred to a committee, which stalled and later reported that it was "unable to obtain satisfactory evidence" justifying expulsion. The issue was resurrected by the same legislator after the regular session began but was again referred to the same committee. This time, however, the committee subsequently rendered a report finding Sheats guilty of "assisting in enrolling men into the service of the United States." A resolution expelling him was then adopted on November 17, but not unanimously. Among the four who voted against the resolution was Augustus Benners.[70]

As Lincoln's year-end deadline was about to expire, an impending battle that mattered to many Alabamians would begin on December 31, 1862, near the Confederate supply depot at Murfreesboro, Tennessee. It pitted the Army of the Cumberland, Buell's former army then at heavily fortified Nashville and now under the command of General William Starke Rosecrans, against the combined armies of Generals Bragg and Kirby Smith, a force now called the Army of Tennessee.[71] Bragg noted in his marching orders that "by this time tomorrow night the fate of Middle Tennessee will be decided."[72] The battle would be more important than that—so important that Jefferson Davis left Richmond shortly before the Battle of Fredericksburg and traveled to Murfreesboro, arriving on December 12. He spoke to the troops there the next day, reportedly telling them that "the critical moment in the history of the Confederacy had arrived, and he relied upon their valor and patriotism to sustain her now more strongly than ever before."[73]

The Mississippi River valley between Memphis and New Orleans, as Davis and most Alabamians knew, was also being threatened by other Union army forces, and its loss would cut the Confederacy in two.[74] Even worse, the Alabama press was already reporting that the resolve of Mississippians to defend their state was weakening.[75] According to a surprisingly candid editorial in the *Mobile Advertiser and Register*, "a desponding spirit has got abroad among the people—that they feel as if they were to be hopelessly overrun by overwhelming numbers of the enemy, and that they have been neglected by their own Government."[76] This sentiment affected members of Alabama units stationed in Mississippi. John Meriwether wrote to his wife that he was "entirely worn out with the life of a soldier" and intended to quit if he could "for I believe I had soon let the infernal Yankees have all I have than be killed off by degrees with cold & filth."[77]

Davis also knew it would be catastrophic if Tennessee were lost again. The Union army could quickly recover north Alabama and then be free to concentrate on taking the Mississippi River valley and then Atlanta without being further concerned about any lengthy closure of its supply lines running back to Ohio and Kentucky. The rest of Alabama, among other places, would be easy prey. The enforcement of Lincoln's Emancipation Proclamation would then gradually end the institution that many had sought to preserve by secession. It was, therefore, imperative that Bragg's army engage and defeat Rosecrans, thus preventing Union army reinforcements in Tennessee from being sent to Mississippi.

But morale among Bragg's men was fragile.[78] A young soldier from Tuscaloosa, Reuben Searcy, wrote to his sister that all of the men "hate Gen'l Braggs' Tyranny and have no confidence in him as a General." It was rumored, he continued, that General Joseph E. Johnston "is expected here to take command every minute, and the soldiers hail his coming with joyful hearts."[79] But Johnston did not appear, and some chose to desert. Searcy wrote to his mother about three from an Alabama regiment who were caught and executed with the remaining soldiers as reluctant witnesses: "Our Brigade was marched out fully accounted—in the midst of a heavy rain to witness their execution. It was hard to witness it."[80] This would be the doomed Searcy's last letter home. Some deserters made it home to Alabama. Sarah Koon, the Pickens County wife of George Koon, a very homesick soldier in Bragg's army who owned no slaves, wrote to him that there were "several of your company coming home and I hear that they ran away." She feared that he might also desert and begged him not to. "If you can't come home like white people, I don't want you to run away. I want you to stand to your post and be a man and not be at home and have to dodge about like you was stealing. I never want to hear that none of my friends in my life say that."[81]

Lincoln's preliminary proclamation may not have spurred slave-owning Unionists to immediately revolt against the Confederacy, but coupled with the slave exemption law, it had the effect of highlighting slavery's central role in the conflict and the real reason Southerners who did not own slaves were being compelled to fight and die. That some of the owners of those slaves were able to remain safe back home had, according to a Mississippi correspondent of Jefferson Davis's, "aroused a spirit of rebellion in some places . . . and bodies of men have banded together to resist; whilst in the army it is said it only needs some daring man to raise the standard to develop a revolt."[82]

With class conflict now threatening to undermine the Confederate armies in the field and a potential rebellion by the poor and less favored on the home front, General Bragg's army attacked the approaching Union army forces near Stones River on the final morning of the nightmarish year of 1862. The slaughter on both sides would continue until January 3, 1863, when Bragg finally ordered another demoralizing retreat, this time to the Duck River southeast of Murfreesboro near Tullahoma, Tennessee.[83] According to an article from a pro-Confederacy Tennessee newspaper reprinted in the *Selma Morning Reporter*, the bloody battle was nonetheless a glorious victory for Bragg and the Confederacy: "Whatever may be said by fire-side Generals about his Kentucky campaign, it must be admitted by all that his campaign in Middle Tennessee has been a decided success, the details of which will ever do him honor."[84] Not even Bragg accepted this false propaganda. He had lost one-third of his men.[85] Thus, the potential morale boost that might have come to Alabamians as a result of Lee's victory at Fredericksburg and the repulse of Sherman at Chickasaw Bayou near Vicksburg was diluted by bad news from Tennessee. "It is useless," wrote one stunned Alabama survivor to his wife in the aftermath of the carnage, "for me to attempt to describe the scenes of a battle field, men with their legs shot off, shot in the head and their brains scattered around them." For him and for many like him, the comfortable vision of war and the romantic view of fighting for one's country were gone forever. "I am," he said, "in low spirits and have been ever since the fight, and at the same time I have more inclination to try to serve God than I ever had in my life because I now know the horrors of a battle and the dangers of same."[86] As another of the demoralized members of Bragg's army would subsequently write to his wife in Alabama, "I'd give all I have in this world to be clear of this war."[87]

In order to prevent these thoughts from being put into action, the *Selma Reporter* warned women against sending letters to soldiers that might encourage them to desert: "Wives! Mothers! Beware what you write to your sons and husbands in the army." Pointing out that the punishment for desertion was death, the editor urged them to avoid sending "that fatal letter" that might tempt the men from their duty. Although most historians see these letters as straightforward evidence of genuine Confederate patriotism, the *Reporter's* editor's warnings call that interpretation into question. The editor instructed that women writing to men in the field instead "encourage them, cheer their hearts, fire their souls, arouse their patriotism, but do not disturb and harass their minds with unavailing murmurs and complaints."[88] Some replies from the soldiers may have been designed to conform to the women's expectations.

But these warnings were often to no avail. Demoralization was quickly combining with smoldering resentment, especially against the elites. The wealthy, wrote another to his wife, were at home "living on the fat of the country, sleeping on their featherbeds" and "charging soldiers' wives exorbitant prices for food and other necessaries. The poor soldiers, however, were forced to sleep on the wet ground and eat beef poor at that" while "our hands is tied behind us and a great ways from home protecting their negroes." Unless things changed, he predicted, there will be a "home rebellion."[89]

8
"The Struggle of the Masters"

> Oh! That this unholy war would cease
> and we would live as the poet says
> "No, never from that hour to
> part we'd live and love so true"
>
> —Malinda Taylor, Tuscaloosa County

Eighteen sixty-three was an election year in Alabama. For those who had opposed secession and civil war, it was the most promising period since the war's inception to push for peace and national reconciliation. Some segments of the general public were increasingly ready to vote for men who would advocate both. Military reports had previously noted that many of the heretofore heavily Democratic "avalanche" counties of north Alabama were now "full of tories,"[1] the center of the most violent opposition to conscription,[2] and the area of operation of guerrilla bands composed of Unionists, draft dodgers, and deserters who were intent on preventing the Confederate government from preying on the people. Even those who had supported secession were disenchanted.[3] David Peter Lewis described to Governor Shorter the horrific conditions under which residents of Lawrence County were then forced to live and which had made them so despondent: "From Mississippi east towards Courtland, our negro cabins are empty, our plantations are grown up in weeds . . . naked chimneys and walls show where dwellings once were; piles of ashes mark spots on which once were gin houses, cribs, or cotton sheds; our rail road, with its bridges and station houses, and our county buildings destroyed." In order to try to eke out a living, he continued, even women who were in a prewar state of "ease, affluence, and refinement" were forced to plow, grub, roll logs and mill."[4] Here was a political base from which to build a party devoted to peace.[5]

But peace advocates still faced political repression and retaliation from Confederate diehards. According to one of many similar postwar accounts, men were "hunted down, and many caught with dogs, handcuffed, side-lined like brutes and drove into the slaughter pens and the poor wives and innocent children left to be fed by the federal Government and charity of the Union men who spurned the foul acts of this foul crowd of men."[6] Confederate guerrilla bands active in the pro-Union counties of Alabama knew not to rely on the local criminal justice system when dealing with Unionists in that region. The result was what the *Memphis Daily Bulletin* called a "perfect reign of terror."[7] The upshot of these activities was the flight of many more north Alabama Unionists who would have voted in the upcoming election but left the state in order to seek protection at the Union army base at Corinth, Mississippi.[8]

The forces there were under the command of Brigadier General Grenville Mellen Dodge, an Iowa resident who was the commander of a division in General Grant's Army of the Tennessee. Situated on the crossroads of the major rail lines that connected the northern portion of the Confederacy with the southern portion (the Mobile and Ohio Railroad) and the eastern portion of the Confederacy with the western portion (the Memphis and Charleston Railroad), Dodge's forces were in a unique position to maintain and protect the railroads and control vital railroad traffic in the region for the Union army.[9] Dodge would be best known for his postwar involvement as chief engineer for the construction of the first transcontinental railroad.[10] But in early 1863 he observed firsthand the plight of Unionists forced to flee for their lives to avoid conscription, political repression, and terrorism in Alabama. One of his widely publicized reports to his superiors contains a vivid and graphic description of their sad lot:

> I will merely state what I know to be true. Abe Canade and Mr. Mitchell were hung two weeks ago for being Union men. They lived on the Hackelborough Settlement, Marion County, Alabama. Mr. Hallwork and daughter, of same county, were both shot for the same cause; the latter instantly killed. The former is yet alive, but will probably die. Peter Lewis and three of his neighbors were hunted down by one hundred bloodhounds and captured. The houses of Messrs. Palmer, Welsly, Williams, the three Wrightmens, and some thirty others were burned over their heads, the women and children turned out of doors, and the community notified that if they allowed them to go into other houses, or fed or harbored them in any manner, that they would be served the same. Mr. Peterson, living at the head of Bull Mountain, was shot. I am now feeding some one hundred of these families, who, with their women and children, some gray-haired old men, and even cripples on crutches, were driven out and made their way here, through the woods and by-ways, without food or shelter—all done for the simple reason they were Union men, or that they had brothers or relations in our army. The statements of these people are almost beyond belief, did we not have the evidence before us. I am informed by them that there are hun-

> dreds of loyal men and women in the woods of Alabama, waiting for an opportunity to escape.[11]

Similar scenes took place across north Alabama, and their consequences would reverberate throughout the postwar period in Alabama.[12]

Motivated by revenge and the desire to end the war and return to their homes, many of the refugees volunteered to actively assist the Union war effort. Under the direct command of General Dodge and funded by his sale of confiscated Confederate cotton, over one hundred refugees served as spies and infiltrated Confederate lines in Alabama, Mississippi, and Tennessee to gather critically important military intelligence.[13] With the assistance of such Alabama Unionist leaders as future Republican governor William Hugh Smith, other refugees were recruited to join what was called the First Alabama Cavalry, USA, a unit that conducted numerous military operations for the Union during the war.[14] In the process, Smith formed an important and historically significant relationship with Union army captain George Eliphaz Spencer, a smart, ambitious New York-born, thirty-one-year-old former Iowa lawyer who would ultimately be placed in command of the First Alabama Cavalry.[15]

Corinth was not the only destination point for Unionist refugees from Alabama. Union sentiment in southeast Alabama manifested itself in a low rate of volunteerism for the Confederate military, considerable conscription avoidance activities, and high desertion rates. According to a letter from Governor Shorter to Jefferson Davis in early 1863, men in Coffee, Covington, Dale, Henry, Pike, and Barbour Counties "availed themselves of the facilities which their territory, generally poor and sparsely populated, affords for escape and concealment."[16] Shorter also reported to the Confederate secretary of war that the Gulf Coast area was a "common retreat of deserters from our army, tories, and runaway negroes."[17] This was confirmed in an article in the *New York Post*, which noted that Alabamians were fleeing to the Union naval base at Pensacola, Florida, where they "frequently join our forces" and "are in every instance well 'pumped' for information, which is communicated to the proper authorities."[18] In the long run, these defections would help undermine the Confederate war effort, but in the meantime every man who left the state resulted in one less vote for peace candidates in the upcoming election.

Ironically, political warfare between Northern Peace Democrats and President Lincoln also undermined Unionist efforts in Alabama. That bitter conflict was welcome news to Confederates in the South, especially those in the press who were supported by government patronage, exempt from conscription, and always on the lookout for fodder for propaganda to pump up morale. "This is a war of opinion as well as of arms," John Forsyth of the *Mobile Advertiser and Register* had earlier declared. "If our military Generals lead the soldiers of liberty to the cannon's mouth on the battlefield, it is the Generals of the Press who plan and fight the great moral battles of the revolution. The one deals in bayonets, bombshells, blood and sinews, and the other marshals the spirit of the revolution, inspires the courage and persuades to the sacrifices of the people."[19] After each battlefield loss by Confederate armies, the pro-Confederacy press had invoked the memory of the Revolutionary War experience where Britain had finally given in to American independence despite winning most of the battles.[20] After each Confederate win, the people were told that their independence was assured.

But after so many battlefield losses in the western theater, the propagandists of the Southern press had been desperate for a new angle from which to encourage continued resistance by a faltering public. The party conflict in the North, therefore, came at the worst possible time for Southern Unionists. Not long after the resurgence of Northern Democrats in the 1862 elections, a south Alabama newspaper declared that the election results "harbinger no good to the Lincoln Government as regards harmony and concert of action in prosecuting the war against us" and will "cripple and embarrass" its "war movements." Therefore, it urged, "let us fight them vigorously and with determination, and we think a change favorable for us will manifest itself before many months elapse."[21] The Southern press also highlighted the fact that in December 1862, Northern Democrats had introduced peace resolutions in Congress following the Union loss at the bloody Battle of Fredericksburg,[22] and that while the issue was still in doubt at Stones River, another Democrat had proposed an armistice and a national convention of all of the states to take place at Louisville, Kentucky, in order to resolve amicably all of the outstanding issues between the warring sides.[23] As the *Selma Reporter* observed, the Northern Peace Democrats' position was that the war would end, the nation would reunite, and the institution of slavery would remain a matter of state determination.[24] It was a seductive appeal that would ironically create a serious undertow to the Alabama peace party in the upcoming election, especially due to its effect on many Unionist slave owners. This stemmed from President Lincoln's Emancipation Proclamation, which caused slaveholding Unionists much consternation. Unless Lincoln could be convinced to withdraw it, peace meant the abolition of slavery, a result many of them had assumed would follow secession. Any possibility of avoiding that result through negotiations would require significant bargaining leverage for the Confederacy. Lincoln would have to be willing to trade away his proclamation in exchange for peace and reunion.

If that were possible, this was the time to sue for peace, while the Confederacy still had significant armies in the field and before any more battles were lost and property destroyed. As a letter to a Mississippi newspaper correctly noted, the loss of middle Tennessee by General Bragg "would place us to a great disadvantage should negotiations for peace be entered into during the spring or summer."[25] The loss of both middle Tennessee and the now hotly contested (and soon to be lost) Mississippi River valley would take away even more leverage from the South. Joshua Callaway, a Confederate soldier from Dallas County stationed in Tennessee, admitted to his wife, Dulcinea, that "if Vicksburg falls the Yankees will rejoice and our cause will be badly crippled if not lost. God forbid that it should ever fall!"[26] But there was little public effort by Alabama politicians or the press to end the fighting by encouraging a constructive response to Northern peace sentiment. The *Selma Daily Reporter* initially dismissed all such expressions of peace by the Northern public as signs of weakness from a vanquished foe, and declared that Northerners were "precisely in the predicament of a bully who had been knocked down and so pummeled by his adversary as to be compelled to beg for quarter."[27] Not everyone accepted this propaganda.

The fact remained, however, that pro-war Republicans, not Peace Democrats, controlled the White House. In a public letter to his brother, who edited the *Huntsville Confederate*, C. C. Clay Jr. conceded that "the indications of a desire for peace are multiplying at the North." But, he cautioned, "this war will continue, in some form, till the end of Lincoln's term [in March 1865], unless there will be foreign intervention, or the Democratic House of Representatives of the Yankee Congress refuse to vote supplies for the army."[28]

Confederates were opposed to negotiations, and to prove peace talks were unnecessary, propagandists created a controversial new fiction. They portrayed the typically heated political campaigns in the North as the first stage of a revolution there that would cause the Midwest to secede and then quickly bring peace and independence to the South. According to the *Selma Daily Reporter*, "it is not merely probable that the West will secede from the East, but it is absolutely certain, if deductions drawn from undoubted premises may be relied on."[29] The following week, it foresaw the "dethronement of the Gorilla [Lincoln] and the dispersion of his Cabinet, and the complete ousting of the Abolition regime from power" as a consequence of the "powerful peace party" in the North.[30]

Demonstrating the continuing persuasiveness of propaganda for some, the same Dallas County soldier who had expressed concern about the implications of losing Vicksburg was energized by this fable. Joshua Callaway wrote to his wife that if the Confederacy could hold out for the next six months, "the defeated & infuriated monster will turn upon itself, gnaw his own vitals and die. The people of the north will become divided, each party will blame the other for the failure and they will make war upon each other for revenge; and anarchy and despotism will reign without a rival throughout the North." The outcome, he assured her, was that the "States will all secede from the old Union, and one by one they will ask admittance into the Confederacy or else form a government to itself, and all that will remain of the once proud fabric of the United States will be the blood chilling history of its bloody dissolution."[31]

The problem this presented for Southern Unionists who were indifferent regarding the preservation of slavery was that it also gave hope to Unionist slaveholders that slavery could be perpetuated as a part of a peace accord if Northern Democrats prevailed. But that might occur only if the war were prolonged until the 1864 presidential election in the North. Hence, an interest in continuing the war at least until then was ironically shared by Confederates as well as proslavery Unionists. In other words, as Thomas Peters wrote years later, the war became "simply a struggle of the former masters of the slaves" to prevent the Emancipation Proclamation from being carried into effect.[32] As long as slaveholding Unionists supported the war for this purpose, peace advocates would have a very difficult time in the 1863 election. All Alabamians would suffer a terrible price for the selfishness of the masters.

IV
THE HARD WAR

Timeline: February 1863–November 1863

February 22, 1863	Union colonel Florence Cornyn's "Destroying Angels" attack Tuscumbia, Alabama.
March 21, 1863	Thomas Hill Watts announces his candidacy for governor of Alabama.
March 27, 1863	Confederate day of "fasting, humiliation and prayer."
April 14, 1863	Union General Grenville Dodge begins a destructive raid from Corinth, Mississippi, into northwest Alabama.
April 28, 1863	Union General Abel Streight's forces reach Thomas Peters's home at Moulton, Alabama.
April 29, 1863	Thomas Peters reaches his home.
May 1, 1863	Port Gibson, Mississippi, falls to Union forces.
May 3, 1863	Streight's forces are captured near the Georgia line by a force under Nathan Bedford Forrest.
May 14, 1863	Jackson, Mississippi, falls to Union forces.
May 22, 1863	Union General Grant begins siege of Vicksburg, Mississippi.
May 28, 1863	Union colonel Florence Cornyn's "Destroying Angels" destroy more property in northwest Alabama.
June 8, 1863	Thomas Hill Watts begins his campaign for governor.
July 3, 1863	Confederate forces are defeated at Gettysburg, Pennsylvania.
July 4, 1863	Confederates surrender at Vicksburg, Mississippi.
July 9, 1863	Confederates surrender at Port Hudson, Louisiana.
July 13, 1863	Union forces begin returning to Huntsville, Alabama.
July 27, 1863	William Lowndes Yancey dies of kidney disease.
August 3, 1863	Thomas Hill Watts defeats Governor John Gill Shorter in the Alabama gubernatorial race.
August 17, 1863	Alabama legislature convenes in special session.
August 22, 1863	Robert Jemison Jr. is elected by the Alabama legislature to the Confederate Senate, replacing the late William Yancey.
September 3, 1863	Union forces occupy Knoxville, Tennessee.
September 4, 1863	Women riot in Mobile over food shortages.
September 8, 1863	Confederate General Bragg evacuates Chattanooga, Tennessee.
September 23, 1863	The Alabama Supreme Court's decisions on conscription are finally released to the public.

September 20, 1863	Union forces are defeated by Braxton Bragg at Chickamauga, Georgia, but Confederates suffer 18,454 casualties and fail to retake Chattanooga.
October 9, 1863	Jefferson Davis arrives at Bragg's headquarters outside besieged Chattanooga.
October 18, 1863	Jefferson Davis speaks at Selma, Alabama.
October 19, 1863	Union guerrillas raid Pikeville, Alabama.
October 20, 1863	Governor-elect Watts speaks at Greenville, Alabama.
October 23, 1863	Governor-elect Watts gives Carnival of Blood speech at Selma.
October 27, 1863	Alabama refugee Dr. Edmund Fowler writes President Lincoln regarding the peace movement in the Alabama legislature.
November 1, 1863	Alabama legislature convenes in regular session.

9
The Destroying Angels

Some Union troops from the Midwest stationed in the South who did not agree with the Lincoln administration's war aims or policies deserted during this period.[1] But many midwesterners deployed in the South believed that Southern elites were to blame for the continuation of the war. They were determined to destroy the basis of elite wealth—as well as the South's war-making capacity—before the 1864 presidential election in order to bring the war to a close and return home. General Dodge had been an enthusiastic supporter of the Emancipation Proclamation as a means of defeating the Confederacy.[2] And as weather conditions became more favorable, he began to execute that proclamation with reinforcements that included the Tenth Missouri Cavalry under the command of an Ohio native and medical doctor, Colonel Florence M. Cornyn.[3] One of Dodge's biggest problems, however, would be controlling the ardently pro-Union Cornyn and preventing the use of controversial terror tactics that had become common during the first part of the war in Missouri, now Dr. Cornyn's home.[4]

This coincided with a change in Union military strategy from one of conciliation toward civilians to hard war concepts—including confiscation or destruction of civilian property and food, and banishment of civilians from their home regions. While Union forces applied pressure on Confederate armies in several areas simultaneously, hoping to defeat them by attrition, raids were made to destroy resources and break the South's will to fight.[5] Unfortunately for north Alabama, where the strongest and most widespread peace sentiment seemed to prevail, that is where Dodge first chose to unleash Cornyn and what became known as his Destroying Angels.[6]

A raid on Tuscumbia would shock Confederates and Unionists alike.[7] The area contained several legitimate military targets and was serving as an important manufacturing center, depot, and source of supply for General Bragg's army in Tennessee. It was also on an important travel corridor by which Confederate forces could be shifted across the Tennessee River between the Mississippi and Tennessee theaters. Dodge had received information that a large cavalry force under Confederate General Earl Van Dorn was moving from north Mississippi to cross the Tennessee River at Tuscumbia and then proceed to Tennessee to harass Union General Rosecrans's supply lines.[8] Dodge attempted to intercept and trap Van Dorn by having Union gunboats sent to Florence and by sending Cornyn's cavalry brigade through Frankfort to Tuscumbia. This brigade consisted of the Tenth Missouri, the Fifth Ohio, an Illinois battalion, and what the *Huntsville Confederate* would later describe as a "Battalion of renegades from Alabama and Mississippi."[9] Although Cornyn and his 1,200 men arrived in time to attack the rear of Van Dorn's column at Tuscumbia at 4 a.m. on Sunday, February 22, 1863, the gunboats were late and Van Dorn was thereby allowed to cross the river and escape the trap.[10]

Colonel Roddey's men had earlier been deployed to Columbia, Tennessee, where they had joined other cavalry units including that of Confederate General Nathan Bedford Forrest.[11] Therefore, Cornyn's men had not thus far faced any significant opposition and were free to turn their attention to the residents of Tuscumbia. Cornyn's force reportedly "arrested every man, searched every house except two, took nearly everything—made the ladies give up all the money and jewelry they had—broke open stores, stole all the money—broke show cases, threw things into the street, broke the blinds from the windows of private houses—pulled palings off the gardens and burned them—tore up flower yards—took all the meat, and totally ruined Tuscumbia." They also "made the men pay them what they called *Tax*, some $1,000, some $500."[12] According to the subsequent report in the Tuscumbia *North Alabamian*, "the scoundrels left town on Wednesday afternoon, taking with them about fifty bales of cotton, all the mules and horses they could find, and as many negroes as they could force off, about sixty in all." Compared to "Cornyn and his set," wrote the *North Alabamian*'s editor, Mitchel and Turchin were "angels."[13]

Cornyn had made Alabama howl long before General Sherman marched through Georgia. Evidence of the raid's psychological impact came fairly quickly. The editor of the Greensboro, Alabama, newspaper dared to advocate a discussion of whether the Union ought to be reconstructed as part of a peace accord.[14] For Unionists that was a very promising sign. Perhaps as a consequence, Union military strategists in Corinth, Memphis, and Nashville made plans for more raids that would, among other things, encourage further growth of the sentiment for peace. On March 22, 1863, Captain George Spencer reported to General Dodge that Union spies had scouted the area between Corinth and Tuscumbia and succeeded in determining the strength and locations of Confederate troops deployed in the region since the Cornyn raid in February.[15] On March 30, Dodge relayed this information up the chain of command of General Grant's Army of the Tennessee and recommended another raid through north Alabama.[16] At about the same time, Colonel Abel D. Streight, who was serving in Tennessee in General Rosecrans's Army of the Cumberland, was proposing an even more audacious move to cut a railroad supply line from Atlanta, Georgia, to General Bragg's army in Tennessee by crossing north Alabama and destroying the Western and Atlantic Railroad at Rome, Georgia.[17] The initiatives of both Dodge and Streight were approved, and at about the same time, General Grant approved another key raid, this through east Mississippi led by another Republican from the Midwest, General Benjamin Henry Grierson.[18]

Dodge was not permitted to act independently in executing his own raid, which was intended to proceed east along the Memphis and Charleston Railroad as far as Decatur.[19] Instead, he was ordered to await the arrival of Streight from Tennessee and then move together with him as far as Tuscumbia. At that point, Streight was to move southeast through Moulton and then east toward Georgia while Dodge screened Streight from attack by Confederate forces moving south.[20] But Dodge impatiently began his movement from Corinth on April 14 before Streight's arrival,[21] and his 6,500 men had little trouble taking the towns of Tuscumbia and Florence and moving through the Tuscumbia Valley to Courtland in Lawrence County. He was, however, blocked at Town Creek by the unexpected arrival of cavalry forces under the command of General Nathan Bedford Forrest, who had been hurried from Tennessee to north Alabama.[22] Nonetheless, at least one, and probably more, of Dodge's spies accompanied his advance before splitting off on their separate missions.[23]

Streight, whose 1,500 men included a number of Alabamians, finally arrived and, although poorly mounted in part on mules (his force was known as the Jackass Brigade), left Tuscumbia on the night of April 26 and reached Moulton on the evening of April 28.[24] Streight's force stopped for a few hours rest immediately across the road from Thomas Peters's home. Peters's wife later recalled that "when the federal soldiers came to our village, there were always Union men, among them, who professed to know my husband and I was never molested."[25] Streight left Moulton late in the night of April 28, and probably not coincidentally, Thomas Peters arrived there on April 29. That same day, General Dodge began his return march to Corinth, leaving a wide swath of destruction in his wake.[26]

Several newspapers that would support Governor Shorter's reelection (as well as some later Alabama historians) tended to focus primarily on Streight's

Raid, specifically the involvement of the teenage heroine, Emma Samson, and Forrest's capture of Streight's force near the Georgia line on May 3.[27] But the incident of most significance was actually Dodge's Raid. The destruction meted out by Dodge between the Alabama state line and Courtland was simply staggering. According to one Union army report, Dodge "rendered useless the garden spot of Alabama for at least one year, besides inflicting a deserved chastisement upon a most unrelenting community of intense rebel sympathizers."[28] In his report, Dodge, whose force included Cornyn's cavalry and the First Alabama Cavalry, listed the accomplishments of the raid: "Destroyed 1,500,000 bushels of corn, besides large quantities of oats, rye, and fodder, and 500,000 pounds of bacon. Captured 150 prisoners, 1,000 head of horses and mules, and an equal number of cattle, hogs, and sheep; also 100 bales of cotton, besides keeping the whole command in meat for three weeks. Destroyed the railroad from Tuscumbia to Decatur; also some 60 flatboats and ferries in the Tennessee River, thereby preventing Van Dorn, in his move, from crossing to my rear; also destroyed five tan-yards and six flouring mills. It has rendered desolate one of the best granaries of the South, preventing them from raising another crop this year, and taking away from them some 1,500 negroes."[29] Dodge's raid, thanks to Cornyn's Destroying Angels, also resulted in the burning of the military school at LaGrange[30] (see figure 11).

This was all certainly welcome news among prowar Northerners, who were weathering another Confederate victory by Robert E. Lee in Virginia, this one at Chancellorsville. The prowar segment of the Northern press, therefore, gave Dodge's efforts significant publicity.[31] The raid also had important political implications in Alabama, coming at the worst possible time for Governor Shorter, who was on the verge of announcing that he would seek reelection. A few weeks later, Alabama newspapers began reporting that Thomas Hill Watts was entering the governor's race.[32] Shortly prior to his own reelection announcement, Shorter responded to these reports by putting the spotlight on Forrest's accomplishment rather than Dodge's. He let it be known that he had demanded that Alabamians who served under Streight, as well as any Union officers found serving with armed slaves, be turned over to him for trial in Alabama state courts. This gained Shorter some positive press, but his demand was rejected by President Davis based on what the Confederate secretary of war called "considerations of public policy."[33]

North Alabama was not the only portion of the state made insecure by the various raids of Union forces at this time. As a result of the fear and confusion caused by Dodge, Streight, and Grierson, the relatively few regular military forces in Alabama were put on high alert,[34] and community leaders even in east Alabama made public appeals for volunteers to join local de-

Figure 11. LaGrange Military School (Courtesy of Alabama Department of Archives and History)

fense forces.[35] Rumors of enemy forces en route to Tuscaloosa reached as far south as Greene County,[36] resulting in consternation in west Alabama as well. Mindful that his academic institution, like LaGrange, had crossed the line to active militarization, University of Alabama president Landon Garland was not operating under any illusions. On May 4, he expressed great concern to Governor Shorter, predicting that "if the enemy should ever reach this place, they would not leave at this University one brick standing upon another."[37] Garland was still a committed Confederate, but his comments to Shorter regarding the spirit of resistance among Tuscaloosans indicate that some in the City of Oaks were not. Several chose to depart the town,[38] leaving the university's Corp of Cadets as the only significant defense force.[39]

Florence Cornyn's cavalry force, meanwhile, blew through scattered defense forces at Florence, Alabama, on May 28, 1863, and proceeded to destroy an estimated $2 million worth of property, including virtually every remaining manufacturing facility in northwest Alabama north of the Tennessee River.[40] "This raid," said the *Daily Huntsville Confederate*, "is pronounced the most successful, of any the enemy have projected, in the injury inflicted upon our people."[41] The destruction of cotton and wool-weaving factories in particular was a "serious matter to the people of this Valley, and our soldiers, who have, to a great extent, been supplied with clothing from these sources."[42] The *Confederate*, which was supporting Governor Shorter's reelection bid, directed public outrage toward Cornyn and "his horde of thieves, robbers, incendiaries and murderers" as well as several Lauderdale County men who had guided Cornyn's force to its targets. The *Confederate*'s editor urged that these "infamous traitors" be "caught and gibbeted on the first convenient limb or sapling." He was adamantly opposed to arresting them and allowing a jury to determine their fate as had already been unsuccessfully attempted. The law, he complained, "has too many loopholes of escape for traitors. A dozen or a hundred credible witnesses to distinct and separate overt acts are insufficient to convict a man of treason under the law."[43]

The havoc created by Dodge and Cornyn placed a serious strain on Confederate morale in Alabama, but so did the even more ominous threat to Vicksburg and other Confederate strongholds on the Mississippi River. Probably aware that the *New York Tribune* and the *New York Herald* had already run a front page story regarding the fortifications at Mobile in their June 4 editions,[44] thus indicating where General Grant would likely next turn his attention after taking Vicksburg, the *Mobile Advertiser and Register* warned that if the Confederate War Department failed to sufficiently reinforce Confederate forces in Mississippi and "avert the indescribable public calamity of the fall of Vicksburg into the hands of the enemy, it will have a load of guilt on its conscience which no Department could well stand under." It urged that the "whole power of the Confederacy ought to be moved to defeat Grant."[45] An anonymous correspondent to the Greensboro *Alabama Beacon* declared that the "safety of the Gulf States trembles in the balance,"[46] and another wrote that Vicksburg was "of more importance to the Confederacy than three Richmond's."[47] Despite these appeals, General Robert E. Lee was planning a move from Virginia in the opposite direction with an ill-advised invasion into Pennsylvania, which his army would begin to execute in mid-June.[48] Lee's soon-to-be irretrievably diminished ranks would not be coming to Vicksburg's rescue, a failure later subjected to considerable criticism.[49]

On July 1, the same day the equally fateful Battle of Gettysburg in Pennsylvania began, a grossly inferior twenty-three thousand man rescue force under Confederate General Joseph E. Johnston marched out of Jackson, Mississippi, to attack General Grant's heavily defended rear, manned by eighty thousand seasoned troops. But before battle could be joined, word came that the Confederate force at Vicksburg had surrendered. Then Johnston's army became the hunted, and Union forces under General Sherman chased him back first to Jackson and then thirty-five miles east to Morton, Mississippi.[50]

The *Clarke County Journal* in Grove Hill, Alabama, ominously predicted that Johnston would "likely . . . make a stand near Meridian," but "if not there then he will fall back to the Bigbee River at Demopolis,"[51] meaning that all of west Alabama from Florence to Tuscaloosa to Mobile was now in jeopardy.[52]

The fall of Vicksburg on July 4, and then Port Hudson days later, were seminal events that triggered, among other things, intense criticism in Alabama of Confederate political and military leaders.[53] Coupled with Cornyn's raids, they also produced a crisis of confidence in Alabama less than a month before the state election. For Unionist slave owners, the critically important question was how could even seasoned negotiators ever regain sufficient leverage to obtain an "honorable" peace—meaning, to them, one that would preserve slavery—without sacrificing even more men to a losing cause. The answer most refused to accept was that this leverage was now gone, never to be regained.

10
The Reconstructionists

> I thank thee for that Lord, and may we soon, yes, very soon have peace. We did not appreciate peace when we were so blessed with [it], but now we feel the want or need of it.
>
> —Diary of Sally Independence Foster, July 12, 1863.

With Confederate forces retreating in both Mississippi and Tennessee and word arriving of Lee's defeat at Gettysburg, a pall of defeatism fell over Alabamians. Joshua Callaway, then serving in General Bragg's army near Chattanooga, wrote to his wife, Dulcinea, that until news of the fall of Vicksburg had reached his company, "we were all cheerful and in good spirits," but "now we are sad and depressed." It was, he wrote, the "most paralyzing stroke that we have ever sustained." The future, he concluded, "does indeed look dark and gloomy."[1] Even George Miller, now serving in General Joseph Wheeler's cavalry in north Georgia, was forlorn. "Our army is considerably depressed at the news of the fate of Vicksburg," he wrote to his fiancée. "Upon hearing of the fall of our great Stronghold [at Vicksburg] I felt myself as tho' I would never live to see peace."[2]

This pessimism was shared by members the civilian population in Alabama from one end of the state to the other. Catherine Fennell wrote that two individuals who had just returned from Huntsville "say that the people on that side of the river think that the South had just as well stop fighting as they think the North will whip us."[3] According to a correspondent who ate dinner in a public house in Tuscaloosa, a "hale hearty old young fellow of forty-two" flatly declared to others in the room that "The game's up" and stated that "Reconstruction [on] whatever terms we can get it, say I." His listeners agreed, and one remarked that "it's time this thing was stopped."[4] Another correspondent wrote from Selma that "some people are already subjugated, although they have yet to hear the first hostile gun fired. The music of the Yankee guns have not yet greeted their ears and they are sadly in want of knee bridles to keep them from assuming an humble attitude and make sorry efforts in whistling to keep up their courage."[5] Augustus Benners wrote that "there is much perplexity and panic,"[6] and Talladega County planter James Mallory posed the rhetorical question on the minds of many in his area: "O the suffering and sorrow, when will it cease."[7] Mariah Cotton all but pleaded with her husband, John, to desert. Faced with the weighty responsibility of operating their 285-acre Coosa County farm as well as raising their seven small children without slave labor, she wrote to John that she hoped "the lorde willbee on your side and gide you saft threw all you trouble and enable you to reach home saft won time mor[.] I hope that happy day will soon com when you can com to see me and you little children[.] I hope the war will com to a close and you can com home to me to stay[.] it would be a day of joy to see you a com home saft again[.] I think if peace was made it wood be the joyfullest times that ever has ben[.]"[8] The editor of the *Selma Daily Reporter* attempted to remain upbeat but later admitted that "many of our people were as completely stunned and stupefied as if a thunderbolt had fallen upon them out of a clear sky."[9] Some had yielded themselves up to "gloom and despondency."[10]

Deserters from Bragg's army flooded the hill and mountain counties in north Alabama,[11] where they joined with emboldened Unionist guerrilla bands that were becoming increasingly active against Confederate conscripting efforts and Confederate sympathizers.[12] According to a later report by the Confederate provost marshal general, some conscription officers in north Alabama cooperated with Unionists there. They, along with the deserters, had joined forces to form what he described as a "secret society organized between the Northern and Southern armies, the object of which is to deplete our ranks by desertion."[13]

Identification of all of the leaders of the Alabama peace movement is now impossible, but after the war Thomas Peters wrote a fascinating letter to Republican Pennsylvania congressman Thaddeus Stevens revealing those of whom Peters was personally aware. In that letter, which Peters marked "Confidential," he listed the names and counties of residence of what he described as "loyal, unconditional Union men of Alabama." In addition to Peters, the list included prominent Alabama lawyers David Peter Lewis of Moulton, David Campbell Humphreys of Huntsville, Richard Sharp Watkins and William Skinner of Franklin County, Circuit Judge William S. Mudd of Jefferson County, and William Hugh Smith of Randolph County. After the war, all of these men would become members of the Republican Party and would be elected or appointed to significant offices in recognition of their wartime service to the Union.[14]

Peters's designation of these men as loyal and *unconditional* Unionists reflected not only their political views in 1860 and 1861 but also their stance during the war. This is to distinguish them from Unionists who acquiesced in or gave at least nominal support to the Confederacy after secession but who now supported reconstruction *conditional* upon the preservation of slavery and other terms. This latter faction of Unionists, called Reconstructionists, wanted to achieve peace but were afraid for the South to reenter the Union without first obtaining these concessions. After all, as a result of wartime inflation, individual slaves were selling for as much as $4,000 apiece in some portions of the South,[15] and Reconstructionists did not want to lose the equity in their investment or be surrounded by freed slaves.

Confederate propagandists did a particularly effective job of playing on those fears in order to discourage reunion and divide peace advocates, ironically turning Lincoln's Emancipation Proclamation into a powerful motivator for white supremacist resistance instead of a means of convincing the Confederates to stop fighting as Lincoln had hoped.[16] The *Mobile Advertiser and Register* predicted that if the South submitted, "the very Yankees will despise your baseness, and will begin the work of plunder with your lands and goods." Therefore, "of all the stark mad fools and empty-headed idiots that we can conceive of on this earth, the Southern submissionist and reconstructionist, at this stage of the game, is the biggest, the starkest and the emptiest. It is the prey proposing a re-alliance with the ravening wolf; it is submission of all you possess to be gobbled up by the invader." This was the Yankee "philosophy and programme of the war—to seize and confiscate the property of the South to save the North from remediless bankruptcy and ruin. It is an evil thing to be stripped of one's possessions, earned by years of anxious care and toil. But is the sting lightened by casting your pride of manhood, your personal honor and your character, as a citizen, upon the sacrificial pile?"[17] "The object of the Lincoln war," the *Advertiser and Register*'s editor continued, "is to rob you of your slaves and confiscate your goods to pay the Yankee war debt and to redeem his countless greenbacks."[18]

As events would demonstrate, one of the most prominent leaders of this Reconstructionist peace-with-slavery faction was New York-born Talladega lawyer Lewis Eliphalet Parsons[19] (see figure 12). He was a secret member of the anti-Confederate Union League,[20] a candidate for the legislature in 1863, and the choice of some to replace C. C. Clay Jr. as one of Alabama's Confederate senators.[21] According to Parsons's mortal political enemy, J. L. M. Curry, Parsons possessed "much outward severity of manner, a graceful address, a shrewd intellect, well cultivated . . . a strong will, inordinate ambition, a study of revenge, immortal hate, and a tortuous policy that disguises the execution of his purpose."[22] In other words, Parsons was a consummate politician, just like Curry.

But neither Parsons nor any other variety of Unionist—Unconditional or Reconstructionist—was brave enough to run for governor in the 1863 state election. Therefore, those intent on ousting Shorter were ultimately forced to

Figure 12. Lewis Parsons (Courtesy of Alabama Department of Archives and History)

pick from the lesser of two south Alabama evils: Thomas Hill Watts, the attorney general of the Confederacy and a staunch prewar Whig, and a late entry, James Ferguson Dowdell of Chambers County, who was then serving in the Confederate army in Mississippi.[23] As an Original Secessionist, Dowdell was as politically dead as Shorter, despite his military service. Almost by default, therefore, the odds-on favorite was Watts. Although he had voted for the secession ordinance, Watts had not come around to publicly promoting secession until after Lincoln's election. During the secession convention, he had been noticeably conciliatory to Unionist delegates. As the Confederate attorney general, he had managed to maintain a relatively low profile, as if biding his time to await the right moment to take advantage of the Alabama Democratic Party's suicidal political course. Watts was also the owner of a plantation near Greenville and a large number of slaves. Other slave owners could rest assured that he would never cut a deal for peace that did not preserve the peculiar institution. While serving as attorney general of the Confederacy, he had expressed the view that conscription was not a violation of the Confederate Constitution[24] and that members of the state militia could be conscripted,[25] thus attempting to ensure that the Confederate war effort would have adequate manpower to continue significant resistance in the field at least through Abraham Lincoln's anticipated defeat in the 1864 presidential election in the North. Watts made no campaign speeches and his public pronouncements were limited to a letter and a proclamation issued before the fall of Vicksburg.[26] Shorter's supporters attempted to paint Watts as a

Reconstructionist, and Watts appears to have avoided denying it, probably in order to garner support from anti-Shorter Unionists within the peace movement. Watts cleverly made no public statements whatsoever after the fall of Vicksburg.[27]

Defeating Governor Shorter was important to the peace movement, but the congressional and state legislative races were at least as important. Adopting the strategy used by peace advocates in North Carolina the prior year, the plan of Alabama Unionists of both varieties was to run opponents against every incumbent who was an Original Secessionist and to blame that class for bringing on the war and the resulting hardships.[28] As if an omen of things to come for the Confederacy, the leading Original Secessionist, William Yancey, became ill from a kidney disease and, according to a Montgomery newspaper, was "exhausted and emaciated."[29] He would be in no condition to canvass the state in behalf of pro-Confederacy candidates and would die on July 27, 1863, a week before the election.[30] The newly elected legislature would, therefore, be in a position to select replacements for both of Alabama's Confederate senators.

Class-based rhetoric was used by even wealthy, slave-owning Unionists to prevail in this election. Lewis Parsons, for example, was making speeches that, according to J. L. M. Curry, were characterized by Parsons's "assiduous cultivation of the mean passions that array classes against each other, his premeditated efforts to dispirit and lower the tone of our people and prepare them to make or accept unacceptable propositions for peace."[31] Similarly divisive tactics were being used in other portions of north Alabama. The *Daily Huntsville Confederate* admitted "reluctantly and sorrowfully, that we have seen lately some indications of a spirit of demagoguery—indications that we had hoped not to witness in the South, at least during the progress of the war, and which are mortifying and disgraceful as they are palpable to the most casual observer." The "most painful feature of the canvass," according to the *Confederate*, were the "appeals to the prejudices and interests of the soldier,"[32] a reference to the failure of the Confederate Congress to increase the pay of common soldiers.[33]

Some incumbents assumed they were insulated from retaliation by the soldier vote because, in contrast to the 1861 elections, most soldiers in the field were not permitted to vote. The stated reason for this arose from a state constitutional requirement that voters cast ballots only in the county, city, or town in which they had resided for the last three months.[34] Unfortunately for those incumbents, however, one subset of soldiers would be able to come home and, if they chose, vote against them. On July 18, the disgruntled and discouraged Confederate soldiers who had been taken prisoner at Vicksburg and then been paroled had been granted furloughs of thirty days by their commanding general. To the chagrin of some Confederates, they would now return home and be permitted to take out any frustrations against the Confederate government at the polls.[35]

The movement against Original Secessionists drew sharp criticism from the still generally pro-Confederacy press, as well as a warning to peace advocates from the *Selma Daily Reporter*. Their "infamous behavior is watched," and "there is a day of reckoning close at hand when they will be made to atone for their recreancy to the South. The people of this Confederacy have suffered too much to think of such baseness as is coupled with the doctrine of reconstruction, and he who aids and abets our enemies in their insane attempts to popularize the idea is a traitor of the deepest dye, and as such he will be dealt with at the proper time."[36] John Forsyth of the *Mobile Advertiser and Register* admitted that "in the spread of this feeling to the masses of the Confederacy"—meaning nonslaveholders—"lies our only danger."[37] There were slave owners "who are ready to submit and anxious for peace and the security of their property on the basis of submission." But, he warned, "it is base to feel and dangerous to be premature in the utterance of such sentiments."[38]

The only extant editorial disagreement in Alabama with these types of threats appeared in the *Livingston Messenger*, and its position would foreshadow the postelection phase of the peace movement. Although denying sympathy for Reconstructionists, the *Messenger*'s editor also denounced any restrictions on individual liberties: "We have no sympathy with this class; but at the same time we dislike to see the freedom of thought and opinion suppressed, and the despotism of Lincoln transplanted to Southern soil." Even more pointedly, the editor declared that "if the Southern confederacy can alone be maintained by muzzling the press, suppressing the freedom of opinion—bullying the people, and similar arbitrary acts, copied from Lincoln, our gallant soldiers are shedding their blood to small purpose. No, if there are Reconstructionists, let them be overcome by reason and argument—let them be silenced by the ballot box, not by a mob or military tyranny."[39]

There were challenges to getting the pro-peace voters to the polls if Alabama's election laws were enforced. On July 15, 1863, President Davis issued a call placing all "white men between the ages of 18 and 45 years, not legally exempt from military service," in the Confederate army, and ordering them to "forthwith repair to the conscript camps established in the respective States of which they may be residents, under pain of being held and punished as deserters in the event of their failure to obey this call."[40] Although this had been authorized in 1862, the Confederate government had not then exercised its power to conscript men over forty. Now, however, many men in this age group would effectively be disfranchised if the nearest conscript camp was not in the county of their residence. A combination of these laws, if rigidly enforced, would certainly have the same effect with regard to what Brigadier General Gideon Pillow estimated on July 28 as "from 8,000 to 10,000 deserters and tory conscripts in the mountains of Alabama."[41] According to one Union army spy, "over half the men from Alabama in Bragg's army are armed and in the mountains, and refuse to go back."[42] On the other hand, even if these men were not permitted to vote, they presented a real threat to the efforts of Confederates to reach the polls.[43] Although the presence of federal military forces at polling places would become a very controversial issue after the war, it was not an uncommon practice for Confederate units to be assigned to superintend elections during this period.[44] Precluding interference and guarding against illegal voters were certainly legitimate goals, but there were expressions of concern that the real reason for this military presence was to assure the "right" result. When the *Selma Daily Reporter* endorsed Thomas Hill Watts two weeks before the election, it declared that "he is the choice of the people, if they be left free and untrammeled in the exercise of the elective franchise"[45] (see figure 13).

These safeguards and tactics may, in part, explain the substantial drop in the statewide vote from 64,672 in 1861 to 38,101 in 1863. But this did not benefit Shorter, who was badly beaten by Watts (28,221 to 9,664).[46] The vast majority of the voters demanded change.[47] "Change is the cry," wrote planter James Mallory, and the change that at least some Alabamians had in mind was peace and reunion.[48] On the day before the election, the *Mobile Advertiser and Register* expressed outrage at the trend of events unfolding in north Alabama: "We hear a multitude of reports horribly detrimental to the character and patriotism of the people in many parts of Mississippi and in portions of North Alabama. Some of these reports are too disgraceful for print. Are a portion of our people gone stark mad under the pressure of temporary and local reverses, and under the potent influence of fear for their property?"[49]

They were certainly "mad," but for different reasons. On Election Day, twelve residents of the aptly named community of "Union" in the Black Belt county of Greene in west Alabama sparked even more controversy by expressly casting ballots for "Reconstruction."[50] The *Eutaw Whig* angrily called them traitors who should be arrested and banished or lynched, and the *Mobile Advertiser and Register* called upon the "civil and military authorities to note, and promptly and properly to deal with the authors of a treason so base and dastardly."[51]

Without citing any authority, some historians, including Walter Fleming, have concluded that six Unionists who favored ending the war at once and

Figure 13. Thomas Hill Watts (Courtesy of Alabama Department of Archives and History)

returning to the Union were elected from Alabama to the Confederate Congress.[52] The number is probably closer to four (of nine), and only two of those could be described as Unconditional Unionists as opposed to Reconstructionists. Another prominent Alabama historian has concluded, again without citing any authority, that the people "sent to Montgomery a legislature made up mostly of obscure men who were quite inclined to sue for peace."[53] But these men were far from obscure or, as events would demonstrate, unconditionally favorable to peace. At this point it was, in fact, questionable whether the election had brought Alabamians any closer to peace.

11
The Slaughter Pen

Many Alabamians were now even more determined to avoid any hard fighting. George Miller, then at home in Talladega on sick leave, wrote to his fiancée in September 1863 that he had been "much disappointed in almost every thing since reaching home and at times regret that I ever returned before the close of the war. From a generous-hearted, patriotic, self-sacrificing people whom I left over two years ago and for whom I have been striving to do battle ever since, I find the majority of the people cold, spineless, apathetic,—a set of demoralized extortionists, ready and willing to drink the very life blood of the widow and rush on when their souls and purses should be open to nourish and protect it."[1] Miller was even more bitter about the skulking of his fellow elites, writing that he was "astonished" to "see the numbers of men at home enjoying ease and comfort when their destiny as freemen or slaves is trembling in the balance. It does seem as tho' all who are not already in the army should hasten to the relief of the country; but the almighty dollar presents a more alluring object than the golden fleece" did to the Greeks. It would suit him, he concluded, if "the destroyer" came and "could fall directly upon them and them alone," but "alas! they are among those who generally make good their escape."[2]

For the well-to-do, a popular means of avoiding bullets was still the hiring of substitutes. Due in part to the expansion of the age of conscription, however, able-bodied substitutes had become very scarce and expensive. As a result, an illicit system of "professional" substitutes had arisen in which those desiring to avoid military service engaged a "substitute broker" who procured men using aliases to act as their substitutes, but only as long as it took the draft dodger to obtain an exemption certificate. The substitute then disappeared.[3] In an effort to combat this scheme, the Confederate War Department issued an order in the fall of 1863 requiring that any conscript furnishing a substitute "would himself become liable immediately upon the services of the substitute being lost to the Government by any cause other than the casualties of war." Until ordered to desist two months later, the always aggressive Confederate General Gideon Pillow applied this order retroactively to include the loss of a substitute's status by conscription. He also placed the problematic burden of proof on the exempted men to establish that their substitute remained in the military service.[4]

"Bomb-proof" military positions and political office were also still popular places of refuge. A disgusted correspondent reported that "on arriving at Montgomery, you'll find one Major, two Captains, and two Lieutenants to furnish transportation, plenty of men to attend to your wants, strong, able-bodied men, able to carry his musket and march his thirty miles daily." The correspondent had a logical solution to the proliferation of what some called "shade officers": "Why not let those fellows who have lost a limb fighting for their country, relieve those who during the war remained at home, and (like a hawk waiting to pounce on his prey), ready to seize the first little city office that will place them at a respectable distance from the Minnie's [rifle bullets]."[5]

The privileged were not the only ones who were evading military service. An Alabama correspondent reported that upon arriving in Chattanooga, one forty-ish conscript remarked that he had rather be a "knot on a dog's tail, than to be a conscript." Others were "staggering into this depot like urchins sent unwillingly to school."[6] Many of these reluctant soldiers did not stay long. According to one Alabama newspaper, poor men were "deserting our army now by the scores."[7] A frustrated General Pillow reported that some deserters were joining recently promoted Brigadier General Philip Roddey's mounted brigade. "I think that fully two-thirds of the commands of Generals Roddey and [James Ronald] Chalmers are composed of deserters from the infantry," a trend Pillow believed was endangering the "very existence" of the infantry.[8]

Some deserters were also joining irregular units to fight for the Union. In Jackson County, which was quickly becoming a depot and thoroughfare for regular Union army troops attempting to get into the rear of Bragg's army at Chattanooga, a "Capt. [Ephraim] Latham," according to the *Daily Huntsville Confederate*, had deserted from the Fiftieth Alabama Infantry after the Battle of Murfreesboro and then recruited "a company of traitors numbering eighty-two men." These men, who were absorbed into what was known as the First Independent Company, Alabama Volunteer Cavalry, would fight in the upcoming battle near Chattanooga, where Latham would be seriously wounded.[9] Other members of this class eschewed any type of formal military service and chose instead to join the growing number of anticonscription guerrilla bands in various parts of the state.[10]

The *Selma Daily Reporter* denigrated these deserters as "either the most dissolute and abandoned characters, or else they are idiots of the lowest type." The *Reporter*'s editor singled out "the Yahoos in North Alabama. What do they know about the great principles for which we contend? The truth is they are little better than the wild beasts with which they herd, and as such, have no more moral influence than a drove of cattle whose instinct is always to fly from danger. They regard the battlefield as a sheer slaughter pen, and not as 'the death bed of fame,' as the poet has it, and as the patriot esteems it."[11] As far as those "Yahoos" were concerned, the impolitic editor of the *Reporter* had it right. They had no interest in climbing into his "death bed of fame" and ignored President Davis's offer of general amnesty and pardon issued on August 1 as a means of trying to entice men back into the ranks.[12]

Most newspapers, however, were more conciliatory and charitable toward the common man. The *Tuscaloosa Observer* advocated that the Confederate Congress levy a tax on slave owners to "save the Confederate currency from further depreciation" and thereby bring the inflation that had preyed on the poor under control. The editor's rationale was remarkably candid: "Tax the planters—tax the slave interest. If our rulers are not all demagogues and time-servers, they will rise up to the exigency of the times, and put the pecuniary burden of the war upon those for whom the war is now waging—the slaveowners—the men who are getting rich by staying at home to make corn crops to sell to soldiers' families at $1.50 per bushel."[13]

Fortunately for the elites, many of the poor were illiterate and could not read the editorial barbs aimed in their direction. It was, nonetheless, suggested that barbecues be conducted at which influential Confederates in the community would raise the specter of racial equality. This strategy had been used very effectively throughout the antebellum period and the secession crisis to sway nonslaveholders to support the position of economic elites. All that was necessary, wrote one newspaper editor, was for the issue of "negro equality" to be "presented to them in the right light to make them as zealous in this war, as any other class."[14] In a public letter issued shortly after his promotion to the rank of brigadier general, Philip Dale Roddey added his voice to this chorus, pointing out that the abolition of slavery, "either immediate or gradual, would render the South a home where no decent white man, *rich or poor*, would live. The [overseas] colonization of millions of negroes, by a nation already exhausted by the greatest war known to history, is impossible; and the experiment will be a fearful one to us, unless we can descend to the level with the negro, even to amalgamation. There will be a war of extermination between the two races," he predicted, "during which the power of the federal government will be thrown into the scale of the negro."[15] Despite this race-baiting, many common folks still showed little desire to fight for the Cause.[16] There was supposedly some interest in local defense in portions of west Alabama. According to the *Eutaw Whig*, the "exempts of Tuscaloosa County are organising rapidly for the purpose of repelling Yankee raids. It is thought over five hundred men and boys, capable of good service, will readily form companies for this purpose."[17] Further east, however, there was little enthusiasm for dying in the last ditch. Confederate Colonel W. H. Jenifer, the young and soon-to-be very controversial new commander of the military post at Selma, initially attempted to scare the civilian population into participating in local defense preparation activities by implying that a Yankee cavalry raid was on its way.[18] The local newspapers played along. "It is believed by many," assured the *Selma Daily Reporter*, that "Selma is the point aimed at by the marauders, and it is therefore especially incumbent upon the people of this city and vicinity to hold themselves in readiness to move at any moment in the work of driving back the vandals—let them come when they will."[19] With the Jackson *Mississippian* newspaper now being published in Selma, where other Mississippi residents had taken refuge,[20] Selmans had a constant reminder of what they might have to do upon the arrival of those vandals. Nonetheless, the civilian population in Selma showed little enthusiasm for working on local defenses. Frustrated, Colonel Jenifer resorted to ridicule when he took a not-so-subtle shot at the business community, declaring that "those who cannot spare the time to leave their offices, or other places of business, to spend a few hours in the fortifications around the city, will be promptly relieved by the patriotic ladies of Selma, who will cheerfully and willingly attend to their business matters while the men are fighting for their protection."[21]

Mobilian Kate Cumming had observed that as far as the traditional social role of women was concerned, war "has cast aside all conventionalities, as it should."[22] Consistent with this, the support of Selma women for the Confederate military was well-known, and Colonel Jenifer had good reason to believe that they would do their part.[23] They had earlier responded to the severe shortage of an essential ingredient for gunpowder, "niter" (then sometimes spelled "nitre"—an oxidizer that had in antebellum times been imported from India and which is mixed with charcoal and sulfur) by retaining the urine from their chamber pots for collection by the local Nitre and Mining Bureau. A local lawyer, Thomas Badger Wetmore, waxed poetic about the practice: "We thought the women did enough at sewing shirts and kissing; but [Selma attorney Jonathan Haralson, the head of the Nitre Bureau] have put the lovely dears to patriotic p[issin]g."[24]

None of this could stay the inexorable advance of the Union army, however, giving Unconditional Unionists further opportunity to push for peace. General Rosecrans was moving across the Cumberland Mountains toward General Bragg and Chattanooga, the gateway to east Alabama and Georgia.[25] A fortnight prior to the election, Governor Shorter had issued a call for a special session of the legislature to begin on August 17, primarily for the purpose of addressing, and hopefully augmenting, the state's defenses.[26] If some historians were correct in their assessment of the strong Unionism of the newly elected legislature, this was the perfect opportunity to provide the evidence. But that certainly did not happen.

The day after General Rosecrans began his move toward Chattanooga, the legislature convened in Montgomery and quickly selected officers for each house. Those officers were almost exclusively former Whigs. Robert Jemison Jr. was elected president of the senate without opposition.[27] The day after Governor Shorter's final address, Lewis Parsons, the presumed peace advocate, offered a joint resolution in the house that made no mention of peace and, instead, shockingly gave a vote of confidence, thanks, and "continued candid support" to Jefferson Davis.[28] This particular resolution did not pass, but one was eventually unanimously adopted, which reaffirmed that Alabama would "never submit to abolition rule" and pledged "to the cause of independence and perpetual separation from the United States all the resources of the State of Alabama." In an obvious jab at the Unconditional Unionists, this same resolution declared it to be "the paramount duty of every citizen in the Confederate States to sustain, invigorate and render effective our gallant armies to the full extent of his ability by encouraging enlistments, by furnishing subsistence to the families of soldiers at prices corresponding with the means of such families, and by upholding the credit and currency of the Confederate Government." To "dishearten the people and the soldiers" was forbidden.[29]

On August 22, 1863, Jemison was elected over John Anthony Winston to the late William Yancey's seat in the Confederate Senate by an overwhelming margin on a single ballot.[30] As the *Montgomery Advertiser* later noted, "In a spirit of magnanimity, the former [Democrat] opponents of Mr. Jemison yielded his election without a contest, when it is well known that, had there been a party organization on their part, his success would have been greatly endangered, if not defeated."[31] Some, like a Columbus, Mississippi, newspaper editor, saw Jemison's selection as "a triumph of Unionism over Secession" and a sign that the "whole legislature are an anti-war party and belong to what is called the conservative, or peace party."[32] And as Joseph C. Bradley, a Reconstructionist legislator from Huntsville, later wrote, Jemison was "elected by union men in our State Legislature" and subsequently discussed strategy with Bradley about "the attempt that the union men intended to make in Ala[bama] to force the State back into the Union" when "our State was ready to act."[33] This may have been true, but on August 25, Jemison nevertheless gave a prowar speech, published throughout the state, in which he declared that the only alternative "now presented to us is, to press forward, arms in hand, until we shall have achieved an honorable and glorious independence, or to tamely and basely submit to the lowest political and social degradation." He pledged a "zealous and unwavering support" for "Southern independence" and implored the people to "press forward to conquer an honorable peace or to honorable graves."[34]

Much has been made by historians of this legislature's supposed sabotage of Alabama's militia structure in the bill that was eventually adopted.[35] But if the majority in this legislature had actually been committed to peace, it would not have passed any militia bill at all. Significantly, they went along with a proposal to impose militia duty on sixteen-and seventeen-year-olds and those between forty-six and sixty, although these two groups—called the "county reserves"—were restricted to use in their home counties.[36] This supposedly pro-peace legislature was not opposed to eating the state's proverbial seed corn either. The militia bill also provided that the "cadets of the University of the State"—apparently regardless of age—were to be organized into a military corp and made subject to the orders of the Governor "for any military services within the State."[37] The university's board of trustees had just recently made provisions to expand the student body to three hundred cadets.[38] According to the board's report, the additional number of students would be accommodated "by the erection of cheap but comfortable shanties," which could be increased to handle four hundred students.[39]

Before adjourning on August 29, this legislature also made it a felony to "feed, harbor, secrete or aid to escape any deserter or straggler from the army or navy of the Confederate States," with the penalty being "such punishment as the jury trying the case shall by their verdict impose." This law also imposed a duty on state civil and militia officials to arrest deserters,[40] possibly a response to a recent controversial decision by a member of the North Carolina Supreme Court holding that that state's militia had no legal authority to arrest deserters from Confederate military service.[41] The new Alabama deserter bill made it the *duty* of the militia as well as civilian officials in Alabama to do so,[42] thereby supplementing the Confederate government's efforts to round them up and put them back on the front lines.[43] As Abraham Lincoln had written a few weeks earlier to New York governor Horatio Seymour explaining his rationale for continuing with the draft in that troubled state, "we are contending with an enemy who, as I understand, drives every able bodied man he can reach into his ranks, very much as a butcher drives bullocks into a slaughter pen."[44]

Finally, a committee of the Alabama house issued a report expressing a willingness to "experiment" with the use of slaves as soldiers in the Confederate army, and the full house overwhelmingly adopted a resolution to that effect.[45] As Margaret Storey noted in her seminal book on Alabama Unionists, the Union army had begun recruiting freed Alabama slaves and organizing them into fighting units shortly after President Lincoln's final Emancipation Proclamation was issued.[46] But up to this point, the Confederacy's use of Alabama slaves had been limited to noncombat roles such as constructing fortifications, most notably around Mobile Bay.[47] There was a doubtful logic in the idea that slaves might fight to remain slaves.[48] For all anyone knew, once armed, the slaves would join forces with the Union army and its growing number of black troops.[49] At the very time this legislature was in session, Union forces were conscripting former slaves in north Alabama (who had recently been freed from slavery by Lincoln's proclamation) and placing them in camps of instruction there to train them to fight and end slavery forever.[50] And in the last several months, the Alabama press had published a public letter from Abraham Lincoln assuring the new recruits that they would not be fighting in vain. Lincoln vowed that his Emancipation Proclamation could not be retracted "any more than the dead can be brought to life."[51] This was followed by reports of a thwarted slave insurrection in Georgia.[52] Historians have estimated that approximately five thousand Alabama slaves enlisted in the Union army,[53] although no statue stands in Alabama in their memory.[54]

Even if a mechanism were established to allow slaves to be enlisted for Confederate service, there was reason to believe their masters would not permit it. A public auction in Mobile demonstrated that what the press called "ordinary field hands" were worth an average of $3,100 each. One newspaper editor noted that "as the enemy advances, the prices for darkies do the same, showing a display of very little fear for the security of such property."[55] Why would slave owners put their increasingly valuable investments in danger? And as the editor of the displaced *Daily Huntsville Confederate* pointed out, white soldiers would "rebel at the idea of being thus reduced to anything approaching terms of equality with negroes" by serving together.[56]

Two years earlier, even the intimation of arming slaves would have been hooted down. But now some Alabama Confederates were desperate and willing to delude themselves into believing that slave soldiers constituted the panacea for augmenting the Confederacy's degraded military power. "The idea strikes us as entirely feasible," wrote the naive editor of the *Selma Reporter*, "for why should not the negro be as docile and obedient under the military law as he is on the plantation at home? And why should he not fight with as much enthusiasm as his master—so far as his capacity will permit—since he has as much stake as any one!"[57] The prior year, the Alabama legislature had quietly authorized the formation of a militia unit in Mobile composed of free, mixed-race, property-owning blacks called Creoles who were assigned to noncombat roles such as guarding government warehouses there.[58] There was obviously support now for accepting them as well as enslaved blacks into the Confederate army. In the end, however, the legislature passed along the decision by adopting a joint resolution submitting to the Confederate Congress "the propriety and policy of using in some effective way a certain percentage of the male slave population of the Confederate States, and to perform such service as Congress may by law direct."[59] [60]

The Alabama press voiced no criticism of this legislature's decisions. On the contrary, they were praised. As John Forsyth of the *Mobile Advertiser and Register* concluded, this legislature was actually "as firm and resolute in its purpose to fight out the war to the bitter end as the most boisterous of those who were full of fight before the first gun was fired."[61] He was particularly pleased that "no man in that body was base coward enough to talk of peace and laying down arms while a Yankee footstep polluted our soil and a Southern claim to freedom was acknowledged."[62]

12
The River of Death

Unlike obedience, loyalty and morale are not traits that can be legislated, and these times were filled with news emphatically suggesting that the war was a lost cause and its continuation a waste of lives and property. Among other things, very dark war clouds were still forming over north Alabama and east Tennessee as General Rosecrans attempted to close the noose around General Bragg's army at Chattanooga in the fall of 1863 (see map 4). "The crossing of the Tennessee River by the federal army at Bridgeport [Alabama]," wrote the editor of the *Selma Daily Reporter*, "is the signal of a terrible conflict, upon the issue of which vibrate the destinies of Georgia and Alabama, if not the balance of the Gulf States."[1] James Thomas Searcy confirmed this in a letter from Chattanooga to his sister in Tuscaloosa. "I had rather the battle would be here than further south in our country. You all at home pray for the success of our arms. It is," he concluded, "a battle fraught with great results at stake."[2] But Bragg did not immediately stand and fight. The Confederacy attempted to stop the Union juggernaut by pouring reinforcements into Bragg's army, but Bragg avoided Rosecrans's trap by evacuating the city. His forces retreated to a location on the south side of then obscure Chickamauga Creek in northwest Georgia.[3]

As Alabamians awaited the battle, evidence of civil unrest continued to multiply. John Forsyth had earlier warned against price gouging on foodstuffs and predicted that "wheat will be a delicate subject to speculate upon this year. There's a perfect volcano of public indignation seething and boiling upon this matter already."[4] That volcano erupted in Forsyth's town on September 4, 1863. A large group of women armed with knives and hatchets marched from Spring Hill Road down Dauphin Street carrying banners with messages such as "Bread or Blood" and "Bread and Peace" and then proceeded to pillage several stores, taking food and clothing. They refused to disperse, even in the face of the Mobile Cadets militia unit, until the mayor and provost marshal promised to address their needs.[5] On the same day as the

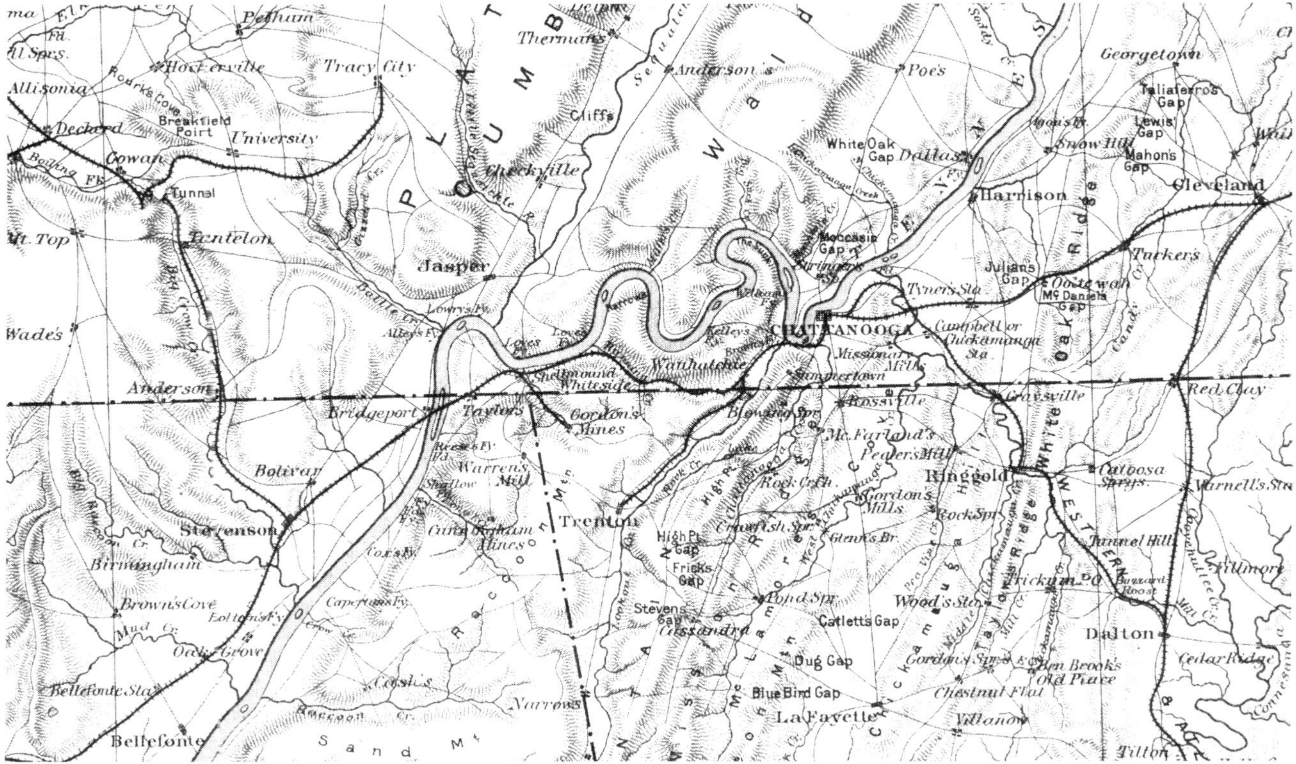

Map 4. Vicinity of Chattanooga and northeast Alabama (*Official Military Atlas of the Civil War*)

Mobile bread riot, a group of what were described as "mechanics and artisans connected with the Government works" reportedly held a public meeting at the Selma city hall with the "avowed object the suppression of extortion as it now exists in our midst." According to press accounts, their targets were the "speculators and extortioners, who are charging such enormous prices for the necessaries of life that it nearly amounts to a prohibition."[6] No violence ensued, but the possibility of a crippling labor strike in the war-related industries in the area could not have been far from anyone's mind. Acts of espionage had already occurred in Selma and more might be in the offing.[7] According to Selma attorney James Quinton Smith, the labor force in Selma consisted of "mostly northern men and foreigners" who were "without loyalty to the South, but who were compelled to work or be conscripted."[8] With inflation now out of control, even more force might have to be used to assure continued production if conditions did not improve. There was talk in the Confederate Congress of imposing martial law in the area because of what one congressman referred to as the "late mob at Selma, Ala."[9]

As the civilian population became increasingly disheartened, friction with the Confederate government was inevitable. Members of Alabama's legal profession were sometimes caught in the middle when they used writs of habeas corpus to free political prisoners or those improperly arrested by Confederate conscript officers. James Quinton Smith was arrested by the post commander at Selma and sent to Mobile to be confined in a military prison after seeking to have that commander held in contempt of court for failing to respond to a writ of habeas corpus questioning the confinement of Smith's client, a local merchant who had been arrested for refusing to receive Confederate money.[10] Fortunately for Smith and others like him, the Confederate Congress had adopted a measure generally known as the "Habeas Corpus Commissioner" law under which commissioners were appointed by the Confederate War Department and charged with the responsibility of investigating the arrest of civilians by the military in order to determine whether there was probable cause to hold them.[11]

Serving as one of these commissioners was physically arduous and potentially dangerous. Among other things, military commanders were less than cooperative. The first Alabamian who was appointed commissioner, Percy Walker of Mobile (Leroy Pope Walker's brother), resigned within ninety days of his appointment.[12] Benjamin Saffold's brother, Milton, was appointed to replace Walker with the assistance of Saffold family friend John Archibald Campbell, then assistant secretary of war.[13] Milton Saffold was initially reluctant to accept the appointment and even asked Campbell for another assignment, but he eventually embraced the task.[14] As Saffold explained after the war, his duties were to "discharge from the Bastiles and military prisons loyal men and women, whom the sedition laws of a manufactured proscriptive sentiment incarcerated therein for alleged disloyal expressions." He recalled that "the secession press and public denounced me for discharging these Union people as a Reconstructionist," a perception that was quite accurate.[15]

Within four days of James Quinton Smith's arrest, Saffold conducted a hearing and ordered Smith's discharge from military custody. Smith then issued a letter to the Selma press lambasting the Selma commander's "utter disregard of statute laws, Constitution and the rights of the citizen there-under," as well as his "contempt of the Courts of Alabama." Smith asserted that "the last spark of expiring liberty" was becoming "extinct."[16]

Saffold's release of Smith and others may explain why military authorities in Alabama began transferring prisoners from Alabama to North Carolina, Mississippi, and other states outside Saffold's jurisdiction. Fortunately for Unionists and Saffold, the Department of War denounced that practice,[17] and John Archibald Campbell later issued a letter to Saffold approving of his course of action and continuing his appointment.[18] At least for the time being, Saffold remained exempt from conscription and in a position to help others.[19]

Even if James Quinton Smith had remained in Alabama under Milton Saffold's protection, the Alabama Supreme Court's extremely important and fateful decisions in a series of conscription and militia-related cases limited legal options considerably. The court rejected challenges to the constitutionality of conscription and approved the state's right to force those who had obtained substitutes to perform militia duties. This substantially limited the legal profession's ability to stop the government from forcing men to fight. Although the official *Alabama Reports* state that the decisions in these cases were rendered during the court's January 1863 Term of Court, newspaper accounts indicate that the opinions were not revealed to the public until, significantly, September 14, 1863, after the state election and after the legislature had adjourned.[20]

The following month, another controversial instance of civilian-military conflict, this time over conscription, occurred in Pike County in southeast Alabama. This region had long exhibited signs of disloyalty to the Confederacy and was, therefore, apparently subject to de facto martial law.[21] Future Alabama Republican Benjamin Gardner, a Troy attorney, wrote to the governor that "an armed guard patrols our square every moment, and the citizens feel that they are under military surveillance."[22] Not surprisingly given this area's lukewarm support for the war effort, local lawyers were from time to time called upon to seek writs of habeas corpus in connection with arrests by conscription officers. The probate judge in Pike County happened to be Benjamin Fitzpatrick's nephew, Bird Fitzpatrick, a Douglas Democrat who did not automatically approve decisions of the Confederate military. Fitzpatrick had crossed the military one too many times. At the behest of Pike County lawyer Alexander Wallace Starke, who had been narrowly defeated in his bid to unseat pro-Confederate James Lawrence Pugh during the congressional elections in August,[23] Judge Fitzpatrick granted a writ of habeas corpus to a man who had been appointed a Confederate tax collector and was arguably therefore exempt from conscription. As had occurred in Selma, that order was ignored by the military. Starke sought and received an order holding the conscript officer in contempt of court, but Confederate soldiers obstructed the county sheriff from executing his arrest, whereupon Fitzpatrick issued an arrest warrant for the local military commander. Future Republican McCaleb Wiley, another local lawyer who had also run against Pugh, interceded to diffuse the confrontation, reportedly as amicus curiae. But by this time Judge Fitzpatrick was so incensed that he ordered Wiley's arrest. The military prevented the sheriff from making this arrest as well, and then arrested *Fitzpatrick*. He was released after a few hours, but the public relations damage was already done.[24] Several Alabama newspapers joined the Troy *Southern Advertiser* in denouncing the Confederate government for the conduct of the soldiers. "Upon the whole," charged the *Advertiser's* editor, "it was one of the most high-handed acts that has been perpetrated in this government—one which is shameful to the country—one which calls for redress, and that quickly."[25] This disregard of civil authority threatened to dramatically expand growing disaffection and increase civil resistance. It therefore played into the hands of those attempting to end the war.[26]

Confederate policies adopted in 1863 in an effort to supply the army ironically also undermined the relationship between the government and its fighting men. The Confederate Congress formally authorized "impressments," or confiscation of goods, produce, horses, mules, slaves and other property for military use in exchange for rapidly depreciating Confederate money. The upshot was that families on the home front were deprived of essential property, and at arbitrarily low prices.[27] Governor Watts recognized the dangers inherent in this practice and warned Confederate secretary of war James Seddon (who had replaced George Randolph) that "if we fail to achieve our independence in this contest, the failure will arise from breaking down the spirits of the People by acts of tyranny by our own officers. The impressments of property," he declared, "only aggravates the price, and creates opposition, to the Government, & our cause."[28]

In addition to what some charged was legalized theft, the hated Confederate tax-in kind law was soon to be implemented. It was adopted early in the year and imposed a tithe on certain farm products even from the wives of soldiers. Available foodstuffs were, as a result, about to become even more scarce and expensive.[29] This tax disproportionately impacted the families of the poor, who needed every kernel of corn and pound of meat they raised in order to survive.[30] Nonslaveholders of moderate means were also resentful. John Cotton's wife, Mariah, had been forced to hire a neighbor's slave to make their crop on their Coosa County farm while John was serving in a cavalry unit. He wrote to her from Tennessee that "it looks hart too think a soldier that has to hire a crop made has to give a tenth of it to the government and him in the field fiting to sustain it." But as if he suspected his mail was being censored, Cotton added that "if the tax would sustain it I would be wiling to pay as much or more."[31] Increasing class tensions, the editor of the *Tuscaloosa Observer* attempted to jawbone local planters to lower the asking price of their corn "and thus put bread into the mouths of the hundreds of helpless women and children whose husbands and whose fathers have gone forth to fight the battles of the country." He particularly challenged "the planters of the Warrior [River] bottoms to rise to the performance of the solemn duty imposed upon them by that bountiful Providence who has blessed them with overwhelming granaries. Give up the idea of adding to your gains," he acidly concluded, "and, for once at least in your lives, act like patriots and Christians."[32]

Despite admonitions to the contrary, poorly fed Alabamians minced no words in describing their plight to family members and friends in the army.[33] In a widely reported letter found on the battlefield following the Battle of Chickamauga, a Talladega man wrote to a soldier in Bragg's army that the war would soon be over and that "all the people in Alabama and Mississippi are holding meetings to see whether they will go back into the Union or not—that the Yankees will whip our Rumps by Christmas—that the woods are full of deserters and paroled men, who swear that they will not go back in the army."[34] Such letters encouraged more desertion. George Koon wrote to his wife, Sarah, from a camp near Chattanooga that dozens of recent desertions had depleted his company down to only thirty men.[35]

But desertion certainly did not place men, or their families, out of danger. Conscription officers supported by cavalry units were sweeping Alabama's counties to recover every man possible for military service. Raids were made in Tuscaloosa and Pickens Counties in September and October 1863, for example, and men who resisted were killed and the wives of those who eluded capture were placed in the county jail and held hostage.[36] These brutal tactics were reportedly also used in Talladega County. "Two women were publicly hung at Talladega" for "refusing to divulge the hiding places of their husbands who had fled at the approach of the conscripting officers. A perfect reign of terror exists in this part of the country. The woods are full of refugees trying to evade the relentless conscripting officers."[37]

Things would not soon improve as the battle began in northwest Georgia near what one Confederate general would call the River of Death.[38] Fighting commenced with the advance of a portion of Bragg's army across the Chickamauga Creek. Before it was all over a few days later, both sides would suffer a huge number of casualties, including a significant number of Alabamians. The dead also included a brother-in-law of Abraham Lincoln who was a Confederate brigade commander.[39] After Rosecrans's army had successfully avoided annihilation by retreating back to Chattanooga, the Alabama press initially proclaimed the Battle of Chickamauga a glorious victory that would soon help bring the war to a close. "Lincoln is whipped and doomed this day," declared the *Selma Daily Reporter*, "and a few more months of manly front at the South will show it to the world."[40] But the truth was that Bragg's army had suffered a staggering 18,454 Confederate casualties, and his victory was incomplete. To retake the Union army stronghold at Chattanooga by force would require fresh troops the Confederacy simply did not have, and more lives that it could not spare. As the *Mobile Advertiser and Register* and other civilian and military commentators noted with obvious frustration, the opportunity for making a successful attack on Rosecrans was during his retreat from the Chickamauga battlefield toward Chattanooga: "The hour when it might have been successfully done has passed," and an attempt to do it now "would be akin to madness."[41] Indeed, it would result in yet another slaughter pen that many deserters were then seeking to avoid.[42]

Bragg had disregarded the advice of his subordinates to pursue Rosecrans into Chattanooga before Rosecrans could stabilize his defenses there. Instead, he chose to lay siege to the city just as General Grant had to the Confederate forces at Vicksburg and Port Hudson.[43] John Cotton wrote to his wife from Bragg's army that "I think ould [General] brag is trying to get them out of chattanooga without a fite[.] if he can it will be best for if we have to whip them out we will lose a many a man and mayby get whipped."[44] Bragg's strategy was mercifully risk averse, but unlike Grant at Vicksburg, he did not have the luxury of time to wait Rosecrans out at Chattanooga. Due in part to the growing number of black troops in the Union army capable of taking over occupation duties in other areas, including north Alabama,[45] as well as the control of key transportation facilities, the North could fairly rapidly reinforce and resupply Chattanooga and launch a new offensive.[46] As a result, according to a Northern newspaper, the Union soldiers in Chattanooga "regard the result of their battles as a virtual triumph, and the rebel prisoners pronounce it a virtual defeat to Bragg."[47]

So did Bragg's subordinate (or insubordinate) officers. The already toxic chemistry between them devolved into an ugly, public controversy over whether Bragg ought to remain in command.[48] The *Mobile Daily Tribune* reprinted an article from the *Charleston Courier* in which a correspondent reported "doubt and disappointment, and the spirit of complaint which I am free to state prevails throughout the army. Officers and men all feel that instead of lying idly today on the borders of Tennessee, we should have been in Nashville, or beyond the broken columns of the federal army retreating before our onward march."[49] A worried Jefferson Davis hurried from Richmond and arrived at Bragg's headquarters on October 9 to mediate between Bragg and his generals.[50] To the chagrin of many, Davis made no change in command. Davis reviewed the troops and addressed them in a brief speech from the porch of a farmhouse on Missionary Ridge.[51] John Cotton wrote to his wife that "ould Jef davis had been up here and made a speech and said peace would bee made in six months."[52] But did any of the rank and file soldiers accept this?

Davis's problems also included the growing peace movement in Alabama, where the legislature was scheduled to convene in its regular session on November 9. He was, as a result, forced to expand his mission beyond his meeting with Bragg and his staff to include a speaking tour in Alabama calculated to pressure legislators to hold the line. For similar reasons, Governor-elect Thomas Hill Watts announced his intention to return from Richmond and address the people. According to the *Huntsville Confederate*, Watts's goal was "to arouse the people to their duties" and promote an "active, energetic, persevering resistance to the aggressions of our enemy. We are glad to hear it. He will, thereby, practically refute the slander that has been inconsiderately or feloniously uttered that he favored reconstruction."[53]

Jefferson Davis made his first speech in Alabama on October 18 from the front door of the Gee House Hotel in Selma where, according to press accounts, he emphasized that the Confederacy's only hope was to conquer a peace by "force of arms." Davis assured his listeners that with more troops, the Union army at Chattanooga that was threatening Alabama could be defeated.[54] Davis subsequently spoke at Demopolis, and the content of his message was likely the same. Not everyone was impressed. Grant Taylor, a Confederate soldier from Tuscaloosa County who had been one of the many parolees from Vicksburg, wrote to his wife from Demopolis that Davis did not "look like anything extra" and in fact his appearance was "similar to a smoked dried herring."[55]

Watts began his own Alabama speaking tour on October 20, 1863, near his large plantation in Butler County with an address at the Baptist church in Greenville. According to the *Greenville Observer*, Watts reminded the overflow audience of "the causes underlying our withdrawal from the old Union," discussed "the history of our struggle for independence," "braced the nerves of the despondent, and encouraged new cheer" by—incredibly—"showing that there was no cause for despondency under heaven."[56] On October 23, Watts made essentially the same speech at Selma's city hall. The *Selma Dispatch* reported that Watts also told the crowd that the Confederacy's prospects "were bright, and brightening hourly, and not many days would elapse before the power of Lincoln would be effectually broken." In a quote reprinted across the South, Watts was said to have declared that President Davis had told him Rosecrans's army "would be compelled to leave Tennessee *before October* went out, and he [Watts] believed it."[57]

Watts also made a fiery denunciation of the doctrine of reconstruction. According to the *Selma Daily Reporter*, he "showed that reconstruction was both absurd and ridiculous, from the fact that there was no longer any Union. Slavery had been abolished, the *habeas corpus* swept away [in the North] and every other constitutional right and indeed the doctrine had been already avowed that the Southern States must be reduced to the condition of Territories." Watts asserted that "to go back to the Yankees as prodigals and traitors would be to give up every civil right. We would not only be a race of beggars, but slaves of the most abject kind. We would not even have the right of trial by jury." Given this, "he preferred to see *every man and woman perish in one grand carnival of blood* rather than accept such a destiny."[58]

Watts then proceeded up the Alabama and Tennessee Rivers Railroad, stopping at Montevallo on October 24 to repeat his now stock speech.[59] By this time, Jefferson Davis was completing his speaking tour through Alabama. After visiting Meridian, Mississippi, Davis had proceeded to Mobile, where he reviewed the troops on October 24 and made another speech.[60] On October 26, the day after Union reinforcements led by Union General Joseph Hooker began crossing the Tennessee River at Bridgeport, Alabama, and moving toward Chattanooga, Davis left Mobile and stopped at Pollard, Alabama, to address Brigadier General James Holt Clanton's brigade.[61]

Clanton was a Montgomery lawyer and protégé of Thomas Hill Watts (see figure 14). In early 1863, following a raid from the Union army's base at Pensacola into Geneva and Coffee Counties,[62] Governor Shorter had ap-

Figure 14. James Holt Clanton (Courtesy of Alabama Department of Archives and History)

pointed Clanton as his special aide-de-camp and then sought and obtained special permission from Jefferson Davis to permit Clanton to recruit men in southeast Alabama subject to conscription, along with deserters, and to form a brigade charged with the defense of that region.[63] In many respects Clanton's task was similar to that of Philip Dale Roddey—to recruit from a population indifferent and oftentimes hostile to the Confederate cause.[64] Clanton had eventually been successful in organizing his brigade but was unsuccessful in creating a motivated, disciplined fighting force. Judging from press accounts, Jefferson Davis must have repeated his peace-is-just-around-the-corner theme at Pollard, because Clanton's men—who would mutiny shortly after Christmas—reportedly gave Davis "one of the most gratifying receptions of his tour."[65] Clanton's men had a very different kind of peace in mind than Davis, however, and they were not alone.

Within a matter of days, Alabama newspapers were reporting that Bragg's siege of Chattanooga was effectively undermined by General Grant's establishment of his "cracker line" back to Bridgeport, Alabama ("cracker line" was a term for a route that provided food and supplies).[66] Even worse, General Sherman and his army were en route from Mississippi toward Chattanooga to help Grant oust Bragg from the mountains encircling that town.[67] The lead elements of Sherman's seventeen thousand men reached Iuka, Mississippi, on October 10, and Sherman himself arrived at Corinth on October 13.[68] The Confederate high command assumed that Sherman's plan was to proceed east to Tuscumbia and then on the Memphis and Charleston Railroad through

Lawrence County to Decatur. A large force of Confederate cavalry, including General Joseph Wheeler's and Roddey's brigades, was busy destroying that span of road and bracing for Sherman's approach.[69] The problem for the Confederates was that this entire cavalry force was south of the now swollen and still rising Tennessee River. Sherman knew this and, as he wrote to General Henry Halleck, was planning to use the Union's naval supremacy to cross that river at Eastport and checkmate the Confederates by simply proceeding through Florence and across north Alabama toward Chattanooga on the north side of the river.[70] To confuse the Confederate commanders south of the river and buy time for the arrival of naval transports, Sherman continued to press one of his divisions south of the river toward Tuscumbia. His plan worked, although the Confederate cavalry's hollow success in repulsing that feint was trumpeted in the Alabama press as a major victory, even though Tuscumbia was briefly occupied.[71] General Wheeler's cavalry force at Courtland was then sent east to Bragg's army and away from Sherman.[72] The remaining forces were, as a result, inadequate to stop Sherman on either side of the Tennessee River. Young Sally Independence Foster, a member of a prominent Florence family, wrote of the overnight stay and the passage of Sherman's army through her town: "They camped on the male college hill and in the college, and back of Mrs. Williams, and a great many places," including in the Foster home. "A large army passed through today; and a great many yesterday," Foster said. She was obviously perturbed that the Yankees were in her town, but she noted that "they have beautiful music. I was awaken[ed] this morning by them leaving, and, also the beautiful music."[73] The only remaining impediments to Sherman's movement across north Alabama was the swollen Elk River in Limestone County west of Athens.[74] But both would soon be overcome.[75]

While Confederate forces in Alabama were focused on Sherman, less well-known smaller operations were initiated. A large Union cavalry force raided through Madison County, reportedly taking large numbers of mules, horses, cattle, and other items.[76] In addition, on October 19, General Dodge reported from Corinth that "three of the [Union] scouts went to Pikeville, Ala," then the county seat of Marion County, Alabama, and "arrested the sheriff of [the] county, took jail keys from him, and released 75 Union prisoners, and all got safely away."[77]

With Sherman's approach, Bragg's army was in great jeopardy. As the army correspondent to the *Mobile Advertiser and Register* reported on October 27, there was "an army gathering for the invasion of Georgia under the supreme guidance of Grant, of 107,000 men."[78] Georgia was not the only target. Both Grant and Sherman fancied Mobile and the strategic Alabama River industrial complex in Selma, and by now their men were in a very bad mood. As Sherman wrote to Admiral David Dixon Porter from Fayetteville, Tennessee, on November 8, "I know our own soldiers are pretty lawless, and will do all I can to repress it, but it results chiefly from the behavior of citizens who sit on porches, peaceable and quiet as we pass, but fall on and wound some poor, footsore fellow who falls behind. Our men are full of the idea that all the people are 'secesh,' and would as leave plunder and kill all as not."[79] Many Southerners would soon pay for this in the continuing "Carnival of Blood."[80]

V
IN SEARCH OF PEACE

Timeline: November 1863–April 1864

November 9, 1863	Alabama legislature convenes in regular session.
November 12, 1863	United States district judge George Washington Lane dies in Kentucky.
November 19, 1863	President Lincoln gives an address at a new military cemetery at Gettysburg, Pennsylvania.
November 24, 1863	Richard Wilde Walker is elected to the Confederate Senate, replacing C. C. Clay Jr.
November 24, 1863	Milton Saffold and William Bibb Figures are elected State Printers, replacing the editors of the *Montgomery Advertiser.*
November 24, 1863	Confederates lose at Lookout Mountain, Tennessee.
November 25, 1863	Confederates lose at Missionary Ridge, Tennessee.
November 28, 1863	Confederates lose at Knoxville, Tennessee.
December 1, 1863	Governor Thomas Hill Watts gives his inaugural address
December 8, 1863	President Lincoln issues his Amnesty Proclamation.
December 8, 1863	Alabama legislature adjourns.
December 10, 1863	The *Mobile Advertiser and Register* notes "apathy and seeming indifference" within the Southern populace.
December 17, 1863	Confederate generals petition the Confederate Congress for changes in military policy.
January 5, 1864	Mutiny by General James Holt Clanton's men.
January 11, 1864	Thirteenth Amendment introduced in the United States Congress.
January 18, 1864	Winston County probate judge is assassinated by Confederate guerrillas.
January 20, 1864	President Lincoln appoints Richard Busteed as Alabama's US district judge.
January 25, 1864	James Quinton Smith urges General U. S. Grant to destroy the military-industrial complex at Selma, Alabama.
February 7, 1864	Resolution calling for peace negotiations introduced in the Confederate Congress.
February 22, 1864	Nathan Bedford Forrest attacks a Union cavalry force near Okolona, Mississippi.

February 25, 1864	The *New York Times* publishes J. L. M. Curry's "Rebel Manifesto."
March 5, 1864	Union meeting held in Huntsville, Alabama.
March 8, 1864	Decatur, Alabama, falls to Union forces.
March 10, 1864	Moulton, Alabama, is temporarily captured by Union forces.
March 11, 1864	Union meeting held in Jackson County, Alabama.
March 13, 1864	Union meeting held in Huntsville, Alabama.
April 12, 1864	Fort Pillow Massacre.
April 26, 1864	General Leonidas Polk implements a new counterinsurgency plan in Alabama.
April 27, 1864	C. C. Clay Jr. is sent to Canada to orchestrate Confederate activities there.

13
"God Close This Terrible War"

Given the real possibility of impending doom, would the supposedly pro-Reconstruction Alabama legislature finally float a trial balloon for peace? As that body convened in regular session on November 9, 1863, it certainly did not appear so. Instead, all of the solons seemed to be focused on whether C. C. Clay Jr. would be replaced as Alabama's other Confederate senator.[1] He would, meaning that another Original Secessionist was ousted from office. But while the various candidates seeking Clay's seat anxiously awaited the vote, the Alabama press was following the worsening situation around Chattanooga and Sherman's march from Florence across north Alabama to link up with Grant.[2] Sherman reached Bridgeport, Alabama, on November 15 and was crossing the Tennessee River there on November 17,[3] thereby increasing Grant's force to over sixty thousand or seventy thousand men versus Bragg's army of slightly more than forty thousand.[4]

The Union army was also tightening its grip on the northern portion of Alabama while laying the groundwork for future operations. Bridgeport in Jackson County had become the principal depot of Grant's army, which was preparing to move against Bragg.[5] The presence of so many Union troops in Jackson County encouraged Unionists there to become even bolder. Williamson R. W. Cobb, who had been elected to the Confederate Congress in 1863, publicly revealed himself as a reunion activist,[6] and other Unionists in the region would soon be organizing to secede from the Confederacy[7] (see figure 15).

Further west in occupied Madison County, such Unionists as Jeremiah Clemens, who had recently returned to Alabama, were also becoming increasingly active in favor of reunion.[8] But Confederate guerrillas and regular army units were still a threat.[9] In addition to encounters with these units, Union cavalry forces under the command of Brigadier General George Crook stationed in and around Huntsville were still busy recruiting slaves to fight as well as confiscating horses, mules, cattle, and food to resupply

Figure 15. Williamson R. W. Cobb (Courtesy of Alabama Department of Archives and History)

the army and deny their use to Confederate forces south of the Tennessee River.[10] According to a letter that appeared in the now Dalton, Georgia–based *Huntsville Confederate*, "Carter, house servant of [Huntsville physician] Robert Fearn, is an officer [in the Union army], and had opened an office for negro recruits."[11]

In Limestone County, forces under General Dodge based just north in Pulaski, Tennessee, were attempting to reconstruct the Tennessee and Alabama Railroad from the Alabama line south to Decatur in Morgan County. The plan was to complete the road from the huge Union army supply base in Nashville while also repairing the Memphis and Charleston Railroad from Decatur east through Huntsville to the depot in Bridgeport, thereby giving Grant's army an additional line of supply for the impending push.[12] Sherman also envisioned a cavalry strike "from Decatur or Eastport at Meridian and Selma."[13] At least at this point, the "march to the sea" Sherman had in mind would be toward the Gulf of Mexico.

General Dodge was, meanwhile, managing his increasingly active spy network in order to provide Sherman and Grant with the critically important intelligence necessary for military planning purposes.[14] Information was acquired from these sources regarding the whereabouts and condition of Charles Christopher Sheats, who had been indicted for treason and then moved to a jail in Montgomery.[15] This led to a decision to take and hold hostage a Huntsville secessionist as security for Sheats's safekeeping until Sheats's release.[16] Dodge was also continuing his efforts to encourage north Alabama Unionists to organize to rid the region of Confederate influence. According to a report in the displaced *Chattanooga Rebel*, "there was a gathering of federals, and Union men and negroes, at Decatur" in mid-November, following which "the federals carried off 1,200 negroes, large quantities of prisoners and everything they could lay their thieving hands upon."[17]

By the evening of November 23, ominous telegraphic reports of Union army offensive activity that morning and afternoon at Chattanooga had reached Montgomery.[18] By midnight, the preliminary step to the assault of Lookout Mountain had begun with an amphibious crossing of the Tennessee River by Union forces.[19] On November 24, General Sherman began his mountain assault on the north side of Missionary Ridge,[20] but it was not initially successful. The assault on the western slope by General George Henry Thomas and his determined Army of the Cumberland the following day did succeed. It was later rumored that the battle was lost by a "panic prevailing in an Alabama brigade."[21] And indeed, faced with the Yankee onslaught, Alabama soldiers were among the many who broke and ran for north Georgia, despite pleas by General Bragg to stop and "fight for your country!"[22]

James Thomas Searcy did not reveal these details in his first letter from Dalton, Georgia, to his family back in Tuscaloosa. He simply called this major loss a "disgraceful affair, the whole of it."[23] In his next, however, he referred to "our skedaddle" and blamed those deployed "where the first break was made." They had "run before any body was hurt" and "so let the others be flanked" that they had to retreat.[24] Ever resolute, Searcy did not desert, but many other members of the Army of Tennessee did.[25]

Word of the disaster reached the general public in the South fairly quickly.[26] The stunned correspondent of one Alabama newspaper did not misrepresent the situation: "The Confederates have sustained today the most ignominious defeat of the whole war—a defeat for which there is but little excuse or palliation. For the first time during our struggle for national independence defeat is chargeable to the troops themselves, and not to the blunders or incompetency of their leaders."[27] Bragg nonetheless took this opportunity to resign, prompting James Searcy to write that "I pity and respect the old man, but most likely it is for the best" because the "majority of the army have lost confidence in him."[28]

Historian Wiley Sword wrote that after the Union victory at Chattanooga, "the grinding, wasting war of attrition prevailed, and the prospects for Confederate independence flickered ever lower, like a solitary candle in a gathering breeze."[29] For Alabama it was worse than that. Coupled with reports that the state was Grant's next target,[30] the debacle's psychological effect was tremendous. The situation prompted James Mallory to express what others may have been thinking at this point: "O God close this terrible war."[31] Grant Taylor, a soldier from Alabama who owned no slaves, prayed for the same result, and he was not alone. Writing from a hospital at Marietta, Georgia, Taylor reported to his wife that after talking with "men here from nearly every southern state" it was clear that they "are generally low spirited and think our cause is gone." As a result, they "do not think it worth while to fight in so hopeless a cause. They feel like they are sacrificing their lives and their all for nothing."[32] John Cotton wrote to his now pregnant wife that "I am sorry to say to you that I am worse out of hart about whipping the yankeys than I have every been[.] There is lots of men says there is no use to fite them any more."[33] At about the same time, Sarah Espy, who was worried sick about her sons serving in the Confederate army, and who was also disconcerted about the number of refugees from Chattanooga now fleeing through her area, expressed this fervent wish: "May the Lord order a close to this cruel war."[34]

As other Confederate soldiers were deciding whether to desert, an opportunity for peace and settlement presented itself. Seven days after Governor Watts's defiant inaugural address, President Lincoln issued what became known as his Amnesty Proclamation. Subject to certain exceptions, most notably civilian officers and agents of the Confederate government, as well as army officers above the rank of colonel, Lincoln offered a full pardon to anyone who had directly or indirectly participated in the rebellion. There was an important catch. The pardon was conditioned on giving an oath in which the recipient swore to abide by and support, among other things, his Emancipation Proclamation and the acts of Congress relating to slaves "so long and so far as not modified or declared void by the decision of the Supreme Court." In that same proclamation, Lincoln also offered to recognize and protect any loyal state government established by as few as 10 percent of the number of residents who had voted in the 1860 election and had taken the oath Lincoln prescribed. In Alabama, that meant the process of reconstruction could be commenced by a mere 9,036 men.[35] Lincoln realized that the slavery proviso would be a bitter pill to swallow, and so he included a sweetener. Angering many Northern abolitionists, Lincoln's proclamation appeared to give his blessing to what could be interpreted as a period of state government-supervised (but employer-administered) involuntary apprenticeship for the slaves. A similar transitional system had been used in the 1830s by the British in the West Indies. Lincoln vaguely called it a "temporary arrangement" consistent with the slaves' "present condition as a laboring, landless, and homeless class."[36]

According to a report to the Confederate Congress by the secretary of war in early December 1863, between one-half and two-thirds of the army were absent from duty.[37] One purpose of Lincoln's Amnesty Proclamation, copies of which were ordered by General Grant to be circulated to front-line Confederate troops,[38] was to accelerate desertions.[39] To the chagrin of Confederate military commanders, Lincoln's plan worked, at least for a few months.[40] George Koon wrote to his wife, Sarah, from Tennessee that he wanted the war to end "for better or worse." He thought that "all the old soldiers are getting tired of this."[41] Koon was quickly becoming bitter. He later wrote to her from a hospital in Virginia about the inflation ravaging the home front, declaring that it was "enough to make every soldier lay down his gun and go home and kill every rich man that is home."[42] The *Milwaukee Daily Sentinel* observed that Lincoln's proclamation "seems to be silently doing its good work in the hearts and minds of those for whom it was designed." According to the *Sentinel*'s editor, a desire among the "rank and file of the rebel army" to "embrace the President's terms" reportedly existed "at Mobile, Alabama, and in Bragg's army," and more would follow as they "begin to realize the fact that [they] are the tools of a junto of traitors and madmen, who, to attain their unholy ends, are willing to wade through seas of blood."[43]

Based at Pollard, Alabama, near the Florida line, Brigadier General Clanton was also aware of trouble brewing in his then nine-regiment brigade.[44] He had somehow discovered that some of his extremely reluctant warriors, who included a significant number of peace movement members, had what James Barrow, one of his privates from Chambers County, described in a letter to his wife, Nancy, as "the spirit of mutiny that has developed itself among our soldiers." There were, Barrow continued, "in all probability not less than three hundred men engaged in it" and "their object seems to have been to lay down their arms and go home in defiance of any authority whatever." They believed "that such a course would tend to produce peace."[45] At first, Clanton assumed that he had effectively handled the situation by having his regimental commanders address their men on December 23, two days before the rumored strike date on Christmas Day.[46] He was mistaken. On January 5, 1864, the same day the *Mobile Advertiser and Register* again lamented the "decay in the patriotism of the people,"[47] at least sixty of Clanton's men at Gonzalez, Florida, mutinied and, according to Clanton's later report, "said they would do no more service" (see map 5). After learning of the incident, Clanton called a mass meeting of his men at Pollard and, according to his report, "made them a speech, and arrested and ironed those who were ringleaders in the contemplated rebellion—the 'Peace Society,' as it is called." Clanton also reported that he had "secured the names, oaths, pass-words, and grips of the concern." One hundred more men, Clanton continued, admitted their

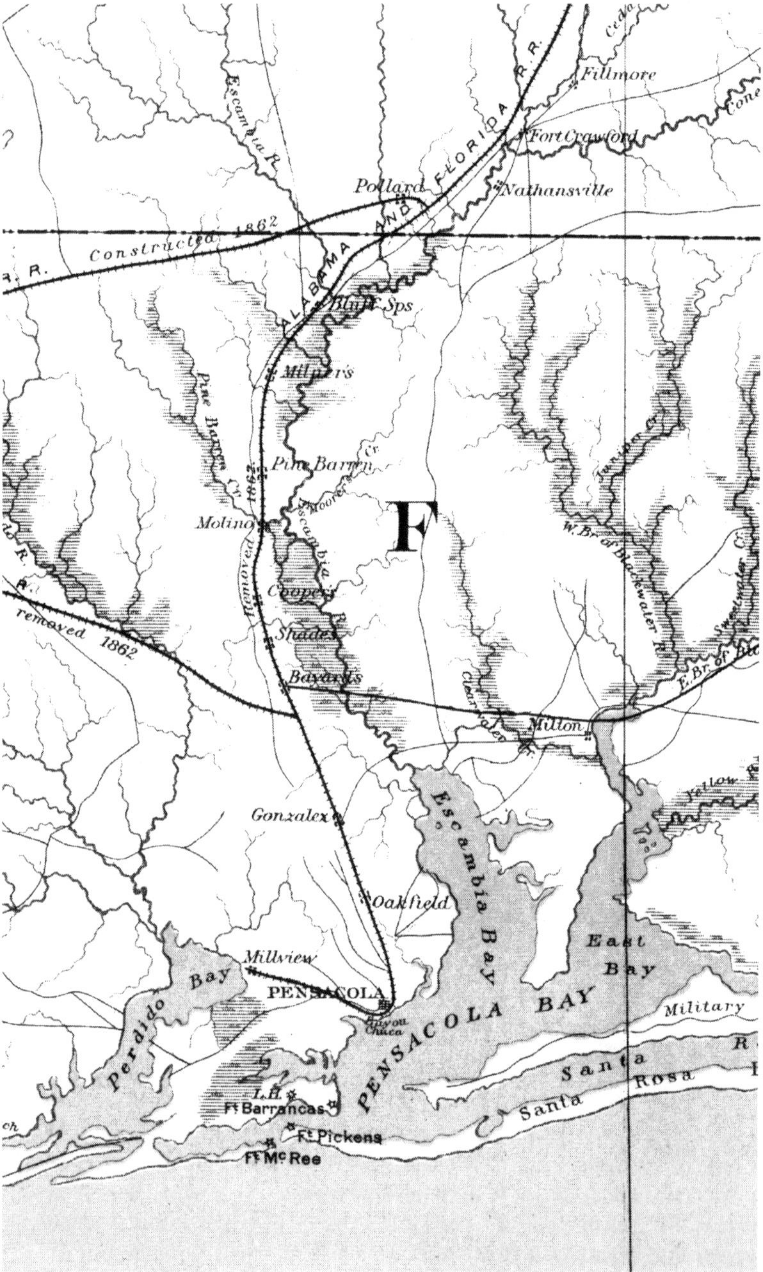

Map 5. Vicinity of Pollard, Gonzalez, and Pensacola (*Official Military Atlas of the Civil War*)

membership in the group, but he did not arrest them after they claimed "they were deceived into it, and ask[ed] pardon."[48]

This incident severely damaged Clanton's already doubtful reputation as a military leader. General Joseph E. Johnston, who had arrived with great fanfare in Dalton, Georgia, to replace Bragg and take command of the Army of Tennessee in late December, was desperate for reinforcements. But he made it clear that he certainly did not want Clanton's men or even Clanton transferred to him.[49] Johnston wrote to Confederate adjutant general Samuel Cooper that "Clanton's troops should be dispersed and sent as far from home as practicable" and that "Clanton's incompetency is proved by their condition." Johnston, who naively assumed that his army had not been infected by the peace bug, recommended that Clanton's men instead be sent to Mississippi, which was under the command of General Leonidas Polk.[50] Confederate secretary of war James Seddon concurred on the ground that this redeployment would permit "less intercourse with a doubtful population, than in North Georgia and East Tennessee."[51] As a result, by January 20, Clanton's Brigade had quietly been reduced to only four regiments.[52] Barring a miracle, even those units would soon be gone.

Similarly, five companies of Philip Dale Roddey's brigade were transferred from north Alabama to serve under Nathan Bedford Forrest in north Mississippi.[53] But in early January, following a series of Union army raids on Florence, the north Alabama congressional delegation and both Senator Clay (whose senate term had not yet ended) and Jemison petitioned Seddon to return them to north Alabama. They also requested that Roddey's remaining force be augmented to guard against raids toward central Alabama and protect the mining and manufacturing establishments now in operation there. Such raids, the petitioners pointed out, would receive "great encouragement in the mountain regions in our State where there is unfortunately in some parts a disaffected population."[54] The balance of Roddey's Brigade was then centered at Tuscumbia, not far from those disloyal "mountain regions," where a portion of that "disaffected population" was moving north toward federal lines and federal protection. General Dodge reported to General Sherman that "if we could make a lodgement at Decatur it would give outlets to a large number of Union people who are seeking our lines and who would join our Alabama regiments."[55] Meanwhile, organized and coordinated Unionist guerrilla attacks were being made in north Alabama as far south as Walker County.[56] Union forces forced Huntsvillians and other north Alabamians to choose between either taking an oath of allegiance to the United States or being banished south of the Tennessee River toward Unionist strongholds in the mountains where their lives would be in grave danger.[57] In attempting to avoid Scylla, Confederates risked Charybdis. The exclusion of present and former Confederate officials from the benefits and protection of Lincoln's Amnesty Proclamation may have influenced Leroy Pope Walker in his decision to leave Huntsville and run the tory gauntlet to seek refuge behind Confederate lines in central Alabama. The inducement of gainful employment by the Confederacy also played a role. Walker was appointed judge of a military court.[58]

Confederate guerrillas were also active during this period, as most infamously evidenced by the kidnapping and assassination of the pro-Union Winston County probate judge, Thomas Pinkney Curtis, on January 18, 1864.[59] Nonetheless, the drift of events in north Alabama toward reunion with the North was obvious. Reports from Jackson County in northeast Alabama, where Unionist guerrillas and federal troops had dominated for some time,[60] indicate that citizens were taking the oath of allegiance in large numbers.[61]

As in the past, one strategy used by Confederates to attempt to reverse this trend was propaganda. This time, however, the source of that propaganda was not simply newspaper editorials and stump speakers. In early 1864, a Richmond, Virginia, company published a novel by the Mobile, Alabama, novelist Augusta Jane Evans titled *Macaria; or, Altars of Sacrifice*. It centered on the decisions of two young Southern women to set aside their desires for marriage and instead unselfishly devote their time and efforts to the Confederacy. Evans, who was also single, dedicated this work of fiction to the Confederate army, referring to herself as "one who, although debarred from the dangers and deathless glory of the 'tented field,' would fain offer a woman's inadequate tribute to the noble patriotism and sublime self-abnegation of her dear and devoted countrymen." Intended by Evans to inspire women to maintain their Confederate nationalism, the book became a best seller in the South and an abomination in the North.[62]

Through her close friend J. L. M. Curry, for whom she had previously ghostwritten political tracts, Evans may have also had input in another work of fiction, issued by the Confederate Congress, during this period. It was called the Confederate Manifesto by the Northern press and was publicly attributed to the pen of Curry. It was a similarly eloquent and lengthy address to Southerners consisting of a justification for secession and war, as well as a discussion of the horrors that would supposedly afflict the South if the North won the war. It constituted a summary of virtually all of the myths that became the backbone of Lost Cause myth and lore. Secession, it was said, was necessary because of Northern hostility to the South's "institutions" and her constitutional rights, and it had occurred with "unanimity and zeal" and a "universality of conviction among the [Southern] people." The North, not the Confederacy, had started the war, and the Confederacy was not fighting to preserve slavery but to avoid the "consequences of subjugation."[63]

Despite all of this, morale remained low, and desertions from the Confederate military were still reaching epidemic levels even in the face of the frequent imposition of the death penalty for those who were captured.[64] To combat this trend, Southerners infected with defeatism needed to know more than just why they fought. On February 1, 1864, President Lincoln called for the conscription of another five hundred thousand men.[65] Unless Confederate loyalists were suicidal, they needed to know they could beat the odds against them and thereby avoid the supposed horrors of reconstruction. They also needed a fanatical hero to emulate. Confederate newspaper editors were willing to please, and Sherman, the Union general, would unwittingly provide the opportunity. For Reconstructionists, that hero's acts would, ironically, make a negotiated peace that included the preservation of slavery even less likely. Those acts would also encourage the Union military to take an even harder line toward the South and Alabama.

14
War Eagle!

War Eagle, fly down the field,
Ever to conquer, never to yield.
War Eagle, fearless and true.

—Kelly Kazek, on the mysterious origin of the Auburn University slogan "War Eagle"

General Sherman, whose army was now based at Vicksburg, Mississippi, had been authorized to make a large-scale raid in February 1864 that appears to have been calculated, in part, to grab headlines while most military forces were still in winter quarters awaiting the late spring campaigns. And he intended to make it without using a supply line, meaning his men would bring some supplies but then essentially live off the food and necessaries of the civilian population. The raid would become a template for his more famous march through Georgia in the fall. Sherman's primary military objective was to further secure control over the Mississippi River by destroying the railroads between Vicksburg and Meridian as well as the Mobile and Ohio Railroad in and around Meridian, thereby hampering Confederate troop and supply movements. But he was also leaving open the option of pushing forward to lightly defended Selma, then being protected by three companies of boys between sixteen and eighteen years of age.[1]

The military assets allotted to Selma's defense were proportionally far less than Selma's role in the war effort justified. Selma—called by the *Montgomery Mail* the "military depot of the South"—was nothing short of a boomtown. With the amount of territory under Confederate control having shrunk dramatically in the preceding months, its productive capacity was even more critically important to the Confederate war effort.[2] It was by no means a military secret that mining operations extracting coal and iron from Jefferson County and Shelby County, and iron-making operations there as well as in Shelby County, Bibb County, and Selma, were providing the materials necessary to manufacture and construct munitions, gunboats, and other essential weapons of war in Selma.[3] Just as significantly, wartime necessity had overriden commercial competition between Alabama cities and corporations that had slowed development of Alabama's railroad grid during the antebellum period. The Selma and Meridian was completed,[4] the South and

North Railroad was finally being constructed north of Selma toward Jefferson County,[5] and the Alabama and Tennessee Rivers Railroad from Selma had reached Blue Mountain (now called Anniston) in Calhoun County and was being extended to Rome, Georgia.[6] Selma had much to gain if it could come out of the war unscathed, and so it had a lot to lose if Sherman's plan succeeded. By the same token, articles in the Northern press about Selma during this period reflect just how important it was as a military target.[7] Taking Selma would not only make Sherman a national hero but would do much to shorten the war. According to General Grant, Sherman's raid was to be followed by a campaign from Chattanooga to Mobile, with Atlanta and Montgomery being "the important intermediate points."[8]

Sherman gave every indication that his ultimate goal was actually to capture Mobile, even to the extent of having his men sew labels on their hats stating "Mobile or Hell."[9] This, as the Washington, DC, *Daily National Republican* later revealed, was a "Ruse de Guerre," a ruse of war.[10] In early February 1864, Sherman's army of over twenty thousand men began its particularly destructive march east from Vicksburg through Jackson and the rest of central Mississippi, sending Alabamians into a state of panic.[11] It was immediately evident that the ruse about Mobile was quite effective, as Governor Watts was convinced to issue an order to noncombatants to leave Mobile.[12] Watts traveled to Mobile and, on the day after Sherman captured Meridian, addressed a worried crowd at the Battle House Hotel. According to local news accounts, Watts "urged upon the men, and if the men could not be found, then that the women shoot down the first person who should attempt to raise the white flag and surrender the city, and that our brave troops fight it out to the bitter end." Watts then declared that "he had rather see the beautiful city of Mobile in ruins, than come under the hated Yankee rule."[13] Two days later—and after returning to the safety of Montgomery—Watts issued another widely reported proclamation calling on all available citizens to form volunteer companies and proceed to Selma, where he would personally "accompany" them to the battlefield.[14]

Some expected the Confederate military to stop Sherman before he reached Alabama.[15] A correspondent in the region reported to a Georgia newspaper that he "saw Confederate soldiers enough in Mississippi to swallow Sherman's army unbuttered."[16] But those who had expected General Polk and his Army of Mississippi to attack Sherman were to be shocked and angered.[17] Rather than confronting Sherman in Mississippi, Polk had evacuated his forces from his base at Meridian and retreated into Alabama across the Tombigbee River at Moscow, Alabama, to Demopolis[18] (see map 6). As a result, Sherman was given free rein to destroy most of Meridian and a large portion

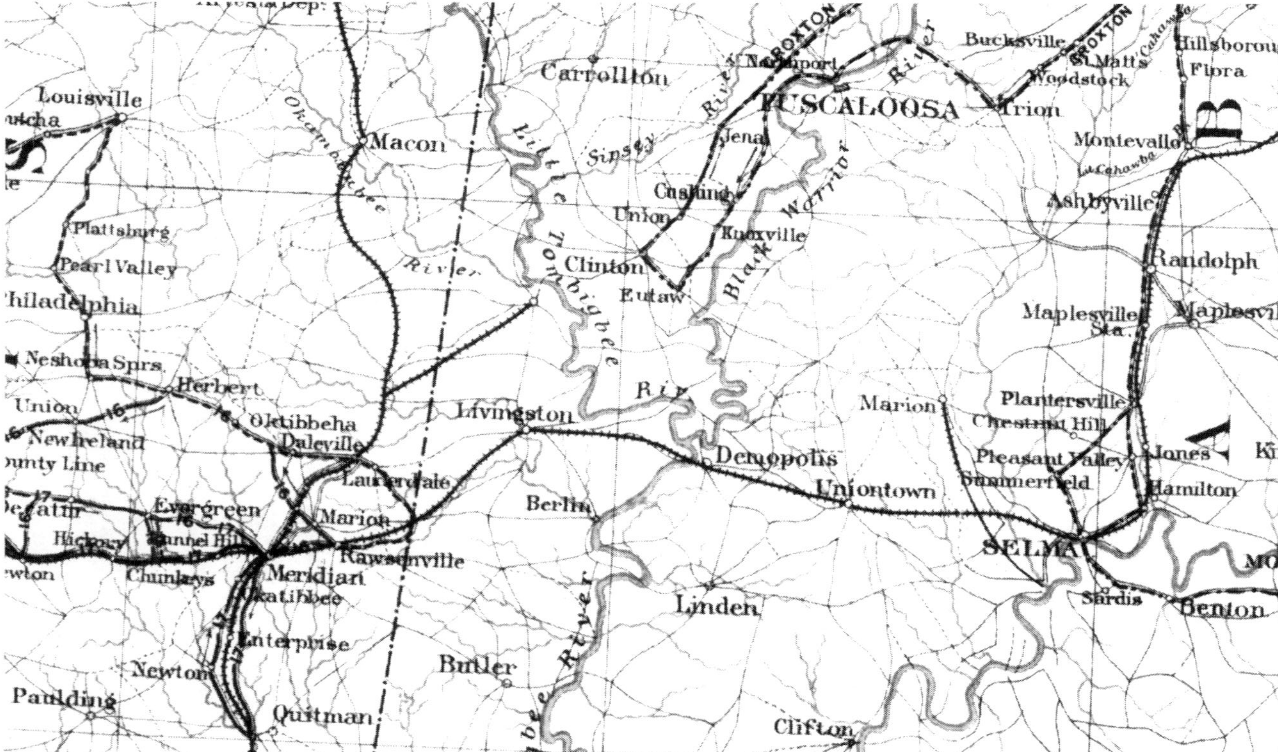

Map 6. Vicinity of Meridian, Mississippi, and west central Alabama (*Official Military Atlas of the Civil War*)

of the Mobile and Ohio Railroad in that vicinity, as well as the Northeast and Southwest Railroad in Sumter County to Gainesville, Alabama, and a portion of the Alabama and Mississippi Railroad toward Demopolis.[19]

As the Mobile press finally correctly guessed, Sherman was now inclined to move further east to engage and destroy Polk's army and then take Selma.[20] The editor of the *Selma Dispatch* observed that "exciting reports of the advance of the Yankees on this place still come in every train, and every wagon and every breeze—keeping the weak kneed in a state of typhoid ague." But he also noted that "from present indications the Yankee General is not making very rapid strides on this place."[21] There was a reason for this. Before proceeding further into Alabama, Sherman first wanted the support of a large cavalry force from Memphis that was supposed to have reached Meridian on February 10.[22] A combination of errors and poor leadership had prevented this force, led by Brigadier General William Sooy Smith, from arriving on time.[23] Tired of waiting for Smith, and with his army having devoured most of the food supplies in the area, Sherman opted simply to declare victory and return to Vicksburg.[24] When word of Sherman's departure from Meridian on February 20 reached Smith at West Point, Mississippi, later that day, Smith ordered a counter march back to Memphis, which began on the morning of February 21.[25]

Then, and only then, came Nathan Bedford Forrest (see figure 16). A recruiting advertisement had earlier appeared in the *Mobile Advertiser and Register* calling on men to "Volunteer for Gen. Forrest, THE WAR EAGLE."[26] A member of an Alabama company under Forrest's command characterized him as "a rash man and fond of going into danger."[27] But like General Polk, Forrest had not attempted to stop Sherman or Smith from moving across Mississippi toward Alabama and did not tangle with Sherman as he moved back toward Vicksburg. Forrest had played no active role in compelling either to leave east Mississippi; his cavalry force merely followed and attacked Smith's receding rear guard on February 22 near Okolona, causing Smith's 7,000 man force to sustain only 150 casualties. Although not fully or accurately reported in the Southern press, Forrest's much smaller force itself suffered 144 casualties, including the death of his brother. All arguably died in vain because Smith would have returned to Memphis even had Forrest not attempted to pursue him.[28]

It was not unusual for the Southern press to belittle Northern gains and make false or exaggerated claims of Confederate victories. That is exactly what happened in this case. A relieved telegrapher at Demopolis appears to have gotten the ball rolling when he telegraphed that "information has been received here that Sherman was retreating via Canton, his campaign having

Figure 16. Nathan Bedford Forrest (Courtesy of Alabama Department of Archives and History)

been defeated by the concentration of our cavalry in front of Gen. Smith, which cut him off from forming a junction via Okolona [Mississippi]. Smith is flying before Forrest, punished every step."[29] Then the public praise for Forrest snowballed. The *Selma Dispatch* said the "redoubtable Forrest" had "come down with an eagle swoop" on the Yankee cavalry.[30] In an editorial titled "The Wizard of the Saddle," the *Atlanta Confederacy* printed these widely republished plaudits: "Forrest's work in Mississippi is, as usual, well done. Does he ever fail? And, wherefore [not]? Because he is a man of genius. If there be one commander in the South who is a representative—who knows nothing but the cause of his race and nation—who hates the enemy with a holy hate—who pursues them with the rapacity of a wolf, and loves nothing about them, but their blood—who never wearies, who never falters—who fights on his own hook and wins battles where other men would lose them—it is Bedford Forrest! Long may he live! He is worth his weight in gold."[31]

The itinerant, Selma-based *Mississippian* (which had been forced to move their press to prevent them from being destroyed by Union forces) reported that "the citizens of Columbus, Mississippi, are wild with joy, and extravagant in their praises of the gallant 'War Eagle.' As a very slight token of their gratitude they have already purchased the finest horse to be found in the country around to present to him. They believe, and justly too, that he has saved them from the ravage of the most brutal part of the Yankee hirelings."[32] John Forsyth and the *Mobile Advertiser and Register* joined the chorus praising

Forrest: "The Confederacy and especially the State of Mississippi, owe it to General Forrest to erect a monument to his heroic energy and courage. What he did for Georgia last year, in throwing his shield between that State and the invading hand of Streight, he has now done for Mississippi and Western Alabama. It was he who defeated the Yankee campaign."[33]

Forrest did his part to contribute to the illusion of his own invincibility. From Demopolis, he telegraphed a staff member (who released the message to the *Atlanta Confederacy*) that "my victory over the enemy was complete," and that the "enemy outnumbered me three to one." He also fudged regarding the casualties on both sides. "The enemy's loss in killed, wounded and captured was about eight hundred, and among them three Colonels killed and one captured." His own loss was only "twenty killed and sixty wounded."[34] Press accounts in the North erroneously reporting that Sherman had actually captured Selma and would soon move on Montgomery helped contribute to the illusion of Sherman's failure.[35] The source of this error appears to have been the pro-Union *Memphis Bulletin*, which relied on "information from a high military authority at Vicksburg" that just might have been a press release prepared and issued by Sherman's staff before he departed Vicksburg.[36]

But whether the illusion matched the truth did not matter to Confederate propagandists. At this point in the war, with Lincoln's Amnesty Proclamation, war weariness, and the expected spring military campaigns causing more and more desertions,[37] the Generals of the Press recognized the need for a hero to promote the Cause. Battlefield victories could give hope, but those were few and far between in the western theater. A dashing warrior hero with whom men could identify was just as important. The common man especially needed someone to emulate who possessed the character traits necessary to persevere against the odds. Thus was born the myth of Nathan Bedford Forrest.[38] He was no common man from a socioeconomic standpoint, having been quite wealthy prior to the war. But he was, like many of those common men, uneducated and not a lawyer or a member of the effete element of the planter elite.[39] Although Forrest had a firm grasp of cavalry tactics, he had joined the Confederate military as a private and was not among that group of West Point graduates like Polk and Bragg who had repeatedly failed to meet expectations.[40] Some military historians still consider him to be a tactical genius.[41]

After the press barrage, Forrest became a household name as well as the Deep South's inspiration and military genius, and an ultrasuccessful recruiter.[42] The Selma *Mississippian* declared that "this victory, won by so few men, is beyond all praise. Its fruits are inestimable."[43] Sick of service under General Wheeler, whom he had variously dubbed an imbecile, the War Child, and little Joe,[44] Alabamian George Miller, then stationed in northwest Georgia, wrote whimsically to his wife that "Gen. Forrest has been winning new laurels—How gratifying it would have been to accompany him—The ground and many of the people would have been familiar, besides the eclat attending so brilliant an expedition."[45] The *Jacksonville Republican* reported that "from every point we hear of recruited strength, good discipline, hope and confidence of success on the part of our armies, and the same spirit has diffused itself among the masses of the people."[46] According to the *Mobile Daily Tribune*, Sherman's raid had been a "magnificent failure" that had "inspired our people with new hope and confidence."[47] The *Mobile Advertiser and Register* agreed and concluded that the "prospect before us is encouraging, and gives promise, under the benign favor of Heaven, of eventual success and independence. Let each and all of us then work and fight as we have never worked and fought before."[48]

The mythical Forrest also became every Confederate's designated role model. Men were told to emulate Forrest, to fight "as he fights."[49] The *Charleston Mercury* described Forrest's manner of warfare by relating a lecture he had given to his men about taking prisoners. " 'Now, boys,' he said, 'War means fight, and fight means kill. What's the use of taking prisoners to eat up your rations?' From that time there was a material falling off in the number of prisoners taken by Forrest's men."[50] The *Atlanta Confederacy* declared that "if every man in the South possessed his spirit of determination, his spirit of vengeance, his energy, his sleeplessness, his patient perseverance, in the one grand object of his present existence—to destroy the enemy wherever he may be found within our Southern borders, the entire swarm of pestilential Yankees would be swept from the country as with a besom of destruction."[51] According to an approving Mississippi newspaper, a Confederate force met a regiment of black Union soldiers near Satartia, Mississippi, on March 3, 1864, and they "killed all except fourteen. Over 800 dead negroes were counted in an enclosure of one acre of grounds."[52]

This mode of warfare would not only become habit-forming but would have fatal consequences for Confederate soldiers when they later expected quarter from Union soldiers.[53] In the end, it would also dramatically affect the Reconstructionists in their efforts to bring about peace with slavery. And that was one goal of Confederates.

15
The Horrors of the Black Flag

Even with Forrest setting the example, however, winning the war was looking less likely, especially if the activities of militant Unionists were not suppressed. Sherman's thrust across Mississippi had not only sent terrified refugees scurrying as far as Montgomery, Alabama—Jefferson Davis's brother Joe was a guest of Robert Jemison Jr. in Tuscaloosa[1]—but it had energized and inspired peace advocates and Unionist guerrilla bands throughout the region. According to a refugee to Nashville who left Montgomery to avoid conscription shortly after Sherman began his return to Vicksburg, "the Union people" had begun to "exhibit a boldness which frightened the rebels" when Sherman first reached Meridian. He contended that if Sherman had advanced as far as Montgomery, "the Union members of the legislature would have assembled, deposed the Governor, taken the oath to support the Constitution of the United States, and ordered an election in counties to fill vacancies, and set the machinery of Government at work at once."[2]

Under the protection of federal forces, Alabama Unionists residing north of the Tennessee River were already engaged in political activities under Lincoln's Ten Percent Plan of reconstruction. In March 1864, a Selma, Alabama, newspaper took note of reports in the Northern press that a convention had been held in Jackson County in northeast Alabama on March 11. At the urging of Unionist Williamson R. W. Cobb, the five hundred participants voted to "carry Jackson County out of the State and Confederacy into the Yankee Government."[3] The following month, south Alabama newspapers quoted similar sources regarding mass meetings in Huntsville on March 5 and March 13 where, at the urging of Huntsville lawyers David Campbell Humphreys and Jeremiah Clemens, resolutions were adopted that denied the legality of Alabama's Ordinance of Secession, deemed the war effort "hopeless," and urged Governor Watts to call the legislature into session to pass legislation for a convention to adopt a new ordinance allowing the state to resume its place in the Union.[4]

In his speech at the Huntsville convention, Humphreys, a slaveholder who had served for a few months in the Confederate army but had recently gone to Nashville and taken the amnesty oath, addressed the still explosive issue of emancipation:[5] "I believe the institution of slavery is gone as a permanent thing—overthrown by the action of the Southern States."[6] But, Humphreys argued, if Alabama would simply return to the Union, "I am confident we shall then have as many years for getting good riddance of this institution as we want."[7] Humphreys gave no details of a gradual emancipation process that might be permitted. But he did assert his belief that "we would receive political cooperation so as to secure the management of that labor by those who were slaves." Probably referring to President Lincoln's proposal regarding an apprenticeship for the slaves, Humphreys added that "there is really no difference, in my opinion, whether we hold them as absolute slaves, or obtain their labor by some other method."[8]

News of these meetings in Jackson and Madison Counties spread like wildfire through the Unionist network in the rest of north Alabama. This network appears to have included the still influential George Smith Houston. Several press accounts reported that evidence introduced in opposition to a court proceeding in Washington filed to confiscate his property there revealed that he had remained loyal to the Union. According to the *Washington Chronicle*, "several of our generals have met with him in Alabama, where, in voluntary obscurity, he was allowed to remain, steadfast in the Union faith. His loyalty is said to be above suspicion."[9] A Mobile newspaper carried a similar account and reported that the legal proceeding was "suspended indefinitely" based on this evidence.[10] Houston's property outside of Alabama was therefore secure, but now his property inside the state, as well as his life, were potentially in great jeopardy, especially if Union occupation forces again withdrew, as had occurred in 1862.

For the time being, however, it appeared that the Union army's occupation north of the Tennessee River was permanent and that it would soon expand south of the river.[11] On March 8, General Dodge advanced south from Athens with the intention of again gaining a solid foothold across the Tennessee River at Decatur, which would become his new base of operations. After a pontoon bridge was erected across the river under Confederate fire that almost took the lives of Dodge and George E. Spencer, Decatur fell on March 8,[12] and Courtland in Lawrence County was captured shortly thereafter. Then Dodge's force quickly moved south and took Moulton on March 10.[13]

Further west in Lauderdale County, the continuous presence of Union military forces since late November 1863 had brought back a semblance of normalcy.[14] As had occurred elsewhere, the citizens there had been given the choice of taking the amnesty oath or being banished. A number of them, including the family of Richard Wilde Walker, had fled south from Florence to Tuscaloosa.[15] Those who remained, according to a letter Walker wrote from the Druid City, were in "uninterrupted" communication with Nashville, and "a good many citizens of Florence have recently been to Nashville."[16] Even some of the Confederate soldiers stationed south of Florence had developed a working relationship with their adversaries. According to a Mobile correspondent, the pickets on both sides of the Tennessee River had agreed not to fire at each other.[17]

Elsewhere, however, the Confederacy was initiating a brutal crackdown on Unionists in the South, and this time significant numbers of regular army units were committed to the operation in east Mississippi, west Tennessee, and Alabama under the command of General Leonidas Polk.[18] The first targets were Unionists and deserters in and around Jones County, Mississippi, south of Meridian—the "Free State of Jones"—who had made several raids in that area in late February.[19] As Alabama newspapers reported, several were killed in firefights, and those who were taken prisoner were summarily executed by hanging.[20] Unionists in that region nonetheless remained resilient and continued to be a problem for the Confederacy.[21]

Next in line would be Unionists in Tennessee. On March 19, while General Dodge was away in Nashville, Tennessee, meeting with Generals Grant and Sherman to discuss the plan of operations for the coming months,[22] Nathan Bedford Forrest left Tupelo, Mississippi, to lead a highly publicized retaliatory raid into west Tennessee and west Kentucky, plundering and terrorizing Unionist communities, most notably Union City, Tennessee, and Paducah, Kentucky, and culminating in a fateful attack on Fort Pillow on the Tennessee side of the Mississippi River.[23]

While Forrest moved toward Tennessee, Unionist guerrillas based in Marion County, Alabama, made two brutal raids against military and civilian targets in Fayette County that drew even more attention to the eroding Confederate situation in north Alabama. On March 24, a guerrilla band reportedly attacked a pro-Confederate family, and the following week, according to a report from the district chief provost marshal in Tuscaloosa, five Confederate soldiers, including one lieutenant, were "found dead tied up to trees, shot through the head." The perpetrators were said to be "deserters and tories."[24] These raids were increasing in frequency and, once again, Confederate civilians were pleading for more men to rid the area of the culprits.[25] General Polk ordered a large force from Mississippi under the overall command of General Stephen Dill Lee sent to central Alabama for this purpose.[26] Lee, who would establish his headquarters at Tuscaloosa, was directed to organize an "expedition against the deserters and tories of North Alabama. He will arrest them," wrote a member of Polk's staff, "and will deal with all such as may be banded together for resistance *in the most summary manner*."[27]

Two days later, the true meaning of that chilling phrase was graphically illustrated during Nathan Bedford Forrest's attack on Fort Pillow; the fort was manned by a force of from five hundred to six hundred men composed mostly of white Southern Unionists who had joined the Union army, as well as four companies of black troops, many from Alabama.[28] After Forrest's demand to surrender was refused, his much larger force stormed Fort Pillow. As an admiring special correspondent to an Alabama newspaper who wrote from the fort under the pseudonym Vidette put it before the political ramifications of the massacre were realized, "indiscriminate slaughter followed—about a hundred prisoners were taken, the balance were slain. The fort ran with blood; many jumped into the [Mississippi] river and were drowned, or shot in the water."[29] Consistent with this account, another Confederate eyewitness reported that "for ten minutes death reigned in the fortification, and along the river bank. Our troops, maddened by excitement, shot down the retreating Yankees, and not until they had attained the waters edge and turned to beg for mercy, did any prisoners fall into our hands. Thus, the whites received quarter but the negroes were shown no mercy."[30]

Because this highly inflammatory event took place on the third anniversary of the beginning of the war, it held great symbolism for both sides. "If the 12th day of April is destined to live in history, as that on which the first gun of this war was sounded," wrote Vidette, "it will remain doubly dear in the memory of every Southerner, as the two-fold anniversary of Southern prowess over Northern despotism. One the first, and the other the third—and allow me to add, emphatically—I hope the *last year* of the war."[31]

Thanks to Forrest, the outnumbered Confederate troops elsewhere were now in significant jeopardy of retaliation.[32] President Lincoln did not immediately rule out the possibility of retribution during his first public remarks about Fort Pillow,[33] and neither did General Sherman, who in less than thirty days would launch his Atlanta Campaign.[34] On the contrary, in a letter to Secretary of War Edwin Stanton, Sherman chillingly predicted that the "Southern army, which is the Southern people . . . will heed the slaughter that will follow as the natural consequence of their own inhuman acts."[35] As a worried soldier caught in the middle wrote to the *Mobile Advertiser and Register* from General Lee's army in Virginia, if retaliation occurred, "we shall of course retaliate, and thus the horrors of the black flag will be superadded to the already aggravated horrors of this cruel war."[36]

Union troops fearful of not receiving quarter if they surrendered were now even more likely to fight to the death, meaning more Confederate casualties would occur.[37] One of General Dodge's spies just in from Tuscaloosa reported Confederate troops bivouacked on the road between Moulton and Decatur, and on April 17, Dodge reported from Decatur that the "enemy made their appearance this a.m. in considerable force, and, as far as I can ascertain, they have got considerable [reinforcements]."[38] Later that day, forces under Generals Roddey and Clanton attacked Decatur, but in contrast to Forrest at Fort Pillow, they were repulsed and driven back toward Moulton.[39]

The Fort Pillow incident sparked a firestorm of controversy in the North, and press accounts from Alabama and elsewhere fed the fire. The *Mobile Advertiser and Register* reprinted an account from the pro-Union *Memphis Argus* charging that the physical facts at Fort Pillow looked "more like indiscriminate butchery than honorable warfare." But the *Advertiser*, which had been one of those suggesting black flag tactics, crassly blamed the "catastrophe of the Yankees at Fort Pillow" on "the cowardice of their negro allies." The incident had, it sniffed, "miraculously vindicated" the institution of slavery.[40] Northern press accounts of the massacre added to Northern rage,[41] and more inflammatory evidence would be compiled by a congressional committee assigned to investigate the incident.[42]

General Polk nonetheless decided to focus on eliminating the disloyal element between Tuscaloosa and the Tennessee River, but he would not be as successful as Forrest. General Stephen Lee first sent several cavalry regiments north from Tuscaloosa to what he referred to as "the infected counties above," while another cavalry brigade was sent east to Elyton in Jefferson County to "operate against disloyal parties."[43] Aware that they were being targeted, the Unionist guerrillas of north Alabama had wisely gone underground, melting into the forests and mountains, where cavalry forces were generally ineffective. "The tories in the mountains are very quiet," reported a lieutenant commanding a company of Confederate scouts in Danville. "I saw none of them."[44] But they were definitely there. Those mountains, according to a report by General Dodge, were full of "deserters and refugees seeking our lines," and together "they hold the mountain district in spite of all efforts of the rebels to catch them. I know of several companies of at least 100 men, each led by our scouts and members of the First Alabama Cavalry."[45]

On April 26, 1864, therefore, Polk announced a new counterinsurgency plan that appears to have been modeled on the principle of a deer drive. General Roddey was ordered by Polk to establish a picket line from the Mississippi state line across northwest Alabama along the southern shore of the Tennessee River to prevent "tories and deserters from escaping to the enemy" on the northern side of the river. At the same time, infantry and cavalry brigades under Lee were ordered to establish a line parallel to the Tennessee River at Tuscaloosa and then begin moving north, sweeping or driving all of the "tories, conscripts, and deserters" toward Roddey's men, who were to intercept them and punish anyone offering armed resistance with "death upon the spot."[46]

The weak links in this plan were Roddey's men, and possibly Roddey himself. Although the forces moving north did net some deserters—several of whom turned out to be Roddey's own men—it is noteworthy that Roddey, whose picket force had significant gaps, never reported capturing any significant numbers at his end.[47] On the contrary, several of Roddey's men, according to the Nashville press, deserted and surrendered at the Union army base in Decatur, joining many other refugees there.[48]

The upshot was that north Alabama Unionists remained a force to be reckoned with for the rest of the war. As a consequence, the Confederacy would be forced to commit increasingly scarce resources to protect the Confederate population from Unionist retribution at a time when every man was necessary in the effort to stop General Sherman.

VI
BOWING DOWN TO MARS

Timeline: May 1864–September 1864

May 2, 1864	Confederate Congress convenes.
May 2, 1864	Judicial elections in Alabama.
May 6, 1864	C. C. Clay Jr. sails for Canada.
May 7, 1864	General Sherman begins movement toward Atlanta, Georgia.
May 14, 1864	Confederate General John Tyler Morgan is arrested for drunkenness and removed from command.
May 27, 1864	William Peters is captured by Union forces and sent to a prison at Rock Island, Illinois.
June 7, 1864	Union Republicans convene in Baltimore, Maryland, and nominate Abraham Lincoln and Andrew Johnson.
June 10, 1864	Nathan Bedford Forrest wins the Battle of Brice's Crossroads in Mississippi.
June 14, 1864	Bishop Leonidas Polk is killed.
June 19, 1864	The CSS *Alabama* is sunk.
June 27, 1864	Confederates prevail at the Battle of Kennesaw Mountain, Georgia.
June 29, 1864	General W. T. Sherman authorizes General Lovell Rousseau to make a cavalry raid through east Alabama.
July 9, 1864	President Lincoln pocket vetoes the Wade-Davis Reconstruction Bill.
July 10, 1864	Rousseau's Raid begins from Decatur, Alabama.
July 14, 1864	Rousseau's raiders repulse Confederates led by James Holt Clanton.
July 14, 1864	Nathan Bedford Forrest is defeated at Harrisburg, Mississippi
July 17, 1864	President Davis replaces Joseph E. Johnston with John Bell Hood.
July 18, 1864	President Lincoln issues his "To Whom It May Concern" Letter.
August 5, 1864	General John Tyler Morgan is reinstated.
August 5, 1864	Union naval forces begin to take control of Mobile Bay.
August 30, 1864	George Brinton McClellan receives the Democratic nomination for the presidency.

September 1, 1864	Atlanta falls to Sherman.
September 6, 1864	Nathan Bedford Forrest is finally ordered to attack Sherman's supply lines in Tennessee.
September 19, 1864	Confederate General Robert Emmett Rodes of Tuscaloosa is killed in Virginia.
September 20, 1864	President Davis begins trip to Alabama.

16
"Retrograde Movements" and "Backward Advances"

Hiram Williams, a very depressed Confederate soldier from Mobile serving in north Georgia, lamented that the "first of May has dawned upon us, the day celebrated in the 'good old times of yore' when Peace-blue-eyed goddess blessed us with her presence," but now "we bow down to Mars, the savage God of War, instead of crowns of flowers and myrtle leaves, we weave a chaplet of sighs and groans, and, crown a ghostly skeleton and bathe our brows with blood from the hearts of our friends and brothers."[1] Williams was not alone in his depression and anxiety. A woman from a prominent Kentucky family who attended church services in Montgomery heard a "beautiful prayer for the success of our Cause, the suffering prisoners, wounded, orphans, and widows, and thanks for our recent victory in Virginia." But, she observed, "though the air trembled with the news of another great victory, the sound brought anguish and desolation to many hearts."[2] Both sides realized that, as Augustus Benners wrote, "the crisis of the War is or seems to be at hand" and the "large armies in Georgia and Va it would seem will decide the contest."[3]

Governor Watts expressed optimism. In response to pleas for corn to help feed starving Alabamians, he offered words of encouragement. "Tell our people there to stand firmly to the cause of liberty and independence," he wrote a political leader in Marshall County. "Two more battles—one in Virginia & one in Georgia, will settle our difficulties, if we are successful. I feel confident we shall whip the Enemy in each fight."[4] Watts was wrong.

In preparation for his impending move from Chattanooga to Atlanta, General Sherman opted to keep a force at Decatur to tie down Confederate forces required to protect Selma and other critically important sources of Confederate industrial output in central and south Alabama.[5] This would prove to be excellent strategy. It cannot be overemphasized that the Confederacy's focus and desire to protect and secure that output was an Achilles heel that would ultimately help cause the devastating and pivotal loss of Atlanta, and in turn play a role in the reelection of President Lincoln.

Confederate General Joseph Johnston had marshalled most of his forces in and around Dalton, Georgia, through which the Western and Atlantic Railroad ran south back to Atlanta and constituted his primary supply line. Not wishing to make a frontal attack at Dalton, Sherman sent a large force west around Johnston's left flank through two mountain gaps[6] (see map 7). As the Alabama press reported, the flanking of Johnston's army caused Johnston to make the first of a series of what the state's newspapers called "retrograde movements" or "backward advances" (the Southern press shunned the more demoralizing term *retreat*).[7]

Although these retreats were nonetheless demoralizing to many Confederate civilians, several soldiers from Alabama in General Johnston's army supported Johnston's decision making, particularly those whose correspondence and diaries also included repeated prayers for peace. J. P. Cannon, a soldier from Lauderdale County, wrote that "from the best information I can get we have about 45,000 men and the report is that Sherman has at least 100,000. If this is correct it is better to fall back, and we have so much confidence in Old Joe [Johnston] that we are willing to be guided by his judgment and wait until he says the time has come to strike." The hope, he continued, was that "by forcing [Sherman] to attack us under disadvantages as he has been doing for some days, and drawing him into the interior, farther from his base, that we can eventually weaken him until we can risk a general engagement."[8] George Miller, the hell-bent-for-glory young officer from Talladega County, had initially written his wife that Johnston had been "out generalled."[9] But even he changed his tune in the next two weeks: "The two grand armies of the west lie confronting one another some 30 miles from Atlanta, each seemingly waiting for the other to attack. We have advantage in position and I hope will wait the longest."[10] These men also assumed that as long as Sherman was occupied in Georgia, he could not move on Alabama.[11]

But all expected that a grand battle would come sooner rather than later, inspiring Hiram Williams to write, "Heaven help the poor careless wretches, who see the moon, shining upon this sinful world for the last time."[12] No one wanted to be one of those wretches, but some did not have to trust God or luck to avoid that fate. Two soldiers from Randolph County who deserted from Johnston's cavalry told a correspondent of a Nashville newspaper that "much disaffection exists among Johnston's soldiers, and desertions occur continually," despite the imposition of capital punishment for those who were caught. "The army," they continued, "is generally exceedingly averse to an engagement, believing that the war is a great outrage, kept up solely by

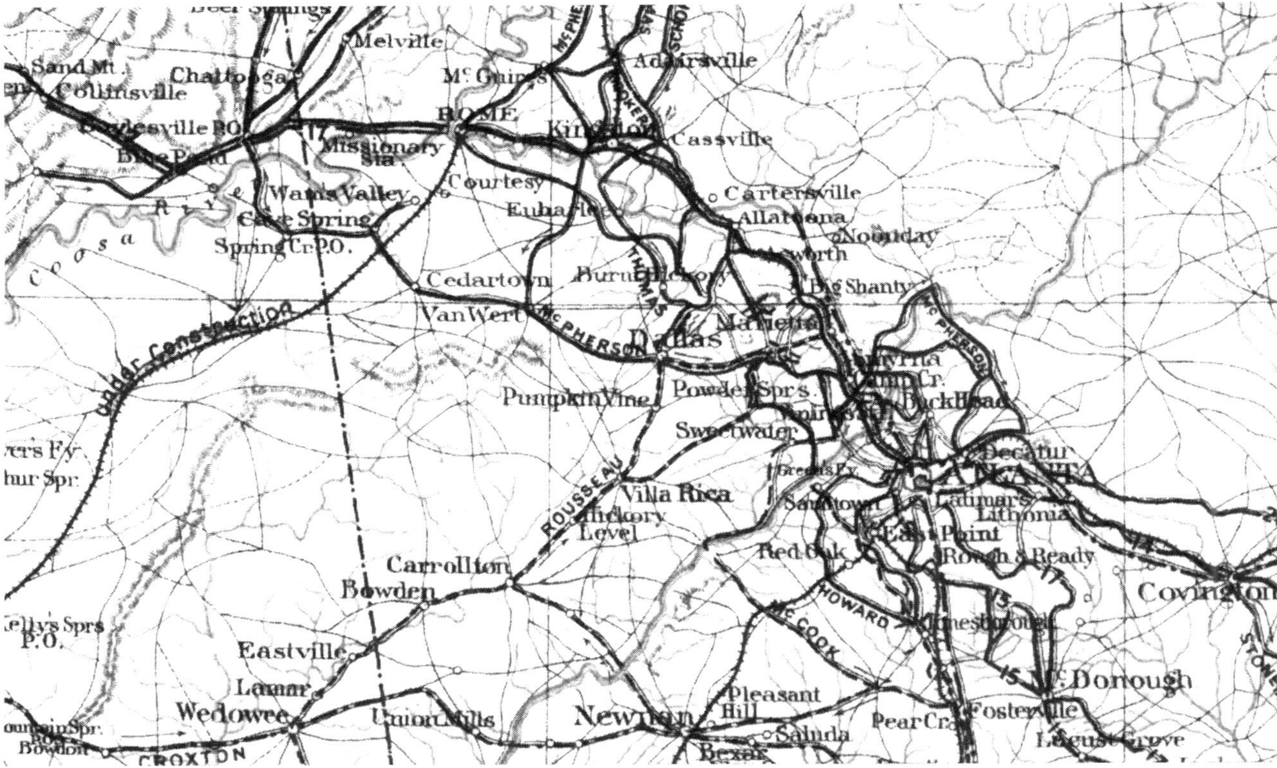

Map 7. Vicinity of northwest Georgia and east Alabama (*Official Military Atlas of the Civil War*)

Southern politicians and military leaders. They are tired of the war and so express themselves freely to each other."[13] This was not propaganda planted in the Yankee press. Governor Watts privately ordered the imprisonment in the state penitentiary of a soldier "charged, tried & convicted, before a general court martial, of the 'Army of Tennessee,' of failing to give information of an intended mutiny."[14]

In nearby Cherokee County, Alabama, Sarah Espy, whose three young sons served in Johnston's army, recorded that a man in her neighborhood who had just returned from Rome, Georgia, had reported that "Rome is nearly deserted" but that he saw "plenty of stripes there." "It seems," she acidly concluded, "our officers have a decided tendency to get out of danger,"[15] inexcusable to her at this critical stage. As Augustus Benners noted, the "fate of the country is quivering in the balance,"[16] and an Alabama newspaper touted this campaign as the "critical and crowning struggle of the war," and one in which "each man feels that his own personal liberty, the sanctity of his home, the honor of his family—all that he holds dearest beneath the stars—are staked upon the issue."[17]

Nonetheless, some on the home front tried to live life as before. A woman who had fled to Tuskegee, Alabama, wrote that she had been invited to "take tea" at the home of a resident, and that when she arrived she was surprised to see other ladies "dressed in evening costume" and "some extravagantly dressed" who "glittered in their diamonds." She was also struck by the lavish supper supplied by the host. It "was a most beautiful table, the center ornamented with a pyramid of flowers in a silver stand, five stands in height and tastefully arranged; the cake was beautifully iced, three varieties, fruit, teacake and pound, calf's foot jelly, turkey, chicken salad, ham, delicious tea; and this is the starvation in the South!" "Nowhere in the South," she continued, "could you find more style, perhaps a greater variety, but nothing more; for wealth, style, beauty and taste no place can surpass it." "If this be a poor dying struggle," she concluded, "Oh! Beautiful South, you are glamorous even in your death!"[18]

But try as those at the home front might, the war continued to raise its ugly head. After the typical initial press reports of telegrams "pouring in upon us the cheering news of Confederate victories—victories decisive of the early independence of this people,"[19] came more ominous news. Among other things, it was evident that the consequences of General Forrest's handiwork at Fort Pillow were coming home to roost. An Alabama newspaper reported that Union prisoners captured in north Georgia had disclosed that they had "*positive orders* to take no prisoners, and from the appearance of our men found dead upon the field, it is plainly evident that they carried out their orders to the very letter. These men were shot through the head; their clothing where the balls penetrated was burnt with powder." It was, the report concluded, "a retaliatory proceeding for the slaughter of a band of armed negroes at Fort Pillow by Gen. Forrest's command."[20]

A newspaper correspondent in Montgomery reported that the "excitement and anxiety in the community is very great,"[21] and a few days later wrote that the "public mind pulsates only to news of the battlefield." There were "croakers" in the community at that early point in the campaign, he admitted, but they "meet little sympathy in the looks or words of the masses."[22] These dissenters may have remained guarded in their activities initially, but this changed after news of Johnston's retreat to Resaca reached Alabama. The correspondent pleaded for someone to "put down those croakers who, like ill omened birds of night sing their doleful songs wherever they may be; and refusing to see anything hopeful or good themselves, are ever trying to infuse the same into others. *We hate these croakers*, and wish there was some special quarter assigned them, where they could only torment each other and surfeit upon the fears and horrors which their diseased imaginations are perpetually conjuring up."[23] This negativism, coupled with an active rumor mill, took their emotional toll. In Tuskegee, the same woman who had written of the luxury and gaiety on display now wrote of "doubt and gloom hanging over the inhabitants of this town. The war news is not so favorable. Oh! God have mercy on us! Many persons have lost sons and brothers and the wails of sorrow can be heard through the town!"[24] The Montgomery correspondent lamented that "drinking shops are multiplying throughout the city," indicating that alcohol consumption "must be on the increase, not withstanding the enormous price charged for the liquid poison."[25] To meet the increased demand for this ancient form of antianxiety medication, opportunistic businessmen in the area began construction of a huge steam-powered distillery reportedly costing $150,000.[26]

Croakers were also active in other parts of Alabama.[27] As Johnston retreated further south toward Atlanta, the editor of a Mobile newspaper attempted to boost sagging morale on the home front. When Sherman's army reached the Chattahoochee River, the *Mobile Advertiser and Register's* editor confidently predicted, "it must have been greatly weakened to guard his long line of communication to Chattanooga." As a result, Sherman "is not likely to bring a very superior force into the action to be fought," while "our troops are accustomed to fight and to defeat more than their equal number." In the end, therefore, Sherman would wear the "crown of a lunatic" rather than a "hero's laurels."[28] Although the *Advertiser and Register's* editor had a point about Sherman's lengthening supply line, few outside Johnston's army saw Johnston's retreats as a sign of strength and ultimate success. Instead, it appeared to some, including Jefferson Davis, that it was Johnston who was trying on the lunatic's crown for size. The *Montgomery Mail* reported public criticism of Johnston's strategy, especially his failure to make a stand at some point above the Etowah River.[29] Some Montgomerians were also complaining about the "inaction" of Governor Watts, especially in light of his bold speeches back in October 1863 in which he had resolutely pledged to drive Union forces out of the state.[30]

As the croakers continued to croak,[31] and prayer meetings in Selma and elsewhere brought no divine intervention or successful change of strategy for the Confederates in north Georgia,[32] the editor of the *Macon Confederate* (in Georgia) suggested what General Johnston had been advocating for some time.[33] On June 3, the *Macon Confederate*'s editor urged that an effort be made to cut Sherman's supply line back to Nashville, Tennessee, and thereby force him to retreat. "The whole campaign seems to have come now to that point." By "massing the forces of Wheeler and Forrest upon the rear of Sherman," he assured, "they can reduce him to the necessity of going back to Chattanooga and thus imperil the safety of his whole army."[34] Given that Sherman's armies outmanned and outgunned Johnston's, the efficaciousness of this strategy was self-evident, especially to Georgians. Wheeler and his comparatively inferior cavalry force were already in north Georgia, but as they noted with dismay, the War Eagle was still in Mississippi.[35]

Forrest had indicated his willingness to go to Tennessee for this purpose as early as April 6,[36] but General Sherman had effectively precluded him from doing so and Georgians could justifiably blame Alabama, and more particularly the industries in and around Montgomery, Selma, and Tuscaloosa, for Atlanta's ultimate demise.[37] Sherman had anticipated threats to his supply line, but he also recognized that the Confederacy seemingly placed as much a priority on the war-related industries in Alabama as on Atlanta. To draw Forrest's attention away from his supply line in middle Tennessee, Sherman sent a series of strong columns of Union cavalry from Memphis, Tennessee, toward Forrest and Alabama. Sherman assumed, quite correctly, that this would tie Forrest down in Mississippi by forcing him to defend that state while also attempting to prevent an invasion of Alabama.[38] When word of an impending raid from Memphis reached Confederate authorities in mid-May 1864, for example, an order sending Forrest into middle Tennessee was quickly suspended by General Polk, who had been transferred to north Georgia as the situation there continued to worsen. Polk instead urged General Stephen Lee that "as large a portion of Forrest's force as possible should be concentrated at Tuscaloosa without delay" and that "you engage yourself actively in preparing for the defense of Selma."[39] As Lee explained the decision to Forrest, "General Johnston has fallen back to Kingston, which leaves central Alabama much exposed from the direction of Rome," and Forrest's forces were necessary to "move toward a raid from Memphis or Rome" and "to protect the prairie country, Selma and Montgomery, about which there is much apprehension."[40] Therefore, despite the prayers of apprehensive and increasingly frantic Atlantans, four thousand of Forrest's men under General Chalmers were instead ordered to Montevallo in central Alabama, and even several hundred of Roddey's men, composing half of his force, were moved to Talladega in east Alabama.[41]

With his rear still secure, Sherman proceeded with his time-consuming but effective flanking movements, thereby maneuvering Johnston out of his prepared positions and reaching a point within twenty-five miles of an increasingly panicky Atlanta in early June.[42] Some Alabama soldiers who had voiced support for Johnston's strategy of retrograde were now losing heart. A soldier from Russell County, Edward Norphlet Brown, wrote to his wife, Fannie, that "I need not tell you I am tired of war. We are all tired—thrice tired. I would give a kingdom to have it stopped."[43] But at least Selma, Montgomery, and the sources of raw materials in central Alabama for manufacturing facilities in both of those towns were all safe for now, a fact which gave little solace to Atlantans.

17
Rousseau's Raid

Other equally significant and fateful maneuvering was going on elsewhere in mid-1864. A few days after a special correspondent to an Alabama newspaper reported from Johnston's army that the "locale of the wizard of the saddle," Forrest, was "a matter of earnest anxiety everywhere" and that "conflicting reports" circulating around headquarters were keeping everyone there "in as deep a mystery as ever enveloped the movement of the Wandering Jew,"[1] a coalition of Republicans and War Democrats were joining hands at the National Union Convention, which convened in Baltimore, Maryland, on June 7.[2] There, Abraham Lincoln was unanimously nominated for reelection on a ticket with Andrew Johnson of Tennessee, who one Alabama newspaper derided as a "renegade demagogue."[3]

A case can be made that Johnson's selection encouraged the Union movement in Alabama and elsewhere in the South. As the *New York Times* put it, Johnson's nomination was "a new proof that the [pro-Republican National Union] party is truly entitled to the grand name it bears, a yet further pledge that the party, in its work of restoring the Union, will know no such thing as sectional antipathy."[4] The *New York Tribune* added that his nomination was "a pledge to the Unionists of the Seceded States that they, at least, are not deemed outcasts from the pale of our Nationality."[5]

In a matter of days after Johnson's nomination, the *Selma Dispatch* reported the discovery of a "treasonable league" called the Peace and Constitutional Union Party, which had been "started in Jefferson and adjoining counties [in central Alabama], having for its object the overthrow of the Confederate Government." According to the *Dispatch*'s editor, agents of this league had been "sent to work in the armies of Georgia and Virginia" and "also to communicate with the enemy."[6] A Confederate investigator in Alabama had earlier reported the results of his "tour of investigation as to the secret treasonable society alleged to exist in this State." The investigator wrote that he was "satisfied that the society embraces more than half the adult males of Randolph, Coosa, and Tallapoosa Counties, a large number in Calhoun and Talladega Counties, and a considerable membership in some of the other counties in Alabama." Lewis Parsons, whom Andrew Johnson would appoint to serve as Alabama's provisional governor in 1865, was believed to be "one of the most prominent members if not the head of this organization."[7] Raising issues about the security of the Confederacy's internal communication network, the fact of this investigation, as well as the existence and contents of this report, almost immediately became known in Nashville, Tennessee, and was reported by a Nashville correspondent to the *Chicago Journal*. "J. Davis' sympathizers in Alabama," the correspondent wrote, "are fully aware of the existence of powerful Union organizations, and they have collected the names of a large number of the leaders and sent them to Richmond, asking the advice of the authorities there as to how best to proceed."[8]

Johnson's rhetoric encouraged Unionists to believe that their continued resistance would be rewarded in the end. In a widely reported, historically significant speech he gave in Nashville shortly after his nomination, Johnson declared that "traitors should take a back seat in the work of restoration" and loyal men "should control the work of re-organization and reformation absolutely," a line that, according to a newspaper account, brought "loud and prolonged applause" from a large audience that likely included many Alabamians.[9] This assurance of simple justice was welcome to all Unconditional Unionists, particularly those members of the traumatized rural white underclass who had been victimized by the terrible consequences of the reckless leadership of those traitors. To others who, like Jeremiah Clemens, had initially opposed the secessionists but had then voted for the adoption of Alabama's secession ordinance or otherwise ostensibly aided the rebellion, Johnson's words potentially sounded the death knell of their political careers. Rather than remaining in Huntsville to provide continuing leadership to the Union movement there, Clemens left Alabama and would live out the remainder of the war in Philadelphia, Pennsylvania.[10]

Andrew Johnson did not stop with generalities about putting loyal Southern Unionists in the front seat of the reconstruction process. As was reported in the Alabama press, he declared in the same speech that "treason must be made odious and traitors must be punished and impoverished."[11] It was a very bold statement reminiscent of Andrew Jackson, and one that many in Alabama and elsewhere took as an article of faith, especially those who had lost family members, homes, and worldly possessions. To many of these victims of secession and war, nothing less than death would suffice.[12]

Given the massacre of white Tennessee Unionists at Fort Pillow and west Tennessee, Nathan Bedford Forrest was probably among those who were very high on Johnson's list. And if General Sherman and others in the Union high command had their way, Forrest would never see the inside of a courtroom. Probably with Johnson's blessing, another Union cavalry force that had left Memphis for Alabama had been given the task of hunting Forrest and his men down and showing no quarter. Among the members of this force were a number of black soldiers who were willing to risk their lives to take Forrest's.[13] But the ensuing Battle of Tishomingo Creek at Brice's Crossroads near Guntown, Mississippi, on June 10 resulted in the defeat of the numerically superior Union force and set off another flurry of man-worship for Forrest by members of the Alabama press and their Southern brethren.[14] An Alabama correspondent in Mississippi was certain that Forrest had stricken the Yankees a "terrible blow, and one that will seriously damage Sherman, if not compel him to fall back to Chattanooga."[15] An Alabama correspondent with Johnston's army in Georgia was just as certain that Forrest would soon be in Sherman's rear, and that when he got there "you will hear of the gnashing of teeth and the rolling of Yankee eyes."[16]

The grim reality was, as Sherman coldly put it in one of his reports, the sacrifice of life in this engagement had succeeded in drawing Forrest from the plan of "striking our roads." To be on the safe side, Sherman had nonetheless ordered that the citizens of Tuscumbia and Florence be notified that if Forrest left Mississippi for Tennessee and crossed the Tennessee River through their communities, the towns would be burned and the people banished north of the Ohio River.[17] Sherman reported to Washington that he would also order another force from Memphis to "go out and follow Forrest to the death, if it cost 10,000 lives and breaks the Treasury. There never will be peace in Tennessee till Forrest is dead."[18] As a result of this new threat from Memphis, General Stephen Lee again concluded that a raid by Forrest into middle Tennessee was "impracticable" for the foreseeable future.[19]

While Johnston (and Georgians) obsessed about cutting Sherman's ever-lengthening supply line, Sherman had his eye on Johnston's even longer line. And he was being pestered by a subordinate in Nashville, Major General Lovell Harrison Rousseau, for permission to strike Selma. On June 19, Rousseau, a prewar Louisville, Kentucky, lawyer,[20] had written Sherman of his wish to pay "my long desired visit to Selma" while Forrest was being kept busy in Mississippi. "With 3,000 men," he claimed, "I could go down and destroy fifty to one hundred millions' worth of property belonging to the rebel government, including a portion of the important road between Selma and Atlanta." The raid Rousseau envisioned would target not only the "manufacturing establishments" at Selma, which were "far more extensive and important than they have at Atlanta," but also "between here and Selma . . . five or six of the most important iron works there are in the Southern Confederacy." Rousseau assured Sherman that "a blow like this now would be of great service to the cause, and might effect [*sic*] your own immediate position."[21]

Sherman's position was actually looking fairly good when Rousseau penned his letter, but he might have nonetheless given Rousseau the go-ahead except for his own bloody setback at Kennesaw Mountain on June 27. Rather than flanking Johnston's fixed fortifications, Sherman had delighted Johnston by finally directing an ill-advised frontal attack. The result was predictable. As one Alabama correspondent described the battle, "the Yankees came up in files of four and five, and we had nothing to do but shoot them down like squirrels."[22] Sherman's loss not only boosted Confederate morale[23] but it also threatened to add to Northern war weariness that, according to the Alabama press, was being encouraged by Northern Peace Democrats as part of their campaign to unseat President Lincoln.[24] The bad news from General Grant's stalemated efforts in Virginia had already provided those Democrats with enough ammunition to orchestrate the postponement of their National Convention until August 29 in order to await the outcome of Grant's and Sherman's campaigns.[25] Sherman did not wish to provide them with any more. Therefore, he wisely returned to his heretofore relatively slow but safe and successful strategy of flanking movements.[26]

But on June 29, five days after an Alabama newspaper reported the immense profits being derived from the operations of the Montgomery and West Point Railroad in supplying Johnston's army,[27] Sherman relented and authorized Rousseau to begin preparations for a lightning cavalry raid from Decatur, Alabama, through east Alabama to destroy the Alabama and Tennessee River Railroad's bridge across the Coosa River, and then to proceed further south to destroy the portion of the Montgomery and West Point Railroad between Tuskegee and Opelika.[28] To Rousseau's dismay, however, Sherman ordered that Selma not be touched. But an advantage of Sherman's plan was that it entailed less risk than that Rousseau had proposed and therefore gave reasonable assurance of positive newspaper headlines in the North. Selma, Sherman wrote, "though important, is more easily defended than the route I have named." As an additional precaution, Sherman expressly prohibited Rousseau from attacking any infantry or fixed defensive positions, and in fact directed that "the party should avoid all fighting possible."[29] As Sherman already knew, however, Rousseau's raid would face only token resistance in north Alabama. By this time, General Roddey and his men had begun leaving north Alabama on June 27 to reinforce Forrest in Mississippi and meet another raid from Memphis.[30] In addition, several counties through which Rousseau would pass were known to be inhabited by large numbers of Unionists who had joined the peace movement.[31] Under these circumstances, Sherman was certainly justified in concluding that if the raid were "managed with secrecy and rapidity the expedition cannot fail of success and will accomplish much good."[32] To be even more on the safe side, however, Sherman suggested that Rousseau "give out that you are going to Selma," thereby tying down any other defensive forces to positions west of Rousseau's actual route.[33]

While Rousseau and his staff busied themselves with consulting refugees from Alabama and planning their raid,[34] other Union forces were in motion that were increasing his chances of success even more. The new Union cavalry force from Memphis had also given out misinformation that it was heading for Selma.[35] In addition, General Sherman had again succeeded in flanking Johnston, forcing the Confederates to retreat to a point south of the Chattahoochee River only a few miles from Atlanta.[36] Signs of increasing defeatism could be seen in at least one east Alabama community, Tuskegee. The owner of a Tuskegee hotel began demanding payment in greenbacks by the guests.[37] Days later, Sherman flanked Johnston yet again by crossing the river, forcing another "retrograde" back to Peachtree Creek on July 9 and, according to one Alabama newspaper editor, bringing the "fate of Atlanta to a crisis."[38]

Those (such as Jefferson Davis) who were caught up in military strategy probably saw it that way, but some of those who had a more direct stake in the matter took it in stride. Whether due to peace movement influence or some other factor, exhausted soldiers in the front lines of both armies in Georgia decided at this point to take an unauthorized break. J. P. Cannon, a soldier from Lauderdale County, wrote that "without consulting the officers we have agreed upon an armistice. All firing between pickets has ceased and consequently we have had a very quiet day, with the exception of the artillery, which is not included in the truce. Johnnies and Yanks have become quite friendly, exchanging many articles, such as tobacco for coffee[,] canteens, etc., but it has to be done on the sly to keep the officers from finding it out as they would hardly sanction so much familiarity." The following day, he noted that it was "a pleasant and quiet Sunday. No doubt the officers are wondering why everything is so silent on the picket-line. Of course, we don't propose to volunteer any information, for we are enjoying the respite, and they might have so little regard for our feelings as to break up the truce."[39]

At least some of those officers knew about that picket truce and did nothing to interfere. In a letter to his wife, the heretofore by-the-book George Miller from Talladega County, wrote that "our pickets and the Yankees had agreed upon a truce." During the day, they sat and conversed, swam and traded.

"After sundown," Miller wrote, "the Yanks assembled on the bank and began to sing songs—national, humorous, and sentimental." Then "squads of Confederates would return the compliment, and each would praise the performance of the other." Although Miller claimed he did not participate, he admitted that the singing "sounded beautiful on the still summer air" and that overall the interaction of the troops was "one of the most impressive I ever witnessed."[40] Tragically, that truce lasted only a few days, and the war would soon lurch forward in north Georgia.

But it resumed without General Johnston when Jefferson Davis fired Johnston and replaced him with John Bell Hood, whom Davis assumed was a more aggressive leader.[41] Johnston, Davis complained, had been too focused on protecting his army.[42] Edward Norphlet Brown, who had avoided fighting in the trenches by virtue of his quartermaster position, ironically expressed relief in this change in command. Johnston, he wrote to his wife back in Russell County, should have engaged Sherman in a grand battle at an early point in the campaign rather than allowing himself to be repeatedly maneuvered back toward Atlanta.[43] But most rank-and-file Alabama soldiers were stunned at this change in command. According to one soldier from Tuscaloosa, word that Johnston had been relieved of command "was received in dead silence, and figuratively speaking 'our hearts went down into our boots,' or whatever happened to be covering our heel." They "believed that President Davis had made a terrible mistake."[44] Davis's decision was also roundly criticized in Alabama for months. Sam Reid of the *Montgomery Advertiser* wrote that the announcement of Johnston's removal "could not have produced a greater shock, or more profound regret, than has been universally felt by his political sacrifice. The asperity of the act of his immolation, by the Executive in Richmond, has fallen as chilling and depressing on the popular heart as a disastrous defeat, while its elating effect upon the enemy has been equal to a victory."[45]

At the same time, the *Mobile Advertiser and Register* was reporting that a large force was being organized at New Orleans to attack Mobile and other portions of south Alabama. The *Advertiser and Register*'s editor hoped that this intelligence would "stimulate Gov. Watts to put into the field the State troops, at once, to reinforce the veterans whose duty it will be to meet this expedition."[46] But the governor had more threats than this with which he would have to deal. Watts was in Tuscaloosa in the process of harvesting a very young crop of troops. After attending the annual session of the Board of Trustees of the University of Alabama on July 9, he had reviewed the university cadets and announced that at the close of commencement exercises graduates would be put into active service.[47] It would not be long before they were on the move to face threats coming from what seemed to be every direction.[48] Published comments about enlisting the university cadets are rare, but probably most Alabamians would have agreed with a Georgia newspaper editor that "we could but regret the necessity which compelled us to send forward such noble youths to battle against the vandals composing the Yankee army. May they be returned safe to their parents, who thus offer upon the altar of liberty their noble boys."[49] Safe behind his exemption from conscription, the editor of the *Selma Dispatch* offered that the "special prayer of many loving hearts will attend them all."[50] They would need divine protection.

Rousseau's raid finally began late on Sunday, July 10, 1864, when he led his approximately 2,500 men from Decatur south into Blount County.[51] They completed the first leg of their trek by reaching Blountsville on July 11 or 12, where they released deserters and runaway slaves from the county jail.[52] Resistance was not to be found and no local militia units were mobilized to stop them in that county or in St. Clair or Talladega Counties the following day.[53] In Asheville, Rousseau audaciously stopped for several hours, long enough to take possession of the local newspaper office and publish a special edition sarcastically (or not) reporting that he was "much pleased with the hospitality and kindness of the citizens of Asheville and the vicinity" and was "well satisfied with the manner in which he was entertained."[54] Coincidentally, reports of the sinking of the Confederate commerce raider CSS *Alabama* off the coast of France first began appearing in the Alabama press at about the same time,[55] and as word began to spread of Rousseau's approach, it would have been impossible for many Alabamians not to see the same fate for the state of Alabama if the war did not end soon. For all south Alabamians knew at this early point in the raid, Rousseau was headed in their direction and the end for them was only a matter of days.

The first real resistance Rousseau met came near daybreak on July 14, the same day Nathan Bedford Forrest and elements of Roddey's Brigade were suffering defeat near Harrisburg, Mississippi.[56] The leader of the opposition to Rousseau was James Holt Clanton, who had apparently been satisfied up to that point with the relatively safe task of organizing short term "ninety days men" in Calhoun County near Blue Mountain.[57] He would later claim in a newspaper interview that his motivation in intervening was to block what he had heard the previous night was an advance by Rousseau on Jacksonville and Blue Mountain.[58] But it is more likely that he had heard rumors that Selma or Montgomery was being targeted and believed that his family and property were in danger. In fact, Clanton's superior officer, Gideon Pillow, had earlier been ordered by General Stephen Lee to move most of the forces from the Blue Mountain area to Montevallo in order to protect Selma.[59]

For whatever reason, Clanton left camp at Blue Mountain on the evening of July 13 with what he said were two hundred men and undertook the proverbial against-all-odds mission that more than anything else would partially redeem his military reputation and capture the imagination of some Confederates. The optimistic *Selma Dispatch* reported that "Gen. Clanton, with a sufficient force to 'gobble them up,' is in pursuit, and we confidently expect to hear good news from that quarter soon."[60] Clanton arrived at a point on the Coosa River known as the Greensport Ferry in Talladega County at dawn on July 14 only to discover that one of Rousseau's regiments had already crossed the river. After learning that a portion of Rousseau's force was also attempting to ford the river at the Ten Island Ford several miles south of his position, Clanton divided his force and sent one hundred men to attempt to block their crossing. Clanton then made a costly attack in which his brother-in-law was killed but that he later claimed forced the Yankees to fall back. Clanton then retreated all the way to Blue Mountain, later claiming that his plan was to block Rousseau's expected drive to that place.[61]

Rousseau crossed the Coosa River at Miller's Ferry without opposition and proceeded toward Talladega, which he reached on July 15.[62] He remained there only a couple of hours, and most newspaper accounts indicate that he was again careful not to harm civilians or their personal property in this area of increasing peace movement activism. The destruction at Talladega was limited to the railroad depot and a gun factory, both clearly legitimate military targets that had been instrumental in supplying Confederate forces in Georgia.[63] According to the *Talladega Reporter*, Rousseau did not bother to destroy the niter works or conscript camp in Talladega, prompting one local wag to suggest that these facilities "kept so many men out of the army, the Yankees were unwilling to destroy them." Before leaving, Rousseau did confiscate Confederate foodstuffs and distribute them to needy whites and blacks, a practice he would continue as he pushed further south.[64]

Rousseau entered Sylacauga on the night of July 15 and then proceeded south down the plank road toward Wetumpka, sending Montgomerians into a panic.[65] He then veered east to Nixburg in Coosa County and crossed the Tallapoosa River on July 16 in the direction of Loachapoka, a station on the critically important Montgomery and West Point Railroad.[66] Fearing that this might be merely a feint, however, the military authorities in Montgomery continued to mobilize the citizenry for local defense at the capital while Rousseau proceeded to destroy the railroad between Loachapoka and Opelika.

Governor Watts, who was still in Tuscaloosa, ordered the remaining draft-eligible University of Alabama cadets into the field under the command of university president Landon Garland before hurrying back to Montgomery.[67] He also issued a proclamation calling out every able-bodied man in the area for local defense, an edict executed by force. According to the Montgomery *Mail*, the bells in Montgomery "were rung, and the citizens turned out in large force and organized at the Courthouse, determined to defend their homes at all hazards."[68] But according to the Montgomery correspondent of a Mobile newspaper, the "several companies having received and inspected their arms, were then served with ammunition and their guns all loaded, they were ready to march, when orders were given to dismiss for the present and all to be in readiness to report at the first sound of the alarm bell," or by seven the next morning, whichever came first.[69] Later that night, military officials received word that the Yankees were not coming to Montgomery and instead were moving east in the direction of Opelika.[70] Despite this, when the men reported for duty the next morning, they were not dispatched to the east in pursuit of Rousseau but were instead dismissed until eleven that morning. After reassembling, they were "kept in the pleasant temperature of 100° Fahrenheit for an hour or so—then dismissed to report again at five." When the Mobile correspondent attempted to find out why they had not been sent toward Opelika, he learned that the commanding general, Jones Mitchell Withers, had gone to take a nap, leaving orders that he was not to be disturbed until five.[71] There has, the disgusted correspondent later wrote, "rarely been a greater farce enacted before the public than the military operations of this city for the last few days."[72]

Montgomery was nonetheless safe, but the same cannot be said for the portion of the Montgomery and West Point Railroad thirty miles east.[73] Once again, however, James Holt Clanton entered the picture.[74] He later explained that after learning Rousseau was not going to Blue Mountain, he had gone south in pursuit and finally made contact with Rousseau's rear guard at Loachapoka on Sunday, July 17. Clanton maintained that, after making an attack, he broke off the engagement and "took the wagon road to Tuskegee to get ahead of the Yankee force going to Chehaw," another station on the railroad east of Opelika. A conflict was avoided when, according to Clanton, a "force unknown to him met and turned [Rousseau and his men] back to Chehaw."[75] This "unknown" force was probably a hastily organized, makeshift regiment of six hundred finally sent from Montgomery. It included approximately forty University of Alabama cadets that Governor Watts had ordered up from their encampment at Selma. Rather than defeating Rousseau, however, they were attacked upon their arrival near Chehaw on July 18 and ultimately forced to retreat.[76] Overall, the outmanned Confederates suffered nearly seventy casualties at Chehaw, including two cadets who were wounded in the engagement.[77]

With Clanton supposedly still in pursuit, Rousseau proceeded to Auburn and Opelika, where he destroyed the railroad and other Confederate property. On the evening of July 19, after being tipped off by local blacks of an approaching Confederate force, Rousseau began making his way north and then into Georgia. Clanton claimed he followed until Rousseau's forces changed course directly toward Sherman's army, "when his [Clanton's] men and horses being entirely broken down, he stopped further pursuit."[78]

Only after Rousseau had crossed the state line into Georgia did Clanton's mentor, Governor Watts, finally issue a proclamation calling on the first-class militia to volunteer for state defense outside the counties of their residence. Most of the second-class militia had already been absorbed through enlistment or conscription into the Confederate army but, declared Watts, these "boys and men, brave boys and brave men" of the first class should "illustrate, by their conduct, that highest order of patriotism which makes all rush to the defense of the imperiled State."[79] As Watts would later reveal, however, few did much rushing toward militia duty anywhere, thereby making Clanton's ineffective intervention appear even more courageous. The failures of Clanton's superior officer, Gideon Pillow, during Rousseau's raid may have had the same effect. Pillow had been at Tuscaloosa with Governor Watts at the time the raid began, and he had returned to his command, which was still at Montevallo. But rather than moving east to intercept Rousseau as ordered by General Stephen Lee, he had moved south to Selma, where his men saw no military action. For this, Pillow was summarily relieved of his command.[80]

One captured Confederate soldier is said to have remarked that Rousseau and his raiders had made a "big hole in Johnston's haversack."[81] And as was the case with Nathan Bedford Forrest in his engagement with William Sooy Smith back in February, Clanton had not saved Alabama or even significantly affected the execution of Rousseau's mission. The Alabama press nonetheless gave Clanton a small taste of the treatment previously accorded the War Eagle, praising the "gallant" exploits of his "little band" and embellishing his role and accomplishments.[82] It was said that during the skirmish at the Coosa River, Clanton's clothing had been almost "riddled" with bullets[83] but that he had "nobly" contended "for every inch of ground."[84] In an interview by an apparently friendly Georgia reporter shortly after the raid, Clanton "modestly" claimed "for himself and his men that their close pursuit prevented the enemy from detaching parties to plunder and destroy the country through which they passed." Clanton and his men had also "so retarded the advance of the raiders and harassed them in the rear, as to afford the people time to rally and stop their progress."[85] In fact, Clanton had had nothing to do with either of those coincidences, which were actually a function of restrictions Sherman imposed on Rousseau.[86]

Although Clanton's ineffective intervention received public notice as far away as South Carolina,[87] the propaganda value of what the *New York Herald*'s front page headlines called "GENERAL ROUSSEAU'S GREAT RAID" gave another timely boost to Abraham Lincoln's bid for reelection.[88] It also made the task of Reconstructionists even more difficult.

18
The Fall of Mobile Bay and Atlanta

The shock of Rousseau's relatively large force slicing through the eastern portion of the state virtually unscathed was still reverberating among Alabama's citizenry when a worried Confederate soldier from Pike County, Alabama, Joel Murphree, warned his wife that there would likely be more raids to come: "Ursula you need not be surprised if you hear of Yankee raiding parties reaching Columbus [Georgia] and Montgomery before a month." He correctly predicted that "all the principal cities of the South will be visited by the enemy before this war closes" and "all our manufacturing establishments will be destroyed."[1]

Much would depend on what happened in Georgia. As the *Selma Morning Reporter* disclosed to its readers, Sherman's forces were close enough to shell Atlanta.[2] James Mallory in Talladega County wrote that he could hear the roar of the cannons from there.[3] An obviously depressed Montgomery correspondent was indignant that Nathan Bedford Forrest had not already been dispatched to cut Sherman's supply line, and he expressed what seems to have been the fervent desire of many to finally "hear the scream of the 'War Eagle' along this line! It is music which the people like and which makes their ears tingle with joy."[4] An anxious Georgia planter stationed in Virginia concurred. "The fable that Forrest is to be turned loose on Sherman's rear must one day become a fact,"[5] he wrote to his wife. Joe Wheeler's cavalry, which had been publicly criticized as "inefficient,"[6] was finally becoming more active in this regard,[7] but he was a poor substitute for the War Eagle.[8]

South Alabama was also under great stress. Just a few months earlier, a Kentucky woman who had fled to Alabama where her husband was stationed described somewhat jealously the beauty of Mobile and how its residents lived: "You meet children and women with waiters of bouquets. The ladies look very handsome with their dark riding dresses and deep pointed cuffs, riding horseback with the officers." Mobile, she wrote, was "quite a feast to the eye."[9] But now the Mobile press was reporting a Rousseau-style raid from the

Figure 17. Battle of Mobile Bay (Courtesy of Alabama Department of Archives and History)

federal base at Pensacola toward the Mobile and Great Northern Railroad[10] and the appearance of a menacing fleet of twenty-three Union naval vessels commanded by Admiral David Farragut just outside Mobile Bay.[11] Although Mobile was subject to the Union naval blockade, it remained a port used by blockade runners and an important defense against Union efforts to penetrate south Alabama using the Alabama River system (see figure 17). However, the vastly outnumbered Confederate fleet at Mobile was ill-equipped to put up a fight. Earlier in the war a Tuscaloosa physician and prolific inventor, John Braham Read, had submitted plans to Confederate authorities for the construction of torpedo boats to which mines would be mounted on spars for the purpose of ramming and sinking Yankee ships.[12] Some were built, but apparently none were deployed at Mobile Bay.[13] A naval officer stationed there had attempted to raise private funds for what he called a "Submarine Torpedo Boat" but had come up several thousand dollars short.[14]

Now it was too late. Nonetheless, the local press advised the public to remain calm and resolute, predicting that any effort to run past Fort Morgan at the mouth of the bay would be a "dangerous experiment in face of the torpedoes which lie across their path and the gauntlet of fire which Fort Morgan can open upon them, together with the no inconsiderable weight of the ordinance with which [Confederate] Admiral [Franklin] Buchanan and his little navy can add in disputing the passage."[15] Buchanan's Mobile squadron was certainly tiny. It included only one ironclad, the ram CSS *Tennessee*, which had been partially constructed in Selma (a ram was a type of ship used to smash into and disable other ships). A few wooden ships provided little support against Union ironclads.[16] On August 5, Farragut launched his initial attack and, after damning the torpedoes, succeeded not only in passing Fort Morgan with two ironclads and fourteen other ships, losing only the USS *Tecumseh* to a torpedo, but also in forcing the evacuation of Fort Powell.[17] Not desiring martyrdom, the Confederate commander of Fort Gaines surrendered on August 7 in what John Forsyth called a "disgraceful capitulation."[18] After being subjected for several days to what an Alabama soldier stationed there called a "most terrific bombardment,"[19] Fort Morgan would follow suit,[20] sending refugees scurrying up the Alabama River for sanctuary in Selma and Montgomery.[21]

Union forces did not immediately invade Mobile in force, instead engaging in a series of probing actions using local blacks as guides. This was very dangerous work. An expedition that crossed the Perdido River and moved in the direction of Mobile Bay was reportedly captured, and the black man who piloted them was executed.[22] But this did not stop other black folks from aiding Union forces or prevent those forces from applying increasing pressure around Mobile or elsewhere in south Alabama.

Signs of desperation and impending doom were now everywhere. In Tuscaloosa, William Russell Smith's wife, Mary, decided to try to get out of the Confederacy before it was too late. Earlier in the year, her mother in Maryland had obtained a pass from President Lincoln permitting Mary Smith to enter federal lines at New Orleans, and it had been sent to her in Tuscaloosa in June. She had then attempted unsuccessfully to obtain a pass from the local Confederate provost marshal. On August 11, however, she left town without one. But someone reported her departure to the Confederate inspector general who happened to be in the area. As a result, Mary was forced to return, but she and William Russell Smith would continue their efforts to get her to safety.[23] Many of those who could not escape physically were doing so mentally. Governor Watts responded to widespread drunkenness in Mobile by ordering the closure of all saloons there.[24]

A correspondent in Montgomery reported that the momentous results of events in Mobile Bay had fallen "with an almost stunning effect upon our community" and "almost banished Richmond and Atlanta from our thoughts."[25] The *Montgomery Mail* took the opportunity to publish a controversial editorial from the Richmond *Sentinel* calling for peace commissioners to be "appointed by either section, and invested with plenary powers of negotiations

[to] meet on neutral territory and discuss the terms of peace."[26] Never accused of unconventional thinking, Alabama governor Thomas Hill Watts instead issued yet another proclamation, this time appealing to every man and boy capable of bearing arms to report at once for the defense of Mobile. The supportive *Montgomery Advertiser* warned that if Mobile fell, "what part of the State will be safe from penetration by our hated vandal foe?"[27]

Noting a "feeling of uneasiness" that was pervasive even in the "money making community" of Selma, the *Selma Dispatch* agreed with Watts and argued that the business community ought to "lock doors and rise the rallying cry, 'Ho, for Mobile!' "[28] As far as can be determined, however, the response of the men of Selma was unsatisfactory.[29] Military officials were forced to order the closure of the saloons in Selma because soldiers passing through were drinking too much. One correspondent wrote to a Georgia newspaper, however, that one of the disappointed soldiers cracked that "this was not true—that he never had enough in his life."[30] At least the Selma women again demonstrated their patriotism, this time by reportedly volunteering "their services at the [cartridge] Laboratory to make cartridges for our gallant armies. Who will imitate these patriotic daughters of the South?" the editor of the *Selma Reporter* inquired.[31] The answer was: very few men.[32]

As a consequence of so many being unwilling to take chances with their lives, the young university cadets, who were away on furlough, were again forced into the breach, this time several days before their furloughs ended.[33] According to the *Selma Dispatch*, the "martial steps and proud bearing of the young patriots as they marched through the streets [of Selma where they had rendezvoused] produced mingled feelings of joyful pride and heart swelling sadness." With more prescience than he probably realized, the *Dispatch*'s editor confessed that it "makes the heart sad to see the noble youth of the land march off to encounter the privations of camp and dangers of the bloody battlefields, but the cause demands the sacrifice."[34] In less than sixty days, more than three-fourths of them contracted malaria while stationed on the Eastern Shore of Mobile Bay at Fort Blakely and had to be withdrawn.[35]

Sarah Espy, who resided near the Alabama-Georgia line, wrote that "we look forward with fearful anticipation of the result of the fighting in Ga. and we fear being run over any way. If our army is conquered there, we know that we are ruined."[36] At about the same time, the outnumbered Confederate soldiers defending Atlanta were being told by their commanders that "the time has come when we must make a grand struggle for our independence, and that the operations of the next few days may go a great way towards deciding the fate of the Confederacy."[37] Given this, where was the War Eagle? As the press would shortly reveal, he was not in Alabama, Georgia, middle Tennessee, east Tennessee, or even Mississippi. Instead, Forrest was busy attacking Memphis, Tennessee.[38]

General Roddey and his brigade were not operating on Sherman's supply line either. They had been ordered back to north Alabama and arrived in Moulton on the evening of August 23. A resident in Russellville wrote that Roddey's return to the Tennessee Valley was a time for rejoicing there because it would supposedly end an anti-Confederate terror campaign that Union troops in Decatur, and Unionist guerrillas in league with them, had been waging for several weeks.[39] Most recently, according to this correspondent, on August 18 "more than four hundred of these fiends in human shape" had entered Moulton prior to dawn, captured the two Confederate enrolling officers there, and murdered them "in cold blood." The raiders also "destroyed all the records and papers of the Judge of Probate and Clerk of the Court's offices." Although not stated in the letter, it was typical of these types of raids to free conscripts and political prisoners from the local jail. Destroying records of pending criminal prosecutions was usually of secondary importance. In any event, lest conscription efforts were resumed in Lawrence County, the raiders had vowed to "give no quarter to officers or men on conscript duty."[40]

With the South's last hope—the Democratic National Convention in Chicago—only a matter of days away, things were looking very bleak for Alabama and the Confederacy, which was quite ironic given that Abraham Lincoln was having feelings of insecurity about his own chances in the election.[41] Edward Norphlet Brown was sure that "Lincoln & his supporters will be defeated in the coming election at the North & a better hearted administration will be placed in power and then peace will follow. This being so," he continued, "the fighting of this revolution will be over in two or three more months & diplomacy will steele [*sic*] the balance."[42] In the days following the fall of Fort Morgan, a Mobile newspaper editor attempted to stress the small number of positives on the battlefield furnishing the convention delegates with "food for reflection." He irrationally predicted that Southerners "have but to hold our own in Virginia, Georgia and Alabama for a *few weeks* to see a change in the political and military situation."[43]

If the rumors in the Northern press of the lobbying activities of C. C. Clay Jr. and other Canadian-based Confederate agents with leaders of the Northern Democratic Party are to be believed, the Mobile editor had at least a scintilla of evidence supporting an equally small degree of optimism regarding the ultimate outcome of the convention and its effect on the war and the South.[44] The party platform declared support for reunion, but unlike the Republican Party's stance in favor of conquering a peace on the battlefield, the Democrats also adopted a plank that the war was a failure and that there ought to be a "cessation of hostilities"—an armistice—"with a view to an ultimate convention of all the States."[45] At this point, the *Montgomery Daily Mail* emphatically instructed that "if the incoming federal administration tender an armistice and propose a convention of the States of both confederations on the basis of the sovereignty of these States, it is our duty to take part in its deliberations."[46]

As it turned out, however, former Union army commander George Brinton McClellan, the presidential candidate nominated by the delegates, neither fit the Confederacy's bill nor supported the Democratic Party's platform. But his position would resonate with Alabama Reconstructionists and worry Confederates. Earlier in the summer, John Forsyth had ironically recommended in an editorial that McClellan receive the Democracy's nomination to run against the Republican "hoosier clown," Lincoln, and his "renegade demagogue" running mate, Andrew Johnson. At that time, Forsyth assured that if Democrats adopted a peace platform but "put McClellan up as the standard-bearer, with his military prestige exalted to the skies by the present campaign of his rival Grant . . . we really believe that the Democrats would sweep the North."[47] But McClellan issued an acceptance letter embracing principles that were actually contrary to the platform, shocking Peace Democrats, Clay, and every other Confederate in the process.[48] In essence, McClellan took a position that was almost identical to that of Southern Reconstructionists and many Northern War Democrats. He would not insist on the abolition of slavery as a goal of the war. Instead, the war would be prosecuted to "re-establish the Union in all its integrity," he wrote, and "Union is the one condition of peace."[49] His letter made no mention of an armistice or a convention of the states, although it did not necessarily rule out those measures. He vaguely declared that "when any one State is willing to return to the Union it should be received at once with a full guarantee of its constitution," meaning slavery.[50] Exactly how and where this willingness to return to the Union was to be determined and expressed was unstated.

The now clearly frustrated and perhaps embarrassed John Forsyth denounced McClellan's nomination, calling him a "political idiot" and "political ass" who should be dropped from the ticket. Forsyth defiantly cried that the South must "stand by our arms and die sooner than become slaves of the inhuman, uncivilized and unchristian people who are striving by force of arms to become our masters."[51]

A portion of Forsyth's exasperation was caused by another shocking event that occurred in the interim between McClellan's nomination and his bombshell letter. The "great flanker," as General Sherman was sometimes called by Forsyth, had made another move, and by the time General Hood figured out what was going on he was forced to abandon Atlanta.[52] Edward Norphlet Brown warned his wife in Russell County that "you will all begin to feel the war in earnest soon as I have no idea that the army will make much of a stop before we get to Macon, Georgia." "I have no other thought now," he later added, "but that we will ultimately be subjugated."[53] A correspondent at Montgomery reported that news of the capitulation of Atlanta caused a "sudden paralysis" to fall on the "public mind" in that town,[54] and this was the case throughout Alabama.[55] Stunned and despondent, Sarah Espy wrote that "it seems that the Lord is indeed shutting us up in the hand of the enemy for they are all around us."[56] Sally Independence Foster was inconsolable that "Florence has had so many of her brave and gallant young gentlemen killed in this dreadful, dreadful war. Oh! my God," she fervently prayed, "do let this horrible war end; and let sweet, sweet 'Peace' reign over our beloved country once more."[57]

The same mood of defeatism was shared by Confederate troops from Alabama serving in Georgia. "When the news was imparted to us it was a death knell to our hopes," wrote J. P. Cannon of Lauderdale County."[58] Hubert Dent, a generally committed young officer from Eufaula, wrote to his wife, Nannie, that the "spirit of our troops is very bad and unless they do better I do not see what is to prevent Sherman from going any where he please."[59] Many blamed their leaders, particularly Jefferson Davis and his replacement of the more careful and experienced Joseph Johnston with the relatively more aggressive John Bell Hood. Malinda Taylor, the wife of a soldier from Tuscaloosa County, had a dark solution for this. She wrote to her husband, Grant, that "I understand that [men in Hoods army] are deserting by 5 hundred a day from Atlanta. I wish evry one would do so until evry man would get home. From what I hear the General you have now is as mean as he can bee. It is a pity," she coldly concluded, "but what someone would point a loaded gun at him."[60]

Worried that mass desertions would dissolve Hood's demoralized army and open Alabama to invasion by Sherman, Governor Watts issued a call for a special session of the Alabama legislature to decide on measures to meet that invasion,[61] and as one wag put it, to petition that body for power to "compel the laggards to do their duty."[62] Watts's intention was, once again, to attempt to convince the legislators to revise the militia law in order to allow him more flexibility in the militiamens' deployment.[63] And as he assured General Hood in response to Hood's plea for troops, "I shall not fail to urge that the Militia may be carried, in case of necessity, even beyond the limits of the State."[64] But given the circumstances, this call for a special session was very risky and actually opened the door for those "laggards" and any of their legislators who were members of the peace movement in Alabama to lay the groundwork for formally putting an end to Alabama's involvement in the war altogether. In an article titled "The New Plan of Peace: How to Divie the South," the editor of the *New York Herald* had recommended the policy of instituting negotiations with the states separately for the purpose of detaching them from the Confederacy.[65] This policy was not only consistent with Lincoln's Ten Percent Plan and McClellan's acceptance letter but ironically also fundamental Confederate government theory. Jeremiah Clemens would soon write from Philadelphia to a friend in Huntsville that if Alabama had had the right to engage in "separate state secession" from the Union in 1861, logic dictated that it could secede from the Confederacy and rejoin the Union.[66] As had preceded Alabama's first secession in 1861, the initial step in the process was to convene the legislature.[67]

For this reason, John Forsyth described Watts's calling of the legislature to convene at this critical juncture "an unsafe experiment, much more likely to result in evil than good."[68] Prevailing public sentiment might for once actually be reflected in the measures to be adopted by their representatives. As Forsyth observed in an important and candid admission, there were now two classes of men in Alabama: "First a class whose hearts have never been in the struggle for independence; and second, a class, who are wearied and worn out with the trials and sacrifices, and dangers of that struggle, and willing to escape it with a patched up treaty of peace, without much regard to Confederate honor or the future well being and interests of these states."[69] The *Selma Reporter* was not afraid to admit that it was currently within at least one of these two classes. In fact, in an obvious rhetorical shot at Forsyth and other diehards, it expressed indignation that "those who oppose the only practicable mode of ending the war are yet unwilling to go to the front and there help to fight it out."[70]

Other Confederates in Alabama recognized the threat of a runaway legislature immediately after the shocking loss of Atlanta had sunk in and the dreaded "croakers" began to "indulge their chronic propensity to grumble and find fault."[71] The idea of calling for a convention of all of the states was also denounced by Confederates as a most "disorganizing and mischievous proposition" that "amounts to the *undoing* of all that has heretofore been done towards the establishment of a Confederate government."[72] It was also pointed out that Republicans controlled the governments of all the Northern states with the exceptions of New York and New Jersey,[73] presumably meaning that any peace terms would be in accordance with Lincoln's formula for peace rather than McClellan's.

Nonetheless, electrifying rumors of possible peace talks between General

Sherman on the one hand, and Georgia governor Joseph Emerson Brown and Confederate vice president Alexander Stephens of Georgia on the other, were already on the street as well as in the press in Alabama and elsewhere throughout the country.[74] Based on newspaper reports of events in Georgia, it seemed to Alabamians that their sister state was on the verge of dropping out of the war and the Confederacy and that Sherman would soon be applying pressure on Alabama to do the same or else. From the Confederacy's standpoint, the situation in Georgia appeared grave. Several days before the fall of Atlanta, the *Montgomery Daily Mail* published a letter from a Georgia newspaper regarding a prominent Georgian traveling in the North claiming to be a peace commissioner appointed by Georgia state officials.[75] At least publicly, Governor Brown distanced himself from this,[76] but Alabamians learned that on September 10, Brown had mysteriously furloughed all of the Georgia militia for thirty days, thereby withdrawing ten thousand men from Hood's already degraded army and sending shockwaves throughout the South.[77] It also became public knowledge that Sherman had proposed a ten-day truce commencing on September 12, supposedly to allow time for the removal of noncombatants from Atlanta (whom Sherman had ordered to leave), and that Hood had agreed to it. This triggered protests from some newspaper editors that Sherman was thereby being permitted to improve his hold, making his repulse from Georgia even more difficult.[78] Based on these incidents and other available information, even Sherman had assumed that Georgians were willing to reach a separate peace. He dispatched Georgia Unionists to invite Brown, Alexander Stephens, and Herschel Johnson to Atlanta for discussions with him.[79]

Whether Sherman also sent peace emissaries to prominent Alabamians is unknown. At least two Alabamians were arrested in Greenville, Alabama, at about this time and charged with what the Greenville *Observer* cryptically called "holding dangerous communications with the enemy." The local circuit judge refused to grant them writs of habeas corpus, and their ultimate disposition is unknown.[80] In any event, Sherman's spies likely made him aware of the looming special session of the Alabama legislature and of the growing defeatism and war weariness in Alabama that his success in Georgia had made even more acute.

Something had to be done by Confederates to prevent Georgia and Alabama from being the next dominoes to fall. The *Selma Reporter* attempted to rally public opinion, but in the process may have done more harm than good: "Atlanta having fallen, it may not be long until this section of Alabama is overrun by the infernal raiders of Sherman's army. They will come like infuriated demons to burn, pillage and devastate." According to the *Re-*

porter, the only alternative was to "arm ourselves to the teeth and calmly await their coming. We may have to quit our homes and sacrifice our household goods—nay, we may have to suffer loss of all our property, but we must fight them to the death, though they be poured upon us in legions like the frogs of Egypt."[81]

Taking heed, James Holt Clanton was suddenly reenergized and attempted to raise men to attack Sherman's railroad supply line in northeast Alabama.[82] By the day the Yankees marched into Atlanta,[83] Jefferson Davis had also finally initiated the process of sending Nathan Bedford Forrest from Mississippi through north Alabama and into Tennessee to attack Union army supply lines there, presumably to somehow miraculously cause Sherman to now withdraw altogether from Georgia.[84] Confederate General Richard Taylor, the newly appointed commander of the Department of Alabama, Mississippi, and East Louisiana, issued the order to Forrest on September 6.[85]

To mislead Sherman's spies about Forrest's intentions, the *Mobile Tribune* reported that Forrest and his men had arrived in that embattled city. The *Tribune*'s editor described the force as a "devil-may-care set of fellows [who] for a time thought they owned the city."[86] But Forrest was actually then moving through north Alabama on his way to middle Tennessee. When he arrived in Cherokee in northwest Alabama on September 18, he was shocked to discover the condition of affairs. At Tuscumbia, Joe Wheeler and the remnants of his cavalry corps were in what Forrest described in reports to Taylor as a "demoralized condition." A large number of Wheeler's men had "deserted and straggled off," and even Wheeler was "disheartened." Forrest also reported that General Roddey was "sick," that his men were "much scattered," and that it was "uncertain what number can be relied on from that quarter." Forrest's ability to round up enough men to accomplish his difficult mission was, as a result, severely hampered.[87] His departure for Tennessee would not improve the security of north Alabama.

In south Alabama, residents of Montgomery and Selma had every reason to believe their towns were on Sherman's short list of targets in the coming months.[88] The conquest of Montgomery and then Mobile following the fall of Atlanta had been General Grant's original plan of action, and Selma had always been on Sherman's mind.[89] Those who were superstitious interpreted the relocation of the wandering *Memphis Appeal* from Atlanta to Montgomery as an evil omen or "avant-courier" of the Yankee horde.[90] With Nathan Bedford Forrest in north Alabama and Tennessee, Tuscaloosa, Selma, Montgomery, and Mobile were now exposed to attack by raiding parties from Memphis, Tennessee, and Georgia as well. And with Mobile's harbor under the exclusive control of the Union navy, jittery Mobilians were certain that an amphibious invasion or siege of their city was only a matter of time, so some were again calling for the slaves to be placed in the Confederate army.[91] John Forsyth was at least initially all for it. "Our white strength is not exhausted—when it is we can put 400,000 strong black arms in the field and stake its brawn and bone upon the issue of that independence which is paramount to every consideration. We may give up black slavery," he shockingly concluded, "but we never can consent to become the white slaves of the hateful Yankee race."[92] Forsyth recovered his senses in the following weeks, however, declaring his vehement disagreement with those who argued that independence was "worth even the sacrifice of the institution for the better security of which we went to war! Let us assure all such dreamers that the *destruction of slavery is reconstruction*—that henceforth for us slavery and independence are '*one and inseparable*.' "[93]

The Confederacy was on the verge of crumbling, and now was the time for it to initiate peace talks. That did not immediately happen, and so for those who were interested in preserving slavery, the terms of peace offered by George McClellan and Northern War Democrats constituted the best deal that could be had. As Confederate assistant secretary of war John Archibald Campbell wrote to a Georgian in a private letter at about this time, the "sentiment of the Northern people in favor of a restoration of the Union is constantly growing," but "any peace on the terms of union will have to be made on the terms of their present Union. No administration at the North can offer more, or could fulfill any agreement to do more."[94] Now more than ever, supporting McClellan's election was essential to the proslavery faction of the Alabama peace apparatus. This Reconstructionist faction's strategy was to encourage the North to vote for McClellan by making it known that, upon his election, the war would end with a negotiated peace and reunion. Or, as Georgia Reconstructionists would somewhat vaguely write of their goal to Confederate vice president Alexander Stephens, "we hold it to be the duty of all good and patriotic men at the South, to take such steps as will encourage [Northern Democrats] and convince the North that we are not unwilling to adjust the difficulties between the two sections *on honorable terms*."[95]

Die-hard Confederates recognized the growing strength of the peace movement in Alabama and elsewhere, as well as the powerful effect of the sirens' song of the McClellan Democrats on Southern slave owners.[96] Hubert Dent, a young officer from Eufaula, Alabama, serving in Hood's army, wrote to his wife asking "what do the people about Eufaula say about the nominees of the Chicago convention? I can't say that I hope for much unless we can check the enemy and even if we succeed in doing that and they are elected we will have another thing to fear and this is the disposition of our people to accept peace on any terms." For this reason, he asserted that if "McClellan is elected and refuses to recognize our independence I believe he and his party would be worse enemies to our cause than Lincoln himself."[97]

As a result of this commonly held fear, C. C. Clay Jr. wrote to Judah Benjamin suggesting that Confederates should "keep our own counsel" and certainly refrain from expressing any preference for McClellan.[98] On September 14, John Forsyth essentially declared that he was a Lincoln man: "Lincoln is far better for us than McClellan, as an open and consistent though a bitter and cruel enemy, is rather to be desired than a fair and hypocritical friend or enemy."[99] In another editorial published on September 18, Forsyth was even more explicit and colorful in explaining his rationale. From McClellan's letter of acceptance, "we gather that he is perhaps the most dangerous adversary we could possibly have to deal with. Conciliation, unluckily, goes very far with our weak-kneed brethren, and with respect to the new nominee it is only the slaver of the anaconda prior to swallowing." "Union or War!," he concluded, "this is the monstrous paradox of Chicago."[100] War it would be, if men like Forsyth continued to have their way. Only an independent slave nation would satisfy them, even if such a course risked the destruction of slavery and the Southern way of life they were attempting to preserve.

Southern Reconstructionists commonly believed, apparently for good reason, that Jefferson Davis was also opposed to McClellan's election because of the boost it would give to the reconstruction movement and, therefore, its adverse impact on Davis's quest for independence.[101] Davis certainly recognized that public opinion was at a crossroads, with reunion in one direction and independence in the other. If morale sank any lower, Sherman was likely to make the result of the national election a moot issue for the Deep South. But Davis also knew that to reverse the trend would require more men. In an effort to address all of these mounting threats to the Confederacy, Davis left Richmond by train on September 20 on a speaking and fact-finding tour through Georgia that would ultimately take him to Montgomery. There he would have a showdown with Alabama's leading Reconstructionists.[102]

VII
THE DEATH THROES OF A REBELLION

Timeline: September 1864–December 1864

September 23, 1864	President Davis speaks in Macon, Georgia, on his way to Alabama.
September 24, 1864	Nathan Bedford Forrest takes Athens, Alabama.
September 25, 1864	Nathan Bedford Forrest takes the Union garrison at Sulphur Branch Trestle north of Athens.
September 25, 1864	President Davis meets with General Hood at Palmetto, Georgia.
September 26, 1864	Alabama legislature convenes in special session.
September 27, 1864	Peace resolutions are introduced in the Alabama legislature.
September 28, 1864	General Hood's army begins moving toward north Georgia.
September 28, 1864	President Davis arrives in Montgomery, Alabama.
September 29, 1864	President Davis addresses the Alabama legislature.
September 30, 1864	President Davis leaves Montgomery.
October 7, 1864	Alabama legislature adjourns its special session.
October 17, 1864	Governor Watts attends a meeting of Southern governors in Augusta, Georgia.
October 19, 1864	Confederates raid St. Albans, Vermont.
October 20, 1864	General Hood's army arrives in Gadsden, Alabama.
October 30, 1864	General Hood's army reaches Tuscumbia, Alabama.
November 7, 1864	Confederate Congress convenes for the last time.
November 8, 1864	President Lincoln is reelected.
November 14, 1864	Alabama legislature convenes in regular session.
November 15, 1864	General Sherman's army burns portions of Atlanta and begins march east.
November 20, 1864	*Chattanooga Rebel* reports the "accidental" death of W. R. W. Cobb.
November 25, 1864	Confederate terrorists attempt to burn downtown New York City.
November 27, 1864	David Campbell Humphreys is arrested by Confederates at Huntsville.
November 30, 1864	Battle of Franklin, Tennessee.
December 1, 1864	*Selma Dispatch* publishes advertisement authored by George Washington Gayle calling for $1 million to be contributed to finance the assassinations of President Lincoln, Andrew Johnson, and William Seward.

December 5, 1864	President Lincoln urges Congress to pass the Thirteenth Amendment.
December 10, 1864	C. C. Clay Jr. leaves Canada.
December 13, 1864	David Campbell Humphreys is released.
December 15, 1864	Alabama legislature adjourns.
December 16, 1864	General Hood's army is routed at Nashville, Tennessee, and flees south toward Alabama.
December 21, 1864	Union forces return to Huntsville, Alabama.
December 26, 1864	Hood's remaining army begins crossing the Tennessee River at Bainbridge Ferry near Florence, Alabama.

19
"On the Wrong Side of the Line of Battle"

Jefferson Davis was not uniformly popular in the Deep South at this point. A Georgian in Robert E. Lee's army referred to him as "our pigheaded President."[1] According to John Forsyth, some members of the Southern press inappropriately seized the occasion of his visit to Georgia to "harshly criticize his blunders and anathematize and deprecate the 'bad luck' he is sure to bring in his train."[2] But some Georgians were optimistic that Davis's coming might lead to a change in military strategy, with Georgia finally being given exclusive priority over Alabama. The *Columbus Sun* reported "intimations that the Government has at last waked up to the importance of holding Georgia."[3]

Davis certainly hinted as much in his speeches on the way to Alabama. The first that received mention in the Alabama press was delivered in the Baptist church in Macon, Georgia, on September 23. Although Davis surprisingly admitted that two-thirds of all Confederate soldiers were absent from the field, most of them without leave, he boldly assured his audience that Sherman's army would "sooner than later" be forced to retreat because of the inability to protect his supply line from Chattanooga. Sherman's army, he assured, would then suffer the same fate "that befell the army of the French Empire in its retreat from Moscow." Sherman's retreat, Davis boldly predicted, would be harassed by the Confederates as did "the Cossacks that of Napoleon, and the Yankee General, like him, will escape with only a body guard."[4]

A Troy, Alabama, newspaper editor expressed displeasure regarding Davis's bold declaration, fearing that it would simply give Sherman and the North even more motivation. He compared it to Leroy Pope Walker's prediction in 1861 that the Confederate flag would soon float over the capitol in Washington. That "imprudent" speech, the editor reminded, had added fuel to the flame kindled by the bombardment of Fort Sumter, "which has been burning intensely ever since." He concluded, "Oh, when will those in power learn wisdom."[5]

But as the public would soon learn, Nathan Bedford Forrest would create the illusion that Davis might be a prophet, bolster public morale, and undermine the peace movement.[6] Huntsville native John Hunt Morgan had been killed a few weeks earlier in Tennessee,[7] leaving the War Eagle as the premier Confederate raider in the Deep South.[8] The *Montgomery Advertiser* was sure that a "brighter day will soon dawn upon the Confederacy." Forrest "of all others is qualified and has the prestige to break and keep broken Sherman's communication, and compel him to take up stakes at Atlanta. The Fort Pillow affair is fresh in the minds of all Yankee garrisons and troops, so that when Forrest is reported advancing their cowardly hearts fail them in anticipation of the doom they certainly expect to know they so richly deserve."[9]

After crossing the Tennessee River at Colbert's Shoals on September 20, Forrest pushed his reputation to new heights by leading his approximately four thousand men across north Alabama toward the Union army garrison on the Tennessee and Alabama Central Railroad at Athens. Like many such garrisons, it was manned primarily by black troops well aware of the fate of the defenders of Fort Pillow earlier in the year. Forrest's primary strategic importance to the Cause at this point was as much what one newspaper editor called the "terror of his name"[10] and its impact on black troops as anything else. Forrest obviously recognized this and made the most of it. His force reached the outskirts of Athens on the evening of September 23, just hours after Jefferson Davis's speech at Macon, and the following morning proceeded to earn the gratitude of local Confederates, who would erect a statue in his honor on the Athens town square many decades later. After an artillery barrage, Forrest threatened to massacre the vastly outnumbered Union force unless its commander surrendered. According to one of Forrest's men, the Union commander "yielded" to Forrest's "persuasive arguments," thereby allowing Forrest to take over one thousand prisoners while suffering only thirty casualties.[11] Among the prisoners Forrest took this time were several hundred black troops, who would be sent to Mobile and put to work on fortifications there.[12] A significant portion of the white troops would be sent to Selma for later imprisonment at Cahaba.[13] Forrest also captured a large amount of desperately needed supplies and weapons and is said to have quipped to the Athenians that "Lincoln being a better quartermaster than Jeff Davis, I patronized him."[14] On Sunday, September 25, Forrest attacked the small Union garrison at the Sulphur Branch Trestle on the Tennessee and Alabama Central Railroad a few miles north of Athens. Once again, he reportedly demanded a surrender, and after having been warned that Forrest was in position to move on the defenders "unconditionally," the "officer in command did not deem it prudent to refuse."[15]

Forrest's reputation was again soaring, thanks to Confederate correspondents and newspaper editors around the South. According to the *Mobile Evening News*, "the 'War Eagle'" was "pouncing down upon [the Yankees] like a vulture. . . . The bravery of Gen. Forrest's troops is the theme of conversation, with the citizens and enemy. The Yankees had it their own way when Gen. Wheeler was in Middle Tennessee, but for the last few days they have had more than a match."[16] As one of Forrest's men would later write, "any man in Forrest's command, with such a leader as Forrest, can make himself a hero by following him."[17] Another of Forrest's men boasted in a letter to a newspaper that the planned "raid upon Sherman's rear will make him retrace his steps from Atlanta, sure. With such a worker and fighter in his rear as the 'War Eagle,' Sherman cannot get his rations. When Gen. Forrest gets done with the railroads in Middle Tennessee and Kentucky, 'somebody will have to suffer for the substantials' of life."[18]

So far, however, Forrest had destroyed a portion of only one of Sherman's transportation lines from Nashville, that between Franklin, Tennessee, and Athens, Alabama.[19] Sherman's army could still receive supplies from Nashville via Chattanooga. To stop that, the Western and Atlantic Railroad between Chattanooga and Atlanta would not only have to be cut but something would have to be done to prevent that road from being rapidly repaired by Union forces. On September 25, the same day Forrest captured Sulphur Branch Trestle, Jefferson Davis arrived to meet with General Hood at his camp near Palmetto, Georgia, twenty-four miles southwest of Atlanta, to address that challenge.

Davis's reception by the troops there was not exactly warm.[20] James Lanning, a soldier from Sylacauga, Alabama, wrote that the members of his brigade "refused to cheer Jeff" because "they did not feel like it."[21] Much of the animosity against Davis arose from his decision to sack Joe Johnston and replace him with Hood. J. P. Cannon, a soldier from Lauderdale County, noted that when Davis rode through, "many of the men called out loudly, 'Give us Johnston,' or, 'Send General Johnston back and we will whip Sherman yet,' and many similar remarks to which the President made no reply."[22]

During Davis's meeting with Hood, an agreement was reached on a plan that would send most of Hood's army back to north Georgia for an assault on the Western and Atlantic Railroad. This was intended to cause massive damage and lure Sherman north toward Tennessee and away from Atlanta.[23] Hood was there to engage and defeat Sherman.[24] In order to provide some added motivation to the Tennessee troops, Davis reportedly told them to "be of good cheer, for within a short while your faces will be turned homeward, and your feet pressing Tennessee soil."[25] Reports of Davis's imprudent disclosure tipped off General Sherman of Hood's move.[26]

The plan had several obvious flaws. Even Kate Cumming, who by 1864 was a nurse stationed in Georgia, wrote that "I do not know any thing about military matters, but it does seem to me that there might be a better plan adopted than that to rid the country of this marauder," Sherman.[27] The plan, to begin with, did not call for the destruction of the estimated ninety days' worth of supplies Sherman had already accumulated and stockpiled in Atlanta.[28] It also failed to account for Sherman's ability, as demonstrated earlier in the year in Mississippi, to simply live off the land and without a fixed supply line. Moreover, by moving Hood from his current position southwest of Atlanta back to north Georgia and then Tennessee, there would be no significant, much less adequate, force that could attempt to block Sherman if he decided to, instead, advance toward east Georgia or south Alabama.[29] As the Selma *Mississippian* would remind all who would read, the "iron and coal interests of Alabama must be protected."[30] And Lincoln's chief of staff, Henry Halleck, would be sending a communication to Sherman on September 26 urging that Sherman's next line of march be "Columbus, Montgomery, and Selma, opening in conjunction with Farragut and Canby, the Alabama River" rather than east toward Savannah, Georgia. "Selma," Halleck reminded Sherman, "is a very important place." Halleck seemed to encourage him to exercise a hard war concept on his way there. "Your mode of conducting war is just the thing we now want. We have tried the kid glove policy long enough."[31]

Davis and Hood were probably well aware of these risks and realized that their plan was a major gamble. But they also recognized that it was consistent with what appears to have been popular opinion among Confederates about what ought to be done, especially those in Georgia and Tennessee.[32] And psychologically, that was what must have seemed necessary to pump up morale at this point, especially within the Confederate Army of Tennessee. As a Northern correspondent in Atlanta would soon observe, Hood's "move, it is true, is a desperate one, but their situation demands desperate remedies. They dare not remain idle and permit this army to dwindle away by desertion or grow despondent in a careful review of their case. An army in camp is always more or less dissatisfied—in the field always in better spirits."[33] A correspondent of the *Montgomery Mail* who was travelling with Hood's army agreed: "No matter what the critics may say—no matter what the books may say—no matter what science may say—we lose more in retreat than we can lose by advancing. The nature of our troops demands action, and they will not bear retrograde."[34]

A bold move that might force Sherman out of Georgia was also necessary to pacify the growing number of anti-Davis politicians in that state and stave off Georgia's capitulation. Not coincidentally, after Davis's meeting with Hood, word reached the public in Alabama that Georgia's Governor Brown and Confederate vice president Stephens (also from Georgia) had decided to reject Sherman's peace overtures.[35] Without their leadership, the Reconstructionists in Georgia would necessarily be forced to await the result of the presidential election in November before the quest for reunion with slavery could be resumed.

Through Davis and Hood's strategy, Georgia might not be the next domino to fall, but Alabamians knew that it left south Alabama wide open to invasion by Sherman.[36] As a result, with its legislature scheduled to convene a special session in Montgomery on September 26, there was still a chance that Alabama would ultimately be compelled to follow Tennessee out of the Confederacy. Under these circumstances, stopping or at least slowing down Alabama's Reconstructionists and their Unconditional Unionist allies was essential to Jefferson Davis. He, along with Confederate senator Benjamin Hill of Georgia, would therefore soon be racing to Montgomery aboard a special train to assure that the Cradle of the Confederacy did not become the Confederacy's grave.[37]

In one of the most striking ironies of the war, by the eve of the meeting of Alabama's legislature in special session on September 26, 1864, some Confederates were even more supportive of the reelection of Abraham Lincoln than ever.[38] According to an Alabama newspaper's Richmond correspondent, the election of Lincoln "will, it is believed in very high circles here, bring about a bloody collision at no very distant day between the [Northern] Peace men and the War men, leading eventually to the withdrawal of the [midwestern] States from the federal Union."[39] On the other hand, the election of McClellan, he continued, was worrisome because it might lead to a similar split from the Confederacy by the Deep South states: "The people of the Gulf States seeing themselves left to the tender mercies of one incompetent commander after another, have already lost heart, and very little more is needed to make them yield to reconstruction in some form. Let McClellan be elected and guarantee their rights as States, and secure them their property, and they will not hesitate a moment about returning to the Union."[40]

Indeed, Alabama Reconstructionists assumed that by making their preference in the election known, and indicating that McClellan's election would lead to peace and reconstruction, they might give him a boost among Northern voters, especially those who were tired of war and not so vindictive that only the abolition of slavery would satisfy them. A gauge for determining how many of those voters there might be was available in the form of state elections in the North that were scheduled to take place on October 11 in

Pennsylvania, Indiana, Ohio, and elsewhere. The meeting of the Alabama legislature was, therefore, the perfect forum from which to send a signal to the North prior to those elections. Jefferson Davis recognized this, and preventing it was one of the reasons why he decided to go to Montgomery.

The legislators who were preparing to convene in Montgomery were aware that Davis was then in Columbus, Georgia, and would be arriving in the next few days.[41] A desire by Confederates to stall until his arrival explains why the house of representatives had such difficulty in achieving a quorum. The senate was barely able to organize by noon, and it was only by what were called "extraordinary exertions" that a quorum was finally found at 4:00 p.m. and the house was organized.[42] By this time, the only matter of significance that could be accomplished was the reading of Governor Watts's annual message. As a result, Reconstructionists would be forced to wait another day before beginning to implement their strategy.

Unwittingly, Watts's brutally frank message may have played into their hands. "The successful advance of the enemy into our sister State, Georgia, and the fall of Atlanta," he said, "have exposed to attack and invasion the northeastern and eastern portions of Alabama. Unless prompt means of defense are provided, the State may become the field for contending armies and the people of Alabama may realize, at their own doors, the deprivations and hardships which bloody war inflicts." To Reconstructionists, the specter of this doom was the strongest motivator for peace on the terms outlined by McClellan. But Watts emphatically ruled out that option: "A reunion under the same government with those who have murdered our sons, outraged our women, destroyed our property with worse than savage malice, would stamp with infamy alike the names of our gallant dead and the living heroes of the war." Instead, Watts asserted, Alabamians had "no alternative but to 'fight on, fight ever,' until liberty and independence shall crown our efforts." To accomplish this, Watts recommended an overhaul of the militia laws that would, among other things, allow him to order the Alabama militia into Georgia and other adjoining states.[43]

The public was definitely not in unanimous support of Watts's proposal. A south Alabama newspaper editor wrote that it was "eminently unwise and improper" to "force the men away from home, wherever it may please his Excellency to order them." These men were desperately needed at home to produce food for the civilian population. Therefore, he hoped that the legislature "will not sanction the policy of the Governor."[44]

Watts's militant stance was not well-received in the legislature. "As one of the evidences of the coolness with which the message was received," wrote one correspondent, "only one hundred and thirty copies [of his address] were ordered printed, against a direct effort to print three thousand copies."[45] Even Confederates worried that Watts's parade-of-horribles rhetoric would encourage an invasion. "To our apprehension," wrote another correspondent, the message "is not calculated to do our cause much service," and Watts should have "avoided altogether such an exposition of our weakness."[46] The anti-Watts sentiment in the legislature did not mean that Alabama legislators had reached a consensus on what to do or how to do it. Following adjournment at five for the evening, a particularly prophetic observer wrote that the "indications of a strife in the Legislature are already cropping out," and the "incongruous elements of that body are little likely to fuse and mingle harmoniously."[47] That would prove to be the understatement of the session, if not the year. In fact, Reconstructionists in the house were poised to shock their Confederate colleagues, Alabamians, and the entire nation and make that observer wish Watts had the power to prorogue the legislature.[48]

By the next morning, however, news of Forrest's capture of Athens had reached Montgomery. This inspired even the *Montgomery Mail* to predict that it was the "beginning of a series of successes which we believe will necessitate the evacuation of Atlanta and the retreat of the federal army."[49] But Forrest's conquest had no apparent impact on Alabama Reconstructionists, at least not yet. The legislature reconvened at ten that morning, and during the call of the counties in the house, the first of a series of extremely controversial resolutions was introduced by an east Alabama member, future Republican J. J. McLemore of Chambers County.[50] McLemore was a thirty-three-year-old Georgia-born newspaper editor who had been elected to the legislature in 1863.[51] The key provision in his resolution advocated "holding a Convention of the various States of both Powers," as proposed by the "Democracy of the United States," to "adjust all the stupendous questions involved and provide for the general welfare, present and prospective of each." But the most dangerous idea contained in McLemore's resolution was that of grounding the convention concept on the proposition of "the sovereignty of the States" and "their individuality and independence." This doctrine could justify Alabama seeking a separate peace.[52] These principles had very recently been endorsed in a letter the prior week by Confederate vice president Alexander Stephens.[53] But Stephens's letter had not even been published in the Georgia press at the time McLemore offered his blockbuster resolution.[54] It is, thus, unclear whether McLemore was following Stephens's lead.

McLemore's initiative ignited a loud controversy. According to one witness, it "caused as much noise and excitement as if a real bomb shell had exploded in the hall of the legislature. I never saw such another scene. The explosion was heard in all the adjoining apartments of State, and soon there was seen a rush for the lobby. The Governor, Judges of the Supreme Court, Attorney General, Senators, official and military dignitaries, with scores of others, flocked to the scene of excitement and trouble, with the anxious inquiry as to the cause of alarm."[55] Press accounts of what happened next are rather cryptic. According to one correspondent, McLemore's "bantling" was subjected to "fierce assaults," although there is no indication that he was physically abused.[56] After a brief period, McLemore is said to have moved that his resolution be tabled, and "quiet once more [was] restored, though doomed to a brief duration."[57]

The real reason why McLemore chose to table his resolution may have been to assure that Lewis Parsons would have time before the scheduled adjournment at 2 p.m. to introduce his own resolutions. When the speaker of the house finally reached Talladega in the call of the counties, Parsons arose and offered a series of resolutions very critical of Lincoln's peace offer, which required both reunion and the abolition of slavery. But they expressed receptiveness to that portion of the Democratic Party's presidential platform offering to "open negotiations with us on the basis of the federal Constitution as it is, and the restoration of the Union under it." Parsons's resolutions did not expressly make reference to the mechanism of a convention of the states. Instead, they proposed that if the Democratic Party were successful in the presidential election, Alabama would be "willing and ready to open negotiations for peace on the basis indicated in the platform adopted by said convention—*our Sister States of this Confederacy being willing thereto*."[58] Parsons may have hoped that adding the emphasized proviso would win over the votes of the undecided, but it did nothing to mute the indignation of the Confederate members. According to one observer, Parsons's proposal caused "another explosion, more loud and terrific than the first."[59] The *Selma Dispatch* reported that his resolution "met with indignant rebuke from all parties."[60] A postwar account would reveal that "on the occasion of his introducing into the legislature, his celebrated resolutions, the propriety of imprisoning him, and even of lynching him for them, was freely canvassed."[61]

Confederates were angry, but they were also scared. In his editorial on Parsons's resolutions, a Georgia editor called the National Democrats' platform on which they were based the "first step towards re-construction of the Union. It is a seductive and winning platform, and we do not hesitate to say we have more fear of it than we have of the armies of Grant and Sherman. It is the 'Trojan horse,' whose admission within our lines must be forbidden, or it will do more for the enemy than all the open warfare of Agamemnon, Ulysses and Achilles." He condemned "the movement" by Parsons and the others as "insidious and seductive" and urged that "its dangerous and loathsome tendency should be exposed at once."[62]

Unlike McLemore, Parsons did not back down. Instead, while falsely denying that he was a Reconstructionist, Parsons argued that the resolutions would strengthen Northern Democrats, help elect McClellan, and thereby bring about peace. Lincoln's reelection, on the other hand, would ensure another four years of war.[63] In a debate that continued until the house adjourned for the day, Parsons's opponents charged that the resolutions actually encouraged more war by sending a message that the South was near capitulation.[64]

By the time Jefferson Davis and Benjamin Hill arrived in Montgomery on the evening of Wednesday, September 28, additional controversial resolutions had been submitted in the house.[65] Two Georgia-born, Macon County legislators who had also been elected in 1863, Joseph C. Head and Augustus B. Fannin,[66] proposed that peace negotiations be initiated and a convention of the states convened.[67] In addition, future Republican Joseph C. Bradley of Madison County introduced a resolution opposing the suspension of the writ of habeas corpus, a direct shot at Davis's policy.[68] But before a vote could be taken on any of these measures, rumors of Hood's new campaign reached Montgomery, and each of the resolutions were tabled until Friday, September 30.[69]

On September 29, President Davis was invited to address a joint session of the Alabama legislature at one o'clock that afternoon.[70] Like any good trial lawyer, Davis accentuated the positives (such as Robert E. Lee's recent success in Virginia) and minimized the negatives in his hour-long speech before reaching the burning issue of peace negotiations. He then claimed that the Confederate government had sought a peace accord with the Lincoln government but had been rebuffed. He also denounced the ideas embodied in the resolutions submitted by Parsons, McLemore, Head, and Fannin as products of self-delusion: "If there be those who hoped to outwit the Yankees, and by smooth words and fair speeches, by the appearance of a willingness to treat or to listen to re-union, hope to elect any certain candidate in the North, they deceive themselves. Victory in the field is the surest element of strength to a peace party. Let us win battles and we shall have overtures soon enough." Davis then all but accused Parsons and the others of treason. "Is there a man in the South in favor of reconstruction?," he reportedly asked, before "drawing a picture of the horrors of re-union." "All that I have to say," he exclaimed, "is that the man who is in favor of this degradation, is on the wrong side of the line of battle."[71]

Predictably, Davis's remarks would resonate in the pro-Confederacy press in and outside Alabama.[72] As a result, Parsons and the others would be subjected to widespread ridicule and accusations of treason and cowardice.[73] But as Davis would quickly discover, support remained strong for a negotiated peace based on whatever the best available terms were, and it came from some surprising places. Late that Thursday night, while Benjamin Hill was addressing a gathering of Montgomerians,[74] Davis met at the Exchange Hotel with Lieutenant General Richard Taylor, his aristocratic, thirty-eight-year-old former brother-in-law and the recently appointed departmental commander of the Alabama, Mississippi, and East Louisiana Department. There they consulted regarding future strategy and the prospects for victory. According to Taylor's postwar account of this meeting, he stunned Davis by frankly and accurately informing him that from a military standpoint, "the best we could hope for was to protract the struggle until spring. It was for statesmen, not soldiers, to deal with the future."[75] Lewis Parsons and the other Alabama legislators advocating peace talks could not have said it any more plainly. As Taylor also later wrote, the philosophy of almost all of the other commanders in the field at that time was to fight "simply to afford statesmanship an opportunity to mitigate the sorrows of inevitable defeat."[76] This revelation may explain the subsequent actions of several western theater commanders, including John Bell Hood.

But as William Russell Smith later noted, Davis had irrevocably substituted stubbornness and personal pride for statesmanship and pragmatism.[77] Even without the benefit of the telescope William Yancey had teasingly left Davis in his will,[78] Davis could easily see that with Nashville, Chattanooga, Memphis, Vicksburg, New Orleans, and now Mobile Bay and Atlanta having fallen, Abraham Lincoln's reelection was a virtual certainty and Confederate defeat was only a matter of time. Yet after leaving Montgomery the next morning, Davis gave more speeches during his return trip to Richmond to trusting war-weary Southerners calculated to give them false hope of victory.[79] As Davis told an audience in Augusta, Georgia, "I go away much more confident than when I came." He assured them that "thirty suns will not set before one foot of an invader will press the soil of Georgia."[80] John Forsyth added to this propaganda by warning that the struggle for independence could not be abandoned because "the deliberate, declared purpose of the enemy is to exterminate the pestilent race of rebels and to replace them with negroes first and Yankees afterwards."[81]

According to the *Nashville Daily Union*, any dissent was also chilled by the continued presence of the Confederate military. The "Southern people are wearied of the war, and are anxious for a peace, even though it involves a return to the Union; but they are, at present, held in chains; and they will continue to be so held, till the military power of Jeff Davis has been broken."[82] Several Southern Unionists, including future Alabama Republican Robert Stell Heflin of Randolph County, confirmed this in a public letter written from occupied Rome, Georgia. They urged Northerners to focus on "the great paramount object of conquering our rebel leaders and restoring the Union. Let who will be elected [president], it is his duty to preserve the Union at all hazards."[83] Meanwhile, the military presence in Montgomery, coupled with Davis's dramatic appearance before the legislature, had the desired effect on all of the resolutions obnoxious to Confederates. One Alabama newspaper pronounced them to be "dead-dead-dead—beyond the hope of resurrection."[84] They were tabled and then ultimately voted down by a vote of 45 to 32.[85]

But that was also the fate of bills that would have revised the militia law, thus defeating the entire purpose for which Governor Watts had called the special session in the first place.[86] A disgusted correspondent of a Georgia newspaper remarked that "Rousseau made his visit to within fifty miles of the Capitol a little too soon, or else the wiseacres lately assembled here were too short."[87] The house also rejected a senate resolution to appoint a joint committee to report on the propriety of commencing the next session of the legislature in January 1865 rather than November 1864.[88] The effect, and perhaps the intent, of this failed measure appears to have been to delay any rash response by Reconstructionists to the result of the Northern presidential election.

After adopting what an observer called a "brave" resolution that it would never "submit to abolition rule,"[89] the legislature adjourned at 9 p.m. on October 7, 1864, leaving Alabama still relatively defenseless should Sherman choose to enter south Alabama.[90] Mindful of Governor Watts's prior pattern, Talladega County planter James Mallory, whose youngest son was ostensibly safe at the University of Alabama, suspected what this meant for that son. He noted that "our son from Tuscaloosa came to stay a few days with us, I fear the old Cadets will be put in the army, O how terrible it is to have the youth of our land killed, corrupted & uneducated."[91]

Before leaving Montgomery to attend a conference of Southern governors in Augusta, Georgia, an embarrassed and mortified Governor Watts made public his final message to the legislature, accusing it of dereliction of duty and predicting that because Alabama was not "properly defended," the legislature's failure to enact his militia bill "may result in the most calamitous consequences to the State."[92] A New York newspaper jeered that the Alabama legislature's refusal to authorize the use of the militia outside the men's home counties was simply a function of "not merely state right rights, but County rights, and we presume town rights and probably ward rights, and then house rights, which would result in the convenient maxim that no man can be called on to fight for any other than his own particular altars and fires—and no more than he chose for those. Behold the beauties of the theory to maintain which the Calhounists rebelled!"[93] Confederates were not amused. The *Richmond Dispatch* reprinted Watts's message of condemnation on its front page in an article titled "A Faithful Governor To A Derelict Legislature."[94]

That did not faze the Reconstructionists. According to a correspondent of the *Mobile News*, the "parting words of the Governor were not very graciously received; some belligerent members grew eloquent in their denunciation of his lecture, and it was proposed to return the obnoxious documents to the Executive inclosed in a black envelope, significant of the wrath of the House." But "upon calling the ayes and noes it was found the House was without a quorum, whereupon it was thought best to adjourn." The correspondent did not stop there. The extra session had ended "without the passage of any law looking to the better protection or defense of the State against the common enemy. The stupid resolutions and speeches of the reconstruction, State negotiating members have been published for the encouragement of the Yankees, and will remain as enduring monuments of their want of patriotism and discretion long after the authors shall have been buried under the overwhelming scorn of an indignant people."[95] A Montgomery correspondent to the *Mobile Advertiser and Register* concurred wholeheartedly: "The Legislature refused to do anything to raise men for the support of the Confederate cause, or for the defence of their own State; but they introduced resolutions which may add, and in all probability will add, many thousands to the army of the enemy. We feel in our inmost soul that ten thousand men in arms against us could not do us a like injury that the introduction of these resolutions will do."[96]

This latter correspondent had a more lenient form of punishment for such acts than other Confederates might have preferred—deportation: "In God's name, let all who want to go back to Yankee rule go; let all who want to renew their affiliation with the destroyers of our property go to them. We say give them a free pass; the country would be greatly benefitted by their absence. Are we never freed of these meddlers and mischief makers? They want the freedom of the South; they want their homes, their slaves, their lives and their liberties protected, and they are constantly throwing obstacles in the way of those who are toiling and fighting to secure these great objects. Truly," he concluded, "they are on the wrong side of the line, and it would be well for the country if they were put on the other."[97]

20
"Rats to Your Holes"

Deportation of Unionists was not sufficient punishment in the eyes of some Confederates. Earlier in the year, a newspaper correspondent had predicted that a day of reckoning with tories and traitors "will come, and the cry will then be 'Rats to your holes.'"[1] Winston County's Unionist probate judge had already been a victim of that fury. But no immediate harm came to Lewis Parsons or the other legislators who had defied Governor Watts, Jefferson Davis, and the Confederacy. This may have been due to fear of a public backlash by citizens yearning for peace. Or it may have been a consequence of General Hood's move toward northwest Georgia on September 28, 1864, which drew General Sherman and possible retribution ever closer to Alabama.[2] According to one disapproving correspondent in Montgomery, Reconstructionists had become confident and almost giddy. John Forsyth in Mobile declared that those who preferred "serving at the altar of mammon to that of country" are "highly elated" and some "are now gloating over the Parsons resolutions."[3]

It infuriated him and other Confederates that, as Reconstructionists had hoped and expected, word of the political turmoil in Alabama and their peace initiatives was now circulating in the press outside the crumbling Confederacy.[4] The pro-McClellan *Chicago Post* cited it as evidence that the "Chicago platform has already raised up a Southern party, worth ten thousand men to the United States armies, and is operating even now as an entering wedge that, with the election of Gen. McClellan will split the Jeff Davis despotism in two. If the people of the North—if all who desire to have this destructive civil war brought to an early and honorable termination—will but remove Abraham Lincoln, it will not be long before the Southern people remove Jeff. Davis too, and peace soon thereafter is inevitable."[5] The Philadelphia *Daily Age* published an editorial titled "Alabama Wants Peace," asserting that the sentiment expressed in the resolutions considered by the Alabama legislature gave "more rational promise of peace than anything that has come from the

South since the beginning of the war." All that was necessary was for Northerners to "choose between the party that offers them honorable peace, on the basis of the old Union, and the party which promises them perpetual and hopeless war for the emancipation of the negro."[6]

But Confederates knew that the plan of Southern Reconstructionists was a gamble. It was predicated not only on McClellan winning the presidential election but also the Northern people being in a compromising—rather than punitive—mood. Confederates could gloat when the early returns from the state elections in Pennsylvania, Ohio, and Indiana seemed to forecast McClellan's defeat.[7] John Forsyth could warn his many readers that "we cannot conciliate the Yankee. They are thirsting for the blood of our freedom. Nothing else," he predicted, "will satisfy them."[8] The *Eutaw Whig and Observer* concurred, charging that the "brotherly love" of the Northern people for the people of the South "is simply the passion of the glutton for the flesh pot. They are a cruel, selfish, cold-blooded, mean and devilish people. We would as soon live in political alliance with the demons of the pit."[9] Anyone still making common cause with them was in grave danger.

Recognizing this and his doubtful political future, Jeremiah Clemens remained in West Philadelphia, Pennsylvania, where he was making the final revisions to the manuscript that would become his next and final novel, *Tobias Wilson: A Tale of the Great Rebellion.*[10] Set in Jackson County in northeast Alabama, it is the story of terrorism by Confederates against Unionists and the cycle of violence this spawned. Among the first Unionists killed was the grandfather of young Tobias Wilson, who was murdered by Confederate guerillas while plowing his field at some point after Union forces temporarily withdrew from north Alabama in 1862.[11] "Two rifle balls had passed through his body," Clemens wrote, "either one of which would have been fatal."[12]

Little did Clemens know that life had very recently imitated his art in Jackson County. This time the Unionist victim was Williamson R. W. Cobb, the colorful, populist leader and longtime political rival of C. C. Clay Jr. Cobb had been elected to the Confederate Congress in 1863 but had never gone to Richmond to take his seat. Instead, he had not only presided over a convention in Jackson County during the spring of 1864 calling for peace and reunion but had been in regular contact with federal authorities in Nashville and Washington since then.[13] A Richmond newspaper claimed that Cobb had also been appointed Alabama's military governor by President Lincoln.[14]

The rumor that Cobb had been appointed Alabama's military governor suggests that Cobb, with the help of the Union army, would soon take power and follow the same pattern utilized by Andrew Johnson in Tennessee to exclude Confederates from state and local government. It is certainly reasonable to assume that Confederates saw Cobb as a serious threat that needed to be neutralized. Whether they planned to murder him or, as in the case of Charles Christopher Sheats, simply arrest and jail him, is unknown. It is undisputed, however, that Cobb was killed at some point in October or early November 1864.[15]

The perpetrators of Cobb's assassination are unknown, but a good bet would be Confederate guerrillas lurking in the region. At about this time, the *Montgomery Daily Advertiser* had singled out for praise a band led by Captain Henry F. Smith of Marshall County for having initiated raids on a large "tory" encampment in Jackson County in late October: "It was the gallant conduct of such men as Captain Smith and Colonel Mead that compelled the Yankees to say that Jackson County had earned her independence."[16] It is also possible that Alabama's most notorious and brutal guerrilla leader, John Pemberton Gatewood, was behind Cobb's bloody death. Gatewood was not one to give quarter to Yankees,[17] and he had a special hatred for Unionists. An admiring reporter wrote during this period that "when he captures tories—who are no better than highway robbers—he metes out summary justice to them." According to the same reporter, Gatewood's "sphere of influence" included Cobb's Jackson County home.[18]

The first report of Cobb's demise, which appeared in the Selma-based *Chattanooga Rebel*, used a thinly veiled metaphor to make clear that Cobb's loyalty to the Union had cost him his life: "Hon. W. R. W. Cobb was killed a few days since in North Alabama, by the accidental discharge of one of his own pistols. He has for some time past been consorting with the Yankees, and was not long since in Nashville. His Yankee friends had presented him a pair of pistols, which he wore on his person. One of them dropped to the ground and went off, the ball penetrating his bowels and coming out his back, causing death."[19] To Unionists, Cobb's death was certainly no accident. "If dead," wrote a newspaper editor in Ohio, "more likely he fell by the pistol of a rebel assassin."[20] Later, the Union army would make at least two retaliatory raids into the area, one that resulted in the burning of almost every building and home in the Marshall County river town of Guntersville,[21] and another that "burnt every house from Paint Rock [in Jackson County] to within four miles of Huntsville."[22]

George Washington Gayle, a lawyer from Cahaba, Alabama, had set his sights quite a bit higher than Cobb. Gayle made a call for blood money by way of a newspaper advertisement placed in the *Selma Dispatch*, and titled "$1,000,000 Wanted To Have Peace by the First of March." The advertisement contained a startling proposal that "if the citizens of the Southern Confederacy will furnish me with the cash, or good security, for the sum of $1,000,000, I will cause the lives of Abraham Lincoln, William H. Seward and Andrew Johnson to be taken." In the advertisement, which was republished throughout the nation by other newspapers, Gayle assured that these assassinations would "satisfy the world that cruel tyrants cannot live in a 'land of liberty,' "—a phrase suspiciously similar to the one that John Wilkes Booth would utter ("sic semper tyrannis") several months later. Gayle also claimed that these assassinations, which would decapitate the federal government, would "give us peace."[23]

Other Unionist leaders in Alabama were being targeted at this time as evidenced by the arrest of Huntsville lawyer David Campbell Humphreys.[24] He was reportedly escorted by two members of General Roddey's staff to Tuscumbia, supposedly to appear before a military court. Ominously, that court was to be presided over by former Confederate secretary of war Leroy Pope Walker.[25] Even more disconcerting for Humphreys was the fact that the judge advocate, or prosecutor, assigned to Walker's court was secessionist J. L. M. Curry, who had taken a bombproof position as "aid pro tempore" on Roddey's staff.[26] Former Confederate congressman Curry certainly had a grudge against the peace movement, and Humphreys was a fitting target for his revenge. If Curry could win a conviction of Humphreys for treason, Humphreys would almost certainly share W. R. W. Cobb's fate.[27]

But while some Confederates seemed bound and determined to make matters worse for the South, others were likely aware that dire personal consequences would follow from such rashness this late in the game. News out of Tennessee indicated that its US district judge would soon be scheduling the trial of men arrested there for treason.[28] Whether Alabama's US district judge would be impaneling grand juries in the near future to indict Alabamians for the same reason would be largely dependent on General Hood's success or failure. If the worst happened, there would be no army to defend Alabama or to protect Confederates who had committed treason, much less war crimes.

As Alice would exclaim in *Alice's Adventures in Wonderland*, the first edition of which was published in 1865, all of a sudden things got "curiouser and curiouser" back in Tuscumbia.[29] Prior to Humphreys's trial in Tuscumbia, General Roddey orchestrated Curry's appointment as commanding officer of one of Roddey's regiments stationed in Corinth, Mississippi.[30] Although this got Curry and some very unfortunate members of Roddey's Brigade to Corinth, where Curry dutifully "drilled the Regiment every day, Sundays excepted,"[31] that still left Leroy Pope Walker to deal with. As it turned out, however, this was not as much of a problem as one might have thought. As early as 1863, Walker had shown that he was keenly interested in how he would be treated during treason trials that all high Confederate leaders, past and present, assumed were looming in the not-too-distant future. According to a postwar letter from Christopher Sheats to Andrew Johnson, Walker had served as one of Sheats's attorneys following Sheats's own arrest for treason, despite criticism within the Huntsville community. According to Sheats, Walker had become a "Peace Advocate."[32]

Walker did not try Humphreys or have him harmed. He instead abruptly adjourned his court and took Humphreys to Montgomery,[33] where Humphreys's arrival was noted with disdain by the *Montgomery Advertiser*: "Our city has recently been *honored* by the arrival of a couple of rather distinguished characters—one of them the notorious R.[obert] S. Tharin and the other, David Humphreys, Esq., of Huntsville." Both "these worthies are now under arrest. What will be done with them we cannot imagine, but fear it will only be a repetition of what has been done in former instances of a similar character,"[34] presumably referring to the success Milton Saffold had had in obtaining the release of civilian political prisoners. The *Advertiser*'s editor obviously had what he considered a more fitting—and probably lethal—outcome for Humphreys and Tharin. But his fear of another potential miscarriage of justice was well-founded. Tharin, the outspoken former Elmore County Unionist who had fled Alabama in 1860, would be released.[35] And according to a report in the *Chicago Journal*, Humphreys was initially "given the freedom of the city parole, and visited the legislature at several of its sittings and learned that the Union sentiment was rapidly on the increase throughout the State."[36]

The legislature had earlier convened in its regular session, but as had occurred at the beginning of the special session earlier in the fall, the house had taken several days to achieve a quorum and this time so had the senate.[37] As one correspondent had joked, the legislative "record was like that of the facetious clerk of the church, 'The Vestry met and nobody came.'"[38] At the capitol, the correspondent continued in a jocular vein, the Confederates turned to God for assistance. Rather than meeting at the capitol, he continued, they had emphasized that "our *whole people* must go up to the solemn temples—or set places—to humble themselves before the Lord our Maker." Furthermore, they said, "He alone must and will decide our fate,"[39] and "if He be with us, and our side, we shall surely triumph. He it is who confounds the counsels of the wicked; who dislocates with a touch their best laid schemes; who holds them back by the pressure of an invisible hand; who makes their chariot wheels to drag heavily; who cuts them down, and lays them low, even in the hour of proud boast; and whose behest is irreversible LAW to angels and to men."[40]

The legislature finally organized, and Governor Watts tendered a message virtually identical to that he had submitted to the special session. He called for an overhaul of the militia system and voiced strong opposition to reconstruction as well as the arming of the slaves to fight for the Confederacy. This time, however, the solons agreed to order the printing of three thousand copies.[41] This was not a signal of an increased degree of cooperation and consensus.[42] Instead, as one observer put it, it was "pretty much, if not entirely—'the same old coon.'"[43] When a south Alabama House member introduced resolutions declaring "unalterable" opposition to reconstruction and favoring independence, "every sort of dodge was resorted to in order to prevent a direct vote on them. The parties most hostile to their passage were vociferous in declaring their opposition to reconstruction! Not a man among them but was perfectly *obstreperous* in his denunciation of such an unpatriotic idea. But they wanted the committee on federal relations to report upon them, and many who were favorable to the resolutions were led to favor the reference, in order to test more fully the fidelity of these parties."[44] This plan of outing the Reconstructionists may have related to a rumored movement by them to undermine Governor Watts's bid for reelection in the 1865 governor's race.[45] Every effort would be made to block Watts's policy initiatives and link him to those of the increasingly despised Jefferson Davis.[46]

There was a noticeable increase in cooperation between the two factions after Humphreys's arrival in Montgomery, culminating in the adoption by a unanimous vote of a carefully worded, watered-down anti-reconstruction resolution declaring Alabama's "unalterable determination" to choose "extermination" over "reconstruction *on the basis heretofore indicated by the Lincoln Government*."[47] This occurred on the same day Governor Watts proclaimed Humphreys's unconditional release, indicating that the adoption of the resolution may have been part of a quid pro quo.[48] Obtaining Humphreys's release may have cost Reconstructionists more than simply the concession of this weak resolution. Indeed, it is noteworthy that no legislator proposed any resolution during this legislative session calling for peace negotiations or for reunion. Unless Governor Watts should call for another special session—a very unlikely event—the legislature would not convene again until November 1865, probably too late for such measures. As evidenced by an editorial in the *Montgomery Daily Advertiser* titled "Backbone and Bottom," legislative silence on these issues was extremely important to Confederates at this juncture.[49] Given this, Confederates may have been even more willing to deal, and it is certainly within the realm of possibility that silence on the issue of peace in the legislature was another term of Humphreys's release.[50]

Reconstructionists actually got more than just Humphreys in the bargain.

A law was adopted imposing stiff fines and jail time for any Confederate conscription officer attempting to force the enrollment of men in the Confederate military who were entitled to exemption.[51] Another law was adopted exempting from service those serving in certain state and local offices and positions.[52] Governor Watts did not veto either of these measures. Furthermore, the house and the senate were still unable to agree on any militia bill before the legislature adjourned.[53] Once again, Watts's legislative program had failed.

And Humphreys was now on his way back home. As a precautionary measure, two prominent Huntsville secessionists had been taken to Nashville as hostages for Humphreys's safety, one of whom was C. C. Clay Jr.'s father, former Alabama governor Clement Comer Clay.[54] They were quickly released, however, when Humphreys returned to Huntsville, with Leroy Pope Walker not far behind displaying a flag of truce.[55] Upon their arrival, they learned that the end for Alabama was near, at least as far as conventional warfare was concerned.

21
"Balls and Parties Are All the Rage"

After some initial success, Jefferson Davis's strategy was not faring very well. Nathan Bedford Forrest had been forced to cut short his raid through middle Tennessee, and his cavalry corps succeeded in avoiding annihilation by a much larger Union cavalry force under General Rousseau only by barely making an escape across the Tennessee River near Florence, Alabama.[1] Although Forrest had not fulfilled expectations that he would single-handedly force Sherman to withdraw from Georgia, his camp released a statement touting the successes of his operation and quoting Forrest's judgment that it was "one of the most successful raids he has ever made."[2] General Hood, meanwhile, had been forced by Sherman's approach to suspend his efforts to destroy the Western and Atlantic Railroad between Atlanta and Chattanooga. But rather than attacking Sherman, the now seemingly gun-shy Hood had meekly receded into east Alabama in the area around Blue Pond and Gaylesville in Cherokee County near the Alabama-Georgia line. He then moved even further west to Gadsden, Alabama, where he arrived on October 20. By then, Joe Wheeler's cavalry had temporarily rejoined Hood and was covering Hood's rear.[3]

Hood's retreat into Alabama was and is very suspicious (see figure 18). He had ordered a press blackout, but information still leaked from his ranks. The editor of the *Charleston Mercury* noted that the "intelligence from the Army of Tennessee, so far, is anything but clear and satisfactory" and for the most part was all "fog and mystery." But what information had been received was "of a rather unwelcome character."[4] President Davis had envisioned that once Sherman was lured north of Atlanta, Hood would attack and defeat him.[5] The conventional wisdom was that if Sherman were defeated somewhere south of the Tennessee River, there would be "little difficulty in crossing the river, and little danger in marching on Nashville and Chattanooga."[6] But, as Hood later explained in his tellingly titled memoir, *Advance and Retreat*, he had polled members of his command and concluded that his army "was not

Figure 18. General John Bell Hood (Courtesy of Alabama Department of Archives and History)

in condition to risk battle against the numbers reported by Wheeler."[7] As will be seen, there is reason to doubt Hood's excuse. Whether Sherman was aware of the previously overly aggressive Texan's caution at this point is unclear, but it is curious that when Sherman reached Gaylesville in Cherokee County, Alabama, he stopped chasing Hood.[8] According to an article in an Alabama newspaper, rumors in the New York press suggested that there was an "understanding" with Sherman that "if he will march through Georgia and take possession of Charleston and Savannah," Alabama, Georgia, and North Carolina would secede from the Confederacy.[9] At least consistent with this seemingly far-fetched suspicion, Sherman chose not to pursue Hood any further and instead made plans for his famous march in the opposite direction to the Atlantic Ocean.[10]

Sherman's men, meanwhile, took full advantage of the farm animals and produce of the farms in the Cherokee County area.[11] A soldier serving under Sherman, Lt. Col. Griffin, wrote to his wife back in Indiana, "Men and animals are living better than they have for a year, much to the disgust of the inhabitants."[12] One person who was anxious for both armies to leave was Sarah Espy, who had been virtually cleaned out of food by hungry, foraging soldiers from both sides. When Hood's army came through, she wrote that "we are overrun with soldiers." She was assigned a "guard of nine men tonight, but the soldiers plundered me notwithstanding." Then Sherman's men came and "stampeded through my fine cornfield" and "the soldiers took what they pleased." To her chagrin, they "killed the remainder of my hogs, even my brood sows which were not fit to eat, and sheep. There is not a living thing on the place except a few chickens. God help us, for we have almost nothing."[13]

Another exasperated Cherokee County woman, South Carolina–born Zillah Haynie Brandon, wrote that while Sherman's men were destroying military targets in the area, including her husband's mill, Sherman declared to her daughter that "God had authorized him to do what he did." Brandon, however, was sure that Sherman's inspiration came from the opposite direction. Referring to the seventh chapter of Revelation, she asserted that Sherman "received his authority from the 'Beast' [the Devil] to whom he is giving his power and strength for 'one hour.'" She placed General Grant in that same category, and added that "it is evident to my mind that Lincoln is one of the heads of the Beast and the above named two of the horns."[14]

Residents of Cherokee County should not have been subjected to these depredations because Hood was not supposed to have retreated into Alabama. If he had not done that, Sherman would not have followed him there. One man who was very suspicious and not a little mistrustful of Hood was General P. G. T. Beauregard, who had earlier been made Hood's departmental commander by Jefferson Davis. Hood appears to have done his best to keep Beauregard in the dark about his plans and even his location. When Beauregard finally found Hood at Gadsden on October 21, Hood claimed that he was planning to move north, cross the Tennessee River at Guntersville, and then proceed into middle Tennessee. As would soon become apparent, however, Hood had not laid the basic, essential, logistical groundwork for such a move, especially in terms of the acquisition of adequate supplies.[15]

For example, despite winter conditions approaching, a significant portion of Hood's soldiers did not have shoes.[16] This is confirmed by Edward Norphlet Brown, who was serving as quartermaster of his brigade. "Shoes and clothing ought by all means to be issued before we march any further," he wrote to his wife from Gadsden. "Many of the men have marched from Dalton here barefoot while some have made sandals of green cowhides. These sandals do tolerably well for a short time but they soon get too hard and become unpleasant to the feet."[17] The government shoe factory at Montgomery turned out 250 pairs of shoes per day,[18] and the press appears to have blamed the failure of supply on the quartermasters in the rear. A correspondent to the *Montgomery Advertiser* complained that Hood's army would have to "wait until some rear quartermaster learns to be a little more industrious and forwards" the shoes before attempting to traverse the "very rocky and rough" roads in north Alabama.[19]

But Hood was the more likely culprit. As historian Frank Vandiver noted, there had been rail access by the recently repaired Montgomery and West Point Railroad to Hood's camp at Palmetto, Georgia, before he moved to north Georgia. He had also had such access by way of the Alabama and Tennessee Rivers Railroad from Selma to Blue Mountain in Alabama, where a full supply depot had been established.[20] But Hood did not stop at Blue Mountain to await resupply. Newspaper reports indicate that while at Gadsden, some shoeless soldiers "were sent to Blue Mountain to get new ones, which had not come up," but then Hood prematurely pushed on into north Alabama toward Gunter's Landing.[21] As a consequence, Hood would have to await supplies from a depot much further away at his ultimate place of encampment.[22] This, in turn, would give Hood a legitimate excuse for not immediately pressing on into Tennessee. The loss of valuable time would play an important role in what would eventually happen to his army.

One plausible hypothesis for explaining Hood's foot-dragging is that at the behest of a segment of his men, he was simply trying to buy more time until the result of the presidential election in the North scheduled to take place on November 8 was known. The Nashville correspondent of the *Chicago Journal* wrote that the "prevailing opinion is, that Hood now sees the utter absurdity of the undertaking which was commenced with such a flourish of trumpets, and feels that Sherman's communications are safe beyond a peradventure; and therefore, all he can do is to make pretenses, until after the Presidential election, when he will return to the heart of the cotton state, to winter."[23]

Joel Murphree wrote to his wife, Ursula, in Troy, Alabama, that it was "universally desired in the army that [McClellan] may be elected."[24] After the fall of Atlanta, another of Hood's men, a lawyer-planter, had explained in a letter to his wife back in Mississippi that "our main hope now is the disagreement existing among the political parties North. If the Democrats are successful," he predicted, "I look for a speedy termination of hostilities and eventually a permanent peace. If McClellan is elected," he continued, "our negroes will not be disturbed I think at all." Moreover, the "negro soldiers will be disbanded and returned to their owners, and the whole subject will be settled by arbitration and not by the sword." But in his mind, the peace would not be permanent. The Yankees will be gone, he predicted, and the "Southwest will set up a new Confederation in a year or so I have no doubt." Thus, he concluded, "I am encouraged by the signs of the time to be hopeful of the future."[25]

But to reach that future, Hood's men would, of course, have to survive, and attacking in Tennessee was unlikely to result in a high survival rate.[26] Instead, he and his men needed to stall for time. Consistent with this hypothesis, Hood and his army of thirty thousand men left Gadsden on October 22 (without Joe Wheeler's cavalry, which remained to harass Sherman), but after arriving at the Tennessee River at Guntersville he inexplicably decided not to cross there despite having previously told Beauregard he would.

Hood then moved further west and, on October 26, 27, and 28, made a half-hearted effort to capture Decatur, which was defended by only three thousand men, including three companies of the Fourteenth US Colored Infantry Regiment. Although both the *Selma Dispatch* and the *Montgomery Mail* reported that Hood took Decatur, the truth was that Hood prematurely terminated his attack there and moved his much larger army west through Lawrence County and into Franklin County, where he reached Tuscumbia on October 30. A portion of his army crossed the Tennessee River into Florence that day, but then Hood stopped. He would remain there for three weeks, long enough for news to arrive on whether McClellan had prevailed.[27] A correspondent to the Selma-based *Chattanooga Rebel* (which, like the *Mississippian*, had had to move its base of operations to Alabama to avoid Union interference) would later note that these would be "three fatal weeks" from an operational standpoint.[28]

Suspiciously, while Hood stood still, another of his men, South Carolina native, Mobile lawyer, and future Alabama Republican Ben Lane Posey, was in Montgomery attempting to lobby for peace. A captain in the Army of Tennessee, Posey had previously written Jefferson Davis to inform him that "this army is in a very bad condition, a condition that promises no success in the future, but a series of disasters that will complete its ruin, and with its ruin, our subjugation is nearly certain." Posey declared that "events may happen any day which will dissolve it, like melted snow."[29] He made a brutally frank speech at the Montgomery County courthouse in which he advocated support for the national peace convention proposed in the National Democratic Party's platform. "The Chicago Convention which represents the peace men of the North," he said, "offers us a means of peace. They request us to meet them in a convention of States, where the question of peace may be discussed between us." To Posey, the time to accept this proposal was now, not later, because continued warfare would only further undermine the South's bargaining position and result in defeat.[30] In conjunction with Posey's efforts, the *Montgomery Mail* editorialized in favor of peace talks, urging the Confederate Congress to "appoint three or five commissioners of national reputation to go to Washington and lay the matter before the United States Government."[31] The *Selma Reporter* went even further, suggesting that if the Confederate Congress failed to act, "the States can, and it should be done promptly and without hesitance."[32]

Whether General Hood had authorized Posey's effort is unknown. No evidence has been found connecting the two in this, or even that anyone publicly accused Hood of stalling for time in the interest of peace. On the contrary, and somewhat humorously, the press in Alabama dutifully portrayed

Hood's erratic and mysterious moves through Alabama as part of some masterful plan that would ultimately bring Sherman to his knees and win the war. The Selma *Mississippian* guessed that this plan was "inspired probably by the genius of the President and Gen. Beauregard" and assured that it was the "boldest and most brilliant move yet made upon the chessboard of war," in the same category as George Washington's crossing of the Delaware River and his defeat of the British at Trenton and Princeton.[33] Responding to claims in the Northern press that Hood was simply running from Sherman, John Forsyth wrote that the "beauty of [the plan]" is that if Hood pursued his course "to the city of Louisville, Kentucky, on the Ohio River, he is all the time and at every foot of his march on Sherman's line of supplies, and able to destroy it as he progresses. Sherman must follow him, or there will be dust kicked up in Kentucky, even across the river, in the 'loyal States,' which will be very unpleasant to Sherman's master, but exceedingly comforting to the civil and military peace men of the Golden Circle."[34] Another Alabama correspondent with the presidential election on his mind dreamed that it "would be a grand thing [for Hood] to enter Nashville before the Northern election takes place, and send the traitor [Andrew] Johnson howling for protection among his abolition confreres!"[35] An apparently less informed Alabama correspondent merely waited "with interest for the next moves on the gigantic chess board. We trust our noble players will soon be able to say to their opponents: 'Check'—when there shall be no further space for a move."[36]

General Beauregard shared those hopes, but at this point he was still in the dark regarding what game Hood was playing, much less Hood's next move.[37] So were Hood's men. Two days after arriving at Tuscumbia, a bewildered Joel Murphree wrote to his wife that "I cannot tell you what move we will make from here" because "we never know when we are going until we get there." A week later, he wrote without a hint of complaint that "we expected to have been in Tennessee before now [but] have remained here I suppose for the purpose of clothing the soldiers, before our departure." Noting that the weather was "very bad indeed," however, he indicated that he "would not be surprised if the trip is totally abandoned and that we go into winter quarters near here soon." This was clearly his fervent hope,[38] and he was not alone. A homesick Edward Norphlet Brown wrote to his wife, Fannie, that the "weather here is beginning to feel very much like winter. It is cloudy, damp & cold. I hope it will not be long before we can go into winter quarters & then I may get the chance to see you & the babies."[39] James Lanning, a soldier from Sylacauga, Alabama, who had been among those who had already crossed the river on a pontoon bridge from Tuscumbia to Florence, noted that "for some reason we did not all cross." At first he assumed that "we will move forward in a day or two." But shortly after the presidential election, he reported it was "rumored that we will fall back to Blue Mountain." That suited him just fine. Just before news of Lincoln's reelection came, he surmised that "we will not advance much farther north this winter but will soon move South of the [Tennessee] River & go into quarters for the winter & hope ere the Winter closes Peace may be made and all honorably discharged from the Service to go home to Stay with our dear ones at home." Furthermore, he concluded, "I do hope the last gun has been fired that will be fired this war [and] that we may all soon learn to have War no more, that Christ may reign Supremely and all will be peace [and] happiness."[40]

Others also had peacetime pursuits on their minds. According to the embarrassing account by an on-the-scene reporter with the pen name of "J.T.G." (whose report somehow made it past Hood's press blackout), Hood and his men were busy making headway on the social scene in Florence. "Balls and parties are all the rage at this time. The splendid rooms of the Male College are crowded every night with men and officers to indulge in a quadrille with the patriotic young ladies of Florence. Last night the Amateur Club of Fenner's battery of New Orleans, gave one of their popular entertainments. The hall was crowded to excess. During the performance Gen. Hood entered the hall and was enthusiastically cheered by the vast audience."[41] The reporter did not fabricate this to spur Hood to action. Sally Independence Foster wrote of her delight that Hood's army "remained with us over three weeks, and there were balls, parties, concerts or theatres up at the male college nearly every night."[42]

The hospitality accorded Hood and his men may not have always been bestowed with purely patriotic motives. A member of Hood's army was puzzled that "Florence has suffered but little from the Yankees," compared to "nearly every [other] county town they have occupied [which] has been burnt." Then he answered his own question: "I cannot say that the citizens are Unionists, but I am informed that many of them swallowed Lincoln's oath, without any grimaces." He also noticed that Yankee but not Confederate money was accepted as legal tender: "Confederate notes would be utterly worthless to us if we had them. We cannot buy a fowl, a pound of beef or flour, in fact nothing, with Confederate currency. I saw this morning a quarter of beef sell for 15 cents payable in Greenbacks. The same man refused $3 per pound in Confederate currency."[43]

Indications of anti-Confederate sentiment can also be seen in the reaction of men in this region to recruiters for Hood's army. That his conscripting officers were ultimately forced to engage in illegal "indiscriminate conscription," meaning in disregard of exemptions authorized by Confederate and state law, is quite revealing.[44] Even then, however, men went to great lengths to avoid serving the dying Cause. The best-known example of this involved future Republican governor David Peter Lewis, who had purchased a mill at Tuscumbia in order to remain exempt from conscription following the resignation of his circuit judgeship and who fled to the Union army base at Decatur and then Nashville when conscripting officers attempted to force him to join Hood's army anyway.[45]

Even for those who were glad to see the return of Confederate forces, the continued presence of so many hungry mouths to feed for an extended period of time was a severe hardship. The portion of Hood's army south of the Tennessee River was forced to subsist on the country,[46] but according to a correspondent on the scene, the "whole Tennessee Valley from Decatur to Tuscumbia is devastated and a scene of desolation. The rich plantations stretched for miles, covered with grass like a vast plain, with here and there the brick chimneys of former elegant mansions destroyed by fire. Everything bears the aspect of grim-visaged war."[47]

Like area Unionists, everyone seemed to be wondering when Hood would finally move on. "Thus far," wrote the editor of the Montgomery-based *Memphis Appeal*, "General Hood has succeeded in mystifying both friend and foe, and as he can very easily direct the conduct of his military superintendent of telegraph, so as to prevent the transmission of intelligence, we may expect to remain befogged until such time as he desires the public to become posted."[48] Even Hood's men were in the dark. "Why we tarry here so long," wrote one from Florence, "I have not the remotest idea."[49] Another wrote that "we are kept so much in the dark in regard to army movements that we know nothing of them until it is too late to be called news. I hardly know what to think of the prospect of going to Middle Tennessee. Sometimes it looks quite flattering, and then again becomes gloomy."[50]

Perhaps to counter negative public reaction to the report indicating that Hood and his men were delaying unnecessarily, a letter was issued—supposedly from his camp—providing a different explanation. The letter's author claimed that the time had been spent in "busy preparation" in an effort to overcome the "obstacles in our way, and in making those preparations suggested by a prudent foresight, which would enable us to reap the fruits of victory and palliate the misfortunes of defeat." He also suggested the following eight causes of delay: "1st, heavy and unusual rain; 2d, a wide and swift river to be bridged; 3d, a railroad to be rebuilt and repaired; 4th, supplies of shoes, clothing, ordnance and provisions to be accumulated; 5th, fortifications to be made to defend our new storehouse of supplies, and the crossing of the river, against raiding parties on either side of the river, and against gunboats in the event of its rise; 6th, insufficiency of rolling stock, and a want of concert between the different railroad companies; 7th, a wide and barren country, which separates us from the well stored granaries of Tennessee; 8th, a vigilant and powerful enemy in our front watching our movements, and ready to take advantage of any false steps." The author explained that he gave these "suggestions for the benefit of those military critics who are so prone to find fault, and so easily disgusted at delay." But he made no effort to defend the items on his list.[51] For example, he did not explain why Hood had not remained near Blue Mountain until the already fully functioning Alabama and Tennessee Rivers Railroad from Selma had supplied all of his needs, such that he could have pushed north as soon as his forces had crossed the river and reached Florence on October 30, thereby obviating the need to remain in Tuscumbia and build fortifications. This would have also opened up those "granaries" in Tennessee to Hood, and done so before the weather turned bad. Finally, although Union soldiers, including Kentuckian General John Thomas Croxton (who had been a lawyer before the war)[52] were certainly keeping an eye on Hood, their force was dwarfed by Hood's and would pull back as soon as Hood began moving north toward Nashville.[53]

In light of all of this, it is certainly possible that the true reason for the manner in which General Hood had conducted this campaign since leaving the Atlanta area was, as a correspondent from Nashville to the *New York Herald* guessed, that he was "awaiting events to develop themselves."[54] Voters in the North as well as Tennessee went to the polls on November 8 to decide whether to stay the course with Lincoln or give McClellan a chance to achieve a different type of peace. Among those voters were the Union soldiers watching Hood's army, who voted in the field and, according to a letter, while "under fire." As the author wrote, "when a regiment has voted it gives a rousing cheer for Abraham Lincoln and goes to its work again with hope and assurance that he will be President of each and all the States of the Union before his present term expires."[55] Hood and others in the South would soon learn that Abraham Lincoln had not only won reelection, he had won big, especially in the electoral college. McClellan lost every state except New Jersey, Delaware, and Kentucky. Lincoln also won 55 percent of the popular vote.[56] Even the midwestern states, where Confederates had predicted a post-election uprising by Peace Democrats,[57] went for Lincoln.[58]

Troops from Alabama and elsewhere were devastated by the news. "It seems that Old Abe is re-elected and there is some probability of another four years of war—isn't it horrible to think of?," wrote George Miller of Talladega to his wife. "The future," he added, "presents a gloomy picture for the homes and fire-sides of the South."[59] Wrote Grant Taylor to his wife back in Tuscaloosa County, "I suppose Old Abe Lincoln is elected again. You need not build any hopes of peace soon for there will be none." On the contrary, "we may look for nothing short of freedom, death, or subjugation." Unfortunately, he noted, "I think this poor little confederacy is about played out."[60] At Florence, one of Hood's men, James Lanning, asked, "when will this cruel war terminate & when will Peace be restored to our now bleeding and distressed country; May God in his mercy take away his Scourging Rod from our land and pour out his blessings upon us abundantly."[61]

While proslavery Reconstructionists in and outside Hood's army were crestfallen, Confederates were delighted, at least publicly. "The advocates of McClellan's reconstruction policy have received a stern and cutting rebuke for their faint heartedness, from the North itself," wrote one Southern newspaper editor. "We are told in unmistakable language that reconstruction is no longer a debatable proposition. The North demands an unconditional surrender on our part of all our rights and privileges as a free and enlightened people." "Our future policy," he continued, "is a plain and positive one. We must gather up every resource of men and means for a continuance of this struggle. We can obtain peace only by conquering it." Therefore, he concluded, "let every man who is able to grasp his rifle go forth thrice armed in spirit to conquer or to die."[62]

And with a justified sense of foreboding, many of Hood's men would thereby usher in one of the darkest phases of the war. In a letter to his wife, Edward Norphlet Brown wrote that he "had not believed all the while that the army would go into Tennessee, and even now it seems almost absurd to me, but I am now forced to believe that the move will be undertaken. How many of us will ever recross the [Tennessee] River no one can tell, but I clearly foresee hard times & disaster to the army. I have," he concluded, "never in my life felt so much opposed to a move." Brown instead wanted peace. He added that "I am certain that it would be no difficult matter to accommodate terms of peace to me this morning. I would accept almost any kind of terms of peace now save those which are dishonorable." Brown signed his letter "from your wayward, sad & dissatisfied . . . Ed."[63]

22
Franklin, Nashville, and Disintegration

Before commencing the march north from Tuscumbia and Florence, General Hood had assured his soldiers that he would—like his predecessor, Joe Johnston—only "fight with equal numbers and choice of ground." But Hood did not or could not fulfill that promise.[1] J. P. Cannon, a Confederate soldier from Lauderdale County, Alabama, wrote about watching as other Confederate brigades marched on Union-occupied Franklin, Tennessee: "Level fields stretched out in front of the enemy and it was a fearful ordeal to charge a fortified position under such disadvantages. When we emerged from the timber we saw our men within 300 yards of the works advancing through the open fields under the most destructive fire we ever witnessed." Then Cannon's own unit came under fire: "We pressed forward and when near enough the infantry opened on us with terrible volleys and it seemed as if not one of us could escape the storm of shells, canister and bullets which were poured into us." Before long, "our single line had become so thinned and nearly every officer killed or disabled. With none to command or lead, it would have simply resulted in a massacre for us to proceed further."[2]

But a terrible massacre of humanity had already occurred. "The next morning," he continued, "a sad scene met our eyes when it was light enough to see. Our dead were literally piled on top of each other at the embankment that alone separated them from the dead federals in the ditch on the opposite side. Dead and wounded were scattered for hundreds of yards in front of the works. The percentage of loss," he sadly concluded, "was equal to, or perhaps greater than, any battle of the war considering the number engaged and the duration of the battle."[3] With a sense of betrayal, another of Hood's men wrote that it "can't be called anything else but cold blooded Murder" on Hood's part.[4]

Back in Alabama, the *Jacksonville Republican*'s first report on the Battle of Franklin (which had taken place on November 30) characterized it as a great rout of the Yankees.[5] Throughout the South, the people were told that the "backbone of the enemy has been broken by a signal defeat; and our army will not give his demoralized forces time to recover. It will press on without intermission, and we doubt whether it will halt short of the Ohio River."[6] Northern propagandists disagreed on the outcome of the battle. On December 1, the *Nashville Daily Union* published a report by Union General John Schofield from Franklin that Hood's army "was repulsed at all points with very heavy loss, probably 5,000, or 6,000."[7] A few days later, the *Selma Dispatch* reported that Hood's dead at Franklin were "piled three deep, and in some places four and five lying across each other. Many of them were shot to pieces, having from 20 to 30 bullet holes through them."[8] Shockingly, among the dead were five Confederate generals, including the popular Irish native Patrick Cleburne.[9]

Due to his losses at Franklin, Hood, who had started out with roughly thirty thousand infantrymen, including a brigade commanded by Edmund Winston Pettus,[10] was down to less than twenty-five thousand as he approached Nashville, which was by now heavily defended thanks to Hood's prolonged delay back at Florence.[11] Some suspected that Hood actually intended to bypass Nashville and march to and take Knoxville so he would be in position to aid General Lee in Virginia.[12] But for weeks the Nashville press had cleverly baited Hood to attack the Tennessee capital, thereby decreasing the chance that Hood would skirt the city in the interest of keeping the only remaining significant Confederate army in the western theater intact.[13] Two days before the Battle of Nashville, however, the *Nashville Daily Union*'s editor prematurely let the cat out of the bag by reprinting an article from the *Cincinnati Enquirer* predicting Hood's fate if he remained at Nashville: "Hood has got his army into a very hopeful situation—that is to say, there is reason to hope that he will be enabled to proceed rapidly with his work of making an end of the rebel military organization in the Southwest." Hood's army, the article continued, "has managed to march as far north as Nashville, only to find itself confronted by a superior force, and to be caught in a spell of the severest wintry weather, without any of the comforts of winter quarters. They were not well supplied when on their railroads, and now, depending upon foraging and wagon trains from Florence, over roads with all the bridges burned, they are in a good condition to enjoy the storms of winter."[14] In other words, Hood's men were right where Union General George Henry Thomas wanted them and would themselves be attacked as soon as the weather improved.

Nathan Bedford Forrest and his cavalry corps had already pulled out and were headed east on a raid toward Murfreesboro. Edward Norphlet Brown, who expressed opposition to an attack by Hood on the Union army's entrenched positions—he wrote that it "would seem the quintescence [*sic*] of folly"—was nonetheless certain that the Confederates could withstand an attack. The men "seem cheerful & as defiant as ever, & if the Vandal horde of Lincoln does not believe it let them come out from their forts & ditches in Nashville & try the poor 'rebs.'"[15] Five days later, Thomas's army obliged, pouncing before Hood could withdraw. As the *Nashville Daily Union* reported with glee, by December 16, the "defeat of the rebels was crushing; indeed, defeat was no name for it—it was a perfect *rout.* Bull Run was eclipsed—eclipsed because old veterans, and not raw recruits, were the subjects of the panic."[16] The *Daily Union*'s editor also had a name for area "rebel sympathizers" who had expected Hood to enter Nashville: "Hood-winked."[17]

This description of the outcome was no exaggeration. As Alabama soldier Joel Murphree wrote to his wife, "this was indeed a stampede."[18] Edward Norphlet Brown called it the largest rout "in modern times."[19] Hood was now in the same position Jefferson Davis had boldly predicted in September for Sherman—the fate "that befell the army of the French Empire in its retreat from Moscow." He was being chased by the Cossacks of the Union army, which included a large cavalry corps commanded by a young Illinois native, General James H. Wilson, whose name would later become anathema to Confederate Alabamians for decades.[20] As Hood and the remnants of his army attempted to race back through mud, freezing rain, and snow to Alabama and cross the icy cold Tennessee River, many of his demoralized men simply deserted and went home. The *Nashville Daily Union* joked that a "large number of Tennesseans have already left the army, declaring that they have only taken Hood at his word; he told them they were to stay in Tennessee, and they are going to do it."[21] Nathan Bedford Forrest, who was attempting to cover Hood's rear during this panicked, embarrassing retreat, would later confirm the mass desertions.[22]

Alabamians deserted too, although one from Lauderdale County, J. P. Cannon, claimed that the "little remnant" of his regiment "was *furloughed* and started home in advance of the command." This was, at best, a creative adaption of the truth. That "furlough" turned out to be permanent, but who could blame them? "Those of us who were on furlough were contentedly enjoying the Christmas days with homefolk. This was the first Christmas we had spent at home for three years." Then, Cannon asserted, the presence of Union forces in northwest Alabama precluded him from crossing the river and moving south although he claimed "we kept a constant vigil."[23] Hood's losses from all causes were substantial and estimated to be a staggering fifteen to twenty thousand men.[24] The Southern press, of course, initially denied this. The *Selma Dispatch* claimed that the Army of Tennessee was "as strong in numbers now as when it crossed the Tennessee."[25] The *Montgomery Adver-*

tiser conceded some losses, but it assured that "a sufficient number of recruits had been received to make up the losses in battle."[26]

The key for Hood, and for Alabama's Confederates, was to get as many of his remaining men and as much war material as possible back across the bloated Tennessee River in Alabama. But that would not be easy.[27] Edward Norphlet Brown wrote to his wife that "the men are worn down." "Thousands of wounded & bare–foot," he continued, "are struggling & struggling on to get across the River. I have seen many bare-foot marching while the blood was oozing from their frost-bitten feet." Brown concluded that "we are in an awful fix & I consider the army ruined."[28]

In addition to the totally demoralized mental state of many of the men, the terrible weather and road conditions, the lack of food, and the pursuing Yankees, Hood's army no longer had a sufficient number of pontoons to construct a bridge reaching across the river.[29] But for once, Hood and his remaining men finally caught a lucky break. After some of General Roddey's men had reoccupied Decatur following its evacuation by Union forces in November, they discovered a number of the enemy's abandoned pontoons there that were part of a temporary bridge spanning the Tennessee River. Hood's engineers were able to float a sufficient number of them about forty miles to Bainbridge Ferry, a river crossing just east of Florence above Little Muscle Shoals and at the foot of Big Muscle Shoals. They miraculously arrived there on Christmas Day. Protected from Union gunboats by the shoals and a dense fog, Hood's engineers hurriedly completed construction of the bridge the following day, and the remnant of his army successfully crossed, thereby escaping certain annihilation by General Wilson's cavalry and the approaching Union army by only about twelve hours.[30] General Thomas's superiors wanted him to immediately launch an attack south from Decatur, but there were no longer sufficient pontoons there to cross the river. Hood's men had wisely taken the pontoons at Bainbridge with them so they could not be used by the Yankees.[31]

The consensus among many Alabamians was that Hood's crushing defeat likely sounded the death knell of the Confederacy. Margaret Gillis blamed it on Jefferson Davis: "Pres. Davis against the views of almost every other man in the Confederacy relieved Joseph E. Johnston from the command of the Ten. Army, and put Hood in his place; and all has gone wrong ever since till now the whole country nearly seems demoralized."[32] Edward Norphlet Brown wrote that Hood's army was "entirely demoralized" and "I think now that the cause of the South is sadly on the wane & I fear we shall be subjugated."[33] His fear was certainly well-founded. Talladega County planter

James Mallory wrote that "we are in an awful condition as a people, two or three hundred thousand of our best men killed or disabled, millions of property destroyed, millions more to go, our slaves rendered useless and a future pest, with a grinding debt on this generation, the people demoralized and wicked beyond any thing, all to gratify a few wild politicians." Even worse, he concluded, "the end is not yet, our only help is God, may he deliver us."[34]

According to a letter to General Grant from a Huntsville Unionist, the "people here, in my opinion, under wise management, are ready for the work of reconstruction. In this opinion our best Union men concur. Hood's disasters," he concluded, "have operated like a charm."[35] Now it would be up to Alabama Unionists to somehow convince Alabama officials to stop the madness before more lives were lost, and the remaining economic gains the state had achieved during the antebellum period were gone. But with a renewed propaganda campaign from the pro-Confederacy press, they had their work cut out for them and not much time to somehow overcome it.[36]

VIII
"THE HOLOCAUST"

Timeline: January 1865–May 1865

January 3, 1865	Hood's army arrives at Corinth, Mississippi.
January 5, 1865	Union troops reach Walker County, Alabama.
January 8, 1865	Landon Garland gives prowar speech in Tuscaloosa.
January 10, 1865	Unionist guerrillas attack Jasper, Alabama, and burn the county courthouse.
January 13, 1865	Preston and Montgomery Blair meet with President Davis to encourage peace talks.
January 14, 1865	*Richmond Sentinel* accuses members of the Confederate House of Representatives of treason.
January 16, 1865	William Russell Smith withdraws from the Confederate House
January 21, 1865	General Sherman orders General Thomas to prepare for an invasion of central and south Alabama.
January 31, 1865	US House approves the Thirteenth Amendment, submitting it to the states for ratification.
February 3, 1865	Hampton Roads Peace Conference fails.
February 11, 1865	Unionist guerrillas burn the St. Clair county courthouse.
February 13, 1865	War meetings of Confederates in Selma, Talladega, and Mobile.
February 14, 1865	Unionist guerrillas raid into Barbour County.
February 20, 1865	Confederate House adopts slave soldier bill.
February 23, 1865	War meeting in Montgomery.
March 1, 1865	Society of Loyal Confederates meets in Mobile.
March 4, 1865	President Lincoln gives second Inaugural Address.
March 11, 1865	War meeting in Tuscaloosa.
March 21, 1865	General Wilson's force begins the invasion of Alabama from Lauderdale County.
March 24, 1865	General Wilson's force reaches Russellville, Alabama.
March 25, 1865	James Holt Clanton is wounded while trying to stop an invasion force from Pensacola, Florida.
March 28, 1865	General Wilson's force reaches Jasper, Alabama.
March 30, 1865	General Wilson's forces reach Elyton, Jefferson County, Alabama.
April 1, 1865	Richmond, Virginia, falls to General Grant.
April 2, 1865	Selma falls to General Wilson's force.

April 3, 1865	Tuscaloosa falls to General John Tyler Croxton's brigade.
April 4, 1865	President Lincoln visits Richmond.
April 9, 1865	General Lee surrenders his army to General Grant at Appomattox, Virginia.
April 12, 1865	Montgomery and Mobile are surrendered to Union forces.
April 14, 1865	President Lincoln is shot by assassin John Wilkes Booth.
April 15, 1865	Lincoln dies.
April 15, 1865	Andrew Johnson is sworn in as president.
April 26, 1865	John Wilkes Booth is killed.
April 26, 1865	General Johnston surrenders his army to General Sherman.
April 27, 1865	The *Sultana* disaster occurs.
May 4, 1865	General Taylor surrenders his army to General Canby.
May 10, 1865	Jefferson Davis is captured in Georgia.
May 12, 1865	C. C. Clay Jr. surrenders in Georgia.
May 25, 1865	Explosion in Mobile, Alabama.
May 29, 1865	President Johnson announces his Reconstruction policy.

23
"Ne-Gotiation" or "Ne-Grotiation"

The mood of Alabamians at this point in the conflict can be readily discerned from their diaries and letters at Christmastime. Hear their voices:

Christmas day. A quiet one, for people cannot now it seems be joyful. The besom of destruction has swept over our land and left but little to be joyful about and yet we should be thankful that it is no worse with us than it is.

—Sarah Espy

You regret very much having to spend another Christmas without me but you cannot regret it more than I did.

—Grant Taylor

Christmas was a very disagreeable rainy day. We went to church and rode home in a hard rain added to which are the distresses of our bleeding country. Oh that Peace could be vouchsafed once more.

—Augustus Benners

Some of our children and grand children spent the day with us, the usual merriment was broken by our dear boys not being with us. Oliver and Frank are in the trenches at Petersburg, Hugh at Mobile. . . . May God close this war to his own glory and preserve our dear boy[s] to return to us in purity & honor.

—James Mallory

What visions of cheer does not the sound of "Merry Christmas" bring in review—happiness, plenty and a forgetting for a few short hours the cares of this weary world! This one has been any thing but merry to us; a gloom has hung over all, that, do what we will, we can not dispel. Our thoughts, whether we will or no, wander to where our armies are struggling to maintain our rights against fearful odds. Alas! when will this strife and bloodshed cease? When will we have peace? "Sweet peace is in her grave!"

—Kate Cumming

Christmas has come again and one of the dullest I have seen, even in the army. We have no roast turkey or other good cheer to welcome in this merry season: not even a glass of eggnog. Some of the citizens have been raising a Christmas dinner for the soldiers: but as our Brigade came from

> Ala., we will probably get none of it, having no particular friends in this country. Our men would provide for themselves if they had money, but the Govern't owed us for pay since June 30th: six months.
>
> —William Fielding

> I thought I had spent dull & gloomy Christmases before, but never one like this. I hope we may be able to rally yet, but it is the "dark day" with us now certain. I am not naturally despondent & have always been confident of success because of the justness of our cause, but I began to think the issue doubtful, though I have not & never will have any doubts as to the "justness" no matter how it terminates. It will be might, not right, that conquers if we are conquered.
>
> —Mary Fielding

> Tomorrow is Christmas. Many may enjoy it & feel gay, but it is no more than any other day in the army.
>
> —Joseph Francis

> Almost every man in this country betwixt the ages of 17 & 45, has his pockets full of Surgeons Certificates, pronouncing him unfit for military duty—This County has been drained.
>
> —Jefferson Buford

For Alabamians, 1865 was truly a critical year. On January 21, General Sherman instructed General Thomas to prepare for the invasion of central and south Alabama, which he envisioned would include "an army of 25,000 infantry and all the cavalry you can get, under Wilson." The plan at this early point was for this force to move from north Alabama to "some point of concentration about Columbus, Miss., and thence march to Tuscaloosa and Selma, destroying [the] former, gathering horses, mules (wagons to be burned), and doing all the damage possible; burning up Selma, that is the navy-yard, the railroad back toward the Tombigbee, and all iron foundries, mills and factories."[1]

In addition, General Grant had ordered Major General Edward Canby to proceed from New Orleans with an amphibious force to take Mobile and then move toward Selma and Montgomery. Canby's plan was to land a portion of this force on the Eastern Shore of Mobile Bay and proceed north to the Confederate garrisons at Spanish Fort and then Fort Blakely. Most of the rest of the force, which was composed of, among others, five thousand black troops as well as Louisiana Unionists under the command of a New Yorker, General Frederick Steele, were to land at Pensacola, make a feint toward Montgomery as far as Pollard, Alabama, and then march west down the Mobile and Great Northern Railroad to link up with Canby and invest Mobile.[2] In order to divert attention from Mobile and give the illusion that Selma and Montgomery were the actual primary targets, Union forces from Pensacola had already begun making raids up the Florida and Alabama Railroad before Steele ever arrived, forcing the Confederates to commit men from the port city away from the area of the main invasion.[3]

There does not appear to have been any other effort by the Union military to keep the basic outline of this plan a closely guarded secret. On the contrary, perhaps to intimidate Alabama into capitulating while at the same time tying down Confederate forces in the Deep South so they could not be sent east to fight against Sherman and Grant, the Northern press teemed with reports about the coming offensive. Generally speaking, those reports were quite accurate.[4] It is clear, therefore, that what would happen in less than ninety days was no surprise to Alabamians.[5] "Indeed," as the Montgomery-based *Memphis Appeal* declared, "there is no excuse for [surprise] now, for the Yankees have themselves boasted so much of their purposes, that such as are unenlightened now as to the dangers which threaten Alabama, will remain ignorant until the gridiron is planted on their faces in the very heart of the State."[6] And the Northern press certainly did boast that taking Alabama would be relatively easy.[7]

A ray of hope for peace advocates in and outside of the Confederate army unexpectedly appeared in January 1865. With great reluctance, Jefferson Davis finally bowed to intense public pressure by agreeing to appoint commissioners to meet with commissioners from the North to discuss peace terms.[8] But the Confederate commissioners he appointed—John Archibald Campbell of Alabama, Confederate Vice President Alexander Stephens of Georgia, and Confederate Senator R. M. T. Hunter of Virginia—were given no leeway by Davis to negotiate beyond a demand for independence. What would become known as the Hampton Roads Peace Conference was intended by Davis as a charade to silence the peace movement and, in the words of the late William Lowndes Yancey, "fire the Southern heart" once again.[9] Davis knew his demand for independence would not be accepted, and when rejected he intended to claim that he had tried and failed to reach a negotiated peace, that Lincoln had not negotiated in good faith, and that continued resistance was the South's only option.[10] After almost four years of war, the peace talks terminated after only four hours when it became obvious Davis had precluded real compromise.[11]

Davis's negotiating position was unrealistic, as he well knew. It was certainly not justified by the Confederacy's strategic position or ability to fight and win its independence. The most glaring problem was that the Confederate army could not match the North's manpower advantage. The solution to this, according to John Forsyth, was to enlist "negro troops" and put them "under the charge of experienced and veteran officers, who could soon initiate them in the principles and practice of the school of the soldiers."[12] This bizarre and highly controversial idea of arming slaves to fight for the Confederacy—and the perpetuation of the institution of slavery—had been the topic of public debate for months before Hood's defeat. In his message to the legislature in November, Governor Watts had opposed what one newspaper called "ne-gotiation" and "ne-grotiation."[13]

At that time, so was John Forsyth. In fact, he had editorially attacked those who proposed that "independence is worth even the sacrifice of the institution for the better security of which we went to war!" and argued that if "the war ended to-morrow, on the basis of the independence of the Confederacy and the ruin of slavery, we believe the present generation would witness the wreck of a nationality purchased at such fearful cost!"[14] Despite this, an Alabama legislator had then introduced a resolution advocating that two hundred thousand slaves between the ages of eighteen and forty-five be enrolled in the Confederate army and placed in the field.[15] His proposal went nowhere. For good reason, many Southern whites still had substantial concerns that once armed, the slaves would simply desert or even turn on the whites, resulting in a bloodbath on the scale of the notorious St. Domingo slave insurrection of the 1790s.[16] The Northern press had wisely played on these fears.[17]

As all knew, the slaves had good cause to settle scores, many old and some of very recent vintage.[18] Rumors were abroad that Governor Watts "had his servants whipped till the blood run"; he ignored the fact that his overseer "didn't show no mercy to the black people."[19] In Tuscaloosa, a slave named Frank who was owned by attorney Washington Moody was tried and convicted in the Circuit Court of Tuscaloosa in the spring of 1864 for "wilfully and maliciously" burning the corn crib of another Tuscaloosa resident. Rather than being sentenced to jail, he was hung.[20] But at least Frank received a semblance of due process. During the summer of 1864, a slave who lived south of Sylacauga and was suspected of murdering his master was reportedly "arrested by the citizens of the neighborhood, tied to a tree, and burned to death."[21] A slave in Greene County suffered the same fate after being accused of having "attacked a school girl." According to the approving *Selma Morning Reporter*, he was "tried by a committee of about forty of the most respectable citizens and condemned to be burned to death on the spot where he attempted the outrage. This sentence was put into execution on

Saturday last, at eleven o'clock, in the presence of the committee and hundreds of negroes."[22]

Mindful of this, Edward Norphlet Brown, who was then moving through South Carolina with the degraded Army of Tennessee—now once again led by General Joseph E. Johnston—wrote to his wife that he was "bitterly opposed" to the idea of arming the slaves. Once armed, they would "fill the woods & swamps" and the "final result of the matter will be the massacre of the negro race" in "self defense."[23] Grant Taylor, then stationed near Mobile at Spanish Fort, wrote to his wife that the question of arming the slaves and having white soldiers "fight side by side with the stinking things" and then setting them free "if we gain independence" was "causing a great deal of excitement" within his brigade. "The men," he continued, "are generally opposed to it and a great many declare they will go home if they are put in ranks with us. That is my notion." As this nonslaveholding soldier indignantly explained, "to think we have been fighting four years to prevent the slaves from being freed [and] now to turn round and free them to enable us to carry on the war. The thing is outrageous." But he also recognized that "the big bugs say things have changed [and] that we must bring the negroes in and make them fight or we will be made slaves ourselves." As far as he was concerned, "if we are reduced to that extremity," then "stop the war at once and let us come home for if we are to depend on the slaves for our freedom it is gone anyway."[24]

After Hood's defeat, however, a change of attitude among some "big bugs," or influential, die-hard Confederates in Alabama and elsewhere, appears to have occurred.[25] At about this time, according to the Alabama press, a letter from Robert E. Lee to a prominent member of the Confederate Congress surfaced in which Lee pointed out the deceptively simple truth that "we must use the negro or the enemy will use him against us."[26] An Alabama soldier in Lee's army noted similar sentiments in his diary. His regiment "did not like the idea" but favored "anything rather than subjugation by the Yankees, & they are willing to submit to any measures deemed necessary to prevent it."[27] Ironically, Nathan Bedford Forrest, the Confederate icon in the western theater and to the North the "Butcher of Fort Pillow," wholeheartedly agreed, telling a Mobile correspondent that the Confederacy ought to put two hundred thousand slaves into the army.[28] Suddenly converted to an ardent supporter of the idea, John Forsyth predicted that it would result in a "magical change in the aspect of the war."[29]

According to the *New York World*, the possibility that the Confederacy might offer slaves freedom in exchange for their agreement to fight was one of the material factors in the US Congress's decision to approve the Thirteenth Amendment when it did in January 1865, ostensibly eliminating that bargaining chip.[30] Perhaps as a consequence, legislation for putting slaves in the army had met substantial resistance in the Confederate Congress, particularly in the Senate.[31] But there was another reason. The issue forced the senators to examine the real reason for secession and war, and the debates were quite revealing. A senator from Virginia noted how Southerners had insisted that the US Congress had no right to interfere with slavery: "If we are right in passing this measure, we were wrong in denying to the old Government the right to interfere with the institution of slavery, and to emancipate slaves." Besides, he continued, "if we offer slaves their freedom, we confess that we were insincere in asserting that slavery is the best state for the negroes themselves."[32] Similarly, a Texas senator argued that "carrying out emancipation by arming the slaves would be destructive of the general organization of the South."[33] Although some claimed during the debates that they were not fighting for slavery, he reportedly admitted that he was "fighting for slavery and nothing else."[34] Of course, these disclosures did nothing to advance the legislation or staunch the desertion of white troops. Even if the legislation were immediately adopted, there was not time to adequately train and deploy the slaves.

Did the slaves have any intention of fighting for the "freedom" they were supposedly to receive in exchange for their lives? A correspondent in Mississippi reported that "I am reliably informed that a great many of them, from counties north of this, are going to Memphis. They have been led to believe that we wish to place them in the front of the battle to protect us from the bullets and this is causing them to leave for the Yankees."[35] To the *Selma Dispatch*, that was not a problem because the slaves were no magic remedy anyway. According to the *Dispatch*'s editor, slaves did not actually have the ability to fight: "The Yankee generals have succeeded in making colored regiments charge breastworks after making them drunk, and placing white soldiers to shoot them down if they turned back." Moreover, "the testimony of our officers in the armies of Virginia and Tennessee goes to show that after breastworks and redoubts have been taken by negro troops they stand like stock to be swept down."[36] But the idea did not go away. Just days after Abraham Lincoln's very conciliatory Second Inaugural Address, the Confederate Congress adopted legislation providing for arming slaves, albeit initially only those whose owners consented to them fighting for the Confederacy.[37]

This very flawed law did not guarantee freedom for the slaves who fought, an omission that amazed some observers. "Thus the negroes are to be asked to fight that their own bondage may be perpetuated and strengthened? Will they be likely to fight for such a cause against a Government that proposed to wipe out slavery? Certainly not," concluded a Northern newspaper editor. "The negroes know better than this. If, therefore, they should be armed, they would desert to our lines whenever and as rapidly as possible. Nothing better illustrates the madness which results from desperation than this new project of the rebel Congress. To arm three hundred thousand soldiers to fight for a cause the chief object of which is to keep in slavery themselves, their parents, their wives and their children, is such a crazy proposition, that none but men in the extremity of despair would bring it forward. And it is to be accepted as evidence of the helplessness of the rebels—stronger and more conclusive evidence than we have."[38]

What would happen to the slaves if their bondage were finally swept away? In the fall of 1864, a Northern newspaper had estimated that, up to that point, 145,000 Alabama slaves had been freed as a consequence of the advances of Union forces during the war.[39] Certainly some, if not most of them, had deserted their masters when given the opportunity, but that was not always the case. On the contrary, there is evidence that in some cases it had been the masters who had deserted their slaves. Elizabeth Meriwether, an intensely committed Confederate woman who had fled from Memphis to Tuscaloosa in 1863 recalled in her memoir that "every day[,] negroes were leaving [Tuscaloosa County] in batches in search of the Yankee army, which always welcomed them, gave them rations and required no work of them. No wonder that under such circumstances the towns in the South were denuded of their negroes. It was not that the negroes *wanted* to leave their former white masters," she claimed, "it was because they were hungry!" Food shortages, she continued, had become so severe that "the white Masters would urge their negroes to run off to the Yankee army—it left more food for the white men and women."[40] And as the slaves who made it through to Union lines had discovered, true freedom was not free of difficulties. According to a report in a Mobile newspaper, the "colored people in Nashville had an immense torch light procession which concluded at the State capitol in honor of Lincoln and Johnson's election." There, Andrew Johnson did not sugarcoat their future in his address to the multitude. Instead, he "counseled his hearers to industry, forbearance, moderation and virtue," "earnestly warned them against the vice of loafing and immoral practices, and advised them to spend their surplus earnings in the education of their children." Freedom, he said, would be a "great struggle," and if "you are not true to yourselves . . . , you don't deserve to be free."[41] If the freedmen chose to join the Union army and fight for the freedom of their family members and the other estimated 290,000 Alabama slaves who had not yet been freed, the rumors about what had occurred at Fort Pillow made clear that they had much more to lose than their freedom.[42]

Through the stray comments by their war-weary masters, those who were still enslaved likely realized that the Confederacy was losing the war and that freedom for them was just around the corner.[43] As reported in the Alabama press, President Lincoln had given them assurances in his Second Inaugural Address that the war would be fought until they were freed.[44] Slaves not guaranteed freedom by the new Confederate law in exchange for fighting for the losing side had absolutely no incentive to fight.[45] By virtue of Alabama law, no promise of emancipation by their masters was enforceable, a fact of which Unionist lawyers likely made the slaves aware. Hence, just as many pro-Confederates feared, it was indeed very likely that slaves involuntarily placed in the army by their masters would simply desert at the first opportunity.[46]

Back in Alabama, some of those who recognized how truly desperate the manpower situation really was nonetheless expressed relief that this act of desperation had finally taken place. John Forsyth, for one, was very glad of it. To him, prolonging the debate over the measure had, under the circumstances, been an act of stupidity: "Two men rise in a sudden and passionate fray in a room. A table is near them and on that table an open knife. One of the combatants grasps the knife, the other refrains from scruples of conscience and considerations of policy. The chances are that the gentleman of so much sensibility will in the end feel the knife he refused to use sticking in his own neck. And who would hesitate to pronounce him a fool."[47] But now, "thank Heaven, that question is decided, albeit tardily, by the Congress," he wrote. "Let the authorities and the people compensate in the energy of the execution of the law for the tardiness of its passage, and all hands go to work with a tremendous will to organize and throw into the field this new and powerful force against the public enemy. We shall then find for the first time in this war that we can raise men faster and in greater number than our enemy, and General Lee has repeatedly assured the country that he only wants the men to be able to force a speedy treaty of peace from the North. Work, work, and push the men to the front," he urged.[48]

The implementation of this new law would not produce a significant number of trained combat soldiers in time to stave off defeat.[49] One possible reason for this was that men like Confederate General John Tyler Morgan, who had radically conservative views regarding the ability of black people to do anything successfully beyond working as field hands, were appointed by Jefferson Davis to recruit and train them.[50] But at least Morgan would have a perfect bomb-proof job in which to ride out the rest of the war, thereby ending his lackluster military career.[51] According to an Ohio newspaper, another reason that this "new scheme for the success of the Confederacy does not seem to work very well" was that even in embattled Virginia, many of the owners of the slaves were not willing to part with them. After two weeks of recruiting, "of the three hundred thousand negroes called for, they have succeeded in raising just two companies, while they are losing about six companies [of white soldiers] by desertion every day." It cited an unidentified Richmond newspaper as having let "the cat out of the bag" that the slaves who had been presented for combat service "had already been in the rebel service as cooks and attendants in the hospitals," and it alleged that even those hoped to "get a chance to desert to the Union lines." Thus, he observed, the "dying Confederacy evidently will not be saved by Sambo."[52]

24
"The Day of Jubilee Am Come!"

Slave soldiers would not save the Confederacy. Some believed there was still a chance to at least prolong the period of their enslavement or stave off unconditional freedom. Fortunately for the slaves, however, too many of Alabama's political leaders remained mindlessly obstinate and self-deluded regarding the state's strategic position.

With time running out, an effort was made by Alabama Unionists to convince Governor Watts to issue a call for a convention or for a special session of the legislature as a first step toward peace talks. But they were rudely rebuffed.[1] Rather than seeking peace, Watts and other die-hard Confederates called for a public meeting in Montgomery to pump up morale by giving false hope of victory and a glimpse of the public's nightmarish fate if reconstruction occurred.[2] During that meeting, which fittingly took place in a theater, Watts displayed his very best Patrick Henry impression, encouraging those in the audience to choose death rather than submitting to "such terms as Lincoln demanded." The military situation, Watts assured, was not really all that bad. "The war had progressed for nearly four years, and none but a jaundiced eye would deny that our successes had been superior to the Northern successes." Apparently there was at least one "jaundiced eye" in the crowd, because when Watts next represented that "we hold more territory now, than we did twelve months ago," some brave soul yelled "Oh, no," prompting Watts to call the dissident a "croaker" and a "tory." Then Watts resumed his argument, portraying the fact that some states had been overrun as actually beneficial to the Cause. Georgia, he said, was now "sounder in republican faith than she was twelve months ago," and South Carolina was not "forgetful of her Sumter and other revolutionary sires" and "will come out of the fire as gold that is purified." Therefore, Watts claimed, there was "no occasion for depression—nothing to justify a disposition to go back to the old Union."[3]

But Watts knew this "disposition" still existed, and he gave the audience his grim vision of what their fate would be if they chose not to fight on: "The Lincoln Congress has usurped the power to abolish slavery. The Federal Constitution requires a vote of 3–4ths of the States to alter that constitution. The Lincoln Congress, professing to regard the Southern States as still in the Union, have submitted to act to alter the Constitution so as to declare slavery forever abolished, to a vote of the loyal States alone. They will not allow the Southern States to vote. You are not regarded as equals. If you would you cannot go back as States, but only as conquered provinces. Who would be your Governor and who your Congressman? Some flat-nosed, thick-lipped Sons of Africa, appointed by your conquerors." Foreshadowing the violent Reconstruction era, Watts vowed that if that occurred "we would be in a perpetual state of war, from the attempt to put our negroes on an equality with us, socially and politically." Under these circumstances, although he loved Alabama "as his mother—and he knew he loved his mother, god bless her!—but if Alabama were to submit, he would leave her forever and would not be willing for his bones to be buried in her soil."[4]

Then Watts turned his rhetorical guns on the peace advocates. "None but a white-livered coward and traitor would submit to such a peace as Lincoln offered," he thundered. But, he continued, "I am told, in whispered words, that we have amongst us men, who are willing to submit to such terms. Great God! are we the sons of Revolutionary Fathers, and have we fallen so low—are we dogs! That we are ready to lick the hand which smites us? Whoever is so base a coward, is unfit to live in a Southern land, is unfit to receive the smiles of Southern women, unfit to be buried in Southern soil! His real home is amongst our foes!" Parroting Jefferson Davis's speech during the special session of the Alabama legislature in the fall, Watts declared that anyone who advocated peace without Confederate independence "is on the wrong side of the line." Watts concluded by invoking Patrick Henry and the Almighty: "And, now, like the tones of an archangel, from people to armies, and from armies to people, the words 'Give me Liberty or give me Death,' come pealing over our broad land, fill our hearts with pride and mingle in the very air we breathe. God grant, that every heart may catch the inspiration of the heaven-born words and that the united voices of a great people, may send back to Heaven, in God-like chorus, 'Give me Liberty, or give me Death!' "[5]

When Alabama Confederates refused to capitulate, Generals Wilson and Canby put in motion their gigantic pincer movement from opposite ends of the state. It was evident that nothing could stop them. The *New York Herald* was more indelicate but just as accurate. From a military standpoint, "Alabama, like South Carolina, is a 'dead cock in the pit.'"[6] The segment of the male population still willing to fight for the Cause was fatally depleted, and Governor Watts knew this.[7]

As the *Montgomery Daily Advertiser* would soon be reporting, General Wilson and his huge cavalry force were moving south from Lauderdale County between Russellville and Jasper in north Alabama and faced even less than token resistance, much less a prepared defensive force.[8] Wilson reached Elyton in Jefferson County on March 30, and his men fanned out to destroy the fledgling iron industry in that region.[9] Before proceeding south to Selma, Wilson dispatched a 1,500-man brigade to Tuscaloosa under the command of Brigadier General John Thomas Croxton, a Kentuckian who had been a lawyer before the war.[10]

Croxton and his men arrived at the Northport side of the Black Warrior River opposite Tuscaloosa at approximately 11 p.m. on April 3 and found that the bridge to Tuscaloosa was still substantially intact.[11] He later reported that a few workers were then in the process of removing some of its floor boards, but only an estimated twenty feet had been taken out. A small force guarded the bridge, and there was no artillery in sight.[12] Croxton ordered a Michigan company to take the bridge and enter the town. This force charged the bridge, and after a very brief exchange of volleys, the guardsmen beat a hasty retreat.[13] Then some university cadets were imprudently brought to town, where they opened fire on the invaders before retreating back to the university and then to Hurricane Creek nine miles to the east. By the time all resistance had ceased, Croxton had suffered dozens of casualties while sealing the fate of the university and other war-related enterprises in the area.[14]

During the night, Croxton's main force in Northport across the river from Tuscaloosa initiated the process of destruction by burning a hat factory.[15] At dawn, these men crossed the bridge and entered Tuscaloosa. As far as can be determined, there was then no resistance and the town was peaceful.[16] Nonetheless, Croxton's men proceeded east toward the university, arriving at 9 a.m., and they then began the fiery destruction of several buildings, including the barracks where the cadets lived, the classrooms where they were taught, and the rotunda that housed the library where they studied. These soldiers did not destroy university facilities that had no apparent connection with military instruction such as the observatory constructed under the oversight of former Professor F. A. P. Barnard in the 1840s or the homes of the president or faculty members. The amount of destruction was actually less than university president Landon Garland had earlier predicted.[17] In the afternoon, Croxton's demolition teams turned their attention to the war-related manufacturing facilities in the downtown area. Among others, the Leach and Avery Foundry, Charles Foster's tanyard, the cotton mill, cotton warehouses, and a niter factory were torched.[18] Coupled with Croxton's destruction of the river bridge upon his departure on April 5 and a war that many Tuscaloosans had opposed, thirty years of commercial development in the City of Oaks had just gone up in smoke.[19]

According to local lore, when Croxton left Tuscaloosa, some gathered at a flagpole in the town with a few soldiers and "danced around the pole, singing *Dixie* and the *Bonny Blue Flag*."[20] But the only Tuscaloosans who had any reason to dance were the slaves, many of whom had celebrated Croxton's arrival. One of Croxton's men recalled that "while we were there the negroes flocked into the city in countless numbers," crying that "the day of jubilee am come!"[21]

There was no reason for Confederate Alabamians to dance anywhere. The essential mining, industrial, and manufacturing facilities in Jefferson, Bibb, and Shelby Counties had been systematically destroyed by General Wilson's main force as it moved from Elyton toward Selma while sweeping aside vastly outnumbered Confederate forces under the command of Nathan Bedford Forrest, Philip Dale Roddey, and others[22] (see map 8). In the process, Forrest had come very near being killed on April 1 at the Battle of Ebenezer Church, approximately twenty-five miles north of Selma.[23] These Confederates then retreated toward what they may have hoped were impregnable fortifications at Selma[24] (see map 9).

Those fortifications, which Forrest first saw on the morning of April 2,[25] were impressive. But unlike Tuscaloosans, the residents of Selma did not have the benefit of a river between them and the oncoming "abolition horde." The Alabama River was south of their town, which hampered any organized retreat. With the aid of slave labor, a giant semicircle of fortifications reaching from bank to bank had been built north of the river. This would require an attacking force from the north (Wilson's direction) to approach over a cleared and flat area, then scale fortifications that included ditches, stockades, and parapet walls, theoretically all under constant fire from soldiers in rifle pits utilizing an inexhaustible supply of munitions produced in Selma.[26] The problem for the Confederates was that there were a grossly inadequate number of soldiers to man these defenses, even with the men under Forrest, Roddey, and others combined.[27] As a result, local civilians were compelled by Forrest to man the trenches.[28]

Not surprisingly, the reluctant civilians of Selma ultimately proved to be the weak links in Selma's defenses. After Wilson began his frontal attack on Sunday, April 2, at approximately 5 p.m., the civilians, according to one of Wilson's troopers, "began to falter and gradually quit their places behind the

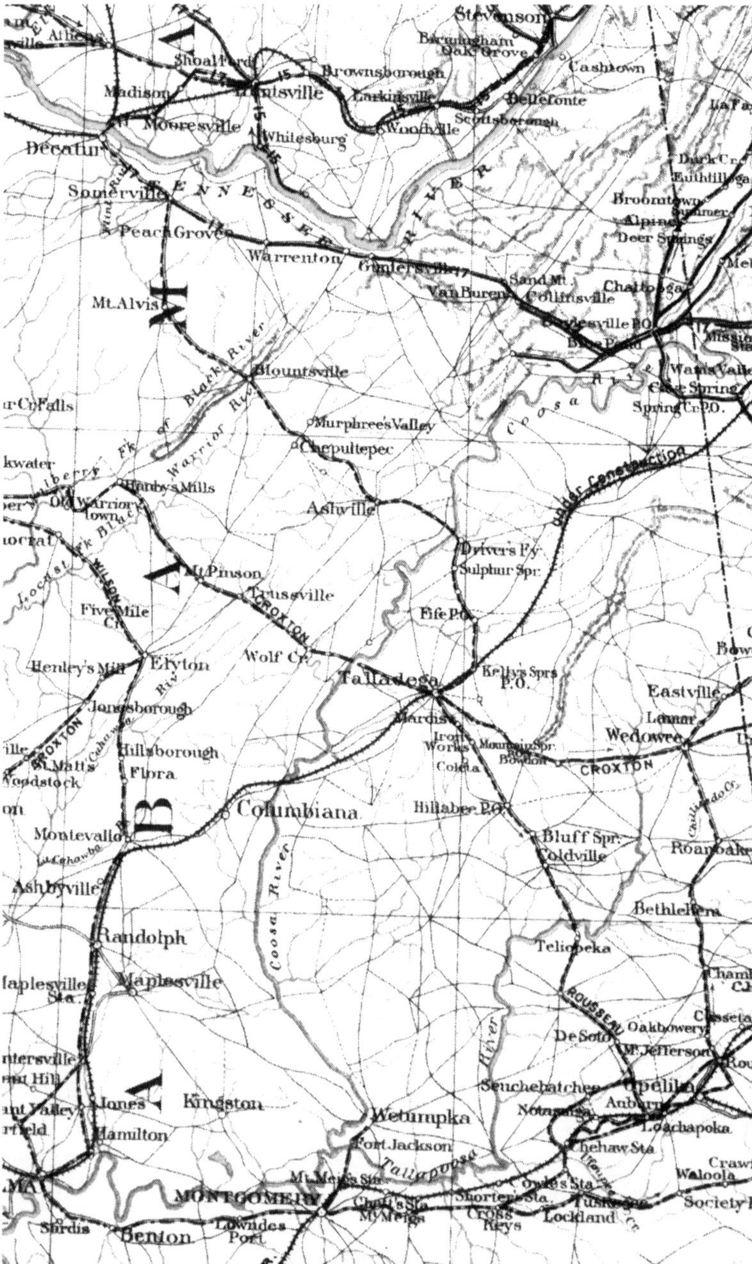

Map 8. Vicinity of central Alabama (*Official Military Atlas of the Civil War*)

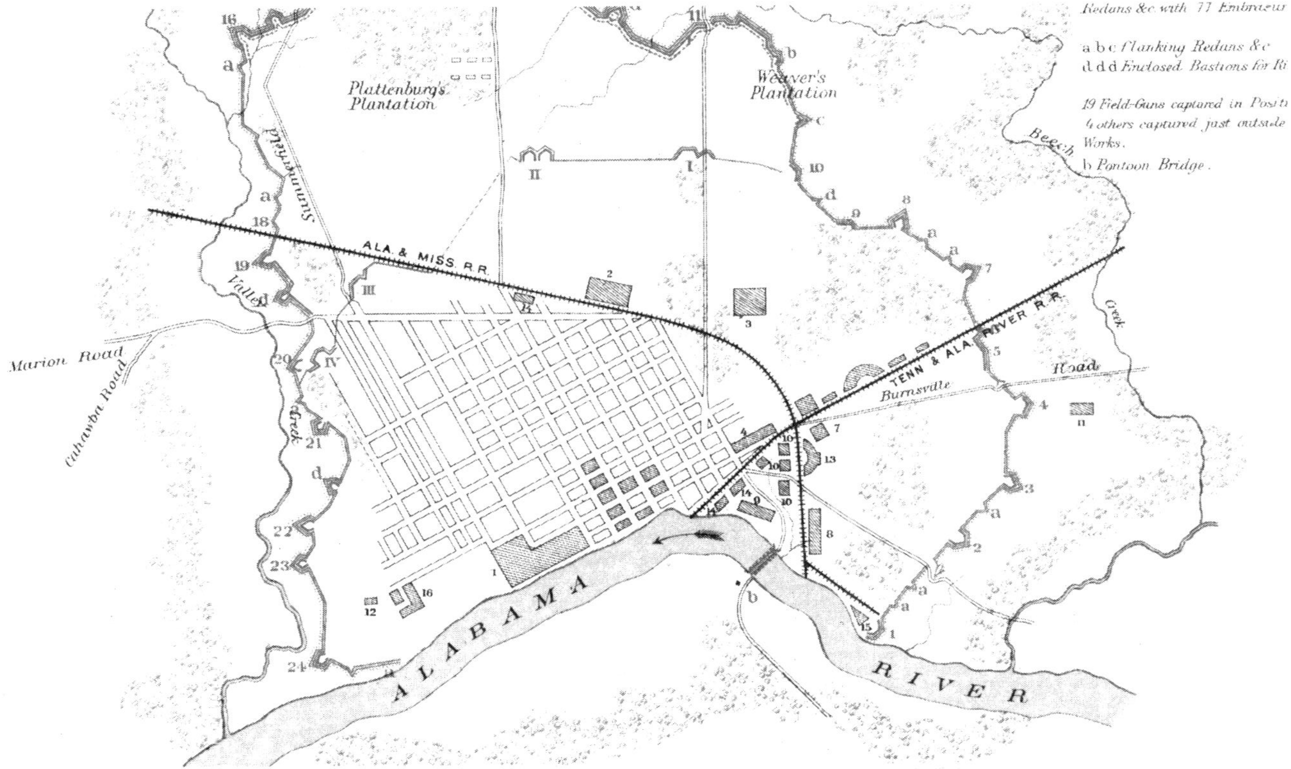

Map 9. Selma's fortifications (*Official Military Atlas of the Civil War*)

breastworks, leaving broad gaps." When Wilson's force hit those gaps, the civilians ran for their lives. The militia threw "away their arms, and were swiftly seeking their horses, and divesting themselves, as they fled, of all that would betray their late connection to the defense of Selma."[29] Several contemporary Southern sources confirm there had been what they called a "disgraceful stampede."[30] The precise length of the "battle" of Selma is unknown, but most contemporary accounts put it somewhere between fifteen minutes and one hour.[31] The engagement ended quickly, but for those who survived, the running away had just begun. The Northern press initially reported that Generals Forrest and Roddey had been captured,[32] but thanks to darkness and confusion, they—along with several other Confederate officers and soldiers—were able to escape.[33]

The Selmans who remained witnessed chaos and pandemonium as retreating Confederate forces set fire to an estimated twenty-five thousand bales of cotton in downtown Selma before they left.[34] The fire spread, wiping out not only a large portion of the business district but also the offices of the local newspapers, several homes, and the Episcopal church. As had occurred in Tuscaloosa to a more limited extent, the poor, including members of the slave population, took advantage and went on a looting spree.[35] The outcome of the nightmare that Sunday night might not have changed even if Wilson's troops had been inclined to stop any of this. But the discovery of large amounts of whiskey presumably made them even more inclined to take out their frustrations on Selma. As a hotbed of secession sentiment and the manufacturing center of weaponry that had brought death to their comrades, relatives, and neighbors, Selma, in their minds, deserved the same treatment accorded to South Carolina.[36] Over the next eight days, 2,700 captured Confederate soldiers and civilian militiamen, who were imprisoned in a cotton warehouse in Selma that had previously housed federal prisoners, were treated to repeated renditions of *Dixie* by Wilson's brass band. Wilson's engineers, meanwhile, executed their plan to destroy the entire industrial complex in the area, including the vitally important railroad tracks, shops, depots, and foundries[37] (see figure 19). When Wilson's force finally left Selma, crossed the Alabama River on a pontoon bridge, and on April 10 began moving east through Lowndes County toward Montgomery, Nathan Bedford Forrest—the man who had become famous for chasing down Abel Streight two years earlier and who the newspapers were confidently reporting would revenge Selma and repulse the invaders—did not follow Wilson.[38] The War Eagle had fought his last.

On April 9, the now unabashedly pro-peace *Montgomery Daily Mail* had published an editorial encouraging the citizens of Montgomery to cease re-

Figure 19. Ruins at Selma (Courtesy of Alabama Department of Archives and History)

sistance and simply acquiesce in the takeover of the capital when Wilson's force arrived.[39] But that very day, Governor Watts issued a public proclamation warning that "base and cowardly fears but invite the enemy to destroy you all." He defiantly declared that the "military authorities here are determined to defend the city of Montgomery" and that "the seat of government shall not be surrendered as long as there is a reasonable hope of defending it."[40]

Wilson and his men therefore initially assumed that they would have a much tougher fight on their hands when they reached the Cradle of the Confederacy.[41] But on April 11, when it became apparent that Watts's final call for volunteers had largely fallen on deaf ears and that Forrest was not riding to the rescue, the Confederate military shocked and angered local Confederates by opting to burn the approximately eighty-five thousand bales of cotton valued at $12 million that was stored there and then skedaddling to Columbus, Georgia. Despite his liberty-or-death declarations of less than a month earlier, Watts was not inclined to stay behind and fight. He was instead among the refugees, including what one newspaper called "original secesh," who left Montgomery with the departing Confederate soldiers. Watts did not stop running in Columbus but instead fled all the way to Eufaula, Alabama.[42]

A correspondent to the *New York Herald* later reported that a "committee of citizens waited upon [Confederate] General Adams previous to the evacuation" and that during their ensuing meeting, Adams "refused to allow the committee to go out and meet the Union Generals."[43] The identity of the members of this committee, which was obviously attempting to obtain permission to surrender Montgomery in order to save it, is unknown.

But given the active and apparently very extensive Union spy network in Alabama, it is likely General Wilson was being kept apprised of these developments in Montgomery, and the fact that the town's mayor, W. L. Coleman, and a delegation of citizens that included Milton Saffold and other Unionists, would surrender the town without a shot being fired. According to one account, after Confederate forces evacuated the town, the "Mayor . . . with a deputation of citizens had made preparations to meet the enemy under a flag of truce, and obtain protection for the undefended city."[44] According to this same account, the delegation left Montgomery on the night of April 11,[45] and other sources indicate that the meeting with the commander of Wilson's forward unit occurred near the Catoma Creek, west of the city on the road to Hayneville, at approximately 3 a.m. on April 12.[46] A correspondent of the *New York Herald* reported that the group was "received with great courtesy," and an agreement was reached to surrender Montgomery.[47]

A few hours later, a squad of mounted Union soldiers reportedly "dashed into Main Street, and rode up to the Capitol, where they formed a line. In about half an hour General [Edward] McCook, at the head of his columns, accompanied by the Mayor and committee of the [City] Council, rode into Court House Square, and from thence to the Capitol. Very soon thereafter the United States flag was floating from the Capitol dome, the Court House, the telegraph office, and from the Exchange Hotel, where General McCook established his headquarters. The flag of truce and the battle flag of the advance were placed one on each side of the Capitol stairs."[48] A Montgomery resident, Sarah Follansbee, wrote that the town was spared, "some said because no defence was made."[49] Later that morning, it was confirmed by a printed placard that "the city of Montgomery having been 'surrendered into a protection of the United States, all private property would be respected, except such as required by military necessity.'"[50]

While the dramas in Tuscaloosa, Selma, and Montgomery were playing out, the fate of Alabama's largest city, Mobile, was also being decided.[51] And General Canby's plan for taking Mobile had been impeccably prepared, in part based on intelligence provided to his staff over the past several months by slaves and spies. According to the *Memphis Bulletin*, some of those spies were operating in plain sight with the aid of members of an old profession: "On the same day two prostitutes obtained a pass, went through the lines in a carriage, and returned with two Federal officers dressed in rebel uniform, whom they drove all through the city, and back through the lines again. The trick was not discovered until the birds had flown. The officers were probably spies, and doubtless obtained all the information they wanted. The women subsequently returned and were placed under arrest."[52] The ultimate fate of these two women is unknown, but the practice on both sides had been to execute spies and several had been hung in the last several months alone.[53]

Part of Canby's strategy included a raid by Union forces from Pensacola to cut the Alabama and Florida Railroad between Pollard and Greenville and thereby prevent Confederates in Montgomery and Mobile from reinforcing each other.[54] The main force at Pensacola, led by Union General Frederick Steele, would meanwhile move toward Pollard and then west toward Mobile. On March 25, General James Holt Clanton and his few remaining regiments had attempted to intercept some of Steele's force in Florida, twenty-five miles south of Pollard, Alabama, possibly assuming that it was merely a raiding party. But Steele had previously sent a detachment east of Clanton's position through Andalusia, Alabama, which had already cut the railroad and captured two trains just south of Evergreen, Alabama, on the morning of March 24. In the process, they had inflicted several casualties, including the son of Governor Watts, Lieutenant John Watts, who was wounded.[55] Clanton realized too late that he was facing not simply another raid, but in fact the lead elements of Steele's twelve-thousand-man invasion force.[56]

General Clanton was not the only one in the dark. On the same day as this confrontation, the very confused or mendacious editor of the Mobile *Army Argus and Crisis* had reported that Clanton was "skirmishing" with the enemy at Pine Barren, Florida, on March 24, but inexplicably discounted the threat: "Many rumors prevailed, none of which we credit. The enemy, it is reported, say that they have delayed the capture of Mobile for two weeks." Therefore, Mobile "is in no real danger. Reports of heavy forces at Pensacola and New Orleans has become stale. Madame Rumor told us that [Union General] Thomas with his whole force would soon be in Alabama, and now we hear that Thomas and his army is in Knoxville, Tennessee. Our readers may rest assured that the Yankee Government has its Virginia programme in hand, and all the fighting of consequence will take place in or near that State."[57]

Clanton would have debated that point after one of Steele's cavalry regiments of Louisiana Unionists had overwhelmed him and his men near Bluff Springs, Florida, capturing over one hundred prisoners.[58] As one of Clanton's panicked soldiers wrote to his father, "the enemy came here twenty thousand strong—nine regiments of cavalry. They charged our brigade and ran over it, capturing 115 men and sixty horses."[59] During the brief engagement, Clanton was very seriously wounded and initial reports were that the wound was mortal.[60] According to one account, he was "shot through the body, between the bowels and the stomach, with a pistol ball."[61] Notwithstanding this, Clanton and his men were truly lucky they did not fall into the hands

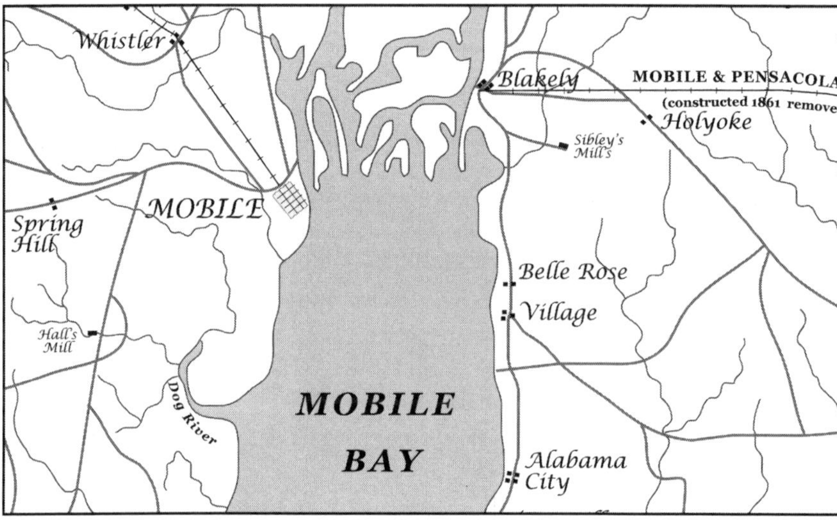

Map 10. Mobile, Mobile Bay, and the Eastern Shore

of Steele's contingent of black infantry troops, many of whom had Fort Pillow on their minds.[62]

As planned, General Canby was basically unmolested during his pounding, thirteen-day siege of Spanish Fort, ultimately forcing the Confederates to evacuate the facility on April 8.[63] Three days before Spanish Fort fell, John Forsyth had bragged to his readers that it would take the Yankees "five years and three months to take Mobile"[64] (see map 10). But on April 9, the same day General Lee surrendered his Army of Northern Virginia to Grant, Canby and Steele teamed their forces in a successful assault on the unfortunate Confederate defenders of Fort Blakely.[65] Thanks to the massacre at Fort Pillow, some of those defenders were shown no quarter by Steele's black infantrymen.[66] According to an Illinois soldier, after the shooting had stopped, some of the captured Confederates "discovered some of their old slaves among the colored soldiers and wanted to be friendly with them." The Confederates even approached them, called them by name, and offered to shake hands. But foreshadowing the impending reshuffle of the social and political deck, the black soldiers rebuffed these overtures. They said "stand bak dar massa, Ise massa now [stand back Master, I am the Master now]."[67]

The fall of Fort Blakely placed Confederate forces in Mobile in jeopardy of being cut off, so on the same day Montgomery was evacuated, General Dabney Maury elected to evacuate Mobile. The mayor, Robert H. Slough, wisely agreed to surrender it to the Union forces.[68] The editor of the Washington, DC, *Daily National Republican* responded to a telegraph report of this news by remarking that "Satan's Kingdom is tumbling down, glory hallelujah."[69] The *Mobile Register* as well as the other Mobile newspapers temporarily ceased publication, and Union General Gordon Granger, the departmental commander, authorized a correspondent of the pro-Union *New Orleans Times* to begin publication of the *Mobile Daily News*, reportedly on John Forsyth's presses.[70] As one might expect, the editorial slant of this new sheet was definitely not Forsythesque. Its editor urged the citizens to "submit cheerfully" to occupation forces.[71]

For committed Confederates in Alabama, that would be very difficult if not impossible. Young Mobile resident Mary Waring, who had long expressed hope that this day would never come, sadly recorded that the Yankee troops marched into her town to the tune of "Yankee Doodle." The next day she could not contain her disgust. "The city is filled with the hated Yanks, who differ in the greatest degree from our poor dear soldiers—the commonest, dirtiest-looking set I ever saw."[72]

But at least the great conflict was finally over after taking over seven hundred thousand lives.[73] Or was it? Even after Abraham Lincoln was tragically shot by an assassin on April 14, 1865, some in the Alabama press maintained that it was not.[74] And for some, the war is still with us even now.

25
Conclusion

In 1877, Jefferson Davis wrote that he wanted future historians to do justice to "our cause and conduct" so a "favorable verdict" could be "rendered by future generations." For this reason, he encouraged the preservation of records that would facilitate that narrow goal.[1] But the words of Talladega planter James Mallory following the crushing Confederate defeat at Nashville bear repeating: "We are in an awful condition as a people, two or three hundred thousand of our best men killed or disabled, millions of property destroyed, millions more to go, our slaves rendered useless and a future pest, with a grinding debt on this generation, the people demoralized and wicked beyond anything, all to gratify a few wild politicians."[2] Mallory was referring to the faction of the legal profession—many of whom were politicos—that had engineered the South's secession in 1860. Led by lawyers like the late William Yancey, who did not live to see the wreck he helped bring about, proponents of secession in Alabama had used the promise of state aid for railroads to secure the passage by the legislature of a resolution requiring the governor to call for the election of delegates to a convention with virtually unlimited powers if a Republican were elected president of the United States in 1860. They had then taken steps to fulfill that condition by undermining the unity of the National Democratic Party.

Another faction of the Alabama legal profession attempted to stop the secessionists, some by appealing to the lame-duck Buchanan administration for federal military intervention and others by throwing up procedural roadblocks such as a requirement of joint, or cooperative, secession by an impossibly large number of other slave states. They had also predicted that secession was a suicidal leap in the dark that would certainly result in civil war, the abolition of slavery, and a probable repeat of the horrors that St. Domingo—the site of a notorious massacre of white citizens and a symbol for some racists of the supposedly inherent incompetence of black-led government—represented in the white supremacist imagination.

But the secession faction was better organized, having worked toward their goal for over a decade. They also had the ability to manipulate the widespread paranoia resulting from John Brown's relatively recent raid and to effectively paint Abraham Lincoln as an abolitionist whose presidency meant the doom of slavery. War with the North, they assured, would be no more than a skirmish. Defeated at the polls, those Alabamians who opposed secession were forced to adopt a reconstruction strategy centered on the 1861 state elections. But that plan was foiled by the Confederate attack on Fort Sumter less than ninety days before those elections. This attack drew Alabama into a war for which its citizens were unprepared emotionally, physically, and materially.

There is little doubt that, at least initially, tens of thousands of Alabamians nonetheless enthusiastically supported the Confederacy and the war effort. How many of them were influenced by the propaganda of John Forsyth and the other Generals of the Press is unknown. Assurances that King Cotton would force foreign recognition and military aid and a quick end to the war, or later that the Midwest would secede, were difficult for some to ignore. But opposition in Alabama to the Confederate government and the war continued. It is actually impossible to determine how many citizens were on either side of the chasm at any particular point. It is, however, apparent that opposition increased with military reverses in Alabama's sister states beginning with the Battle of Shiloh, coupled with the sudden occupation of north Alabama, the death toll, and increasing home front hardships. Defeatism and a desire for peace existed even among many who had initially supported the Confederacy. Absent this opposition, the Confederacy would not have been forced to enact at an early point in the war coercive laws allowing deportation of "alien enemies" and sequestration of property, conscription of reluctant civilians for military service, and the suspension of the authority of courts to issue writs of habeas corpus in aid of political prisoners and the conscripted.

One wonders what might have happened if President Lincoln had issued his Emancipation Proclamation a year later than he did. Yankee raids punished north Alabama in the spring of 1863. Then the pivotal loss of Vicksburg and the Confederate defeat at Gettysburg in July 1863 established favorable conditions for the peace movement in Alabama to take over the state in the August 1863 state elections. But after the proclamation took effect on January 1, 1863, fear that a separate peace would require emancipation of the slaves split the slave-owning leadership of the peace movement. Some chose to aid the war effort until the Confederacy achieved enough success on the battlefield to reacquire sufficient bargaining leverage to negotiate away any emancipation requirement.

This "struggle of the masters," as Thomas Peters called it, was doomed to fail. Those on the home front continued to sink further into grinding poverty while Alabama soldiers who did not desert and hide in the mountains and forests of Alabama were put through a meat grinder in Georgia and elsewhere in 1864. Hopes by proslavery peace advocates that Lincoln would lose the 1864 presidential election to a proslavery Peace Democrat had proved false. And the shocking losses subsequently suffered by the Army of Tennessee at Franklin and Nashville left Alabama basically undefended.

Despite this, too many of the politicians James Mallory called "wild" were deaf to pleas for peace. The Generals of the Press, led by John Forsyth, continued to spew out misleading prowar propaganda, just as they had since the war began. Governor Thomas Hill Watts's intransigence was particularly senseless. If he had called the Alabama legislature into special session in January 1865, or at any point before Wilson's Raid began in late March, the damage and destruction inflicted at Tuscaloosa and Selma might have been avoided. But Watts did not, and instead he ridiculed those who advised otherwise.

Neither did God "close this terrible war" as James Mallory had often prayed. And that was a providential boon to the hundreds of thousands of Alabama slaves. Indeed, the secessionists' gamble to save the peculiar institution backfired. But for Confederate diehards like Watts and their proslavery peace advocate coadjutors, legal slavery in some form might have continued for years. But freedom had arrived with the Union troops, reportedly leading one black Alabama woman who was baptized in Huntsville in the following weeks to come forth from the water shouting "freed from slavery, freed from sin—bless God and General Grant."[3]

In so many other ways, the "few wild politicians" had brought destruction to Alabama and tens of thousands of its citizens to their death or the brink of death. Alabama's first elected postwar governor, Robert Miller Patton, stated in his inaugural address that "for four years [the war] swept over our land like a sulphurous sirocco, and scarcely a locality in the South escaped its devastating blast."[4] Historian Kenneth Noe compared the war to "a natural disaster, a tsunami of four years' duration that brought suffering, stole lives, divided families, destroyed property 'gained by honest toil,' wrecked communities and left nothing as it was before."[5]

The suffering in Alabama did not end with the surrender of the Confederate armies. The confusing and oftentimes violent maelstrom known as Reconstruction would follow as Alabamians slowly and reluctantly adjusted to the terms and conditions of defeat.[6] Former Confederates had to face the possibility of punishment, particularly after the tragic assassination of President Lincoln in April 1865 enraged the North even further.[7] All Alabamians, white and black, would have to find some way to avoid starvation while re-orienting their relationships—economic, social, and political—initially under federal supervision and control.[8] Without sufficient financial resources, Alabamians would also be forced to somehow repair their dislocated economy.

Given what happened, it is difficult to see how our generation can reach the verdict Jefferson Davis had sought. The true Cause—the preservation of slavery—and the actions of Davis and his Alabama supporters cannot be squared with common sense or modern morals. But even judging by the result-oriented standards prevailing in Davis's era, one cannot escape the conclusion that the conduct of those who brought about secession and war to preserve slavery produced nothing but disaster. Any politician who caused that would be hard-pressed to merit a favorable verdict from an unbiased jury.

Notes

Foreword

1. James M. McPherson, *Battle Cry of Freedom: The Civil War Era* (New York: Oxford University Press, 1988), ix.

2. Francis Mitchell Grace, "What a Civilian Saw during the War," 3, Randolph Collection, MFS 648, Samford University Special Collections, Birmingham, Alabama.

Introduction

1. *Cleveland Morning Leader*, April 10, 1865, 4.

2. See, e.g., Ben H. Severance, *Portraits of Conflict: A Photographic History of Alabama in the Civil War* (Fayetteville: University of Arkansas Press, 2012). The term *Civil War* is used in this book because that is what Confederates often called it. See, e.g., Nathan Bedford Forrest to Soldiers, May 9, 1865, *The War of the Rebellion: A Compilation of the Official Records of the Union and Confederate Armies* (Washington, DC: Government Printing Office, 1880–1901) (hereinafter "Official Records"), series 1, vol. 49 (Part II), 1289; William Warren Rogers Sr., Robert David Ward, Leah Rawls Atkins, and Wayne Flynt, *Alabama: The History of a Deep South State* (Tuscaloosa: University of Alabama Press, 1994), 222 (on Jefferson Davis). The term *War between the States* was not used until after the war ended, and even then was not generally used until much later.

3. Relying on the letters and diaries by the soldiers to discern the motivations and sentiments of the civilian population is also inherently problematic. We cannot now determine the extent to which their comments are the result of programming by their superiors or the propaganda of the wartime press. Relying on letters *to* the soldiers is equally problematic. There is no way to determine whether comments of the authors were constrained by propaganda and other influences.

4. Walter Lynwood Fleming's dated *Civil War and Reconstruction in Alabama* (London: P. Smith, 1905) used a topical rather than a narrative approach. Malcolm McMillan's very fine *The Disintegration of a Confederate State* (Macon, GA: Mercer University Press, 1986) is narrower than this study. For recent treatment of certain important

aspects of the war experience in Alabama, see the excellent collection of essays in Kenneth W. Noe, ed., *The Yellowhammer War: The Civil War and Reconstruction in Alabama* (Tuscaloosa: University of Alabama Press, 2013).

5. See, e.g., Herbert James Lewis, *Clearing the Thickets: A History of Antebellum Alabama* (New Orleans: Quid Pro Books, 2013); J. Mills Thornton III, *Politics and Power in a Slave Society: Alabama, 1800–1860* (Baton Rouge: Louisiana State University Press 1978); Sarah Woolfolk Wiggins, *The Scalawag in Alabama Politics, 1865–1881* (Tuscaloosa: University of Alabama Press, 1977).

6. Wayne Cline, *Alabama Railroads* (Tuscaloosa: University of Alabama Press, 1997), 42; William G. Thomas, *The Iron Way: Railroads, the Civil War, and the Making of Modern America* (New Haven, CT: Yale University Press, 2011), 70–72, 133.

7. Robert H. McKenzie, "Reconstruction of the Alabama Iron Industry, 1865–1880," *Alabama Review* XXV (July 1972): 178–79; Mildred Beale, "Charles Teed Pollard: Industrialist," *Alabama Historical Quarterly* 2 (Summer 1940): 189–207; Curtis J. Evans, *The Conquest of Labor: Daniel Pratt and Southern Industrialization* (Baton Rouge: Louisiana State University Press, 2001), 50; Angela Lakweta, "The Eclectic Industrialism of Antebellum Baldwin County," *Alabama Review* 65 (January 2012): 3–6; Beth English, *A Common Thread: Labor, Politics, and Capital Mobility in the Textile Industry* (Athens: University of Georgia Press, 2006), 40–41; Fred Bateman and Thomas Weiss, *Deplorable Scarcity: The Failure of Industrialization In the Slave Economy* (Chapel Hill: University of North Carolina Press, 2002), 12, 149; Randall Martin Miller, *The Cotton Mill Movement in Antebellum Alabama* (New York: Arno, 1978); Rogers Sr. et al., *Alabama*, 174–81; William Warren Rogers Jr., *Confederate Home Front: Montgomery during the Civil War* (Tuscaloosa: University of Alabama Press, 1999), 49; Albert Burton Moore, *History of Alabama* (Tuscaloosa: Alabama Book Store, 1951), 283–318; Randall M. Miller, "Daniel Pratt's Industrial Urbanism: The Cotton Mill Town in Ante-Bellum Alabama," *Alabama Historical Quarterly* XXXIV (Spring, 1972): 5–35.

8. John F. Kvach, *DeBow's Review: The Antebellum Vision of a New South* (Lexington: University Press of Kentucky, 2013), 45, 70, 90, 104, 111, 114, 116–19, 153; Cline, *Alabama Railroads*, 42; James Harold Clark, "History of the North East and South West Railroad to 1872" (master's thesis, University of Alabama, 1949); Ethel Marie Armes, *The Story of Coal and Iron in Alabama* (Birmingham, AL: Chamber of Commerce, 1910), 58–124; Kincaid A. Herr, *The Louisville & Nashville Railroad*, 1850–1963 (Lexington: University Press of Kentucky, 2000), 46–47; A. Davis Smith and T. A. DeLand, *North Alabama, Historical and Biographical* (Birmingham, AL: Smith & Deland, 1888), 45–46; James R. Bennett, *Tannehill and the Growth of the Alabama Iron Industry: Including the Civil War in West Alabama* (Saline, MI Alabama Historic Ironworks Commission, 1999), 5–281; Douglas A. Blackmon, *Slavery by Another Name: The Re-enslavement of Black People in America from the Civil War to World War II* (New York Doubleday, 2008), 19. Regarding outside interest in Alabama's natural resources during the antebellum period, see James Dunwoody Brownson DeBow, *The Industrial Resources, Etc., of the Southern and Western States: Embracing a View of Their Com-*

merce, Agriculture, Manufactures, Internal Improvements; Slave and Free Labor, Slavery Institutions, Products, Etc., of the South (New Orleans: DeBow's Review, 1852), I: 57–62.

9. Regarding the effect of sectional conflict on international money markets, see Jay Sexton, *Debtor Diplomacy: Finance and American Foreign Relations in the Civil War Era 1837–1873* (New York: Clarendon Press, 2005), 79–80; Evans, *Conquest of Labor*, 193–94; Henry M. McKiven, *Iron and Steel: Class, Race, and Community in Birmingham, Alabama, 1875–1920* (Chapel Hill: University of North Carolina Press, 1995), 8–10; Thomas, *Iron Way*, 133, 137.

10. Thornton, *Politics and Power in a Slave Society*, 281.

11. *Livingston Journal*, July 20, 1867, 2. (Tuscaloosa) *Independent Monitor*, March 25, 1868, 2; (Selma) *Alabama State Sentinel*, June 20, 1867, 2.

12. *Montgomery Mail*, reprinted in *Charleston Mercury*, March 13, 1860, 1.

13. Thomas, *Iron Way*, 135–41.

14. Lewy Dorman, *Party Politics in Alabama from 1850 through 1860* (Tuscaloosa: University of Alabama Press, 1995), 82–83; Thornton, *Politics and Power in a Slave Society*, 340–41; Cline, *Alabama Railroads*, 43; Evans, *Conquest of Labor*, 193–99; Wallace Hettle, *The Peculiar Democracy: Southern Democrats in Peace and Civil War* (Athens: University of Georgia Press, 2001), 45–48.

15. *Montgomery Mail*, May 15, 1865; Mary Fielding, "Mary Fielding's Diary," in "*To Lochaber Na Mair*": *Southerners View the Civil War*, ed. Faye Acton Axford, 159 (Athens, AL: Athens Publishing, 1986); Richard Barksdale Harwell, ed., *Kate: The Journal of a Confederate Nurse* (Baton Rouge: Louisiana State University Press, 1998), 302; Wendy Hamand Venet, ed., *Sam Richard's Civil War Diary: A Chronicle of the Atlanta Home Front* (Athens: University of Georgia Press, 2009), 270. See also David Williams, *Rich Man's War: Class, Caste, and Confederate Defeat in the Lower Chattahoochee Valley* (Athens: University of Georgia Press, 1998), 126. As has been noted by others, myths regarding constitutional issues and states' rights were publicly used to obscure the preservation of slavery as the real purpose of the war. See Richard E. Beringer, Herman Hataway Archer Jones, William N. Still Jr., *Why the South Lost the Civil War* (Athens: University of Georgia Press, 1991), 403–17; Glenn Linden and Virginia Linden, eds., *Disunion, War, Defeat, and Recovery in Alabama: The Journal of Augustus Benners, 1850–1885* (Macon, GA: Mercer University Press, 2007), 137; Dwight Franklin Henderson, ed., *The Private Journal of Georgiana Gholson Walker 1862–1865 with Selections From the Post-War Years, 1865–1876* (Tuscaloosa, AL: Confederate Pub. Co., 1963), 110; Donald E. Collins, *Death and Resurrection of Jefferson Davis*, (Lanham, MD: Rowman & Littlefield Publishers, 2005), 17–18; Virginia K. Jones, ed., "The Journal of Sarah G. Follansbee," *Alabama Historical Quarterly* 27 (Fall–Winter 1965): 232; Joshua Burns Moore, "Daily Journal of Joshua Burns Moore," 84, Alabama Department of Archives and History, Montgomery; Grady McWhiney, Warner O. Moore Jr., and Robert F. Pace, eds., "*Fear God and Walk Humbly*": *The Agricultural Journals of James Mallory, 1843–1877* (Tuscaloosa: University of Alabama Press, 1997), 343; Private Journal of Sarah R. Espy, 1859–1868, 97, Alabama Department of Archives and History, Montgomery; *Montgomery Mail*, May 15, 1865.

16. Rogers et al., *Alabama*, 227.

17. McWhiney, Moore, and Pace, eds., "*Fear God and Walk Humbly,*" 343.

18. *Huntsville Advocate*, June 13, 1866, 2, June 27, 1866, 2; Wiggins, *Scalawag in Alabama Politics*, 5–14; Margaret M. Storey, *Loyalty and Loss: Alabama's Unionists in the Civil War and Reconstruction* (Baton Rouge: Louisiana State University Press, 2004), 170–92; Allen Johnston Going, *Bourbon Democracy in Alabama, 1874–1890* (Tuscaloosa: University of Alabama Press, 1951), 1; Fleming, *Civil War and Reconstruction in Alabama*, 316.

19. Wiggins, *Scalawag in Alabama Politics*, 18–20; Going, *Bourbon Democracy in Alabama*, 2; Fleming, *Civil War and Reconstruction in Alabama*, 473–91.

20. The 1870 Alabama census revealed that there were 521,384 white men and women and 475,510 black men and women. The potential voting age population in 1860 was 206,275, with 113,871 being white men and 92,404 black men. It is assumed that the ratios remained the same or probably decreased between 1860 and 1870. C. Vann Woodward, *The Burden of Southern History* (Baton Rouge 2008), 99; David Hardin, *After the War: The Lives and Images of Major Civil War Figures After the Shooting Stopped* (Lanham, MD: Rowman and Littlefield, 2010), 289; Clara Mary Lauderdale, "Population of Alabama Between 1860 and 1870" (master's thesis, University of Wisconsin, 1912), 9; Fleming, *Civil War and Reconstruction in Alabama*, 491 (104,518 blacks registered to vote in 1867); *Montgomery Daily Advertiser*, December 22, 1866, 2 (the 1866 state census revealed a decrease of whites since 1860 of 9,267).

21. Wiggins, *Scalawag in Alabama Politics*, 19–36; Fleming, *Civil War and Reconstruction in Alabama*, 505–12; Michael W. Fitzgerald, "'He Was Always Preaching the Union': The Wartime Origins of White Republicanism during Reconstruction," in *Yellowhammer War*, ed. Kenneth W. Noe, 235.

22. Wiggins, *Scalawag in Alabama Politics*, 34–42; Going, *Bourbon Democracy in Alabama*, 2; Fleming, *Civil War and Reconstruction in Alabama*, 735–47. Like Smith, many of the Unionists were Democrats and lawyers—albeit of a different faction—prior to the war. Some had been members of the prewar opposition Whig Party. To illustrate the role and activities of these Unionists and future Republicans, particular attention is given in this book to the three antebellum Alabama lawyers who were elected as Republicans to the Alabama Supreme Court in 1868: E. W. Peck of Tuscaloosa in central Alabama, Thomas Minott Peters of Moulton in north Alabama, and Benjamin Franklin Saffold of Selma in south Alabama. Peck, a member of the antebellum Whig Party, was a native of New York who settled in Alabama in the 1820s, was very involved in the Protestant Episcopal Church, and before the war became one of the most successful lawyers in the state. Joel D. Kitchens, "E. W. Peck: Alabama's First Scalawag Chief Justice," *Alabama Review* 54 (January 2001): 3; Paul M. Pruitt Jr., "Scalawag Dreams: Elisha Woolsey Peck's Career, and Two of His Speeches, 1867–1869," *Alabama Review* 66 (July 2013): 211–39. Peters, another Whig, was born in Tennessee to northern-born parents who later settled in north Alabama. After graduating from the University of Alabama in the 1830s, he likewise was a successful lawyer and educator, as well as a serious botanist and a determined railroad promoter and

commercial booster. James Edmonds Saunders, *Early Settlers of Alabama* (New Orleans: L. Graham & Son, printers, 1899), 75, 110–11; Paul Horton, "Lightning Rod Scalawag: The Unlikely Political Career of Thomas Minott Peters," *Alabama Review* 64 (2011): 116. Benjamin Saffold, a Democrat and the youngest of the three, was a son of a member of the state's first constitutional convention, former Alabama Supreme Court chief justice Reuben Saffold. Like Benjamin's brother, Montgomery lawyer Milton Saffold, he was to-the-manor-born in every sense. After graduating from the University of Alabama at the top of his class in the 1840s, he was practicing law in Selma when the war began. Wiggins, *Scalawag in Alabama Politics*, 20, 128–29, 136; Albert James Pickett, *History of Alabama and Incidentally of Georgia and Mississippi, From Earliest Period* (Sheffield, AL: R. C. Randolph, 1896), 635, 656–58; Val L. McGee, *Selma: A Novel of the Civil War* (Oxford, MS: Yoknapatawpha Press, 2008), 381–82. Peck, Peters, and Saffold were prominent men and slave owners but were also vocal opponents of secession. After the war, they became important leaders of the Republican Party in Alabama who supported black suffrage and, therefore, were figuratively dead to Democrats and most early historians except as occasional targets of derision and ridicule. Following their experiences and those of their communities through secession and war provides insight both into the plight of Unionists and the origins of the Republican Party in Alabama, as well as important regional differences within the state. Regarding the Whig Party, see Lawrence Frederick Kohl, *The Politics of Individualism: Parties and the American Character in the Jacksonian Era* (New York: Oxford University Press, 1989); J. Mills Thornton, *Politics and Power in a Slave Society: Alabama, 1800–1860* (Baton Rouge: Louisiana State University Press, 1978) ; Dorman, *Party Politics in Alabama*; Thomas B. Alexander, "The Basis of Alabama's Ante-Bellum Two-Party System," *Alabama Review* 19 (October, 1966): 243–76.

23. Wiggins, *Scalawag in Alabama Politics*, 66–71; Going, *Bourbon Democracy in Alabama*, 3–4; Fleming, *Civil War and Reconstruction in Alabama*, 750–53.

24. Wiggins, *Scalawag in Alabama Politics*, 72–83; Going, *Bourbon Democracy in Alabama*, 5–7; Fleming, *Civil War and Reconstruction in Alabama*, 754–55.

25. Patrick R. Cotter, *After Wallace: The 1986 Contest for Governor and Political Change in Alabama* (Tuscaloosa: University of Alabama Press, 2013), 218 (regarding the election of Republican Guy Hunt).

26. The state's bonded indebtedness had ballooned as a result of postwar efforts to finance an economic recovery and regeneration, and now that indebtedness was in default. As a consequence, whites faced the potential of higher taxes to pay those debts and Democrats were quite effective in placing the blame on the Republicans. Wiggins, *Scalawag in Alabama Politics*, 86; Going, *Bourbon Democracy in Alabama*, 7–10.

27. Wiggins, *Scalawag in Alabama Politics*, 92–102; Going, *Bourbon Democracy in Alabama*, 12–18; Fleming, *Civil War and Reconstruction in Alabama*, 770–97.

28. William Warren Rogers Sr., *The One-Gallused Rebellion: Agrarianism in Alabama, 1865–1896* (Baton Rouge: Louisiana State University Press, 1970). xx.

29. Regarding Hayne, see George W. Bungay, *Traits of Representative Men* (New York: Fowler & Wells, 1882), 280–86.

30. *Montgomery Advertiser and Mail,* May 5, 1872, 2. Regarding Burke, see Edmund Burke, *Reflections on the Revolution in France* (New York: Alfred A. Knopf, 2015), 84. ("But the age of chivalry is gone.")

31. Donald E. Collins, *The Death and Resurrection of Jefferson Davis* (Lanham, MD, Rowman and Littlefield, 2005), 155–56.

32. *Montgomery Advertiser and Mail,* May 5, 1872, 2.

33. See also William J. Cooper Jr., *Jefferson Davis and the Civil War Era* (Baton Rouge: Louisiana State University Press, 2008), which notes that Davis was also a leader in revising the history of the Cause to exclude slavery as the reason for secession and war.

34. Jefferson Davis to Rev. J. William Jones, May 15, 1877, in William J. Cooper, ed., *Jefferson Davis: The Essential Writings,* 417–18 (New York: Random House, 2004). See also William J. Cooper, *Jefferson Davis, American* (New York: Vintage Books, 2001), 669. Alabama Democrats voiced no objections. After all, their legacies were also on the line. But it was not just that the legacies of men were at stake if the whole truth were told. It was their profession. The largest percentage of the leaders of the secession movement were, like Jefferson Davis and Alabama's most vocal secessionist, William Lowndes Yancey, members of the powerful legal profession. Pat Boyd Rumore, *From Power to Service: The Story of Lawyers in Alabama* (Montgomery: Alabama State Bar, 2010), 38–68; *Confederate Politicians of Alabama, 1861–1865* (n.p., n.d.), 2–30, available at Tuscaloosa Public Library, Tuscaloosa, Alabama. Each of Alabama's wartime governors was also a lawyer. When the war ended, most of the leaders were economically and politically ruined in the short run. J. Mills Thornton, "Alabama's Presidential Reconstruction Legislature," in *A Political Nation: New Directions in Mid-Nineteenth Century American Political History,* ed. Gary W. Gallagher and Rachel A. Sheldon, 171–72 (Charlottesville: University of Virginia Press, 2012) (noting the postwar reduction in the number of lawyers in the Alabama legislature). But by pushing the white supremacy agenda in later years, many younger lawyer-secessionists were able to reinvent and redeem themselves, unite the white majority, and thereby achieve fame, and in some cases, high political office. They included John Tyler Morgan (see Joseph A. Fry, *John Tyler Morgan and the Search for Southern Autonomy* [Knoxville: University of Tennessee 1992], and Thomas Adams Upchurch, "Senator John Tyler Morgan and the Genesis of Jim Crow Ideology, 1889–1891," *Alabama Review* 57 [April, 2004]: 110); Edmund Winston Pettus of Dallas County (see Thelma Caine Berry, "The Life of Edmund Winston Pettus" [master's thesis, Auburn University, 1941]); James Holt Clanton (see Arthur W. Bergeron Jr., "James Holt Clanton," in *The Confederate General,* ed. William C. Davis [New York: Free Press, 1991], I: 189–91, and William H. Davidson, "Brigadier General James Holt Clanton: Alabama's Rash Gallant," *Alabama Lawyer* 29 [1959]: 285); Thomas Hill Watts of Montgomery (Emma Beall Culver, *Thomas Hill Watts: A Statesman of the Old Regime* [Montgomery, Alabama Historical Society, Reprint No. 19, 1904]); and J. L. M. Curry of Talladega County (see Jessie Pearl Rice, *J. L. M. Curry: Southerner, Statesman and Educator* [New York: Kings Crown Press, 1949]).

35. *Montgomery Mail*, May 5, 1860, 2.

36. Robert Penn Warren, *The Legacy of the Civil War* (Lincoln: University of Nebraska Press, 1998), 54. See also John Witherspoon DuBose, *Alabama's Tragic Decade: Ten Years of Alabama, 1865–1874* (Birmingham, AL: Webb Book Co., 1940), 20–21, 26, 49–50; Brooks D. Simpson, "Continuous Hammering and Mere Attrition: Lost Cause Critics and the Military Reputation of Ulysses S. Grant," in Gary W. Gallagher and Alan T. Nolan, eds., *The Myth of the Lost Cause and Civil War History* (Bloomington: Indiana University Press, 2000), 147; Wesley Moody, *Demon of the Lost Cause: Sherman and Civil War History* (Columbia: University of Missouri Press, 2011), 1–2; Charles Reagan Wilson, *Baptized in Blood: The Religion of the Lost Cause, 1865–1920* (Athens: University of Georgia Press, 2009), 37–38; Amy L. Heyse, *Teachers of the Lost Cause: The United Daughters of the Confederacy and the Rhetoric of Their Catechisms* (College Park: University of Maryland Press, 2006).

37. Joseph Moreau, *Schoolbook Nation: Conflicts over American Textbooks from the Civil War to the Present* (Ann Arbor: University of Michigan Press, 2003), 52–81; James M. McPherson, "Long-Legged Yankee Lies: The Southern Textbook Crusade," in *Memory of the Civil War in American Culture*, ed. Alice Fahs, 64–78 (Chapel Hill: University of North Carolina Press, 2004); Fred Arthur Bailey, "The Textbooks of the Lost Cause: Censorship and the Creation of Southern State Histories," *Georgia Historical Quarterly* LXXV (Fall, 1991): 507–33; Karen L. Cox, *Dixie's Daughter: The United Daughters of the Confederacy and the Preservation of Confederate Culture* (Gainesville: University Press of Florida, 2003), 124.

38. (Huntsville) *Southern Advocate*, May 22, 1850, 3. Regarding Manly, see also Harold Wilson, "Basil Manly, Apologist for Slavocracy," *Alabama Review* 15 (January 1962): 38; A. James Fuller, *Chaplain to the Confederacy: Basil Manly and Baptist Life in the Old South* (Baton Rouge: LSU Press, 2000); and Thomas McAdory Owen, *Dr. Basil Manly: The Founder of the Alabama Historical Society* (Montgomery, AL: Alabama Historical Society Reprint, 1904). Regarding the use of history in this manner and its effect, see Michael Kammen, *Mystic Chords of Memory: The Transformation in American Culture* (New York: Knopf, 1991), 120–31; Robert Partin, "The Use of History," *Alabama Review* 19 (April, 1966): 109–24.

39. Fleming, *Civil War and Reconstruction in Alabama*, 61–244. Fleming's examination of the war amounted to only 173 of the book's 809 pages.

40. Michael C. C. Adams, *Living Hell: The Dark Side of the Civil War* (Baltimore: Johns Hopkins University Press, 2014), 184.

41. Gallagher and Nolan, eds., *Myth of the Lost Cause and Civil War History*, 1–8.

42. Fleming, *Civil War and Reconstruction in Alabama*, iii; Tommy Stevenson, "A Different War, A Different South, Than We've Known," *Tuscaloosa News*, December 4, 1994, 9A. See, e.g., Malcolm Cook McMillan, *The Land Called Alabama* (Austin, TX: Steck-Vaughn, 1968), 222–23 (in discussing the reasons for Confederate defeat, the only Alabama politician singled out for criticism was Governor Thomas Hill Watts, a prewar Whig); Moore, *History of Alabama*, 427–28 (Moore was certain that when Alabama went to war, "all hearts were in the cause"), 438, 444, 455.

43. Michael C. C. Adams, *Living Hell: The Dark Side of the Civil War* (Baltimore: Johns Hopkins University Press, 2014).

Chapter 1

Epigraph. Grant Taylor to Malinda Taylor, January 11, 1865, in *This Cruel War: The Civil War Letters of Grant and Malinda Taylor, 1862–1865*, ed. Ann Kicker Blomquist and Robert A. Taylor (Macon, GA: Mercer University Press, 2000), 322–23.

1. (Montgomery) *Alabama State Journal*, May 4, 1875, 1 (publishing a letter from Montgomery lawyer Walter Lawrence Bragg); E. R. Mattoon, "The Lawyer as a Social Force," *Alabama Lawyer* 15 (January, 1954): 55, 62–65; Dorman, *Party Politics in Alabama*, 172.

2. Dorman, *Party Politics in Alabama*, 172.

3. Eric H. Walther, *William Lowndes Yancey and the Coming of the Civil War* (Chapel Hill: University of North Carolina Press, 2006), 4–73, 226–27 (Huntsville) *Democrat*, January 22, 1845, 3.

4. *Mobile Register and Journal*, October 4, 1848, 2. See also *Mobile Register and Journal*, June 28, 1848, 2.

5. *Montgomery Advertiser*, July 28, 1863, 2.

6. *Mobile Daily Advertiser and Register*, December 15, 1866, 2. See also *Mobile Daily Advertiser and Register*, December 19, 1866, 2. Regarding Forsyth, see Lonnie A. Burnett, *The Pen Makes a Good Sword: John Forsyth of the Mobile Register* (Tuscaloosa: University of Alabama Press, 2006).

7. Lonnie A. Burnett, "Precipitating a Revolution: Alabama's Democracy in the Election of 1860," in *Yellowhammer War*, ed. Kenneth W. Noe, 15–33.

8. *Mobile Daily Register*, May 3, 1859, 2.

9. William Stanley Hoole, *Alabama Tories, the First Alabama Cavalry, U.S.A., 1862–1865* (Tuscaloosa, AL: Confederate Pub. Co., 1960), 8, 10. See, generally, Kenneth M. Stampp, *The Peculiar Institution: Slavery in the Antebellum South* (New York: Knopf, 1956), 30–32; Gerald Gunderson, "The Origin of the American Civil War," *Journal of Economic History* 34 (Dec. 1974): 915, 922–24; James L. Huston, *Calculating the Value of the Union: Slavery, Property Rights, and the Economic Origins of the Civil War* (Chapel Hill: University of North Carolina Press, 2003), 24–26; and Adam Rothman, *Slave Country: American Expansion and the Origins of the Deep South* (Cambridge, MA: Harvard University Press, 2005), 21–22; Kvach, *DeBow's Review*, 122.

10. (Mobile) *Nationalist*, September 20, 1866, 1.

11. William W. Freehling, *The Road to Disunion: Secessionists at Bay: 1776–1854* (New York: Oxford University Press, 1991), 133–34, 150–52.

12. George C. Rable, *But There Was No Peace: The Role of Violence in the Politics of Reconstruction* (Athens: University of Georgia Press, 2007), 16–32. Alfred N. Hunt, *Haiti's Influence on Antebellum America* (Baton Rouge: Louisiana State University Press, 1988), 9–36; David P. Geggus, *The Impact of the Haitian Revolution in the Atlantic World* (Columbia: University of South Carolina Press, 2001), 4; G. Ward Hubbs, *Guarding*

Greensboro: A Confederate Company in the Making of a Southern Community (Athens: University of Georgia Press, 2003), 57–72.

13. Hunt, *Haiti's Influence on Antebellum America*, 16–40; Ira Berlin, *Many Thousands Gone: The First Two Centuries of Slavery in North America* (Cambridge, MA: Belknap Press of Harvard University Press, 1998), 221–27.

14. (New Orleans) *Daily Picayune*, June 15, 1862, 2.

15. (Tuscaloosa) *Flag of the Union*, November 21, 1835, 2; *Selma Free Press*, October 3, 1839, 1; *Mobile Register and Journal*, December 20, 1844, 2; (New Orleans) *Daily Picayune*, September 17, 1839, 2, June 19, 1853, 2; (Mobile) *Weekly Herald and Tribune*, June 18, 1853.

16. (Tuscaloosa) *Flag of the Union*, September 22, 1841, 3; (Mobile) *Weekly Herald and Tribune*, March 22, 1853, March 29, 1853, April 1, 1853, April 7, 1853, April 23, 1853, April 27, 1853, April 28, 1853, May 7, 1853; *Montgomery Advertiser and State Gazette*, June 12, 1856, 2.

17. *Mobile Commercial Register and Patriot*, May 22, 1839, 2; *Mobile Register and Journal*, December 20, 1844, 2; (Tuscaloosa) *Independent Monitor*, February 10, 1848, 2; *Montgomery Advertiser and State Gazette*, May 18, 1857, 2, September 23, 1857, 2, April 27, 1859, 2; *Montgomery Daily Advertiser*, March 2, 1851, 2, April 6, 1866, 4, May 11, 1867, 2; (Greensboro) *Alabama Beacon*, April 26, 1873, 1; (Huntsville) *Southern Advocate*, March 3, 1859, 1, May 5, 1859, 1. See also Hunt, *Haiti's Influence on Antebellum America*, 2, 5, 28, 42, 89, 109, 114, 117, 123–25; Lydia Maria Francis Child, *The Right Way, The Safe Way* (New York: American Anti-Slavery Society, 1860; repr. 1969), 86–88; E. N. Elliott, *Cotton Is King and Pro-Slavery Arguments* (Augusta, GA: Pritchard, Abbott & Loomis, 1860), 409–12; Ira Berlin, *Slaves without Masters: The Free Negro in the Antebellum South* (New York: Pantheon, 1974), 82, 89, 131–39; David Brion Davis, *Inhuman Bondage: The Rise and Fall of Slavery in the New World* (Oxford: Oxford University Press, 2006), 158, 270; Stephen John Hartnett, *Democratic Dissent & the Cultural Fictions of Antebellum America* (Urbana: University of Illinois Press, 2002), 42; Winthrop Jordan, *White Over Black: American Attitudes toward the Negro, 1550–1812* (Chapel Hill: University of North Carolina Press, 1968), 375–402; Cal M. Logue, "Rhetorical Ridicule of Reconstruction Blacks," *Quarterly Journal of Speech* 62 (December 1976): 400.

18. *Mobile Daily Register*, quoted in (Montgomery) *Advertiser and State Gazette*, February 26, 1851, 1.

19. Elizabeth R. Varon, *Disunion!: The Coming of the American Civil War, 1789–1859* (Chapel Hill: University of North Carolina Press, 2008), 273–91.

20. *Montgomery Advertiser and State Gazette*, September 15, 1857, 4.

21. (Huntsville) *Southern Advocate*, September 30, 1858, 2; (Greensboro) *Alabama Beacon*, April 6, 1860, 2; *Moulton Democrat*, July 16, 1858, 1. Slaughter reportedly committed suicide on August 9, 1860. *Atlanta Confederacy*, August 10, 1860, reprinted in *Charleston Mercury*, August 13, 1860, 1.

22. See, generally, Varon, *Disunion!*, 326–35; Tony Horwitz, *Midnight Rising: John Brown and the Raid that Sparked the Civil War* (New York: Henry Holt, 2011); Allen C. Guelzo, *Fateful Lightning: A New History of the Civil War and Reconstruction* (New York:

Oxford University Press, 2012), 116–20; *Charleston Mercury*, October 19, 1859, 1–3, October 20, 1859, 1, October 31, 1859, 1, November 1, 1859, 1.

23. *Montgomery Daily Mail*, June 2, 1860, 2.

24. Ibid. See also Hubbs, *Guarding Greensboro*, 86; Davis Blake Carter, *The Story Uncle Minyard Told: A Family's 200 Year Migration across the South* (Spartanburg, SC: Reprint Co., Publishers, 1994), 203 (regarding fears generated in Coosa County as a result of the raid).

25. (Tuscaloosa) *Independent Monitor*, December 17, 1859, 2.

26. *Mobile Daily Register*, October 19, 1859, 2.

27. See, generally, James L. Huston, *The Panic of 1857 and the Coming of the Civil War* (Baton Rouge: Louisiana State University Press, 1987), 220–22.

28. (Tuscaloosa) *Independent Monitor*, October 29, 1859, 2; *Montgomery Advertiser and State Gazette*, October 26, 1859, 3; *Memphis Daily Appeal*, January 10, 1860, 1; *Charleston Mercury*, October 25, 1859, 4.

29. (Huntsville) *Southern Advocate*, November 9, 1859, 3.

30. *Mobile Daily Register*, October 25, 1859, 2.

31. See, generally, James Terry Southern, "Constructing/Inventing John Brown: A Study of the Political Texts" (PhD diss., University of Alabama, 1995), 149.

32. Private Journal of Sarah R. Espy, 1859–1868, 3–4.

33. (Tuscaloosa) *Independent Monitor*, December 10, 1859, 2.

34. Ibid., November 26, 1859, 2.

35. *Montgomery Daily Mail*, November 28, 1859, 2.

36. (Huntsville) *Southern Advocate*, September 23, 1858, 3. "Vigilance committees" were local groups of citizens who constituted themselves as watchdogs over the community. Anyone suspected of being antislavery or anti-secession were likely to be arrested by them and punished.

37. *Selma Reporter*, reprinted in (Tuscaloosa) *Independent Monitor*, December 17, 1859, 2. The fate of the peddler is unknown.

38. (Tuscaloosa) *Independent Monitor*, November 19, 1859, 2.

39. (Greensboro) *Alabama Beacon*, December 2, 1859, 2. See also Hubbs, *Guarding Greensboro*, 86–91.

40. *New York Observer*, reprinted in (Huntsville) *Southern Advocate*, December 7, 1859, 2.

41. (Tuscaloosa) *Independent Monitor*, December 17, 1859, 2.

42. Walther, *William Lowndes Yancey and the Coming of the Civil War*, 236; *Charleston Mercury*, December 9, 1859, 1.

43. (Huntsville) *Southern Advocate*, October 19, 1859, 3.

44. *Montgomery Advertiser and State Gazette*, October 9, 1859, 2, October 19, 1859, 2, November 2, 1859, 2; *Mobile Daily Register*, October 21, 1859, 1.

45. (Tuscaloosa) *Independent Monitor*, February 25, 1860, 2.

46. Ibid., October 22, 1859, 2, November 5, 1859, 2; *Montgomery Advertiser and State Gazette*, October 19, 1859, 2.

47. *Montgomery Advertiser and State Gazette*, October 19, 1859, 4, November 2, 1859, 1.

48. Walter M. Jackson, *The Story of Selma* (Birmingham, AL: Birmingham Print Co., 1954), 124; (Selma) *Alabama State Sentinel*, September 11, 1860.

49. (Greensboro) *Alabama Beacon*, April 6, 1860, 2.

50. (Tuscaloosa) *Independent Monitor*, October 22, 1859, 2.

51. Logrolling had been common in connection with state aid over the previous several years. *Montgomery Advertiser and State Gazette*, June 21, 1856, 2.

52. *Ala. Acts*, No. 31, 25 (February 23, 1860). See (Tuscaloosa) *Independent Monitor*, March 10, 1860, 2; *Charleston Mercury*, January 27, 1860, 1, January 30, 1860, 1. See, generally, Helen Eckinger, "The Militarization of the University of Alabama," *Alabama Review* 66 (July 2013): 164, 169–70. The university was the second collegiate military school in Alabama. The first was at LaGrange College in northwest Alabama. *Ala. Acts* No. 253, 275 (February 6, 1858), ibid., No. 111, 90 (January 26, 1860).

53. *Ala. Acts*, No. 68, 54 (February 18, 1860), No. 39, 31 (February 24, 1860), and No. 132, 110 (February 24, 1860).

54. Ibid., No. 45, 36 (February 24, 1860); (Huntsville) *Southern Advocate*, February 29, 1860, 3; (Greensboro) *Alabama Beacon*, March 2, 1860, 2; *Mobile Daily Register*, February 28, 1860, 2; *Charleston Mercury*, March 6, 1860, 1, March 12, 1860, 4.

55. *Ala. Acts*, Joint Resolutions (February 24, 1860) (emphasis added).

56. *Mobile Daily Register*, November 17, 1859, 1; (Tuscaloosa) *Independent Monitor*, November 26, 1859, 1.

57. (Tuscaloosa) *Independent Monitor*, February 4, 1860, 1 (publishing a report regarding Alabama's bonded indebtedness); Writer's Program, *Alabama: A Guide to the Deep South* (St. Clair Shores, MI: Somerset Publishers, 1973), 68.

58. *Montgomery Daily Mail*, February 21, 1860, 2.

59. (Tuscaloosa) *Independent Monitor*, February 25, 1860, 2.

60. Ibid., March 3, 1860, 2.

61. *Alabama House Journal*, 474 (February 22, 1860); Thornton, *Politics and Power in a Slave Society*, 405–8.

62. (Montgomery) *Confederation*, reprinted in *Mobile Daily Register*, May 12, 1860, 1.

63. (New Orleans) *Daily Picayune*, October 30, 1860, 2.

64. (Tuscaloosa) *Independent Monitor*, January 21, 1860, 2; (Greensboro) *Alabama Beacon*, January 27, 1860, 1; *Charleston Mercury*, January 14, 1860, 1, January 16, 1860, 1. See also Walther, *William Lowndes Yancey and the Coming of the Civil War*, 237–38; *Charleston Mercury*, May 3, 1860, 1.

65. (Huntsville) *Southern Advocate*, October 24, 1860, 2.

66. (Tuscaloosa) *Independent Monitor*, February 4, 1860, 2; *Mobile Daily Register*, January 19, 1860, 2.

67. (Tuscaloosa) *Independent Monitor*, February 18, 1860, 2. See also (Tuscaloosa) *Independent Monitor*, March 10, 1860, 1–2, March 17, 1860, 2, March 24, 1860, 2, April 7, 1860, 1.

68. (Tuscaloosa) *Independent Monitor*, March 17, 1860, 2. See also (Selma) *Alabama State Sentinel*, July 29, 1860.

69. *Charleston Mercury*, May 19, 1860, 4.

70. David B. Chesebrough, *Clergy Dissent in the Old South, 1830–1865* (Carbondale:

Southern Illinois University Press, 1996), 16–17; James W. Silver, *Confederate Morale and Church Propaganda* (Tuscaloosa, AL: Confederate Pub. Co., 1957).

71. Fuller, *Chaplain to the Confederacy*, 290–93. And when one remembers how reliant churches are on financial contributions from their members—many of whom are lawyers, business people, and others of prominence in the community—it is just as easy to conclude that the slant of the sermons of many of these ministers of the gospel of disunion was procured by assurances of charitable giving.

72. (Tuscaloosa) *Independent Monitor*, March 31, 1860, 2.

73. James Benson Sellers, *History of the University of Alabama* (Tuscaloosa: University of Alabama Press, 1953), 260–61; Suzanne Rau Wolfe, *The University of Alabama, A Pictorial History* (Tuscaloosa: University of Alabama Press, 1983), 38–41; Eckinger, "Militarization of the University of Alabama," 164, 170.

74. *United States v. Gould*, 25 F.Cas. 1375 (S.D. Ala., 1860); (Greensboro) *Alabama Beacon*, May 4, 1860, 1; (Huntsville) *Southern Advocate*, May 9, 1860, 4. See also *Montgomery Daily Mail*, April 23, 1860, 2; (New Orleans) *Daily Picayune*, July 12, 1860, 6.

75. (New Orleans) *Daily Picayune*, July 12, 1860, 6; *New York Times*, July 9, 1860, 1; *Montgomery Daily Mail*, April 23, 1860, 2.

76. James D. Lockett, "The Last Ship That Brought Slaves from Africa to America: The Landing of the Clotilde at Mobile in the Autumn of 1859," *Western Journal of Black Studies* 22 (Fall 1998), 159. See also *New York Times*, August 1, 1860, 6; (New Orleans) *Daily Picayune*, July 12, 1860, 6, July 28, 1860, 1; *Montgomery Weekly Post*, July 18, 1860, 1; *Hayneville* (Alabama) *Chronicle*, July 19, 1860, 3; and Ronald T. Takaki, *A Pro-Slavery Crusade: The Agitation to Reopen the African Slave Trade* (New York: Free Press, 1971).

77. *New York Times*, April 21, 1860, 4 (regarding the *Wanderer*). See also Erik Calonius, *The Wanderer: The Last American Slave Ship and the Conspiracy That Set Its Sails* (New York: St. Martin's Press, 2006), 172–73, 230–31.

78. *Mobile Daily Register*, April 28, 1860, 1; (Huntsville) *Southern Advocate*, May 2, 1860, 3, May 16, 1860, 2; *Montgomery Daily Mail*, April 28, 1860, 2; *Charleston Mercury*, May 1, 1860, 1. See also James Leonidas Murphy, "Alabama and the Charleston Convention of 1860," in *Studies in Southern and Alabama History*, ed., George Petrie, (Montgomery: Alabama Historical Society, 1905), 252–55.

79. *New York Times*, June 25, 1860, 4. See also William B. Hesseltine, *Three against Lincoln* (Baton Rouge: Louisiana State University Press, 1960), 265–78, 301; Murphy, "Alabama and the Charleston Convention," 265.

80. *Brooklyn Eagle*, November 8, 1860, 2 (discussing Yancey's views); *New York Times*, June 7, 1860, 2 (publishing a letter from Yancey); *Charleston Mercury*, April 30, 1860, 1. Damon Wells, *Stephen Douglas: The Last Years, 1857–1861* (Austin: University of Texas Press, 1971), 244–46, 251.

81. *Charleston Mercury*, July 13, 1860, 1.

82. *Mobile Daily Register*, May 11, 1860, 2.

83. Ibid. See also (Huntsville) *Southern Advocate*, May 16, 1860, 3, June 20, 1860, 2, June 27, 1860, 3; *New York Times*, June 7, 1860; *Montgomery Weekly Mail*, July 24, 1860.

84. Montgomery *Confederation*, reprinted in *Daily Columbus* (Georgia) *Enquirer*, May 5, 1860, 2.

85. (Huntsville) *Southern Advocate*, August 15, 1860, 2. For earlier criticism, see *Mobile Register and Journal*, June 28, 1848, 2.

86. Diary of Miss Catherine M. Fennell, 14, Huntsville/Madison County Public Library, Huntsville, Alabama.

87. William C. Harris, *Leroy Pope Walker: Confederate Secretary of War* (Tuscaloosa: Confederate Pub. Co., 1962), 15. See also (Tuscumbia) *North Alabamian*, reprinted in *Montgomery Advertiser and State Gazette*, November 14, 1860, 1 (publishing Walker's letter dated October 15, 1860).

88. R. S. Tharin, *Arbitrary Arrests in the South* (New York: J. Bradburn, 1863), 62.

89. Fuller, *Chaplain to the Confederacy*, 290.

90. Private Journal of Sarah R. Espy, 10.

91. Ibid., 18–19.

92. Linden and Linden, eds., *Disunion, War, Defeat, and Recovery in Alabama*, 57.

Chapter 2

1. Margaret Josephine Miles Gillis Diary, November 15, 1860, SPR 5, Alabama Department of Archives and History, Montgomery.

2. *Montgomery Advertiser and State Gazette*, December 12, 1860.

3. (Washington, DC) *National Republican*, January 1, 1861, 2; *Decatur Daily*, April 10, 2005.

4. Thomas Peters, "A Cry Out of Alabama," (Boston) *Littell's Living Age* 98, January 26, 1861, 194; (New York) *Commercial Advertiser*, December 29, 1860, 1; *Salem Register*, December 31, 1860, 2; Thomas M. Peters to James Buchanan, December 6, 1860, James Buchanan Papers, State Historical Society of Pennsylvania, Harrisburg, Pennsylvania; William W. Freehling, *The Road to Disunion: Secessionists Triumphant 1854–1861* (New York: Oxford University Press, 2007), 2: 501, 582.

5. (Montpelier) *Vermont Watchman and State Journal*, February 9, 1866.

6. *New York Times*, December 5, 1860, 1.

7. (Selma) *Daily State Sentinel*, November 21, 1867, 2.

8. (Selma) *Alabama State Journal*, December 5, 1860, 2; (Selma) *Alabama State Sentinel*, December 1, 1860; *Daily Selma Messenger*, April 14, 1867, 2; Alston Fitts, *Selma: Queen City of the Black Belt* (Selma, AL: Clairmont Press, 1989), 37–38.

9. Fleming, *Civil War and Reconstruction in Alabama*, 28. Most later Alabama historians have expressly or implicitly accepted Fleming's theory without question. See, e.g., Thornton, *Politics and Power in a Slave Society*, 347, 421–22, 424, 430; Clarence Phillips Denman, *The Secession Movement in Alabama* (Montgomery, AL: Alabama State Dept. of Archives and History, 1933), 93–94 (citing no authority).

10. Chauncey Samuel Boucher, "The Secession and Co-Operation Movements in South Carolina, 1848 to 1852," *Washington University Studies* V (April 1918): 67–138; Freehling, *Road to Disunion: Secessionists at Bay 1776–1854*, I: 510–33; *Charleston Mer-*

cury, February 27, 1851, 2, March 8, 1851, 2; *Charleston Courier*, September 20, 1851, 2. This strategy had also been used in Alabama. Fleming, *Civil War and Reconstruction in Alabama*, 14–15.

11. (Huntsville) *Southern Advocate*, October 3, 1866, 3.

12. Huntsville lawyer-Unionist-Cooperationist Jeremiah Clemens wrote to Kentucky US senator J. J. Crittenden that "my object is not merely to contribute my mite toward saving the Union, but I desire at the same time to obtain ample security for our just rights." He stressed that he believed "redress could be obtained in the Union" but that this would require both time and an understanding by the North that "their fanaticism has passed the limits of patient endurance." Jeremiah Clemens to J. J. Crittenden, November 24, 1860, Crittenden Collection, Library of Congress, Washington, DC; Address of William W. Boyce to the Citizens of York, Chester, Fairfield, Richland, Sumter, and Kershaw Districts, reprinted in (Columbia, SC) *Daily Phoenix*, December 14, 1865, 2.

13. (Selma) *Alabama State Sentinel*, December 15, 1860.

14. Fitts, *Selma*, 38.

15. (Selma) *Alabama State Sentinel*, December 1, 1860.

16. See, e.g., Joseph W. Danielson, *War's Desolating Scourge: The Union's Occupation of North Alabama* (Lawrence: University Press of Kansas, 2012), 5. Part of the interpretive problem in Alabama stems from postwar political rhetoric that first surfaced in 1872. That was an election year in which former Cooperationist David Peter Lewis was the Republican nominee for governor and the Democratic nominee was former secessionist Thomas Hord Herndon. Democrats attempted to undermine Lewis's support in north Alabama by claiming that, like Herndon, Lewis had actually been a proponent of secession in 1860 and 1861 rather than a Unionist. See, e.g., (Huntsville) *Democrat*, September 27, 1872, 2. Lewis denied this and in the end won the election. (Montgomery) *Alabama State Journal*, September 8, 1872, 2; Wiggins, *Scalawag in Alabama Politics*, 79–83.

17. Freehling, *Road to Disunion: Secessionists Triumphant, 1854–1861*, 395–96.

18. *Charleston Mercury*, December 27, 1860, 1; *Montgomery Weekly Mail*, December 10, 1860.

19. (Greensboro) *Alabama Beacon*, December 21, 1860, 1.

20. D. P. Lewis to Thomas Hill Watts, February 9, 1863, Papers of Governor Watts, Alabama Department of Archives and History, Montgomery.

21. (Selma) *Alabama State Sentinel*, December 19, 1860, 1; *Livingston* (Alabama) *Journal*, April 27, 1867, 2; (Selma) *Daily State Sentinel*, December 2, 1867 3.

22. (Selma) *Alabama State Sentinel*, December 19, 1860, 1, December 20, 1860, 3. See, generally, *Daily Selma Messenger*, April 14, 1867, 2.

23. (Greensboro) *Alabama Beacon*, December 21, 1860, 3 ("A Col. Baker introduced a series of resolutions, but the manifestations were so decidedly against them that he withdrew them."); (Selma) *Alabama State Sentinel*, December 19, 1860, 1.

24. *Mobile Daily Advertiser and Register*, December 19, 1866, 2.

25. Beringer et al., *Why the South Lost the Civil War*, 87–88. See also (Greensboro) *Alabama Beacon*, May 2, 1874, 2; (Selma) *Alabama State Sentinel*, October 24, 1867, 2.

26. *Montgomery Mail*, reprinted in *Charleston Mercury*, October 24, 1860, 1. *Charleston Mercury*, November 19, 1860, 1, December 28, 1860, 1.

27. *Eutaw Observer*, reprinted in *Montgomery Advertiser and State Gazette*, November 21, 1860.

28. *Charleston Mercury*, January 24, 1861, 2 (estimating that in Alabama, 26,286 voted for "co-operation").

29. Michael J. Dubin, *United States Presidential Elections, 1788–1860: The Official Results of County and State* (Jefferson, NC: McFarland, 2011), 159.

30. Fitts, *Selma*, 38; Fry, *John Tyler Morgan and the Search for Southern Autonomy*, 12; William L. Barney, *Secessionist Impulse: Alabama and Mississippi in 1860* (Tuscaloosa: University of Alabama Press, 2004), 247.

31. Barney, *Secessionist Impulse*, 273; Danielson, *War's Desolating Scourge*, 12; (Huntsville) *Southern Advocate*, cited in *Montgomery Weekly Post*, January 2, 1861, 4; Faye Acton Axford, ed., *The Journals of Thomas Hubbard Hobbs* (Tuscaloosa: University of Alabama Press, 1976), 225.

32. Dubin, *United States Presidential Elections*, 160.

33. Fuller, *Chaplain of the Confederacy*, 290–91; Barney, *Secessionist Impulse*, 276–78; Jerry C. Oldshue, "Secession Movement in Tuscaloosa County, Alabama" (master's thesis, University of Alabama, 1961), 57, 67–69, 71–77; Secretary of State Election Files, Delegates to State Convention 1860, SG2475, Alabama Department of Archives and History, Montgomery.

34. William R. Smith, *The History and Debates of the Convention of the People of Alabama* (Montgomery, AL: White, Pfister, 1861), 22. Regarding Sheats, see Donald B. Dodd and Wynelle S. Dodd, *Winston: An Antebellum and Civil War History of a Hill County of North Alabama* (Jasper, AL: C. Elliot, 1972), 76–77 (stating that Sheats was only twenty-two at the time); Wesley S. Thompson, *The Free State of Winston: A History of Winston County, Alabama* (Winfield, AL: Parell Press, 1968), 2–4, 29–30.

35. (New Orleans) *Daily Picayune*, December 25, 1860, 1, December 27, 1860, 1, 5. See also, Robert Saunders, *John Archibald Campbell, Southern Moderate* (Tuscaloosa: University of Alabama Press, 1997), 137–41. Regarding Mobile County during this period, see John A. Campbell to Daniel Chandler, November 12, 1860 in "Papers of Hon. John A. Campbell—1861–1865," *Southern Historical Society Papers* 62 (September 1917), 23; *Montgomery Advertiser and State Gazette*, November 28, 1860, 1; (New Orleans) *Daily Picayune*, November 13, 1860, 2, December 11, 1860, 6, December 15, 1860, 6, December 19, 1860, 5, December 20, 1860, 1, December 21, 1860, 8; *Charleston Mercury*, November 19, 1860, 3, December 4, 1860, 3, December 12, 1860, 4, December 19, 1860, 3, December 29, 1860, 1.

36. Augusta Jane Evans to Mrs. L. V. V. French, January 13, 1861, in *A Southern Woman of Letters: The Correspondence of Augusta Jane Evans Wilson*, ed. Rebecca Grant Sexton (Columbia, SC: Parell Press, 2002), 28–30. Regarding Evans, see William

Perry Fidler, *Augusta Evans Wilson, 1835–1909: A Biography* (Tuscaloosa: University of Alabama Press, 1951); Johanna Nicol Shields, *Freedom in a Slave Society: Stories from the Antebellum South* (Cambridge: Cambridge University Press, 2012), 83–92, 256–64. Regarding the views of some Alabama women, see Jennifer Ann Newman Treviño, "'The Aggressions of the North Can Be Borne No Longer': White Alabamian Women during the Secession Crisis and Outbreak of War," in *Yellowhammer War*, ed. Kenneth W. Noe, 34–54.

37. Diary of Colonel Daniel Robinson Hundley, January 1, 1861, SPR III, Alabama Department of Archives and History, Montgomery.

38. Private Journal of Sarah R. Espy, 20.

39. Elizabeth Rhodes Diary, December 31, 1860, Auburn University Library, Special Collections and Archives, Auburn, Alabama.

40. *New York Times*, January 12, 1861, 3.

Chapter 3

1. William W. Freehling, *Prelude to Civil War: The Nullification Controversy in South Carolina, 1816–1836* (New York: Oxford University Press, 1992), 260–300.

2. LeRoy P. Graf, Ralph W. Haskins, and Paul H. Bergeron, eds. *The Papers of Andrew Johnson* (Knoxville: University of Tennessee Press, 1976), IV: 10, 13. See also, George C. Rable, "Anatomy of a Unionist: Andrew Johnson in the Secession Crisis," *Tennessee Historical Quarterly* 32 (Winter 1973): 332, 342–44.

3. *Memphis Avalanche*, quoted in (New Orleans) *Daily Picayune*, December 28, 1860, 3; *Montgomery Weekly Advertiser*, December 28, 1860; Rable, "Anatomy of a Unionist," 343–45.

4. Thomas M. Peters to Andrew Johnson, January 15, 1861, in Graf, et al, *Papers of Andrew Johnson*, ed., IV: 173; Paul Horton, "Submitting to the Shadow of Slavery: The Secession Crisis and Civil War in Alabama's Lawrence County," *Civil War History* 44 (June 1998): 111, 117; Allan Nevins, *The Emergence of Lincoln* (New York: Scribner, 1950), II: 424.

5. Tharin, *Arbitrary Arrests in the South*, 102; Wiggins, *Scalawag in Alabama Politics*, 6.

6. C. Vann Woodward, *The Burden of Southern History* (Baton Rouge: Louisiana State University Press, 1968), 99; *Charleston Mercury*, January 24, 1861, 2.

7. *Charleston Mercury*, January 24, 1861, 2. See Robert Leckie, *None Died in Vain: The Saga of the American Civil War* (New York: HarperCollins, 1990), 87 (stating that secessionists received 35,600 votes and Cooperationists 28,100 but citing no authority).

8. Joseph C. Bradley to Andrew Johnson, March 8, 1861, in *Papers of Andrew Johnson*, ed. Graf, et al., IV: 370–71.

9. (Montgomery) *Alabama State Journal*, September 8, 1872, 2. See also *Montgomery Weekly Post*, January 30, 1861, 3, March 19, 1861, 2.

10. *Montgomery Advertiser and State Gazette*, January 4, 1861, 2.

11. *Charleston Mercury*, January 3, 1861, 1. Regarding the growing crisis at Charleston, see *Charleston Mercury*, January 5, 1861, 1. See also Freehling, *Road to Disunion*, 2: 476–524; David Detzer, *Allegiance: Fort Sumter, Charleston, and the Beginning of the Civil War* (New York: Harcourt, 2001), 162–210; William C. Davis, *First Blood: Fort Sumter to Bull Run* (Alexandria, VA: Time-Life Books, 1983).

12. *Charleston Mercury*, January 5, 1861, 1; Freehling, *Road to Disunion*, 2: 482–83.

13. *Charleston Mercury*, January 10, 1861, 3; *New York Times*, January 12, 1861, 3; Freehling, *Road to Disunion*, 2: 483.

14. *Mobile Register*, January 5, 1861; (New Orleans) *Daily Picayune*, January 5, 1861, 6, 10, January 10, 1861, 5; *New York Times*, January 12, 1861, 3; *Montgomery Advertiser and State Gazette*, January 9, 1861, 1, January 15, 1861, 2; *Charleston Mercury*, January 10, 1861, 3; *Cleveland Morning Leader*, January 12, 1861, 2; Freehling, *Road to Disunion*, 2: 484; Arthur William Bergeron, "The Confederate Defense of Mobile, 1861–1865" (PhD diss., Louisiana State University, 1980), 9–10. See also *Nobel & Bro. v. Cullom*, 44 Ala. 554, 579 (1870) (an opinion by Thomas Peters discussing this preemptive strike).

15. *Montgomery Weekly Post*, January 8, 1860.

16. Clement Anselm Evans, ed., *Confederate Military History: A Library of Confederate States History* (Atlanta, GA: Confederate Pub. Co. 1899), XII: 34–36; Fuller, *Chaplain to the Confederacy*, 290–92.

17. *Tuskaloosa Gazette*, December 8, 1900, 4; *Montgomery Advertiser and State Gazette*, December 26, 1860, 1; *Charleston Mercury*, January 8, 1861, 3; Smith, *History and Debates of the Convention of the People of Alabama*, 23; Barney, *Secessionist Impulse*, 298; Edwin I. Hatch, "William McLin Brooks, 1815–1893," *Alabama Lawyer* 16 (July, 1955): 324–35.

18. Mildred Easby-Smith, *William Russell Smith of Alabama, His Life and Works* (Philadelphia: Dolphin Press, 1931), 98.

19. Ibid., 100; *Montgomery Advertiser and State Gazette*, January 9, 1861.

20. *Charleston Mercury*, March 16, 1861, 1.

21. *Nashville Daily Union*, April 15, 1865, 2 (publishing a letter from Clemens explaining his strategy during this period). Clemens resigned from that position on October 30, 1861. Jere Clemens to A. B. Moore, October 30, 1861, Papers of Governor Moore, Alabama Department of Archives and History, Montgomery.

22. James Edmonds Saunders, *Early Settlers of Alabama* (New Orleans: Graham & Son, printers, 1899), 1: 111.

23. *Montgomery Advertiser and State Gazette*, January 9, 1861; *Charleston Mercury*, January 9, 1861, 3; Smith, *History and Debates of the Convention of Alabama*, 43–49.

24. Smith, *History and Debates of the Convention of Alabama*, 77–78; *Official Journal of the Constitutional Convention of Alabama, 1861* (Montgomery, AL: Shorter and Reid, 1861), 12.

25. Smith, *History and Debates of the Convention of Alabama*, 55–56.

26. A. B. Moore to Capt. R. A. Rodes, January 8, 1861, Governor Moore Papers,

Alabama Department of Archives and History, Montgomery; *Montgomery Advertiser and State Gazette*, January 15, 1861; *Charleston Mercury*, January 10, 1861, 3, January 12, 1861, 2; (New Orleans) *Daily Picayune*, January 11, 1861, 6; *Montgomery Weekly Post*, January 16, 1861, 2; Freehling, *Road to Disunion*, II: 484–88.

27. (New Orleans) *Daily Picayune*, January 10, 1861, 5–6; *Charleston Mercury*, January 10, 1861, 1; Freehling, *Road to Disunion*, II: 486–88.

28. *Charleston Mercury*, January 9, 1861, 1.

29. Ibid., January 10, 1861, 1.

30. Ibid., January 11, 1861, 3; Smith, *History and Debates of the Convention of Alabama*, 57.

31. Smith, *History and Debates of the Convention of Alabama*, 58–63, 67, 69.

32. Ibid., 70–72, 74.

33. *New York Times*, January 23, 1861, 4; *Cleveland Morning Leader*, January 25, 1861, 2.

34. Smith, *History and Debates of the Convention of Alabama*, 76–90.

35. *Ordinances and Constitution of the State of Alabama, with the Constitution of the Provisional Government and of the Confederate States of America* (Montgomery, AL: Barrett, Wimbish & Co., Steam Printers and Binders, 1861), 3–4, 118; Axford, ed., *Journals of Thomas Hubbard Hobbs*, 226; *New York Times*, January 28, 1861, 2; *Charleston Mercury*, January 12, 1861, 3; (New Orleans) *Daily Picayune*, January 12, 1861, 6; *Montgomery Advertiser and State Gazette*, January 12, 1861; *New York Herald*, January 12, 1861, 3; *Memphis Daily Appeal*, February 14, 1861, 1. See also Thornton, *Politics and Power in a Slave Society*, 430.

36. W. H. Mitchell to his wife, January 11, 1861, in *Alabama: A Documentary History to 1900*, by Lucille Griffith, 382–83 (Tuscaloosa: University of Alabama Press, 1972); Fuller, *Chaplain to the Confederacy*, 293; Easby-Smith, *William Russell Smith*, 103; Rogers, *Confederate Home Front*, 20–21.

37. Linden and Linden, eds., *Disunion*, 58.

38. Easby-Smith, *William Russell Smith*, 102.

39. Thomas M. Peters to Andrew Johnson, *Papers of Andrew Johnson*, ed. Graf, et al., IV: 173; Horton, "Submitting to the Shadow of Slavery," 119; Nevins, *Emergence of Lincoln*, II: 424. Peters also wrote to Stephen Douglas. Thomas M. Peters to Stephen A. Douglas, January 16, 1861, Stephen Douglas Papers, University of Chicago Library.

40. Hugh Lawson Clay to C. C. Clay Jr., January 11, 1861, Clay Papers, David M. Rubenstein Rare Book and Manuscript Library, Duke University, Durham, NC; Denman, *Secession Movement in Alabama*, 149; Elbert L. Watson, "The Story of Nickajack," *Alabama Review* 20 (January 1967), 17.

41. (Montgomery) *Alabama State Journal*, September 8, 1872, 2. Axford, ed., *Journals of Thomas Hubbard Hobbs*, 226.

42. *Montgomery Advertiser and State Gazette*, January 12, 1861; *Charleston Mercury*, January 28, 1861, 1.

43. Smith, *History and Debates of the Convention of Alabama*, 160–61; *Memphis Daily*

Appeal, January 29, 1861, 2; *Montgomery Daily Advertiser*, October 2, 1872, 2; (Montgomery) *Alabama State Journal*, October 16, 1872, 1.

44. Thornton, *Politics and Power in a Slave Society*, 427–28, 435; Easby-Smith, *William Russell Smith*, 116; Axford, ed., *Journals of Thomas Hubbard Hobbs*, 227.

45. (Tuscaloosa) *Independent Monitor*, February 1, 1861; (New Orleans) *Daily Picayune*, January 25, 1861, 6; *Nashville Daily Union*, April 15, 1865, 2.

46. (New Orleans) *Daily Picayune*, February 8, 1861, 10; *Charleston Mercury*, January 23, 1861, 3.

47. Axford, ed., *Journals of Thomas Hubbard Hobbs*, 228–29 (a Union flag was raised at the Limestone County courthouse on January 22); (Huntsville) *Democrat*, February 20, 1861, 3; *Charleston Mercury*, February 26, 1861, 1; George C. Rable, *The Confederate Republic: A Revolution against Politics* (Chapel Hill: University of North Carolina Press, 1994), 45

48. James L. Pugh to William P. Miles, January 24, 1861, quoted in Barney, *Secessionist Impulse*, 304–5. See also *Charleston Mercury*, December 11, 1860, 4.

49. Benjamin Fitzpatrick et al. to Isaac W. Hayne, January 15, 1861, in *The Papers of Jefferson Davis: 1861*, ed. Lynda Lasswell Crist, 7: 10–12 (Baton Rouge: Louisiana State University Press, 1992); David M. Potter, *Lincoln and His Party in the Secession Crisis* (Baton Rouge: Louisiana State University Press, 1995), 359; Saunders, *John Archibald Campbell*, 143. See also *Charleston Mercury*, January 31, 1861, 1, February 18, 1861, 4.

50. See, e.g., *Charleston Mercury*, January 25, 1861, 1, February 2, 1861, 1, February 12, 1861, 1; *Montgomery Advertiser and State Gazette*, March 13, 1861; *Selma Weekly Issue*, reprinted in (Washington, DC) *Daily National Intelligencer*, February 27, 1861. See also, (London) *Times*, February 19, 1861, 7 (reporting a speech by William Yancey on this subject); Potter, *Lincoln and His Party in the Secession Crisis*, 219–32. See, generally, Rable, *Confederate Republic*, 44.

Chapter 4

1. Private Journal of Sarah R. Espy, 22.

2. Saunders, *John Archibald Campbell*, 145.

3. See *Montgomery Weekly Post*, January 30, 1861, 1.

4. Saunders, *John Archibald Campbell*, 144.

5. Potter, *Lincoln and His Party in the Secession Crisis*, 254, 358–59.

6. (Huntsville) *Democrat*, February 20, 1861, 3; *Cleveland Morning Leader*, June 7, 1865, 2; *Harper's Weekly*, reprinted in *Highland* (Ohio) *Weekly News*, April 6, 1865, 2; Crist, ed., *Papers of Jefferson Davis*, 7: 42.

7. Donald Stoker, *The Grand Design: Strategy and the U.S. Civil War* (New York: Oxford University Press, 2010), 232.

8. Davis and Lasswell, eds., *Papers of Jefferson Davis*, 7: 49. See also Paul D. Escott, *The Confederacy: The Slaveholders' Failed Venture* (Santa Barbara, CA: Praeger, 2010), 2.

9. William Warren Rogers Jr., "Safety Lies Only in Silence: Secrecy and Sub-

version in Montgomery's Unionist Community," in *Enemies of the Country: New Perspectives on Unionists in the Civil War South*, ed. John C. Inscoe and Robert C. Kenzer (Athens: University of Georgia Press, 2001), 172–87.

10. David Hubbard to Andrew B. Moore, February 23, 1861, Governor Moore Papers, quoted in Thornton, *Politics and Power in a Slave Society*, 438.

11. Wiggins, *Scalawag in Alabama Politics*, 53; Ezra J. Warner and W. Buck Yearns, *Biographical Register of the Confederate Congress*, 150–51 (Baton Rouge: Louisiana State University Press, 1975); *Journal of the Congress of the Confederate States of America, 1861–1865* (Washington, DC: Government Printing Office, 1904), I: 143, 159.

12. William C. Davis, *Look Away!: A History of the Confederate States of America* (New York: Simon & Schuster, 2002), 82–83; Rable, *Confederate Republic*, 72; Escott, *Confederacy*, 9; *Charleston Mercury*, February 22, 1861, 3; *Montgomery Advertiser and State Gazette*, February 27, 1861, 1; (New Orleans) *Daily Picayune*, February 22, 1861, 2.

13. *Tuscaloosa Flag of the Union*, April 25, 1838, 2, October 31, 1838, 2; *Charleston Mercury*, April 19, 1839, 2, April 22, 1857, 2, May 5, 1857, 2, May 11, 1857, 2; *Mobile Register and Journal*, June 14, 1849, 2; *Florence Gazette*, July 21, 1849, 3; (Huntsville) *Southern Advocate*, June 11, 1851, 3, June 25, 1851, 3, March 19, 1856, 3, April 9, 1856, 2, June 11, 1856, 3, April 2, 1857, 3, April 30, 1857, 3, June 4, 1857, 3; Robert C. Black, *The Railroads of the Confederacy* (Chapel Hill: University of North Carolina Press, 1998), 139.

14. *Charleston Mercury*, February 8, 1861, 1. Fort Pickens guarded Pensacola, Florida's harbor, which was served by the Alabama and Florida Railroad, whose owners in Montgomery saw similar benefits if Pickens were neutralized.

15. *Charleston Mercury*, February 18, 1861, 4.

16. Ibid., February 12, 1861, 1.

17. Ibid., February 12, 1861, 4. See also ibid., February 13, 1861, 4, February 15, 1861, 4, February 18, 1861, 1, 4, February 22, 1861, 1, February 23, 1861, 1, February 25, 1861, 1.

18. Ibid., February 23, 1861, 1.

19. Ibid., March 5, 1861, 3; (New Orleans) *Daily Picayune*, March 5, 1861, 1, March 29, 1861, 12; *Daily Columbus* (Georgia) *Enquirer*, March 6, 1861, 2.

20. *Charleston Mercury*, March 5, 1861, 3, March 13, 1861, 3; *Daily Columbus* (Georgia) *Enquirer*, March 16, 1861, 2.

21. *Charleston Mercury*, March 7, 1861, 1.

22. Private Journal of Sarah R. Espy, 24.

23. *Nashville Democrat*, reprinted in (Washington, DC) *National Republican*, February 8, 1861, 2; *Nashville Union and American*, January 26, 1861, 2.

24. Potter, *Lincoln and His Party in the Secession Crisis*, 312–13; William W. Freehling and Craig Simpson, eds., *Showdown in Virginia: The 1861 Convention and the Fate of the Union* (Charlottesville: University of Virginia Press, 2010).

25. Axford, ed., *Journals of Thomas Hubbard Hobbs*, 230–31. A similar rally had earlier been orchestrated by secessionists in Lawrence County, *Montgomery Weekly Post*, February 27, 1861, 2; (Montgomery) *Alabama State Journal*, September 8, 1872, 2, and

another would occur in Madison County. Thornton, *Politics and Power in a Slave Society*, 438–39.

26. Axford, ed., *Journals of Thomas Hubbard Hobbs*, 231–32. The nature of the guarantees they expected Republicans to give is unclear. See also (Athens) *Union Banner*, March 20, 1861, cited in *Daily Columbus* (Georgia) *Enquirer*, March 29, 1861, 2; (Athens) *Union Banner*, reprinted in *Daily Columbus* (Georgia) *Enquirer*, April 4, 1861, 2.

27. (Tuscumbia) *North Alabamian*, March 22, 1861, reprinted in (Warren, Ohio) *Western Reserve Chronicle*, April 3, 1861, 2; *Daily Columbus* (Georgia) *Enquirer*, March 29, 1861, 2.

28. *Moulton Democrat*, March 1, 1861, reprinted in *Athens* (Tennessee) *Post*, March 8, 1861, 2.

29. *Montgomery Weekly Post*, March 19, 1861, 2; (Tuscaloosa) *Independent Monitor*, March 29, 1861, 1, 2, April 5, 1861, 1.; (Greensboro) *Alabama Beacon*, March 29, 1861, 2, April 5, 1861, 2; *Daily Columbus* (Georgia) *Enquirer*, March 20, 1861, 2.

30. (Tuscaloosa) *Independent Monitor*, reprinted in (Washington, DC) *Daily National Intelligencer*, February 27, 1861, and *Weekly Raleigh* (North Carolina) *Register*, March 6, 1861, *Daily Nashville Patriot*, March 8, 1861, 2, *Athens* (Tennessee) *Post*, March 8, 1861, 2. See also (Tuscaloosa) *Independent Monitor*, February 1, 1861, 2.

31. *Tuscaloosa Observer*, April 3, 1861, 2; (Tuscaloosa) *Independent Monitor*, March 29, 1861, 2; Easby-Smith, *William Russell Smith*, 118. See, generally, *Charleston Mercury*, March 27, 1861, 1.

32. Easby-Smith, *William Russell Smith*, 118–23. See also, Rable, *Confederate Republic*, 77.

33. (Tuscumbia) *North Alabamian*, reprinted in *Daily Nashville Patriot*, March 8, 1861, 2.

34. *Daily Columbus* (Georgia) *Enquirer*, March 26, 1861, 2.

35. *Montgomery Advertiser and State Gazette*, November 14, 1860, 1. *Charleston Mercury*, September 17, 1860, 4.

36. *New York Times*, January 24, 1861, 2.

37. *Montgomery Weekly Post*, March 20, 1861, 1; *Charleston Mercury*, March 18, 1861, 3; (Greensboro) *Alabama Beacon*, March 22, 1861, 3; *Selma Morning Reporter*, April 9, 1861, 2.

38. (Huntsville) *Southern Advocate*, October 22, 1846, 3; (Tuscaloosa) *Independent Monitor*, March 12, 1841, 3.

39. (Huntsville) *Southern Advocate*, April 2, 1861, reprinted in *Daily Columbus* (Georgia) *Enquirer*, April 7, 1861, 2; *Selma Morning Reporter*, August 9, 1861, 2; (New Orleans) *Daily Picayune*, March 29, 1861, 12; *New York Times*, April 6, 1861, 1; (Selma) *Alabama State Sentinel*, June 29, 1860; *Daily Columbus* (Georgia) *Enquirer*, March 29, 1861, 2; (Dalton, Georgia) *Huntsville Confederate*, reprinted in *Charleston Mercury*, January 28, 1864, 1; *Journal of the Executive Proceedings of the Senate of the United States* (Washington, DC: Government Printing Office, 1887), 344 (March 26, 1861). Regarding Cobb, see David Ritchey, "Williamson R.W. Cobb: Rattler of Tinware and Crockery for Peace," *Alabama Historical Quarterly* 36 (Summer 1974): 112.

40. Axford, ed., *Journals of Thomas Hubbard Hobbs*, 234. See, e.g., *Selma Morning Reporter*, March 4, 1861, 2; (Greensboro) *Alabama Beacon*, April 12, 1861, 2, April 26, 1861, 2; (New Orleans) *Daily Picayune*, March 29, 1861, 12, April 9, 1861, 1.

41. *Montgomery Mail*, March 30, 1861, reprinted in *Nashville Union and American*, April 3, 1861, 2.

42. *Daily Columbus* (Georgia) *Enquirer*, March 30, 1861, 2.

43. *Charleston Mercury*, March 9, 1861, 4.

44. Ibid., March 6, 1861, 1.

45. Ibid., February 12, 1861, 1, February 13, 1861, 4, February 15, 1861, 4, February 18, 1861, p 1, 4, February 23, 1861, 1, February 25, 1861, 1.

46. *Mobile Mercury*, reprinted in *Charleston Mercury*, February 18, 1861, 4.

47. *Montgomery Daily Advertiser*, April 15, 1893.

48. *New York Times*, March 24, 1864, 5; *New York World*, reprinted in *Daily Columbus* (Georgia) *Enquirer*, April 15, 1864, 2; McPherson, *Battle Cry of Freedom*, 273; W. A. Swanberg, *First Blood: The Story of Fort Sumter* (New York: Scribner, 1957), 286; (Washington, DC) *Daily National Republican*, March 25, 1864, 1 (quoting a speech in Huntsville, Alabama, by Jeremiah Clemens on March 12, 1864). Regarding Gilchrist, see Thomas McAdory Owen, *History of Alabama and Dictionary of Alabama Biography* (Chicago: S.J. Clarke, 1921), 3: 654, William Garrett, *Reminiscences of Public Men in Alabama: For Thirty Years* (Atlanta: Plantation Publ. Co. Press, 1872), 500–501, and *Charleston Mercury*, July 14, 1852, 2.

49. *Charleston Mercury*, April 13, 1861, 1, April 18, 1861, 1; *Selma Reporter*, reprinted in *Memphis Daily Appeal*, April 14, 1861, 2; *Montgomery Weekly Advertiser*, April 13, 1861; (New Orleans) *Daily Picayune*, March 24, 1861, 5, March 26, 1861, 5, April 4, 1861, 1, April 8, 1861, 4, April 13, 1861, 1, April 15, 1861, 1.

50. *Tuskaloosa Gazette*, May 6, 1886, 1.

51. *Charleston Mercury*, February 12, 1861, 1, February 22, 1861, 1.

52. L. P. Walker to P. G. T. Beauregard, April 10, 1861, reprinted in Malcolm C. McMillan, ed., *The Alabama Confederate Reader* (Tuscaloosa: University of Alabama Press, 1963).

53. *Charleston Mercury*, April 13, 1861, 1.

54. (Montgomery) *Confederation*, April 14, 1861, reprinted in *Daily Columbus* (Georgia) *Enquirer*, April 17, 1861, 2 (the reporter was a correspondent to the *Pensacola Observer*), *Charleston Mercury*, April 18, 1861, 1; (New Orleans) *Daily Picayune*, April 16, 1861, 1; *Mobile Tribune*, reprinted in (New Orleans) *Daily Picayune*, April 18, 1861, 1, 4. See, generally, Mark E. Neely Jr., *Southern Rights: Political Prisoners and the Myth of Confederate Constitutionalism* (Charlottesville: University of Virginia Press, 1999), 1; Patricia G. McNeely, Debra Reddin van Tuyll, and Henry H. Schulte, *Knights of the Quill: Confederate Correspondents and Their Civil War Reporting* (West Lafayette, IN: Purdue University Press, 2010), 181–86; Kenneth W. Noe, *Reluctant Rebels: The Confederates Who Joined the Army after 1861* (Chapel Hill: University of North Carolina Press, 2010), 153–54.

55. *Charleston Mercury*, April 15, 1861, 3; *Montgomery Weekly Advertiser*, April 13, 1861. See also, Detzer, *Allegiance*, 284–85.

56. *Daily Columbus* (Georgia) *Enquirer*, May 14, 1861, 2. See, generally, David Detzer, *Dissonance: The Turbulent Days between Fort Sumter and Bull Run* (Orlando, FL: Harcourt, 2006), 224–30; (New Orleans) *Daily Picayune*, April 16, 1861, 1.

57. (Troy) *Southern Advertiser*, September 30, 1864, 2.

58. *Charleston Mercury*, April 15, 1861, 3, April 18, 1861, 3; *Montgomery Weekly Advertiser*, April 17, 1861; Geoffrey Perret, *Lincoln's War: The Untold Story of America's Greatest President As Commander In Chief* (New York: Random House, 2004), 33 (discussing Lincoln's fear of invasion); Michael Burlingame, *Abraham Lincoln: A Life* (Baltimore: Johns Hopkins University Press, 2008), II: 132–33 (also on Lincoln's fear of invasion); Kenneth Winkle, *Lincoln's Citadel: The Civil War in Washington, D.C.*, (New York: W. W. Norton, 2013), 142–52.

59. *New York Times*, January 12, 1861, 4. For a discussion of Northern public opinion, see Russell McClintock, *Lincoln and the Decision for War: The Northern Response to Secession* (Chapel Hill: University of North Carolina Press, 2008), 227–37.

60. Richard B. Harwell, ed., *Kate: The Journal of a Confederate Nurse* (Baton Rouge: Louisiana State University Press, 1959), 25.

61. Elizabeth Rhodes Diary, April 13, 1861, Auburn University Library Special Collections, Auburn, Alabama.

62. Private Journal of Sarah R. Espy, 25–26.

63. *Montgomery Weekly Mail*, April 12, 1861, 1.

64. Ibid., April 18, 1861, 2.

65. (Baltimore) *Sun*, February 5, 1861, 1; *Albany* (New York) *Evening Journal*, February 8, 1861, 2.

66. Diary of Daniel Robinson Hundley, May 18-May 31, 1861, June 9, 1861, SPR 111, Alabama Department of Archives and History, Montgomery.

67. Saunders, *John Archibald Campbell*, 152–53 (Campbell's letter of resignation was dated April 26, 1861). See also (New Orleans) *Daily Picayune*, May 8, 1861, 1.

68. See, e.g., Willis Brewer, *Alabama, Her History, Resources, War Record, and Public Men: From 1540 to 1872* (Montgomery, AL: Barrett & Brown, 1872), 241; Owen, *History of Alabama and Dictionary of Alabama Biography*, 3: 582; Samuel L. Webb and Margaret E. Armbrester, *Alabama Governors: A Political History of the State* (Tuscaloosa: University of Alabama Press, 2001), 47–48.

69. See, e.g., Ruth Ketring Nuermberger, *Clays of Alabama: A Planter-Lawyer Politician Family* (Lexington: University of Kentucky Press, 1958), 189–90. Fitzpatrick later turned down an appointment to serve in an official capacity in connection with the impressments of private property. T. H. Watts to Hon. B. Fitzpatrick, November 19, 1864, and Benjamin Fitzpatrick to Thomas H. Watts, November 28, 1864, Papers of Governor Watts, Alabama Department of Archives and History, Montgomery.

70. (Huntsville) *Democrat*, June 12, 1861, 4; *Daily Columbus* (Georgia) *Enquirer*, June 11, 1861, 1 (listing Jemison's stated reasons for his withdrawal).

71. *Tuscaloosa Observer*, April 3, 1861, 3. See, generally, John Christopher Schwab, *The Confederate States of America 1861–1865: A Financial and Industrial History of the South during the Civil War* (New York: Burt Franklin, 1968), 6–7.

72. *Tuscaloosa Observer*, April 3, 1861, 3. See also (Tuscaloosa) *Independent Monitor*,

March 29, 1861, 2, May 17, 1861, 2. See, generally, (Huntsville) *Democrat*, April 24, 1861, 3 (George Beirne was appointed a commissioner in north Alabama).

73. See, generally, Hermoine Dannelly Jackson, "Life and Times of Robert Jemison, Jr. during the Civil War and Reconstruction" (master's thesis, University of Alabama, 1942), 68 (stating that Jemison purchased Confederate bonds).

74. (Huntsville) *Democrat*, June 12, 1861, 3–4; Robert M. Patton to Governor Andrew Barry Moore, June 28, 1861, Governor Moore Papers, Alabama Department of Archives and History, Montgomery; (Greensboro) *Alabama Beacon*, July 19, 1861, 2; Owen, *History of Alabama and Dictionary of Alabama Biography*, 4: 1328; Diary of Daniel Robinson Hundley, June 28, 1861, SPR 111, Alabama Department of Archives and History, Montgomery.

75. *Mobile Advertiser and Register*, September 24, 1861, 2; Nuermberger, *Clays of Alabama*, 186.

76. Owen, *History of Alabama and Dictionary of Alabama Biography*, 3: 932.

77. (Huntsville) *Southern Advocate*, April 24, 1861, 3. See also *Montgomery Weekly Mail*, April 19, 1861, April 29, 1861; (Greensboro) *Alabama Beacon*, August 23, 1861, 2; *Mobile Advertiser and Register*, October 6, 1861, 1. See also, John C. Carter, ed., *Welcome the Hour of Conflict: William Cowan McClellan and the 9th Alabama* (Tuscaloosa, 2007), 18–19 (regarding Houston); Easby-Smith, *William Russell Smith of Alabama*, 134–41.

Chapter 5

1. Moore, *History of Alabama*, 428.

2. McMillan, *Disintegration of a Confederate State*, 22; Griffith, *Alabama*, 421; Rogers et al., *Alabama*, 229.

3. *Mobile Advertiser and Register*, October 1, 1864, 2.

4. William McLin Brooks to Jefferson Davis, May 18, 1861, quoted in David Williams, *Bitterly Divided: The South's Inner Civil War* (New York: New Press, 2008), 48, and Escott, *Confederacy*, 23.

5. Williams, *Bitterly Divided*, 50.

6. William Warren Rogers Jr., "Safety Lies Only in Silence: Secrecy and Subversion in Montgomery's Unionist Community," in *Enemies of the Country: New Perspectives on Unionists in the Civil War South*, ed. John C. Inscoe and Robert C. Kenzer, 172.

7. Michael W. Fitzgerald, "From Unionists to Scalawags: Elite Dissent in Civil War Mobile," *Alabama Review* 55 (Spring 2002): 106–21.

8. (Tuscaloosa) *Reconstructionist*, quoted in (Selma) *Alabama State Sentinel*, September 26, 1867, 3, and *New York Herald*, November 29, 1867.

9. (Tuscaloosa) *Independent Monitor*, December 18, 1867, 2.

10. United States Senate Reports, No. 22, "Alabama Testimony in Ku Klux Report," 42nd Cong., 2nd Sess., vol. IX: 1850, 1864–65, 1977, 1980 (hereafter cited as "Alabama Testimony").

11. "Alabama Testimony," 1977.

12. "Alabama Testimony," 1864–1865, 1977, 1980.

13. Lewis E. Parsons to Andrew Johnson, October 4, 1865, in Graf, et al., ed., *Pa-*

pers of Andrew Johnson, 9: 186–87. See also J. A. Elmore to L. E. Parsons, September 13, 1865, and Price Williams to S. H. Dixon, September 16, 1865, Papers of Governor Parsons, Alabama Department of Archives and History, Montgomery.

14. Nicholas Davis to Andrew Johnson, June 17, 1865, quoted in Christine Dee, "Trying James Hickman: The Politics of Loyalty in a Civil War Community," *Alabama Review* 58 (April 2005): 83, 103. See also Fitzgerald, "From Unionists to Scalawags," 106, 108–15; Storey, *Loyalty and Loss*, 63–65.

15. Daily Journal of Joshua Burns Moore, 88.

16. *Daily Columbus* (Georgia) *Enquirer*, June 21, 1861, 2.

17. See, generally, McMillan, *Disintegration of a Confederate State*, 22; Thompson, *Free State of Winston*, 27–32; Dodd and Dodd, *Winston*, 82.

18. Compare Thompson, *Free State of Winston*, 3, 31 (stating that it occurred in 1861) and Wiggins, *Scalawag in Alabama Politics*, 6 (same), with Bessie Martin, *A Rich Man's War, A Poor Man's Fight: Desertion of Alabama Troops from the Confederate Army* (Tuscaloosa: University of Alabama Press, 2003), 100 (asserting that it occurred in 1862); Dodd and Dodd, *Winston*, 87–88 (same); Alan Sewell, "Disent: The Free State of Winston," *Civil War Times Illustrated* 20 (December 1981): 30 (same); Donald B. Dodd, "The Free State of Winston," *Alabama Heritage* 28 (Spring, 1993): 12–14 (same); Charles Rice, *Hard Times: The Civil War in Huntsville and North Alabama* (Huntsville, AL: Old Huntsville, 1995), 144. Regarding Alabama Unionists generally, see Margaret M. Storey, "Civil War Unionists and the Political Culture of Loyalty in Alabama, 1860–1861," *Journal of Southern History* 69 (February 2003): 71. Note: (same) means that one author's conclusion is the same as that of the previously cited author.

19. See J. H. Vail to A. B. Moore, July 8, 1861, Petition of Citizens of Byler Road to A. B. Moore, July 8, 1861, L. W. Hampton to A. B. Moore, July 9, 1061, Governor Moore Papers, Alabama Department of Archives and History, Montgomery. See also, Dodd and Dodd, *Winston*, 81; Thompson, *Free State of Winston*, 27–32.

20. Thompson, *Free State of Winston*, 3–4; Dod and Dodd, *Winston*, 88. That idea may have been voiced by those in attendance as a spoof in response to a report in the pro-secession Huntsville *Democrat* regarding a March 2 meeting in Franklin County, Tennessee, where a resolution was adopted declaring the county out of the Union when Tennessee voters had initially refused to vote in favor of a referendum calling for a secession convention. (Huntsville) *Democrat*, March 27, 1860, 4.

21. Thompson, *Free State of Winston*, 4; Dodd and Dodd, *Winston*, 88.

22. (Huntsville) *Democrat*, February 12, 1862, 4; Hugh C. Bailey, "Disloyalty in Early Confederate Alabama," *Journal of Southern History* 23 (November 1957): 522–24; Thompson, *Free State of Winston*, 32–39; Dodd and Dodd, *Winston*, 83.

23. James Bell to Henry Bell, April 21, 1861, Governor Moore Papers, Alabama Department of Archives and History, Montgomery. See also, Dodd and Dodd, *Winston*, 79; Joel Sanford Mize, *Unionists of the Warrior Mountains of Alabama* (Lakewood, CO: Dixie Historical Research and Education Publication, 2004), Vol. B: 136–38; Bruce Levine, *The Fall of the House of Dixie: The Civil War and the Social Revolution that Transformed the South* (New York: Random House, 2013), 71.

24. (Huntsville) *Democrat*, March 6, 1861, 3.

25. Williams, *Bitterly Divided*, 48.

26. A. B. Moore to Josephus Hampton, July 12, 1861, Governor Moore Papers, Alabama Department of Archives and History, Montgomery. One reason for Moore's reluctance to bring the hammer down was probably the looming state elections that would, among other things, decide the legislators who would then select Alabama's first two Confederate senators. Moore aspired to the seat informally allotted to south Alabama, but to win it he would need north Alabama's support in order to beat William Yancey. *Mobile Advertiser and Register*, October 22, 1861, 2; *Charleston Courier*, October 17, 1861, 1.

27. Axford, ed., *Journals of Thomas Hubbard Hobbs*, 235–39.

28. George S. Houston to A. B. Moore, August 1, 1861, August 21, 1861, Governor Moore Papers, Alabama Department of Archives and History, Montgomery.

29. *Mobile Advertiser and Register*, July 24, 1861, 1; *Charleston Mercury*, July 22, 1861, 1.

30. (Carrollton) *West Alabamian*, August 14, 1861, 2. A "charge bayonets" means a charge of a body of soldiers with bayonets fixed on the ends of their rifles.

31. Ibid., October 30, 1861, 2.

32. *Richmond Enquirer*, July 26, 1861.

33. *Montgomery Advertiser and State Gazette*, June 19, 1861, 3.

34. David Detzer, *Donnybrook: The Battle of Bull Run, 1861* (Orlando, FL: Harcourt, 2004), 435–36 (stating that Confederate casualties officially totalled 1,969, including 387 killed and 1,582 wounded, but suggesting it was much higher); Easby-Smith, *William Russell Smith*, 132 (stating that Union Army losses were 481 killed and 1,011 wounded; Confederate losses were 269 killed and 1,483 wounded).

35. *Mobile Advertiser and Register*, August 8, 1861, 1. This term is meant to be "minié balls," conical-headed rifle bullets commonly used during this period.

36. Ibid., July 26, 1861, 2 (reporting the death of ten men from a Lauderdale County company).

37. Ibid., July 27, 1861, 2.

38. *Montgomery Mail*, July 24, 1861, reprinted in (New Orleans) *Daily Picayune*, July 27, 1861; *Mobile Advertiser and Register*, August 2, 1861, 2.

39. *Mobile Advertiser and Register*, July 30, 1861, 1.

40. *Selma Daily Reporter*, July 25, 1861, 2. In one of the many ironies of the war, the death toll of the Governor's Guards would have been greater but for the efforts of a slave to save the life of his master. According to a newspaper account, a "federal soldier was in the act of bayoneting the captain, when the faithful boy fell upon the soldier with his bowie-knife and killed him. The captain escaped with a scratch." *Memphis Daily Appeal*, August 10, 1861, 2.

41. Hubbs, ed., *Voices from Company D: Diaries by the Greensboro Guards, Fifth Alabama Infantry Regiment, Army of Northern Virginia* (Athens: University of Georgia Press, 2003), 23.

42. *Mobile Advertiser and Register*, July 24, 1861, 2; C. Vann Woodward, ed., *Mary Chesnut's Civil War* (New Haven, CT: Yale University Press, 1981), 111.

43. *Mobile Advertiser and Register*, July 25, 1861, 1. See also, (Huntsville) *Democrat*, July 24, 1861, 3.

44. *Mobile Advertiser and Register*, July 27, 1861, 1.

45. The military historian Bevin Alexander concluded that the Confederates could have consolidated their victory, captured Washington, and possibly ended the war at this point. Bevin Alexander, *How the South Could Have Won the Civil War: The Fatal Errors That Led to Confederate Defeat* (New York: Crown Publishers, 2007), 8–32.

46. *Mobile Advertiser and Register*, August 3, 1861, 1.

47. Gary W. Gallagher, *The Confederate War* (Cambridge, MA: Harvard University Press, 1997), 17–18.

48. See, e.g., Gary W. Gallagher, *Becoming Confederates: Paths to a New National Loyalty* (Athens, University of Georgia Press, 2013), 2–6, 93; Kristopher A. Teters, "Fighting for the Cause? An Examination of the Motivations of Alabama's Confederate Soldiers from a Class Perspective," in *Yellowhammer War*, ed. Kenneth W. Noe, 99. In the end, one is left to speculate on the key factors. There were, of course, no scientific opinion polls conducted during the war. And the available collections of letters and diaries from this period are insufficient to create an adequate sample size. This may explain why some historians have wisely avoided making conclusions in this interpretational thicket. See, e.g., Rable, *Confederate Republic*, 2, 45–46. Regarding the concept of Confederate nationalism, see Noe, *Reluctant Rebels*, 24–25.

49. See, e.g., J. P. Morgan to Governor Moore, August 8, 1861, Papers of A. B. Moore, Alabama Department of Archives and History, Montgomery (reporting the arrest of a merchant in Montevallo); *Charleston Mercury*, August 24, 1861, 3 (arrest of business agent in Eufaula); *Daily Columbus* (Georgia) *Enquirer*, June 1, 1861, 3, August 1, 1861, 3, August 3, 1861, 3, August 15, 1861, 3, September 3, 1861, 3, December 20, 1861, 3, June 2, 1862, 2; (Eufaula) *Spirit of the South*, reprinted in *Daily Columbus* (Georgia) *Enquirer*, June 4, 1862, 2.

50. *Journal of the Congress of the Confederate States of America*, I: 319–20, 327, 388–89, 798, 803, 833. See also *Montgomery Advertiser and State Gazette*, August 14, 1861, 2, August 21, 1861; *Mobile Advertiser and Register*, August 16, 1861, 2, August 17, 1861, 1, August 21, 1861, 1, August 21, 1861, 1, October 8, 1861, 1; *Charleston Mercury*, August 17, 1861, 1; *Huntsville Independent*, September 14, 1861, 4; (Greensboro) *Alabama Beacon*, August 23, 1861, 2; (Huntsville) *Democrat*, August 21, 1861, 4.

51. *Daily Columbus* (Georgia) *Enquirer*, September 23, 1861, 2, September 25, 1861, 2, September 26, 1861, 2. See, generally, Daniel W. Hamilton, *The Limits of Sovereignty: Property Confiscations in the Union and the Confederacy during the Civil War* (Chicago: University of Chicago Press, 2007), 82–110.

52. *Mobile Advertiser and Register*, September 3, 1861, 1, September 8, 1861, 2, September 20, 1861, 1, October 8, 1861, 1; (Huntsville) *Democrat*, September 25, 1861, 3; *Selma Daily Reporter*, November 20, 1861, 2 (publishing a notice from a receiver in Selma). See also Noel C. Fisher, *War at Every Door: Partisan Politics and Guerrilla Violence in East Tennessee, 1860–1869* (Chapel Hill: University of North Carolina Press, 1997), 50; Peter Maslowski, *Treason Must Be Made Odious, Military Occupation and Wartime Reconstruction in Nashville, Tennessee*, 1862–65 (Millwood, NY: KTO Press, 1978), 12–13.

53. *Montgomery Weekly Advertiser*, January 26, 1862.

54. Fleming, *Civil War and Reconstruction in Alabama*, 178. See, e.g., *Mobile Adver-*

tiser and Register, September 13, 1861, 1, September 20, 1861, 1, October 1, 1861, 2, October 2, 1861, 2 (reporting that Judge Jones appointed John N. Malone of Limestone County to serve as the receiver for the Northern District of Alabama), October 5, 1861, 1, October 29, 1861, 2, October 30, 1861, 1; (Huntsville) *Democrat*, April 10, 1861, 4 (announcing the Terms of Court), September 25, 1861, 3 (Malone's appointment); and (New Orleans) *Daily Picayune*, December 5, 1861, 2. Regarding sequestration cases in other states, see, e.g., *Daily Columbus* (Georgia) *Enquirer*, February 6, 1862, 2 (Tennessee), March 19, 1862, 3 (Georgia). Assuring that decisions by the district courts would not be frustrated by appeals, the Confederate Congress also repealed a law adopted in the spring of 1861 that would have led to the creation of a Confederate Supreme Court. The orders of district judges were, therefore, not appealable. *Mobile Advertiser and Register*, August 20, 1861, 4.

55. Fleming, *Civil War and Reconstruction in Alabama*, 131.

56. See, e.g., *Charleston Mercury*, August 8, 1861, 1 (reporting the embarkation of Union soldiers at Norfolk, Virginia), August 29, 1861, 1 (same from Hampton Roads, Virginia); *Montgomery Advertiser and State Gazette*, August 6, 1861 (reporting the call in the North for five hundred thousand additional troops).

57. *Charleston Mercury*, July 24, 1861, 1.

58. Ibid.

59. *Montgomery Advertiser and State Gazette*, August 10, 1861.

60. Easby-Smith, *William Russell Smith*, 137.

61. Diary of Daniel Robinson Hundley, October 27, November 1, November 23, December 6, December 31, 1861, SPR 111, Alabama Department of Archives and History, Montgomery.

62. Linden and Linden, eds., *Disunion*, 70.

63. *Mobile Advertiser and Register*, October 12, 1861, 1.

64. See, e.g., *Charleston Mercury*, January 25, 1861, 1., January 30, 1861, 4, February 4, 1861, 1, February 21, 1861, 1; *Montgomery Advertiser and State Gazette*, March 3, 1861.

65. See, e.g., *Mobile Advertiser and Register*, August 11, 1861, 2, August 17, 1861, 3, August 28, 1861, 2, September 10, 1861, 1, October 11, 1861, 1; (Huntsville) *Democrat*, October 16, 1861, 4; *Huntsville Independent*, August 3, 1861, 4.

66. *Mobile Advertiser and Register*, August 28, 1861, 2.

67. (Selma) *Alabama State Sentinel*, December 19, 1860, 1. See, generally, Dean B. Mahin, *One War at a Time: The International Dimensions of the American Civil War* (Washington, DC: Brassey's, 1999), 56–58, 208.

68. Kvach, *DeBow's Review*, 144.

69. *Martin v. Hewitt*, 44 Ala. 418, 428 (1870).

70. *Mobile Advertiser and Register*, October 22, 1861, 2; (Huntsville) *Democrat*, October 30, 1861, 3; Mahin, *One War at a Time*, 58; Walther, *William Lowndes Yancey and the Coming of the Civil War*, 321, 326. Unbeknownst to him, President Davis was at that very time appointing replacements, John Slidell of Louisiana and James Mason of Virginia. Mahin, *One War at a Time*, 58.

71. Walther, *William Lowndes Yancey and the Coming of the Civil War*, 326; (Huntsville) *Democrat*, October 30, 1861, 3.

72. Walther, *William Lowndes Yancey and the Coming of the Civil War*, 328. The role of political hell raiser was tailor-made for Yancey, but the same could not be said for C. C. Clay Jr. After resigning from the US Senate in January, Clay had not immediately returned to Alabama. Whether due to his physical health or concerns about what kind of reception he would receive in Huntsville, Clay did not arrive home until late February. He had then left Huntsville for St. Paul, Minnesota, of all places, supposedly due to continuing problems associated with asthma. After the declaration of war, Clay returned to Alabama, but not to fight. He even declined an offer by his friend, Jefferson Davis, to become secretary of war, thus opening the door for Leroy Pope Walker. Now false rumors were being circulated that Clay was terminally ill. Both Yancey and Clay were eventually elected to the senate, but their impact would be minimal. *Nashville Union and American*, March 6, 1861, 3; Nuermberger, *Clays of Alabama*, 182–87; *Montgomery Weekly Post*, April 9, 1861; *Anderson* (South Carolina) *Intelligencer*, January 31, 1861, 2; Nuermberger, *Clays of Alabama*, 184, 187, 189–90 and 190 n7; (Huntsville) *Democrat*, June 12, 1861, 4, October 30, 1861, 4, November 27, 1861, 4; (New Orleans) *Daily Picayune*, November 26, 1861, 1. See, generally, McMillan, *Disintegration of a Confederate State*, 77–78.

73. *Mobile Advertiser and Register*, August 14, 1861, 1.

74. (Huntsville) *Democrat*, August 21, 1861, 1.

75. Emily Beck Moxley to William M. Moxley, September 3, 1861, in *Oh, What a Loansome Time I Had: The Civil War Letters of Major William Morel Moxley, Eighteenth Alabama Infantry, and Emily Beck Moxley*, ed. Thomas Cutrer, 29 (Tuscaloosa: University of Alabama Press, 2002).

76. William Moxley to Emily Moxley, December 17, 1861, in *Oh, What a Loansome Time I Had*, ed. Thomas Cutrer, 84.

77. G. W. Mark to George Milan, November 10, 1861, reprinted in *Belmont* (Ohio) *Chronicle*, January 2, 1862, 2.

Chapter 6

1. Stoker, *Grand Design*, 19, 26, 120–21, 232 ("The year 1862 proved a disastrous one for the Confederacy.").

2. Rable, *Confederate Republic*, 118; Stoker, *Grand Design*, 51, 107–9.

3. Bradley R. Clampitt, *The Confederate Heartland: Military and Civilian Morale in the Western Confederacy* (Baton Rouge: Louisiana State University Press, 2011), 2.

4. Escott, *Confederacy*, 25–29.

5. (New Orleans) *Daily Picayune*, November 23, 1861, 1, November 24, 1861, 2, November 26, 1861, 1.

6. *Mobile Advertiser and Register*, October 25, 1861, 2, October 29, 1861, 2.

7. (Huntsville) *Democrat*, November 13, 1861, 3; (New Orleans) *Daily Picayune*, November 10, 1861, 2, November 12, 1861, 2, November 14, 1861, 1; *Daily Columbus*

(Georgia) *Enquirer*, October 16, 1861, 2, January 23, 1862, 2. See also Noel C. Fisher, *War at Every Door: Partisan Politics and Guerrilla Violence in East Tennessee, 1860–1869* (Chapel Hill: University of North Carolina Press, 1997), 52–61.

8. See, generally, (New Orleans) *Daily Picayune*, November 15, 1861, 2, November 17, 1861, 4, November 22, 1861, 1; *Fayetteville* (North Carolina) *Observer*, November 25, 1861; (Huntsville) *Democrat*, December 25, 1861, 1; *Selma Daily Reporter*, December 7, 1861, 2; *Montgomery Weekly Advertiser*, January 19, 1861; *Daily Columbus* (Georgia) *Enquirer*, November 22, 1861, 2. See also Stephen V. Ash, ed., *Secessionists and Other Scoundrels: Selections from Parson Brownlow's Book* (Baton Rouge: Louisiana State University Press, 1999), 93–99, 126.

9. William Best Hesseltine, *Civil War Prisons: A Study in War Psychology* (Columbus: Ohio State University Press, 1930).

10. *Richmond Dispatch*, reprinted in *Fayetteville* (North Carolina) *Observer*, November 25, 1861; *Memphis Daily Appeal*, December 11, 1861, 3; (Greensboro) *Alabama Beacon*, December 13, 1861, 2; *New York Herald*, December 23, 1861, 2; (New Orleans) *Daily Picayune*, December 20, 1861, 1; Ted Genoways and Hugh H. Genoways, ed., *A Perfect Picture of Hell: Eyewitness Accounts by Civil War Prisoners from the 12th Iowa* (Iowa City: University of Iowa Press, 2001), 11, 37, 58–59.

11. Jackson, "Life and Times of Robert Jemison, Jr.," 25–26.

12. A. C. Myers to Maj. J. L. Calhoun, December 10, 1861, Official Records, Series 2, Vol. 3, 751.

13. (Tuscaloosa) *Independent Monitor*, reprinted in *Selma Daily Reporter*, November 6, 1861, 2; *Memphis Daily Appeal*, December 21, 1861, 3; *Daily Columbus* (Georgia) *Enquirer*, April 8, 1862, 2 (the name of the new business was "Kirkman, Hay & Co.").

14. See, generally, Hesseltine, *Civil War Prisons*, 62–63; Official Records, Series 2, Vol. 3, 751–52. There is evidence that the Drish Warehouse in Tuscaloosa was also used at one point.

15. *New York Herald*, December 23, 1861, 2.

16. *Lowell* (Massachusetts) *Daily Citizen and News*, December 31, 1861. See also *Memphis Daily Appeal*, December 11, 1861, 3; *Milwaukee Daily Sentinel*, August 31, 1865, 2.

17. Henry James Walker, *Let Us Keep the Feast: The History of Christ Episcopal Church, Tuscaloosa, Alabama, 1828–1998* (Tallahassee, FL: Sentry Press, 2000), 49 (mentioning burial of one of the prisoners); *Providence* (Rhode Island) *Evening Press*, November 7, 1862, 3 (the prisoner, who had suffered what was called "bleeding at the lungs," was taken to a private dwelling where he was treated before his death).

18. *Tuscaloosa Observer*, reprinted in *Selma Daily Reporter*, December 7, 1861, 2.

19. (Tuscaloosa) *Independent Monitor*, reprinted in *Selma Daily Reporter*, January 14, 1862, 2.

20. *Montgomery Weekly Advertiser*, January 7, 1862, January 14, 1862; (New Orleans) *Daily Picayune*, December 18, 1861, 1, December 20, 1861, 1, January 12, 1862, 2; *Selma Daily Reporter*, January 3, 1862, 2. Regarding their arrival in Tuscaloosa, see *Tuscaloosa Observer*, December 13, 1861, reprinted in *Memphis Daily Appeal*, December

19, 1861, 2. See also *Tuscaloosa Observer*, January 8, 1862, reprinted in *Memphis Daily Appeal*, January 14, 1862, 2 (escape by two prisoners); *Daily Nashville Union*, June 6, 1862, 2 (listing the names of several of the Tennesseans).

21. Robert P. Blount to J. P. Benjamin, January 19, 1862, Official Records, Series 1, Vol. 7, 840.

22. McMillan, *Disintegration of a Confederate State*, 52; *Tuscaloosa Observer*, December 24, 1861, cited in (New Orleans) *Daily Picayune*, January 3, 1862, 1.

23. (New Orleans) *Daily Picayune*, January 12, 1862, 4, January 23, 1862, 2; *Montgomery Weekly Advertiser*, January 7, 1862, January 19, 1862, January 25, 1862. See also (Savannah, Georgia) *Daily Morning News*, March 12, 1862 (reporting that 500 prisoners of war from Tuscaloosa had been paroled and were on their way by rail to Norfolk); *Semi-Weekly Raleigh* (North Carolina) *Register*, March 29, 1862 (reporting that 217 prisoners taken at Fort Donelson were en route for Tuscaloosa); *Montgomery Weekly Advertiser*, February 2, 1862 (twenty prisoners being sent from Knoxville); Braxton Bragg to J. P. Benjamin, February 12, 1862, Official Records, Series 2, Vol. 3, 795 (stating that two prisoners had recently tried to escape but "had to surrender in a starving condition"); John Gill Shorter to General L. Polk, February 26, 1862, Official Records, Series 2, Vol. 3 (refusing additional prisoners); H. W. Walter, General Orders No. 2, March 5, 1862, and John Adams to Thomas Jordan, March 18, 1862, Official Records, Series 2, Vol. 3, 814, 825 (more prisoners being sent to Tuscaloosa from Memphis); *Montgomery Weekly Advertiser*, March 11, 1862 (reporting the parole of prisoners from Tuscaloosa); *Boston Herald*, May 7, 1862, 4 (reporting an account by a Tennessee prisoner regarding overcrowding during the period December 21, 1861, to January 8, 1862); T. O. H. P. Burnham, *The Stars and Stripes in Rebeldom: A Series of Papers Written by Federal Prisoners in Richmond, Tuscaloosa, New Orleans and Salisbury, N.C.* (Boston: T. O. H. P. Burnham, 1862).

24. Proclamations of Governor A. B. Moore, November 21, 1861 and November 22, 1861, Papers of Governor Moore, Alabama Department of Archives and History, Montgomery.

25. Sarah Woolfolk Wiggins, ed., *The Journals of Josiah Gorgas 1857–1878* (Tuscaloosa: University of Alabama Press, 1995), 43.

26. See, e.g., (New Orleans) *Daily Picayune*, March 9, 1862, 5 (reprinting a letter from Huntsville).

27. L. W. Jenkins to Gov. John Gill Shorter, December 8, 1861, Papers of Governor Shorter, Alabama Department of Archives and History, Montgomery. See also A. Kaiser to Gov. John Gill Shorter, December 3, 1861 and R. Kinsey to Gov. John Gill Shorter, December 6, 1861, Papers of Governor Shorter, Alabama Department of Archives and History, Montgomery. "Huranghing" here probably means that the men were shouting "hurrah" for Lincoln.

28. Robert P. Blount to Judah P. Benjamin, January 19, 1862, Official Records, Series I, Vol. 7, 840.

29. (New Orleans) *Daily Picayune*, November 23, 1861, 1, November 26, 1861, 1. See also *Montgomery Weekly Advertiser*, January 4, 1862, January 7, 1862, January 26,

1862; Grady McWhiney, *Braxton Bragg and Confederate Defeat* (New York: Columbia University Press, 1969), 196–97.

30. (Huntsville) *Democrat,* January 16, 1862, 3.

31. (New Orleans) *Daily Picayune,* January 18, 1862, 2. See also *Montgomery Weekly Advertiser,* January 24, 1862.

32. L. P. Walker to J. P. Benjamin, February 17, 1862, Official Records, Series 1, Vol. 7, 888–89.

33. (New Orleans) *Daily Picayune,* January 17, 1862, 2 (stating that 36,000 Alabamians were in the field); (Huntsville) *Democrat,* February 12, 1862, 4 (stating that 75,000 were not).

34. *Selma Alabama Reporter,* February 11, 1862; *Richmond Examiner,* February 5, 1862, 2; Official Records, Series 4, Vol. 1, 941, 1048–49, 1053–54 (the Act providing this financing was adopted on February 15, 1862).

35. (Selma) *Alabama State Sentinel,* cited in (New Orleans) *Daily Picayune,* January 12, 1862, 2.

36. Black, *Railroads of the Confederacy,* 153–58; *New York Herald,* reprinted in *Nashville Daily Union,* November 27, 1862, 1; (New Orleans) *Daily Picayune,* February 13, 1862, 1.

37. James M. McPherson, *War on the Waters: The Union and Confederate Navies, 1861–1865* (Chapel Hill: University of North Carolina Press, 2012): 74–75; Kendall D. Gott, *Where the South Lost the War: An Analysis of the Fort Henry-Fort Donelson Campaign, February 1862* (Mechanicsburg, PA: Stackpole Books, 2003), 75–106 (also noting at 18–19 that the Confederate government gave priority to the eastern theater).

38. *Montgomery Weekly Advertiser,* February 7, 1862, February 9, 1862, March 15, 1862; (New Orleans) *Daily Picayune,* February 8, 1862, 2, February 14, 1862, 1; (Greensboro) *Alabama Beacon,* February 14, 1862, 3, February 21, 1862, 2; *Selma Daily Reporter,* February 21, 1862, 2; *Daily Columbus* (Georgia) *Enquirer,* February 10, 1862, 2, February 11, 1862, 2, December 12, 1862, 2. Regarding Foote, see Spencer Tucker, *Andrew Foote: Civil War Admiral on Western Waters* (Annapolis, MD: Naval Institute Press, 2000). Regarding the implications of the fall of Fort Henry, see Edwin C. Bearss, *Fall of Fort Henry* (Dover, TN: Eastern National Park and Monument Association, Fort Donelson National Military Park, 1992); B. Franklin Cooling, *Forts Henry and Donelson—The Key to the Confederate Heartland* (Knoxville, TN: Eastern Press, 1987).

39. *Memphis Daily* Appeal, reprinted in (Huntsville) *Democrat,* February 19, 1862, 4 and (New Orleans) *Daily Picayune,* February 14, 1862, 1.

40. *New York Times,* February 13, 1862, 1; *Cincinnati Daily Press,* February 12, 1862, 3; (Washington, DC) *National Republican,* February 13, 1862, 2; *New York Daily Tribune,* February 13, 1862, 4.

41. (New Orleans) *Daily Picayune,* February 9, 1862, 2, February 11, 1862, 2, February 12, 1862, 2, February 14, 1862, 1; *Selma Daily Reporter,* February 17, 1862, 2.

42. (New Orleans) *Daily Picayune,* February 14, 1862, 1; *Memphis Daily Appeal,* reprinted in (Richmond) *Daily Dispatch,* February 17, 1862, 2.

43. (Huntsville) *Democrat*, February 12, 1862, 3; *Montgomery Weekly Advertiser*, February 15, 1862; (New Orleans) *Daily Picayune*, February 11, 1862, 2, February 12, 1862, 2–3, February 14, 1862, 1; *Harper's Weekly*, March 1, 1862, 140; (Greensboro) *Alabama Beacon*, February 14, 1862, 3; *Daily Columbus* (Georgia) *Enquirer*, February 10, 1862, 2; *Memphis Avalanche*, February 11, 1862, reprinted in *Daily Columbus* (Georgia) *Enquirer*, February 15, 1862, 2; (Philadelphia) *North American and United States Gazette*, February 14, 1862. See, generally, Edwin C. Bearss, "A Federal Raid Up the Tennessee River," *Alabama Review* 17 (October 1964): 261; Storey, *Loyalty and Loss*, 87; Fleming, *Civil War and Reconstruction*, 115–16; McMillan, *Alabama Confederate Reader*, 143–44. Regarding Phelps, see Jay Slagle, *Ironclad Captain: Seth Ledyard Phelps and the U.S. Navy, 1841–1864* (Kent, OH: Kent State University Press, 1996), 168–69; McPherson, *War on the Waters*, 75; Earl J. Hess, *The Civil War in the West: Victory and Defeat from the Appalachians to the Mississippi* (Chapel Hill: University of North Carolina Press, 2012), 35.

44. Daily Journal of Joshua Burns Moore, 27–28, Alabama Department of Archives and History, Montgomery.

45. Private Journal of Sarah R. Espy, 39.

46. Diary of Miss Catherine M. Fennell, 26.

47. Mrs. P. E. Collins to Gov. John G. Shorter, March 1, 1862, Papers of Governor Shorter, Alabama Department of Archives and History, Montgomery. See also, Petition to Governor Shorter, April 1, 1862, Papers of Governor Shorter, Alabama Department of Archives and History, Montgomery.

48. Linden and Linden, eds., *Disunion*, 75.

49. *Nashville Union and American*, reprinted in (New Orleans) *Daily Picayune*, February 16, 1862, 2.

50. *Tuscumbia Constitution*, February 21, 1862, 2. "Paid in Confederate bacon" does literally mean that his payment came in the form of meat.

51. *Selma Daily Reporter*, March 19, 1862, 1.

52. *Montgomery Weekly Advertiser*, March 19, 1862; (New Orleans) *Daily Picayune*, March 16, 1862, 2 (referring to spies near Decatur, Alabama), March 22, 1862, 2 (referring to the arrest of a Decatur man).

53. Diary of Thomas Bragg, March 19, 1862, Southern Historical Collection, University of North Carolina.

54. *Montgomery Advertiser and State Gazette*, reprinted in *Selma Daily Reporter*, March 4, 1862, 1.

55. *Selma Daily Reporter*, March 8, 1862, 2.

56. Ray Mathis, *John Horry Dent: South Carolina Aristocrat on the Alabama Frontier* (Tuscaloosa: University of Alabama Press, 1979), 204.

57. Mathis, *John Horry Dent*, 204.

58. (New Orleans) *Daily Picayune*, February 12, 1862, February 18, 1862, 2; *Montgomery Weekly Advertiser*, February 23, 1862; William B. Feis, *Grant's Secret Service: The Intelligence War from Belmont to Appomattox* (Lincoln: University of Nebraska Press, 2004), 71; Stoker, *Grand Design*, 121–22.

59. (New Orleans) *Daily Picayune*, February 28, 1862, 2.

60. (Huntsville) *Democrat*, February 19, 1862, 3; *Montgomery Weekly Advertiser*, February 23, 1862; (New Orleans) *Daily Picayune*, February 18, 1862, 2, February 20, 1862, 1, February 28, 1862, 2; *Selma Daily Reporter*, February 22, 1862, 2; *Daily Columbus* (Georgia) *Enquirer*, February 24, 1862, 2; Feis, *Grant's Secret Service*, 73.

61. Emily Moxley to William Moxley, February 24, 1862, in *Oh, What a Loansome Time I Had*, ed. Thomas Cutrer, 129.

62. Larry J. Daniel, *Soldiering in the Army of Tennessee: A Portrait of Life in a Confederate Army* (Chapel Hill: University of North Carolina, 1991), 127.

63. Diary of Miss Catherine M. Fennell, 26.

64. Private Journal of Sarah R. Espy, 40.

65. Linden and Linden, eds., *Disunion*, 76.

66. Noe, *Reluctant Rebels*, 102–5.

67. *Cincinnati Gazette*, reprinted in *Montgomery Weekly Advertiser*, January 22, 1862. See also *Montgomery Weekly Advertiser*, February 25, 1862.

68. *Montgomery Weekly Advertiser*, February 23, 1862.

69. Ibid.

70. *Mobile Tribune*, reprinted in *Daily Columbus* (Georgia) *Enquirer*, March 6, 1862, 2. As a worried Confederate colonel in Knoxville, Tennessee, had written the secretary of war in January, there would be "many cases of serious guilt wherein the prisoner will be turned over to the civil courts to be bailed out and tried by his peers." D. Ledbetter to J. P. Benjamin, January 11, 1862, Official Records, Series 2, Vol. 1, 870.

71. See, generally, John B. Robbins, "The Confederacy and the Writ of Habeas Corpus," *Georgia Historical Quarterly* 55 (Summer 1971): 83–86; Rable, *Confederate Republic*, 145.

72. *Montgomery Weekly Advertiser*, March 9, 1862 (North Alabama), March 30, 1862 (Mobile), April 9, 1862 (Montgomery), May 6, 1862 (Montgomery); *Selma Daily Reporter*, July 10, 1862, 2 (in Selma, attorney Thomas B. Wetmore was appointed provost marshal). See also, Arthur W. Bergeron, *Confederate Mobile* (Jackson: University Press of Mississippi, 1991), 23.

73. Easby-Smith, *William Russell Smith*, 141.

74. A. M. Barclay to John G. Shorter, March 10, 1862, quoted in Dodd and Dodd, *Free State of Winston*, 87; Thompson, *Free State of Winston*, 45.

75. R. W. Walker to Governor Shorter, March 10, 1862, quoted in Dodd and Dodd, *Free State of Winston*, 87.

76. *Montgomery Weekly Advertiser*, March 19, 1862. See also *Mobile Advertiser and Register*, reprinted in *Daily Columbus* (Georgia) *Enquirer*, April 30, 1862, 2 (sale of cotton in north Alabama). *Daily Columbus* (Georgia) *Enquirer*, March 19, 1862, 3. See also *Atlanta Confederacy*, reprinted in *Daily Columbus* (Georgia) *Enquirer*, April 10, 1862, 2 (indicating that cotton was also being sold through Tennessee by "traitorous Georgians").

77. B. R. Johnson to Col. Thomas Jordan, April 21, 1862, reprinted in Official Re-

cords, Series I, Vol. 10, (Part 2), 161–63, 174–75, 431. See also Frank L. Owsley, "Defeatism in the Confederacy," *North Carolina Historical Review* 3 (July 1926): 446, 452; Dodd and Dodd, *Free State of Winston*, 87.

78. Stoker, *Grand Design*, 121; McWhiney, *Braxton Bragg and Confederate Defeat*, 202–5; Bergeron, *Confederate Mobile*, 22–23; *Selma Daily Reporter*, March 4, 1862; *Montgomery Weekly Advertiser*, March 8, 1862.

79. *Augusta* (Georgia) *Chronicle*, March 4, 1862, 3.

80. Linden and Linden, eds., *Disunion*, 77.

81. Feis, *Grant's Secret Service*, 81.

82. McWhiney, *Braxton Bragg and Confederate Defeat*, 204.

83. Feis, *Grant's Secret Service*, 81–82; McWhiney, *Braxton Bragg and Confederate Defeat*, 208–9; *Montgomery Weekly Advertiser*, March 22, 1862; (New Orleans) *Daily Picayune*, March 6, 1862, 2, March 12, 1862, 2.

84. (New Orleans) *Daily Picayune*, March 14, 1862, 2, March 20, 1862, 3, March 21, 1862, 2.

85. (Tuscumbia) *North Alabamian*, March 15, 1862, reprinted in (New Orleans) *Daily Picayune*, March 20, 1862, 2. *Montgomery Weekly Advertiser*, March 22, 1862, March 25, 1862.

86. *Montgomery Weekly Advertiser*, March 25, 1862; *Mobile Advertiser and Register*, April 4, 1862, 21; McMillan, *Disintegration of a Confederate State*, 47–48.

87. (New Orleans) *Daily Picayune*, April 1, 1862, 2. See also Official Records, Series 1, Vol. 10 (Part II), 487 (a letter from Roddey dated May 4, 1862, signed "Captain, Tishomingo Rangers"). Regarding Roddey, see Zack C. Waters, "General Philip D. Roddey: 'Defender of North Alabama,'" *Alabama Heritage* 110 (Fall 2013): 24–33; William C. Scott Jr., "Philip Dale Roddey: Confederate General from Alabama," *Journal of Muscle Shoals History* 15 (1999): 37; Owen, *History of Alabama and Dictionary of Alabama Biography*, 4: 1454.

88. Stoker, *Grand Design*, 128.

89. *Mobile Advertiser and Register*, April 6, 1862, 2, April 8, 1862, 1–2, April 9, 1862, 1–2, April 11, 1862, 1; *Montgomery Weekly Advertiser*, April 8, 1862, April 11, 1862, April 22, 1862; (New Orleans) *Daily Picayune*, April 8, 1862, 2, 4, April 10, 1862, 2. See, generally, Joseph Allan Frank, *"Seeing the Elephant": Raw Recruits at the Battle of Shiloh* (Urbana: University of Illinois Press, 2003); James R. Arnold, *Shiloh, 1862: The Death of Innocence* (London: Praeger, 2004); Timothy T. Isbell, *Shiloh & Corinth: Sentinels of Stone* (Jackson: University Press of Mississippi 2007); McWhiney, *Braxton Bragg and Confederate Defeat*, 247–49; Jack Hurst, *Nathan Bedford Forrest: A Biography* (New York: A. A. Knopf, 1994), 67–94; Feis, *Grant's Secret Service*, 99–106; James Lee McDonough, *Shiloh: In Hell Before Night* (Knoxville: University of Tennessee Press, 1977), 129, 177, 198–99 (mentioning the Alabama units in this battle).

90. David T. Gleeson, *The Green and the Gray: The Irish in the Confederate States of America* (Chapel Hill: University of North Carolina Press, 2013), 176; Rogers et al., *Alabama*, 201.

91. *Montgomery Weekly Advertiser*, August 8, 1862; *Mobile Advertiser and Register*, April 6, 1862, 2; *Daily Columbus* (Georgia) *Enquirer*, April 8, 1862, 2, April 17, 1862, 2; Stoker, *Grand Design*, 128.

92. Richard M. McMurry, ed., *An Uncompromising Secessionist: The Civil War of George Knox Miller, Eighth (Wade's) Confederate Cavalry* (Tuscaloosa: University of Alabama Press, 2007), 66–67.

93. Michael B. Ballard, *The Civil War in Mississippi: Major Campaigns and Battles* (Jackson: University Press of Mississippi, 2011), 13.

94. DuBose, *Alabama's Tragic Decade*, 13.

95. *Martin v. Hewitt*, 44 Ala. 418, 427 (1870).

96. *Daily Columbus* (Georgia) *Enquirer*, April 18, 1862, 2. See, generally, Genoways and Genoways, eds., *Perfect Picture of Hell*, 10–11, 37, 55–58 (regarding these prison facilities).

97. *Montgomery Weekly Advertiser*, March 19, 1862; (New Orleans) *Daily Picayune*, August 12, 1862, 2, August 23, 1862, 2 (regarding the Suez Canal). See, generally, Frank Lawrence Owsley, *King Cotton Diplomacy: Foreign Relations of the Confederate States of America* (Tuscaloosa: University of Alabama Press, 2008).

98. *Mobile Advertiser and Register*, October 2, 1861; (New Orleans) *Daily Picayune*, January 17, 1862, 2; (Huntsville) *Democrat*, February 12, 1862, 4. About 127,000 would reach military age during the war. Rogers et al., *Alabama*, 197. But see Thomas Leonard Livermore, *Numbers and Losses in the Civil War in America, 1861–1865* (Bloomington: Indiana University Press, 1957), 21 (stating that in 1860 there were 99,967 men of military age in Alabama).

99. (Greensboro) *Alabama Beacon*, April 25, 1862, 2. See also *Daily Columbus* (Georgia) *Enquirer*, April 3, 1862, 2, April 4, 1862, 2, April 21, 1862, 2 (noting conflict over this bill), May 1, 1862, 2 (same); Rable, *Confederate Republic*, 139–44; Noe, *Reluctant Rebels*, 105; Margaret M. Storey, "The Crucible of Reconstruction: Unionists and the Struggle for Alabama's Postwar Home Front," in *The Great Task Remaining Before Us: Reconstruction as America's Continuing Civil War*, ed. Paula A. Cimbala and Randall M. Miller, 72–73 (New York: Fordham University Press, 2010); Albert Burton Moore, *Conscription and Conflict in the Confederacy* (New York: Macmillan, 1924), 12–26; Daniel, *Soldiering in the Army of Tennessee*, 127–28; Walther, *William Lowndes Yancey and the Coming of the Civil War*, 339–41; (Greensboro) *Alabama Beacon*, May 2, 1862, 3; *Mobile Advertiser and Register*, April 16, 1862, 2, April 22, 1862, 2, April 26, 1862, 1; (New Orleans) *Daily Picayune*, April 17, 1862, 2, April 23, 1862, 2; *Montgomery Weekly Advertiser*, April 20, 1862; Escott, *Confederacy*, 30–31, 47–48.

100. *Richmond Whig*, April 18, 1862, 2.

101. (New Orleans) *Daily Picayune*, April 13, 1862, 2; *Mobile Advertiser and Register*, April 17, 1862, 1–2, April 22, 1862, 2, May 13, 1862, 2; *Montgomery Weekly Advertiser*, April 22, 1861; (Washington, DC) *Daily National Intelligencer*, May 2, 1862. See, generally, Stoker, *Grand Design*, 129; George C. Bradley and Richard L. Dahlen, *From Conciliation to Conquest: The Sack of Athens and the Court-Martial of Colonel John B. Turchin* (Tuscaloosa: University of Alabama Press, 2006), 96–98; Charles Rice, *Hard*

Times, 57–60; Mark Grimsley, *The Hard Hand of War: Union Military Policy toward Southern Civilians (1861–1865)* (Cambridge: Cambridge University Press, 1995), 79; Stephen Chicoine, *John Basil Turchin and the Fight to Free the Slaves* (Westport, CT: Praeger, 2003), 47–52; Paul Horton, "Submitting to the Shadow of Slavery," 111, 121–27.

102. Nancy M. Rohr, ed., *Incidents of the War: The Civil War Journal of Mary Jane Chadick* (Huntsville, AL: Silver Threads Publishing, 2005), 30.

103. Daily Journal of Joshua Burns Moore, 33–36.

104. George Goldthwaite to R. Jemison Jr., April 9, 1862, Official Records, Series I, Vol. 52 (Part 2), 299–300; Official Records, Series I, Vol. 10 (Part 2), 431; Dodd and Dodd, *Free State of Winston*, 90–91. Regarding that convention, see *Montgomery Advertiser*, reprinted in *Daily Columbus* (Georgia) *Enquirer*, May 2, 1862, 2.

105. *Montgomery Weekly Advertiser*, April 20, 1862. (New Orleans) *Daily Picayune*, April 13, 1862, 2; *Mobile Advertiser and Register*, April 17, 1862, 1.

106. Bradley and Dahlen, *From Conciliation to Conquest*, 98.

107. *Mobile Advertiser and Register*, April 11, 1862, 1, April 22, 1862, 2, April 24, 1862, 2.

108. *Mobile Advertiser and Register*, April 29, 1862, 2; Linden and Linden, eds., *Disunion*, 81–82. See also (New Orleans) *Daily Picayune*, April 30, 1862, 2, May 1, 1862, 2; *New York Times*, May 1, 1862, 1. See, generally, Hess, *Civil War in the West*, 75–79; Stoker, *Grand Design*, 134–35.

109. See, generally, Michael D. Pierson, *Mutiny at Fort Jackson: The Untold Story of the Fall of New Orleans* (Chapel Hill: University of North Carolina Press, 2008).

110. Arthur Freemantle, quoted in Escott, *Confederacy*, 58.

111. *Montgomery Advertiser*, reprinted in *New York Times*, May 4, 1862, 2.

112. John W. Cotton to Mariah Hindsman Cotton, May 1, 1862, in Lucille Griffith, ed., *Yours Till Death: Civil War Letters of John W. Cotton* (Tuscaloosa: University of Alabama Press, 1951), 2.

113. *Montgomery Weekly Advertiser*, May 1, 1862.

114. *Montgomery Weekly Advertiser*, May 6, 1862. See also *Mobile Advertiser and Register*, May 11, 1862, 1 (discussing what would happen to Andrew Johnson "should the Lincoln army be routed in the battle impending near Corinth"); *New York Times*, May 22, 1862, 5 (discussing the effect of threatened retribution on pro-Union political expression in the South), May 27, 1862, 4 (same).

115. William B. Campbell to Gov. A. Johnson, May 8, 1862, Graf et al., *Papers of Andrew Johnson*, 5: 370.

116. *Montgomery Weekly Advertiser*, April 9, 1862, May 3, 1862 (attack on Tuscumbia); *Charleston Courier*, June 14, 1862; *Selma Daily Reporter*, May 31, 1862, 1; (Washington, DC) *Daily National Intelligencer*, May 2, 1862; *Mobile Advertiser and Register*, June 6, 1862, 1, May 14, 1862, 2, May 15, 1862, 2, June 6, 1862, 1; Bradley and Dahlen, *From Conciliation to Conquest*, 99–106; Chicoine, *John Basil Turchin and the Fight to Free the Slaves*, 62–64.

117. Bradley and Dahlen, *From Conciliation to Conquest*, 99–106. See also *Mobile*

Advertiser and Register, May 11, 1862, 1; *Daily Columbus* (Georgia) *Enquirer*, May 9, 1862, 2.

118. *Montgomery Weekly Advertiser*, May 3, 1862.

119. Ibid., May 11, 1862, 1. See also *Montgomery Weekly Advertiser*, April 13, 1862; *Mobile Advertiser and Register*, April 16, 1862, 1.

120. Hess, *Civil War in the West*, 66; Stoker, *Grand Design*, 130.

121. C. C. Clay Jr. to John Gill Shorter, May 30, 1862, Papers of Governor Shorter, Alabama Department or Archives and History, Montgomery.

122. See, e.g., Nuermberger, *Clays of Alabama*, 213 (citing a letter from C. C. Clay Jr.); *Mobile Advertiser and Register*, May 24, 1862, 2, May 31, 1862, 3, February 6, 1863, 1, December 12, 1863, 2; *Montgomery Weekly Advertiser*, May 24, 1862, June 3, 1862; ibid., August 30, 1866, 2; (Greensboro) *Alabama Beacon*, June 6, 1862, 2; *New York Times*, June 8, 1862, 3. But see *Selma Daily Reporter*, June 27, 1862, 2 (refuting the contention that Clemens had defected). See also Dee, "Trying James Hickman," 83, 91–95 and 95n39; Charles Rice, *Hard Times*, 234; Danielson, *War's Desolating Scourge*, 30; Shields, *Freedom in a Slave Society*, 276–79.

123. *New York Times*, June 29, 1862, 3; *Huntsville Reveille*, June 19, 1862, 1, 3.

124. O. M. Mitchel to E. M. Stanton, May 4, 1862, Official Records, Series 1, Vol. 10 (Part II), 162–63.

125. *Selma Morning Reporter*, August 15, 1862, 1. Regarding the collaboration of slaves with Union forces prior to President Lincoln's issuance of the final Emancipation Proclamation, see Storey, *Loyalty and Loss*, 144–53.

126. Bradley and Dahlen, *From Conciliation to Conquest*, 102.

127. Carter, *Welcome the Hour of Conflict*, 167; Bradley and Dahlen, *From Conciliation to Conquest*, 124.

128. Bradley and Dahlen, *From Conciliation to Conquest*, 100, 104.

129. *Selma Daily Reporter*, March 6, 1862.

130. *Montgomery Weekly Advertiser*, April 19, 1862, April 26, 1862, May 3, 1862, May 7, 1862, May 10, 1862; *Mobile Advertiser and Register*, May 3, 1862, 1; *Selma Daily Reporter*, March 6, 1862, 2.

131. *Selma Daily Reporter*, May 23, 1862, 1.

132. *Mobile Advertiser and Register*, May 14, 1862, 2, May 15, 1862, 2; *Montgomery Weekly Advertiser*, May 20, 1862; *Charleston Courier*, June 14, 1962; Bradley and Dahlen, *From Conciliation to Conquest*, 104–6.

133. Bradley and Dahlen, *From Conciliation to Conquest*, 106–8; McMillan, *Alabama Confederate Reader*, 147–58, 180; Chicoine, *John Basis Turchin and the Fight to Free the Slaves*, 61–73, 77, 88; Danielson, *War's Desolate Scourge*, 49–56.

134. Bradley and Dahlen, *From Conciliation to Conquest*, 109–22; William A. Blair, *With Malice toward Some: Treason and Loyalty in the Civil War Era* (Chapel Hill: University of North Carolina Press, 2014), 134–37.

135. Linden and Linden, eds., *Disunion*, 81; *Montgomery Weekly Advertiser*, May 3, 1862, May 20, 1862; *Mobile Advertiser and Register*, May 18, 1862, 2; *Louisville Daily Journal*, October 23, 1862, 4; (New Orleans) *Daily Picayune*, April 10, 1862, 2.

136. *Montgomery Weekly Advertiser*, February 18, 1862, March 22, 1862; (New Orleans) *Daily Picayune*, March 1, 1862, 1; John G. Shorter to G. W. Randolph, March 27, 1862, Official Records, Series 4, Vol. 1, 1028–29.

137. *Montgomery Weekly Advertiser*, March 22, 1862, March 28, 1862, April 8, 1862, May 20, 1862; *Mobile Advertiser and Register*, May 20, 1862, 1.

138. *Tuscaloosa Observer*, reprinted in (Greensboro) *Alabama Beacon*, May 23, 1862, 3.

139. Matthew William Clinton, *Matt Clinton's Scrapbook* (Northport, AL: Portals, 1979), 167–68; *New York Herald*, June 4, 1862, 4; *Macon* (Georgia) *Telegraph*, September 2, 1865, 3; *Milwaukee Sentinel*, August 31, 1865, 2. Regarding Andersonville Prison, see William Marvel, *Andersonville: The Last Depot* (Chapel Hill: University of North Carolina Press, 1994); Hesseltine, *Civil War Prisons*, 63–64, 115, 237–38, 247.

140. *Nashville Union*, June 4, 1862, reprinted in *Weekly Wisconsin Patriot*, June 21, 1862, 6. See also Genoways and Genoways, eds., *Perfect Picture of Hell*, 58–62, 86, 103, 108–9, 116, 251.

141. Clinton, *Matt Clinton's Scrapbook*, 167–68.

142. Owen, *History of Alabama and Dictionary of Alabama Biography*, 4: 1022; Clinton, *Matt Clinton's Scrapbook*, 162–63; Walker, *Let Us Keep the Feast*, 51.

143. *Tuscaloosa Observer*, reprinted in *Memphis Daily Appeal*, April 30, 1862, 2; *Montgomery Weekly Advertiser*, April 6, 1863. See also "Alabama Testimony," 1976 (Newton Whitfield testified that Dr. Sewell Jones Leach and Charles Foster, the tanner, among others, were Northern natives who did not sympathize with the rebellion).

144. Clinton, *Matt Clinton's Scrapbook*, 159, 165, 252; *Daily Columbus* (Georgia) *Enquirer*, April 8, 1862, 2; Walker, *Let Us Keep the Feast*, 151, 159. It should be noted that contracts with the Confederacy were not necessarily a product of free will. The government paid for production at a rate of 50 percent of market price. A refusal to contract on this basis could lead to nationalization of a manufacturing facility. J. Whiting to Lewis J. Parsons, August 22, 1865, Papers of Governor Parsons, Alabama Department of Archives and History, Montgomery; James A. Seddon to Gov. T. H. Watts, February 10, 1864, Papers of Governor Watts, Alabama Department of Archives and History, Montgomery.

145. Clinton, *Matt Clinton's Scrapbook*, 159, 131; G. Ward Hubbs, *Tuscaloosa: Portrait of An Alabama County: An Illustrated History* (Northridge, CA: Windsor Publications, 1987), 40.

146. Regarding refugees to Tuscaloosa during the Civil War, see, e.g., Hubbs, *Tuscaloosa*, 40; Clinton, *Matt Clinton's Scrapbook*, 232, 239.

147. The Yankee prisoners in Tuscaloosa recognized this tenuous cash nexus, and perhaps with the aid of the aforementioned "Yankee Sympathizers," they began a counterfeiting operation which, according to the *New York Times*, produced "Confederate Shinplasters" of better quality than the "genuine article." With tongue in cheek, the *Times* excused their "heinous offence of counterfeiting" by pointing out that the men had been in a "community where the people have so reversed the action of their moral faculties as to regard patriotism and honesty as crimes, while stealing is a virtue and perjury an honor." The discovery of this scheme may have been

what led to a tightening of security by Wirz that resulted in the shooting of one of the prisoners who reportedly had violated a rule prohibiting prisoners from looking out the window, a measure designed in part to limit communication with sympathetic locals. If so, it did not work. Possibly with the aid of those locals, sixty of the prisoners reportedly escaped in early May 1862, although most, if not all, were later captured. They were not returned to Tuscaloosa but were instead transferred along with the balance of the prisoners to Montgomery and then to Chattanooga, where they were paroled for exchange. *New York Times*, June 15, 1862, 4. But see *Tuscaloosa Observer*, reprinted in *Memphis Daily Appeal*, August 20, 1862, 1 (denying that Confederate money could be counterfeited); *New York Herald*, June 4, 1862, 4 (stating that the shooting occurred on April 15, 1862). Regarding Wirz's activities in Tuscaloosa, see *Nashville Daily Union*, November 1, 1862, 2; (Greensboro) *Alabama Beacon*, May 30, 1862, 2; *New York Herald*, June 4, 1862, 4; William R. Morales, *The 41st Alabama Infantry Regiment, Confederate States of America: A Narrative History of the Civil War Regiment From West Central Alabama* (Wyandotte, OK: Greguth, 2011), 23; *Selma Daily Reporter*, June 3, 1862, 1; Genoways and Genoways, eds., *Perfect Picture of Hell*, 31, 99.

148. Neely, *Southern Rights*, 33–34; *Selma Daily Reporter*, July 10, 1862, 2, July 11, 1862, 2, July 16, 1862, 2.

149. *Montgomery Weekly Advertiser*, August 21, 1862, September 23, 1862; *Nashville Daily Union*, November 27, 1862, 1; *New York Herald*, November 20, 1862, 5; McWhiney, *Braxton Bragg and Confederate Defeat*, 262; Black, *Railroads of the Confederacy*, 156–57.

150. Official Records, Series 4, Vol. 2, 200 (reprinting the Act adopted October 2, 1862); *Ala. Acts*, No. 118, 143–44 (November 4, 1862).

151. Ernest Barnwell Johnston Jr., "Selma Alabama as a Center of Confederate War Production, 1860–1865" (bachelor's thesis, Harvard College, 1952). See, generally, Ivan Musicant, *Divided Waters: The Naval History of the Civil War* (New York, Castle Books, 2000), 69, 307–8; William W. Still, "Selma and the Confederate States Navy," *Alabama Review* 15 (January 1962): 19; Jackson, *Story of Selma*, 197; Frank Everson Vandiver, *Ploughshares Into Swords: Josiah Gorgas and Confederate Ordnance* (College Station: Texas A&M University Press, 1994), 148, 169, 171, 240; Blackmon, *Slavery by Another Name*, 19–21, 23–24; *Ala. Acts*, No. 109, 120 (December 5, 1862) (incorporating the Selma Iron Foundry Company), No. 112, 124 (November 20, 1862) (amending the charter of the Shelby County Iron Manufacturing Company), No. 173, 176 (November 17, 1862); *Ware v. Jones*, 61 Ala. 288 (1878); N. P. Banks to Gen. H. W. Halleck, December 24, 1862, Official Records, Series 1, Vol. 15, 618.

152. *Selma Morning Reporter*, February 28, 1863, 1. See also Emory M. Thomas, *Confederacy as a Revolutionary Experience* (Englewood Cliffs, NJ: Prentice-Hall, 1971), 88.

153. *Montgomery Weekly Advertiser*, May 9, 1862, May 13, 1862, May 16, 1862; *Greenville Observer*, May 7, 1862, reprinted in *Selma Daily Reporter*, May 12, 1862, 1; *Mobile Tribune*, reprinted in *Daily Columbus* (Georgia) *Enquirer*, May 14, 1862, 2; McMillan, *Disintegration of a Confederate State*, 37.

154. *Montgomery Weekly Advertiser*, May 24, 1862, June 6, 1862; (New Orleans) *Daily Picayune*, May 29, 1862, 2.

155. *New York Times*, June 14, 1862, 4.

156. *Daily Columbus* (Georgia) *Enquirer*, May 30, 1862, 2.

157. Ibid., June 2, 1862, 2. See also Donald, *Lincoln*, 363.

158. See *Montgomery Weekly Advertiser*, May 10, 1862, May 13, 1862, May 20, 1862, May 22, 1862; *Mobile Advertiser and Register*, May 13, 1862, 2. Regarding Butler, see James Fairfax McLaughlin, *American Cyclops: The Hero of New Orleans, and Spoiler of Silver Spoons* (Baltimore: Kelly and Piet, 1868); Robert Werlich, *"Beast" Butler: The Incredible Career of Major General Benjamin Franklin Butler* (Washington, DC: Quaker Press, 1962); Chester G. Hearn, *When the Devil Came Down to Dixie: Ben Butler in New Orleans* (Baton Rouge: Louisiana State University Press, 1997); Hess, *Civil War in the West*, 83–91. Butler was the military commander in New Orleans after it fell in 1862. After unruly behavior from Confederate citizens (especially women), toward Union soldiers, Butler issued an order stating that any women seen on the streets would be dealt with as prostitutes; whether this order was actually carried out is unknown. Confederate propagandists used Butler's conduct as a means of encouraging resistance, knowing that women would encourage the men in their lives to continue fighting.

159. *Eutaw Whig*, quoted in *Montgomery Weekly Advertiser*, May 16, 1862. *Selma Daily Reporter*, June 5, 1862, 2.

160. Diary of Miss Catherine M. Fennell, 34.

161. *Montgomery Weekly Advertiser*, May 22, 1862, May 28, 1862.

162. *Mobile Advertiser and Register*, May 20, 1862, 2.

163. *Montgomery Weekly Advertiser*, May 29, 1862; *Daily Columbus* (Georgia) *Enquirer*, May 30, 1862, 3.

164. *Montgomery Advertiser*, reprinted in *New York Times*, May 31, 1862, 2.

165. Margaret Josephine Miles Gillis Diary, July 8, 1862, SPR 5, Alabama Department of Archives and History, Montgomery.

166. Linden and Linden, eds., *Disunion*, 84. See (Selma) *Alabama State Sentinel*, August 6, 1862; *Montgomery Weekly Advertiser*, June 10, 1862, June 11, 1862; (Greensboro) *Alabama Beacon*, June 6, 1862, 2; *Selma Daily Reporter*, June 3, 1862, 2, June 5, 1862, 2, June 9, 1862, 2; *Mobile Advertiser and Register*, June 3, 1862, 2; (New Orleans) *Daily Picayune*, June 14, 1862, 1.

Chapter 7

1. Fleming, *Civil War and Reconstruction*, 78–83. Noe, ed., *Yellowhammer War*, 2 ("90,000 to 120,000").

2. The 1860 Alabama census indicated that there were 106,000 Alabama men of military age. Of these, an estimated 36,000 were in the field. *Mobile Advertiser and Register*, October 2, 1861; (New Orleans) *Daily Picayune*, January 17, 1862, 2;

(Huntsville) *Democrat*, February 12, 1862, 4; McMillan, *Disintegration of a Confederate State*, 23 (27,000 as of December 1861).

3. *Selma Daily Reporter*, April 21, 1862, 1.

4. Noe, *Reluctant Rebels*, 209.

5. Ibid., 13, 108, 121.

6. *Selma Reporter*, reprinted in *Boston Daily Advertiser*, June 25, 1862, 2.

7. Moore, *Conscription and Conflict in the Confederacy*, 130.

8. *Selma Reporter*, reprinted in *Boston Daily Advertiser*, June 25, 1862, 2; (New Orleans) *Daily Picayune*, June 13, 1862, 1; *Mobile Advertiser and Register*, June 3, 1862, 2; *Selma Daily Reporter*, June 5, 1862, 2; *Daily Columbus* (Georgia) *Enquirer*, June 5, 1862, 2, June 6, 1862, 3; *New York Times*, May 31, 1862, 4, June 1, 1862, 4, June 5, 1862, 8; McWhiney, *Braxton Bragg and Confederate Defeat*, 257–58; Feis, *Grant's Secret Service*, 109.

9. *Selma Daily Reporter*, June 9, 1862, 2; *Montgomery Weekly Advertiser*, June 10, 1862; (New Orleans) *Daily Picayune*, June 26, 1862, 1. See also *New York Times*, June 9, 1862, 4, June 12, 1862, 1; Hess, *Civil War in the West*, 60.

10. Stoker, *Grand Design*, 132–33.

11. Alan Sewell, "Dissent: The Free State of Winston," *Civil War Times Illustrated* 20 (December, 1981): 30, 35–36; McMillan, *Alabama Confederate Reader*, 172–76; Dodd and Dodd, *Free State of Winston*, 93–95; Charles Rice, *Hard Times*, 146–47; Glenda McWhirter Todd, *First Alabama Cavalry, U.S.A.: Homage to Patriotism* (Bowie, MD: Heritage Books, 1999), 5–7; (Dalton, Georgia) *Huntsville Confederate*, March 26, 1863, 3; Fleming, *Civil War and Reconstruction in Alabama*, 126, 154; *Alabama House Journal*, 121–22 (1862). But see Thompson, *Free State of Winston*, 47–48 (crediting Bill Looney of Looney's Tavern). See, generally, Official Records, Series 1, Vol. 16 (Part I), 785–91, Series 1, Vol. 16 (Part II), 125, Series 2, Vol. 5, 589.

12. *Montgomery Weekly Advertiser*, June 24, 1862. See also *Montgomery Weekly Advertiser*, July 30, 1862.

13. A. D. Streight to Capt. W. H. Schlater, July 16, 1862, Official Records, Series 1, Vol. 16 (Part II), 789. Regarding Streight, see Robert L. Willett Jr., *The Lightning Mule Brigade: Abel Streight's 1863 Raid into Alabama* (Carmel, IN: Guild Press, 1999), 17–19; Storey, *Loyalty and Loss*, 87, 102–3, 127.

14. See, e.g., Fleming, *Civil War and Reconstruction in Alabama*, 117; Hoole, *Alabama Tories*, 14 (also stating that 2,066 served in the First Alabama Cavalry, USA).

15. James B. Fry to General George H. Thomas, July 11, 1862, Official Records Series 1, Vol. 16 (Part II), 124.

16. George H. Thomas to Col. J. B. Fry, July 12, 1862, Official Records, Series 1, Vol. 16 (Part II), 132.

17. A. D. Streight to Capt. W. H. Schlater, Official Records, Series I, Vol. 16 (Part 1), 785–90; O. P. Morton to E. M. Stanton, May 11, 1863, Official Records, Series 2, Vol. 5, 589.

18. Official Records, Series 1, Vol. 17 (Part II), 648–49, 656–58. See, generally, Kenneth W. Noe, *Perryville: This Grand Havoc of Battle* (Lexington: University of Kentucky Press, 2001), 22–30; McWhiney, *Braxton Bragg and Confederate Defeat*, 266–74; Feis, *Grant's Secret Service*, 111.

19. Hess, *Civil War in the West*, 94–105; Escott, *Confederacy*, 50–53; Stoker, *Grand Design*, 175–91.

20. D. C. Buell to General J. D. Morgan, July 29, 1862, Official Records, Series 1, Vol. 16 (Part II), 225.

21. Thomas Jordan, Special Orders No. 123, July 17, 1862, Series I, Vol. 16 (Part II), 648–49, 767–68.

22. W. S. Rosecrans to Major General Buell, July 29, 1862, J. K. Mizner to Col. J. B. Fry, July 29, 1862, James D. Morgan to Major General Buell, August 10, 1862, Official Records, Series 1, Vol. 16 (Part II), 225, 227, 303–4; James D. Morgan to Brigadier General Elliott, July 31, 1862, August 1, 1862, and August 3, 1862, Official Records, Series 1, Vol. 52 (Part I), 266–68; Frank C. Armstrong to Major Thomas L. Snead, July 26, 1862, Official Records, Series 1, Vol. 16 (Part I), 827–28.

23. D. C. Buell to Maj. Gen. William Nelson, August 10, 1862, Official Records, Series I, Vol. 16 (Part II), 304.

24. *Daily Columbus* (Georgia) *Enquirer*, September 2, 1862, 2, September 5, 1862, 2; *Montgomery Weekly Advertiser*, September 9, 1862; *Chattanooga Rebel*, August 14, 1862, 2, reprinted in *Daily Columbus* (Georgia) *Enquirer*, September 16, 1862, 2; McWhiney, *Braxton Bragg and Confederate Defeat*, 281–91; Clifton R. Hall, *Andrew Johnson: Military Governor of Tennessee* (Princeton, NJ: Princeton University Press, 1916), 59–61; Noe, *Perryville*, 47; Charles Rice, *Hard Times*, 120–21; McMillan, *Alabama Confederate Reader*, 176–79; Samuel Jones to Governor Shorter, September 8, 1862, Official Records, Series 1, Vol. 16 (Part II), 802 (reporting that there were no United States troops in north Alabama east of Decatur).

25. C. C. Clay Jr. to John Gill Shorter, September 27, 1862, Papers of Governor Shorter, Alabama Department of Archives and History, Montgomery.

26. Dee, "Trying James Hickman," 94–112; Storey, *Loyalty and Loss*, 57–59, 64.

27. (New Orleans) *Daily Picayune*, September 21, 1862, 2 (referring to Clemens and Lane); *Jacksonville Republican*, September 25, 1862, reprinted in McMillan, *Alabama Confederate Reader*, 180 (referring to Lane); *Montgomery Weekly Advertiser*, September 9, 1862; *Selma Morning Reporter*, November 20, 1862, 1 (Lane); Dee, "Trying James Hickman," 94.

28. James Oakes, *Freedom National: The Destruction of Slavery in the United States, 1861–1865* (New York: W. W. Norton, 2013), 423.

29. Official Records, Series 1, Vol. 17 (Part II), 213.

30. Official Records, Series 2, Vol. 4, 496–97; *Montgomery Weekly Advertiser*, September 10, 1862.

31. Fleming, *Civil War and Reconstruction in Alabama*, 404n2; Naomi Peters Claim, Lawrence County, Disallowed and Barred claims, RG 233, Southern Claims Commission, 1871–1880, NARA Microfiche M 1407, National Archives, Washington, DC; Horton, "Submitting to the Shadow of Slavery," 122.

32. Joseph Bradley to Gov. John Gill Shorter, October 9, 1862, Papers of Governor Shorter, Alabama Department of Archives and History, Montgomery; (Dalton, Georgia) *Huntsville Confederate*, March 26, 1863, 3; (Grove Hill) *Clarke County Journal*, June 4, 1863, 2; *Alabama House Journal*, 121–22 (November 17, 1862); (Montgomery)

Alabama State Journal, September 2, 1872, reprinted in *Little Rock Daily Republican*, October 12, 1872; (Tuscaloosa) *Blade*, October 3, 1872; Sewell, "Free State of Winston," 36; Rice, *Hard Times*, 147–51; T. A. Deland and A. David Smith, eds., *Northern Alabama: Historical and Biographical* (Birmingham, AL: Smith and Deland, 1888), 327.

33. *Jacksonville Republican*, September 25, 1862, reprinted in McMillan, *Alabama Confederate Reader*, 180; Dee, "Trying James Hickman," 97–101.

34. (Greensboro) *Alabama Beacon*, November 27, 1865, 2.

35. *Mobile Weekly Advertiser and Register*, November 1, 1862. See also, Shields, *Freedom in a Slave Society*, 278–79.

36. *New York Times*, November 19, 1862, 2.

37. *Selma Morning Reporter*, October 2, 1862, 1; (New Orleans) *Daily Picayune*, October 15, 1862, 2; Moore, *Conscription and Conflict in the Confederacy*, 138–41.

38. *Mobile Tribune*, reprinted in the *Montgomery Daily Mail*, October 25, 1862, reprinted in Dodd and Dodd, *Free State of Winston*, 91n26.

39. Horton, "Submitting to the Shadow of Slavery," 132–33.

40. Marilyn Davis Barefield, *Historical Records of Randolph County, Alabama: 1832–1900* (Birmingham, AL: M. D. Barefield, 1995), 83; Randolph County Heritage Book Committee, *The Heritage of Randolph County, Alabama* (Randolph County, AL: Heritage Pub. Consultants, 1998), 256; McMillan, *Disintegration of a Confederate State*, 41; A. R. Hill to John Gill Shorter, November 29, 1862, Papers of Governor Shorter, Alabama Department of Archives and History, Montgomery.

41. Private Journal of Sarah R. Espy, 48.

42. Diary of Catherine M. Fennell, 41–42.

43. *Selma Morning Reporter*, October 2, 1862, 1; Burrus M. Carnaman, *Act of Justice: Lincoln's Emancipation Proclamation and the Law of War* (Lexington: University Press of Kentucky, 2007), 75; Harold Holzer, Edna Greene Medford, and Frank J. Williams, *The Emancipation Proclamation: Three* Views (Baton Rouge: Louisiana State University Press, 2006), 62–70; Roland C. McConnell, "From Preliminary to Final Emancipation Proclamation: The First Hundred Days," *Journal of Negro History* 48 (October 1963): 260; George C. Rable, *God's Almost Chosen Peoples: A Religious History of the American Civil War* (Chapel Hill: University of North Carolina Press, 2010), 192–97. For reaction in the South, see, e.g., (Greensboro) *Alabama Beacon*, October 10, 1862, 3; (New Orleans) *Daily Picayune*, October 9, 1862, 2 (publishing an article from the *Louisville Journal*), October 18, 1862, 1 (publishing a letter from Tennessean T. A. R. Nelson), November 1, 1862, (same); William Ben Campbell to Andrew Johnson, November 2, 1862, Graf et al., ed., *Papers of Andrew Johnson*, 5: 46–47; (New Orleans) *Daily Picayune*, December 18, 1862, 2 (reprinting a portion of a letter that appeared in the *New York Herald*). See, generally, William K. Klingaman, *Abraham Lincoln and the Road to Emancipation 1861–1865* (New York: Viking Press, 2001), 81; Sellers, *History of the University of Alabama*, 274–75 (discussing Landon Garland's fears of a slave insurrection in October of 1862).

44. Bertis English, "Freedom's Church: Sociocultural Construction, Reconstruction, and Post-Reconstruction in Perry County, Alabama's African American Churches," in *Yellowhammer War*, ed. Kenneth W. Noe, 259.

45. (New Orleans) *Daily Picayune*, October 9, 1862, 2, October 18, 1862, 1, November 1, 1862, 2; Sellers, *History of the University of Alabama*, 274–75.

46. (Greensboro) *Alabama Beacon*, October 10, 1862, 3; Timothy B. Smith, *Corinth 1862: Siege, Battle, Occupation* (Lawrence: University Press of Kansas, 2012); (New Orleans) *Daily Picayune*, October 12, 1862, 4, October 16, 1862, 2; Evans, *Confederate Military History* 7: 265–67; Peter Cozzens, *The Darkest Days of the War: The Battles of Iuka & Corinth* (Chapel Hill: UNC Press, 1997), 254–70.

47. (New Orleans) *Daily Picayune*, October 21, 1862, 1, October 31, 1862, 1, November 1, 1862, 1, December 12, 1862, 1; (Greensboro) *Alabama Beacon*, October 24, 1862, 1; *Selma Morning Reporter*, October 29, 1862, 1, November 10, 1862, 1; Burnett, *Pen Makes a Good Sword*, 137; McWhiney, *Braxton Bragg and Confederate Defeat*, 293–336; Noe, *Perryville*.

48. C. C. Clay Jr. to G. W. Randolph, October 24, 1862, Official Records, Series 4, Vol. 2, 141.

49. James Phelan Sr. to Jefferson Davis, December 9, 1862, Official Records, Series 1, Vol. 17 (Part II), 792. Regarding Lee, see Escott, *Confederacy*, 38–41.

50. Anonymous woman to Gov. Watts, July, 1864, Papers of Governor Watts, Alabama Department of Archives and History, Montgomery.

51. *Montgomery Weekly Advertiser*, May 20, 1862; (Greensboro) *Alabama Beacon*, May 23, 1862, 2–3; *Mobile Advertiser and Register*, May 20, 1862, 1; *Alabama House Journal*, 91–92 (1862); McMillan, *Disintegration of a Confederate State*, 41–43; Sellers, *History of the University of Alabama*, 269.

52. (Greensboro) *Alabama Beacon*, October 17, 1862, 2, December 5, 1862, 2; *Selma Morning Reporter*, January 19, 1863, 2. See, generally, Moore, *Conscription and Conflict in the Confederacy*, 68n33, 70–71.

53. *Selma Daily Reporter*, May 20, 1862, 2 (publishing an advertisement for a substitute), November 20, 1862, 1; *(Greensboro) Alabama Beacon*, December 5, 1862, 2; *Augusta* (Georgia) *Chronicle*, June 4, 1863, 1. See, generally, Moore, *Conscription and Conflict in the Confederacy*, 27–51; Noe, *Reluctant Rebels*, 114–18.

54. C. C. Clay Jr. to G. W. Randolph, October 21, 1862, Official Records, Series 4, Vol. 2, 140.

55. J. B. Moore to Thomas H. Watts, June 15, 1864, Papers of Governor Watts, Alabama Department of Archives and History, Montgomery.

56. Malinda Taylor to Grant Taylor, May 8, 1862, in *This Cruel War*, ed. ed.s Blomquist and Taylor, 14–15.

57 Noe, *Reluctant Rebels*, 175.

58. Sterling Price to Brig. Gen. Thomas Jordan, August 31, 1862, Official Records, Series 1, Vol. 16 (Part I), 884.

59. Scott, "Philip Dale Roddey," 40,

60. (Montgomery) *Alabama State Journal*, October 23, 1872, 1. See also Moore, *Daily Journal of Joshua Burns Moore*, 53–54.

61. Brewer, *Alabama*, 682–83; Diary of Sally Independence Foster, Archives and Special Collections, Collier Library, University of North Alabama.

62. Daily Journal of Joshua Burns Moore, 63–64.

63. Nina Leftwich, *Two Hundred Years at Muscle Shoals, Being an Authentic History of Colbert County 1700–1900 with Special Emphasis on the Stirring Events of the Early Times* (Tuscumbia, AL: American Legion Post #31, 1998)). 211.

64. (Tuscumbia) *North Alabamian*, June 4, 1886, 3 (announcing a reunion of this group).

65. Naomi Peters Claim, Southern Claims Commission; Horton, "Submitting to the Shadow of Slavery," 122–24; *Memorial Record of Alabama*, 2: 407; Smith and DeLand, *Northern Alabama Historical and Biographical*, 73.

66. Dodd Dodd, *Free State of Winston*, 96–97; *Selma Reporter*, reprinted in (Washington, DC) *Daily National Intelligencer*, February 19, 1863, 3; Noe, ed., *Yellowhammer War*, 6 (estimating that 10,000 deserters hid in north Alabama); McMillan, *Disintegration of a Confederate Sate*, 58–59 (same).

67. *Montgomery Daily Advertiser*, December 20, 1862, 2 (publishing Yancey's speech to the Alabama legislature on December 3, 1862).

68. *Ala. Acts*, Act No. 12: p. 26, No. 11: p. 25, No. 143: pp. 155, 165, and No. 178: p. 179 (1862); ibid., No. 26, p. 42 (1862); ibid., No. 30, p. 47 (1862); ibid., No. 149, p. 162 (1862); ibid., No. 150, p. 162 (1862).

69. Ibid., Joint Resolution, 201–2 (1862).

70. *Alabama House Journal*, 4, 24, 27, 56, 66–67, 105, 121–23 (1862–1863). Interestingly, Benners did not discuss or even mention this episode in his journal. Sheats was later indicted for treason and denied bail but was never brought to trial. (Dalton, Georgia) *Huntsville Confederate*, March 26, 1863, 3; (Dalton, Georgia) *Huntsville Confederate*, reprinted in *Daily Columbus* (Georgia) *Enquirer*, February 19, 1864, 2; (Grove Hill) *Clarke County Journal*, June 4, 1863, 2.

71. Early J. Hess, *Banners to the Breeze: The Kentucky Campaign, Corinth and Stones River* (Lincoln: University of Nebraska Press, 2000), 177–231; Steven E. Woodworth, *Six Armies in Tennessee: The Chickamauga and Chattanooga Campaigns* (Lincoln: University of Nebraska Press, 1998), 2–4; Peter Cozzens, *No Better Place to Die: The Battle of Stones River* (Urbana: University of Illinois Press, 1990).

72. (New Orleans) *Daily Picayune*, January 14, 1863, 1.

73. (New Orleans) *Daily Picayune*, December 27, 1862, 1, January 1, 1863, 1. See, generally, *Mobile Advertiser and Register*, December 23, 1862, 1; George C. Rable, *Fredericksburg! Fredericksburg!* (Chapel Hill: University of North Carolina Press, 2002), 328–29.

74. (Grove Hill) *Clarke County Journal*, January 8, 1863, 2 (reporting Davis's speech in Mobile on December 30, 1862). See also *Daily Columbus* (Georgia) *Enquirer*, June 21, 1862, 2, July 14, 1862, 2, August 12, 1862, 2, August 16, 1862, 2.

75. James Phelan to Jefferson Davis, December 9, 1862, Official Records, Series 1, Vol. 17 (Part II), 790; *Mobile Advertiser and Register*, December 13, 1862, 2; Robert W. Dubay, *John Jones Pettus, Mississippi Fire-Eater: His Life and Times, 1813–1867* (Jackson: University Press of Mississippi, 2008), 153, 157.

76. *Mobile Advertiser and Register*, December 14, 1862, 2.

77. John S. Meriwether to Alice, December 21, 1862, quoted in Noe, *Reluctant Rebels*, 177.

78. Daniel, *Soldiering in the Army of Tennessee*, 126–29.

79. Reuben Searcy to Evie Searcy, November 20, 1862, Papers of James T. Searcy, Alabama Department of Archives and History, Montgomery. Johnston was appointed departmental commander at this point but not placed in direct command of the Army of Tennessee. Stoker, *Grand Design*, 234.

80. Reuben Searcy to Mother, December 26, 1862, Papers of James T. Searcy, Alabama Department of Archives and History, Montgomery.

81. Sarah E. L. Koon to George A. Koon, November 19, 1862, in *Family History: Kuhns-Koon-Koons-Kohn-Coon: Kith and Kin: Suber-Wedaman-Miller-Folk-Hickman-Craft-Cash*, by Kathleen S. Brown, 38 (Gordo, AL: K.S. Brown, 1990). A couple of weeks later she wrote to him that a local man "said he wished you all would pick up your guns and come home," and that others were returning. She also made him aware that she had heard "they are catching the men with dogs" before again warning him not to desert. Sarah Koon to George A. Koon, December 7, 1862, in, *Family History*, by Kathleen S. Brown, 42. Her correspondence, which also consistently wished that he was at home with her and their children, could not have failed to cause Koon to be conflicted. Koon did not desert and died in 1864 in a Virginia hospital.

82. James Phelan to Jefferson Davis, December 9, 1862, Official Records, Series 1, Vol. 17 (Part II), 790.

83. *Selma Morning Reporter*, January 10, 1863, 2. See, generally, (New Orleans) *Daily Picayune*, January 9, 1863, 1, January 13, 1863, 2, January 14, 1863, 1, January 17, 1863, 1, January 18, 1863, 1; McWhiney, *Braxton Bragg and Confederate Defeat*, 352–74; Morales, *41st Alabama Infantry Regiment*, 127; Stoker, *Grand Design*, 222.

84. *Winchester Bulletin*, reprinted in *Selma Morning Reporter*, January 10, 1863, 2. *Mobile News*, reprinted in (New Orleans) *Daily Picayune*, January 22, 1863, 2.

85. Stoker, *Grand Design*, 222, 237.

86. Morales, *The 41st Alabama Infantry Regiment*, 122.

87. Ibid., 146–47.

88. *Selma Reporter*, reprinted in *Macon Daily Telegraph*, February 13, 1863, 4.

89. Morales, *41st Alabama*, 146–47.

Chapter 8

Epigraph. Malinda Taylor to Grant Taylor, October 21, 1862, in *This Cruel War*, ed.s Blomquist and Taylor, 112–13 (a letter from a Tuscaloosa County woman whose husband was serving near Mobile, Alabama).

1. B. R. Johnson to Col. Thomas Jordan, April 21, 1862, Official Records, Series 1, Vol. 10 (Part II), 431.

2. (Grove Hill) *Clarke County Journal*, February 5, 1863, 2; W. L. Walthall to John A. Campbell, November 24, 1862, Official Records, Series 4, Vol. 2, 207–8; John Gill Shorter to George W. Randolph, September 19, 1862, Official Records, Series 4, Vol. 2, 87.

3. John Gill Shorter to James A. Seddon, December 23, 1862, Official Records, Series 4, Vol. 2, 258.

4. David Peter Lewis to Gov. Watts, February 9, 1863, Papers of Governor Watts, Alabama Department of Archives and History, Montgomery.

5. See, generally, Frank L. Owsley, "Defeatism in the Confederacy," *North Carolina Historical Review* 3 (July 1926): 446, 452–55; Georgia Lee Tatum, *Disloyalty in the Confederacy* (Lincoln: University of Nebraska Press, 2000), 26, 54–63.

6. (Montgomery) *Alabama State Sentinel*, October 17, 1867, 2. See also (Montgomery) *Alabama State Sentinel*, August 31, 1867, 2; (Montgomery) *Alabama State Journal*, October 22, 1871, 2.

7. *Memphis Daily Bulletin*, February 11, 1863. See also G. M. Dodge to Colonel Roddey, January 17, 1863, Official Records, Series 2, Vol. 5, 185.

8. G. M. Dodge to Col. Roddey, January 17, 1863, Official Records, Series 2, Vol. 5, 185; Thompson, *Free State of Winston*, 55.

9. For discussion of refugee life, see Mary Elizabeth Massey, *Refugee Life in the Confederacy* (Baton Rouge: Louisiana State University Press, 2001), 46, 86; Steven V. Ash, *When the Yankees Came: Conflict and Chaos in the Occupied South, 1861–1865* (Chapel Hill: University of North Carolina Press, 1995), 111–12, 178. For the life of Grenville Dodge, see Stanley P. Hirshson, *Grenville M. Dodge: Soldier, Politician, Railroad Pioneer* (Bloomington: Indiana University Press, 1967); Steven E. Woodworth, *Grant's Lieutenants: From Cairo to Vicksburg* (Lawrence: University Press of Kansas, 2001), 183–98; Feis, *Grant's Secret Service*, 125–29.

10. Hirshson, *Grenville M. Dodge*, 132–72; Woodworth, *Grant's Lieutenants*, 183–87; Stephen E. Ambrose, *Nothing Like It in the World: The Men Who Built the Transcontinental Railroad*, 1863–1869 (New York: Simon & Schuster, 2000), 18, 31–33.

11. G. M. Dodge to Capt. R. M. Sawyer, January 24, 1863, Official Records, Series I, Vol. 23, Part II, 11. See also *Memphis Daily Bulletin*, March 12, 1863, 1; *New York Times*, March 8, 1863, 8 (referring to Dodge's report); *New Haven Daily Palladium*, March 4, 1863 (publishing a letter from a Union soldier in Corinth); Bella Zilfa Spencer, *Tried and True or Love and Loyalty: A Story of the Great Rebellion* (Springfield, MA: W. J. Holland, 1866), iii–ix (a book written by the wife of George Eliphaz Spencer).

12. (Montgomery) *Alabama State Sentinel*, October 10, 1867, 2; Storey, *Loyalty and Loss*, 86.

13. Woodworth, *Grant's Lieutenants*, 191–96; Feis, *Grant's Secret Service*, 126–29, 166–67; Hirshson, *Grenville M. Dodge*, 60, 67–68, 73–74; George Sibley Johns, *Philip Henson, the Southern Union Spy* (St. Louis: Nixon-Jones Print Co., 1887), 33–47, 73 (a biography of one of Dodge's spies, who was born in Jackson County); Harnett T. Kane, *Spies for the Blue and Gray* (Garden City, NY: Hanover House, 1954), 198; Storey, *Loyalty and Loss*, 154–59.

14. Woodworth, *Grant's Lieutenants*, 193; Feis, *Grant's Secret Service*, 128; Fleming, *Civil War and Reconstruction in Alabama*, 125; James Alex Baggett, *The Scalawags: Southern Dissenters in the Civil War and Reconstruction* (Baton Rouge: Louisiana State University Press, 2004), 73, 161; Storey, *Loyalty and Loss*, 103; Hirshson, *Grenville M. Dodge*, 119; Hoole, *Alabama Tories*, 17, 33; Richard Nelson Current, *Lincoln's Loyalists: Union Soldiers from the Confederacy* (Boston: Northeastern University Press, 1992), 103–6;

(Tuscumbia) *North Alabamian and Times*, April 14, 1870, 3, October 18, 1870, 2, October 27, 1870, 1, November 3, 1870, 1; (Montgomery) *Alabama State Sentinel*, July 4, 1867, 1 (a biographical sketch of Smith); (Montgomery) *Alabama State Journal*, October 16, 1874, 2 (publishing a letter from Smith); (Tuscaloosa) *Independent Monitor*, October 25, 1870, 1, November 1, 1870, 2. See also John R. Phillips, "The Diary of a Union Soldier from Alabama," *Alabama Heritage* 28 (Spring 1993): 20–25; Dodd, "Free State of Winston," 8, 10, 13–19.

15. Spencer would later be stereotyped by political opponents and historians as the prototypical grasping and scheming carpetbagger politician in his role as one of Alabama's Reconstruction Era US senators. Wiggins, *Scalawag in Alabama Politics*, 39, 57–61; Woodworth, *Grant's Lieutenants*, 196; Hirshson, *Grenville M. Dodge*, 64, 73–74, 119, 129, 159; Current, *Lincoln's Loyalists*, 30–32; Hoole, *Alabama Tories*, 29, 32; Sarah Van V. Woolfolk, "George E. Spencer: A Carpetbagger in Alabama," *Alabama Review* 19 (January 1966): 41–42; *New York Times*, August 15, 1863, 5; *Washington Post*, February 20, 1893, 1; Official Record, Series 1, Vol. 30, 118; Michael W. Fitzgerald, "Republican Factionalism and Black Empowerment: The Spencer-Warner Controversy and Alabama Reconstruction, 1868–1880," *Journal of Southern History* 64 (August, 1998): 473; Terry L. Seip, "Of Ambition and Enterprise: The Making of Carpetbagger George E. Spencer," in *Yellowhammer War*, ed. Kenneth W. Noe, 191–219.

16. John Gill Shorter to Jefferson Davis, January 10, 1863, Official Records, Series 1, Vol. 15, 939.

17. John Gill Shorter to James A. Seddon, January 14, 1863, Official Records, Series 1, Vol. 15, 946.

18. *New York Post*, January 14, 1863, reprinted in (New Orleans) *Daily Picayune*, January 29, 1863, 2. See also (New Orleans) *Delta*, cited in (New Orleans) *Daily Picayune*, February 15, 1863, 4.

19. *Mobile Advertiser and Register*, May 29, 1862, 2.

20. Ibid., reprinted in *Selma Daily Reporter*, March 4, 1862, 1. See also (New Orleans) *Daily Picayune*, April 8, 1862, 2 (comparing the Battle of Shiloh to those at Saratoga and Yorktown).

21. (Grove Hill) *Clarke County Journal*, November 13, 1862, 2. *Mobile Advertiser and Register*, December 19, 1863, 2; *Selma Reporter*, reprinted in (Houston, Texas) *Tri-Weekly Telegraph*, April 13, 1863, 2.

22. (Grove Hill) *Clarke County Journal*, January 1, 1863, 2; *Mobile Advertiser and Register*, December 28, 1862, 1; (New Orleans) *Daily Picayune*, January 4, 1863, 1.

23. (New Orleans) *Daily Picayune*, January 22, 1863, 2.

24. *Selma Reporter*, reprinted in *Memphis Daily Appeal*, May 1, 1863, 1; *New York Times*, February 18, 1863, 4, March 17, 1863, 4; (New Orleans) *Daily Picayune*, March 14, 1863, 2. See, generally, Joseph E. Stevens, *1863: The Rebirth of a Nation* (New York: Bantam Books, 1999), 71–74; Bruce Tap, *Over Lincoln's Shoulder: The Committee on the Conduct of the War* (Lawrence: University of Kansas Press, 1998), 143, 149; Van der Linden, *Dark Intrigue*, 54–65; Jerome Mushkat, *Fernando Wood: A Political Biography* (Kent, OH: Kent State University Press, 1990), 130–51.

25. (New Orleans) *Daily Picayune*, March 14, 1863, 2.

26. J. K. Callaway to Dulcinea Callaway, May 19, 1863, in *The Civil War Letters of Joshua K. Callaway*, ed. Judith Lee Hallock, 91 (Athens: University of Georgia Press, 1997): 91.

27. *Selma Morning Reporter*, January 10, 1863, 2.

28. Ibid., February 6, 1863, 2.

29. Ibid., February 7, 1863, 2.

30. Ibid., February 12, 1863, 2. See also *Selma Daily Reporter*, February 20, 1863, 2. See also *Mobile Advertiser and Register*, February 12, 1863, 2; (Grove Hill) *Clarke County Journal*, January 20, 1863 (Lawrence: University of Kansas Press, 1998), 63; (Grove Hill), *Clarke County Journal*, February 5, 1863, 2, February 19, 1863, 2, February 25, 1863, 2.

31. J. K. Callaway to Dulcinea Callaway, April 5, 1863, in *Civil War Letters of Joshua Callaway*, ed. Judith Lee Hallock, 79.

32. *Morgan, Adm'r v. Nelson, Adm'r*, 43 Ala. 586 (1869).

Chapter 9

1. *New York Herald*, February 9, 1863; *Milwaukee Daily Sentinel*, March 4, 1863; *Boston Daily Advertiser*, March 25, 1863; *Daily Cleveland Herald*, April 16, 1863; *Milwaukee Daily Sentinel*, February 16, 1863 ("A Voice from Rosecrans's Army"), February 24, 1863, April 4, 1863 ("Wisconsin Soldiers on the Copperheads"), February 25, 1863; *New Haven* (Connecticut) *Daily Palladium*, February 18, 1863 ("What Indiana and Ohio Soldiers Think of the Copperheads"), February 28, 1863; *New York Tribune*, reprinted in (Philadelphia) *North American and United States Gazette*, February 27, 1863; *Bangor* (Maine) *Daily Whig & Courier*, February 28, 1863, March 23, 1863; *Wisconsin State Register*, March 14, 1863; *Scioto* (Ohio) *Gazette*, March 24, 1863; *Daily Cleveland Herald*, April 15, 1863; *Ripley* (Ohio) *Bee*, April 16, 1863.

2. Grenville M. Dodge to John A. Kasson, November 22, 1862, Lincoln Papers, Library of Congress. See also Hubert H. Wubben, *Civil War Iowa and the Copperhead Movement* (Ames: Iowa State University Press, 1980), 111, 126.

3. *Milwaukee Daily Sentinel*, March 9, 1863.

4. Regarding Cornyn, see *New York Times*, August 23, 1863, 6, September 13, 1863, 4; *New York Herald*, August 15, 1863; *St. Louis Globe-Democrat*, August 8, 1880, May 21, 1882, 17, May 28, 1882, 4; Florence M. Cornyn to "General," July 9, 1863, Official Records, Series 1, Vol. 24 (Part II), 663.

5. Stoker, *Grand Design*, 411.

6. Arthur James Lyon Fremantle, *Three Months in the Southern States: April–June, 1863* (London: Tantor Media, 1863 [2012]), 142–43 (containing a reprint of a newspaper article).

7. Regarding Cornyn's raiders, see Sean Michael O'Brien, *Mountain Partisans: Guerrilla Warfare in the Southern Appalachians, 1861–1865* (Westport, CT: Praeger, 1999), 87; William Lindsey McDonald, *A Walk through the Past—People and Places of Florence and Lauderdale County, Alabama* (Killen, AL: Heart of Dixie Pub., 2003), 108.

8. G. M. Dodge to Major-General Rosecrans, February 23, 1863, Series 1, Vol. 23 (Part 1), 64.

9. (Dalton, Georgia) *Huntsville Confederate*, March 5, 1863, reprinted in *Mobile Advertiser and Register*, March 12, 1863, 1.

10. C. S. Hamilton to Major-General Hurlburt, February 25, 1863 and G. M. Dodge to Major General Rosecrans, February 23, 1863, Official Records, Series 1, Vol. 23 (Part I), 63–64.

11. G. M. Dodge to Major-General Rosecrans, February 23, 1863, Official Re cords, Series 1, Vol. 23 (Part 1), 64; Patton Keith Pickens, "A History of the Fifth Alabama Cavalry Regiment CSA," *Journal of Muscle Shoals History* 15 (1999): 93, 95.

12. (Greensboro) *Alabama Beacon*, April 3, 1863, 2. See also Diary of Sally Independence Foster, February 28, 1863; *Huntsville Advocate*, reprinted in *Montgomery Daily Advertiser*, March 8, 1863, 1, 3; (Dalton, Georgia) *Huntsville Confederate*, March 5, 1863, reprinted in *Mobile Advertiser and Register*, March 12, 1863, 1, March 17, 1863, 2; (New Orleans) *Daily Picayune*, March 13, 1863, 2.

13. *Mobile Advertiser and Register*, March 17, 1863, 2. See also Leftwich, *Muscle Shoals*, 199–201, 207; Jill K. Garrett, *A History of Florence, Alabama* (Columbia, TN: J. K. Garrett, 1968), 35; Daily Journal of Joshua Burns Moore, 68–69.

14. (Greensboro) *Alabama Beacon*, February 27, 1863, 2.

15. Geo. E. Spencer to Brig. Gen. Grenville M. Dodge, March 22, 1863, Official Records, Series 1, Vol. 24 (Part III), 129–30.

16. G. M. Dodge to Capt. Henry Binmore, March 30, 1863, Official Records, Series 1, Vol. 24 (Part III), 155–56.

17. Th. J. Wood, to Brig. Gen. James Garfield, April 6, 1863, Official Records, Series 1, Vol. 23 (Part II), 213–14; Willett, *Lightning Mule Brigade*, 21.

18. D. Alexander Brown, *Grierson's Raid: A Cavalry Adventure of the Civil War* (Urbana: University of Illinois Press, 1981), 23–25; William H. Leckie and Shirley A. Leckie, *Unlikely Warriors: General Benjamin H. Grierson and His Family* (Norman: University of Oklahoma Press, 1984), 83–87. See also *Mobile Advertiser and Register*, April 26, 1863, 2.

19. G. M. Dodge to Henry Binmore, April 4, 1863, Official Records, Series 1, Vol. 23 (Part II), 214–15.

20. W. S. Rosecrans to Major General Hurlburt, April 5, 1863, Official Records, Series 1, Vol. 23 (Part II), 215; S.A. Hurlburt to Maj. Gen. W.S. Rosecrans, April 9, 1863, Series 1, Vol. 23 (Part II), 223; W. S. Rosecrans to Maj. Gen. H. W. Halleck, April 12, 1863 and to Major General Hurlburt, April 12, 1863, Official Records, Series 1, Vol. 23 (Part II), 232; Willett, *Lightning Mule Brigade*, 21.

21. S. A. Hurlburt to General Rosecrans, April 13, 1863, Official Records, Series 1, Vol. 23 (Part II), 236, 243, 254; R. J. Oglesby to General S. A. Hurlburt, May 3, 1863, Official Records, Series 1, Vol. 23 (Part I), 245–46.

22. *Mobile Advertiser and Register*, April 28, 1863, 1, May 3, 1863, 2, May 5, 1863, 2; *New York Herald*, May 5, 1863, 7; (New Orleans) *Daily Picayune*, May 7, 1863, 1; (Savannah, Georgia) *Daily Morning News*, May 7, 1863; *Memphis Daily Appeal*, May 7, 1863, 2; Grenville M. Dodge, *Battle of Atlanta and Other Campaigns* (Council Bluffs,

IA: Monarch Printing Co., 1910), 114–19; Feis, *Grant's Secret Service*, 146; Hirshson, *Grenville M. Dodge*, 71–73; Hurst, *Nathan Bedford Forrest*, 117–24.

23. Johns, *Philip Henson*, 40.

24. Willett, *Lightning Mule Brigade*, 72–73, 96–97; (New Orleans) *Daily Picayune*, May 16, 1863, 4.

25. Testimony of Naomi Peters, Naomi Peters Claim, Southern Claims Commission. Union men led by a brother of William Hugh Smith went to the jail in Moulton and released several inmates who had been imprisoned for refusing to fight in the Confederate army. They then set about to forage for supplies from the corn cribs of those who supported the Confederacy. Willett, *Lightning Mule Brigade*, 99–100.

26. Willett, *Lightning Mule Brigade*, 100; Testimony of Thomas Peters, Naomi Peters Claim, Southern Claims Commission; R. J. Oglesby to General S. A. Hurlburt, May 3, 1863, Official Records, Series 1, Vol. 23 (Part I), 245. A conclusion that there was some connection between Peters and the Union military's movements is difficult to avoid. Indeed, it is likely that one of the many purposes of these raids was to sow Union men like him across north Alabama who could use their influence in the upcoming state elections and further encourage the peace movement.

27. (Greensboro) *Alabama Beacon*, May 8, 1863, 3; *Mobile Advertiser and Register*, May 8, 1863, 1, May 9, 1863, 2, May 10, 1863, 4, May 15, 1863, 1, May 16, 1863, 2, June 25, 1863, 1; *Montgomery Daily Advertiser*, May 9, 1863, 1; (Savannah, Georgia) *Daily Morning News*, May 7, 1863; Fleming, *Civil War and Reconstruction in Alabama*, 67–68; Griffith, *Alabama*, 398–405; Rogers et al., *Alabama*, 210–13.

28. R. J. Oglesby to General S. A. Hurlburt, May 3, 1863, Official Records, Series 1, Vol. 23 (Part I), 245.

29. G. M. Dodge to Capt. S. Wait, May 5, 1863, Official Records, Series 1, Vol. 23 (Part I), 246, 249. See also Florence M. Cornyn to Capt. George E. Spencer, May 16, 1863, Official Records, Series 1, Vol. 23 (Part I), 251–58; *New York Herald*, May 11, 1863.

30. *Mobile Advertiser and Register*, June 24, 1863, 2, July 4, 1863, 1; (New Orleans) *Daily Picayune*, July 12, 1863, 4; *Milwaukee Daily Sentinel*, May 13, 1863; *New York Times*, May 17, 1863. See also Leftwich, *Muscle Shoals*, 207.

31. *New York Herald*, May 11, 1863; *Cincinnati Gazette*, reprinted in *Milwaukee Daily Sentinel*, May 13, 1863; *New York Times*, May 17, 1863; *New York Commercial*, reprinted in (New Orleans) *Daily Picayune*, June 2, 1863, 2; Danielson, *War's Desolating Scourge*, 118–24. Regarding the battle, see Gary W. Gallagher, *Chancellorsville: The Battle and Its Aftermath* (Chapel Hill: University of North Carolina Press, 1996); Ben H. Severance, "Confederate Alabama's Finest Hour: The Battle of Salem Church, May 3, 1863," in *Yellowhammer War*, ed. Kenneth W. Noe, 55–70.

32. (Dalton, Georgia) *Daily Huntsville Confederate*, May 20, 1863, 1; (Grove Hill) *Clarke County Journal*, May 21, 1863, 2, May 24, 1863, 2.

33. John Gill Shorter to James A. Seddon, May 8, 1863, Official Records, Series 2, Vol. 5, 946–47; (Grove Hill) *Clarke County Journal*, May 28, 1863, 2; *Mobile Advertiser and Register*, June 11, 1863, 2; James A. Seddon to John Gill Shorter, May 23, 1863,

Official Records, Series 2, Vol. 5, 955. Regarding Shorter's announcement for reelection, see (Grove Hill) *Clarke County Journal*, June 4, 1863, 2; (Greensboro) *Alabama Beacon*, June 5, 1863, 2; Donald Bradford Dodd, "Unionism in Confederate Alabama" (PhD diss., University of Georgia, 1969), 63–64.

34. *Mobile Advertiser and Register*, May 5, 1863, 2, May 10, 1863, 2; (Grove Hill) *Clarke County Journal*, May 21, 1863, 2.

35. *Montgomery Advertiser*, reprinted in (Greensboro) *Alabama Beacon*, May 15, 1863, 2.

36. Linden and Linden, eds., *Disunion*, 101; (Greensboro) *Alabama Beacon*, May 8, 1863, 3.

37. L. C. Garland to J. G. Shorter, May 4, 1863, quoted in Sellers, *History of the University of Alabama*, 275.

38. L. C. Garland to J. G. Shorter, May 7, 1863, cited in Sellers, *History of the University of Alabama*, 276.

39. Sellers, *History of the University of Alabama*, 276.

40. (Dalton, Georgia) *Daily Huntsville Confederate*, May 30, 1863, 2, June 5, 1863, 2; (New Orleans) *Daily Picayune*, June 9, 1863, 1, June 16, 1863, 1, July 12, 1863, 4; *Mobile Advertiser and Register*, June 2, 1863, 2, June 16, 1863, 2; (Grove Hill) *Clarke County Journal*, June 11, 1863, 2; *Daily Cleveland* (Ohio) *Herald*, June 15, 1863. See also Leftwich, *Muscle Shoals*, 56, 62–63; McDonald, *A Walk through the Past*, 110–11; Richard C. Sheridan, "Civil War Manufacturing in the Tennessee Valley," *Journal of Muscle Shoals History* 15 (1999): 50, 56, 62–63; S. L. Phelps to D. D. Porter, June 3, 1863, Official Records, Series 1, Vol. 25, 130; Florence M. Cornyn to Brig. Gen. Grenville M. Dodge, Official Records, Series 1, Vol. 23, Part 1, 349; G. M. Dodge to General Rosecrans, June 1, 1863, Official Records, Series 1, Vol. 23 (Part II), 381; S. A. Hurlburt to Maj. Gen. H. W. Halleck, June 2, 1863, Official Records, Series 1, Vol. 24 (Part III), 377.

41. (Dalton, Georgia) *Daily Huntsville Confederate*, June 11, 1863, 2.

42. Ibid., May 30, 1863, 2. See also William L. McDonald, "The Day They Set Fire to the Mills," *Journal of Muscle Shoals History* 7 (1979): 61.

43. (Dalton, Georgia) *Daily Huntsville Confederate*, June 10, 1863, 2. The editor was referring to the surprising acquittal by a local jury of a Huntsville businessman who sold cotton to Northern cotton brokers in 1862 and was indicted for treason by a Confederate grand jury. Christine Dee, "Trying James Hickman: The Politics of Loyalty in a Civil War Community," *Alabama Review* 58 (April, 2005): 91–112.

44. *New York Tribune*, June 4, 1863, 1; *New York Herald*, June 4, 1863, 1.

45. *Mobile Advertiser and Register*, June 12, 1863, 2. Grant did, in fact, advocate a move on Mobile after taking Vicksburg. Stoker, *Grand Design*, 311.

46. (Greensboro) *Alabama Beacon*, June 19, 1863, 2.

47. Ibid., June 26, 1863, 3.

48. *Mobile Advertiser and Register*, June 26, 1863, 2, June 28, 1863, 2, July 18, 1863, 2, July 29, 1863, 2; (New Orleans) *Daily Picayune*, July 8, 1862, 2. See, generally, Clifford Dowdey, *Death of a Nation: The Story of Lee and His Men at Gettysburg* (New York: Butternut and Blue, 1988); Kent Masterson Brown, *Retreat from Gettysburg: Lee, Logistics, and the Pennsylvania Campaign* (Chapel Hill: University of North Carolina Press,

2005); Thomas E. Schott, *Alexander H. Stephens of Georgia: A Biography* (Baton Rouge: Louisiana State University Press, 1988), 378; Allen C. Guelzo, *Gettysburg: The Last Invasion* (New York: Alfred A. Knopf, 2013); Escott, *Confederacy*, 75–76.

49. *Montgomery Advertiser*, reprinted in *Mobile Advertiser and Register*, July 29, 1863, 2; *Charleston Mercury*, July 11, 1863, 1, July 30, 1863, 1; (Grove Hill) *Clarke County Journal*, July 23, 1863, 2; Stoker, *Grand Design*, 251, 303–5.

50. Morales, *41st Alabama*, 173–75; Feis, *Grant's Secret Service*, 171–74; Craig L. Symonds, *Joseph E. Johnston: A Civil War Biography* (New York: W. W. Norton, 1994), 215–16, 219; *Mobile Advertiser and Register*, July 7, 1863, 2, July 11, 1863, 2, July 14, 1863, 2, July 18, 1863, 2, July 22, 1863, 2, July 28, 1863, 2; (Grove Hill) *Clarke County Journal*, July 16, 1863, 2; (Greensboro) *Alabama Beacon*, July 17, 1863, 2.

51. (Grove Hill) *Clarke County Journal*, July 16, 1863, 2.

52. *Charleston Mercury*, July 15, 1863, 1. See, generally, Hess, *Civil War in the West*, 134–59.

53. See, e.g., *Mobile Advertiser and Register*, July 14, 1863, 2, July 16, 1863, 1–2, July 28, 1863, 2; (Grove Hill) *Clarke County Journal*, July 16, 1863, 2, July 23, 1863, 2. See, generally, Escott, *Confederacy*, 78–87.

Chapter 10

1. J. K. Callaway to Dulcinea Callaway, July 11, 1863, in *War Letters of Joshua K. Callaway*, ed. Judith Lee Hallock, 110–11.

2. George K. Miller to Cellie Hopkins, July 10, 1863, in *Uncompromising Secessionist*, ed. Richard M. McMurry, 142. For similar expressions, see Noe, *Reluctant Rebels*, 183.

3. Diary of Miss Catherine M. Fennell, 45.

4. *Mobile Advertiser and Register*, August 1, 1863, 1. See also *Louisville Daily Journal*, August 27, 1863, 1.

5. *Mobile Advertiser and Register*, August 1, 1863, 2. See also ibid., July 23, 1863, 2.

6. Linden and Linden, eds., *Disunion*, 108.

7. McWhiney, Moore, and Pace, eds., "*Fear God and Walk Humbly,*" 323.

8. Mariah Cotton to John Cotton, July 16, 1863, in *Yours Till Death*, ed. Lucille Griffith, 76–77.

9. *Selma Daily Reporter*, July 15, 1863, 2.

10. Ibid., July 11, 1863, 2.

11. Gideon J. Pillow to Col. Benjamin S. Ewell, July 28, 1863, and Gideon J. Pillow to Brigadier General Mackall, July 14, 1863, Official Records, Series 4, Vol. 2, 638, 680.

12. Dodd, "Unionism in Confederate Alabama," 65–67; Williams, *Bitterly Divided*, 123, 143, 154, 157, 169; (Dalton, Georgia) *Huntsville Confederate*, April 23, 1863, cited in (Washington, DC) *Daily National Intelligencer*, May 13, 1863 (referring to Sand Mountain tory bands); *New York Herald*, August 12, 1863, 4.

13. B. J. Hill to Col. E. J. Harvie, March 25, 1864, Official Records, Series 1, Vol.

32 (Part III), 681–82. See also H. W. Walter to General B. Bragg, May 8, 1864, Official Records, Series 4, Vol. 3, 393. Regarding the peace society, see, generally, Owsley, "Defeatism in the Confederacy," 446, 451–55; Nathaniel C. Hughes and Roy P. Stonesifer, *The Life and Wars of Gideon Pillow* (Chapel Hill: University of North Carolina Press, 1993), 269–70.

14. Beverly Wilson Palmer, *The Selected Papers of Thaddeus Stevens: April 1865-August 1868* (Pittsburgh: University of Pittsburgh Press, 1998), 2: 88–90.

15. *Daily Columbus* (Georgia) *Enquirer*, September 10, 1863, 2.

16. *Selma Daily Reporter*, July 17, 1863, 2. See also *Reluctant Rebels*, Kenneth W. Noe, 47.

17. *Mobile Advertiser and Register*, July 23, 1863, 2. See also *Mobile Advertiser and Register*, August 2, 1863, 2; *Selma Morning Reporter*, August 1, 1863, 2; *Daily Columbus* (Georgia) *Enquirer*, September 19, 1863, 2.

18. *Mobile Advertiser and Register*, August 2, 1863, 2.

19. DuBose, *Alabama's Tragic Decade*, 38–41.

20. *New York Times*, June 24, 1871, 1.

21. H. W. Walter to General B. Bragg, May 8, 1864, Official Records, Series 4, Vol. 3, 394; Statement of Jefferson Falkner and Abner R. Hill, Official Records, Series 4, Vol. 3, 398.

22. J. L. M. Curry to Robert Jemison Jr., October 23, 1863, Robert Jemison Papers, Hoole Special Collections Library, University of Alabama, Tuscaloosa.

23. (Grove Hill) *Clarke County Journal*, April 16, 1863, 2; Owen, *History of Alabama and Dictionary of Alabama Biography*, 3: 502.

24. Daniel P. Currie, "Through the Looking Glass: The Confederate Constitution in Congress, 1861–1865," *Virginia Law Review* 90 (September 2004): 1257, 1281.

25. William L. Shaw, "The Confederate Conscription and Exemption Acts," *American Journal of Legal History* 6 (October 1962): 368, 392.

26. T. H. Watts to Levi W. Walker, March 21, 1863, reprinted in (Dalton, Georgia) *Daily Huntsville Confederate*, May 20, 1863, 1, *Selma Morning Reporter*, July 11, 1863, 1; T. H. Watts, "To the People of Alabama," June 8, 1863, reprinted in (Dalton, Georgia) *Daily Huntsville Confederate*, June 21, 1863, 1 and *Jacksonville* (Alabama) *Republican*, July 11, 1863, 1.

27. *Selma Daily Reporter*, September 25, 1863, 2; Levine, *Fall of the House of Dixie*, 207–8.

28. John Clisby to Governor Shorter, July 22, 1863, Gov. Shorter Papers, Alabama Department of Archives and History, Montgomery; *Jacksonville* (Alabama) *Republican*, July 11, 1863, 2. This very strategy had been used in North Carolina in 1862 to purge Original Secessionists from political office in that state. See, generally, Paul D. Escott, *Many Excellent People: Power and Privilege In North Carolina, 1850–1900* (Chapel Hill: University of North Carolina Press, 1985), 47, 49, 60–76; Edgar E. Folk and Bynum Shaw, *W. W. Holden: A Political Biography* (Winston-Salem, NC: J. F. Blair, 1982), 156–65, 207–16, 244–45.

29. *Montgomery Advertiser*, reprinted in *Mobile Advertiser and Register*, July 14, 1863, 2.

30. Walther, *William Lowndes Yancey and the Coming of the Civil War*, 368–70.

31. J. L. M. Curry to Robert Jemison Jr., October 23, 1863, Jemison Papers, Hoole Special Collections Library, University of Alabama, Tuscaloosa.

32. (Dalton, Georgia) *Daily Huntsville Confederate*, July 29, 1863, 2,

33. *Jacksonville* (Alabama) *Republican*, July 11, 1863, 1, July 18, 1863, 2.

34. *Montgomery Weekly Advertiser*, September 20, 1863; *Mobile Advertiser and Register*, June 13, 1863.

35. *Mobile Advertiser and Register*, July 31, 1863, 2, August 1, 1863, 1–2. This is not intended to suggest the soldiers would necessarily vote for defeatist candidates.

36. *Selma Daily Reporter*, July 16, 1863, 2.

37. *Mobile Advertiser and Register*, July 30, 1863, 2.

38. Ibid., July 11, 1863, 2. See also, ibid., July 21, 1863, 2, July 30, 1863, 2; (Dalton, Georgia) *Daily Huntsville Confederate*, July 29, 1863, 2.

39. *Livingston Messenger*, July 11, 1863, reprinted in *Mobile Advertiser and Register*, July 21, 1863, 2.

40. *Selma Daily Reporter*, July 23, 1863, 2; *Mobile Advertiser and Register*, July 22, 1863, 1; *Clarke County* (Alabama) *Journal*, July 23, 1863, 2.

41. Gid. J. Pillow to Col. Benjamin S. Ewell, July 28, 1863, Official Records, Series 4, Vol. 2, 680–81.

42. S. A. Hurlburt to H. W. Halleck, August 1, 1863, Official Records, Series 1, Vol. 24 (Part III), 571.

43. See J. N. Galleher to Brigadier General A. E. Jackson, July 29, 1863, Official Records, Series 1, Vol. 23 (Part II), 936.

44. G. M. Dodge to Major-General Hurlbut, July 29, 1863, Official Records, Series 1, Vol. 24 (Part III) 562; W. T. Walthall to Lieut. Col. G. W. Lay, August 6, 1863, Official Records, Series 4, Vol. 2, 726–27.

45. *Selma Daily Reporter*, July 19, 1863, 2.

46. McMillan, *Disintegration of a Confederate State*, 68.

47. Compare, (Montgomery) *Alabama State Journal*, 109 (1863) with the (Huntsville) *Democrat*, September 11, 1861, 4 and *Mobile Weekly Advertiser*, August 31, 1861, 4.

48. McWhiney, Moore, and Pace, eds., "*Fear God and Walk Humbly*," 325.

49. *Mobile Advertiser and Register*, August 2, 1863, 2.

50. Ibid., August 11, 1863, 2.

51. Ibid., August 11, 1863, 2. See also ibid., August 30, 1863, 2; *Selma Morning Reporter*, August 14, 1863, 1. Regarding the "Union" community, see John Stanley Rich, "The Place-Names of Greene and Tuscaloosa Counties, Alabama" (PhD diss., University of Alabama, 1979).

52. See, e.g., Tatum, *Disloyalty in the Confederacy*, 61; Owsley, "Defeatism in the Confederacy," 452; Fleming, *Civil War and Reconstruction in Alabama*, 138–39; Levine, *Fall of the House of Dixie*, 208–9.

53. McMillan, *Disintegration of a Confederate State*, 65. See also *Montgomery Weekly Advertiser*, August 5, 1863 (charging, before significant numbers of election returns

had been received, that Unionists had "brought out obscure candidates for Congress, and in some instances, for the legislature, against men of the most approved capacity and devotion to the cause").

Chapter 11

1. George Miller to Cellie Hopkins, September 30, 1863, in *An Uncompromising Secessionist*, ed. Richard M. McMurry, 148.

2. George Miller to Cellie Hopkins, September 15, 1863, in *An Uncompromising Secessionist*, ed. Richard M. McMurry, 146–47.

3. *Mobile Advertiser and Register*, October 30, 1863; *Augusta* (Georgia) *Chronicle*, June 4, 1863, 1.

4. *Mobile Advertiser and Register*, October 13, 1863, 1, October 27, 1863, 1. See also *Daily Columbus* (Georgia) *Enquirer*, October 16, 1863, 2; James A. Seddon to Brigadier General Pillow, October 27, 1863, Official Records, Series 4, Vol. 2, 911–12.

5. *Macon* (Georgia) *Daily Telegraph*, June 22, 1863, 3. One soldier referred to these men as "useless shade officers." *Selma Reporter*, reprinted in (Augusta) *Daily Constitutionalist*, December 7, 1864, 2.

6. *Mobile Advertiser and Register*, reprinted in (New Orleans) *Daily Picayune*, August 23, 1863, 4; *Augusta* (Georgia) *Chronicle*, June 4, 1863, 1.

7. *Mobile Advertiser and Register*, August 15, 1863, 2.

8. Gideon J. Pillow to General S. Cooper, August 28, 1863, Official Records, Series 4, Vol. 2, 774–75. See also *Charleston Mercury*, August 8, 1863, 2 (stating that Roddey was promoted to brigadier general effective August 3, 1863); *Mobile Advertiser and Register*, August 11, 1863, 2, September 9, 1863, 2 (publishing a letter from Roddey); *Selma Daily Reporter*, September 3, 1863, 2 (publishing a list of deserters from the 17th Alabama Infantry Regiment).

9. *Daily* (St. Louis) *Missouri Republican*, August 26, 1863, 2; (Dalton, Georgia) *Daily Huntsville Confederate*, October 29, 1863, 1. See also *Mobile Advertiser and Register*, August 26, 1863, 2, September 20, 1863, 1; J. A. Garfield to Brigadier General King, September 4, 1863, Official Records, Series 1, Vol. 30 (Part III), 343 (referring to Lieutenant Ephraim Latham); Storey, *Loyalty and Loss*, 98, 103–4 (calling this unit the "First Tennessee & Alabama Independent Vidette Cavalry").

10. John Gill Shorter to General H. Cobb, August 4, 1863, Official Records, Series 1, Vol. 28 (Part II), 273–74; Gideon J. Pillow to Brigadier General Mackall, July 14, 1863, Official Records, Series 4, Vol. 2, 638; *Mobile Advertiser and Register*, August 26, 1863, 1 (discussing a "tory band" in Jackson County), September 20, 1863, 1 (same); *Jacksonville Republican*, October 17, 1863, 2 (Talladega County); *Talladega Reporter*, reprinted in *Daily Columbus* (Georgia) *Enquirer*, October 14, 1863, 2 (same); *Selma Dispatch*, reprinted in (Augusta) *Daily Constitutionalist*, July 28, 1863, 2 (central Alabama); Williams, *Bitterly Divided*, 123, 143, 154, 157, 169.

11. *Selma Daily Reporter*, September 18, 1863, 2.

12. Regarding that address, see (Grove Hill) *Clarke County Journal*, August 13, 1863, 2; *Selma Morning Reporter*, August 9, 1863, 2; (Greensboro) *Alabama Beacon*, September 4, 1863, 4; *Jacksonville Republican*, August 15, 1863, 2.

13. *Tuscaloosa Observer*, September 23, 1863, reprinted in *Nashville Daily Union*, October 10, 1863, 2 and *Hartford Daily Courant*, October 21, 1863, 3.

14. *Mobile Advertiser and Register*, August 15, 1863, 2.

15. Ibid., September 9, 1863, 2. One wonders whether Roddey's promotion—which effectively permitted him to receive even more deserters from the commands of others—was a quid pro quo for this prowar public appeal. In any event, growing Roddey's force meant diminishing that of others.

16. John Gill Shorter to General Joseph E. Johnston, August 4, 1863, Official Records, Series 1, Vol. 26 (Part III), 139–40; *Mobile Advertiser and Register*, August 20, 1863, 1; (Grove Hill) *Clarke County Journal*, August 27, 1863, 2 (publishing the opinion of the probate judge of Montgomery County adverse to the petitioner in *Ex parte McCants*).

17. *Eutaw Whig*, reprinted in *Selma Morning Reporter*, August 14, 1863, 2.

18. *Selma Morning Reporter*, August 12, 1863, 1; (Savannah, Georgia) *Daily Morning News*, August 17, 1863; *Selma Daily Reporter*, August 12, 1863, 2; *Selma Morning Reporter*, August 4, 1863, 1 (publishing the announcement of Jenifer's appointment), August 12, 1863, 1, August 13, 1863, 2.

19. *Selma Daily Reporter*, August 12, 1863, 2.

20. (New Orleans) *Daily Picayune*, August 16, 1863, 4; *Selma Daily Reporter*, July 21, 1863, 2; (Selma) *Mississippian*, reprinted in *Macon Telegraph*, May 11, 1864, 1.

21. (Savannah, Georgia) *Daily Morning News*, August 17, 1863.

22. Harwell, ed., *Kate*, 58.

23. *Chattanooga Daily Rebel*, November 1, 1862, 1 (giving up carpets to make blankets for the soldiers).

24. Vandiver, *Plowshares into Swords*, 107; Jackson, *Story of Selma*, 199–201. See also Bell I. Wiley, *Life of Johnny Reb: The Common Soldier of the Confederacy* (Baton Rouge: Louisiana State University Press, 2000), 304–5; Jack Kelly, *Gunpowder: Alchemy, Bombards, and Pyrotechnics* (New York: Basic Books, 2004), 198–201; Rogers et al., *Alabama*, 195–96.

25. Stoker, *Grand Design*, 320–21.

26. *Selma Daily Reporter*, July 23, 1863, 2; *Mobile Advertiser and Register*, July 24, 1863, 2, August 20, 1863, 1; (Grove Hill) *Clarke County Journal*, August 6, 1863, 1.

27. *Alabama House Journal*, 30 (August 22, 1863); *Mobile Advertiser and Register*, August 25, 1863, 2; *Selma Morning Reporter*, August 19, 1863, 1.

28. *Alabama House Journal*, 17–18 (August 18, 1863). See also *Alabama Senate Journal*, 20–21, August 18, 1863 (an identical joint resolution was offered in the Senate); (New Orleans) *Daily Picayune*, September 2, 1863.

29. *Ala. Acts*, Joint Resolutions, 52–53 (August 26, 1863); *Mobile Daily Tribune*, September 23, 1863, 1.

30. *Alabama Senate Journal*, 29 (August 22, 1863); *Alabama House Journal*, 30 (August

22, 1863); *Mobile Advertiser and Register*, August 25, 1863, 1–2; *Selma Daily Reporter*, August 27, 1863, 2; *Montgomery Advertiser*, August 22, 1863, reprinted in *Charleston Mercury*, August 26, 1863, 1.

31. (Dalton, Georgia) *Daily Huntsville Confederate*, September 7, 1863, 1. See also *Charleston Mercury*, August 24, 1863, 1 (also stating that Jemison's election was "an act of party magnanimity").

32. *Columbus Republic*, reprinted in *Mobile Advertiser and Register*, September 13, 1863, 2. See also *Selma Daily Reporter*, September 22, 1863, 2, September 25, 1863, 2.

33. Joseph C. Bradley to Andrew Johnson, September 28, 1865, *Papers of Andrew Johnson*, ed. Graf, et al., 9: 142.

34. *Alabama Senate Journal*, 40–41 (August 25, 1863). See also *Selma Daily Reporter*, August 29, 1863, 2; *Selma Morning Reporter*, August 27, 1863, 1, August 29, 1863, 2; *Mobile Advertiser and Register*, August 29, 1863, 1; *Daily Columbus* (Georgia) *Enquirer*, August 28, 1863, 2.

35. See, e.g., McMillan, *Disintegration of a Confederate State*, 66–67 (referring to the new system as "absurd and certainly cumbersome"); Fleming, *Civil War and Reconstruction in Alabama*, 90–91 (alleging that the new system made the militia "worthless to the Confederacy" and "practically useless").

36. *Ala. Acts*, No. 1, 3 (August 29, 1863); *Montgomery Weekly Advertiser*, September 15, 1863; *Clarke County* (Alabama) *Journal*, September 3, 1863, 2.

37. *Ala. Acts*, No. 1, Section 12, 8 (August 29, 1863).

38. (Dalton, Georgia) *Daily Huntsville Confederate*, December 17, 1863, 1; *Mobile Daily Tribune*, November 13, 1863, 1, December 22, 1863, 2; *Mobile Advertiser and Register*, November 13, 1863, 1.

39. *Alabama House Journal*, 221–22 (December 5, 1863).

40. *Ala. Acts*, No. 3, 13 (August 29, 1863).

41. (Dalton, Georgia) *Daily Huntsville Confederate*, June 9, 1863, 1.

42. *Ala. Acts*, No. 3, 13 (August 29, 1863).

43. *Mobile Evening News*, September 18, 1863, 2.

44. Abraham Lincoln to Horatio Seymour, August 7, 1863, reprinted in (New Orleans) *Daily Picayune*, August 21, 1863, 2.

45. *Alabama House Journal*, 39–42, 61 (1863).

46. Storey, *Loyalty and Loss*, 114–22.

47. *Selma Morning Reporter*, October 25, 1862, 1. See also *Boston Herald*, November 25, 1863, 4 (slave labor used to mine coal in Alabama). See, generally, Sean Michael O'Brien, *Mobile, 1865: Last Stand of the Confederacy* (Westport, CT: Praeger, 2001), 21.

48. Putting a gun in their hands and expecting them to fight to preserve a slave society that countenanced such brutal practices as burning slaves at the stake who were suspected of crimes of violence and hangings for property crimes was a quantum leap past engrained societal boundaries. See, e.g., *Mobile Advertiser and Register*, December 18, 1862, 2 (Pike County slave burned), September 6, 1863, 2 (Randolph County slave to be hung).

49. (Greensboro) *Alabama Beacon*, November 4, 1864, 2. See also (New Orleans)

Daily Picayune, March 5, 1863, 2, March 6, 1863, 2, December 1, 1863, 2, June 26, 1863, 1; *Daily Columbus* (Georgia) *Enquirer*, February 20, 1864, 2; *Mobile Advertiser and Register*, November 9, 1864, 2.

50. (Dalton, Georgia) *Daily Huntsville Confederate*, November 25, 1863, 2, reprinted in *Daily Columbus* (Georgia) *Enquirer*, November 28, 1863, 2. See also ibid., December 20, 1863, 1; *Jacksonville Republican*, January 2, 1864, 2; (Grove Hill) *Clarke County Journal*, December 24, 1863, 2; (Dalton, Georgia) *Daily Huntsville Confederate*, December 5, 1863, 2; *Mobile Advertiser and Register*, December 19, 1863, 1.

51. *Mobile Daily Tribune*, September 10, 1863, 1.

52. (New Orleans) *Daily Picayune*, November 10, 1863, 2.

53. Oakes, *Freedom National*, 388. Regarding black Union soldiers, see, generally, Keith P. Wilson, *Campfires of Freedom: The Camp Life of Black Soldiers during the Civil War* (Kent, OH: Kent State University Press, 2002); George W. Williams, *A History of the Negro Troops in the War of the Rebellion 1861–1865* (New York: Bergman Publishers, 1968).

54. Adams, *Living Hell*, 188.

55. *Mobile Advertiser and Register*, December 13, 1863, 2.

56. (Dalton, Georgia) *Daily Huntsville Confederate*, August 19, 1863, 2. (Greensboro) *Alabama Beacon*, November 4, 1864, 2. See Grant Taylor to Malinda Taylor, January 11, 1865, in *This Cruel War*, ed. ed.s Blomquist and Taylor, 322–23.

57. *Selma Reporter*, August 5, 1863, 2. See also (Grove Hill) *Clarke County Journal*, September 3, 1863, 2; *Mobile Advertiser and Register*, August 6, 1863, 2, August 15, 1863, 2; *Selma Reporter*, August 6, 1863, 2, August 13, 1863, 2, and (Greensboro) *Alabama Beacon*, September 4, 1863, 2.

58. O'Brien, *Mobile, 1865*, 21 (noting that the "Creole Guards," as they were known, were allowed to be enlisted in the army in the fall of 1864); Bergeron, *Confederate Mobile*, 104–6. The Creoles had actually been formed into independent military companies in early 1862. (New Orleans) *Daily Picayune*, January 28, 1862, 2.

59. *Ala. Acts*, Joint Resolutions, 52 (August 29, 1863).

60. *Montgomery Mail*, reprinted in *Mobile Advertiser and Register*, December 12, 1863, 2, November 15, 1864, 2. Several generals in the Army of Tennessee petitioned the Confederate Congress to authorize the enlistment of blacks in noncombat positions. *Daily Columbus* (Georgia) *Enquirer*, January 6, 1864, 1; *Mobile Advertiser and Register*, December 31, 1863, 2. See, generally, Colin Edward Woodward, *Marching Masters: Slavery, Race, and the Confederate Army during the Civil War* (Charlottesville: University of Virginia Press, 2014), 155–79.

61. *Mobile Advertiser and Register*, August 25, 1863, 2.

62. Ibid., September 13, 1863, 2.

Chapter 12

1. *Selma Daily Reporter*, August 29, 1863, 2.

2. James T. Searcy to Stella Searcy, September 3, 1863, Papers of James T. Searcy, Alabama Department of Archives and History, Montgomery.

3. Stoker, *Grand Design*, 322–23; Morales, *41st Regiment*, 187–93. See also *Mobile Daily Tribune*, September 15, 1863, 1 (reporting the fall of Chattanooga); (New Orleans) *Daily Picayune*, September 19, 1863, 2 (same); *Daily Columbus* (Georgia) *Enquirer*, September 17, 1863, 1, September 19, 1863, 2 (same).

4. *Mobile Advertiser and Register*, June 14, 1863, reprinted in *Macon* (Georgia) *Telegraph*, June 18, 1863, 2.

5. *New Orleans Era*, September 21, 1863, reprinted in *New York Times*, October 1, 1863, 4. See also *Mobile Daily Tribune*, September 8, 1863, 2, September 13, 1863, 2; (Grove Hill) *Clarke County Journal*, September 17, 1863, 2 (regarding "Speculation and Extortion"); *Mobile Advertiser and Register*, October 1, 1863, 1. See, generally, Burnett, *Pen Makes a Good Sword*, 141; Bergeron, *Confederate Mobile*, 101–2; Andrew F. Smith, *Starving the South: How the North Won the Civil War* (New York: St. Martin's Press, 2011), 61–63; George C. Rable, *Civil Wars: Women and the Crisis of Southern Nationalism* (Urbana: University of Illinois Press, 1989), 108–11; Williams, *Bitterly Divided*, 93; Guelzo, *Fateful Lightning*, 326–27; Escott, *Confederacy*, 60.

6. *Selma Dispatch*, reprinted in *Memphis Daily Appeal*, September 11, 1863, 1; *Selma Morning Reporter*, September 5, 1863, 2, September 9, 1863, 1; *Mobile Daily Tribune*, September 9, 1863, 2. Regarding the problem of price gouging during this period, see also *Daily Columbus* (Georgia) *Enquirer*, September 3, 1863, 1.

7. *Atlanta Southern Confederacy*, September 15, 1862, reprinted in (Augusta) *Daily Constitutionalist*, September 17, 1862, 1. On February 25, 1864, an explosion mysteriously occurred at the arsenal. *Macon* (Georgia) *Telegraph*, February 27, 1864, 2.

8. James Q. Smith to Maj. Gen. U. S. Grant, January 25, 1864, Official Records, Series 1, Vol. 32 (Part II), 215.

9. *Macon* (Georgia) *Telegraph*, October 21, 1863, 2.

10. *Selma Daily Reporter*, September 24, 1863, 2; *Boston Herald*, January 12, 1864, 2 (stating that the merchant's last name was "Evans").

11. *Selma Morning Reporter*, November 13, 1862, 1. See, generally, Neely, *Southern Rights*, 80–87; William Morrison Robinson, *Justice in Grey: A History of the Judicial System of the Confederate States of America* (New York: Russell & Russell, 1968), 387–411; Escott, *Confederacy*, 69.

12. *Selma Morning Reporter*, November 13, 1862, 1.

13. M. J. Saffold to John A. Campbell, March 16, 1863, Official Records, Series 2, Vol. 5, 852; James A. Seddon to J. G. Shorter, October 27, 1863, Official Records, Series 4, Vol. 2, 910–11; James A. Seddon to Major General Maury, October 27, 1863, Official Records, Series 2, Vol. 6, 432; *Selma Morning Reporter*, March 23, 1863, 2; *Montgomery Daily Advertiser*, May 9, 1863, 2; Neely, *Southern Rights*, 85.

14. M. J. Saffold to John A. Campbell, March 16, 1863, Official Records, Series 2, Vol. 5, 852.

15. (Mobile) *Nationalist*, September 20, 1866, 1.

16. *Selma Daily Reporter*, September 24, 1863, 2. The reaction of the Selma military to Smith's withering criticism may explain why Smith soon left Alabama to seek refuge behind Union lines at Nashville, Tennessee. There he joined Andrew Johnson's growing Unionist organization, and after the war Johnson would place

Smith in a position to have his revenge. See, generally, James Q. Smith to Maj. Gen. U. S. Grant, January 25, 1864, Official Records, Series 1, Vol. 32 (Part II), 214; James Q. Smith to Henry Stansberry, September 28, 1866, National Archives, Washington, DC.

17. James A. Seddon to Major General Maury, October 27, 1863, Official Records, Series 2, Vol. 6, 432.

18. J. A. Campbell to M. J. Saffold, October 29, 1863, Official Records, Series 2, Vol. 6, 444.

19. (Livingston) *Independent*, October 24, 1863. Meanwhile, Jenifer was replaced as post commander at Selma.

20. Compare *Mobile Advertiser and Register*, September 22, 1863, 1 and November 12, 1863, 2, with *Ex parte Hill*, Ala. 429 (1863), *Ex parte Stringer*, 38 Ala. 457 (1863), and *Ex parte Hill*, 38 458 (1863). See, generally, William Henderson Brantley, *Chief Justice Stone of Alabama* (Birmingham, AL : Birmingham Publishing Co., 1943), 156–59.

21. Martin, *Rich Man's War*, 49–52, 115.

22. Benjamin Gardner to John Gill Shorter, October 11, 1863 quoted in Neely, *Southern Rights*, 55.

23. *Selma Morning Reporter*, September 24, 1863, 1; Owen, *History of Alabama and Dictionary of Alabama Biography*, 4: 1614.

24. (Grove Hill) *Clarke County Journal*, June 4, 1863, 2; (Troy) *Southern Advertiser*, reprinted in *Mobile Evening Telegraph*, October 27, 1863, 2 and *Mobile Daily Tribune*, October 28, 1863, 1. See, generally, Neely, *Southern Rights*, 55.

25. (Troy) *Southern Advertiser*, October 27, 1863, 2. See also *Mobile Daily Tribune*, October 27, 1863, 2, October 28, 1863, 1, November 1, 1863, 1; (Grove Hill) *Clarke County Journal*, November 5, 1863, 2; *Selma Morning Dispatch*, November 6, 1863, 2; *Memphis Daily Appeal*, October 29, 1863, 1; *Mobile Advertiser and Register*, October 27, 1863, 2.

26. See, generally, Paul D. Escott, *Military Necessity: Civil-Military Relations in the Confederacy* (Westport, CT: Praeger Security International, 2006), 81–82, 175–78.

27. Emory M. Thomas, Lesley J. Gordon, John C. Inscoe, eds., *Inside the Confederate Nation: Essays In Honor of Emory M. Thomas* (Baton Rouge: Louisiana State University Press, 2005), 133; Stephanie McCurry, *Confederate Reckoning: Power and Politics in the Civil War South* (Cambridge, MA: Harvard University Press, 2010), 155–67; Richard Cecil Todd, *Confederate Finance* (Athens: University of Georgia Press, 1954), 165–67; Jeffrey Rogers Hummel, *Emancipating Slaves, Enslaving Free Men: A History of the American Civil War* (Chicago: Open Court, 1996), 229–30.

28. Thomas H. Watts to James A. Seddon, January 19, 1864, Papers of Governor Watts, Alabama Department of Archives and History, Montgomery.

29. *Mobile Advertiser and Register*, September 4, 1863, 2; (Savannah, Georgia) *Daily Morning News*, August 13, 1863 (publishing a letter by James Lawrence Pugh); *Weekly Raleigh* (North Carolina) *Register*, August 26, 1863 (reporting complaints); Rable, *Confederate Republic*, 192–93; Escott, *Confederacy*, 61.

30. Sarah Koon to George Koon, November 15, 1863, November 29, 1863, January 30, 1864, in Brown, *Family History*, 54–55, 58; Martin, *A Rich Man's War, A Poor Man's Fight*, 93–94. See, generally, Douglas B. Ball, *Financial Failure and Confederate Defeat* (Urbana: University of Illinois Press, 1991), 232–35.

31. John Cotton to Mariah Cotton, October 28, 1863, in *Yours Till Death*, ed. Lucille Griffith, 91.

32. *Tuscaloosa Observer*, reprinted in (Grove Hill) *Clarke County Journal*, October 15, 1863, 2. See also *Tuscaloosa Observer*, reprinted in *Selma Morning Reporter*, August 9, 1863, 2; (Livingston) *Independent*, September 19, 1863 (blaming planters for depreciation of Confederate money and inflation of prices).

33. *Jacksonville* (Alabama) *Republican*, September 19, 1863, 2.

34. (Dalton, Georgia) *Daily Huntsville Confederate*, October 7, 1863, 2; *Mobile Advertiser and Register*, October 13, 1863, 1; *Daily Columbus* (Georgia) *Enquirer*, October 11, 1863, 2.

35. George Koon to Sarah Koon, September 5, 1863, in Brown, *Family History*, 12.

36. Sarah Koon to George Koon, September 13, 1863, September 20, 1863, October 11, 1863, October 18, 1863, in Brown, *Family History*, 45–50. See, generally, Williams, *Bitterly Divided*, 113.

37. (New York) *Evening Post*, November 23, 1863, 2.

38. William B. Bate to Maj. R. A. Hatcher, October 9, 1863, Official Records, Series 1, Vol. 30 (Part II), 387.

39. (Greensboro) *Alabama Beacon*, October 9, 1863, 1; Morales, *41st Regiment*, 193–203; Stephen W. Berry, *House of Abraham Lincoln and the Todds, A Family Divided* (Boston: Mariner Books, 2009), 144–47. See, generally, (Greensboro) *Alabama Beacon*, September 25, 1863, 3 (reporting the wounding of Thomas Hord Herndon), October 23, 1863, 3 (the death of Sydenham Moore's oldest son); *Mobile Daily Tribune*, September 26, 1863, 1; *Mobile Advertiser and Register*, September 29, 1863, 1–2, October 1, 1863, 1, October 2, 1863, 2, October 23, 1863, 1; (Grove Hill) *Clarke County Journal*, October 1, 1863, 2; Patrick Abbazia, *Chickamauga Campaign, December 1862—November 1863* (New York: Gallery Books, 1988), 65–99.

40. *Selma Daily Reporter*, September 22, 1863, 2. See also *Mobile Daily Tribune*, September 23, 1863, 1; (Greensboro) *Alabama Beacon*, September 25, 1863, 3, October 9, 1863, 3; *Selma Daily Reporter*, September 26, 1863, 2; *Mobile Advertiser and Register*, October 4, 1863, 2, October 10, 1863, 2; (Grove Hill) *Clarke County Journal*, October 15, 1863, 2; *Jacksonville Republican*, September 19, 1863, 2. See, generally, Hess, *Civil War in the West*, 189–92.

41. *Mobile Advertiser and Register*, reprinted in (Savannah, Georgia) *Daily Morning News*, October 22, 1863. See also *Chattanooga Rebel*, October 9, 1863, reprinted in (Washington, DC) *Daily National Intelligencer*, October 24, 1863 ("In a word, we have lost ten or twelve thousand men without gaining an equivalent in producing territory.").

42. Daniel, *Soldiering in the Army of Tennessee*, 135–36.

43. *Mobile Advertiser and Register*, reprinted in (Savannah, Georgia) *Daily Morning*

News, October 22, 1863; Abbazia, *Chickamauga Campaign*, 102–37; Hess, *Civil War in the West*, 195.

44. John Cotton to Mariah Cotton, September 29, 1863, in *Yours Till Death*, ed. Lucille Griffith, 86.

45. *Jacksonville Republican*, December 26, 1863, 2 ("several negro regiments" were stationed near Huntsville); *Mobile Daily Tribune*, October 13, 1863, 1 (two regiments of black troops at Pensacola); *Mobile Advertiser and Register*, October 13, 1863, 1 (same); (Grove Hill) *Clarke County Journal*, October 15, 1863, 2 (at Charleston, South Carolina).

46. *Daily Columbus* (Georgia) *Enquirer*, October 6, 1863, 2.

47. *Milwaukee Daily Sentinel*, October 13, 1863. See also *New Haven* (Connecticut) *Daily Palladium*, September 26, 1863, citing the *Richmond Examiner*.

48. See, e.g., *Daily Columbus* (Georgia) *Enquirer*, October 16, 1863, 1, October 31, 1863, 2, November 1, 1863, 2; Hess, *Civil War in the West*, 192–95; Stroker, *Grand Design*, 325.

49. *Mobile Daily Tribune*, October 27, 1863, 1. See also (Dalton, Georgia) *Daily Huntsville Confederate*, October 14, 1863, 2.

50. (Dalton, Georgia) *Daily Huntsville Confederate*, October 14, 1863, 2; *Mobile Advertiser and Register*, October 16, 1863, 1, December 30, 1863, 1; *Jacksonville Republican*, October 17, 1863, 2, October 24, 1863, 2; David C. Smith, *Campaign to Nowhere: The Results of General Longstreet's Move Into Upper East Tennessee* (Strawberry Plains, TN: Strawberry Plains Press, 1999), 215–16; Morales, *41st Regiment*, 212–13; Craig L. Symonds, "War and Politics: Jefferson Davis Meets the Army of Tennessee," in *Gateway to the Confederacy: New Perspectives on the Chickamauga and Chattanooga Campaigns, 1862–1863*, ed. Evan C. Jones and Wiley Sword, 159–71 (Baton Rouge: Louisiana State University Press, 2014), 159–71.

51. *Mobile Daily Tribune*, October 13, 1863, 1; *Mobile Advertiser and Register*, October 13, 1863, 1, October 16, 1863, 1; (Dalton, Georgia) *Daily Huntsville Confederate*, October 14, 1863, 2; *Selma Daily Reporter*, October 27, 1863, 2.

52. John Cotton to Mariah Cotton, October 25, 1863, in *Yours Till Death*, ed. Lucille Griffith, 90.

53. (Dalton, Georgia) *Huntsville Confederate*, reprinted in *Mobile Advertiser and Register*, October 10, 1863, 1.

54. *Charleston Mercury*, October 20, 1863, 1; *Mobile Daily Tribune*, October 21, 1863, 2; *Selma Dispatch*, October 17, 1863, reprinted in (Richmond) *Daily Dispatch*, October 24, 1863, 1; (Augusta, Georgia) *Daily Constitutionalist*, October 20, 1863, 1; *Richmond Examiner*, October 20, 1863, 1; (Savannah, Georgia) *Daily Morning News*, October 22, 1863; *Daily Columbus* (Georgia) *Enquirer*, October 20, 1863, 2; John Beauchamp Jones, *A Rebel War Clerk's Diary at the Confederate States Capital* (Philadelphia: J. B. Lippincott, 1866), 76.

55. Grant Taylor to Malinda Taylor, October 18, 1863, in *This Cruel War*, ed.s Blomquist and Taylor, 186. See also (Dalton, Georgia) *Daily Huntsville Confederate*, October 24, 1863, 1–2. (Davis spoke at Demopolis while on his way to Meridian.)

56. *Selma Morning Reporter*, October 24, 1863, 1. See also (Livingston) *Independent*, October 31, 1863; *Charleston Mercury*, November 5, 1863, 1.

57. *Memphis Daily Appeal*, October 29, 1863, 1. See also, *Mobile Daily Tribune*, October 27, 1863, 2, October 28, 1863, 1; *Mobile Advertiser and Register*, October 27, 1863, 2; (Dalton, Georgia) *Daily Huntsville Confederate*, October 29, 1863, 1; *Daily Columbus* (Georgia) *Enquirer*, October 29, 1863, 2; *Edgefield* (South Carolina) *Advertiser*, November 11, 1863, 1.

58. *Memphis Daily Appeal*, October 29, 1863, 1. See also *Mobile Daily Tribune*, October 27, 1863, 2; *Mobile Advertiser and Register*, October 27, 1863, 2; *Selma Daily Reporter*, October 24, 1863, 2; *Mobile Evening Telegraph*, October 27, 1863, 2.

59. *Mobile Daily Tribune*, October 28, 1863, 1.

60. (New Orleans) *Daily Picayune*, November 7, 1863, 2; *Mobile Advertiser and Register*, October 27, 1863, 2.

61. *Mobile Advertiser and Register*, October 27, 1863, 2. Regarding Hooker, see Walter H. Hebert, *Fighting Joe Hooker* (Lincoln: University of Nebraska Press, 1944), 252–60 (Hooker had arrived at Stevenson, Alabama, on October 2).

62. (New Orleans) *Daily Picayune*, January 18, 1863, 1.

63. John Gill Shorter to Jefferson Davis, January 10, 1863, Official Records, Series 1, Vol. 15, 939; John Gill Shorter to James A. Seddon, January 14, 1863, Official Records, Series 1, Vol. 15, 946; John Gill Shorter to James A. Seddon, March 5, 1863, Series 4, Vol. 2, 419–20; McMillan, *Disintegration of a Confederate State*, 60. See also Tatum, *Disloyalty in the Confederacy*, 63–66; (New Orleans) *Daily Picayune*, January 29, 1863, 2 (reporting that Pensacola was a destination for deserters from Alabama and Florida), February 15, 1863, 4 (same).

64. John Gill Shorter to Jefferson Davis, January 10, 1863, Official Records, Series 1, Vol. 15, 939. See also, Williams, *Bitterly Divided*, 169.

65. *Mobile Advertiser and Register*, October 29, 1863, 2; (New Orleans) *Daily Picayune*, November 15, 1863, 1. See, generally, Brigadier General Asboth to Brig. Gen. Charles P. Stone, November 23, 1863, Official Records, Series 1, Vol. 26 (Part I), 817–18 (reporting Clanton's position); Fleming, *Civil War and Reconstruction in Alabama*, 139–41 (regarding the mutiny).

66. *Mobile Daily Tribune*, November 1, 1863, 1; *Mobile Advertiser and Register*, November 3, 1863, 1; (Grove Hill) *Clarke County Journal*, November 19, 1863, 2.

67. Jno. A. Rawlins to Maj. Gen. W. T. Sherman, September 25, 1863, Official Records, Series 1, Vol. 30 (Part III), 842. Sherman had every reason to be in a very bad mood when he reached Alabama. While visiting Sherman at Vicksburg, Sherman's eldest son, nine-year-old Willie, had contracted fever and dysentery, and by October 3, the day Sherman arrived by boat at Memphis, Tennessee, on the first leg of his journey east, Willie had died. Sherman was devastated. To General Henry Halleck, Sherman wrote that Willie's "loss to me is more than words can express," and to his friend, Admiral David Dixon Porter, Sherman confided that Willie "was my pride and hope of life, and his loss takes from me the great incentive to excel, and now I must work on purely and exclusively for love of country and professional pride." It would only

be natural for Sherman to blame the war for Willie's illness and death. Shortly before Sherman left camp in Mississippi, he had written to Halleck regarding his opinion about how the conflict should be brought to an end: "War is upon us; none can deny it. It is not the act of the Government of the United States but a faction. The government was forced to accept the issue or submit to a degradation fatal and disgraceful to all the inhabitants. In accepting war it should be pure and simple as applied to the belligerents. I would keep it so till all traces of the war are effaced; till those who appealed to it are sick and tired of it, and come to the emblem of our nation and sue for peace. I would not coax them or even meet them half way, but make them so sick of war that generations would pass before they would again appeal to it."

Once the initial shock over Willie's loss subsided, Sherman would implement this philosophy with a vengeance. W. T. Sherman to Henry Halleck, October 4, 1863, Official Records, Series 1, Vol. 30 (Part IV), 73; W. T. Sherman to Admiral D. D. Porter, October 14, 1863, Official Records (Naval), Series 1, Vol. 25, 469; W. T. Sherman to Maj. Gen. H. W. Halleck, September 17, 1863, Official Records, Series 1, Vol. 30 (Part III), 698.

68. P. J. Osterhaus to Capt. R. M. Sawyer, October 10, 1863, W. T. Sherman to General Grant, October 15, 1863, Official Records, Series 1, Vol. 30 (Part IV), 239, 380; W. T. Sherman to Brig. Gen. J. A. Rawlins, October 14, 1863, Official Records, Series 1, Vol. 30 (Part IV), 355.

69. *Daily Columbus* (Georgia) *Enquirer*, October 27, 1863, 2, November 1, 1863, 2; E. A. Carr to Major General Hurlburt, October 3, 1863, U. S. Grant to Maj. Gen. S.A. Hurlburt, October 8, 1863; F. P. Blair Jr. to Major General Sherman, October 10, 1863; W. T. Sherman to Brig. Gen. J. A. Rawlins, October 14, 1863, Official Records, Series 1, Vol. 30 (Part IV), 55, 170, 237–38, 356; P. D. Roddey to General Bragg, October 21, 1863, Official Records, Series 1, Vol. 30 (Part II), 728–30; P. D. Roddey to General Wheeler, October 24, 1863, Official Records, Series 1, Vol. 31 (Part III), 587.

70. W. T. Sherman to Maj. Gen. H. W. Halleck, October 18, 1863, W. T. Sherman to Maj. Gen. S. A. Hurlburt, October 18, 1863, Official Records, Series 1, Vol. 30 (Part IV), 451; W. T. Sherman to Maj. Gen. Frank Blair Jr., General Dodge and General Hurlburt, October 20, 1863; W. T. Sherman to Brig. Gen. Grenville M. Dodge, October 22, 1863, Official Records, Series 1, Vol. 3 (Part IV), 675–76, 699 ("I will checkmate them").

71. *Mobile Advertiser and Register*, October 28, 1863, 1, November 5, 1863, 2, November 7, 1863, 1, November 13, 1863, 1, November 21, 1863, 1; (New Orleans) *Daily Picayune*, October 31, 1863, 3. See also Stephen D. Lee to Maj. George William Brent, October 21, 1863, Stephen D. Lee to Col. B. S. Ewell, October 22, 1863, Stephen D. Lee to Lt. Col. George William Brent, October 28, 1863, Official Records, Series 1, Vol. 3 (Part IV), 26–29; Herman Hattaway, *General Stephen D. Lee* (Jackson, University Press of Mississippi, 1976), 103–4.

72. George Wm. Brent to Major-General Wheeler, October 17, 1863, Official Records, Series 1, Vol. 3 (Part IV), 27–28. See also Edward G. Longacre, *A Soldier to the Last* (Washington, DC: Potomac Books, 2007), 129; Dyer, *"Fightin' Joe" Wheeler*, 139.

73. Diary of Sally Independence Foster, November 3, 1863.

74. W. T. Sherman to Admiral D. D. Porter, November 8, 1863, Official Records (Naval), Series 1, Vol. 25, 539; S. D. Lee to Col. B. S. Ewell, November 6, 1863, Official Records, Series 1, Vol. 31 (Part III), 640.

75. *Daily Columbus* (Georgia) *Enquirer*, November 21, 1863, 2.

76. (Dalton, Georgia) *Huntsville Confederate*, reprinted in *Mobile Daily Tribune*, October 31, 1863, 1. See also *Mobile Advertiser and Register*, November 5, 1863, 2, November 6, 1863, 1; *Selma Morning Reporter*, November 6, 1863, 1; *Selma Morning Dispatch*, November 6, 1863, 2; *Montgomery Advertiser*, reprinted in *Daily Columbus* (Georgia) *Enquirer*, October 31, 1863, 2, (Dalton, Georgia) *Daily Huntsville Confederate*, November 11, 1863, 2.

77. G. M. Dodge to "Harris," October 19, 1863, Official Records, Series 1, Vol. 30 (Part IV), 477. See also, Storey, *Loyalty and Loss*, 158.

78. *Mobile Advertiser and Register*, November 3, 1863, 1.

79. W. T. Sherman to Admiral D. D. Porter, November 8, 1863, Official Records, Series 1, Vol. 25, 539, 541; Stoker, *Grand Design*, 345–47.

80. "Carnival of Blood" was Thomas Hill Watts's term for the war. *Selma Daily Reporter*, October 24, 1863 2.

Chapter 13

1. Nuermberger, *Clays of Alabama*, 224–26. See also *Mobile Daily Tribune*, November 11, 1863, 2 (supporting Clay's reelection), November 15, 1863, 1.

2. *Mobile Advertiser and Register*, November 17, 1863, 1.

3. Hugh Ewing to Maj. W. D. Green, November 28, 1863, Official Records, Series 1, Vol. 31 (Part II), 630–32.

4. Feis, *Grant's Secret Service*, 183; Woodworth, *Six Armies in Tennessee*, 178.

5. M. C. Meigs to Hon. E. M. Stanton, November 16, 1863, Official Records, Series 1, Vol. 31 (Part III), 162.

6. *Mobile Advertiser and Register*, December 27, 1863, 3, April 7, 1864, 1.

7. *Selma Morning Reporter*, March 23, 1864, 2; *Mobile Advertiser and Register*, March 27, 1864, 2, May 8, 1864, 2; *New York Times*, June 12, 1864, 2.

8. (Grove Hill) *Clarke County Journal*, December 24, 1863, 2; *Jacksonville Republican*, January 2, 1864, 2; *Daily Columbus* (Georgia) *Enquirer*, December 20, 1863, 1.

9. (Dalton, Georgia) *Daily Huntsville Confederate*, December 5, 1863, 2, December 8, 1863, 2, December 14, 1863, 2; Williams, *Bitterly Divided*, 125–26.

10. *Mobile Advertiser and Register*, December 4, 1863, 2; *Jacksonville Republican*, December 26, 1863, 2, January 2, 1864, 2; *Daily Columbus* (Georgia) *Enquirer*, December 20, 1863, 2. See also, (Dalton, Georgia) *Daily Huntsville Confederate*, December 5, 1863, 2, December 8, 1863, 2. George Crook to Maj. Gen. J. J. Reynolds, December 3, 1863, Official Records, Series 1, Vol. 31 (Part III), 320; J. Morris Young to Capt. R. P. Kennedy, November 18, 1863, Official Records, Series 1, Vol. 31 (Part I), 567.

11. (Dalton, Georgia) *Huntsville Confederate*, reprinted in *Charleston Mercury*, January 28, 1864, 1.

12. G. M. Dodge to Major-General Sherman, November 15, 1863, Official Rec-

ords, Series 1, Vol. 31 (Part III), 162 and G. M. Dodge to Maj. Gen. U. S. Grant, November 21, 1863, Official Records, Series 1, Vol. 31 (Part III), 220; W. T. Sherman to Maj. John A. Logan, December 21, 1863, Official Records, Series 1, Vol. 31 (Part III), 459.

13. W. T. Sherman to Maj. Gen. H. W. Halleck, November 18, 1863, Official Records, Series 1, Vol. 31 (Part III), 185.

14. G. M. Dodge to Maj. Gen. Grant, December 15, 1863, Official Records, Series 1, Vol. 31 (Part III), 412.

15. Rice, *Hard Times*, 149; (Dalton, Georgia) *Huntsville Confederate*, reprinted in *Charleston Mercury*, January 28, 1864, 1.

16. William D. Whipple to Brig. Gen. George Crook, December 9, 1863, Official Records, Series 1, Vol. 31 (Part III), 366. Sheats was later released on bail, and William McDowell was then released. (Dalton, Georgia) *Huntsville Confederate*, reprinted in *Charleston Mercury*, January 28, 1864, 1.

17. *Chattanooga Rebel*, December 2, 1863, reprinted in *Daily Huntsville Confederate*, December 2, 1863, 2.

18. See, generally, James Lee McDonough, *Chattanooga: Death Grip on the Confederacy* (Knoxville: University of Tennessee Press, 1989), 110–14.

19. *Mobile Advertiser and Register*, November 26, 1863, 2, December 10, 1863, 1. Regarding Pettus, see, (Greensboro) *Alabama Beacon*, October 9, 1863, 3; Berry, "Life of Edmund Winston Pettus," 22; Garrett, *Reminiscences of Public Men in Alabama*, 382; Owen, *History of Alabama and Dictionary of Alabama Biography*, 4: 1351–52. See, generally, McDonough, *Chattanooga*, 118–19.

20. (Dalton, Georgia) *Daily Huntsville Confederate*, December 12, 1863, 2; McDonough, *Chattanooga*, 120.

21. (Troy) *Southern Advertiser*, April 28, 1865, 2.

22. Wiley Sword, *Mountains Touched with Fire: Chattanooga Besieged, 1863* (New York: St. Martin's Press, 1995), 291, 308–12.

23. James T. Searcy to Reuben Searcy, November 28, 1863, Papers of James T. Searcy, Alabama Department of Archives and History, Montgomery.

24. James T. Searcy to Stella Searcy, December 1, 1863, Papers of James T. Searcy, Alabama Department of Archives and History, Montgomery.

25. Daniel, *Soldiering in the Army of Tennessee*, 137–39; Noe, *Reluctant Rebels*, 185.

26. *Mobile Advertiser and Register*, November 26, 1863, 2, November 27, 1863, 2, November 29, 1863, 1–2, December 1, 1863, 1, December 3, 1863, 1, December 12, 1863, 2; *Mobile Daily Tribune*, November 29, 1863, 1, December 5, 1863, 2; (Dalton, Georgia) *Daily Huntsville Confederate*, November 26, 1863, 2; (Livingston) *Independent*, November 28, 1863, December 5, 1863; Feis, *Grant's Secret Service*, 187–89; Hess, *Civil War in the West*, 192–98.

27. *Mobile Advertiser and Register*, December 1, 1863, 1. See also *Mobile Advertiser and Register*, December 27, 1863, 2 (a firsthand account by Ben Lane Posey), December 31, 1863, 2 (same).

28. J. T. Searcy to Stella Searcy, December 2, 1863, Papers of James T. Searcy, Ala-

bama Department of Archives and History, Montgomery. See, generally, Stoker, *Grand Design*, 333.

29. Wiley Sword, "'Our Fireside in Ruins': Consequences of the 1863 Chattanooga Campaign," in *Gateway to the Confederacy*, ed. Evan C. Jones and Wiley Sword, 241.

30. (New Orleans) *Daily Picayune*, November 27, 1863, 1.

31. McWhiney, Moore, and Pace, eds., *"Fear God and Walk Humbly,"* 328.

32. Grant Taylor to Malinda Taylor, December 6, 1863, in *This Cruel War*, eds. Bloomquist and Taylor, 205.

33. John Cotton to Mariah Cotton, December 14, 1863, in *Yours Till Death*, ed. Lucille Griffith, 98.

34. Private Journal of Sarah R. Espy, 71.

35. *Mobile Daily Advertiser and Register*, December 22, 1863, 2; *Mobile Daily Tribune*, December 20, 1863, 1; (Dalton, Georgia) *Daily Huntsville Confederate*, December 24, 1863, 2; *Daily Columbus* (Georgia) *Enquirer*, December 19, 1863, 2; (New Orleans) *Daily Picayune*, December 19, 1863, 1; Roy P. Basler, ed., *The Collected Works of Abraham Lincoln* (New Brunswick, NJ: Rutgers University Press, 1953), VII: 53–56. See, generally, Jonathan Truman Dorris, *Pardon and Amnesty under Lincoln and Johnson* (Chapel Hill: University of North Carolina Press, 1977), 34–38; John Hope Franklin, *Reconstruction after the Civil War* (Chicago: University of Chicago Press, 1994), 16–17; Stevens, *1863*, 403–5.

36. Basler, ed., *Collected Works of Abraham Lincoln*, VII: 55. See also Paul D. Escott, *"What Shall We Do with the Negro?": Lincoln, White Racism and Civil War America* (Charlottesville: University of Virginia Press, 2009), 102–6; Henry Mayer, *All on Fire: William Lloyd Garrison and the Abolition of Slavery* (New York: Norton, 2008), 562 (regarding criticism by abolitionists); (Boston) *Liberator*, December 18, 1863, 202 (same). See, generally, James Walvin, *England, Slaves and Freedom, 1776–1838* (Jackson: University Press of Mississippi, 1986), 165; Michael Craton, *Slavery, Abolition, and Emancipation* (London: Longman, 1976), 325 (discussing the British system of apprenticeship); Eric Foner, *Reconstruction: America's Unfinished Revolution, 1863–1877* (New York: Perennial Classics, 2002), 201–2 (discussing postwar apprenticeship systems that were a component of the now-infamous Black Codes).

37. *Mobile Advertiser and Register*, December 10, 1863, 1.

38. George H. Thomas to Maj. R. M. Sawyer, March 10, 1864, Official Records, Series 1, Vol. 32 (Part I), 7; J. Longstreet to J. G. Foster, January 8, 1864, Official Records, Series 3, Vol. 4, 50–53.

39. Dorris, *Pardon and Amnesty*, 37–38, 86.

40. Bessie Martin, *Desertion of Alabama Troops from the Confederate Army: A Study in Sectionalism* (New York, Columbia University Press, 1932), 26–27, 33, 244–45; Mark A. Weitz, *More Damning Than Slaughter: Desertion in the Confederate Army* (Lincoln: University of Nebraska Press, 2005), 234–76.

41. George Koon to Sarah Koon, February 8, 1864, in Brown, *Family History*, 21.

42. George Koon to Sarah Koon, April 24, 1864, in Brown, *Family History*, 26.

43. *Milwaukee Daily Sentinel*, January 25, 1864.

44. Dabney H. Maury to James A. Seddon, December 28, 1863, Official Records, Series 1, Vol. 26 (Part II), 548.

45. James H. Barrow to Nancy E. Barrow, January 8, 1864, in *Word from Camp Pollard, C.S.A.*, ed. William H. Davidson, 140 (West Point, GA: Davidson, 1978); James H. Barrow to Nancy E. Barrow, in January 10, 1864, in *Word from Camp Pollard, C.S.A.*, ed. William H. Davidson, 152. See also Dabney H. Maury to James A. Seddon, December 28, 1863, Official Records, Series 1, Vol. 26 (Part II), 548.

46. C. J. L. Cunningham to Capt. R. S. Abercrombie, December 26, 1863, Official Records, Series 1, Vol. 26 (Part II), 550.

47. *Mobile Advertiser and Register*, January 5, 1864, 2.

48. Jas. H. Clanton to Col. George G. Garner, January 6, 1864, Official Records, Series 1, Vol. 26 (Part II), 552. See also Brig. Gen. Asboth to Brig. Gen. Charles P. Stone, January 10, 1864, Official Records, Series 1, Vol. 35 (Part I), 453–54.

49. *Mobile Daily Tribune*, December 27, 1863, 1; *Mobile Advertiser and Register*, December 27, 1863, 3; (Greensboro) *Alabama Beacon*, January 1, 1864, 2; Stoker, *Grand Design*, 340–42.

50. J. E. Johnston to General S. Cooper, January 15, 1864, Official Records, Series 1, Vol. 26 (Part II), 553.

51. J. A. Seddon to General Dabney H. Maury, January 9, 1864, Official Records, Series 1, Vol. 26 (Part II), 551. See, generally, Tatum, *Disloyalty in the Confederacy*, 64–66; Owsley, "Defeatism in the Confederacy," 455.

52. Official Records, Series 1, Vol. 32 (Part II), 582.

53. T. H. Watts to Lieut. Gen. Leonidas Polk, January 30, 1864, Official Records, Series 1, Vol. 26 (Part (II), 554.

54. Petition of Thomas J. Foster et al., January 1864, Official Records, Series 1, Vol. 32 (Part II), 515; *Montgomery Advertiser*, January 8, 1864, 1.

55. G. M. Dodge to Maj. Gen. W. T. Sherman, January 12, 1864, Official Records, Series 1, Vol. 32 (Part II), 74.

56. Dodd, "Unionism in Confederate Alabama," 68; *Mobile Advertiser and Register*, February 17, 1864, 2.

57. (Dalton, Georgia) *Huntsville Confederate*, reprinted in *Charleston Mercury*, January 28, 1864, 1 and *Daily Columbus* (Georgia) *Enquirer*, February 10, 1864, 1; *Mobile Advertiser and Register*, January 30, 1864, 1; *Montgomery Daily Advertiser*, reprinted in *Daily Columbus* (Georgia) *Enquirer*, January 26, 1864, 1. See also *Daily Columbus* (Georgia) *Enquirer*, February 17, 1864, 1. ("One notorious [Alabama] tory, named John Wessen, rode up to his neighbor, Lewis Moore, a true Southern man, and blew his brains out."); Rohr, ed., *Incidents of the War*, 131.

58. Brewer, *Alabama*, 355.

59. Storey, *Loyalty and Loss*, 167; Dodd, "Unionism in Confederate Alabama," 72; Rice, *Hard Times*, 150; Thompson, *Free State of Winston*, 81–86; Williams, *Bitterly Divided*, 125–26. Regarding other Confederate guerrilla activity in north Alabama in early 1864, see J. I. Alexander to Major General Logan, January 2, 1864, Official Records, Series 1, Vol. 32 (Part II), 11; James E. Saunders to Maj. Gen. Joseph Wheeler,

January 30, 1864, Official Records, Series 1, Vol. 52 (Part II), 612–14; Thomas Hill Watts to Lt. Col. Lockhart, February 6, 1864, Papers of Governor Watts, Alabama Department of Archives and History, Montgomery.

60. (Dalton, Georgia) *Huntsville Confederate*, reprinted in *Daily Columbus* (Georgia) *Enquirer*, February 18, 1864, 1.

61. *Cincinnati Gazette*, February 1, 1864.

62. Augusta Jane Evans, *Macaria; or, the Altars of Sacrifice* (1864; reprinted Baton Rouge: Louisiana State University, 1992); *Charleston Mercury*, September 14, 1864, 3. See, generally, Jennifer Lynn Gross, "Augusta Jane Evans: Alabama's Confederate *Macaria*," in *Yellowhammer War*, ed. Kenneth W. Noe, 125–48; Anne Sophie Riepma, *Fire & Fiction: Augusta Jane Evans in Context* (Amsterdam: Rodopi, 2000), 59–108; Shields, *Freedom in a Slave Society*, 258–64. Any debate over the year *Macaria* was first published is settled by a card from its publisher in the Richmond *Daily Dispatch* explaining why publication was delayed until early 1864. (Richmond) *Daily Dispatch*, December 10, 1863, 2.

63. *Mobile Advertiser and Register*, February 26, 1864, 2; *New York Times*, February 25, 1864, 1. For the text of this address, see *Mobile Advertiser and Register*, February 25, 1864, 1; *Mobile Daily Tribune*, February 28, 1864, 1–2; Address of Congress to the People of the Confederate States, Official Records, Series 4, Vol. 2, 126–37. If press accounts were accurate, one Alabama woman who also doggedly continued to do her duty was, ironically, the sister-in-law of Abraham Lincoln and sister of Mary Todd Lincoln. Martha Todd White had married a Selma physician in the 1850s, and when the war began, she and her other sister Elodie had received national attention for their pro-Confederate activities in Alabama. In 1864, Martha further embarrassed Lincoln and his administration by reportedly smuggling $40,000 worth of gold from the North to the South during a trip with her mother to Kentucky and Washington, DC. It was, wrote the *Richmond Examiner*, "a remarkable instance of woman's ingenuity." *Richmond Examiner*, March 2, 1864, 1; Berry, *House of Abraham*, 157–65. See also *Columbus* (Georgia) *Daily Enquirer*, March 8, 1864, 2; *Milwaukee Sentinel*, March 22, 1864, 1; (New Haven, Connecticut) *Columbian Register*, April 2, 1864, 3.

64. *Richmond Enquirer*, reprinted in *Mobile Advertiser and Register*, February 28, 1864, 1; (New Orleans) *Daily Picayune*, March 11, 1864, 4.

65. Stokes, *Grand Design*, 349.

Chapter 14

1. Thomas H. Rosser to Col. Thomas M. Jack, January 27, 1864, Official Records, Series 1, Vol. 32 (Part II), 626; W. T. Sherman to Maj. Gen. H. W. Halleck, January 12, 1864, Official Records, Series 1, Vol. 32 (Part II), 75; *Charleston Mercury*, February 18, 1864, 1; *Richmond Examiner*, November 26, 1863, 2.

2. *Montgomery Mail*, reprinted in *Richmond Daily Whig*, May 6, 1864, 4.

3. *Chattanooga Daily Rebel*, March 11, 1863, 2; *Macon* (Georgia) *Telegraph*, February 27, 1863, 1, March 7, 1863, 2; *Charleston Mercury*, March 4, 1863, 1; *Cleveland*

Plain Dealer, March 20, 1863, 2; (Atlanta) *Daily Constitutionalist*, April 3, 1863, 3; *New York Herald*, June 4, 1863, 1; *Augusta Chronicle*, August 20, 1863, 2; *Alexandria Gazette*, October 13, 1863, 2; *Philadelphia Inquirer*, April 6, 1864, 4; *Nashville Union*, reprinted in (New York) *Evening Post*, May 11, 1864, 4; A. T. Jones to Charles B. Mitchell, April 26, 1864, Rare Book Collection, University of North Carolina at Chapel Hill.

4. *Alexandria* (Virginia) *Gazette*, February 14, 1863, 1.

5. *Mobile Advertiser and Register*, April 21, 1864, 2. See also *Mobile Advertiser and Register*, March 25, 1864, 2.

6. *Jacksonville Republican*, May 21, 1864, 2.

7. *Hartford* (Connecticut) *Press*, reprinted in (New Orleans) *Daily Picayune*, April 21, 1864, 1 and *Vermont Chronicle*, April 9, 1864, 3; *New York Herald*, June 4, 1863, 1; *New Haven Palladium*, November 13, 1863, 2; (New York) *Evening Post*, November 23, 1863, 2.

8. U. S. Grant to Maj. Gen. George H. Thomas, January 19, 1864, Official Records, Series 1, Vol. 32 (Part II), 143.

9. *Mobile Advertiser and Register*, February 12, 1864, 1; (New Orleans) *Daily Picayune*, February 27, 1864, 1; *Charleston Mercury*, February 16, 1864, 1. See, generally, Buckley Thomas Foster, *Sherman's Mississippi Campaign* (Tuscaloosa: University of Alabama, 2006), 15–27; Grimsley, *Hard Hand of War*, 162–64.

10. (Washington, DC) *Daily National Republican*, March 5, 1864, 1.

11. *Mobile Advertiser and Register*, February 6, 1864, 1, February 12, 1864, 1, February 14, 1864, 2, February 16, 1864, 1, February 19, 1864, 1; *Clarke County* (Alabama) *Journal*, February 11, 1864, 2, February 18, 1864, 2; *Mobile Daily Tribune*, January 28, 1864, 2, February 7, 1864, 1, February 11, 1864, 2, February 25, 1864, 2; *Charleston Mercury*, February 6, 1864, 1, February 12, 1864, 2; *New York Tribune*, February 10, 1864, 4; *Macon* (Georgia) *Telegraph*, March 23, 1864, 2; Mary Elizabeth Mitchell Journal, 54, Southern Historical Collection, University of North Carolina, Chapel Hill.

12. *Mobile Advertiser and Register*, February 16, 1864, 1; *Mobile Daily Tribune*, February 25, 1864, 2; *Charleston Mercury*, February 17, 1864, 1, February 20, 1864, 1.

13. *Mobile Advertiser and Register*, February 16, 1864, 2. See also (Grove Hill) *Clarke County Journal*, February 18, 1864, 2; *Charleston Mercury*, February 20, 1864, 1

14. *Mobile Advertiser and Register*, February 21, 1864, 1; (Grove Hill) *Clarke County Journal*, February 25, 1864, 2; *Charleston Mercury*, February 25, 1864, 1.

15. (Selma) *Mississippian*, February 10, 1864, reprinted in *Daily Columbus* (Georgia) *Enquirer*, February 14, 1864, 1; *Charleston Mercury*, February 17, 1864, 1.

16. *Macon* (Georgia) *Telegraph*, February 10, 1864, reprinted in *Daily Columbus* (Georgia) *Enquirer*, February 11, 1864, 1.

17. *Mobile Tribune*, February 27, 1864, reprinted in *Daily Columbus* (Georgia) *Enquirer*, March 1, 1864, 1; *Charleston Mercury*, March 12, 1864, 1; Linden and Linden, eds., *Disunion*, 113 ("there is great excitement about our army falling back in Miss and fears of the federal army destroying by raids").

18. (Selma) *Mississippian*, February 17, 1864, reprinted in *Daily Columbus* (Georgia) *Enquirer*, February 20, 1864, 1; *Charleston Mercury*, February 22, 1864, 1, Feb-

ruary 23, 1864, 2; *Daily Columbus* (Georgia) *Enquirer*, February 17, 1864, 1; *Memphis Appeal*, reprinted in *Daily Columbus* (Georgia) *Enquirer*, February 19, 1864, 2; *Macon Telegraph*, February 17, 1864, 2; W. M. Brooks to Gov. Thomas H. Watts, February 17, 1864, Papers of Governor Watts, Alabama Department of Archives and History, Montgomery; Noe, *Reluctant Rebels*, 185.

19. *Selma Reporter*, reprinted in *Mobile Advertiser and Register*, February 23, 1864, 1, March 5, 1864, 2 and *Memphis Daily Appeal*, February 19, 1864, 2; *Clarke County* (Alabama) *Journal*, February 25, 1864, 2; *Mobile Daily Tribune*, February 28, 1864, 2; *Daily Columbus* (Georgia) *Enquirer*, February 28, 1864, 1, March 4, 1864, 1; *Chicago Journal*, reprinted in *Milwaukee Daily Sentinel*, March 14, 1864; *Charleston Mercury*, February 29, 1864, 1; (New Orleans) *Daily Picayune*, March 25, 1864, 5; (Atlanta) *Daily Constitutionalist*, February 24, 1864, 2; Foster, *Sherman's Mississippi Campaign*, 62, 90, 100–108, 150–52.

20. *Mobile Tribune*, February 17, 1864, reprinted in *Daily Columbus* (Georgia) *Enquirer*, February 20, 1864, 1.

21. *Selma Dispatch*, February 18, 1864, reprinted in *Macon Telegraph*, February 26, 1864, 1.

22. W. T. Sherman to Brig. Gen. R. P. Buckland, February 28, 1864, Official Records, Series 1, Vol. 32 (Part II), 492–93; Foster, *Sherman's Mississippi Campaign*, 32.

23. Foster, *Sherman's Mississippi Campaign*, 25, 126–35, 148–49; *Charleston Mercury*, February 20, 1864, 1.

24. *Mobile Advertiser and Register*, February 24, 1864, 2; *Mobile Daily Tribune*, February 25, 1864, 2; (Selma) *Mississippian*, February 26, 1864, reprinted in *Daily Columbus* (Georgia) *Enquirer*, March 1, 1864, 1; *Daily Columbus* (Georgia) *Enquirer*, February 25, 1864, 2, February 26, 1864, 2. W. T. Sherman to Brig. Gen. R. P. Buckland, February 28, 1864, Official Records, Series 1, Vol. 32 (Part II), 493; Foster, *Sherman's Mississippi Campaign*, 120–22, 162–65.

25. Foster, *Sherman's Mississippi Campaign*, 136.

26. *Mobile Advertiser and Register*, January 29, 1864, 1.

27. R. E. Corry to Lizzie, November 25, 1863, quoted in Noe, *Reluctant Rebels*, 168.

28. S. D. Lee to Lieut. Col. T. M. Jack, April 18, 1864, Official Records, Series 1, Vol. 32 (Part I), 367; *Mobile Advertiser and Register*, February 26, 1864, 2, March 5, 1864, 1–2, March 6, 1864, 2, March 8, 1864, 1; *Charleston Mercury*, March 2, 1864, 1; *Daily Columbus* (Georgia) *Enquirer*, February 24, 1864, 2, February 26, 1864, 2. See, generally, Hurst, *Nathan Bedford Forrest*, 147–55; Brian Steel Wills, *A Battle from the Start: The Life of Nathan Bedford Forrest* (New York: Harper Perennial, 1993), 158–67; Paul Ashdown and Edward Caudill, *The Myth of Nathan Bedford Forrest* (Lanham, MD: Rowman and Littlefield, 2005), 26–27; Foster, *Sherman's Mississippi Campaign*, 136–47, 169.

29. *Daily Columbus* (Georgia) *Enquirer*, February 26, 1864, 2.

30. *Selma Dispatch*, February 25, 1864, reprinted in (Augusta) *Daily Constitutionalist*, February 28, 1864, 2.

31. *Atlanta Confederacy*, reprinted in *Mobile Advertiser and Register*, March 6, 1864, 2. See also *Memphis Appeal*, October 2, 1864, reprinted in *Mobile Advertiser and Register*, October 5, 1864, 2; *Charleston Mercury*, June 20, 1864, 1.

32. (Selma) *Mississippian*, March 1, 1864, reprinted in *Daily Columbus* (Georgia) *Enquirer*, March 4, 1864, 1 and (Athens, Georgia) *Southern Watchmen*, March 9, 1864, 2. For other references to Forrest as the "War Eagle," see *Mobile Advertiser and Register*, July 28, 1864, 2, October 5, 1864, 1, October 12, 1864, 1, October 13, 1864, 1, November 12, 1864, 2, December 7, 1864, 2; *New York Herald*, April 13, 1865, 1; *Atlanta Intelligencer*, reprinted in *Charleston Mercury*, February 22, 1864, 1, June 6, 1864, 1, July 7, 1864, 2; (Montgomery) *Memphis Appeal*, reprinted in *Macon* (Georgia) *Telegraph*, July 6, 1864, 1.

33. *Mobile Advertiser and Register*, reprinted in *Daily Columbus* (Georgia) *Enquirer*, March 8, 1864, 2. See also *Mobile Evening News*, March 2, 1864, reprinted in (New Orleans) *Daily Picayune*, March 13, 1864, 2; *Memphis Appeal*, reprinted in (New Orleans) *Daily Picayune*, March 23, 1864, 1. See also *Mobile Daily Tribune*, March 9, 1864, reprinted in (New Orleans) *Daily Picayune*, March 20, 1864, 8; *Mobile Advertiser and Register*, March 5, 1864, 2 and March 6, 1864, 2; *Marion Commonwealth*, cited in *Daily Columbus* (Georgia) *Enquirer*, June 10, 1864, 2.

34. *Atlanta Confederacy*, reprinted in *Daily Columbus* (Georgia) *Enquirer*, March 6, 1864, 1; *Charleston Mercury*, March 4, 1864, 1, March 7, 1864, 1.

35. See, e.g., *New York Tribune*, February 29, 1864, 1.

36. See *New York Times*, February 27, 1864, reprinted in (New Orleans) *Daily Picayune*, March 8, 1864, 1; *New York Tribune*, reprinted in *Mobile Advertiser and Register*, March 16, 1864, 1; *New York Herald*, March 21, 1864; *Boston Herald*, March 7, 1864, 4; *Vermont Watchman and State Journal*, March 4, 1864.

37. *Daily Columbus* (Georgia) *Enquirer*, March 9, 1864, 2, April 16, 1864, 2.

38. John Allan Wyeth, *That Devil Forrest: Life of General Nathan Bedford Forrest* (Baton Rouge: Louisiana State University Press, 1989), xi.

39. *Mobile Advertiser and Register*, July 2, 1864, 2.

40. Ibid., May 21, 1864, 1; *Charleston Mercury*, June 20, 1864, 1; Ashdown and Caudill, *Myth of Nathan Bedford Forrest*, 72–73.

41. Stoker, *Grand Design*, 415.

42. *Memphis Appeal*, reprinted in *Daily Columbus* (Georgia) *Enquirer*, May 22, 1864, 1. See, generally, Clampitt, *Confederate Heartland*, 22–23.

43. (Selma) *Mississippian*, March 1, 1864, reprinted in *Daily Columbus* (Georgia) *Enquirer*, March 4, 1864, 1.

44. George Knox Miller to Celestine Miller, January 2, 1864, in *An Uncompromising Secessionist*, ed. Richard M. McMurry, 165.

45. George Knox Miller to Celestine Miller, April 10, 1864; George Knox Miller to Celestine Miller, April 10, 1864, 189.

46. *Jacksonville Republican*, March 12, 1864, 2.

47. *Mobile Daily Tribune*, February 28, 1864, 2, March 1, 1864, 2. See also *Mobile Advertiser and Register*, March 2, 1864, reprinted in (New Orleans) *Daily Picayune*, March 13, 1864, 2 and March 3, 1864, 2.

48. *Mobile Advertiser and Register*, March 3, 1864, 2. See also *Daily Columbus* (Georgia) *Enquirer*, March 19, 1864, 2 ("we have everything to encourage us in the campaign of this year" and "the Yankee prospect is decidedly gloomy"); *Charleston Mercury*, March 16, 1864, 1, March 17, 1864, 1.

49. *Mobile Advertiser and Register*, March 5, 1864, 2. See also (Meridian) *Daily Clarion*, March 28, 1865, 2.

50. *Charleston Mercury*, March 10, 1864, 1.

51. *Atlanta Confederacy*, reprinted in *Mobile Advertiser and Register*, March 9, 1864, 1.

52. *Brandon* (Mississippi) *Republican*, March 10, 1864, reprinted in *Daily Columbus* (Georgia) *Enquirer*, March 25, 1864, 1.

53. Adams, *Living Hell*, 168, 171.

Chapter 15

1. Mary Elizabeth Mitchell Journal, 51; *Mobile Advertiser and Register*, March 12, 1864, 2; Jackson, "Life and Times of Robert Jemison, Jr.," 71.

2. *Chicago Journal*, reprinted in *Mobile Advertiser and Register*, May 11, 1864, 2.

3. *Selma Morning Reporter*, March 23, 1864, 2; Williams, *Bitterly Divided*, 237–38. See also *Mobile Advertiser and Register*, March 27, 1864, 2; *Clarke County* (Alabama) *Journal*, March 21, 1864, 2, March 31, 1864, 2; *Daily Columbus* (Georgia) *Enquirer*, March 27, 1864, p 1; *Charleston Courier*, reprinted in *Daily Columbus* (Georgia) *Enquirer*, April 8, 1864, 2; Robert Dunnavant, *Decatur, Alabama: Yankee Foothold in Dixie, 1861–1865* (Athens, AL: Pea Ridge Press, 1995), 91, 141; Edward McPherson, *The Political History of the United States of America During the Great Rebellion* (Washington, DC: Philip & Solomons, 1865), 402 (stating that Cobb was expelled from the Confederate Congress on November 17, 1864, for his peace activities); Rev. Milus E. Johnston, *The Sword of "Bushwacker" Johnston* (Huntsville, AL: Flint River Press, 1992), 106 (stating that Cobb died on November 1, 1864, of an "apparently accidental" gunshot); Owen, *History of Alabama and Dictionary of Alabama Biography*, 3: 357–58 (same); Martin, *Desertion of Alabama Troops from the Confederate Army*, 110n192 ("In 1864, Cobb was expelled from Congress for giving aid and comfort to the enemy," Journal of Congress, Vol. VII, 275–78); *Daily Columbus* (Georgia) *Enquirer*, May 11, 1864, 1.

4. *Mobile Advertiser and Register*, April 23, 1864, 1; (Greensboro) *Alabama Beacon*, April 15, 1864, 3. See also *New York World*, reprinted in *Daily Columbus* (Georgia) *Enquirer*, April 15, 1864, 2; *New York Times*, March 24, 1864, 5 (reporting the proceedings at the meeting), April 23, 1864, 1; (New Orleans) *Daily Picayune*, April 8, 1864, 2; Rice, *Hard Times*, 232–38; Dunnavant, *Decatur, Alabama*, 141; Fleming, *Civil War and Reconstruction in Alabama*, 144–45; James H. Clanton to Gov. T. H. Watts, April 5, 1864, Official Records, Series I, Vol. 32 (Part III), 750–51 (James Holt Clanton's report to Governor Watts about coverage of the Huntsville meeting in a Nashville newspaper); Wallace Hettle, *The Peculiar Democracy: Southern Democrats in Peace and Civil War* (Athens: University of Georgia Press, 2001), 135; Danielson, *War's Desolating Scourge*, 132.

5. Report of the Committee, Part III, 65–67 (congressional testimony of Humphreys in 1866); (Huntsville) *Southern Advocate*, April 24, 1861, 3; *Selma Morning Reporter*, March 4, 1864, 1.

6. Graf et al., eds., *Papers of Andrew Johnson*, 6: 549 (Johnson was more emphatic, telling his audience that "the institution is dead."). See also *Mobile Advertiser and Register*, April 17, 1864, 2; (New Orleans) *Daily Picayune*, April 22, 1864, 2.

7. *New York Times*, March 24, 1864, 5.

8. (Montgomery) *Alabama State Sentinel*, May 30, 1867, 2. See also James Holt Clanton to Governor Thomas Hill Watts, April 5, 1864, Official Records, Series I, Vol. 32 (Part III), 750; Fleming, *Civil War and Reconstruction in Alabama*, 145; *New York Times*, February 14, 1864, 3 (publishing a letter from Humphreys urging restoration of the Union in order to "secure to the State the right to dispose of its labor system in a way and manner that will accord with the circumstances surrounding us"). See, generally, Walter L. Fleming, "The Peace Movement in Alabama during the Civil War," *South Atlantic Quarterly* 2 (April 1903): 114, 122–24; Levine, *Fall of the House of Dixie*, 205–6.

9. *Washington Chronicle*, reprinted in *Chattanooga Daily Gazette*, June 19, 1864.

10. *Mobile Advertiser and Register*, June 30, 1864, 1.

11. *Selma Reporter*, reprinted in *Daily Columbus* (Georgia) *Enquirer*, April 24, 1864, 1.

12. G. M. Dodge to Brig. Gen. J. A. Rawlins, March 8, 1864, Official Records, Series 1, Vol. 32 (Part III), 38; (New Orleans) *Daily Picayune*, April 6, 1864, 2.

13. G. M. Dodge to Lt. Col. Bowers, March 11, 1864, Official Records, Series 1, Vol. 32 (Part I), 492. See also *Montgomery Advertiser*, March 15, 1864, reprinted in *Daily Columbus* (Georgia) *Enquirer*, March 16, 1864, 2; *Charleston Mercury*, March 19, 1864, 1; *Nashville Daily Times and True Union*, March 26, 1864, 2; Dunnavant, *Decatur, Alabama*, 92.

14. *Mobile Daily Tribune*, January 31, 1864, 3; *Charleston Mercury*, January 8, 1864, 1.

15. *Montgomery Weekly Advertiser*, February 10, 1864, 1.

16. R. W. Walker to D. L. Dalton, April 14, 1864, Official Records, Series 1, Vol. 32 (Part III), 824. See also G. M. Dodge to Major-General McPherson, April 17, 1864, Official Records, Series 1, Vol. 32 (Part II), 388 (indicating that Roddey's family was also in Tuscaloosa).

17. *Mobile Daily Tribune*, April 26, 1864, 2.

18. Fleming, *Civil War and Reconstruction in Alabama*, 67.

19. L. Polk to General S. Cooper, March 3, 1864 and A.H. Polk to Lt. Col. T.F. Sevier, March 3, 1864, Official Records, Series 1, Vol. 32 (Part III), p 579–81; (New Orleans) *Daily Picayune*, March 11, 1864, 1; *Mobile Tribune*, reprinted in *Daily Columbus* (Georgia) *Enquirer*, February 28, 1864, 2, March 6, 1864, 1; (Selma) *Mississippian*, reprinted in *Philadelphia Inquirer*, March 15, 1864, 2.

20. *Mobile Advertiser and Register*, April 27, 1864, 2, May 6, 1864, 1; (Grove Hill) *Clarke County Journal*, March 17, 1864, 2; *Daily Columbus* (Georgia) *Enquirer*, March 22, 1864, 1, April 8, 1864, 1; (New Orleans) *Daily Picayune*, March 24, 1864, 2. See also Dabney H. Maury to Col. T. M. Jack, March 15, 1864 and H. Maury to Major-

General Maury, March 12, 1864, Official Records, Series 1, Vol. 32 (Part III), 632–33; L. Polk to General S. Cooper, Official Records, Series 1, Vol. 32 (Part I), 499; W. Wirt Thomson to Hon. James A. Seddon, March 29, 1864, Official Records, Series 1, Vol. 32 (Part III), 711.

21. James Hamilton to Col. T. M. Jack, March 31, 1864, Official Records, Series 1, Vol. 32 (Part III), 727–28. See, generally, Victoria E. Bynum, *The Free State of Jones: Mississippi's Longest Civil War* (Chapel Hill: University of North Carolina Press, 2001).

22. (New Orleans) *Daily Picayune*, March 25, 1864, 5.

23. *Mobile Advertiser and Register*, April 22, 1864, 2, April 26, 1864, 2, April 28, 1864, 1; (Greensboro) *Alabama Beacon*, April 15, 1864, 3; *Daily Columbus* (Georgia) *Enquirer*, April 3, 1864, 2, April 6, 1864, 2, April 12, 1864, 1, April 17, 1864, 1–2; *Jacksonville Republican*, April 9, 1864, 2, April 23, 1864, 2; *Charleston Mercury*, April 2, 1864, 1, April 7, 1864, 1.

24. T. H. Baker to Maj. J. C. Denis, April 4, 1864 and D. P. Walston to Lieut. Col. T. H. Baker, April 2, 1864, Official Records, Series 1, Vol. 32 (Part III), 745–47.

25. Ibid. See, generally, Dodd, "Unionism in Confederate Alabama," 75–77.

26. L. Polk to Maj. Gen. S. D. Lee, April 8, 1864, Official Records, Series 1, Vol. 32 (Part II), 758.

27. T. M. Jack to Unknown, April 10, 1864, Official Records, Series 1, Vol. 32 (Part III), 770 (emphasis added).

28. S. A. Hurlburt to Maj. W. F. Bradford, March 28, 1864, and N. B. Forrest to Major-General Lee, April 10, 1864, Official Records, Series 1, Vol. 32 (Part III), 177, 770; (New Orleans) *Daily Picayune*, April 22, 1864, 2 (stating that the force included "Companies A, B, C and D of the 1st Alabama (colored) or 6th US heavy artillery, and companies A, B, D and E of the 13th Tennessee cavalry"). See also Williams, *History of the Negro Troops*, 257; Andrew Ward, *River Run Red: The Fort Pillow Massacre in the American Civil War* (New York: Viking, 2005), 128, 141–42; Hurst, *Nathan Bedford Forrest*, 164–65; Dunnavant, *Decatur, Alabama*, 101; *Mobile Advertiser and Register*, April 29, 1864, 1. Cf., (New Orleans) *Daily Picayune*, May 5, 1864, 1 (reporting the presence of the First Alabama Cavalry at Decatur), April 29, 1864, 1 (noting concern that it would be "impossible to keep colored troops in the service unless we protected them the same as white troops"); *Mobile Advertiser and Register*, June 2, 1864, 1 (noting that after Forrest's expedition through west Tennessee, no "tory command" existed there and "Not a tory dare show his head"); Storey, *Loyalty and Loss*, 115 (stating that the 106th US Colored Infantry was organized in Decatur in the spring and summer of 1864). Black troops were also fortifying Decatur, Alabama, under the command of Grenville Dodge. As the *Savannah News* would later classify Fort Pillow, Decatur, with both the First Alabama Cavalry, USA., and the 106th US Colored Infantry deployed there, was also a "mongrel garrison," the destruction of which could be effectively used to suppress the spirit of volunteerism of Southern whites and blacks to the Union military, and instead stimulate desertions.

29. *Mobile Advertiser and Register*, April 17, 1864, 2; *Jacksonville Republican*, April

23, 1864, 2. See also *Mobile Advertiser and Register*, April 15, 1864, 2, April 19, 1864, 1, April 21, 1864, 2, April 28, 1864, 1, April 30, 1864, 1, May 29, 1864, 2.

30. *Mobile Advertiser and Register*, April 26, 1864, 2. See also, *Daily Columbus* (Georgia) *Enquirer*, April 21, 1864, 2; *Charleston Mercury*, April 18, 1864, 1.

31. *Mobile Advertiser and Register*, April 30, 1864, 1.

32. *Charleston Mercury*, April 26, 1864, 1. See also Brian Steel Wills, *The River Was Dyed with Blood: Nathan Bedford Forrest and Fort Pillow* (Norman: University of Oklahoma Press, 2014), 162–83.

33. (New Orleans) *Daily Picayune*, April 29, 1864, 2, *Daily Columbus* (Georgia) *Enquirer*, April 24, 1864, 2, May 27, 1864, 2; *Charleston Mercury*, June 28, 1864, p. 2.

34. *Jacksonville Republican*, March 12, 1864, 2.

35. W. T. Sherman to E. M. Stanton, April 23, 1864, Official Records, Series 1, Vol. 32 (Part III), 464. See also Ward, *Run Red*, 311, 329–30, 335; *Nashville Daily Times and True Union*, April 20, 1864, 1 (calling for retaliation), May 24, 1864, 2 (reporting an instance of retaliation by black troops near Natchez); *Scioto* (Ohio) *Gazette*, April 18, 1864 (reporting a desire for retaliation among black soldiers stationed at Memphis); *Daily Cleveland Herald*, June 3, 1864 (reporting the retaliation near Natchez); (Washington, DC) *Daily National Intelligencer*, May 23, 1865 (reporting that force had to be used to prevent black troops in Memphis from retaliating against paroled Confederate prisoners after the war); *Richmond Examiner*, reprinted in *Daily Columbus* (Georgia) *Enquirer*, May 25, 1864, 2.

36. *Mobile Advertiser and Register*, reprinted in *Daily Columbus* (Georgia) *Enquirer*, June 5, 1864, 2.

37. See, e.g., *Daily Columbus* (Georgia) *Enquirer*, June 15, 1864, 2.

38. G. M. Dodge to Major-General McPherson, April 17, 1864, Official Records, Series 1, Vol. 32 (Part II), 388.

39. James C. Veatch to Brigadier General Dodge, April 18, 1864, Official Records, Series 1, Vol. 32 (Part I), 671; *Chicago Journal*, reprinted in *Milwaukee Daily Sentinel*, April 29, 1864; Dunnavant, *Decatur, Alabama*, 94; (New Orleans) *Daily Picayune*, May 5, 1864, 1.

40. *Mobile Advertiser and Register*, April 19, 1864, 1. See also *Daily Columbus* (Georgia) *Enquirer*, April 22, 1864, 2; (New Orleans) *Daily Picayune*, April 20, 1864, 2.

41. *Daily Columbus* (Georgia) *Enquirer*, May 7, 1864, 1; *Liberty* (Missouri) *Tribune*, April 22, 1864, 4; *Memphis Argus*, reprinted in *Charleston Mercury*, April 23, 1864, 1; *Charleston Mercury*, April 26, 1864, 1.

42. *Daily Columbus* (Georgia) *Enquirer*, May 1, 1864, 1–2.

43. S. D. Lee to Lt. Col. T. M. Jack, April 19, 1864, Official Records, Series 1, Vol. 32 (Part III), 795–96; S. W. Ferguson to Maj. Gen. S. D. Lee, April 23, 1864, Official Records, Series 1, Vol. 32 (Part III), 812.

44. A. B. Coffey to Brig. Gen. Ferguson, April 21, 1864, Official Records, Series 1, Vol. 32 (Part III), 812–13. See also D. W. Jones to Capt. Thomas B. Sykes, April 27, 1864, Official Records, Series 1, Vol. 32 (Part I), 671–72; J. J. Perry to Capt. T. B. Sykes, April 30, 1864, Official Records, Series 1, Vol. 32 (Part III), 860; S. D. Lee to Lt. Col. T. M. Jack, April 30, 1864, Official Records, Series 1, Vol. 32 (Part III), 858–59.

45. G. M. Dodge to Maj. Gen. J. B. McPherson, April 6, 1864, Official Records, Series 1, Vol. 32 (Part III), 274. See also James C. Bates to Ma, March 4, 1864, in *A Texas Cavalry Officer's Civil War: The Diary and Letters of James C. Bates*, ed. Richard Lowe (Baton Rouge: Louisiana State University Press, 1999), 290–91 (a letter written from a camp near Tuscaloosa).

46. L. Polk to Major-General French, April 26, 1864, Official Records, Series 1, Vol. 32 (Part III), 824–26; Douglas West to Maj. J. D. Bradford, May 2, 1864, Official Records, Series 1, Vol. 38 (Part IV), 657–58; Martin, *Desertion of Alabama Troops from the Confederate Army*, 44, 202–3; Dodd, "Unionism In Confederate Alabama," 77–79.

47. S. D. Lee to Lt. Col. T. M. Jack, April 30, 1864, Official Records, Series 1, Vol. 32 (Part III), 859.

48. *Nashville Daily Times & True Union*, April 9, 1864, 2; Dodd, "Unionism in Confederate Alabama," 79–80. See also, John D. Stevenson to Col. Sawyer, May 6, 1864, Official Records, Series 1, Vol. 38 (Part IV), 50 (reporting the arrival in Decatur of "caravans of refugees" as well as "100 recruits and deserters"); *Nashville Daily Times and True Union*, April 21, 1864, 1 (reporting from Decatur that "refugees are coming in daily, in large numbers"), June 29, 1864, 1 (discussing the Nashville Refugee Aid Society, which had established "Refugee Barracks" in January of 1864 and by June of 1864 had aided 12,000 refugees).

Chapter 16

1. Lewis N. Wynne and Robert A. Taylor, eds., *This War So Horrible* (Tuscaloosa: University of Alabama Press 1993). 52–53.

2. Diary of Frances Woolfolk Wallace, 29, Southern Historical Collection, University of North Carolina at Chapel Hill.

3. Linden and Linden, eds., *Disunion*, 120.

4. Thomas H. Watts to L. S. Sheffield, April 25, 1864, Papers of Governor Watts, Alabama Department of Archives and History, Montgomery. See also, T.H. Watts to Dr. F.W. Sykes, May 18, 1864, Papers of Governor Watts, Alabama Department of Archives and History, Montgomery.

5. W. T. Sherman to General McPherson, May 1, 1864 and James B. McPherson to Brig. Gen. John D. Stevenson, May 1, 1864, Official Records, Series 1, Vol. 38 (IV), 8–9; Dunnavant, *Decatur, Alabama*, 99–101.

6. Hirshon, *Grenville Dodge*, 93–95; John R. Scales, *Sherman Invades Georgia* (Annapolis, MD: Naval Institute Press, 2006), 161–63; Albert Castel, *Decision in the West: The Atlanta Campaign of 1864* (Lawrence: University of Kansas Press, 1992), 121–39; Stephen Davis, *Atlanta Will Fall: Sherman, Joe Johnston, and the Yankee Heavy Battalions* (Wilmington, DE: Scholarly Resources, 2001), 38–41.

7. *Mobile Advertiser and Register*, May 18, 1864, 1, May 27, 1864, 1, May 28, 1864, 2; *Selma Morning Dispatch*, May 25, 1864, 2; (New Orleans) *Daily Picayune Extra*, May 23, 1864; *Daily Columbus* (Georgia) *Enquirer*, May 18, 1864, 2, May 21, 1864, 1, May 22, 1864, 1, May 24, 1864, 1; James Lee McDonough and James Pickett Jones. *War So Terrible: Sherman and Atlanta* (New York: Norton, 1987), 110–18.

8. Noel Crowson and John V. Brogden, eds., *Bloody Banners and Barefoot Boys: "A History of the 27th Regiment Alabama Infantry CSA," The Civil War Memoirs and Diary Entries of J.P. Cannon M.D.* (Shippensburg, PA: Burd Street Press, 1997), 67, 69, 71, 74, 79.

9. George Knox Miller to Celestine Miller, May 13, 1864, in *An Uncompromising Secessionist*, ed. Richard M. McMurry, 201.

10. George Knox Miller to Celestine Miller, June 2, 1864, in *An Uncompromising Secessionist*, ed. Richard M. McMurry, 213. See also Edward Norphlet Brown to Fannie Brown, May 22, 1864, Edward Norphlet Brown Letters, Alabama Department of Archives and History, Montgomery. Regarding the level of morale under Johnston, see Daniel, *Soldiering in the Army of Tennessee*, 140–43.

11. For discussion of the effects of retreats on soldiers in Johnston's army, see Stephen M. Hood, *John Bell Hood: The Rise, Fall, and Resurrection of a Confederate General* (El Dorado, CA: Savas Beatie, 2013), 27–30.

12. Wynne and Taylor, ed., *This War So Horrible*, 76.

13. *Nashville Daily Union*, reprinted in (New York) *Evening Post*, May 11, 1864, 4.

14. Order of Thomas Hill Watts, April 30, 1864, Papers of Governor Watts, Alabama Department of Archives and History, Montgomery.

15. Private Journal of Sarah R. Espy, 79.

16. Linden and Linden, eds., *Disunion*, 122.

17. *Mobile Advertiser and Register*, May 3, 1864, 2. The pressure was too much for some. Brigadier General John Tyler Morgan of Alabama was commanding a brigade in Wheeler's cavalry, but the only record of Morgan's conduct in any of the initial days of fighting in the campaign reflects that he was arrested for drunkenness while on duty on May 14 and removed from command. At least Morgan was on duty. The same cannot be said for Brigadier General James Holt Clanton. Rather than going straight from north Alabama to north Georgia as he had been ordered, Clanton had furloughed most of his men. None of these embarrassing incidents made the newspapers back in Alabama. Nonetheless, little news from north Georgia inspired confidence among Confederates. McMurry, ed., *An Uncompromising Secessionist*, 220; Fry, *John Tyler Morgan and the Search for Southern Autonomy*, 21–22; Edward G. Longacre, *A Soldier to the Last: Maj. Gen. Joseph Wheeler in Blue and Gray* (Washington, DC: Potomac Books, 2007), 151; *Mobile Advertiser and Register*, May 3, 1864, 2; S. D. Lee to Brig. Gen. Gideon J. Pillow, June 1, 1864, Official Records, Series 1, Vol. 3, (Part IV), 754.

18. Diary of Frances Woolfolk Wallace, 34–35.

19. *Mobile Advertiser and Register*, May 8, 1864, p 2.

20. Ibid., May 8, 1864, 2; *Daily Columbus* (Georgia) *Enquirer*, May 4, 1864, 2. See also (Grove Hill) *Clarke County Journal*, May 12, 1864, 2 (also reporting instances of retaliation at a prison at Point Lookout, Maryland).

21. *Mobile Advertiser and Register*, May 11, 1864, 2.

22. Ibid., May 14, 1864, 2.

23. Ibid., May 18, 1864, 1.

24. Diary of Frances Woolfolk Wallace, 38.

25. *Mobile Advertiser and Register*, May 19, 1864, 2.

26. Ibid., June 19, 1864, 1, July 13, 1864, 4 *Charleston Mercury*, June 24, 1864, 1.

27. *Mobile Advertiser and Register*, May 27, 1864, 2.

28. Ibid., May 25, 1864, 2. *Daily Columbus* (Georgia) *Enquirer*, May 25, 1864, 2, May 31, 1864, 2.

29. *Montgomery Mail*, cited in *Mobile Advertiser and Register*, May 28, 1864, 2.

30. *Mobile Advertiser and Register*, May 31, 1864, 2.

31. Ibid., June 9, 1864, 2.

32. *Selma Morning Reporter*, June 1, 1864, 1; *Mobile Advertiser and Register*, June 2, 1864, 1; Daniel Coleman Diary, 34, Huntsville-Madison County Library, Huntsville, Alabama (discussing a "great revival of religion" in Tuscumbia).

33. Richard M. McMurry, *Atlanta 1864: Last Chance for the Confederacy*. Lincoln: University of Nebraska Press, 2000, 98–99; Stoker, *Grand Design*, 356–57, 359.

34. *Macon Confederate*, reprinted in *Mobile Advertiser and Register*, June 7, 1864, 1. See also *Charleston Mercury*, May 26, 1864, 2, June 1, 1864, 1, June 6, 1864, 2.

35. *Daily Columbus* (Georgia) *Enquirer*, May 18, 1864, 2, May 20, 1864, 1, May 22, 1864, 1, June 2, 1864, 2. *Charleston Mercury*, July 16, 1864, 1, July 22, 1864, 1, September 26, 1864, 1. Other Confederates noted this paradox. Clayton E. Jewett, ed., *Rise and Fall of the Confederacy: The Memoir of Senator Williamson S. Oldham, CSA* (Columbia: University of Missouri Press, 2006), 37, 192. (Confederate Senator Williamson Oldham of Texas concluded that a mistake was made when Forrest was not sent to Tennessee at this point.)

36. N. B. Forrest to Gen. Joseph E. Johnston, April 6, 1864, Official Records, Series 1, Vol. 52 (Part II), 653; Davis, *Atlanta Will Fall*, 66, 71; *Charleston Mercury*, July 26, 1864, 2.

37. Cf. McMurry, *Atlanta 1864*, 134–36.

38. Jas. B. McPherson to Maj. Gen. C. C. Washburn, April 20, 1864, Official Records, Series 1, Vol. 32 (Part III), 430; U. S. Grant to Major General Sherman, April 21, 1864, Official Records, Series 1, Vol. 32 (Part III), 437; W. T. Sherman to General Washburn, April 21, 1864, Official Records, Series 1, Vol. 32 (Part III), 441; W. T. Sherman to Gen. C. C. Washburn, April 28, 1864, Official Records, Series 1, Vol. 32 (Part III), 527; W. T. Sherman to Gen. C. C. Washburn, April 28, 1864, Official Records, Series 1, Vol. 32 (Part III), 527; C. C. Washburn to Maj. Gen. W. T. Sherman, April 30, 1864, Official Records, Series 1, Vol. 32 (Part III), 545. See also McMurry, *Atlanta 1864*, 98.

39. L. Polk to Maj. Gen. S. D. Lee, May 17, 1864; S. D. Lee to Gen. J. E. Johnston, May 17, 1864, N. B. Forrest to Gen. S. D. Lee, May 17, 1864, Official Records, Series 1, Vol. 38 (Part IV), 723; S. D. Lee to Gen. S. Cooper, May 18, 1864, Official Records, Series 1, Vol. 39 (Part II), 606.

40. S. D. Lee to Maj. Gen. N. B. Forrest, May 20, 1864, Official Records, Series 1, Vol. 38 (Part IV), 729–30.

41. S. D. Lee to General Bragg, May 22, 1864, Official Records, Series 1, Vol. 38

(Part IV), 734; S. D. Lee to Brig. Gen. Pillow, May 23, 1864, Official Records, Series 1, Vol. 39 (Part II), 617.

42. McMurry, *Atlanta 1864*, 85–95.

43. Edward Norphlet Brown to Fannie Brown, June 20, 1864, Edward Norphlet Brown Letters, Alabama Department of Archives and History, Montgomery.

Chapter 17

1. *Mobile Advertiser and Register*, June 7, 1864, 1.

2. *New York Times*, June 7, 1864, 4, June 8, 1864, 1. See, generally, David Johnson, *Decided on the Battlefield: Grant, Sherman, Lincoln, and the Election of 1864* (Amherst, NY: Prometheus Books, 2012), 60–75; *Mobile Advertiser and Register*, June 8, 1864, p 2.

3. *Mobile Advertiser and Register*, June 14, 1864, 2, June 23, 1864, 2; *New York Times*, June 9, 1864, 1; (Washington, DC) *Daily National Intelligencer*, June 9, 1964. For other Johnson bashing by the Southern press at this time, see *Daily Columbus* (Georgia) *Enquirer*, June 16, 1864, June 18, 1864, 2, June 30, 1864, 1, July 1, 1864, 2, July 12, 1864, 2; *New York Herald*, reprinted in *Mobile Advertiser and Register*, June 23, 1864, 2 and cited in (Greensboro) *Alabama Beacon*, June 24, 1864, 3; Edward C. Kirkland, *Peacemakers of 1864* (New York, Macmillan 1927), 48. See also George Fort Milton, *Age of Hate: Andrew Johnson and the Radicals* (New York: Coward-McCann, 1930).

4. *New York Times*, June 22, 1864, 4.

5. *New York Tribune*, reprinted in *Chattanooga Daily Gazette*, June 15, 1864.

6. *Selma Dispatch*, reprinted in *Mobile Advertiser and Register*, June 28, 1864, 1. See also *Daily Columbus* (Georgia) *Enquirer*, July 6, 1864, 2.

7. H. W. Walter to Gen. B. Bragg, May 8, 1864, Official Records, Series 1, Vol. 3, 393–94.

8. *Chicago Journal*, reprinted in Mobile Advertiser and Register, May 11, 1864, 2.

9. *Nashville Times and True Union*, reprinted in (Philadelphia) *North American and United States Gazette*, June 16, 1864; *Daily* (Georgia) *Columbus Enquirer*, July 1, 1864, 1.

10. Rohr, ed., *Incidents of War*, 148 (Clemens and his family left Alabama in April 1864); *Mobile Advertiser and Register*, June 23, 1864, 2. See also *New York Times*, October 17, 1864, 2 (publishing a portion of a letter written by Clemens from Philadelphia supporting Lincoln's reelection); (Washington, DC) *Daily National Republican*, November 2, 1864, 2 (stating that Clemens was scheduled to speak at a Union League meeting in Philadelphia).

11. *Mobile Advertiser and Register*, July 1, 1864, 2; *Nashville Times and True Union*, reprinted in (Philadelphia) *North American and United States Gazette*, June 16, 1864; *Daily Columbus* (Georgia) *Enquirer*, July 1, 1864, 1.

12. *Mobile Daily* News, July 21, 1865, 6. See also *Ashville Vidette*, reprinted in (Meridian, Miss.) *Daily Clarion*, March 28, 1865, 2; Storey, *Loyalty and Loss*, 192–93; Blackmon, *Slavery by Another Name*, 25–26; Private Journal of Sarah R. Espy, 100

13. *Mobile Advertiser and Register*, June 15, 1864, 1, June 17, 1864, 2 (reporting that prisoners had revealed that Selma was their ultimate target), June 19, 1864, 1, June 25, 1864, 1; *Charleston Mercury*, June 28, 1864, 1.

14. *Mobile Advertiser and Register*, June 14, 1864, 1, June 15, 1864, 1, June 16, 1864, 1, June 17, 1864, 1, June 19, 1864, 1, June 24, 1864, 2, June 25, 1864, 1, June 26, 1864, 1, July 2, 1864, 2, July 10, 1864, 1; (Greensboro) *Alabama Beacon*, June 24, 1864, 3; (Grove Hill) *Clarke County Journal*, June 16, 1864, 2; *Daily Columbus* (Georgia) *Enquirer*, June 11, 1864, 2, June 12, 1864, 2, June 15, 1864, 2, June 16, 1864, 2, June 17, 1864, 2, June 18, 1864, 2, June 22, 1864, 2, June 28, 1864, 2, July 3, 1864, 2. See also, S.D. Lee to Gen. S. Cooper, June 11, 1864 and June 12, 1864, Official Records, Series 1, Vol. 39 (Part I), 221. See, generally, Stewart L. Bennett, *The Battle of Brice's Crossroads* (Charleston, SC: History Press, 2012), 30–124.

15. *Mobile Advertiser and Register*, June 15, 1864, 1.

16. *Mobile Advertiser and Register*, June 22, 1864, 1.

17. W. T. Sherman to Gen. William Sooy Smith, June 12, 1864, Official Records, Series 1, Vol. 38 (Part IV), 462.

18. W. T. Sherman to Hon. E. M. Stanton, June 15, 1864, Official Records, Series 1, Vol. 39 (Part III), 121. See also *Mobile Advertiser and Register*, June 24, 1864, 1 (reporting rumors of another expedition from Memphis), July 2, 1864, 2.

19. P. Ellis to Gen. P. D. Roddey, June 18, 1864, Official Records, Series 1, Vol. 39 (Part II), 655.

20. *Daily Columbus* (Georgia) *Enquirer*, July 24, 1864, 1.

21. Lovell H. Rousseau to Maj. Gen. W. T. Sherman, June 19, 1864, Official Records, Series 1, Vol. 38 (Part IV), 530–31.

22. *Mobile Advertiser and Register*, July 3, 1864, 1.

23. *Mobile Advertiser and Register*, July 1, 1864, 1, July 10, 1864, 1.

24. *Mobile Advertiser and Register*, July 1, 1864, 2, July 3, 1864, 1, July 9, 1863, 2, July 16, 1864, 1, July 16, 1864, 2, July 17, 1864, 2. See, generally, Hess, *Civil War in the West*, 216.

25. *Mobile Advertiser and Register*, July 1, 1864, 2; *Daily Columbus* (Georgia) *Enquirer*, July 1, 1864, 1–2.

26. Hess, *Civil War in the West*, 216–17.

27. *Mobile Advertiser and Register*, June 24, 1864, 2, June 29, 1864, 1, and reprinted in *Charleston Mercury*, July 7, 1864, 2.

28. W. T. Sherman to Maj. Gen. L. H. Rousseau, June 29, 1864, and June 30, 1864, Official Records, Series 1, Vol. 38 (Part II), 909–10.

29. W. T. Sherman to Maj. Gen. L. H. Rousseau, June 30, 1864, Official Records, Series 1, Vol. 38 (Part II), 910.

30. W. T. Sherman to General Rousseau, July 2, 1864, Official Records, Series 1, Vol. 38 (Part V), 19; James E. Saunders to Major General Forrest, June 28, 1864, Official Records, Series 1, Vol. 38 (Part IV), 804.

31. *Mobile Advertiser and Register*, June 28, 1864, 1; *Selma Dispatch*, reprinted in (Augusta) *Daily Constitutionalist*, June 23, 1864, 1.

32. W. T. Sherman to Gen. Rousseau, July 6, 1864, Official Records, Series 1, Vol. 38 (Series V), 71.

33. W. T. Sherman to Maj. Gen. L. H. Rousseau, July 7, 1864, Official Records, Series 1, Vol. 38 (Part V), 82.

34. *New York Times*, July 26, 1864, 1.

35. *Mobile Advertiser and Register*, July 2, 1864, 2, July 9, 1864, 1; *Daily Columbus* (Georgia) *Enquirer*, July 6, 1864, 2.

36. *Mobile Advertiser and Register*, July 7, 1864, 1–2, July 8, 1864, 1, July 10, 1864, 102, July 16, 1864, 1; *Daily Columbus* (Georgia) *Enquirer*, July 6, 1864, 2.

37. Diary of Frances Woolfolk Wallace, 54.

38. *Mobile Advertiser and Register*, July 10, 1864, 2, July 12, 1864, 1. See also *Daily Columbus* (Georgia) *Enquirer*, July 12, 1864, 2, July 14, 1864, 2; McMurry, *Atlanta 1864*, 110–17.

39. Crowson and Brogden, eds., *Bloody Banners and Barefoot Boys*, 84.

40. George Knox Miller to Celestine Miller, July 12, 1864 in McMurry, ed., *An Uncompromising Secessionist*, 235.

41. *Charleston Mercury*, July 20, 1864, 1, August 6, 1864, 1; Hess, *Civil War in the West*, 222–23.

42. Stoker, *Grand Design*, 362.

43. Edward Norphlet Brown to Fannie Brown, July 23, 1864, Edward Norphlet Brown Letters, Alabama Department of Archives and History, Montgomery.

44. Dr. George Little and Dr. James R. Maxwell, *A History of Lumsden's Battery C.S.A.* (Tuscaloosa, AL: R. E. Rhodes Chapter United Daughters of the Confederacy, 1988), 45–46.

45. *Montgomery Advertiser*, reprinted in *Charleston Mercury*, July 26, 1864, 1 (editorial by "Ora"); *Charleston Mercury*, July 26, 1864, 2 (identifying Reid as "Ora"). Regarding the sentiment of other soldiers, see Daniel, *Soldiering in the Army of Tennessee*, 143.

46. *Mobile Advertiser and Register*, July 10, 1864, 1. See also *Daily Columbus* (Georgia) *Enquirer*, April 17, 1864, 2 (reportedly, Admiral Farragut was preparing an expedition against Mobile), July 6, 1864, 2 (reporting that General Canby was organizing a force to threaten Mobile or Demopolis).

47. *Montgomery Weekly Advertiser*, August 19, 1864, 2.

48. *Selma Dispatch*, reprinted in *Daily Columbus* (Georgia) *Enquirer*, July 31, 1864, 2; *Daily Columbus* (Georgia) *Enquirer*, August 3, 1864, 3.

49. *Daily Columbus* (Georgia) *Enquirer*, August 3, 1864, 2.

50. *Selma Dispatch*, reprinted in *Daily Columbus* (Georgia) *Enquirer*, July 31, 1864, 2.

51. *New York Herald*, July 23, 1864, 1; *New York Times*, July 26, 1864, 1, August 3, 1864, 8. See, generally, Edwin C. Bearss, "Rousseau's Raid on the Montgomery and West Point Railroad," *Alabama Historical Quarterly* 25 (Spring & Summer, 1963): 7–48; Rogers et al., *Alabama*, 216–17.

52. Dunnavant, *Decatur, Alabama*, 105; *New York Times*, August 3, 1864, 8.

53. N. B. Rowe to Gov. Watts, July 22, 1864, Papers of Governor Watts, Alabama Department of Archives and History, Montgomery; *Mobile Advertiser and Register*, July 19, 1864, 1, July 20, 1864, 1, July 21, 1864, 1, July 26, 1864, 1.

54. *Asheville Vidette*, quoted in *Mobile Advertiser and Register*, July 21, 1864, 1; *Selma Reporter*, reprinted in *Mobile Advertiser and Register*, July 29, 1864, 2; *New York Times*, August 3, 1864, 8.

55. *Mobile Advertiser and Register*, July 12, 1864, 1; (Grove Hill) *Clarke County Journal*, July 21, 1864, 2; *Daily Columbus* (Georgia) *Enquirer*, July 13, 1864, 1, July 14, 1864, 1; Rogers et al., *Alabama*, 218.

56. *Mobile Advertiser and Register*, July 22, 1864, 1; *Daily Columbus* (Georgia) *Enquirer*, July 30, 1864, 1.

57. J. M. Withers to President Davis, July 14, 1864, Official Records, Series 1, Vol. 39 (Part II), 711. See also, Greg Starnes, "Grey Troops at Blue Mountain," *Alabama Heritage* 111 (Winter 2014): 28–31.

58. *Mobile Advertiser and Register*, July 31, 1864, 2.

59. Hughes and Stonesifer, *Life and Wars of Gideon J. Pillow*, 291.

60. *Selma Dispatch*, July 15, 1864, reprinted in (Augusta) *Daily Constitutionalist*, July 20, 1864, 1.

61. *Mobile Advertiser and Register*, July 29, 1864, 2, July 31, 1864, 2, August 3, 1864, 1; (Selma) *Mississippian*, July 16, 1864, reprinted in *Mobile Advertiser and Register*, July 19, 1864, 1; *Selma Reporter*, July 18, 1864, reprinted in *Mobile Advertiser and Register*, July 21, 1864, 1. Upon arriving at Blue Mountain, however, he told a train conductor a different story: that Rousseau's force had "taken advantage of the darkness of the night to avoid him," and thereby escaped his grasp. The truth was that, as a soldier in Rousseau's force later reported, Clanton and his men were "completely routed" and, remembering that discretion was the better part of valor, returned to their camp. (Selma) *Mississippian*, July 16, 1864, reprinted in *Mobile Advertiser and Register*, July 19, 1864, 1; *New York Times*, July 31, 1864, 6.

62. *New York Times*, August 3, 1864, 8; *Selma Reporter*, July 16, 1864, reprinted in *Mobile Advertiser and Register*, July 19, 1864, 1; *Montgomery Advertiser*, July 17, 1864, reprinted in *Mobile Advertiser and Register*, July 20, 1864, 1; *Talladega Democratic Watchtower*, reprinted in *Daily Columbus* (Georgia) *Enquirer*, August 2, 1864, 2.

63. *New York Times*, August 3, 1864, 8; (Selma) *Mississippian*, July 16, 1864, reprinted in *Mobile Advertiser and Register*, July 19, 1864, 1; *Selma Reporter*, July 18, 1864, reprinted in *Mobile Advertiser and Register*, July 21, 1864, 1; *Talladega Reporter*, reprinted in *Mobile Advertiser and Register*, August 2, 1864, 1 and August 11, 1864, 2.

64. *Talladega Reporter*, reprinted in *Mobile Advertiser and Register*, August 2, 1864, 1. But see (Selma) *Mississippian*, reprinted in (Augusta) *Daily Constitutionalist*, July 20, 1864, 1.

65. *Montgomery Advertiser*, July 17, 1864, reprinted in *Mobile Advertiser and Register*, July 20, 1864, 1; *New York Times*, August 17, 1864, 8.

66. *Montgomery Advertiser*, July 19, 1864, reprinted in *Mobile Advertiser and Register*, July 21, 1864, 1; *Mobile Advertiser and Register*, July 19, 1864, 1; *Selma Reporter*, July 18, 1864, reprinted in *Mobile Advertiser and Register*, July 21, 1864, 1.

67. *Daily Columbus* (Georgia) *Enquirer*, July 31, 1864, 2, August 3, 1864, 2.

68. *Montgomery Mail*, July 18, 1864, reprinted in *Mobile Advertiser and Register*, July 20, 1864. See also *Montgomery Advertiser*, July 19, 1864, reprinted in *Mobile Advertiser and Register*, July 21, 1864, 1; *New York Times*, August 7, 1864, 8; *Mobile Advertiser and Register*, November 20, 1864, 1 (publishing Watts's message, which included a pas-

sage regarding the university cadets). See, generally, Rogers, *Confederate Home Front*, 122–23.

69. *Mobile Advertiser and Register*, July 20, 1864, 1.

70. *Montgomery Advertiser*, July 19, 1864, reprinted in *Mobile Advertiser and Register*, July 21, 1864, 1.

71. *Mobile Advertiser and Register*, July 20, 1864, 1.

72. *Mobile Advertiser and Register*, July 23, 1864, 2.

73. Rogers, *Confederate Home Front*, 123; *Columbus* (Georgia) *Sun*, reprinted in *Charleston Mercury*, July 25, 1864, 1.

74. *Montgomery Advertiser*, July 25, 1864, reprinted in *Mobile Advertiser and Register*, July 23, 1864, 1.

75. *Mobile Advertiser and Register*, July 31, 1864, 2. See also *Mobile Advertiser and Register*, August 3, 1864, 1.

76. *Montgomery Mail*, reprinted in *Mobile Advertiser and Register*, July 23, 1864, 1; *Daily Columbus* (Georgia) *Enquirer*, July 30, 1864, 1.

77. T. H. Watts to James A. Seddon, July 29, 1864, Papers of Governor Watts, Alabama Department of Archives and History, Montgomery; *Montgomery Advertiser*, reprinted in *Mobile Advertiser and Register*, July 27, 1864, 2; *Selma Morning Reporter*, July 27, 1864, 1; *Montgomery Mail*, reprinted in *Mobile Advertiser and Register*, July 23, 1864, 1; *Montgomery Mail*, July 19, 1864, reprinted in *Mobile Advertiser and Register*, July 20, 1864, 1, November 20, 1864, 1; *Montgomery Advertiser*, July 19, 1864, reprinted in *Mobile Advertiser and Register*, July 21, 1864, 1; *Columbus* (Georgia) *Enquirer*, July 28, 1864, 2; *Mobile Advertiser and Register*, July 19, 1864, 1, July 20, 1864, 2, July 21, 1864, 1; *New York Times*, July 31, 1864, 6, August 3, 1864, 8. See also Rogers, *Confederate Home Front*, 123.

78. *Mobile Advertiser and Register*, July 31, 1864, 2. See also *Mobile Advertiser and Register*, August 3, 1864, 8; *Daily Columbus* (Georgia) *Enquirer*, reprinted in *Charleston Mercury*, July 28, 1864, 2; Williams, *Bitterly Divided*, 186; Griffith, *Alabama*, 405–6.

79. *Selma Morning Reporter*, July 27, 1864, 1. See also (Greensboro) *Alabama Beacon*, July 29, 1864, 3; *Mobile Advertiser and Register*, July 29, 1864, 1; *Daily Columbus* (Georgia) *Enquirer*, July 29, 1864, 1, August 13, 1864, 1.

80. *Mobile Advertiser and Register*, August 4, 1864, 2; *Mobile Daily Tribune*, July 29, 1864, 2; Hughes and Stonesifer, *Life and Wars of Gideon J. Pillow*, 291–92.

81. *New York Times*, August 3, 1864, 8.

82. *Montgomery Advertiser*, July 19, 1864, reprinted in *Mobile Advertiser and Register*, July 21, 1864, 1.

83. *Selma Reporter*, July 18, 1864, reprinted in *Mobile Advertiser and Register*, July 21, 1864, 1.

84. *Selma Reporter*, July 16, 1864, reprinted in *Mobile Advertiser and Register*, July 19, 1864, 1.

85. *Daily Columbus* (Georgia) *Enquirer*, July 24, 1864, 2, reprinted in *Mobile Advertiser and Register*, July 31, 1864, 2.

86. Regarding other comments about Clanton by this Georgia newspaper, see *Daily Columbus* (Georgia) *Enquirer*, July 24, 1864, 1–2, July 30, 1864, 1, July 30, 1864,

2, August 2, 1864, 2, August 3, 1864, 2, August 4, 1864, 2 (publishing a poem about Clanton's dead brother in-law), August 5, 1864, 2, August 11, 1864, 2.

87. *Charleston Mercury*, July 28, 1864, 2.

88. *New York Herald*, July 23, 1864, 1. See also *New York Times*, July 26, 1864, 1, July 31, 1864, 6, August 3, 1864, 8.

Chapter 18

1. Joel Murphree to Ursula Murphree, July 19, 1864, in Joel Murphree, "Autobiography of Civil War Letters of Joel Murphree of Troy, Alabama," ed. H. E. Sterkx, *Alabama Historical Quarterly* 19 (Spring, 1957): 184.

2. *Selma Morning Reporter*, July 27, 1864.

3. McWhiney, Moore and Pace, eds., "*Fear God and Walk Humbly*," 338.

4. *Mobile Advertiser and Register*, July 28, 1864, 2.

5. Edgeworth Bird to Sallie Bird, August 4, 1864, in John Rozier, ed., *The Granite Farm Letters: The Civil War Correspondence of Edgeworth & Sallie Bird* (Athens: University of Georgia Press, 1988), 180.

6. *Mobile Advertiser and Register*, July 7, 1864, 1, August 26, 1864, 1.

7. *Mobile Advertiser and Register*, July 29, 1864, 1; *Daily Columbus* (Georgia) *Enquirer*, July 31, 1864, 1.

8. Regarding assessments of Wheeler, see Edward Norphlet Brown to Fannie Brown, August 14, 1864 and August 21, 1864, Edward Norphlet Brown Letters, Alabama Department of Archives and History, Montgomery.

9. Diary of Frances Woolfolk Wallace, 21–22.

10. *Mobile Tribune*, reprinted in *Daily Columbus* (Georgia) *Enquirer*, August 3, 1864, 2, and on August 1.

11. *Mobile Advertiser and Register*, August 3, 1864, 2.

12. John B. Read to Governor Bonham, August 12, 1863, Official Records, Series 1, Vol. 28 (Part II), 277. Regarding Read, see also G. Ward Hubbs, "John B. Read's Okra Paper," *Alabama Review* 43 (October 1990): 289–96; *Mobile Advertiser and Register*, March 22, 1865, 2 (another invention was the "Read Shell"); *Tuscaloosa Observer*, reprinted in *Charleston Mercury*, July 17, 1860, 1 (same).

13. R. Thomas Campbell, *Hunters of the Night: Confederate Torpedo Boats in the War Between the States* (Shippensburg, PA: Burd Street Press, 1990).

14. *Mobile Daily Tribune*, August 25, 1864, 2.

15. *Mobile Advertiser and Register*, August 3, 1864, 2.

16. Bergeron, *Confederate Mobile*, 70, 138–51.

17. *Mobile Advertiser and Register*, August 6, 1864, 1, August 7, 1864, 2, August 11, 1864, 1; *Mobile Daily Tribune*, August 6, 1864, 2.

18. *Mobile Advertiser and Register*, August 9, 1864, 1; *Montgomery Daily Mail*, August 6, 1864, 2.

19. Diary of Hurieosco Austill, 14–19, Alabama Department of Archives and History, Montgomery.

20. See, generally, Burnett, *Pen Makes a Good Sword*, 142–43; (Washington, DC) *Daily National Republican*, August 15, 1864, 2.

21. *Montgomery Daily Mail*, August 19, 1864, 2. See, generally, *Daily Columbus* (Georgia) *Enquirer*, August 7, 1864, 2, August 9, 1864, 1, August 10, 1864, 1–2, August 11, 1864, 1, August 12, 1864, 1, August 13, 1864, 2, August 16, 1864, 1–2, August 17, 1864, 2, August 18, 1864, 1, August 19, 1864, 2, August 21, 1864, 1, August 24, 1864, 1, August 27, 1864, 1–2, September 1, 1864, 2, September 3, 1864, 1; Rogers et al., *Alabama*, 218–19.

22. *Charleston Mercury*, August 27, 1864, 2. See, generally, Bergeron, *Confederate Mobile*, 165–67.

23. Easby-Smith, *William Russell Smith*, 158–60. Regarding the pass system in Alabama during this phase of the war, see *Mobile Advertiser and Register*, October 27, 1864, 1.

24. Mayor R. H. Slough to T. H. Watts, September 1, 1864, Papers of Governor Watts, Alabama Department of Archives and History, Montgomery.

25. *Mobile Advertiser and Register*, August 11, 1864, 1. See also *Montgomery Daily Mail*, August 7, 1864, 1.

26. *Montgomery Daily Mail*, August 17, 1864, 2.

27. *Montgomery Advertiser*, reprinted in *Mobile Advertiser and Register*, August 11, 1864, 2.

28. *Selma Dispatch*, reprinted in *Mobile Daily Tribune*, August 12, 1864, 2.

29. See, e.g., *Mobile Daily Tribune*, September 29, 1864, 1 (reprinting Governor Watts's message to the Alabama legislature in which he reported that the response to his call was "small"); McMillan, *Disintegration of a Confederate State*, 99 (same).

30. (Augusta) *Daily Constitutionalist*, September 15, 1864, 1.

31. *Selma Reporter*, reprinted in *Montgomery Daily Mail*, August 18, 1864, 2. *Cf.*, *Selma Reporter*, cited in *Daily Columbus* (Georgia) *Enquirer*, October 18, 1864, 2 (discussing the existence of a labor shortage at this "Laboratory").

32. Boys and girls were reportedly put to work at the laboratory. *Selma Reporter*, reprinted in *Charleston Mercury*, November 1, 1864, 2.

33. *Mobile Advertiser and Register*, July 26, 1864, 2; *Montgomery Daily Mail*, August 6, 1864, 2.

34. *Selma Dispatch*, August 2, 1864, reprinted in *Mobile Advertiser and Register*, August 4, 1864, 2.

35. *Mobile Advertiser and Register*, September 29, 1864, 1.

36. Private Journal of Sarah R. Espy, 83.

37. Crowson and Brogden, eds., *Bloody Banners and Barefoot Boys*, 87.

38. *Mobile Advertiser and Register*, August 23, 1864, p 1–2, August 31, 1864, 2; *Montgomery Daily Mail*, August 28, 1864, 2; *Daily Columbus* (Georgia) *Enquirer*, August 26, 1864, 1, September 3, 1864, 2; *Charleston Mercury*, August 26, 1864, 1; Hurst, *Nathan Bedford Forrest*, 212–15.

39. R. S. Granger to Gen. George H. Thomas, August 24, 1864, Official Records, Series 1, Vol. 38 (Part V), 652; *Montgomery Weekly Advertiser*, September 14, 1864, 3.

40. *Montgomery Weekly Advertiser*, September 14, 1864, 3.

41. Donald, *Lincoln*, 529–30; Oscar A. Kinchen, *Confederate Operations in Canada*

and the North (North Quincy, MA: Christopher Pub. House, 1970), 87; Stoker, *Grand Design*, 375.

42. Edward Norphlet Brown to Fannie Brown, August 25, 1864, Edward Norphlet Brown Letters, Alabama Department of Archives and History, Montgomery.

43. *Mobile Advertiser and Register*, August 26, 1864, 2. *Daily Columbus* (Georgia) *Enquirer*, September 1, 1864, 1.

44. The *New York Times* was certain that "Mr. Clay brought with him from Richmond the draft of a Platform and Address to be adopted by that Convention, and that the special object of his Embassy was to arrange with the leaders of the Democratic Party for its adoption." *New York Times*, August 22, 1864, 4. *Bangor* (Maine) *Daily Whig & Courier*, August 25, 1864. See, generally, Nuermberger, *Clays of Alabama*, 250.

45. *Mobile Advertiser and Register*, September 3, 1864, 2, September 4, 1864, 2; *Selma Morning Reporter*, September 3, 1864, 2; *Montgomery Daily Mail*, September 8, 1864, 2; *Daily Columbus* (Georgia) *Enquirer*, September 6, 1864, 1.

46. *Montgomery Daily Mail*, September 11, 1864, 2.

47. *Mobile Advertiser and Register*, June 14, 1864, 2. See also *Mobile Advertiser and Register*, September 4, 1864, 2 (initially expressing satisfaction with McClellan's nomination).

48. *Mobile Advertiser and Register*, September 4, 1864, 2, September 10, 1864, 1; Nuermberger, *Clays of Alabama*, 251; *Mobile Advertiser and Register*, September 14, 1864, 2, September 15, 1864, 2; *Montgomery Mail*, September 14, 1864, 2, September 20, 1864, 1; *Milwaukee Daily Sentinel*, September 26, 1864; *Daily Columbus* (Georgia) *Enquirer*, September 2, 1864, 2, September 8, 1864, 1–2, September 10, 1864, 2, September 20, 1864, 1, September 21, 1864, 2, September 22, 1864, 2, September 24, 1864, 1; Kinchen, *Confederate Operations in Canada and the North*, 94–97; Johnson, *Decided on the Battlefield*, 178–82.

49. *Mobile Advertiser and Register*, September 13, 1864, 2; (New Orleans) *Daily Picayune*, September 26, 1864, 2.

50. *Mobile Advertiser and Register*, September 13, 1864, 2, September 20, 1864, 1.

51. *Mobile Advertiser and Register*, September 14, 1864, 2. See also *Mobile Advertiser and Register*, September 15, 1864, 2. *Memphis Appeal*, reprinted in *Daily Columbus* (Georgia) *Enquirer*, September 24, 1864, 1.

52. *Mobile Advertiser and Register*, August 30, 1864, 2, September 6, 1864, 2, September 10, 1864, 1; *Montgomery Weekly Advertiser*, September 6, 1864, 4; *Daily Columbus* (Georgia) *Enquirer*, September 6, 1864, 1–2, September 7, 1864, 2; *Charleston Mercury*, September 7, 1864, 1, McMurry, *Atlanta 1864*, 174.

53. Edward Norphlet Brown to Fannie Brown, September 3, 1864, September 10, 1864, Edward Norphlet Brown Letters, Alabama Department of Archives and History, Montgomery.

54. *Mobile Advertiser and Register*, September 7, 1864, 1.

55. See also *Montgomery Weekly Advertiser*, September 14, 1864, 2 (noting "despondency").

56. Private Journal of Sarah R. Espy, 86.

57. Diary of Sally Independence Foster, September 30, 1864.

58. Crowson and Brogden, eds., *Bloody Banners and Barefoot Boys*, 93.

59. Stouten Hubert Dent to "Nannie," September 7, 1864, in Gerald Mathis and Douglas C. Purcell, eds., *In the Land of the Living: Wartime Letters by Confederates from the Chattahoochee Valley of Alabama and Georgia* (Troy, AL: Troy State University Press, 1981), 109.

60. Blomquist and Taylor, eds., *This Cruel War*, 132. But see Daniel, *Soldiering in the Army of Tennessee*, 143–46 (suggesting that little opposition to Hood actually existed).

61. *Mobile Advertiser and Register*, September 9, 1864, 2; *Montgomery Weekly Advertiser*, September 9, 1864, 4.

62. *Mobile Advertiser and Register*, September 10, 1864, 1.

63. *Mobile Advertiser and Register*, September 10, 1864, 1.

64. T. H. Watts to Gen. John B. Hood, September 19, 1864, Papers of Governor Watts, Alabama Department of Archives and History, Montgomery.

65. *New York Herald*, August 30, 1864, reprinted in *Mobile Daily Tribune*, September 24, 1864, 2.

66. *Philadelphia Press*, October 14, 1864, reprinted in (San Francisco) *Daily Evening Bulletin*, November 10, 1864, and *New York Times*, October 17, 1864, 2.

67. See, generally, Fleming, *Civil War and Reconstruction in Alabama*, 145–46.

68. *Mobile Advertiser and Register*, September 29, 1864, 1.

69. *Mobile Advertiser and Register*, October 1, 1864, 2.

70. *Selma Reporter*, quoted in *Daily Columbus* (Georgia) *Enquirer*, September 23, 1864, 2.

71. *Mobile Advertiser and Register*, September 6, 1864, 1.

72. *Mobile Advertiser and Register*, September 7, 1864, 2.

73. *Mobile Advertiser and Register*, September 13, 1864, 1.

74. *Mobile Daily Tribune*, September 24, 1864, 2, September 29, 1864, 1, September 29, 1864, 1; *Mobile Advertiser and Register*, September 21, 1864, 1; *Daily Columbus* (Georgia) *Enquirer*, September 20, 1864, 2, September 24, 1864, 2, October 16, 1864, 1; *New York Herald*, September 26, 1864; *New York Times*, September 22, 1864, 1, September 26, 1864, 1, September 27, 1864, 1, September 28, 1864, 8, October 8, 1864, 8; *Richmond Dispatch*, September 20, 1864, reprinted in *Milwaukee Daily Sentinel*, September 27, 1864; *Newark* (Ohio) *Advocate*, September 30, 1864.

75. *Montgomery Daily Mail*, August 26, 1864, 2 (the Georgian was Charles G. Baylor), August 28, 1864, 2. See also, *Selma Morning Reporter*, November 10, 1864, 1.

76. *Mobile Advertiser and Register*, November 9, 1864, 1.

77. *Mobile Advertiser and Register*, September 13, 1864, 2, September 25, 1864, 1; *Charleston Mercury*, September 15, 1864, 3; Joseph H. Parks, *Joseph E. Brown of Georgia* (Baton Rouge: Louisiana State University Press, 1977), 294–95.

78. *Mobile Advertiser and Register*, September 11, 1864, 2, September 13, 1864, 1 (publishing the communications between Sherman and Hood); *Daily Columbus* (Georgia) *Enquirer*, September 11, 1864, 2, September 13, 1864, 1, September 14, 1864, 1, September 17, 1864, 1–2.

79. *Mobile Advertiser and Register*, November 6, 1864, 2, November 19, 1864, 2;

Daily Columbus (Georgia) *Enquirer*, September 24, 1864, 2, September 25, 1864, 2, September 29, 1864, 1–2, September 30, 1864, 1; *Charleston Mercury*, September 19, 1864, 2; Parks, *Joseph E. Brown of Georgia*, 295–97; Schott, *Alexander H. Stephens of Georgia*, 425–28; David Williams, Teresa Crisp Williams, and David Carlson, *Plain Folk In a Rich Man's War: Class and Dissent in Confederate Georgia* (Gainesville: University Press of Florida, 2002), 180–82, 185–86 (discussing efforts of Georgia peace activists during this period); Thomas Conn Bryan, *Confederate Georgia* (Athens: University of Georgia Press, 1964), 163–64.

80. *Greenville Observer*, reprinted in (New Orleans) *Daily Picayune*, October 2, 1864, 5. Earlier in the summer a woman had been arrested in Tuskegee for trying to send Sherman a letter requesting him to move on that town. Diary of Frances Woolfolk Wallace, 46.

81. *Selma Reporter*, reprinted in *Richmond Examiner*, September 15, 1864, 2.

82. R. S. Granger to Major-General Steedman, September 14, 1864, Official Records, Series 1, Vol. 39 (Part II), 379.

83. McMurry, *Atlanta 1864*, 175.

84. Jefferson Davis to Maj. Gen. D. H. Maury, September 2, 1864, Official Records, Series 1, Vol. 39 (Part II), 812; Jefferson Davis to General Richard Taylor, September 6, 1864, Official Records, Series 1, Vol. 39 (Part II), 818.

85. R. Taylor to Jefferson Davis, September 7, 1864, Official Records, Series 1, Vol. 39 (Part II), 818–19 (Taylor was appointed to this post on August 15); W. F. Bullock Jr., to Brig. Gen. Daniel W. Adams, September 9, 1864, Official Records, Series 1, Vol. 39 (Part II), 826.

86. *Mobile Tribune*, September 8, 1864, reprinted in *Daily Columbus* (Georgia) *Enquirer*, September 11, 1868, 1.

87. N. B. Forrest to Lt. Gen. R. Taylor, September 18, 1864, and September 20, 1864, Official Records, Series 1, Vol. 39 (Part II), 845, 859. See also Longacre, *A Soldier to the Last*, 176–77; *Mobile Advertiser and Register*, September 16, 1864, 2 (defending Wheeler), September 20, 1864, 2 (same), September 22, 1864, 2 (same); *Daily Columbus* (Georgia) *Enquirer*, September 20, 1864, 1.

88. *Mobile Advertiser and Register*, September 24, 1864, 2.

89. See also Noah Andre Trudeau, *Southern Storm: Sherman's March to the Sea* (New York, 2008), 34; U. S. Grant to Maj. Gen. George H. Thomas, January 19, 1864, Official Records, Series 1, Vol. 32 (Part II), 142–43.

90. *Mobile Advertiser and Register*, September 15, 1864, 1. See also *Montgomery Daily Mail*, September 7, 1864, 2; *Daily Columbus* (Georgia) *Enquirer*, September 24, 1864, 2; Rogers, *Confederate Home Front*, 125; Barbara G. Ellis, *The Moving Appeal: Mr. McClanahan, Mrs. Dill, and the Civil War's Great Newspaper Run* (Macon, GA: Mercer University Press, 2003), 316–24.

91. *Mobile Advertiser and Register*, September 20, 1864, 1, September 24, 1864, 1, October 12, 1864, 2.

92. *Mobile Advertiser and Register*, October 14, 1864, 2. See also *Mobile Advertiser and Register*, October 27, 1864, 2.

93. *Mobile Advertiser and Register*, November 15, 1864, 2. *Charleston Mercury*, No-

vember 19, 1864, 1, January 3, 1865, 1, January 13, 1865, 1, January 26, 1865, 1, February 5, 1865, 1. In contradiction: *Mobile Daily Tribune*, December 1, 1864, 2; *Montgomery Advertiser*, reprinted in *Richmond Daily Dispatch*, December 1, 1864, 1.

94. J. A. Campbell to Joel A. Bellups, September 13, 1864, in *Syracuse* (New York) *Journal*, reprinted in (New Orleans) *Daily Picayune*, March 5, 1865, 3.

95. Isaac Scott et al. to A. H. Stephens, reprinted in *Mobile Advertiser and Register*, November 3, 1864, 1.

96. See, e.g., *Mobile Advertiser and Register*, September 16, 1864, 2 (publishing a letter from a Richmond correspondent).

97. Stouten Hubert Dent to "Nannie," September 7, 1864, in Mathis and Purcell, eds., *In the Land of the Living*, 109. (Troy) *Southern Advertiser*, October 14, 1864, 2.

98. C.C. Clay Jr. to J. P. Benjamin, September 12, 1864, Official Records, Series 4, Vol. 3, 636.

99. *Mobile Advertiser and Register*, September 14, 1864, 2.

100. *Mobile Advertiser and Register*, September 18, 1864, 2. See also *Mobile Advertiser and Register*, October 7, 1864, 2, October 14, 1864, 2, October 15, 1864, 2, October 18, 1864, 2.

101. Stoker, *Grand Design*, 376; Schott, *Alexander Stephens of Georgia*, 429; Larry E. Nelson, *Bullets, Ballots and Rhetoric: Confederate Policy for the United States Presidential Contest of 1864* (Tuscaloosa: University of Alabama Press, 1980), 28, 128–37, 161.

102. *Mobile Advertiser and Register*, September 29, 1864, 2; *Daily Columbus* (Georgia) *Enquirer*, September 25, 1864, 1, September 25, 1864, 2.

Chapter 19

1. Edgeworth Bird to Saida Bird, August 10, 1864, in John Rozier, ed., *The Granite Farm Letters: The Civil War Correspondence of Edgeworth & Sallie Bird* (Athens: University of Georgia Press, 1988), 185.

2. *Mobile Advertiser and Register*, quoted in *Daily Columbus* (Georgia) *Enquirer*, October 2, 1864, 2. The *Charleston Mercury* was one of Davis's most bitter critics. *Charleston Mercury*, September 26, 1864, 1.

3. *Columbus* (Georgia) *Sun*, quoted in *Jacksonville Republican*, September 22, 1864, 2.

4. *Mobile Advertiser and Register*, September 28, 1864, 1. See also *Mobile Advertiser and Register*, September 24, 1864, 2, October 6, 1864, 2; *Montgomery Daily Mail*, September 27, 1864, 1; *Daily Columbus* (Georgia) *Enquirer*, September 27, 1864, 2; *Charleston Mercury*, September 24, 1864, 1, September 27, 1864, 1. See also Rable, *Confederate Republic*, 274. Those who were familiar with Napoleon's retreat from Moscow in 1812 and the roles of "General Weather" and "General Starvation" in that winter debacle certainly must have been dubious. Bountiful crops were then being harvested in Georgia and Alabama, and prevailing temperatures in Georgia were in the seventies and eighties. Adam Zamoyski, *Moscow 1812: Napoleon's Fatal March* (London: Harper Collins: 2004); *Daily Columbus* (Georgia) *Enquirer*, September 18, 1864, 2.

5. (Troy) *Southern Advertiser*, September 30, 1864, 2.

6. Robert Dunnavant, *The Railroad War: N.B. Forrest's 1864 Raid through Northern Alabama and Middle Tennessee* (Athens, AL: Pea Ridge Press: 1994).

7. *Jacksonville Republican*, September 15, 1864, 2; *Montgomery Daily Mail*, September 7, 1864, 2; *Daily Columbus* (Georgia) *Enquirer*, September 7, 1864, 1, September 13, 1864, 2.

8. *Montgomery Daily Mail*, September 11, 1864, 2.

9. *Montgomery Advertiser*, reprinted in *Richmond Enquirer*, September 27, 1864, reprinted in (New Orleans) *Daily True Delta*, October 13, 1864, 2.

10. *Mobile Advertiser and Register*, August 31, 1864, 2.

11. *Mobile Advertiser and Register*, October 5, 1864, 1. See also *Mobile Advertiser and Register*, September 27, 1864, 1, October 20, 1864, 1; (Richmond) *Daily Dispatch*, September 28, 1864, 1; *Newark* (Ohio) *Advocate*, September 30, 1864; *New York Times*, September 29, 1864, 1; *Nashville Daily Times and True Union*, September 26, 1864, 2; N. B. Forrest to Lt. Gen. R. Taylor, September 24, 1864, Official Records, Series 1, Vol. 39 (Part II), 870; Hurst, *Nathan Bedford Forrest*, 216–18.

12. *Daily Columbus* (Georgia) *Enquirer*, October 11, 1864, 2, October 23, 1864, 1.

13. *Selma Dispatch*, October 6, 1864, reprinted in *Daily Columbus* (Georgia) *Enquirer*, October 11, 1864, 2.

14. Mary Fielding, "Mary Fielding Diary, 25 September—28 December 1864," in Faye Acton Axford, ed., "*To Lochaber Na Mair*": *Southerners View the Civil War* (Athens, AL, 1986), 144.

15. *Mobile Advertiser and Register*, October 5, 1864, 1. See also *Mobile Advertiser and Register*, October 6, 1864, 1; *Selma Reporter*, reprinted in *Mobile Daily Tribune*, October 2, 1864, 1; *Daily Columbus* (Georgia) *Enquirer*, September 30, 1864, 1.

16. *Daily Columbus* (Georgia) *Enquirer*, October 16, 1864, 2.

17. *Mobile Advertiser and Register*, November 12, 1864, 1.

18. *Mobile Advertiser and Register*, October 5, 1864, 1. See also *Daily Columbus* (Georgia) *Enquirer*, October 4, 1864, 2.

19. *Daily Columbus* (Georgia) *Enquirer*, October 7, 1864, 2.

20. *Charleston Mercury*, October 12, 1864, 1.

21. Civil War Diary of James Montgomery Lanning, 5, Huntsville-Madison County Public Library, Huntsville, Alabama.

22. Crowson and Brogden, eds., *Bloody Banners and Barefoot Boys*, 96. See, generally, Clampitt, *Confederate Heartland*, 75–6, 104–5.

23. *Mobile Advertiser and Register*, October 6, 1864, 2, October 7, 1864, 1, October 20, 1864, 2.

24. Stoker, *Grand Design*, 380.

25. *Mobile Daily Tribune*, October 2, 1864, 1; *Daily Columbus* (Georgia) *Enquirer*, September 30, 1864, 1–2. See, generally, Castel, *Decision in the West*, 551–52; *Daily Columbus* (Georgia) *Enquirer*, October 1, 1864, 2.

26. Hood, *John Bell Hood*, 82.

27. Richard Barksdale Harwell, ed., *Kate: The Journal of a Confederate Nurse* (Baton Rouge, 1998), 238.

28. *Mobile Advertiser and Register*, October 5, 1864, 2.

29. *Daily Columbus* (Georgia) *Enquirer*, October 8, 1864, 2.

30. (Selma) *Mississippian*, October 29, 1864, reprinted in *Daily Columbus* (Georgia) *Enquirer*, November 1, 1864, 2.

31. H. W. Halleck to Major-General Sherman, September 26, 1864, Official Records, Series 1, Vol. 39 (Part II), 480.

32. *Mobile Advertiser and Register*, September 20, 1864, 1 (publishing a letter from Ben Lane Posey), October 20, 1864, 2 (same).

33. Ibid., October 22, 1864, 2.

34. Ibid., October 26, 1864, 1. For a spirited defense of Hood by one of his decedents, see Hood, *John Bell Hood*, 69–88.

35. *Milledgeville Confederate Union*, September 27, 1864, reprinted in *Mobile Advertiser and Register*, October 1, 1864, 2; *Daily Columbus* (Georgia) *Enquirer*, reprinted in *Mobile Advertiser and Register*, October 2, 1864, 1; *Charleston Mercury*, October 3, 1864, 1; Rable, *Confederate Republic*, 271; Schott, *Alexander H. Stephens of Georgia*, 427–28; Parks, *Joseph E. Brown of Georgia*, 296–98.

36. *Daily Columbus* (Georgia) *Enquirer*, October 8, 1864, 2.

37. *Mobile Daily Tribune*, October 2, 1864, 2; *Daily Columbus* (Georgia) *Enquirer*, September 25, 1864, 2, October 1, 1864, 2.

38. Clampitt, *Confederate Heartland*, 101–2.

39. *Mobile Advertiser and Register*, September 25, 1864, 1. See also *Mobile Advertiser and Register*, October 29, 1864, 2, November 9, 1864, 2; *Daily Columbus* (Georgia) *Enquirer*, October 8, 1864, 2, October 16, 1864, 2, October 20, 1864, 1, November 2, 1864, 2, November 13, 1864, 2. See, generally, Nelson, *Bullets, Ballots and Rhetoric*, 159.

40. *Mobile Advertiser and Register*, September 16, 1864, 2. See also ibid., October 29, 1864, 2.

41. *Mobile Daily Tribune*, September 29, 1864, 1–2.

42. Ibid., September 29, 1864, 1–2. See also *Mobile Advertiser and Register*, September 29, 1864, 1; *Montgomery Daily Mail*, September 27, 1864, 2; *Daily Columbus* (Georgia) *Enquirer*, September 29, 1864, 1.

43. *Mobile Advertiser and Register*, September 29, 1864, 1; *Mobile Daily Tribune*, September 29, 1864, 1; *Montgomery Daily Mail*, September 27, 1864, 2; *Daily Columbus* (Georgia) *Enquirer*, September 24, 1864, 1. See, generally, McMillan, *Disintegration of a Confederate State*, 101–4.

44. (Troy) *Southern Advertiser*, October 7, 1864, 2.

45. *Mobile Daily Tribune*, September 29, 1864, 1. The printing of official documents was done at state expense by the public printer elected by the legislature. The number of copies printed was also a legislative decision. Sometimes the decision of the number of copies to be printed was indicative of the degree of support for the author or his policies. By writing "only one hundred and thirty copies [of his address] were ordered printed, against a direct effort to print three thousand copies," the reporter is portraying this episode as an insult to Watts, whose supporters wanted his address widely disseminated. They made a "direct effort" to have that done, but Watts's opponents rallied against him and voted to print far fewer copies.

46. *Mobile Advertiser and Register*, September 29, 1864, 1.

47. Ibid., September 29, 1864, 1–2.

48. *Mobile Advertiser and Register*, September 30, 1864, 1.

49. *Montgomery Daily Mail*, September 27, 1864, 2.

50. Wiggins, *Scalawag in Alabama Politics*, 138, 142, 145.

51. Brewer, *Alabama*, 164.

52. *Mobile Daily Tribune*, October 9, 1864, 2.

53. *Daily Columbus* (Georgia) *Enquirer*, October 5, 1864, 2, October 8, 1864, 1 (the letter was dated September 25, 1864); *Nashville Daily Press*, October 20, 1864, 2. See also *Mobile Advertiser and Register*, October 18, 1864, 2, October 21, 1864, 2; *Nashville Daily Press*, October 19, 1864, 1; *New York Herald*, October 30, 1864, 5.

54. *Daily Columbus* (Georgia) *Enquirer*, October 5, 1864, 2; *Charleston Mercury*, October 5, 1864, 1; Nelson, *Bullets, Ballots and Rhetoric*, 140–42; Schott, *Alexander H. Stephens of Georgia*, 426–27.

55. *Mobile Daily Tribune*, September 30, 1864, 1.

56. Ibid.

57. Ibid. See also *Mobile Daily Tribune*, September 30, 1864, 2. See, generally, *Daily Columbus* (Georgia) *Enquirer*, October 1, 1864, 1.

58. *New York Times*, October 29, 1864, 1 (emphasis added). See also *Mobile Daily Tribune*, September 30, 1864, 2; *Daily Columbus* (Georgia) *Enquirer*, October 1, 1864, 1, October 2, 1864, 1–2. See, generally, Nelson, *Bullets, Ballots and Rhetoric*, 135.

59. *Mobile Daily Tribune*, September 30, 1864, 1.

60. *Selma Dispatch*, reprinted in *Daily Columbus* (Georgia) *Enquirer*, October 8, 1864, 2.

61. *Mobile Daily News*, June 29, 1865, 2.

62. *Daily Columbus* (Georgia) *Enquirer*, October 2, 1864, 2.

63. *Mobile Daily Tribune*, September 30, 1864, 1; *Mobile Advertiser and Register*, October 13, 1864, 1.

64. *Mobile Daily Tribune*, September 30, 1864, 1, October 9, 1864, 2; *Mobile Advertiser and Register*, October 1, 1864, 2.

65. *Montgomery Advertiser*, September 29, 1864, reprinted in *Daily Columbus* (Georgia) *Enquirer*, October 1, 1864, 2.

66. Brewer, *Alabama*, 345; Garrett, *Reminiscences of Public Men in Alabama*, 729.

67. *Mobile Advertiser and Register*, October 1, 1864, 1.

68. Ibid., October 2, 1864, 1.

69. *Mobile Advertiser and Register*, September 30, 1864, 1; *Mobile Daily Tribune*, October 2, 1864, 1; *Daily Columbus* (Georgia) *Enquirer*, October 1, 1864, 1, October 2, 1864, 2.

70. *Mobile Advertiser and Register*, October 2, 1864, 1; *Mobile Daily Tribune*, October 2, 1864, 1; *Daily Columbus* (Georgia) *Enquirer*, October 2, 1864, 1.

71. (Montgomery) *Memphis Appeal*, October 1, 1864, reprinted in (New Orleans) *Daily Picayune*, October 7, 1864, 1; *Montgomery Mail*, reprinted in *Mobile Advertiser and Register*, October 2, 1864, 1; *Daily Columbus* (Georgia) *Enquirer*, October 4, 1864, 1 and *Fayetteville* (North Carolina) *Observer*, October 10, 1864; *Mobile Advertiser and Reg-*

ister, October 2, 1864, 1; *Mobile Daily Tribune*, October 2, 1864, 1–2; *Edgefield* (South Carolina) *Advertiser*, October 5, 1864, 1. See also Dunbar Rowland, *Jefferson Davis: Constitutionalist* (Jackson, MS: Printed for the Mississippi Department of Archives and History, 1923), IV: 345–47; Hudson Strode, *Jefferson Davis: Tragic Hero* (New York: Harcourt, Brace, 1964), III: 91–94; Cooper, *Jefferson Davis, American*, 489–90; Rable, *Confederate Republic*, 274; Crist, ed., *Papers of Jefferson Davis*, 11: 74–75.

72. One exception was the *Charleston Mercury*, whose editor ridiculed Davis by reciting from the Robert Burns poem titled "To a Louse." Ibid., October 4, 1864, 1.

73. *Mobile Daily Tribune*, September 30, 1864, 2, October 2, 1864, 2, October 9, 1864, 2; (Talladega) *Democratic Watchtower*, October 11, 1864, 1; *Mobile Advertiser and Register*, September 30, 1864, 1–2, October 5, 1864, 2, October 9, 1864, 1, October 13, 1864, 1, October 14, 1864, 2, October 18, 1864, 2, October 21, 1864, 1–2.

74. *Mobile Daily Tribune*, October 2, 1864, 1.

75. Richard Taylor, *Destruction and Reconstruction: Personal Experiences of the Late War* (Edinburgh: Blackwood and Sons, 1879), 196–97, 206. See also T. Michael Parrish, *Richard Taylor: Soldier Prince of Dixie* (Chapel Hill: University of North Carolina Press, 1992), 3, 10, 12, 405–6, 413.

76. Taylor, *Destruction and Reconstruction*, 197.

77. Easby-Smith, *William Russell Smith of Alabama*, 161.

78. Davis, *Look Away!*, 354.

79. *Mobile Daily Tribune*, September 30, 1864, 2; *Charleston Mercury*, October 6, 1864, 1, October 7, 1864, 1.

80. *Daily Columbus* (Georgia) *Enquirer*, October 9, 1864, 1.

81. *Mobile Daily Advertiser and Register*, January 6, 1865, 2.

82. *Nashville Daily Union*, October 30, 1864, 2.

83. *Milwaukee Sentinel*, October 25, 1864, 2.

84. *Mobile Advertiser and Register*, October 5, 1864, 2.

85. *Montgomery Mail*, October 8, 1864, reprinted in *Daily Columbus* (Georgia) *Enquirer*, October 11, 1864, 1, October 16, 1864, 1; McMillan, *Disintegration of a Confederate State*, 105. See also *Mobile Advertiser and Register*, October 9, 1864, 2. This vote demonstrated significant support for peace talks.

86. *Mobile Advertiser and Register*, October 7, 1864, 1, October 9, 1864, 1; *Mobile Daily Tribune*, October 9, 1864, 1.

87. *Augusta Chronicle*, October 15, 1864, 2.

88. *Mobile Advertiser and Register*, October 7, 1864, 1.

89. McPherson, *Political History of the United States during the Great Rebellion*, 456; Martin, *Desertion of Alabama Troops from the Confederate Army*, 216.

90. *Mobile Daily Advertiser and Register*, October 11, 1864, 1, October 13, 1864, 1; *Montgomery Mail*, October 8, 1864, reprinted in *Daily Columbus* (Georgia) *Enquirer*, October 11, 1864, 1.

91. McWhiney, Moore, and Pace, eds., "*Fear God and Walk Humbly*," 340.

92. (Washington DC) *Daily National Intelligencer*, November 1, 1864; *Nashville Daily Times & True Union*, November 5, 1864, 1; *Daily Columbus* (Georgia) *Enquirer*,

October 19, 1864, 1; Jeanne Hall Lynch, "Thomas Hill Watts, Civil War Governor of Alabama, 1863–1865" (Master's Thesis, Auburn University, 1957), 71; Fleming, "Peace Movement in Alabama During the Civil War," 120–21; Davis, *Look Away!*, 156–57.

93. *New York Tribune*, March 20, 1865, 4.

94. *Richmond Dispatch*, October 20, 1864, 1.

95. *Mobile News*, reprinted in *Nashville Daily Union*, November 4, 1864, 1.

96. *Mobile Advertiser and Register*, October 13, 1864, 1.

97. *Mobile News*, reprinted in *Nashville Daily Union*, November 4, 1864, 1.

Chapter 20

1. *Atlanta Intelligencer*, reprinted in *Daily Columbus* (Georgia) *Enquirer*, July 6, 1864, 2.

2. *Mobile Advertiser and Register*, October 5, 1864, 2, October 6, 1864, 102, October 7, 1864, 1, October 9, 1864, 1, October 11, 1864, 2, October 12, 1864, 1–2, October 15, 1864, 1–2, October 16, 1864, 1, October 20, 1864, 1; *Selma Dispatch*, October 13, 1864, reprinted in *Mobile Advertiser and Register*, October 15, 1864, 1; Trudeau, *Southern Storm*, 38; Castel, *Decision In the West*, 552–53.

3. *Mobile Advertiser and Register*, October 13, 1864, 1. Although certainly speculative, it is possible that Reconstructionists were also relieved that Sherman was not actually planning to march through Alabama and had negotiated for Sherman's pledge to spare Alabama from further destruction in exchange for an open call for peace in the legislature. As the arrest of a female Union spy in Selma on October 28 indicates, Sherman had his agents in Alabama at this time. *Selma Dispatch*, October 27, 1864, reprinted in *Mobile Advertiser and Register*, October 30, 1864, 1.

4. See, e.g., *Chattanooga Daily Gazette*, November 5, 1864; (New Orleans) *Daily Picayune*, October 7, 1864, 2; *Lowell Daily Citizen and News*, October 31, 1864; *New York Times*, October 23, 1864, 3, October 29, 1864, 1; *Milwaukee Daily Sentinel*, November 3, 1864; *New York Herald*, October 30, 1864, 5. See also *Raleigh Progress*, reprinted in *Mobile Advertiser and Register*, October 27, 1864, 2; (San Francisco) *Daily Evening Bulletin*, December 5, 1864, 2; (New Orleans) *Daily True Delta*, October 7, 1864, 2; *New York Herald*, October 8, 1864, 4; *Philadelphia Inquirer*, October 10, 1864, 8; (Washington, DC) *Daily Constitutional Union*, October 29, 1864, 2.

5. *Chicago Post*, reprinted in *Nashville Daily Press*, November 8, 1864, 2. (Portland, Maine) *Eastern Argus*, November 2, 1864, 2.

6. (Philadelphia) *Daily Age*, October 31, 1864, 2.

7. (Greensboro) *Alabama Beacon*, November 4, 1864, 2; *Mobile Advertiser and Register*, October 18, 1864, 1, October 20, 1864, 2, October 21, 1864, 2; October 23, 1864, 1; *New York Times*, October 20, 1864, 1.

8. *Mobile Advertiser and Register*, October 18, 1864, 2.

9. *Eutaw Whig and Observer*, reprinted in *Mobile Advertiser and Register*, October 22, 1864, 2.

10. *Nashville Daily Union*, December 27, 1864, 3, January 26, 1865, 1, March 10, 1865, 2, April 15, 1865, 2; (Philadelphia) *Daily Evening Bulletin*, May 23, 1865, 4 (Clemens had lived in West Philadelphia since the fall of 1864). See Jeremiah Clemens, *Tobias Wilson: A Tale of the Great Rebellion* (Philadelphia: J.B. Lippincott & Co., 1865).

11. Clemens, *Tobias Wilson*, 26–46.

12. Ibid, 46. According to one account, Clemens's book was "founded on fact." *Nashville Daily Union*, April 15, 1865, 2.

13. See, e.g., *New York Tribune*, reprinted in *Chattanooga Daily Gazette*, August 14, 1864; *New Haven* (Connecticut) *Daily Palladium*, August 10, 1864.

14. *Richmond Daily Dispatch*, December 8, 1864, 1. ("W. R. W. Cobb, the traitor, at the time of his death, was about to assume the military governorship of Huntsville.") It is possible that Clemens was the source of information for an editorial in a Philadelphia newspaper about Cobb's subsequent expulsion from the Confederate Congress:

> We all remember that Mr. Cobb was the last member of the United States Congress from the South to leave his seat at Washington when the rebellion was inaugurated. He was always a strong Union man, and he lifted his voice and used all his influence, which was great, to prevent the secession of the Southern States. With Alexander H. Stephens, Jere Clemens, John M. Botts, and other distinguished Southerners, he saw nothing but ruin to the South in case of a war for separation. To win him over effectually to the side of rebellion, after his return home he was chosen to the Rebel Congress in his district, but his lukewarmness in the cause, has created the suspicion that his heart still yearned for the old Union—the old flag. Hence his arraignment before the House on the charge of disloyalty and his summary expulsion.
>
> Mr. Cobb is a man highly respected, has a large circle of influential friends throughout the South, and can prove a sharp thorn in the Confederate side. There is no doubt but that he is loyal at heart, and *his influence, which may soon be exerted, in view of Sherman's operations, may tell with fearful effect upon the Rebel cause in Alabama and Georgia.*

(Philadelphia) *Evening Telegraph*, November 21, 1864, 2 (emphasis added).

15. *Mobile Advertiser and Register*, November 20, 1864, 1 (making reference to a report of Cobb's death in the *Chattanooga Rebel*); Owen, *History of Alabama and Dictionary of Alabama Biography*, 3: 358 (placing the date of Cobb's death as November 1, 1864).

16. *Montgomery Daily Advertiser*, reprinted in *Mobile Advertiser and Register*, November 11, 1864, 2.

17. *Mobile Advertiser and Register*, October 30, 1864, 2. While marching through Cherokee County, Alabama, which was Gatewood's base of operations, a soldier in John Bell Hood's army observed that the "roadside is lined with Yankee graves, their four by six homestead, as soldiers term the burial spot of a Yankee." *Daily Columbus* (Georgia) *Enquirer*, October 26, 1864, 2.

18. *Mobile Daily Advertiser and Register*, October 30, 1864, 2, and reprinted in *Daily Columbus* (Georgia) *Enquirer*, November 4, 1864, 2 and *Vicksburg Daily Herald*, March 25, 1864, 2. See also *Nashville Daily Union*, February 5, 1865, 2, March 29, 1865, 2; (Washington, DC) *Daily National Intelligencer*, February 24, 1865, 2; *Belmont* (Ohio) *Chronicle*, February 23, 1865, 1; *Huntsville Advocate*, October 12, 1865, 4; Larry David Stephens, *John P. Gatewood, Confederate Bushwhacker* (Gretna, LA: Pelican, 2012); Jonathan Dean Sarris, *A Separate Civil War: Communities in Conflict in the Mountain South* (Charlottesville, VA: University of Virginia Press, 2006), 135–38.

19. (Selma) *Chattanooga Rebel*, reprinted in *Montgomery Daily Advertiser*, November 20, 1864, 1 and *Daily Columbus* (Georgia) *Enquirer*, November 22, 1864, 1. See also *Mobile Advertiser and Register*, November 20, 1864, 1 (referring to the *Rebel's* report); *Richmond Daily Dispatch*, November 29, 1864, 1 (reprinting the *Rebel's* report but not attributing it to the *Rebel*); *Augusta Chronicle*, November 26, 1864, reprinted in *New York Times*, December 2, 1864, 8 (same); *Edgefield* (South Carolina) *Advertiser*, November 30, 1864, 1 (same); *Shreveport* (Louisiana) *News*, January 10, 1865, 2 (same). See, generally, Owen, *History of Alabama and Dictionary of Alabama Biography*, 3: 358 (adopting this tale); *Mobile Advertiser and Register*, February 22, 1865, 2 (repeating it).

20. *Fremont* (Ohio) *Journal*, December 9, 1964, 2.

21. *Selma Reporter*, reprinted in (New Orleans) *Daily Picayune*, February 15, 1865, 1.

22. (Selma) *Chattanooga Rebel*, reprinted in (New Orleans) *Daily Picayune*, February 14, 1865, 1. *Richmond Daily Dispatch*, March 3, 1865, 1.

23. *Selma Dispatch*, December 1, 1864, reprinted in *White Cloud Kansas Chief*, February 9, 1865, 2; (Washington DC) *Daily Republican*, reprinted in *Daily Cleveland Herald*, June 24, 1865; and Jackson, *Story of Selma*, 208–9. See, e.g., *Cork* (Ireland) *Examiner*, February 7, 1865, available at http//:www.irelandoldnews.com/ Cork/1865 /FEB.html; *Cleveland* (Ohio) *Morning Leader*, January 23, 1865, 2,; *Fremont* (Ohio) *Journal*, January 27, 1865, 2; (Pennsylvania) *Jeffersonian*, February 16, 1865, 1; *White Cloud Kansas Chief*, February 9, 1865, 2; (Washington DC) *Daily Republican*, reprinted in *Daily Cleveland Herald*, June 24, 1865; *Brownlow's Knoxville Whig and Rebel Ventilator*, February 1, 1865, 2; *Highland* (County, Ohio) *Weekly News*, February 9, 1865, 1.

24. *Nashville Daily Press*, January 7, 1865, 2; (Greensboro) *Alabama Beacon*, July 27, 1865, 2.

25. *Nashville Daily Press*, January 7, 1865, 2; O. Edward Cunningham, "Captain Frank B. Gurley, Fourth Alabama Cavalry, C.S.A.: Murderer or Victim," *Alabama Review* 28 (January, 1975): 83–103.

26. *Selma Morning Reporter*, November 20, 1864, 1; *Mobile Advertiser and Register*, February 7, 1865, 1; Erwin Anderson Alderman and Armistead Churchill Gordon, *J.L.M. Curry: A Biography* (New York: MacMillan, 1911), 182–83.

27. *Montgomery Advertiser*, December 16, 1864, reprinted in *Mobile Advertiser and Register*, December 20, 1864, 2.

28. *Brownlow's Knoxville Whig and Rebel Ventilator*, November 30, 1864, 2.

29. Lewis Carroll, *Alice's Adventures in Wonderland* (New York: Phillip Warner, 1914), 14.

30. *Mobile Advertiser and Register*, February 7, 1865, 1. Although Curry was, accord-

ing to his biographers, "scarcely more than a civilian in experience," each of the officers of the regiment mysteriously waived their right to promotion to the position and unanimously requested that Curry be made their commanding officer with the rank of lieutenant colonel. Alderman and Gordon, *J.L.M. Curry*, 182–83.

31. Alderman and Gordon, *J.L.M. Curry*, 183.

32. C. C. Sheats to Andrew Johnson, July 25, 1865, Leroy Pope Walker Papers, 1817–1884, File 2, Alabama Department of Archives and History, Montgomery.

33. *Nashville Daily Press*, January 7, 1865, 2.

34. *Montgomery Advertiser*, December 16, 1864, reprinted in *Mobile Advertiser and Register*, December 20, 1864, 2.

35. R. S. Tharin to Col. L. P. ?, September, 1865, Papers of Governor Parsons, Alabama Department of Archives and History, Montgomery. After the war, Tharin became a Baptist minister in Baltimore, Maryland. (Philadelphia) *Evening Telegraph*, December 24, 1866, 3.

36. *Chicago Journal*, reprinted in *Milwaukee Daily Sentinel*, January 12, 1865 and (Philadelphia) *North American and United States Gazette*, January 26, 1865.

37. *Mobile Advertiser and Register*, November 18, 1864, 1; *Daily Columbus* (Georgia) *Enquirer*, November 18, 1864, 1.

38. *Mobile Advertiser and Register*, November 20, 1864, 1.

39. Ibid., November 13, 1864, 2.

40. Ibid., November 16, 1864, 2.

41. Ibid., November 18, 1864, 1, November 20, 1864, 2; *Montgomery Advertiser*, reprinted in *Richmond Daily Dispatch*, December 1, 1864, 1; *New York Times*, December 4, 1864, 3.

42. *Mobile Advertiser and Register*, November 29, 1864, 1.

43. Ibid., November 29, 1864, 2.

44. Ibid., November 29, 1864, 2. See also ibid., November 29, 1864, 1, December 1, 1864, 1.

45. See ibid., December 6, 1864, 1; *Daily Columbus* (Georgia) *Enquirer*, December 3, 1864, 2.

46. See, e.g., *Mobile Advertiser and Register*, November 29, 1864, 1 (questioning the number of conscription-age cadets allowed to attend the University of Alabama), November 29, 1864, 2 (opposing further suspensions of the writ of habeas corpus), December 3, 1864, 1 (same). The copies of Watts's message to the legislature were possibly going to be used against him in the campaign, explaining why so many were to be printed by the public printers, Reconstructionists Milton Saffold and William Bibb Figures. In response, Confederates may have hoped that by forcing votes on pro-independence measures, Reconstructionist leaders such as Lewis Parsons would be neutralized as potential gubernatorial candidates.

47. *Ala. Acts*, Joint Resolutions, 185 (December 13, 1864) (emphasis added). See also *Mobile Advertiser and Register*, December 18, 1864, 1, December 20, 1864, 2; (Mobile) *Army Argus and Crisis*, December 24, 1864, 1.

48. Proclamation of T. H. Watts, December 15, 1864, Papers of Governor Watts,

Alabama Department of Archives and History, Montgomery; McMillan, *Disintegration of a Confederate State*, 63.

49. *Montgomery Daily Advertiser*, reprinted in *Daily Columbus* (Georgia) *Enquirer*, November 25, 1864, 2.

50. But by acceding to, or perhaps offering, these terms, Reconstructionists were not exactly giving away the store. Peace advocates in the Confederate house had already agreed to a similar anti-reconstruction resolution but then offered resolutions calling for peace negotiations. *Journal of the Congress of the Confederate States of America, 1861–1865* (Washington, DC: G.P.O, 1904–1905), 7: 360–64; *Highland* (Ohio) *Weekly News*, December 1, 1864, 2; *Daily Columbus* (Georgia) *Enquirer*, December 2, 1864, 1; *Nashville Daily Union*, December 23, 1864, 1.

51. *Ala. Acts*, No. 89, 76 (December 12, 1864).

52. Ibid., No. 103, 83 (December 13, 1864).

53. *Mobile Advertiser and Register*, December 18, 1864, 1, December 20, 1864, 2.

54. Ibid., January 25, 1865, 1; *Nashville Daily Press*, January 7, 1865, 2; *Baltimore American*, January 10, reprinted in (Greensboro) *Alabama Beacon*, January 27, 1865, 2; Robert Ould to Lt. Col. John E. Mulford, January 18, 1865, Official Records, Series 2, Vol. 8, 86–87; *Nashville Daily Union*, December 30, 1864, 2 (reporting that three citizens were arrested and sent to Nashville); Nuermberger, *Clays of Alabama*, 216.

55. *Nashville Daily Press*, January 7, 1865, 2; Nuermberger, *Clays of Alabama*, 216; (Philadelphia) *North American and United States Gazette*, January 26, 1865.

Chapter 21

1. *Mobile Advertiser and Register*, October 12, 1864, 1, October 18, 1864, 2; *Charleston Mercury*, October 17, 1864, 1, October 18, 1864, 1, November 1, 1864, 2; Hurst, *Nathan Bedford Forrest*, 221.

2. *Mobile Advertiser and Register*, October 7, 1864, 2.

3. Ibid., October 12, 1864, 1, October 15, 1864, 2, October 16, 1864, 1, October 20, 1864, 2, October 22, 1864, 2, October 28, 1864, 2, October 29, 1864, 1–2, October 30, 1864, 2; *Jacksonville Republican*, November 17, 1864, 2; *Daily Columbus* (Georgia) *Enquirer*, October 11, 1864, 1–2, October 12, 1864, 1, October 16, 1864, 1, October 25, 1864, 1, October 26, 1864, 1–2, October 30, 1864, 1–2; *Richmond* (Virginia) *Dispatch*, October 28, 1864, 1; *Sunbury* (Pennsylvania) *American*, November 12, 1864, 2; Jack H. Lepa, *Breaking the Confederacy: The Georgia and Tennessee Campaigns of 1864* (Jefferson, N.C.: McFarland, 2005), 132–34; Wiley Sword, *Embrace an Angry Wind: The Confederacy's Last Hurrah: Spring Hill, Franklin, and Nashville* (New York: Harper Collins, 1992), 54–57, 63; Castel, *Decision in the West*, 553; Trudeau, *Southern Storm*, 41–42.

4. *Charleston Mercury*, October 19, 1864, 1.

5. T. Harry Williams, *P. G. T. Beauregard: Napoleon in Gray* (Baton Rouge: Louisiana State University Press, 1955), 242–43; Lepa, *Breaking the Confederacy*, 131; Sword, *Embrace an Angry Wind*, 71.

6. *Charleston Mercury*, October 31, 1864, 1.

7. John Bell Hood, *Advance and Retreat* (Secaucus, NJ: Blue and Grey Press, 1985), 262–64. See also Sword, *Embrace an Angry Wind*, 71.

8. *Jacksonville Republican*, November 17, 1864, 2; *Charleston Mercury*, November 4, 1864, 1, November 10, 1864, 1.

9. *Mobile Advertiser and Register*, November 29, 1864, 2. See, generally, *Sunbury* (Pennsylvania) *American*, November 12, 1864, 2.

10. Trudeau, *Southern Storm*, 38–44; Sword, *Embrace an Angry Wind*, 61.

11. Hess, *Civil War in the West*, 251.

12. Lt. Col. Griffin to his wife, October 22, 1864, in Arville L. Funk, "A Hoosier Regiment in Alabama," *Alabama Historical Quarterly* 27 (Spring and Summer, 1965): 92.

13. Private Journal of Sarah R. Espy, 87–88.

14. Zillah Haynie Brandon Diary, 372, December 9, 1864, SPR 262, Alabama Department of Archives and History, Montgomery.

15. Williams, *Beauregard*, 243–44; Sword, *Embrace an Angry Wind*, 63–74; Lepa, *Breaking the Confederacy*, 174–75; Frank E. Vandiver, "General Hood as Logistician," *Military Affairs* 16 (Spring 1952): 1–11. But see Hood, *John Bell Hood*, 89–94.

16. *Mobile Advertiser and Register*, November 24, 1864, 2; *Daily Columbus* (Georgia) *Enquirer*, October 23, 1864, 2, November 1, 1864, 1–2, November 18, 1864, 1 (quoting a letter stating that "there were not less than five thousand barefooted soldiers" under Hood's command at Tuscumbia); (Montgomery) *Memphis Appeal*, reprinted in *Daily Columbus* (Georgia) *Enquirer*, October 25, 1864, 1 (opining that circumstances "should spur the quartermaster's department to extraordinary exertions"); (Athens, Georgia) *Southern Watchman*, November 23, 1864, 4; (Philadelphia) *Evening Telegraph*, October 26, 1864, 1; *Savannah* (Georgia) *Republican*, reprinted in (Philadelphia) *Evening Telegraph*, November 4, 1864 ("Whole regiments are barefooted."); (Washington, DC) *Daily National Republican*, November 7, 1864, 1; *Montgomery Advertiser*, October 19, 1864, reprinted in (Washington, DC) *Daily National Republican*, October 29, 1864; *Montgomery Advertiser*, reprinted in *Daily Columbus* (Georgia) *Enquirer*, October 22, 1864, 2.

17. Edward Norphlet Brown to Fannie Brown, October 21, 1864, Edward Norphlet Brown Letters, Alabama Department of Archives and History, Montgomery.

18. (Philadelphia) *Evening Telegraph*, December 14, 1864, 1.

19. *Montgomery Advertiser*, reprinted in *Daily Columbus* (Georgia) *Enquirer*, October 22, 1864, 2. See also *Charleston Mercury*, October 26, 1864, 1, October 28, 1864, 1, October 29, 1864, 1, November 4, 1864, 1.

20. Vandiver, *Ploughshares into Swords*, 219; *Augusta Chronicle*, October 15, 1864, 2; (Augusta) *Daily Constitutionalist*, October 26, 1864, 1; *Selma Reporter*, reprinted in *Daily Columbus* (Georgia) *Enquirer*, October 30, 1864, 2; *Jacksonville Republican*, October 20, 1864, 2 (discussing a military order that the latter road be extended to Jacksonville).

21. *Montgomery Advertiser*, October 19, 1864, reprinted in (Washington, DC) *Daily*

National Republican, October 29, 1864; *Selma Reporter*, reprinted in *Daily Columbus* (Georgia) *Enquirer*, October 30, 1864, 2.

22. (Savannah) *Republican*, reprinted in *Richmond Examiner*, November 1, 1864, 3.

23. *Chicago Journal*, reprinted in *Milwaukee Daily Sentinel*, November 9, 1864, 2. Hood most certainly knew of his own unpopularity within his army after the debacle in Georgia and that a surge in desertions was a real possibility if they again perceived he was not sensitive to their interests. The editor of a Georgia newspaper had described Hood's army as a "huge ganglionic nerve through the fibres of which is continually flowing as much intelligence and individuality as can be found in any mass of the community. The troops are accustomed to measure causes and events for themselves, and to apply a judgment to men and actors, which, if not infallible, is at least generally correct." Many of Hood's men had assessed their predicament quite correctly and come to a very logical conclusion. *Savannah Republican*, reprinted in *Charleston Mercury*, July 22, 1864, 1.

24. Joel Murphree to Ursula Murphree, November 18, 1864, in "Autobiography and Civil War Letters of Joel Murphree of Troy, Alabama," ed. H. E. Sterkx, 200. Harvey Luttrell to Susan Luttrell, September 3, 1864, in John D. Miller, "An Alabama Merchant in Civil War Richmond: The Harvey Wilkerson Luttrell Letters, 1861–1865," *Alabama Review* 58 (July 2005): 200; Gary Wilson, ed., "The Diary of John S. Tucker: Confederate Soldier From Alabama," *Alabama Historical Quarterly* XLIII (Spring 1981): 30; (New York) *Evening Post*, October 25, 1864, 2.

25. William L. Nugent to Eleanor Nugent, September 10, 1864, in *My Dear Nellie: The Civil War Letters of William L. Nugent to Eleanor Smith Nugent*, ed. William M. Cash and Lucy Somerville Howorth, 203 (Jackson: University Press of Mississippi, 1977).

26. *Charleston Mercury*, October 31, 1864, 1 (urging that Hood avoid Tennessee until Sherman was defeated in Alabama).

27. Jill K. Garrett, ed., *Confederate Diary of Robert D. Smith* (Columbia, TN: Capt. James Madison Sparkman Chapter, United Daughters of the Confederacy, 1975), 79–82; *Selma Dispatch*, November 1, 1864, reprinted in *Daily Columbus* (Georgia) *Enquirer*, November 5, 1864, 1; *Mobile Advertiser and Register*, October 26, 1864, 1, October 30, 1864, 1–2, November 5, 1864, 1, November 8, 1864, 2, November 9, 1864, 1, November 10, 1864, 1, November 11, 1864, 2, November 13, 1864, 1, November 16, 1864, 1, November 24, 1864, 2, November 26, 1864, 2, November 27, 1864, 1; *Mobile Daily Tribune*, November 25, 1864, 1; *Milwaukee Daily Sentinel*, November 10, 1864 (mentioning the presence of black troops at Decatur); *Nashville Daily Times and True Union*, November 10, 1864, 1 (same); *Montgomery Mail*, November 3, 1864, cited in *Daily Columbus* (Georgia) *Enquirer*, November 6, 1864, 1; (Montgomery) *Memphis Appeal*, November 6, 1864, reprinted in *Daily Columbus* (Georgia) *Enquirer*, November 8, 1864, 1; *Daily Columbus* (Georgia) *Enquirer*, November 9, 1964, 1, November 11, 1864, 1, November 12, 1864, 1; *Edgefield* (South Carolina) *Advertiser*, November 9, 1864, 1; *Charleston Mercury*, November 12, 1864, 1. See also Sword, *Embrace an Angry Wind*, 64–74; Williams, *Beauregard*, 244–45; Hood, *John Bell Hood*, 92–94 (defending Hood).

28. (Selma) *Chattanooga Rebel*, reprinted in (Augusta) *Daily Constitutionalist*, December 15, 1864, 2.

29. Ben Lane Posey to Jefferson Davis, September 22, 1864, in Jerry Frey, *Three Quarter Cadillac*, 149–51 (Sandy, UT: Aardvark Global Publishing, 2008).

30. *Mobile Daily News*, July 7, 1865, 1.

31. *Montgomery Mail*, reprinted in (Washington, DC) *Daily National Intelligencer*, November 12, 1864, 3; *Philadelphia Inquirer*, November 5, 1864, 4.

32. *Selma Reporter*, reprinted in *Augusta Chronicle*, November 16, 1864, 1.

33. (Selma) *Mississippian*, reprinted in *Mobile Advertiser and Register*, November 9, 1864, 2.

34. Ibid., October 28, 1864, 2.

35. Ibid., October 30, 1864, 1.

36. Ibid., October 27, 1864, 1.

37. Ibid., November 16, 1864, 1, November 24, 1864, 2, November 27, 1864, 1; (Athens, Georgia) *Southern Banner*, November 30, 1864, 2; *Daily Columbus* (Georgia) *Enquirer*, November 19, 1864, 2, November 29, 1864, 2; Sword, *Embrace an Angry Wind*, 65–68.

38. Joel Murphree to Ursula Murphree, November 1, 1864, and November 8, 1864, in "Autobiography and Civil War Letters of Joel Murphree," ed. H. E. Sterkx, 197–98.

39. Edward Norphlet Brown to Fannie Brown, November 51, 1864, Edward Norphlet Brown Letters, Alabama Department of Archives and History, Montgomery.

40. Civil War Diary of James Montgomery Lanning, 13–17. See, generally, Clampitt, *Confederate Heartland*, 113–14 (other soldiers also believed Hood's army would simply go into winter quarters).

41. *Daily Columbus* (Georgia) *Enquirer*, November 29, 1864, 2. See also *Canton* (Mississippi) *Citizen*, November 14, 1864, reprinted in *Mobile Advertiser and Register*, November 16, 1864, 1; *Montgomery Advertiser*, November 11, 1864, reprinted in *Charleston Mercury*, December 14, 1864, 2.

42. Diary of Sally Independence Foster, November 6, 1864.

43. *Daily Columbus* (Georgia) *Enquirer*, November 19, 1864, 2. The condition of Florence was far from pristine. Edward Norphlet Brown to Fannie Brown, November 14, 1864, Edward Norphlet Brown Letters, Alabama Department of Archives and History, Montgomery.

44. *Richmond Daily Dispatch*, December 3, 1864, 1.

45. Daily Journal of Joshua Burns Moore, 89; (Montgomery) *Alabama State Journal*, September 8, 1872; (Selma) *Southern Argus*, September 6, 1872, 2, September 20, 1872, 2; *Montgomery Advertiser and Mail*, August 31, 1872, 2, September 10, 1872, 2, September 26, 1872, 2; *Huntsville Daily Democrat*, September 27, 1872, 2; (Greensboro) *Alabama Beacon*, September 21, 1872, 2; *Mobile Daily Register*, September 19, 1872, 2; (Tuscumbia) *North Alabamian and Times*, reprinted in *Shelby County Guide*, September 19, 1872, 2 and *Montgomery Advertiser and Mail*, September 6, 1872, 2; *Florence Journal*, September 19, 1872, 2; *Lauderdale Times*, August 27, 1872, 2; *Jackson-*

ville Republican, September 14, 1872, 2; (Macon) *Georgia Weekly Telegraph & Georgia Journal & Messenger*, September 17, 1872.

46. *Mobile Advertiser and Register*, November 13, 1864, 1.

47. *Richmond Daily Dispatch*, November 16, 1864, 1. Clampitt, *Confederate Heartland*, 113.

48. (Montgomery) *Memphis Appeal*, reprinted in *Charleston Mercury*, November 19, 1864 and *Richmond Daily Dispatch*, November 23, 1864, 1. See also *Mobile Advertiser and Register*, November 24, 1864, 2, November 27, 1864, 1.

49. *Montgomery Daily Advertiser*, November 28, 1864, 2.

50. *Montgomery Mail*, reprinted in *Richmond Daily Dispatch*, November 23, 1864, 1.

51. *Mobile Advertiser and Register*, November 24, 1864, 2, reprinted in (Montgomery) *Memphis Appeal*, November 29, 1864, and in *Daily Columbus* (Georgia) *Enquirer*, December 2, 1864, 1.

52. *Cincinnati Gazette*, reprinted in (Philadelphia) *Evening Telegraph*, November 18, 1864, 1.

53. Some have attempted to blame the delay on Nathan Bedford Forrest's failure to promptly link up with Hood at Florence. But Hood already had the services of a division of cavalry under General William H. "Red" Jackson. Hood, *John Bell Hood*, 100 (blaming Forrest but making this admission).

54. *New York Herald*, reprinted in *Richmond Daily Dispatch*, December 3, 1864, 1.

55. (Washington, DC) *Daily National Republican*, November 22, 1864, 2.

56. *Mobile Advertiser and Register*, November 11, 1864, 2, November 13, 1864, 1–2, November 15, 1864, 1. See, generally, Johnson, *Decided on the Battlefield*, 225–29.

57. *Mobile Advertiser and Register*, November 9, 1864, 2.

58. *New York Tribune*, November 9, 1864, reprinted in *New Haven Daily Palladium*, November 9, 1864.

59. George Knox Miller to Celestine Miller, November 15, 1864, in *An Uncompromising Secessionist*, ed. Richard M. McMurry, 259.

60. Grant Taylor to Malinda Taylor, November 16, 1864, in *This Cruel War*, eds. Ann Kicker Blomquist and Robert A. Taylor, 303–4.

61. Civil War Diary of James Montgomery Lanning, 18.

62. *Shreveport* (Louisiana) *News*, November 29, 1864, 2.

63. Edward Norphlet Brown to Fannie Brown, November 10, 1864, Edward Norphlet Brown Letters, Alabama Department of Archives and History, Montgomery.

Chapter 22

1. Clampitt, *Confederate Heartland*, 120.

2. Crowson and Brogden, eds., *Bloody Banners and Barefoot Boys*, 99–100.

3. Ibid.

4. Norman D. Brown, ed., *One of Cleburne's Command: The Civil War Reminiscences and Diary of Captain Samuel T. Foster, Granbury's Texas Brigade, CSA* (Austin: Uni-

versity of Texas Press, 1980), 150–51. See, generally, Hess, *Civil War in the West*, 252–55; Hood, *John Bell Hood*, 164–75.

5. *Jacksonville Republican*, December 8, 1864, 2.

6. (Athens, Georgia) *Southern Banner*, December 14, 1864, 1. See also *Mobile Advertiser and Register*, December 6, 1864, 1–2.

7. *Nashville Daily Union*, December 1, 1864, 2. Citing a source who had been in Tennessee at the time, an article would later appear in the *Selma Dispatch* revealing that the "battle near Franklin was fought against the real wishes of General Hood, but he yielded to the demands of his men. The Tennessee regiments, particularly, were clamorous for the fight, and threatened to mutiny unless they were allowed to attack the federals then and there." They should have listened to Hood. *Selma Dispatch*, December 15, 1864, reprinted in *Nashville Daily Union*, January 7, 1865, 1.

8. *Selma Morning Dispatch*, December 20, 1864, 2.

9. (Selma) *Chattanooga Rebel*, reprinted in *Augusta Chronicle*, December 20, 1864, 1; *Mobile Advertiser and Register*, December 25, 1864, 1; *Montgomery Advertiser*, December 17, 1864, reprinted in *Nashville Daily Union*, January 7, 1865, 1. See, generally, *Nashville Daily Union*, December 1, 1864, 2, December 2, 1864, 2; *Mobile Advertiser and Register*, December 6, 1864, 1–2; W. J. Wood, *Civil War Generalship: The Art of Command* (Westport, CT: Praeger, 1997), 203–5. (Hood's total casualties at Franklin actually exceeded 6,000.)

10. Berry, "Life of Edmund Winston Pettus," 25–26; Sword, *Embrace an Angry Wind*, 444.

11. *Selma Morning Dispatch*, January 10, 1865, 2.

12. *New York Times*, cited in *Nashville Daily Union*, December 1, 1864, 1.

13. *Nashville Daily Union*, November 1, 1864, 3; *Nashville Daily Union*, November 26, 1864, 2; *Nashville Daily Union*, December 6, 1864, 2.

14. *Cincinnati Enquirer*, reprinted in *Nashville Daily Union*, December 13, 1864, 2.

15. Edward Norphlet Brown to Fannie Brown, December 10, 1864, Edward Norphlet Brown Letters, Alabama Department of Archives and History, Montgomery.

16. *Nashville Daily Union*, December 17, 1864, 2.

17. Ibid., December 20, 1864, 2. See, generally, *Montgomery Advertiser*, reprinted in *Selma Morning Dispatch*, January 7, 1865, 2 and (New Orleans) *Daily Picayune*, January 18, 1865, 1; *Selma Reporter*, December 30, 1864, reprinted in *Nashville Daily Union*, January 8, 1865, 2.

18. Joel Murphree to Ursula Murphree, December 28, 1864, in "Autobiography and Civil War Letters of Joel Murphree of Troy, Alabama," ed. H. E. Sterkx, 202.

19. Edward Norphlet Brown to Fannie Brown, December 24, 1864, Edward Norphlet Brown Letters, Alabama Department of Archives and History, Montgomery.

20. *Mobile Advertiser and Register*, September 28, 1864, 1. See, generally, Jerry Keenan, *Wilson's Cavalry Corps: Union Campaigns in the Western Theatre, October, 1864 through Spring 1865* (Jefferson, NC: McFarland, 1998), 113–25.

21. *Nashville Daily Union*, December 27, 1864, 2.

22. N. B. Forrest to Lt. Gen. R. Taylor, January 2, 1865, Official Records, Series 1, Vol. 45 (Part II), 756–57. See, generally, (Washington, DC) *Daily National Intelligencer*,

January 3, 1865; *Selma Morning Dispatch*, January 10, 1865, 2; (New Orleans) *Daily Picayune*, January 21, 1865, 1; *Chicago Tribune*, reprinted in *Charleston Mercury*, January 27, 1865, 1. *Mobile Advertiser and Register*, December 24, 1864, 2, December 28, 1864, 2, December 31, 1864, 2; *Selma Morning Dispatch*, January 7, 1865, 2; *Charleston Mercury*, January 20, 1865; *Nashville Daily Press*, December 17, 1864, 2; (New Orleans) *Daily Picayune*, December 27, 1864, 2, December 31, 1864, 2; *New York Times*, January 7, 1865, 1, 4. See, generally, Anne J. Bailey, *Chessboard of War: Sherman and Hood in the Autumn Campaigns of 1864* (Lincoln: University of Nebraska Press, 2000), 91–111, 132–68; Sword, *Embrace an Angry Wind*, 321–426; Lepa, *Breaking the Confederacy*, 193–206; Derek Smith, *In the Lion's Mouth: Hood's Tragic Retreat From Nashville, 1864* (Mechanicsburg, PA: Stackpole Books, 2011), 229; Hess, *Civil War in the West*, 255–58; Hood, *John Bell Hood*, 176–201.

23. Crowson and Brogden, eds., *Bloody Banners and Barefoot Boys*, 106.

24. *New York Tribune*, January 11, 1865, 1; (Washington, DC) *Daily National Republican*, December 23, 1864, 2; *Cincinnati Commercial*, reprinted in *Cleveland Morning Leader*, January 10, 1865, 1–2; (Washington, DC) *Daily National Intelligencer*, January 3, 1865 ("The rebels acknowledge they lost half their army while in Tennessee."); *Chicago Journal*, reprinted in *Milwaukee Daily Sentinel*, January 12, 1865 (quoting a Union Army officer's estimate of 20,000); Smith, *In the Lion's Mouth*, 258–59.

25. *Selma Morning Dispatch*, January 10, 1865, 2.

26. *Montgomery Advertiser*, reprinted in (New Orleans) *Daily Picayune*, January 18, 1865, 1.

27. *Montgomery Mail*, reprinted in (New Orleans) *Daily Picayune*, January 17, 1865, 1.

28. Edward Norphlet Brown to Fannie Brown, December 24, 1864, Edward Norphlet Brown Letters, Alabama Department of Archives and History, Montgomery.

29. (Philadelphia) *Evening Telegraph*, December 27, 1864, 1; *Gallipolis* (Ohio) *Journal*, December 29, 1864, 2; *Burlington* (Vermont) *Free Press*, December 30, 1864, 2; *Fremont* (Ohio) *Journal*, December 30, 1864, 3; Smith, *In the Lion's Mouth*, 186–87, 237.

30. *Montgomery Mail*, reprinted in (New Orleans) *Daily Picayune*, January 17, 1865, 1; *New York Tribune*, January 9, 1865, 1, January 12, 1865, 1; *Chicago Tribune*, reprinted in *Charleston Mercury*, January 27, 1865, 1; *Nashville Daily Union*, December 30, 1864, 2; *Burlington* (Vermont) *Free Press*, January 6, 1865, 1; *New York Daily Tribune*, January 12, 1865, 1; *Philadelphia Daily Evening Bulletin*, January 6, 1865, 1, January 16, 1865, 2; *Washington* (DC) *Herald*, January 3, 1915, 35; Smith, *In the Lion's Mouth*, 154, 186–87, 205–6, 219, 226–35; Keenan, *Wilson's Cavalry Corps*, 122.

31. *New York Tribune*, January 9, 1865, 1; *Richmond Daily Dispatch*, January 10, 1865, 2; *Nashville Daily Union*, January 6, 1865, 3; William J. Palmer to Major Moe, January 5, 1865, Official Records, Series 1, Vol. 45 (Part II), 521 (the 80 pontoons were later destroyed by Union forces); Smith, *In the Lion's Mouth*, 234–41; Keenan, *Wilson's Cavalry Corps*, 122.

32. Margaret Josephine Miles Gillis Diary, January 22, 1865, 149, SPR 5, Alabama Department of Archives and History, Montgomery.

33. Edward Norphlet Brown to Fannie Brown, December 24, 1864, Edward Norphlet Brown Letters, Alabama Department of Archives and History, Montgomery.

34. McWhiney, Moore and Pace, eds., "*Fear God and Walk Humbly,*" 343.

35. Peter M. Dox to U. S. Grant, January 14, 1865, in *The Papers of Ulysses S. Grant,* ed. John Y. Simon, 13: 505 (Carbondale, IL: Southern Illinois University Press, 1967).

36. George C. Rable, "Despair, Hope, and Delusion: The Collapse of Confederate Morale Reexamined," in *The Collapse of the Confederacy,* ed. Mark Grimsley and Brooks D. Simpson, 129–67 (Lincoln: University of Nebraska Press, 2001).

Part VIII

Epigraph. William Stanley Hoole and Elizabeth Hoole McArthur, *The Yankee Invasion of West Alabama, March–April, 1865* (Tuscaloosa, AL: Confederate Pub. Co., 1985), 60, 76–77 (referring to the burning of the University of Alabama in 1865 as "utterly useless destruction" and a "holocaust," despite favorably comparing the university to West Point and therefore ignoring the contradiction (that he himself raised) that was inherent in the fact that the Union considered the university not just an institute of higher education but also one of the Confederacy's strategic military assets); *Cincinnati Daily Gazette,* May 14, 1881, 6. (A correspondent alleged that it was "almost as bad as the act of the Mohammedan who fired the Alexandrian Library"—despite the fact that most historians date the burning of the library to several centuries before Muhammad was even born.)

Chapter 23

Epigraph 1. Private Journal of Sarah R. Espy, 91.

Epigraph 2 Grant Taylor to Malinda Taylor, January 4, 1865, in *This Cruel War,* eds. Ann Kicker Blomquist and Robert A. Taylor, 321.

Epigraph 3. Linden and Linden, eds., *Disunion, War, Defeat, and Recovery in Alabama,* 128.

Epigraph 4. McWhiney, Moore, and Pace, eds., "*Fear God and Walk Humbly,*" 343.

Epigraph 5. Harwell, ed., *Kate: The Journal of a Confederate Nurse,* 246.

Epigraph 6. William Eppa Fielding, "William Eppa Fielding's Diary, 29 July 1864–February 1865," in "*To Lochaber Na Mair": Southerners View the Civil War,* ed. Faye Acton Axford, 136 (Athens, AL: Athens Publishing, 1986).

Epigraph 7. Mary Fielding, "Mary Fielding Diary," in "*To Lochaber Na Mair": Southerners View the Civil War,* ed. Faye Acton Axford, 151 (Athens, AL: Athens Publishing, 1986).

Epigraph 8. Joseph Francis to Sister Willie, December 24, 1864, in James P. Pate, ed., *When This Evil War Is Over: The Correspondence of the Francis Family, 1860–1865* (Tuscaloosa: University of Alabama Press, 2006), 203.

Epigraph 9. Jefferson M. Buford to Governor Watts, December 28, 1864, Papers of Governor Watts, Alabama Department of Archives and History, Montgomery.

1. W. T. Sherman to Maj. Gen. George H. Thomas, January 21, 1865, Official Records, Series 1, Vol. 45 (Part II), 621–22.

2. Chester G. Hearn, *Mobile Bay and the Mobile Campaign: The Last Great Battles*

of the Civil War (Jefferson, NC: McFarland, 1998), 146–58; Sean Michael O'Brien, *Mobile 1865: Last Stand of the Confederacy* (Westport, CT: Praeger, 2001), 58–65; Max L. Heyman Jr., *Prudent Soldier: A Biography of Major General E.R.S. Canby 1817–1873* (Glendale, CA: Arthur H. Clark, 1959), 223–32; George S. Burkhardt, *Confederate Rage, Yankee Wrath: No Quarter in the Civil War* (Carbondale, IL: Southern Illinois University Press, 2007), 236–37.

3. *Montgomery Advertiser*, reprinted in Mobile *Advertiser and Register*, March 1, 1865, 1. See also *Mobile Advertiser and Register*, March 6, 1865, 2; (Tuscaloosa) *Observer*, March 8, 1865, 1, and *Selma Morning Dispatch*, March 12, 1865, 2; (Tuscaloosa) *Observer*, March 8, 1865, 2; (New Orleans) *Daily Picayune*, March 4, 1865, 2; *New York Times*, reprinted in *Milwaukee Daily Sentinel*, March 4, 1865 and *Nashville Daily Times and True Union*, March 6, 1865, 2. See also *Columbus* (Georgia) *Enquirer*, February 12, 1865, reprinted in *Mobile Advertiser and Register*, February 16, 1865, 1, February 19, 1865, 2, February 24, 1865, 2.

4. *Cleveland Morning Leader*, January 9, 1865, 2, January 11, 1865, 1–2; *New York Tribune*, January 11, 1865, 4, February 10, 1865, 4; *Hartford Daily Courant*, March 2, 1865, 2; *Mobile Advertiser and Register*, February 7, 1865, 1, March 18, 1865, 1; *Richmond Daily Dispatch*, January 11, 1865, 2, January 14, 1865, 2, March 3, 1865, 4; *Milwaukee Daily Sentinel*, March 4, 1865; *New York Times*, reprinted in *Nashville Daily Times and True Union*, March 6, 1865, 2; *Philadelphia Press*, March 1, 1865, 1; *Chicago Tribune*, reprinted in *Charleston Mercury*, January 27, 1865, 1; (Alexandria) *Soldiers' Journal*, January 18, 1865, 4; *Boston Herald*, February 13, 1865, 4; *Montgomery Daily Mail*, January 24, 1865, 1. See also *Montgomery Daily Advertiser*, March 3, 1865, 2; *Selma Reporter*, reprinted in (Grove Hill) *Clarke County Journal*, January 26, 1865, 2; *Mobile Advertiser and Register*, February 7, 1865, 1; *Richmond Whig*, February 7, 1865, reprinted *New York Times*, February 10, 1865, 4. See also Linden and Linden, eds., *Disunion, War, Defeat and Recovery in Alabama*, 133, 136.

5. (Tuscaloosa) *Observer*, March 15, 1865, 1–2; *Selma Dispatch*, reprinted in *Augusta Chronicle*, February 23, 1865, 3; (Selma) *Chattanooga Rebel*, March 21, 1865, 1.

6. (Montgomery) *Memphis Appeal*, reprinted in *Mobile Advertiser and Register*, February 18, 1865, 2.

7. *Cleveland Morning Leader*, January 9, 1865, 2; *Chicago Journal*, reprinted in *Milwaukee Daily Sentinel*, February 8, 1865 and *New York Times*, February 8, 1865, February 10, 1865, 4. See also, *New York Times*, February 10, 1865, 4, quoting the *Richmond Whig; Nashville Daily Press*, February 18, 1865, 1 (discussing the assembly of a cavalry force at Gravelly Springs); *Nashville Daily Times and True Union*, March 6, 1865, 2 (publishing an article titled "The Plan of the Approaching Campaign—Occupation of Mobile the First Object—Cahawba, Selma, Montgomery and Columbus, Ga., the Next Points"); *Boston Herald*, February 13, 1865, 4; *Mobile Daily Advertiser and Register*, February 15, 1865, 2 (discussing reports from the Memphis press of an impending movement on Alabama).

8. *Mobile Advertiser and Register*, January 29, 1865, 2, February 8, 1865, 1; (Grove Hill) *Clarke County Journal*, February 1, 1865, 2; (Washington, DC) *Daily National Intelligencer*, February 1, 1865; (New Orleans) *Daily Picayune*, January 27, 1865, 2, Feb-

ruary 7, 1865, 2; *Daily Cleveland Herald*, January 19, 1865; *Fayetteville Observer*, January 30, 1865; *Edgefield Advertiser*, February 1, 1865, 1.

9. James B. Conroy, *Our One Common Country: Abraham Lincoln and the Hampton Roads Peace Conference of 1865* (Guilford, CT: Lyons Press 2014), 113–17, 211, 216–20; Escott, *Confederacy*, 123–24; Rable, *Confederate Republic*, 292–93; *Cleveland Morning Leader*, February 11, 1865, 2, June 26, 1865, 1, December 18, 1865, 2; *New York Times*, cited in (New Orleans) *Daily Picayune*, February 12, 1865, 2; *Nashville Daily Press*, February 7, 1865, 1; *Cleveland Morning Leader*, June 12, 1865, 1.

10. Escott, *Confederacy*, 123–25; Paul J. Zingg, "John Archibald Campbell and the Hampton Road Conference: Quixotic Diplomacy, 1865," *Alabama Historical Quarterly* XXXVI (Spring 1974): 25–28; *Mobile Advertiser and Register*, January 29, 1865, 2. *Richmond Sentinel*, January 30, 1865, reprinted in (New Orleans) *Daily Picayune*, February 11, 1865, 1; *Selma Reporter*, reprinted in (Grove Hill) *Clarke County Journal*, February 9, 1865, 2.

11. See, generally, *Mobile Advertiser and Register*, February 11, 1865, 1; (New Orleans) *Daily Picayune*, February 16, 1865, 2 (publishing the reports of the commissioners); *Cleveland Morning Leader*, June 12, 1865, 1 (regarding Davis's instructions to the Confederate commissioners prior to the conference, and efforts by them to change his mind); *Augusta Chronicle and Sentinel*, June 17, 1865 (publishing an article said to be based on Alexander Stephens's account of the conference), reprinted in *Nashville Daily Union*, June 29, 1865, 1 and *Cleveland Morning Leader*, June 26, 1865, 1; *Nashville Daily Union*, March 30, 1866, 4 (publishing Seward's February 7, 1865, letter to Charles Francis Adams about the conference).

12. *Mobile Advertiser and Register*, reprinted in (New Orleans) *Daily Picayune*, January 19, 1865, 1.

13. *Greeneville Observer*, cited in *Mobile Advertiser and Register*, November 24, 1864, 1. In his message to the Confederate Congress in November of 1864, Davis recommended the use of the slaves only as laborers, and expressly rejected the policy of arming them. Report of the Committee on Military Affairs, Confederate House of Representatives, Official Records, Series 1, Vol. 3, 1144–49. See, generally, Rable, *Confederate Republic*, 288.

14. *Mobile Advertiser and Register*, November 15, 1864, 2. See also *Mobile Advertiser and Register*, November 9, 1864, 2, November 12, 1864, 2, November 15, 1864, 2, November 16, 1864, 1, November 18, 1864, 1 (publishing Davis's message), November 20, 1864, 1, November 22, 1864, 1; (Greensboro) *Alabama Beacon*, November 4, 1864, 2; *Nashville Daily Press*, November 16, 1864, 1; *Mobile Daily Tribune*, December 1, 1864, 2. See, generally, Rable, *Confederate Republic*, 287–92; Nelson, *Bullets, Ballots, and Rhetoric*, 167; Bruce C. Levine, *Confederate Emancipation: Southern Plans to Free and Arm Slaves during the Civil War* (New York: Oxford University Press, 2006).

15. *Mobile Advertiser and Register*, November 12, 1864, 2.

16. (Greensboro) *Alabama Beacon*, January 27, 1865, 2; (Richmond) *Daily Dispatch*, February 28, 1865, 3 (Georgia's governor opposed the concept). Regarding St. Domingo and its effect on Southern thought, see Matthew J. Clavin, *Toussaint Louverture*

and the American Civil War: The Promise and Peril of a Second Haitian Revolution (Philadelphia, 2010).

17. See, e.g., *Cleveland Morning Leader*, February 16, 1865, 2; *New York Tribune*, January 11, 1865, 1; (New Orleans) *Daily Picayune*, January 6, 1865, 1; *Nashville Daily Union*, February 12, 1865, 2, February 17, 1865, 2; *Fremont* (Ohio) *Journal*, February 10, 1865, 1.

18. *White Cloud Kansas Chief*, January 19, 1865, 3.

19. Andrew Ward, *The Slaves' War: The Civil War in the Words of Former Slaves* (Boston: Mariner Books, 2008), 22.

20. *Montgomery Daily Advertiser*, April 16, 1864, 1.

21. *New York Times*, August 3, 1864, 8.

22. *Selma Morning Reporter*, July 28, 1864, 1. See also *Mobile Advertiser and Register*, February 7, 1865, 1 ("Judge Lynch" in Greenville, Alabama); (New Orleans) *Daily Picayune*, February 15, 1865, 1 (same).

23. Edward Norphlet Brown to Fannie Brown, March 16, 1865, Edward Norphlet Brown Letters, Alabama Department of Archives and History, Montgomery.

24. Grant Taylor to Malinda Taylor, January 11, 1865, in Blomquist and Taylor, eds., *This Cruel War*, eds. 322–23. Linden and Linden, eds., *Disunion, War, Defeat, and Recovery in Alabama*, 131.

25. Jefferson Davis to John Forsyth, February 21, 1865, Official Records, Series 1, Vol. 3, 1110; *Mobile Tribune*, reprinted in (New Orleans) *Daily Picayune*, January 18, 1865, 1; *Mobile Advertiser and Register*, February 19, 1865, 1; *Fremont* (Ohio) *Journal*, February 24, 1865, 4; *Edgefield* (South Carolina) *Advertiser*, March 8, 1865, 3; Clampitt, *Confederate Heartland*, 141–47. Governor Watts, however, never changed his mind. *Montgomery Daily Advertiser*, March 3, 1865, 1.

26. *Mobile Advertiser and Register*, January 20, 1865, 2, January 21, 1865, 1; (Greensboro) *Alabama Beacon*, March 31, 1865, 1; *Richmond Enquirer*, January 12, 1865, reprinted in *New York Daily Tribune*, January 16, 1865, 1; *Edgefield Advertiser*, February 8, 1865, 2; (Richmond) *Daily Dispatch*, February 20, 1865, 1, February 21, 1865, 1. See also, (Richmond) *Daily Dispatch*, February 24, 1865, 1 (publishing Lee's second letter on this topic), February 27, 1865, 1.

27. Civil War Diary of Samuel Pickens, 186, in Hubbs, ed., *Voices from Company D*, 355.

28. *Mobile Advertiser and Register*, reprinted in (Richmond) *Daily Dispatch*, February 8, 1865, 2; *Cleveland Morning Leader*, February 13, 1865, 1; *Nashville Daily Union*, February 26, 1865, 1.

29. *Mobile Advertiser and Register*, reprinted in (New Orleans) *Daily Picayune*, January 21, 1865, 1.

30. *New York World*, reprinted in *Holmes County* (Ohio) *Farmer*, February 9, 1864, 2.

31. *Richmond Daily Dispatch*, February 9, 1865, 3; *Cleveland Morning Leader*, March 2, 1865, 3.

32. (New Orleans) *Daily Picayune*, March 21, 1865, 1. See also, (New Orleans) *Daily Picayune*, March 19, 1865, 1, March 24, 1865, 1.

33. *Nashville Daily Union*, February 17, 1865, 2.

34. *Nashville Daily Press*, February 7, 1865, 1. See, generally, (Richmond) *Daily Dispatch*, February 9, 1865, 3, February 20, 1865, 1 (advocating passage of the legislation), February 21, 1865, 1 (same).

35. *Mobile Advertiser and Register*, March 29, 1865, 2.

36. *Selma Dispatch*, reprinted in (Montgomery) *Memphis Appeal*, March 6, 1865, 1.

37. General Order, No. 14, Official Records, Series 4, Vol. 3, 1161–62. See also (New Orleans) *Daily Picayune*, March 24, 1865, 1; *Cleveland Morning Leader*, March 2, 1865, 3 (Alabama senator Richard Wilde Walker had been a supporter of the bill); *New York Tribune*, March 13, 1865, 1; Woodward, *Marching Masters*, 155–76.

38. *Cleveland Morning Leader*, March 13, 1865, 2.

39. (Philadelphia) *North American*, reprinted in *Mobile Advertiser and Register*, October 21, 1865, 1.

40. Elizabeth Avery Meriwether, *Recollections of 92 Years, 1824–1916* (Nashville: Tennessee Historical Commission, 1958), 113.

41. *Mobile Daily Tribune*, November 25, 1864, 2. See also, Graf, et al., ed., *Papers of Andrew Johnson*, 7: 281–82 (this speech occurred on November 12, 1864).

42. See also, *Mobile Advertiser and Register*, November 9, 1864, 1–2 (publishing information regarding the fate of the "first negro soldiers ever captured by the Army of Tennessee").

43. See, generally, Clarence L. Mohr, *On the Threshold of Freedom: Masters and Slaves in Civil War Georgia* (Baton Rouge: Louisiana State University Press, 2001); Andrew Ward, *Slaves' War: The Civil War in the Words of Former Slaves* (Boston: Mariner Books, 2008).

44. "Yet, if God wills that it continue until all the wealth piled by the bondsman's two hundred and fifty years of unrequited toil shall be sunk, and until every drop of blood drawn with the lash shall be paid by another drawn with the sword, as was said three thousand years ago, so still it must be said 'the judgments of the Lord are true and righteous altogether.'" *Mobile Advertiser and Register*, March 19, 1865, 2.

45. Ben Ames Williams, ed., *A Diary from Dixie* (Cambridge, MA: Harvard University Press, 2002), 456.

46. *Mobile Advertiser and Register*, March 16, 1865, 2 ("He would hunger for the flesh pots of Egypt very soon."); *Richmond Examiner*, reprinted in *Nashville Daily Times and True Union*, March 30, 1865, 2 (reporting that at camps in Virginia, "guards are posted at every avenue of escape" and "the colored soldiers are kept under strict surveillance," but "many get away in spite of all precaution"). Even if successful in obtaining committed and loyal soldiers, the fact that the Confederacy would now undermine its food supply by taking the slaves out of the fields and putting them into military camps certainly did not concern the North. As President Lincoln quipped in a widely reported public speech to a very animated audience, "I do know [slaves] cannot fight and stay at home and make bread too [Laughter and applause]. And as one is about an important as the other, then I do not care which they do. [Renewed applause.]" *Nashville Daily Union*, March 24, 1865, 4; (New Orleans) *Daily Picayune*,

March 30, 1865, pl. 1; *Cleveland Morning Leader*, March 23, 1865, 2; *Burlington* (Vermont) *Free Press*, March 24, 1865, 4.

47. *Mobile Advertiser and Register*, March 15, 1865, 2.

48. *Mobile Advertiser and Register*, March 15, 1865, 2.

49. McCurry, *Confederate Reckoning*, 350–57; Woodward, *Marching Masters*, 176–79.

50. *Montgomery Daily Mail*, April 8, 1865, 2; John Witherspoon DuBose, *General Joseph Wheeler and the Army of Tennessee* (La Crosse, WI: Brookhaven Press, 2005), 258 (stating that Morgan was put in charge of a training camp in the "canebrake region of Alabama"); Fry, *John Tyler Morgan and the Search for Southern Autonomy*, 22.

51. *Cf.*, Woodward, *Marching Masters*, 177 (suggesting that those who trained black recruits did so to avoid battle); Edward Norphlet Brown to Fannie Brown, March 16, 1865, Edward Norphlet Brown, Alabama Department of Archives and History, Montgomery, Alabama (Brown, who was "bitter opposed" to the arming of slaves but who also feared being "ordered into the ranks," wrote to his wife that "I have a notion . . . of making application for authority to raise a negro Regt.").

52. *Cleveland Morning Leader*, March 29, 1865, 2. Woodward, *Marching Masters*, 177–79.

Chapter 24

1. Fleming, *Civil War and Reconstruction*, 146; (New Orleans) *Daily Picayune*, February 6, 1865, 2; *Chicago Tribune*, reprinted in (Philadelphia) *North American and United States Gazette*, February 10, 1865; *New York Times*, February 10, 1865, 4; *Chicago Journal*, reprinted in *Milwaukee Daily Sentinel*, February 8, 1865; (New Orleans) *Daily Picayune*, February 16, 1865, 2; *Huntsville Advocate*, June 13, 1866, 2, June 27, 1866, 2; *Chicago Journal*, reprinted in *Weekly Perrysburg* (Ohio) *Journal*, February 1, 1865, 2; *Cleveland Morning Leader*, January 12, 1865, 2; *Chicago Tribune*, reprinted in (Philadelphia) *North American and United States Gazette*, February 10, 1865.

2. *Montgomery Daily Advertiser*, February 22, 1865, 2.

3. *Montgomery Daily Advertiser*, March 3, 1865, 1.

4. *Montgomery Daily Advertiser*, March 3, 1865, 1.

5. *Montgomery Daily Advertiser*, March 3, 1865, 1. See also, (New Orleans) *Daily Picayune*, March 25, 1865, 3; *Mobile Advertiser and Register*, February 28, 1865, 1, March 1, 1865, 1, March 3, 1865, 1, March 14, 1865, 1; (New Orleans) *Daily Picayune*, March 25, 1865, 3. See, generally, Rogers, *Confederate Home Front*, 137; McMillan, *Disintegration of a Confederate State*, 120.

6. *New York Herald*, April. 3, 1865, 4.

7. Since the first of the year, Watts had privately told everyone requesting protection from Yankee and Tory raids that he had no troops to provide. T. H. Watts to S. P. Wood and John V. Sutherlin, January 18, 1865, to Stephen McBrown, February 2, 1865, to Gen. Richard Taylor, March 6, 1865, Papers of Governor Watts, Alabama Department of Archives and History, Montgomery, Alabama.

8. *Montgomery Daily Advertiser*, March 28, 1865; Keenan, *Wilson's Cavalry Corps*,

152; James P. Jones, *Yankee Blitzkrieg: Wilson's Raid through Alabama and Georgia* (Lexington: University of Kentucky Press, 2000), 13, 27–9; Charles A. Misulia, *Columbus, Georgia, 1865: The Last True Battle of the Civil War* (Tuscaloosa: University of Alabama Press, 2010), 13; Thomas Crofts, *History of the Service of the Third Ohio Veteran Volunteer Cavalry in the War for the Preservation of the Union from 1861–1865* (Toledo, Ohio: Blue Acorn Press, 1910), 188; Benjamin F. McGee, *History of the 72d Indiana Volunteer Infantry of the Mounted Lightning Brigade* (Lafayette, IN: S. Vater & Co., 1882), 519–27. See also *Nashville Daily Times and True Union*, March 31, 1865, 1; *New York Times*, April 4, 1865, 9; (Washington, DC) *National Tribune*, June 18, 1903, 3; *Hawkins v. Nelson*, 40 Ala. 553 (1867) (a case involving a horse "liberated" by Wilson's forces in Walker County).

9. Keenan, *Wilson's Cavalry Corps*, 162.

10. John T. Croxton to Maj. John M. Bacon, May 1865, Official Records, Series 1, Vol. 49 (Part I), 418–19 (hereinafter "Croxton's Report"); Rex Miller, *Croxton's Raid* (Depew, N.Y.: Patrex Press, 1992), 29; Jones, *Yankee Blitzkrieg*, 59–60. See also William Forse Scott, *The Story of a Cavalry Regiment: The Career of the Fourth Iowa Veteran Volunteers from Kansas to Georgia, 1861–1865* (New York: G. P. Putnam and Sons, 1892), 434, 515; Richard R. Hancock, *Hancock's Diary: A History of the Second Tennessee Confederate Cavalry* (Nashville, TN: Brandon Printing Co., 1887), 550; Iowa Adjutant General's Office, *Roster and Record of Iowa Soldiers in Miscellaneous Organizations of the Mexican War, Indian Campaigns, War of the Rebellion, and the Spanish-American and Philippine Wars: Together With Historical Sketches of Volunteer Organizations, 1861–1866* (Des Moines: E. H. English, State Printer, E. D. Chassell, State Binder, 1910) 4: 1518; Thomas C. McCorvey, "Southern Cadets in Action," *Century Magazine* XXXIX (November, 1889): 152–53; James Harrison Wilson, *Recollections of Military Operations in the War For the Union, the Spanish War, the Boxer Rebellion, etc.* (New York: D. Appleton and Company, 1912). 2: 205.

11. On his way from Elyton, Croxton had skirmished with Red Jackson's much larger force near what is now Vance on the morning of April 1 before turning back and moving north toward the Black Warrior River. Official Records, Series 1, Vol. 49 (Part 1) ("Croxton's Report"), 420–21; (Greensboro) *Alabama Beacon*, April 5, 1865, 2. See also Waldon Spicer Loving, *Coming Like Hell: The Story of the 12th Tennessee Cavalry, Richardson's Brigade, Forrest's Cavalry Corps, Confederate States Army, 1862–1865* (San Jose, CA: Writers Club Press, 2002), 138–39; Hubbs, *Tuscaloosa*, 43–44; Hancock, *Hancock's Diary*, 550–51; Iowa Adjutant General's Office, *Roster and Record of Iowa Soldiers during the War of the Rebellion*, 1518–19; Miller, *Croxton's Raid*, 32–33; Jones, *Yankee Blitzkrieg*, 60–62, 145–46; Keenan, *Wilson's Cavalry Corps*, 204–6. Croxton's later report indicates that rather than chancing another advance on Tuscaloosa from the south side of the Black Warrior River, he improvised a plan that called for his force to cross the river at a ferry approximately forty miles east of Tuscaloosa, move west, and then attempt to recross the river at Northport. Croxton's Report, 121. See also Hubbs, *Tuscaloosa*, 44; Miller, *Croxton's Raid*, 33; Keenan, *Wilson's Cavalry Corps*, 206; Loving, *Coming Like Hell*, 138. However, he had no bridging equipment or pon-

toons, and at this time of year, the river was swollen with spring rains and therefore treacherous. According to a letter from one of Croxton's troopers describing the first crossing, the water was "unfordable" but the ferry flat boat was apparently operational. The craft was so small that it was relegated to transporting the equipment, while the men and horses were forced to swim across. Charles Wooster to "Brother John," June 25, 1865, *Alabama Historical Quarterly* 64 (Fall 1982), 109, 113; Croxton's Report, 421. See also Iowa Adjutant General's Office, *Roster and Record of Iowa Soldiers*, 1519. In the process, several men and horses drowned. Miller, *Croxton's Raid*, 35; Jones, *Yankee Blitzkrieg*, 145–47; Croxton's Report, 421. Significantly, this crossing was accomplished without resistance from their enemy. Croxton and his men certainly must have hoped this would be the case when they attempted to recross the river at Northport.

12. (Washington, DC) *National Tribune*, April 23, 1891, 1; Croxton's Report, 421. See also Hubbs, *Tuscaloosa*, 44; Charles Wooster to "Brother John," June 25, 1865, 114; Miller, *Croxton's Raid*, 37–39; Jones, *Yankee Blitzkrieg*, 147–49; Keenan, *Wilson's Cavalry Corps*, 206; John S. Lupold and Thomas L. French Jr., *Bridging Deep South Rivers: The Life and Legend of Horace King* (Athens: University of Georgia Press, 2004): 206–7; McCorvey, "Southern Cadets in Action," 152.

13. Miller, *Croxton's Raid*, 37; Jones, *Yankee Blitzkrieg*, 148.

14. *Croxton's Report*, 421. See also Hubbs, *Tuscaloosa*, 44–45; Miller, *Croxton's Raid*, 38–39, 42–44, 46; Jones, *Yankee Blitzkrieg*, 148–50; Keenan, *Wilson's Cavalry Corps*, 206; McCorvey, "Southern Cadets in Action," 152; Sellers, *History of the University of Alabama*, 283–85; Owen, *History of Alabama and Dictionary of Alabama Biography*, 2: 1363; *Montgomery Advertiser*, March 21, 1905, 10, May 5, 1907, 7.

15. Miller, *Croxton's Raid*, 38; Jones, *Yankee Blitzkrieg*, 150–51.

16. Miller, *Croxton's Raid*, 51; Keenan, *Wilson's Cavalry Corps*, 206.

17. Hubbs, *Tuscaloosa*, 45; Sellers, *History of the University of Alabama*, 275, 285–87; Miller, *Croxton's Raid*, 46–49; Jones, *Yankee Blitzkrieg*, 151; Clark E. Center Jr., "The Burning of the University of Alabama," *Alabama Heritage* 16 (Spring, 1990): 30; Robert O. Mellown and Gene Byrd, "F.A.P. Barnard and Alabama's First Observatory," *Journal of Alabama Academy of Science* 57 (January, 1986): 39.

18. *Mobile Advertiser and Register*, April 9, 1865, 2.

19. (Greensboro) *Alabama Beacon*, April 5, 1865, 2; Miller, *Croxton's Raid*, 53–54; Jones, *Yankee Blitzkrieg*, 153; Keenan, *Wilson's Cavalry Corps*, 207 (also noting that the Pickens County courthouse at Carrollton was later burned by Wilson's men); Lupold and French, *Bridging Deep South Rivers*, 207–8 (the bridge was later rebuilt by the famous black bridge builder, Horace King). See also Scott W. Owens, "The Federal Invasion of Pickens County, April, 1865: Croxton's Sipsey River Campaign," *Alabama Review* 62 (April, 2009), 83 (discussing the activities of Croxton's raiders after they left Tuscaloosa). The destruction of the bridge later spawned litigation that reached the Alabama Supreme Court. See *Tuskaloosa Bridge Co. v. Olmstead*, 41 Ala. 9 (1867); Jackson, "Life and Times of Robert Jemison, Jr.," 135–36. See also Robert K. Bell, "Reconstruction in Tuscaloosa County" (Master's thesis, University of Alabama,

1933), 8. Similarly, the destruction of the library at the University of Alabama and the postwar efforts to restore it—which included the establishment of a lottery—also reached the Court after the war. See *Broadbent v. Tuskaloosa Scientific and Art Association*, 45 Ala. 170 (1871) and *Tuskaloosa Scientific and Art Association v. Green*, 48 Ala. 346 (1872).

20. Miller, *Croxton's Raid*, 54; Jones, *Yankee Blitzkrieg*, 153.

21. (Washington, DC) *National Tribune*, April 23, 1891, 1.

22. (Selma) *Chattanooga Rebel*, April 1, 1865, reprinted in *Mobile Advertiser and Register*, April 5, 1865, 2; *Columbia* (South Carolina) *Phoenix*, April 8, 1865, 6; (Greensboro) *Alabama Beacon*, April 5, 1865, 2; *Mobile Advertiser and Register*, April 5, 1865, 2. See also Wilson, *Under the Old Flag*, 2: 207–25; Hurst, *Nathan Bedford Forrest*, 249–50; Parrish, *Richard Taylor*, 433–34; Fitts, *Selma*, 55–57; Jones, *Yankee Blitzkrieg*, 63–83; Keenan, *Wilson's Cavalry Corps*, 165–169; J.H. Wilson to Brig. Gen. William D. Whipple, May 3, 1865, Official Records, Series 1, Vol. 49 (Part I), 350–51 (hereinafter "Wilson's Report"); McKenzie, "Reconstruction of the Alabama Iron Industry," 180–81.

23. Saunders, *Early Settlers of Alabama*, 76.

24. Jones, *Yankee Blitzkrieg*, 81. See, generally, *Meridian* (Mississippi) *Clarion*, reprinted in *Mobile Advertiser and Register*, April 5, 1865, 2.

25. Jones, *Yankee Blitzkrieg*, 82; Hurst, *Nathan Bedford Forrest*, 250; Jackson, *Story of Selma*, 215.

26. *New York Herald*, April 22, 1865, 8; J. H. Wilson to Brig. Gen. William D. Whipple, June 29, 1865, Official Records, Series 1, Vol. 49 (Part I), 360–61; Jones, *Yankee Blitzkrieg*, 79–80.

27. (Mobile) *Army Argus and Crisis*, April 8, 1865, 4. See also Jones, *Yankee Blitzkrieg*, 82; Fitts, *Selma*, 58; Jackson, *Story of Selma*, 215–16.

28. *Selma Union*, reprinted in (New Orleans) *Daily Picayune*, April 23, 1865, 3; Fitts, *Selma*, 57–58; Keenan, *Wilson's Cavalry Corps*, 169; Parrish, *Richard Taylor*, 435; Jackson, *Story of Selma*, 216.

29. Hancock, *Hancock's Diary*, 558. See also Wills, *A Battle from the Start*, 310.

30. *Macon Daily Telegraph and Confederate*, April 6, 1865, 2; (Columbia) *South Carolina Phoenix*, April 10, 1865, 3; *Columbus* (Georgia) *Sun*, April 5, 1865, reprinted in *Edgefield* (South Carolina) *Advertiser*, April 12, 1865, 1. See also (Mobile) *Army Argus and Crisis*, April 8, 1865, 1; *Meridian* (Mississippi) *Clarion*, reprinted in *Mobile Advertiser and Register*, April 5, 1865, 2; *Mobile Advertiser and Register*, April 19, 1865, 2; (New Orleans) *Daily Picayune*, April 23, 1865, 3; Jones, *Yankee Blitzkrieg*, 83–91; Hurst, *Nathan Bedford Forrest*, 251; Fitts, *Selma*, 58–59; Keenan, *Wilson's Cavalry Corps*, 171–72; Jackson, *Story of Selma*, 216; Parrish, *Richard Taylor*, 435.

31. *Macon* (Georgia) Telegraph, May 28, 1865, 2; New *York Herald*, April 22, 1865, 8; *Selma Union*, reprinted in (New Orleans) *Daily Picayune*, April 23, 1865, 2 and *New Orleans Times*, April 25, 1865, 7; *Mobile Daily News*, July 13, 1865, 4; Hurst, *Nathan Bedford Forrest*, 251; William Stanley Hoole, ed., *History of Shockley's Alabama Escort Company* (Tuscaloosa, AL: Confederate Pub. Co., 1983), 11; Elbridge Colby, "Wilson's Cavalry Campaign of 1865," II *Journal of the American Military History Founda-*

tion (1928), 211. For a list of casualties among the defenders, see *Montgomery Daily Mail*, April 21, 1865.

32. *New York Herald*, April 13, 1865, 1; (Washington, DC) *Daily National Intelligencer*, April 13, 1865; *New Haven Daily Palladium*, April 12, 1865; *Cleveland Morning Leader*, April 14, 1865, 2.

33. *Louisville* (KY) *Daily Journal*, April 30, 1865, 1; *Columbia* (South Carolina) *Phoenix*, April 10, 1865, 3; *New York Herald*, April 13, 1865, 1; *Boston Herald*, April 24, 1865, 4; Jones, *Yankee Blitzkrieg*, 90; Hurst, *Nathan Bedford Forrest*, 251–53; Jackson, *Story of Selma*, 218; Wilson's Report, 351.

34. Wilson's Report, 351; *Montgomery Mail*, April 7, 1865, reprinted in (Augusta) *Daily Constitutionalist*, April 12, 1865, 1.

35. *Montgomery Advertiser*, reprinted in (Troy) *Southern Advertiser*, April 28, 1865, 2; *Edgefield* (South Carolina) *Advertiser*, April 19, 1865, 4 (citing the comments of a woman who escaped Selma); (Selma) *Chattanooga Rebel*, April 14, 1865, reprinted in (Greensboro) *Alabama Beacon*, April 21, 1865, 2; *Mobile Advertiser and Register*, April 9, 1865, 2; *Columbia* (South Carolina) *Phoenix*, April 10, 1865, o. 3. See also Jones, *Yankee Blitzkrieg*, 92–95; Keenan, *Wilson's Cavalry Corps*, 172–73; Fitts, *Selma*, 59; *Milwaukee Daily Sentinel*, April 11, 1865, April 15, 1865; (New Orleans) *Daily Picayune*, April 23, 1865, 3; *Mobile Daily News*, May 5, 1865, 1. During this wild melee, a slave was shot and killed by a prominent Selman, Fielding Vaughan, Jackson, *Story of Selma*, 10, 13, 14, 164 (mentioning Vaughan), for which Vaughan was indicted for murder after the war. Vaughan later applied to the Alabama Supreme Court for bail, but in an opinion by Benjamin Saffold the application was denied. *Ex parte Vaughan*, 44 Ala. 417 (1870). Perhaps responding to one of Vaughan's legal arguments, Saffold made it clear that wartime did not justify homicide. He opined that "we would be loth to hold that there had been any time, in the history of the State, when the crime of murder was not amenable to the civil law." *Id*, 418.

36. *Jackson* (Mississippi) *News*, reprinted in *Houston* (Texas) *Tri-Weekly*, May 1, 1865, 4; Edgefield (South Carolina) *Advertiser*, April 12, 1865, 1, April 19, 1865, 4 (citing the contents of a letter); (Selma) *Messenger*, reprinted in *Cincinnati Enquirer*, July 27, 1865, 1. See, generally, Jones, *Yankee Blitzkrieg*, 90–95; Fitts, *Selma*, 59–60; Keenan, *Wilson's Cavalry Corps*, 172–73.

37. *Montgomery Daily Mail*, April 6, 1865, reprinted in *Anderson* (South Carolina) *Intelligencer*, April 20, 1865, 1; *Jackson* (Miss.) *News*, reprinted in *Mobile Advertiser and Register*, April 9, 1865, 2; *Chattanooga* (Selma) *Rebel*, April 15, 1865, reprinted in *Montgomery Daily Mail*, April 21, 1865, 1; *Jackson* (Miss.) *News*, April 14, 1865, reprinted in (New Orleans) *Daily Picayune*, April 23, 1865, 3; *New York Herald*, reprinted in *Daily Cleveland Herald*, April 24, 1865; *Cincinnati Commercial*, reprinted in *Boston Herald*, April 24, 1865, 4; *Montgomery Daily Advertiser*, April 21, 1865, 2; *Mobile Daily News*, May 5, 1865, 1; (Selma) *Chattanooga Rebel*, April 14, 1865, reprinted in (Greensboro) *Alabama Beacon*, April 21, 1865, 8; (New Orleans) *Daily Picayune*, April 23, 1865, 3; *Columbia* (South Carolina) *Phoenix*, April 10, 1865, 3; *Milwaukee Daily Sentinel*, April 11, 1865, April 15, 1865; (Augusta) *Daily Constitutionalist*, April 26, 1865, 3; Jones, *Yankee Blitzkrieg*, 95–100; Keenan, *Wilson's Cavalry Corps*, 175–76; Fitts, *Selma*, 60; Wilson's

Report, 351; John Hardy, *Selma: Her Institutions, and Her Men* (Selma, AL: Bert Neville and Clarence DeBray, 1957). 51–53.

38. (Mobile) *Army Argus and Crisis*, April 8, 1865, 1. See also *Mobile Advertiser and Register*, April 5, 1865, 2; Wills, *Battle from the Start*, 310–12.

39. *Montgomery Daily Mail*, April 9, 1865, 1.

40. *Montgomery Daily Mail*, April 11, 1865, April 18, 1865, 2. See also *Columbus* (Georgia) *Sun*, April 6, 1865, reprinted in *Anderson* (South Carolina) *Intelligencer*, April 20, 1865, 1; *Augusta Chronicle*, April 11, 1865, 2; (Augusta) *Daily Constitutionalist*, April 12, 1865, 1.

41. *Montgomery Daily Advertiser*, April 18, 1865, 2.

42. Rogers, *Confederate Home Front*, 145–47; *Columbus Times*, reprinted in (Troy) *Southern Advertiser*, April 21, 1865, 2; *Columbus* (Georgia) *Sun*, April 5, 1865, reprinted in *Edgefield* (South Carolina) *Advertiser*, April 12, 1865, 1; *Columbus* (Georgia) *Sun*, April 12, 1865, reprinted in *Edgefield* (South Carolina) *Advertiser*, April 19, 1865, 1; (Augusta, Georgia) *Daily Chronicle & Sentinel*, April 16, 1865; *Montgomery Daily Advertiser*, April 18, 1865, 2; *Mobile Daily News*, May 4, 1865, 1; *New York Herald*, May 15, 1865, 1, reprinted in *Boston Herald*, May 17, 1865, 5; *Nashville Daily Press*, April 25, 1865, 1; *New York Herald*, reprinted in *Cleveland Leader*, May 16, 1865, 1 ("Fortunately the wind was from the east, and blew the flames away from the City.").

43. *New York Herald*, reprinted in *Cleveland Leader*, May 16, 1865, 1.

44. *Montgomery Daily Advertiser*, April 18, 1865, 2. See also *New York Herald*, May 15, 1865, 1, reprinted in *Boston Herald*, May 17, 1865, 5. See, generally, Rogers, *Confederate Home Front*, 145–47.

45. *Montgomery Daily Advertiser*, April 18, 1865, 2. The delegation included Coleman, Milton Saffold, Saffold's brother-in-law (Dr. James Berney), businessman Josiah Morris and others.

46. Rogers, *Confederate Home Front*, 147; Jones, *Yankee Blitzkrieg*, 111–12; McMillan, ed., *Alabama Confederate Reader*, 420–21; Wilson's Report, 352.

47. *New York Herald*, May 15, 1865, 1, reprinted in *Boston Herald*, May 17, 1865, 5, and *Milwaukee Daily Sentinel*, May 19, 1865.

48. See also, (Selma) *Chattanooga Rebel*, April 15, 1865, reprinted in *Montgomery Daily Mail*, April 21, 1865, 1; *Philadelphia Press*, April 13, 1865, 2, April 18, 1865, 2, April 28, 1865, 2, May 5, 1865, 2.

49. Jones, ed., "Journal of Sarah G. Follansbee," 232.

50. *Montgomery Daily Advertiser*, April 18, 1865, 3. See also McMillan, *Disintegration of a Confederate State*, 119–20; Keenan, *Wilson's Cavalry Corps*, 182; Jones, *Yankee Blitzkrieg*, 111.

51. Bergeron, *Confederate Mobile*, 173–92; Terrance J. Winschel, ed., *The Civil War Diary of a Common Soldier: William Wiley of the 77th Illinois Infantry* (Baton Rouge: Louisiana State University Press, 2001), 143–54.

52. *Memphis Bulletin*, March 28, 1865, reprinted in (Washington, DC) *Daily National Republican*, April 7, 1865.

53. See, e.g., *Brownlow's Knoxville Whig and Rebel Ventilator*, March 15, 1865, 2 (Union spy executed); *Fremont Journal*, February 10, 1865, 4, February 24, 1865, 2

(Confederate spy disguised as woman); *Nashville Daily Union*, February 2, 1865, 3 (Confederate spy to be hung), February 15, 1865, 3 (same); *Cleveland Morning Leader*, January 24, 1865, 4 (the wife of a Union spy killed by "bushwhackers" also became a spy for the Union); (Richmond) *Daily Dispatch*, February 20, 1865, 2 (Confederate spy to be hung), February 28, 1865, 2 (same), March 1, 1865, 2 (describing the hanging of a Confederate spy in New York). See, generally, Lisa Tendrich Frank, *Women in the Civil War* (Santa Barbara, Cal.: ABC-CLIO, 2008), 29–35.

54. *Mobile News*, March 21, 1865, reprinted in *Montgomery Advertiser*, March 28, 1865, reprinted in *Mobile Advertiser and Register*, April 5, 1865, 1; *Nashville Daily Press*, April 13, 1865, 1; George F. Pearce, *Pensacola During the Civil War: A Thorn in the Side of the Confederacy* (Gainesville: University Press of Florida, 2000). 225–27; Bergeron, *Confederate Mobile*, 174.

55. *Mobile Advertiser and Register*, March 26, 1865, 1, March 28, 1865, 1, March 29, 1865, 2; *Montgomery Advertiser*, March 28, 1865, reprinted in *Mobile Advertiser and Register*, April 5, 1865, 1; *Richmond Whig*, reprinted in *New York Daily Tribune*, April 3, 1865, 4; (Columbia) *Daily South Carolinian*, March 31, 1865.

56. Pearce, *Pensacola During the Civil War*, 225–27; *St. Louis Dispatch*, reprinted in *Mobile Daily Register*, October 29, 1871, 3; *Nashville Daily Press*, April 13, 1865, 1; *Mobile Evening News*, March 21, 1865, reprinted in (New Orleans) *Daily Picayune*, April 1, 1865, 1; *Chicago Tribune*, reprinted in *Cleveland Morning Leader*, April 11, 1865, 2.

57. (Mobile) *Army Argus and Crisis*, March 25, 1865, 1. At this time, according to an eyewitness, there was "constant alarm in the city" and desertions were "numerous." (Washington, DC) *Daily National Republican*, April 7, 1865, 2.

58. Hearn, *Mobile Bay and the Mobile Campaign*, 151–53; *Montgomery Advertiser*, March 28, 1865, reprinted in *Mobile Advertiser and Register*, April 5, 1865, 1; *Mobile Advertiser and Register*, April 1, 1865, 1.

59. *Daily Columbus* (Georgia) *Enquirer*, reprinted in *Montgomery Daily Mail*, April 11, 1865.

60. *Nashville Daily Press*, April 13, 1865, 1; *Columbia* (South Carolina) *Phoenix*, April 6, 1865, 1. See, generally, Davidson, *Word from Camp Pollard*, 281.

61. *Montgomery Daily Mail*, April 11, 1865. See also *Nashville Daily Press*, April 13, 1865, 1; (Mobile) *Army Argus and Crisis*, April 1, 1865, 1; *Mobile Advertiser and Register*, March 25, 1865, 1, March 26, 1865, 2, April 1, 1865, 1; (New Orleans) *Daily Picayune*, April 4, 1865, 4.

62. Burkhardt, *Confederate Rage, Yankee Wrath*, 237–38.

63. (Mobile) *Army Argus and Crisis*, April 1, 1865, 1, April 8, 1865, 1; *Milwaukee Daily Sentinel*, April 14, 1865; *Charleston Courier*, April 20, 1865, 1; Bergeron, *Confederate Mobile*, 176–83; O'Brien, *Mobile, 1865*, 173–82.

64. *Mobile Advertiser and Register*, April 5, 1865, 2.

65. Bergeron, *Confederate Mobile*, 182–87; O'Brien, *Mobile, 1865*, 185–200; Stoker, *Grand Design*, 401.

66. Burkhardt, *Confederate Rage*, 237–39; Michael W. Fitzgerald, "Another Kind of Glory: Black Participation and Its Consequences in the Campaign for Confederate Mobile," *Alabama Review* 54 (October 2001): 243, 256–61; Michael W. Fitzgerald,

Urban Emancipation: Popular Politics in Reconstruction Mobile, 1860–1890 (Baton Rouge: LSU Press, 2002), 25; Richard A. Baumgartner, ed., *Blood & Sacrifice: The Civil War Journal of a Confederate Soldier* (Huntington, WV: Blue Acorn Press, 1994), 218. See, generally, *Mobile Daily News*, June 5, 1865, 4; *Urbana* (Ohio) *Union*, April 19, 1865, 2.

67. Winschel, ed., *Civil War Diary of a Common Soldier*, 150–51.

68. *New York Times*, April 24, 1865, 1; *Mobile Daily News*, April 13, 1865; (Washington, DC) *Daily National Intelligencer*, April 19, 1865, April 27, 1865; *Montgomery Daily Advertiser*, April 22, 1865, 2; *Cleveland Morning Leader*, April 27, 1865, 1 (publishing the mayor's letter); *Charleston Courier*, April 27, 1865, 1; (Washington, DC) *Daily National Republican*, May 1, 1865, 2; Bergeron, *Confederate Mobile*, 188–91; O'Brien, *Mobile, 1865*, 209–13.

69. (Washington, DC) *Daily National Republican*, April 7, 1865, 2.

70. *Charleston Courier*, April 27, 1865, 1; *Shreveport News*, May 2, 1865, 2.

71. *Mobile Daily News*, April 13, 1865, reprinted in *New York Tribune*, May 2, 1865, 7.

72. Mary Douglas Waring Diary, 30–31, Alabama Department of Archives and History, Montgomery.

73. J. David Hacker, "A Census-Based Count of the Civil War Dead," *Civil War History* 57 (December, 2011): 307–48.

74. *Clayton Banner*, reprinted in (Troy) *Southern Advertiser*, April 28, 1865, 2.

Chapter 25

1. Jefferson Davis to Rev. J. William Jones, May 15, 1877, in *Jefferson Davis: The Essential Writings*, ed. William J. Cooper Jr., 417–18.

2. McWhiney, More, and Pace, eds., "*Fear God and Walk Humbly,*" 343.

3. *Nashville Daily Union*, July 30, 1865, 2.

4. *Inaugural Address of Robert M. Patton, Governor of Alabama* (Montgomery, AL: Reid & Screws, State Printers, 1865).

5. Noe, *Reluctant Rebels*, 210. Fleming, *Civil War and Reconstruction in* Alabama, 251–61.

6. Sarah Woolfolk Wiggins, "Alabama's Reconstruction after 150 Years," in Noe, ed., *Yellowhammer War*, ed. Kenneth W. Noe, 177–86.

7. Harriet E. Amos Doss, "Every Man Should Consider His Own Conscience: Black and White Alabamians' Reactions to the Assassination of Abraham Lincoln, 1865–1867," in *Yellowhammer War*, ed. Kenneth W. Noe, 165–76.

8. Jason J. Battles, "Labor, Law, and the Freedmen's Bureau in Alabama, 1865–1867," in *Yellowhammer War*, ed. Kenneth W. Noe, 240–57.

Bibliography

Primary Sources

Unpublished

Alabama Department of Archives and History

Joseph Dill Alison Diary
Eliza Frances Andrews Diary
Charles Jacob Armstrong Diary
Hurieosco Austill Diary
Alpheus Baker Diary
Zillah Haynie Brandon Diary
Edward Norphlet Brown Letters
John Joel Chappell Diary
Edward Crenshaw Diary
Sarah Lowe Davis Diary
Sarah R. Espy Journal
Thomas L. Faulkner Diary
James Finch Diary
John Jefferson Flowers Diary
Margaret Josephine Miles Gillis Diary
William Proctor Gould Diary
Francis R. Hanson Diary
Hilary Abner Herbert, Grandfather Talks about His Life under Two Flags: Reminiscences
James G. Hudson Diary
Daniel Robinson Hundley Diary
John Washington Inzer Diary
James B. Irvine Diary
A. M. Jordan Diary
William Lowery Diary
Charles L. Lumsden Diary
James H. McMath Journal

Andrew Barry Moore Papers
Daily Journal of Joshua Burns Moore
Papers of Governor Lewis J. Parsons
Robert Miller Patton Papers
Sally Randall Perry Diary
C. A. Ryder Diary
James Thomas Searcy Papers
Stephen Vaughn Shipman Diary
John Gill Shorter Papers
James Osgood Story Diary
Robert Branch Tarpley Diary
John S. Tucker Diary
Paul Turner Vaughn Diary
Mary D. Waring Diary
Leroy Pope Walker Papers
Thomas Hill Watts Papers
E. D. Willett Diary
Henry Felix Wilson Diary

Archives and Special Collections, Collier Library, University of North Alabama

Sally Independence Foster Diary

Auburn University Library of Special Collections and Archives

Elizabeth Rhodes Diary

David M. Rubenstein Rare Book and Manuscript Library, Duke University

C. C. Clay Jr. Papers

Hoole Special Collections Library, University of Alabama

Robert Jemison Jr. Papers
Basil Manly Papers

Huntsville-Madison County Public Library

Daniel Coleman Diary
Catherine M. Fennell Diary
James Montgomery Lanning Diary

Library of Congress, Washington, DC

Lincoln Papers

National Archives and Records Administration Washington, DC

Records of the Southern Claims Commission, Denied Claims
Attorney General Henry Stansberry Papers

Samford University Special Collections, Birmingham, Alabama

Randolph Collection

Southern Historical Collection, Wilson Library, University of North Carolina

Thomas Bragg Diary
John Archibald Campbell Papers
John J. Crittenden Papers
Mary Elizabeth Mitchell Journal
Frances Woolfolk Wallace Diary

State Historical Society of Pennsylvania

James Buchanan Papers

University of Chicago Library

Stephen Douglas Papers

University of North Carolina at Chapel Hill

Rare Book Collection

Published

Axford, Faye Acton, ed. *The Journals of Thomas Hubbard Hobbs*. Tuscaloosa: University of Alabama Press, 1976.

Basler, Roy P., ed. *The Collected Works of Abraham Lincoln*. 2 vol.s New Brunswick, NJ: Rutgers University Press, 1953.

Baumgartner, Richard A., ed. *Blood & Sacrifice: The Civil War Journal of a Confederate Soldier*. Huntington, WV: Blue Acorn Press, 1994.

Benners, Augustus, *Journal of Augustus Benners*, in Glenn and Virginia Linden, eds. *Disunion, War, Defeat, and Recovery in Alabama: The Journal of Augustus Benners, 1850–1885*. Macon, GA: Mercer University Press, 2007.

Bird, Edgeworth and Sallie Bird. *The Granite Farm Letters: The Civil War Correspondence of Edgeworth & Sallie Bird*. John Rozier, ed. Athens: University of Georgia Press, 1988.

Blassingame, John W., and John R. McKivigan. *The Frederick Douglass Papers*. New Haven, CT: Yale University Press, 1991.

Blomquist, Ann Kicker, and Robert A. Taylor, eds. *This Cruel War: The Civil War Letters of Grant and Malinda Taylor, 1862–1865*. Macon, GA: Mercer University Press, 2000.

Blue, Ellen. "Diary of Ellen Blue," in *The Works of Matthew Blue, Montgomery's First Historian*, ed. Mary Ann Neeley. Montgomery, AL: NewSouth Books, 2010.

Brown, Kathleen S. *Family History: Kuhns—Koon—Koons—Kohn—Coon: Kith and Kin: Suber-Wedaman-Miller-Folk-Hickman-Craft-Cash*. Gordo, AL: K. S. Brown, 1990.

Brown, Norman D., ed. *One of Cleburne's Command: The Civil War Reminiscences and Diary of Captain Samuel T. Foster, Granbury's Texas Brigade, CSA*. Austin: University of Texas Press, 1980.

Campbell, John Archibald. "Papers of Hon. John A. Campbell, 1861–1865," *Southern Historical Society Papers* 4 (October, 1917), 62.

Cash, William M., and Lucy Somerville Howorth, eds. *My Dear Nellie: The Civil War Letters of William L. Nugent to Eleanor Smith Nugent.* Jackson: University Press of Mississippi, 1977.

Clemens, Jeremiah. *Tobias Wilson: A Tale of the Great Rebellion.* Philadelphia: J. B. Lippincott & Co., 1865.

Crist, Lynda Lasswell, ed., *The Papers of Jefferson Davis: 1861.* 8 Vol.s. Baton Rouge: Louisiana State University Press, 1992.

Crowson, Noel, and John V. Brogden, eds. *Bloody Banners and Barefoot Boys: "A History of the 27th Regiment Alabama Infantry CSA," The Civil War, Memoirs and Diary Entries of J.P. Cannon, M.D.* Shippensburg, PA: Burd Street Press, 1997.

Cutrer, Thomas W., ed. *Oh, What a Loansome Time I Had: The Civil War Letters of Major William Morel Moxley, Eighteenth Alabama Infantry, and Emily Beck Moxley.* Tuscaloosa: University of Alabama Press, 2002.

Fielding, Mary. "Mary Fielding's Diary," in "*To Lochaber Na Mair": Southerners View the Civil War,* ed. Faye Acton Axford. Athens, AL: Athens Publishing Company, 1986.

Folmar, John Kent, ed. *From That Terrible Field: Civil War Letters of James M. Williams, Twenty-First Alabama Infantry Volunteers.* Tuscaloosa: University of Alabama Press, 1981.

Fremantle, Arthur James Lyon. *Three Months in the Southern States: April–June, 1863.* London: Tantor Media, 1863 (2012).

Funk, Arville L. "A Hoosier Regiment in Alabama," *Alabama Historical Quarterly* 27 (Spring and Summer, 1995): 92.

Garrett, Jill K., ed. *Confederate Diary of Robert D. Smith.* Columbia, TN: Capt. James Madison Sparkman Chapter, United Daughters of the Confederacy, 1975.

Genoways, Ted, and Hugh H. Genoways. *A Perfect Picture of Hell: Eyewitness Accounts by Civil War Prisoners from the 12th Iowa.* Iowa City: University of Iowa Press, 2001.

Graf, LeRoy P., Ralph W. Haskins, and Paul H. Bergeron, eds. *The Papers of Andrew Johnson.* 16 vols. Knoxville: University of Tennessee Press, 1967–2000.

Griffith, Lucille, ed. *Yours Till Death: Civil War Letters of John W. Cotton.* Tuscaloosa: University of Alabama Press, 1951.

Hague, Parthenia. *A Blockaded Family: Life in Southern Alabama during the Civil War.* Boston: Houghton Miffin, 1988.

Hallock, Judith Lee, ed. *The Civil War Letters of Joshua K. Callaway.* Athens: University of Georgia Press, 1997.

Hancock, Richard R. *Hancock's Diary: A History of the Second Tennessee Confederate Cavalry.* Nashville, TN: Brandon Printing Co., 1887.

Harwell, Richard Barksdale, ed. *Kate: The Journal of a Confederate Nurse.* Baton Rouge: Louisiana State University Press, 1998.

Henderson, Dwight Franklin, ed. *The Private Journal of Georgiana Gholson Walker 1862–1865 with Selections from the Post-War Years, 1865–1876.* Tuscaloosa, AL: Confederate Pub. Co., 1963.

Jewett, Clayton E., ed. *Rise and Fall of the Confederacy: The Memoir of Senator Williamson S. Oldham, CSA*. Columbia: University of Missouri Press, 2006.

Jones, John Beauchamp. *A Rebel War Clerk's Diary of the Confederate States Capital*. Philadelphia: J. B. Lippincott, 1866.

Jones, Virginia K., ed. "The Journal of Sarah G. Follansbee," *Alabama Historical Quarterly* 27 (Fall and Winter, 1965), 213–39.

Kazek, Kelly. *Hidden History of Auburn*. Charleston, SC: History Press, 2011, 118–25.

Linden, Glenn, and Virginia Linden, eds., *Disunion, War, Defeat, and Recovery in Alabama: The Journal of Augustus Benners, 1850–1885* (Macon, GA: Mercer University Press, 2007), 137.

Lowe, Richard, ed. *A Texas Cavalry Officer's Civil War: The Diary and Letters of James C. Bates*. Baton Rouge: Louisiana State University Press, 1999.

Mathis, Gerald Ray, and Douglas C. Purcell. *In the Land of the Living: Wartime Letters by Confederates from the Chattahoochee Valley of Alabama and Georgia*. Troy, AL: Troy State University Press, 1981.

Maxwell, James Robert. *Autobiography of James Robert Maxwell of Tuskaloosa, Alabama*. Baltimore: Gateway Press, 1996.

McMurry, Richard M., ed. *An Uncompromising Secessionist: The Civil War of George Knox Miller, Eighth (Wade's) Confederate Cavalry*. Tuscaloosa: University of Alabama Press, 2007.

McWhiney, Grady, Warner O. Moore Jr., and Robert F. Pace, eds. "*Fear God and Walk Humbly": The Agricultural Journals of James Mallory, 1843–1877*. Tuscaloosa: University of Alabama Press, 1997.

Meriwether, Elizabeth Avery, *Recollections of 92 Years, 1824–1916*. Nashville: Tennessee Historical Commission, 1958.

Miller, John D. "An Alabama Merchant in Civil War Richmond: The Harvey Wilkerson Luttrell Letters, 1861–1865," *Alabama Review* 58 (July 2005): 200.

Palmer, Beverly Wilson, ed. *The Selected Papers of Thaddeus Stevens: April 1865–August 1868*. Pittsburgh: University of Pittsburgh Press: 1998.

Pate, James P. *When This Evil War Is Over: The Correspondence of the Francis Family*. Tuscaloosa: University of Alabama Press, 2006.

Patton, Robert Miller. *Inaugural Address of Robert M. Patton, Governor of Alabama*. Montgomery, AL: Reid and Screws, State Printers, 1865.

Peters, Thomas M. "A Cry Out of Alabama," *Littell's Living Age* 98 (January 26, 1861): 194.

Phillips, John R. "The Diary of a Union Soldier from Alabama," *Alabama Heritage* 28 (Spring 1993): 20.

Redkey, Edwin S., ed. *A Grand Army of Black Men: Letters from African American Soldiers in the Union Army, 1861–1865*. Cambridge: Cambridge University Press, 1992.

Report of the Joint Committee on Reconstruction at the First Session Thirty-Ninth Congress (Washington, DC: Government Printing Office, 1866).

Rohr, Nancy M., ed. *Incidents of the War: The Civil War Journal of Mary Jane Chadick*. Huntsville, AL: Silver Threads Publishing, 2005.

Sexton, Rebecca Grant, ed. *A Southern Woman of Letters: The Correspondence of Augusta Jane Evans Wilson*. Columbia, SC: Parell Press, 2002.

Simon, John Y., ed. *The Papers of Ulysses S. Grant*. 32 vol.s. Carbondale: Southern Illinois University Press, 1967.

Smith, William R. *The History and Debates of the Convention of the People of Alabama*. Montgomery, AL: White, Pfister, 1861.

Sterkx, H. E., ed., "Autobiography and Civil War Letters of Joel Murphree of Troy, Alabama, 1864–1865," *Alabama Historical Quarterly* 19 (Spring 1957): 170–208.

Tharin, R. S. *Arbitrary Arrests in the South*. New York: J. Bradburn, 1863.

Venet, Wendy Hamand, ed. *Sam Richard's Civil War Diary: A Chronicle of the Atlanta Home Front*. Athens: University of Georgia Press, 2009.

Williams, Ben Ames, *A Diary from Dixie*. Cambridge, Mass.: Harvard University Press, 2002.

Wilson, Gary, ed. "The Diary of John S. Tucker: Confederate Soldier from Alabama," *Alabama Historical Quarterly* XLIII (Spring 1981): 30.

Winschel, Terrance J., ed., *The Civil War Diary of a Common Soldier: William Wiley of the 77th Illinois Infantry*. Baton Rouge: Louisiana State University Press, 2001.

Woodward, C. Vann, ed., *Mary Chesnut's Civil War*, New Haven, CT: Yale University Press, 1981.

Wooster, Charles, letter to "Brother John," June 25, 1865. *Alabama Historical Quarterly* 64 (Fall 1982).

Wynne, Lewis N. and Robert A., eds. Taylor. T*his War So Horrible: The Civil War Diary of Hiram Smith Williams*. Tuscaloosa: University of Alabama Press, 1993).

Public Documents

Alabama Acts (Montgomery, AL: Shorter and Reid, 1859–64).

Broadbent v. Tuskaloosa Scientific and Art Association, 45 Ala. 170 (1871)

Ex parte Hill, 38 458 (1863)

Ex parte Hill, Ala. 429 (1863)

Ex parte Stringer, 38 Ala. 457 (1863)

Ex parte Vaughan, 44 Ala. 417 (1870)

Hawkins v. Nelson, 40 Ala. 553 (1867)

Journal of the Congress of the Confederate States of America, 1861–1865 (Washington, DC: Government Printing Office, 1904–1905)

Journal of the Executive Proceedings of the Senate of the United States (Washington, DC: Government Printing Office, 1887)

Journal of the House of Representatives of the State of Alabama (Alabama House Journal) (Montgomery, AL: Shorter and Reid, 1859–64)

Journal of the Senate of the State of Alabama (Montgomery: Shorter and Reid, 1859–64).

Martin v. Hewitt, 44 Ala. 418 (1870)

Morgan, Adv'r v. Nelson, Adm'r, 43 Ala. 586 (1869)

Nobel & Bro. v. Cullom, 44 Ala. 554 (1870)

Official Journal of the Constitutional Convention of Alabama, 1861 (Montgomery, AL: Shorter & Reid, State Printers, 1861)
Ordinances and Constitution of the State of Alabama, with the Constitution of the Provisional Government of the Confederate States of America (Montgomery, AL, Barrett, Wimbish & Co., Steam Printers and Binders, 1861)
Secretary of State Election Files, Delegates to State Convention 1860, SG 2475, Alabama Department of Archives and History, Montgomery, Alabama
Tuskaloosa Bridge Co. v. Olmstead, 41 Ala. 9 (1867)
Tuskaloosa Scientific and Art Association v. Green, 48 Ala. 346 (1872)
United States v. Gould, 25 F.Cas. 1375 (S.D. Ala., 1860)
United States Senate Reports, No. 22, "Alabama Testimony in Ku Klux Klan Report," 42nd Cong., 2nd Sess., Vol. IX
The War of the Rebellion: A Compilation of the Official Records of the Union and Confederate Armies (Washington, DC: Government Printing Office, 1887)
Ware v. Jones, 61 Ala. 288 (1878)

Newspapers

Many of these newspapers had daily, weekly, morning, and/or evening editions at different times during the period covered here.

Albany (New York) *Evening Journal*
Alexandria Gazette
(Alexandria) *Soldiers' Journal*
Anderson (SC) *Intelligencer*
Asheville Vidette
Ashtabula (OH) *Weekly Telegraph*
(Athens, GA) *Southern Banner*
(Athens, GA) *Southern Watchmen*
(Athens, GA) *Union Banner*
Athens (TN) *Post*
Atlanta Confederacy
Atlanta Constitutionalist
Atlanta Intelligencer
Augusta (GA) *Chronicle*
Augusta (GA) *Chronicle and Sentinel*
Augusta (GA) *Constitutionalist*
(Baltimore) *Sun*
Bangor (ME) *Daily Whig & Courier*
Belmont (OH) *Chronicle*
Boston Daily Advertiser
Boston Herald
(Boston) *Liberator*
Brandon (MS) *Republican*

Brooklyn Eagle
Brownlow's Knoxville Whig and Rebel Ventilator
Buffalo Advertiser
Burlington (VT) *Free Press*
Canton (MS) *Citizen*
(Carrollton) *West Alabamian*
Charleston Courier
Charleston Mercury
Chattanooga Daily Gazette
Chattanooga Rebel
Chicago Journal
Chicago Post
Chicago Times
Chicago Tribune
Cincinnati Commercial
Cincinnati Daily Press
Cincinnati Enquirer
Cincinnati Gazette
Clayton Banner
Cleveland Leader
Cleveland Plain Dealer
(Columbia) *Daily South Carolinian*
Columbia Democrat and Bloomsburg (PA) *General Advertiser*
Columbia (SC) *Phoenix*
Columbus Republic
Columbus (GA) *Sun*
Columbus (GA) *Times*
Daily Cleveland Herald
Daily Columbus (GA) *Enquirer*
Daily Huntsville Confederate
Daily Missouri Republican
Daily Nashville Patriot
Daily Nashville Union
(Dalton, GA) *Huntsville Confederate*
Decatur Daily
Demopolis Herald
Edgefield (SC) *Advertiser*
(Eufaula) *Spirit of the South*
Eutaw Observer
Eutaw Whig
Eutaw Whig and Observer
Fayetteville (NC) *Observer*
Florence Gazette

Florence Journal
Fremont (OH) *Journal*
Gainesville Independent
Gallipolis (OH) *Journal*
(Greensboro) *Alabama Beacon*
(Grove Hill) *Clarke County Journal*
Harper's Weekly
Hartford Daily Courant
Hartford (CT) *Press*
Hayneville Chronicle
Highland (OH) *Weekly News*
Holmes County (OH) *Farmer*
(Houston, TX) *Tri-Weekly Telegraph*
Howard (MO) *Union*
Huntsville Advocate
Huntsville Chronicle
(Huntsville) *Democrat*
Huntsville Independent
Huntsville Reveille
(Huntsville) *Southern Advocate*
Jackson (MS) *News*
Jacksonville Republican
Lauderdale Times
Liberty (MO) *Tribune*
Livingston Independent
Livingston Journal
(London) *Times*
Louisville (KY) *Daily Journal*
Lowell Daily Citizen and News
Macon (GA) *Confederate*
Macon (GA) *Telegraph*
Macon Telegraph and Confederate
Macon (GA) *Weekly Telegraph & Georgia Journal and Messenger*
Marion Commonwealth
Memphis Avalanche
Memphis Daily Appeal
Memphis Daily Bulletin
Meridian (MS) *Clarion*
Milledgeville Confederate Union
Milwaukee Sentinel
(Mobile) *Army Argus and Crisis*
Mobile Commercial Register and Patriot
Mobile Advertiser

Mobile Advertiser and Register
Mobile Evening Telegraph
Mobile Mercury
(Mobile) *Nationalist*
Mobile News
Mobile Register
Mobile Register and Journal
Mobile Tribune
(Mobile) *Weekly Herald and Tribune*
Montana Post
Montgomery Advertiser
Montgomery Advertiser and Mail
(Montgomery) *Advertiser and Register*
(Montgomery) *Advertiser and State Gazette*
(Montgomery) *Alabama State Journal*
(Montgomery) *Alabama State Sentinel*
(Montgomery) *Confederation*
Montgomery Daily Advertiser
Montgomery Daily Mail
Montgomery Mail
Montgomery Weekly Mail
Montgomery Weekly Post
Moulton Democrat
Nashville Daily Press
Nashville Daily Press and Times
Nashville Daily Times and True Union
Nashville Democrat
Nashville Union
Nashville Union and American
Newark (OH) *Advocate*
(New Haven) *Columbian Register*
New Haven Daily Palladium
(New Orleans) *Daily Picayune*
(New Orleans) *Daily True Delta*
New Orleans Era
New Orleans Times
New York Commercial
New York Commercial and Advertiser
New York Herald
New York Observer
New York Post
New York Times
New York Tribune
New York World

Opelika Weekly Southern Era
(Pennsylvania) *Jeffersonian*
(Philadelphia) *Daily Age*
Philadelphia Daily Evening Bulletin
(Philadelphia) *Evening Telegraph*
(Philadelphia) *Inquirer*
(Philadelphia) *North American and United States Gazette*
Philadelphia Press
(Portage) *Wisconsin State Register*
(Portland, ME) *Eastern Argus*
Providence (Rhode Island) *Evening Press*
Raleigh Progress
Richmond Dispatch
Richmond Enquirer
Richmond Examiner
Richmond Sentinel
Richmond Whig
Ripley (OH) *Bee*
Salem Register
(San Francisco) *Daily Evening Bulletin*
(Savannah, GA) *Daily Morning News*
Savannah (GA) *Republican*
Scioto (OH) *Gazette*
(Selma) *Alabama State Sentinel*
(Selma) *Chattanooga Rebel*
Selma Dispatch
(Selma) *Daily State Sentinel*
Selma Federal Union
Selma Free Press
Selma Messenger
(Selma) *Mississippian*
Selma Reporter
(Selma) *Southern Argus*
Selma Union
Selma Weekly Issue
Semi-Weekly Raleigh Register
Shelby (Columbiana) *County Guide*
Shreveport News
(St. Albans) *Vermont Transcript*
St. Louis Globe-Democrat
Sunbury (PA) *American*
Talladega Democratic Watchtower
Talladega Reporter
(Troy) *Southern Advertiser*

(Tuscaloosa) *Blade*
(Tuscaloosa) *Flag of the Union*
(Tuscaloosa) *Independent Monitor*
Tuscaloosa News
(Tuscaloosa) *Observer*
Tuscumbia Constitution
(Tuscumbia) *North Alabamian*
(Tuscumbia) *North Alabamian and Times*
Tuskaloosa Gazette
Urbana (OH) *Union*
Vermont (Bellows Falls) *Chronicle*
Vermont (Montpelier) *Watchman and State Journal*
Washington Chronicle
(Washington, DC) *Daily Constitutional Union*
Washington (DC) *Herald*
(Washington, DC) *National Intelligencer*
(Washington, DC) *National Republican*
(Washington, DC) *National Tribune*
Washington Post
Weekly Perrysburg (OH) *Journal*
Weekly Raleigh Register
Western Reserve (Warren, OH) *Chronicle*
White Cloud Kansas Chief
Wisconsin State Register
Winchester (TN) *Bulletin*

Secondary Sources

BOOKS, DISSERTATIONS, AND THESES

Abbazia, Patrick. *Chickamauga Campaign, December 1862—November 1863*. New York: Gallery Books, 1988.

Adams, Michael C. C. *Living Hell: The Dark Side of the Civil War*. Baltimore: Johns Hopkins University Press, 2014.

Alderman, Edwin Anderson, Armistead C. Gordon. *J. L. M. Curry: A Biography*. New York: MacMillan, 1911.

Alexander, Bevin. *How the South Could Have Won the Civil War: The Fatal Errors That Led to Confederate Defeat*. New York: Crown Publishers, 2007.

Ambrose, Stephen E. *Nothing Like It in the World: The Men Who Built the Transcontinental Railroad, 1863–1869*. New York: Simon & Schuster, 2000.

Amos, Harriet E. *Cotton City: Urban Development in Antebellum Mobile*. Tuscaloosa: University of Alabama Press, 1985.

Armes, Ethel Marie. *The Story of Coal and Iron in Alabama*. Birmingham, AL: Chamber of Commerce, 1910.

Arnold, James R. *Shiloh, 1862: The Death of Innocence*. London: Praeger, 2004.

Ash, Stephen V., ed. *Secessionists and Other Scoundrels: Selections from Parson Brownlow's Book*. Baton Rouge: Louisiana State University Press, 1999.

——. *When the Yankees Came: Conflict and Chaos in the Occupied South, 1861–1865*. Chapel Hill: University of North Carolina Press, 1995.

Ashdown, Paul, and Edward Caudill. *The Myth of Nathan Bedford Forrest*. Lanham, MD: Rowman and Littlefield, 2005.

Baggett, James Alex. *The Scalawags: Southern Dissenters in the Civil War and Reconstruction*. Baton Rouge: LSU Press, 2004.

Bailey, Anne J. *The Chessboard of War: Sherman and Hood in the Autumn Campaigns of 1864*. Lincoln: University of Nebraska Press, 2000.

Bailey, Richard. *Neither Carpetbaggers Nor Scalawags: Black Officerholders during the Reconstruction of Alabama, 1867–1878*. Montgomery, AL: R. Bailey, 1991.

Ball, Douglas B. *Financial Failure and Confederate Defeat*. Urbana: University of Illinois Press, 1991.

Ballard, Michael B. *The Civil War in Mississippi: Major Campaigns and Battles*. Jackson: University Press of Mississippi, 2011.

Barefield, Marilyn Davis. *Historical Records of Randolph County, Alabama: 1832–1900*. Birmingham, AL: M. D. Barefield, 1995.

Barney, William L. *The Secessionist Impulse in Alabama and Mississippi in 1860*. Tuscaloosa: University of Alabama Press, 2004.

Bateman, Fred, and Thomas Weiss. *Deplorable Scarcity: The Failure of Industrialization in the Slave Economy*. Chapel Hill: University of North Carolina Press 2002.

Bates, William Carnes, ed., *The Stars and Stripes in Rebeldom: A Series of Papers Written by Federal Prisoners (Privates) in Richmond, Tuscaloosa, New Orleans, and Salisbury, N.C.* (Boston: T. O. H. P. Burnham, 1862).

Bearss, Edwin C. *Fall of Fort Henry*. Dover, TN: Eastern National Park and Monument Association, Fort Donelson National Military Park, 1992.

Bell, Robert K. "Reconstruction in Tuscaloosa County." Master's thesis, University of Alabama, 1933.

Bennett, James R. *Tannehill and the Growth of the Alabama Iron Industry: Including the Civil War in West Alabama*. Saline, MI: Alabama Historic Ironworks Commission, 1999.

Bennett, Stewart L. *The Battle of Brice's Crossroads*. Charleston, SC: History Press, 2012.

Bergeron, Arthur W. "The Confederate Defenses of Mobile, 1861–1865." PhD diss., Louisiana State University, 1980.

——. *Confederate Mobile*. Jackson: University Press of Mississippi, 1991.

Beringer, Richard E., Herman Hataway, Archer Jones, and William N. Still Jr. *The Elements of Confederate Defeat: Nationalism, War Aims, and Religion*. Athens: University of Georgia Press, 1988.

——. *Why the South Lost the Civil War*. Athens: University of Georgia Press, 1991.

Berlin, Ira. *Many Thousands Gone: The First Two Centuries of Slavery in North America*. Cambridge, MA: Belknap Press of Harvard University Press, 1998.

——. *Slaves without Masters: The Free Negro in the Antebellum South*. New York: Pantheon Books, 1974.

Berney, Saffold. *Handbook of Alabama: A Complete Index to the State, with Map*. Mobile, AL: Mobile Register Printing, 1878.

Berry, Stephen W. *House of Abraham: Lincoln and the Todds, A Family Divided by War*. Boston: Mariner Books, 2009.

Berry, Thelma Caine. "The Life of Edmund Winston Pettus." Master's thesis, Auburn University, 1941.

Black, Robert C. *Railroads of the Confederacy*. Chapel Hill: University of North Carolina Press, 1998.

Blackmon, Douglas A. *Slavery by Another Name: The Re-enslavement of Black People in America from the Civil War to World War II*. New York: Doubleday, 2008.

Blair, William A. *With Malice toward Some: Treason and Loyalty in the Civil War Era*. Chapel Hill: University of North Carolina Press, 2014.

Blum, Edward J. *Reforging the White Republic: Race, Religion, and American Nationalism, 1865–1898*. Baton Rouge: Louisiana State University Press, 2005.

Boyko, John. *Blood and Daring: Canada and the American Civil War*. Toronto: Alfred A. Knopf, 2013.

Bradley, George C., and Richard L. Dahlen. *From Conciliation to Conquest: The Sack of Athens and the Court-Martial of Colonel John B. Turchin*. Tuscaloosa: University of Alabama Press, 2006.

Brantley, William H. *Chief Justice Stone of Alabama*. Birmingham, AL: Birmingham Pub. Co., 1943.

Brewer, Willis. *Alabama, Her History, Resources, War Records, and Public Men: From 1540–1872*. Montgomery, AL: Barrett & Brown, 1872.

Brown, D. Alexander. *Grierson's Raid: A Cavalry Adventure of the Civil War*. Urbana: University of Illinois Press, 1981.

Brown, Kent Masterson. *Retreat from Gettysburg: Lee, Logistics, and the Pennsylvania Campaign*. Chapel Hill: University of North Carolina Press, 2005.

Bryan, Thomas Conn. *Confederate Georgia*. Athens: University of Georgia Press, 1964.

Buckley, Thomas Foster. *Sherman's Mississippi Campaign*. Tuscaloosa: University of Alabama Press, 2006.

Bungay, George W. *Traits of Representative Men*. New York: Fowler & Wells, 1882.

Burke, Edmund. *Reflections on the Revolution in France*. New York: Alfred A. Knopf, 2015.

Burkhardt, George S. *Confederate Rage, Yankee Wrath: No Quarter in the Civil War*. Carbondale: Southern Illinois University Press, 2007.

Burlingame, Michael. *Abraham Lincoln: A Life*. Baltimore: Johns Hopkins University Press, 2008.

Burnham, T. O. H. P., compiler and publisher. *The Stars and Stripes in Rebeldom: A Series of Papers Written by Federal Prisoners (Privates) in Richmond, Tuscaloosa, New Orleans, and Salisbury, N.C., With Appendix*. Boston: T. O. H. P. Burnham, 1862.

Burnett, Lonnie A. *The Pen Makes a Good Sword: John Forsyth of the Mobile Register*. Tuscaloosa: University of Alabama Press, 2006.

Bynum, Victoria E. *The Free State of Jones: Mississippi's Longest Civil War*. Chapel Hill: University of North Carolina Press, 2001.

Cabaniss, Allen. *The University of Mississippi: Its First Hundred Years*. Hattiesburg: University College Press of Mississippi, 1971.

Calonius, Erick. *The Wanderer: The Last American Slave Ship and the Conspiracy that Set Its Sails*. New York: St. Martin's Press, 2006.

Campbell, R. Thomas. *Hunters of the Night: Confederate Torpedo Boats in the War between the States*. Shippensburg, PA: Burd Street Press, 1990.

Carnahan, Burrus M. *Act of Justice: Lincoln's Emancipation Proclamation and the Law of War*. Lexington: University Press of Kentucky, 2007.

Carroll, Lewis. *Alice's Adventures in Wonderland*. New York: Phillip Warner, 1914, 1865.

Carter, Dan T. *When the War Was Over: The Failure of Self-Reconstruction in the South, 1865–1867*. Baton Rouge: Louisiana State University Press, 1985.

Carter, Davis Blake. *The Story Uncle Minyard Told: A Family's 200 Year Migration across the South*. Spartanburg, SC: Reprint Co., 1994.

Carter, John C., ed. *Welcome the Hour of Conflict: William Cowan McClellan and the 9th Alabama*. Tuscaloosa: University of Alabama Press, 2007.

Castel, Albert. *Decision in the West: The Atlanta Campaign of 1864*. Lawrence: University Press of Kansas, 1992.

Chesebrough, David B. *Clergy Dissent in the Old South, 1830–1865*. Carbondale: Southern Illinois University Press, 1996.

Chicoine, Stephen. *John Basil Turchin and the Fight to Free the Slaves*. Westport, CT: Praeger, 2003.

Child, Lydia Maria Francis. *The Right Way, The Safe Way*. New York: American Anti-Slavery Society, 1860; repr. 1969.

Chodes, John J. *Jabez L. M. Curry: Confederate Educator, Trojan Horse*. New York: Algora, 2005.

Cimprich, John. *Slavery's End in Tennessee, 1861–1865*. Tuscaloosa: University of Alabama Press, 2002.

Clampitt, Bradley R. *The Confederate Heartland: Military and Civilian Morale in the Western Confederacy*. Baton Rouge: Louisiana State University Press, 2011.

Clark, James Harold. "History of the North East and South West Railroad to 1872." Master's thesis, University of Alabama, 1949.

Clark, John B. *Populism in Alabama*. Auburn, AL: Auburn Print Co., 1927.

Clark, John Elwood. *Railroads in the Civil War: The Impact of Management on Victory and Defeat*. Baton Rouge: Louisiana State University Press, 2004.

Clay-Clopton, Virginia. *A Belle of the Fifties: Memoirs of Mrs. Clay of Alabama*. Tuscaloosa: University Press of Alabama, 1999.

Cline, Wayne. *Alabama Railroads*. Tuscaloosa: University of Alabama Press, 1997.

Clinton, Mathew William. *Matt Clinton's Scrapbook*. Northport, AL: Portals, 1979.

Colby, Elbridge. "Wilson's Cavalry Campaign of 1865," II *Journal of the American Military History Foundation* (1928).

Collins, Donald E. *The Death and Resurrection of Jefferson Davis*. Lanham, MD: Rowman and Littlefield, 2005.

Confederate Politician of Alabama, 1861–1865 (n.p., n.d.).

Conroy, James B. *Our One Common Country: Abraham Lincoln and the Hampton Roads Peace Conference of 1865*. Guilford, CT: Lyons Press, 2014.

Cooling, B. Franklin. *Forts Henry and Donelson—The Key to the Confederate Heartland*. Knoxville, TN: Easton Press, 1987.

Cooling, Benjamin Franklin, III. *To the Battles of Franklin and Nashville and Beyond: Stabilization and Reconstruction in Tennessee and Kentucky, 1864–1866*. Knoxville: University of Tennessee Press, 2011.

Cooper, William J., Jr. *Jefferson Davis, American*. New York: Vintage Books, 2001.

——. *Jefferson Davis and the Civil War Era*. Baton Rouge: Louisiana State University Press, 2008.

——, ed. *Jefferson Davis: The Essential Writings*. New York: Random House, 2004.

Cotter, Patrick R. *After Wallace: The 1986 Contest for Governor and Political Change in Alabama*. Tuscaloosa: University of Alabama Press, 2013.

Cox, Karen L. *Dixie's Daughter: The United Daughters of the Confederacy and the Preservation of Confederate Culture*. Gainesville: University Press of Florida, 2003.

Cozzens, Peter. *The Darkest Days of the War: The Battles of Iuka & Corinth*. Chapel Hill: University of North Carolina Press, 1997.

——. *No Better Place to Die: The Battle of Stones River*. Urbana: University of Illinois Press, 1990.

Craton, Michael. *Slavery, Abolition and Emancipation*. London: Longman, 1976.

Crofts, Thomas. *History of the Service of the Third Ohio Veteran Volunteer Cavalry in the War for the Preservation of the Union from 1861–1865*. Toledo, OH: Blue Acorn Press, 1910.

Current, Richard Nelson. *Lincoln's Loyalists: Union Soldiers from the Confederacy*. Boston: Northeastern University Press, 1992.

Daniel, Larry J. *Soldiering in the Army of Tennessee: A Portrait of Life in the Confederate Army*. Chapel Hill: University of North Carolina Press, 1991.

Danielson, Joseph W. *War's Desolating Scourge: The Union's Occupation of North Alabama*. Lawrence: University Press of Kansas, 2012.

Davidson, William H. *Word from Camp Pollard, C.S.A.* West Point, GA: Davidson, 1978.

Davis, Andrew McFarland. *The Origins of the National Banking System*. Washington, DC: Government Printing Office, 1910.

Davis, David Brion. *Inhuman Bondage: The Rise and Fall of Slavery in the New World*. Oxford: Oxford University Press, 2006.

Davis, George B., Leslie J. Perry, Joseph W. Kirkley, and Calvin D. Cowles, eds., *The Official Military Atlas of the Civil War* (New York: Amo Press/Crown Publishers, 1978).

Davis, Stephen. *Atlanta Will Fall: Sherman, Joe Johnston, and the Yankee Heavy Battalions*. Wilmington, DE: Scholarly Resources, 2001.

Davis, Susan Lawrence. *Authentic History, Ku Klux Klan 1865–1877*. New York: American Library Service, 1924.

Davis, William C., ed. *The Confederate General*. New York: National Historical Society, 1991.

——. *First Blood: Fort Sumter to Bull Run.* Alexandria, VA: Time-Life Books, 1983.

——. *Look Away!: A History of the Confederate States of America.* New York: Simon & Schuster, 2002.

Dean, Eric T., Jr. "Post-Traumatic Stress" 396–422 In *The Civil War Veteran: A Historical Reader*, edited by Larry M. Logue and Michael Barton. New York: New York University Press, 2007.

——. *Shook Over Hell: Post-Traumatic Stress, Viet Nam, and the Civil War.* Cambridge, MA: Harvard University Press, 1997.

DeBow, James Dunwoody Brownson. *The Industrial Resources, Etc., of the Southern and Western States: Embracing a View of Their Commerce, Agriculture, Manufacturers, Internal Improvements; Slave and Free Labor, Slavery Institutions, Products, Etc., of the South.* New Orleans: DeBow's Review, 1852.

Deland, T. A., and A. David Smith, eds., *Northern Alabama: Historical and Biographical.* Birmingham, AL: Smith and DeLand, 1888.

Denman, Clarence P. *The Secession Movement in Alabama.* Montgomery: Alabama State Dept. of Archives and History, 1933.

Detzer, David. *Allegiance: Fort Sumter, Charleston, and the Beginning of the Civil War.* New York: Harcourt, 2001.

——. *Dissonance: The Turbulent Days between Fort Sumter and Bull Run.* Orlando, FL: Harcourt, 2006.

——. *Donnybrook: The Battle of Bull Run, 1861.* Orlando, FL: Harcourt, 2004.

Dodd, Donald B. "Unionism in Confederate Alabama." PhD diss., University of Georgia, 1969.

Dodd, Donald B., and Amy Bartlett-Dodd. *The Free State of Winston* Charleston, SC: Arcadia Publishing, 2000.

Dodd, Donald B., and Wynelle S. Dodd. *Winston: An Antebellum and Civil War History of a Hill County of North Alabama.* Jasper, AL: C. Elliot, 1972.

Dodge, Grenville M. *Battle of Atlanta and Other Campaigns.* Council Bluffs, IA: Monarch Printing Co., 1910.

Donald, David H. *Lincoln.* New York: Simon & Schuster, 1995.

Dorman, Lewy. *Party Politics in Alabama from 1850 through 1860.* Tuscaloosa: University of Alabama Press, 1995.

Dorris, Jonathan Truman. *Pardon and Amnesty under Lincoln and Johnson.* Chapel Hill: University of North Carolina Press, 1977.

Dowdey, Clifford. *Death of a Nation: The Story of Lee and His Men at Gettysburg.* New York: Butternut and Blue, 1988.

Dubay, Robert W. *John Jones Pettus, Mississippi Fire-Eater: His Life and Times, 1813–1867.* Jackson: University Press of Mississippi, 2008.

Dubin, Michael J. *United States Presidential Elections, 1788–1860: The Official Results of County and State.* Jefferson, NC: McFarland, 2011.

DuBose, John Witherspoon. *Alabama's Tragic Decade: Ten Years of Alabama 1865–1874.* Birmingham, AL: Webb Book Co., 1940.

——. *General Joseph Wheeler and the Army of Tennessee.* La Crosse, Wis.: Brookhaven Press, 2005.

Dunnavant, Robert. *Decatur, Alabama: Yankee Foothold in Dixie, 1861–1865*. Athens, AL: Pea Ridge Press, 1995.

———. *The Railroad War: N.B. Forrest's 1864 Raid through Northern Alabama and Middle Tennessee*. Athens, AL: Pea Ridge Press, 1994.

Dyer, John Percy, *"Fightin' Joe" Wheeler*. Baton Rouge: LSU Press, 1941.

Easby-Smith, Mildred. *William Russell Smith of Alabama, His Life and Works*. Philadelphia: Dolphin Press, 1931.

Elliott, E. N. *Cotton Is King and Pro-Slavery Arguments*. Augusta, GA: Pritchard, Abbott & Loomis, 1860.

Ellis, Barbara G. *The Moving Appeal: Mr. McClanaham, Mrs. Dill, and The Civil War's Great Newspaper Run*. Macon, GA: Mercer University Press, 2003.

Emberton, Carole. *Beyond Redemption: Race, Violence, and the American South after the Civil War*. Chicago: University of Chicago Press, 2013.

English, Bertis. "Civil Wars and Civil Beings: Violence, Religion, Race, Politics, Education, Culture and Agrarianism in Perry County, Alabama, 1860–1875." PhD diss., Auburn University, 2006.

———. "Freedom's Church: Sociocultural Construction, Reconstruction, and Post-Reconstruction in Perry County, Alabama's African American Churches." In *The Yellowhammer War: The Civil War and Reconstruction in Alabama*, ed. Kenneth W. Noe, 258–80. Tuscaloosa: University of Alabama Press, 2013.

English, Beth. *A Common Thread: Labor, Politics and Capital Mobility in the Textile Industry*. Athens: University of Georgia Press, 2006.

Escott, Paul D. *The Confederacy: The Slaveholders' Failed Venture*. Santa Barbara, CA: Praeger, 2010.

———. *Many Excellent People: Power and Privilege In North Carolina, 1850–1900*. Chapel Hill: University of North Carolina Press, 1985.

———. *Military Necessity: Civil-Military Relations in the Confederacy*. Westport, CT: Praeger Security International, 2006.

———. *"What Shall We Do With the Negro?": Lincoln, White Racism and Civil War America*. Charlottesville: University of Virginia Press, 2009.

Evans, Augusta Jane, *Macaria; or, the Altars of Sacrifice* (1864; reprinted Baton Rouge: Louisiana State University, 1992);

Evans, Clement A., ed. *Confederate Military History: A Library of Confederate States History*. 12 vol.s. Atlanta: Confederate Pub. Co., 1899.

Evans, Curtis J. *The Conquest of Labor: Daniel Pratt and Southern Industrialization*. Baton Rouge: Louisiana State University Press, 2001.

Feis, William B. *Grant's Secret Service: The Intelligence War from Belmont to Appomattox*. Lincoln: University of Nebraska Press, 2004.

Fermer, Douglas. *James Gordon Bennett and the New York Herald: A Study of Editorial Opinion in the Civil War Era 1854–1867*. London: Royal Historical Society, 1986.

Fidler, William Perry. *Augusta Evans Wilson, 1835–1909: A Biography*. Tuscaloosa: University of Alabama Press, 1951.

Fisher, Noel C. *War at Every Door: Partisan Politics and Guerrilla Violence in East Tennessee, 1860–1869*. Chapel Hill: University of North Carolina Press, 1997.

Fitts, Alston. *Selma: Queen City of the Blackbelt*. Selma, AL: Clairmont Press, 1989.

Fitzgerald, Michael W. *Splendid Failure: Postwar Reconstruction in the American South*. Chicago: Ivan R. Dee, 2007.

——. *Urban Emancipation: Popular Politics in Reconstruction Mobile, 1860–1890*. Baton Rouge: Louisiana State University Press, 2002.

Fleming, Thomas J. *A Disease in the Public Mind: A New Understanding of Why We Fought the Civil War*. New York: Da Capo Press, 2013.

Fleming, Walter Lynwood. *Civil War and Reconstruction in Alabama*. London: P. Smith, 1905.

Folk, Edgar Estes, and Bynum Shaw. *W. W. Holden, A Political Biography*. Winston-Salem, NC: J. F. Blair, 1982.

Foner, Eric. *Reconstruction: America's Unfinished Revolution, 1863–1877*. New York: Perennial Classics, 2002.

Foster, Buck T. *Sherman's Mississippi Campaign*. Tuscaloosa: University of Alabama Press, 2006.

Frank, Joseph Allan. *"Seeing the Elephant": Raw Recruits at the Battle of Shiloh*. Urbana: University of Illinois Press, 2003.

Frank, Lisa Tendrich. *Women in the Civil War*. Santa Barbara, CA: ABC-CLIO, 2008.

Franklin, John Hope. *Reconstruction after the Civil War*. Chicago: University of Chicago Press, 1994.

Freehling, William W. *Prelude to Civil War: The Nullification Controversy in South Carolina, 1816–1836*. New York: Oxford University Press, 1992.

——. *The Road to Disunion: Secessionists at Bay: 1776–1854*. 2 vol.s. New York: Oxford University Press, 1991.

——. *The Road to Disunion: Secessionists Triumphant, 1854–1861*. New York: Oxford University Press, 2007.

——. *The South vs. the South: How Anti-Confederate Southerners Shaped the Course of the Civil War*. New York: Oxford University Press, 2001.

Freehling, William W., and Craig Simpson, eds. *Showdown in Virginia: The 1861 Convention and the Fate of the Union*. Charlottesville: University of Virginia Press, 2010.

French Jr., Thomas L. *Bridging Deep South Rivers: The Life and Legend of Horace King*. Athens: University of Georgia Press, 2004.

Frey, Jerry. *Three Quarter Cadillac: Common Sense for the Common Good*. Sandy, UT: Aardvark Global Publishing, 2008.

Fry, Joseph A. *John Tyler Morgan and the Search for Southern Autonomy*. Knoxville: University of Tennessee Press, 1992.

Fuller, A. James. *Chaplain to the Confederacy: Basil Manly and Baptist Life in the Old South*. Baton Rouge: Louisiana State University Press, 2000.

Gallagher, Gary W. *Becoming Confederates: Path to a New National Loyalty*. Athens: University of Georgia Press, 2013.

——. *Chancellorsville: The Battle and Its Aftermath*. Chapel Hill: University of North Carolina Press, 1996.

——. *The Confederate War*. Cambridge, MA: Harvard University Press, 1997.

Gallagher, Gary W., and Alan T. Nolan, eds. *The Myth of the Lost Cause and Civil War History*. Bloomington: Indiana University Press, 2001.

Gambill, Edward L. *Conservative Ordeal: Northern Democrats and Reconstruction, 1865–1868*. Ames: Iowa State University Press, 1981.

Garrett, Jill K. *A History of Florence, Alabama*. Columbia, TN: J. K. Garrett, 1968.

Garrett, William. *Reminiscences of Public Men in Alabama: For Thirty Years*. Atlanta: Plantation Publ. Co. Press, 1872.

Geggus, David P. *The Impact of the Haitian Revolution in the Atlantic World*. Columbia: University of South Carolina Press, 2001.

Genoways, Ted, and Hugh H. Genoways, eds. *A Perfect Picture of Hell: Eyewitness Accounts by Civil War Prisoners from the 12th Iowa*. Iowa City: University of Iowa Press, 2001.

Gleeson, David T. *The Green and the Gray: The Irish in the Confederate States of America*. Chapel Hill: University of North Carolina Press, 2013.

Going, Allen Johnston. *Bourbon Democracy in Alabama, 1874–1890*. Tuscaloosa: University of Alabama Press, 1951.

Goodrich, Thomas, and Debra Goodrich Bisel. *The Day Dixie Died: Southern Occupation, 1865–1866*. Mechanicsburg, PA: Stackpole Books, 2001.

Gott, Kendall D. *Where the South Lost the War: An Analysis of the Fort Henry–Fort Donelson Campaign, February, 1862*. Mechanicsburg, PA: Stackpole Books, 2003.

Griffith, Lucille, *Alabama: A Documentary History to 1900*. Tuscaloosa: University of Alabama Press, 1972.

Grimsley, Mark. *The Hard Hand of War: Union Military Policy toward Southern Civilians (1861–1865)*. Cambridge: Cambridge University Press, 1995.

Guelzo, Allen C. *Fateful Lightning: A New History of the Civil War and Reconstruction*. New York: Oxford University Press, 2012.

———. *Gettysburg: The Last Invasion*. New York: Alfred A. Knopf, 2013.

Hacker, Louis M. *The Triumph of American Capitalism: The Development of Forces in American History to the End of the Nineteenth Century*. New York: McGraw-Hill, 1947.

Hall, Clifton R. *Andrew Johnson: Military Governor of Tennessee*. Princeton, NJ: Princeton University Press, 1916.

Hamilton, Daniel W. *The Limits of Sovereignty: Property Confiscations in the Union and the Confederacy during the Civil War*. Chicago: University of Chicago Press, 2007.

Hardin, David. *After the War: The Lives and Images of Major Civil War Figures after the Shooting Stopped*. Lanham, MD: Rowman and Littlefield, 2010.

Harris, William C. *Leroy Pope Walker: Confederate Secretary of War*. Tuscaloosa, AL: Confederate Pub. Co., 1962.

Hartnett, Stephen John. *Democratic Dissent & the Cultural Fictions of Antebellum America*. Urbana: University of Illinois Press, 2002.

Hattaway, Herman, *General Stephen D. Lee* (Jackson, University Press of Mississippi, 1976).

Haughton, Andrew. *Training, Tactics and Leadership in the Confederate Army of Tennessee*. New York: Routledge, 2000.

Hearn, Chester G. *Mobile Bay and the Mobile Campaign: The Last Great Battles of the Civil War.* Jefferson, NC: McFarland, 1998.

——. *When the Devil Came Down to Dixie: Ben Butler in New Orleans.* Baton Rouge: Louisiana State University Press, 1997.

Hebert, Walter H. *Fighting Joe Hooker.* Lincoln: University of Nebraska Press, 1944.

Herr, Kincaid A. *The Louisville & Nashville Railroad, 1850–1963.* Lexington: University Press of Kentucky, 2000.

Hess, Earl J. *Banners to the Breeze: The Kentucky Campaign, Corinth and Stones River.* Lincoln: University of Nebraska Press, 2000.

——. *The Civil War in the West: Victory and Defeat from the Appalachians to the Mississippi.* Chapel Hill: University of North Carolina Press, 2012.

Hesseltine, William Best. *Civil War Prisons: A Study in War Psychology.* Columbus: Ohio State University Press, 1930.

——. *Three against Lincoln: Murat Halstead Reports the Caucuses of 1860.* Baton Rouge: Louisiana State University Press, 1960.

Hettle, Wallace. *The Peculiar Democracy: Southern Democrats in Peace and Civil War.* Athens: University of Georgia Press, 2001.

Heyman, Max L., Jr. *Prudent Soldier: A Biography of Major General E. R. S. Canby 1817–1873.* Glendale, CA: Arthur H. Clark, 1959.

Heyse, Amy L. *Teachers of the Lost Cause: The United Daughters of the Confederacy and the Rhetoric of Their Catechisms.* College Park: University of Maryland Press, 2006.

Hirshson, Stanley P. *Grenville M. Dodge: Soldier, Politician, Railroad Pioneer.* Bloomington: Indiana University Press, 1967.

Holzer, Harold, Edna Greene Medford, Frank J. Williams. *The Emancipation Proclamation: Three Views.* Baton Rouge: Louisiana State University Press, 2006.

Hood, John Bell. *Advance and Retreat.* Secaucas, NJ: Blue and Grey Press, 1985.

Hood, Stephen M. *John Bell Hood: The Rise, Fall, and Resurrection of a Confederate General.* El Dorado Hills, CA: Savas Beatie, 2013.

Hoole, William Stanley. *Alabama Tories, the First Alabama Cavalry, U.S.A., 1862–1865.* Tuscaloosa, AL: Confederate Pub. Co., 1960.

——, ed. *History of Shockley's Alabama Escort Company.* Tuscaloosa, AL: Confederate Pub. Co., 1983.

Hoole, William Stanley, and Elizabeth Hoole McArthur. *The Yankee Invasion of West Alabama, March–April, 1865.* Tuscaloosa, AL: Confederate Pub. Co., 1985.

Horwitz, Tony. *Midnight Rising: John Brown and the Raid that Sparked the Civil War.* New York: Henry Holt, 2011.

Howard, Gene L. *Death at Cross Plains: An Alabama Reconstruction Tragedy.* Tuscaloosa: University of Alabama Press, 1984.

Hubbs, G. Ward. *Guarding Greensboro: A Confederate Company in the Making of a Southern Community.* Athens: University of Georgia Press, 2003.

——. *Tuscaloosa: Portrait of An Alabama County: An Illustrated History.* Northridge, CA: Windsor Publications, 1987.

——. *Voices from Company D: Diaries by the Greensboro Guards, Fifth Alabama Infantry Regiment, Army of Northern Virginia.* Athens: University of Georgia Press, 2003.

Hughes, Nathaniel C., and Roy P. Stonesifer. *The Life and Wars of Gideon Pillow.* Chapel Hill: University of North Carolina Press, 1993.

Hummel, Jeffrey Rogers. *Emancipating Slaves, Enslaving Free Men: A History of the American Civil War.* Chicago: Open Court, 1996.

Hunt, Alfred N. *Haiti's Influence on Antebellum America.* Baton Rouge: Louisiana State University Press, 1988.

Hurst, Jack. *Nathan Bedford Forrest: A Biography.* New York: A.A. Knopf, 1994.

Huston, James L. *Calculating the Value of the Union: Slavery, Property Rights, and the Economic Origins of the Civil War.* Chapel Hill: University of North Carolina Press, 2003.

——. *The Panic of 1857 and the Coming of the Civil War.* Baton Rouge: Louisiana State University Press, 1987.

Iowa Adjutant General's Office. *Roster and Record of Iowa Soldiers in Miscellaneous Organizations of the Mexican War, Indian Campaigns, War of the Rebellion, and the Spanish-American and Philippine Wars: Together With Historical Sketches of Volunteer Organizations, 1861–1866.* 6 vol.s. Des Moines, IA: E. H. English, State Printer, E.D. Chassell, State Binder, 1910.

Isbell, Timothy T. *Shiloh and Corinth: Sentinels of Stone.* Jackson: University Press of Mississippi, 2007.

Jackson, Hermoine Dannelly. "The Life and Times of Robert Jemison, Jr., during the Civil War and Reconstruction." Master's thesis, University of Alabama, 1942.

Jackson, Walter M. *The Story of Selma.* Birmingham, AL: Birmingham Print Co., 1954.

Johns, George Sibley. *Philip Henson, the Southern Union Spy.* St. Louis: Nixon-Jones Print Co., 1887.

Johnson, David. *Decided on the Battlefield: Grant, Sherman, Lincoln, and the Election of 1864.* Amherst, NY: Prometheus Books, 2012.

Johnston, Ernest Barnwell, Jr., "Selma, Alabama, as a Center of Confederate War Production, 1860–1865." Bachelor's thesis, Harvard College, 1952.

Johnston, Milus E. *The Sword of "Bushwacker" Johnston.* Huntsville, AL: Flint River Press, 1992.

Jones, Howard. *Blue & Gray Diplomacy: A History of Union and Confederate Foreign Relations.* Chapel Hill: University of North Carolina Press, 2010.

Jones, James P., *Yankee Blitzkrieg: Wilson's Raid through Alabama and Georgia.* Lexington: University Press of Kentucky, 2000).

Jordan, Winthrop. *White Over Black: American Attitudes toward the Negro, 1550–1812.* Chapel Hill: University of North Carolina Press, 1968.

Kammen, Michael. *Mystic Chords of Memory: The Transformation of Tradition in American Culture.* New York: Knopf, 1991.

Kane, Harnett T. *Spies for the Blue and Gray.* Garden City, NY: Hanover House, 1954.

Kazek, Kelly. *Hidden History of Auburn.* Charleston, SC: History Press, 2011.

Keehn, David C. *Knights of the Golden Circle: Secret Empire, Southern Secession, Civil War.* Baton Rouge: Louisiana State University Press, 2013.

Keenan, Jerry. *Wilson's Cavalry Corps: Union Campaigns in the Western Theatre, October, 1864 through Spring 1865*. Jefferson, NC: McFarland, 1998.

Kelly, Jack. *Gunpowder: Alchemy, Bombards and Pyrotechnics*. New York: Basic Books, 2004.

Kinchen, Oscar A. *Confederate Operations in Canada and the North*. North Quincy, MA: Christopher Pub. House, 1970.

Kirkland, Edward C. *Peacemakers of 1864*. New York: MacMillan, 1927.

Klingaman, William K. *Abraham Lincoln and the Road to Emancipation 1861–1865*. New York: Viking Press, 2001.

Klingberg, Frank W. *The Southern Claims Commission*. Berkeley: University of California Press, 1955.

Kohl, Lawrence Frederick. *The Politics of Individualism: Parties and the American Character in the Jacksonian Era*. New York: Oxford University Press, 1989.

Kolchin, Peter. *First Freedom: The Responses of Alabama's Blacks to Emancipation and Reconstruction*. Westport, CT: Greenwood Press, 1972.

Kvach, John F. *DeBow's Review: The Antebellum Vision of the New South*. Lexington: University Press of Kentucky, 2013.

Lauderdale, Clara Mary. "Population of Alabama between 1860 and 1870." Master's thesis, University of Wisconsin, 1912.

Leckie, Robert. *None Died in Vain: The Saga of the American Civil War*. New York: HarperCollins, 1990.

Leckie, William H. and Shirley A. Leckie. *Unlikely Warriors: General Benjamin H. Grierson and His Family*. Norman: University of Oklahoma Press, 1984.

Leftwich, Nina. *Two Hundred Years at Muscle Shoals, Being an Authentic History of Colbert County 1700–1900 with Special Emphasis on the Stirring Events of the Early Times*. Tuscumbia, AL: American Legion Post # 31, 1998.

Leonard, Elizabeth D. *Lincoln's Avengers: Justice, Revenge, and Reunion after the Civil War*. New York: W. W. Norton, 2004.

Lepa, Jack H. *Breaking the Confederacy: The Georgia and Tennessee Campaigns of 1864*. Jefferson, NC: McFarland, 2005.

Levine, Bruce. *Confederate Emancipation: Southern Plans to Free and Arm Slaves during the Civil War*. New York: Oxford University Press, 2006.

———. *The Fall of the House of Dixie: The Civil War and the Social Revolution That Transformed the South*. New York: Random House, 2013.

Lewis, Herbert James. *Clearing the Thickets: A History of Antebellum Alabama*. New Orleans: Quid Pro Books, 2013.

Little, Dr. George, and Dr. James R. Maxwell. *A History of Lumsden's Battery C.S.A.* Tuscaloosa, AL: R. E. Rhodes Chapter United Daughters of the Confederacy, 1988.

Livermore, Thomas Leonard. *Numbers and Losses in the Civil War in America, 1861–1865*. Bloomington: Indiana University Press, 1957.

Longacre, Edward G. *A Soldier to the Last: Maj. Gen. Joseph Wheeler in Blue and Gray*. Washington, DC: Potomac Books, 2007.

Longfellow, Henry Wadsworth. *Hyperion A Romance.* Book IV. New York, 1839. Paraphrased in *Nashville Daily Union,* June 8, 1865, 2.

Loving, Waldon Spicer. *Coming Like Hell: The Story of the 12th Tennessee Cavalry, Richardson's Brigade, Forrest's Cavalry Corps, Confederate States Army, 1862–1865.* San Jose, CA: Writers Club Press, 2002.

Lupold, John S., and Thomas L. French Jr. *Bridging Deep South Rivers: The Life and Legend of Horace King.* Athens: University of Georgia Press, 2004.

Mahin, Dean B. *One War at a Time: The International Dimensions of the American Civil War.* Washington, DC: Brassey's, 1999.

Martin, Bessie. *Desertion of Alabama Troops from the Confederate Army: A Study in Sectionalism.* New York: Columbia University Press, 1932.

——. *A Rich Man's War, A Poor Man's Fight: Desertion of Alabama Troops from the Confederate Army.* Tuscaloosa: University of Alabama Press, 2003.

Marvel, William. *Andersonville: The Last Depot.* Chapel Hill: University of North Carolina Press, 1994.

Maslowski, Peter. *Treason Must Be Made Odious, Military Occupation and Wartime Reconstruction in Nashville, Tennessee, 1862–65.* Millwood, NY: KTO Press, 1978.

Massey, Mary Elizabeth. *Refugee Life in the Confederacy.* Baton Rouge: Louisiana State University Press, 2001.

Mathis, Ray. *John Horry Dent, South Carolina Aristocrat on the Alabama Frontier.* Tuscaloosa: University of Alabama Press, 1979.

Mayer, Henry. *All on Fire: William Lloyd Garrison and the Abolition of Slavery.* New York: W. W. Norton, 2008.

McClintock, Russell. *Lincoln and the Decision for War: The Northern Response to Secession.* Chapel Hill: University of North Carolina Press, 2008.

McCurry, Stephanie. *Confederate Reckoning: Power and Politics in the Civil War South.* Cambridge, MA: Harvard University Press, 2010.

McDonald, William Lindsey. *A Walk through the Past—People and Places of Florence and Lauderdale County, Alabama.* Killen, AL: Heart of Dixie, 2003.

McDonough, James Lee. *Chattanooga: Death Grip on the Confederacy.* Knoxville: University of Tennessee Press, 1984.

——. *Shiloh: In Hell before Night.* Knoxville: University of Tennessee Press, 1977.

McDonough, James Lee, and James Pickett Jones. *War So Terrible: Sherman and Atlanta.* New York: Norton, 1987.

McGee, Benjamin F. *History of the 72d Indiana Volunteer Infantry of the Mounted Lightning Brigade.* LaFayette, IN: S. Vater & Co., Printers, 1882.

McGee, Val. L. *Selma: A Novel of the Civil War.* Oxford, MS: Yoknapatawpha Press, 2008.

McKiven, Henry M. *Iron & Steel: Class, Race, and Community in Birmingham, Alabama, 1875–1920.* Chapel Hill: University of North Carolina Press, 1995.

McLaughlin, James Fairfax. *The American Cyclops: The Hero of New Orleans, and Spoiler of Silver Spoons.* Baltimore: Kelly and Piet, 1868.

McMillan, Malcolm Cook, ed. *The Alabama Confederate Reader*. Tuscaloosa: University of Alabama Press, 1963.

———. *The Disintegration of a Confederate State: Three Governors and Alabama's Wartime Home Front, 1861–1865*. Macon, GA: Mercer University Press, 1986.

———. *The Land Called Alabama*. Austin, TX: Steck-Vaughn, 1968.

McMurry, Richard M. *Atlanta 1864: Last Chance for the Confederacy*. Lincoln: University of Nebraska Press, 2000.

McNeely, Patricia G., Debra Redding van Tuyll, and Henry H. Schulte. *Knights of the Quill: Confederate Correspondents and Their Civil War Reporting*. West Lafayette, IN: Purdue University Press, 2010.

McPherson, Edward. *The Political History of the United States of America during the Great Rebellion*. Washington, DC: Philip & Solomons, 1865.

McPherson, James M. *Battle Cry of Freedom: The Civil War Era*. New York: Oxford University Press, 1988.

———. *War on the Waters: The Union and Confederate Navies, 1861–1865*. Chapel Hill: University of North Carolina Press, 2012.

McWhiney, Grady. *Braxton Bragg and Confederate Defeat*. New York: Columbia University Press, 1969.

Memorial Record of Alabama: A Concise Account of the State's Political, Military, Professional and Industrial Progress, Together with the Personal Memoirs of Many of Its People. Spartanburg, SC: Reprint Company, 1976.

Menaster, Kimberly. "Political Violence in the American South: 1882–1890." Master's thesis, Massachusetts Institute of Technology, 2009.

Miller, Randall Martin. *The Cotton Mill Movement in Antebellum Alabama*. New York: Arno Press, 1978.

Miller, Rex. *Croxton's Raid*. Depew, NY: Patrex Press, 1992.

Milton, George Fort. *Age of Hate: Andrew Johnson and the Radicals*. New York: Coward-McCann, 1930.

Misulia, Charles A. *Columbus, Georgia, 1865: The Last True Battle of the Civil War*. Tuscaloosa: University of Alabama Press, 2010.

Mize, Joel Sanford. *Unionists of the Warrior Mountains of Alabama*. Lakewood, CO: Dixie Historical Research and Education Publication, 2004.

Mohr, Clarence L. *On the Threshold of Freedom: Masters and Slaves in Civil War Georgia*. Baton Rouge: Louisiana State University Press, 2001.

Moody, Wesley. *Demon of the Lost Cause: Sherman and Civil War History*. Columbia: University of Missouri Press, 2011.

Moore, Albert Burton. *Conscription and Conflict in the Confederacy*. New York: Macmillan, 1924.

———. *History of Alabama*. 2 vol.s. Tuscaloosa: Alabama Book Store, 1951.

Morales, William R. *The 41st Alabama Infantry Regiment, Confederate States of America: A Narrative of the Civil War Regiment from West Central Alabama*. Wyandotte, OK: Greguth Pub., 2001.

Moreau, Joseph. *Schoolbook Nation: Conflicts over American Textbooks from the Civil War to the Present.* Ann Arbor: University of Michigan Press 2003.

Mushkat, Jerome. *Fernando Wood: A Political Biography.* Kent, OH: Kent State University Press, 1990.

Musicant, Ivan. *Divided Waters: The Naval History of the Civil War.* New York: Castle Books, 2000.

Neely, Mark E. *Southern Rights: Political Prisoners and the Myth of Confederate Constitutionalism.* Charlottesville: University Press of Virginia, 1999.

Nelson, Larry E. *Bullets, Ballots and Rhetoric: Confederate Policy for the United States Presidential Contest of 1864.* Tuscaloosa: University of Alabama Press, 1980.

Nevins, Allan. *The Emergence of Lincoln.* New York: Scribner, 1950.

Newman, Jennifer Ann. "Writing, Religion and Women's Identity in Civil War Alabama." PhD diss., Auburn University, 2009.

Noe, Kenneth W. *Perryville: This Grand Havoc of Battle.* Lexington: University of Kentucky Press, 2001.

——. *Reluctant Rebels: The Confederates Who Joined the Army after 1861.* Chapel Hill: University of North Carolina Press, 2010.

——, ed. *The Yellowhammer War: The Civil War and Reconstruction in Alabama.* Tuscaloosa: University of Alabama Press, 2013.

Nuermberger, Ruth Ketring. *The Clays of Alabama: A Planter-Lawyer-Politician Family.* Lexington: University of Kentucky Press, 1958.

Oakes, James. *Freedom National: The Destruction of Slavery in the United States, 1861–1865.* New York: W. W. Norton, 2013.

O'Brien, Sean Michael. *Mobile 1865: Last Stand of the Confederacy.* Westport, CT: Praeger, 2001.

——. *Mountain Partisans: Guerrilla Warfare in the Southern Appalachians, 1861–1865.* Westport, CT: Praeger, 1999.

Oldshue, Jerry C. "The Secession Movement in Tuscaloosa County, Alabama." Master's thesis, University of Alabama, 1961.

Owen, Thomas McAdory. *Basil Manly: The Founder of the Alabama Historical Society.* Montgomery, AL: Alabama Historical Society, 1904).

——. *History of Alabama and Dictionary of Alabama Biography.* 4 vol.s. Chicago: S.J. Clarke, 1921.

Ownsbey, Betty J. *Alias "Paine": Lewis Thorton Powell, the Mystery Man of the Lincoln Conspiracy.* Jefferson, NC: McFarland, 1993.

Owsley, Frank Lawrence. *King Cotton Diplomacy: Foreign Relations of the Confederate States of America.* Tuscaloosa: University of Alabama Press, 2008.

Parks, Joseph H. *Joseph E. Brown of Georgia.* Baton Rouge: Louisiana State University Press, 1977.

Parrish, T. Michael. *Richard Taylor: Soldier Prince of Dixie.* Chapel Hill: University of North Carolina Press, 1992.

Perret, Geoffrey. *Lincoln's War: The Untold Story of America's Greatest President as Commander in Chief.* New York: Random House, 2004.

Pickett, Albert James. *History of Alabama and Incidentally of Georgia and Mississippi, from Earliest Period*. Sheffield, AL: R.C. Randolph, 1896.

Pierson, Michael D. *Mutiny of Fort Jackson: The Untold Story of the Fall of New Orleans*. Chapel Hill: University of North Carolina Press, 2008.

Rable, George C. *But There Was No Peace: The Role of Violence in the Politics of Reconstruction*. Athens: University of Georgia Press, 2007.

——. *Civil Wars: Women and the Crisis of Southern Nationalism*. Urbana: University of Illinois Press, 1989.

——. *The Confederate Republic: A Revolution against Politics*. Chapel Hill: University of North Carolina Press, 1994.

——. *Fredericksburg! Fredericksburg!* Chapel Hill: University of North Carolina Press, 2002.

——. *God's Almost Chosen Peoples: A Religious History of the American Civil War*. Chapel Hill: University of North Carolina Press, 2010.

Randolph County Heritage Book Committee. *The Heritage of Randolph County, Alabama*. Randolph County, AL: Heritage Pub. Consultants, 1998.

Reid, Brian Holden. *Robert E. Lee: Icon for a Nation*. Amherst, NY: Prometheus Books, 2007.

Rice, Charles. *Hard Times: The Civil War in Huntsville and North Alabama*. Huntsville, AL: Old Huntsville, 1995.

Rice, Jessie Pearl. *J. L. M. Curry: Southerner, Statesman and Educator*. New York: Kings Crown Press, 1949.

Rich, John Stanley. "The Place Names of Greene and Tuscaloosa Counties, Alabama." PhD diss., University of Alabama, 1979.

Riepma, Anne Sophie. *Fire & Fiction: Augusta Jane Evans in Context*. Amsterdam: Rodopi, 2000.

Rogers, William Warren, Jr. *Black Belt Scalawag: Charles Hays and the Southern Republicans in the Era of Reconstruction*. Athens: University of Georgia Press, 1993.

——. *Confederate Home Front: Montgomery during the Civil War*. Tuscaloosa: University of Alabama Press, 1999.

Rogers, William Warren, Sr. *The One-Gallused Rebellion: Agrarianism in Alabama, 1865–1896*. Baton Rouge: Louisiana State University Press, 1970.

Rogers, William Warren, Sr., Robert David Ward, Leah Rawls Atkins, and Wayne Flynt. *Alabama: The History of a Deep South State*. Tuscaloosa: University of Alabama Press, 1994.

Rohr, Nancy M., ed. *Incidents of the War: The Civil War Journal of Mary Jane Chadick*. Huntsville, AL: Silver Threads Publishing, 2005.

Rothman, Adam. *Slave Country: American Expansion and the Origins of the Deep South*. Cambridge, MA: Harvard University Press, 2005.

Rowland, Dunbar. *Jefferson Davis: Constitutionalist*. 10 vol.s. Jackson: Printed for the Mississippi Department of Archives and History, 1923.

Ruhlman, Fred F. *Captain Henry Wirz and Andersonville Prison: A Reappraisal*. Knoxville: University of Tennessee Press, 2006.

Rumore, Pat Boyd. *From Power to Service: The Story of Lawyers in Alabama.* Montgomery: Alabama State Bar, 2010.

Sarris, Jonathan Dean. *A Separate Civil War: Communities in Conflict in the Mountain South.* Charlottesville: University of Virginia Press, 2006.

Saunders, James Edmonds. *Early Settlers of Alabama.* New Orleans: L. Graham & Son, printers, 1899.

Saunders, Robert, Jr. *John Archibald Campbell, Southern Moderate: 1811–1889.* Tuscaloosa: University of Alabama Press, 1997.

Scales, John R. *Sherman Invades Georgia.* Annapolis, MD: Naval Institute Press, 2006.

Schott, Thomas E. *Alexander H. Stephens of Georgia: A Biography.* Baton Rouge: Louisiana State University Press, 1988.

Schultz, Duane. *The Dahlgren Affair: Terror and Conspiracy in the Civil War.* New York: W. W. Norton, 1998.

Schwab, John Christopher. *The Confederate States of America 1861–1865: A Financial and Industrial History of the South during the War.* New York: Burt Franklin, 1968.

Scott, William Forse. *The Story of a Cavalry Regiment: The Career of the Fourth Iowa Veteran Volunteers from Kansas to Georgia, 1861–1865.* New York: G. P. Putnam, 1892.

Sellers, James Benson. *History of the University of Alabama.* Tuscaloosa: University of Alabama Press, 1953.

Severance, Ben H. *Portraits of Conflict: A Photographic History of Alabama in the Civil War.* Fayetteville: University of Arkansas Press, 2012.

Sexton, Jay. *Debtor Diplomacy: Finance and American Foreign Relations in the Civil War Era 1837–1873.* New York: Clarendon, 2005.

Shields, Johanna Nicol. *Freedom in a Slave Society: Stories from the Antebellum South.* Cambridge: Cambridge University Press, 2012.

Silver, James W. *Confederate Morale, and Church Propaganda.* Tuscaloosa, AL: Confederate Pub. Co., 1957.

Slabaugh, Arlie R. *Confederate States Paper Money: Civil War Currency from the South.* Iola, WI: Krause Publications, 2011.

Slagle, Jay. *Ironclad Captain: Seth Ledyard Phelps and the U.S. Navy, 1841–1864.* Kent, OH: Kent State University Press, 1996.

Smith, A. Davis, and T. A. DeLand. *Northern Alabama, Historical and Biographical.* Birmingham, AL: Smith & Deland, 1888.

Smith, Andrew F. *Starving the South: How the North Won the Civil War.* New York: St. Martin's Press, 2011.

Smith, David C. *Campaign to Nowhere: The Results of General Longstreet's Move into Upper Tennessee.* Strawberry Plains, TN: Strawberry Plains Press, 1999.

Smith, Derek. *In the Lion's Mouth: Hood's Tragic Retreat from Nashville, 1864.* Mechanicsburg, PA: Stackpole Books, 2011.

Smith, Timothy B. *Corinth 1862: Siege, Battle, Occupation.* Lawrence: University Press of Kansas, 2012.

Southern, James Terry. "Constructing/Inventing John Brown: A Study of the Political Texts." PhD diss., University of Alabama, 1995.

Spencer, Bella Zilfa. *Tried and True or Love and Loyalty: A Story of the Great Rebellion.* Springfield, MA: W. J. Holland, 1866.

Stampp, Kenneth Milton. *The Peculiar Institution: Slavery in the Antebellum South.* New York: Knopf, 1956.

Stephens, Larry David. *John P. Gatewood, Confederate Bushwhacker.* Gretna, LA: Pelican, 2012.

Stevens, Joseph E. *1863: The Rebirth of a Nation.* New York: Bantam Books, 1999.

Stoker, Donald. *The Grand Design: Strategy and the U.S. Civil War.* New York: Oxford University Press, 2010.

Storey, Margaret M. *Loyalty and Loss: Alabama's Unionists in the Civil War and Reconstruction.* Baton Rouge: Louisiana State University Press, 2004.

Strode, Hudson. *Jefferson Davis: Tragic Hero.* 3 vol.s. New York: Harcourt, Brace, 1964.

Sutherland, Daniel E. *A Savage Conflict: The Decisive Role of Guerrillas in the American Civil War.* Chapel Hill: University of North Carolina Press, 2009.

Swanberg, W. A. *First Blood: The Story of Fort Sumter.* New York: Scribner, 1957.

Sword, Wiley. *Embrace an Angry Wind: The Confederacy's Last Hurrah: Spring Hill, Franklin, and Nashville.* New York: Harper Collins, 1992.

——. *Mountains Touched with Fire: Chattanooga Besieged, 1863.* New York: St. Martin's Press, 1995.

Symonds, Craig L. *Joseph E. Johnston: A Civil War Biography.* New York: W. W. Norton, 1994.

Takaki, Ronald T. *A Proslavery Crusade: The Agitation to Reopen the African Slave Trade.* New York: Free Press, 1971.

Tap, Bruce. *Over Lincoln's Shoulder: The Committee on the Conduct of the War.* Lawrence: University of Kansas Press, 1998.

Tatum, Georgia Lee. *Disloyalty in the Confederacy.* Lincoln: University of Nebraska Press, 2000.

Taylor, Frazine K. *Researching African American Genealogy in Alabama: A Resource Guide.* Montgomery, AL: NewSouth Books, 2008.

Taylor, Richard. *Destruction and Reconstruction: Personal Experiences of the Late War.* Edinburgh: Blackwood and Sons, 1879.

Thomas, Emory M. *The Confederacy as a Revolutionary Experience.* Englewood Cliffs, NJ: Prentice-Hall, 1971.

Thomas, Emory M., Lesley J. Gordon, and John C. Inscoe, eds. *Inside the Confederate Nation: Essays in Honor of Emory M. Thomas.* Baton Rouge: Louisiana State University Press, 2005.

Thomas, William G. *The Iron Way: Railroads, the Civil War, and the Making of Modern America.* New Haven, CT: Yale University Press, 2011.

Thompson, Wesley S. *The Free State of Winston: A History of Winston County, Alabama.* Winfield, AL: Parell Press, 1968.

Thornton, J. Mills, III. *Politics and Power in a Slave Society: Alabama, 1800–1860.* Baton Rouge: Louisiana State University Press, 1978.

Todd, Glenda McWhirter. *First Alabama Cavalry, U.S.A.: Homage to Patriotism*. Bowie, MD: Heritage Books, 1999.

Todd, Richard Cecil. *Confederate Finance*. Athens: University of Georgia Press, 1954.

Towns, Peggy Allen. *Duty Driven: The Plight of North Alabama's African Americans during the Civil War*. Bloomington, IN: Authorhouse, 2012.

Trelease, Allen W. *White Terror: The Ku Klux Klan Conspiracy and Southern Reconstruction*. New York: Harper and Row, 1971.

Trudeau, Noah Andre. *Southern Storm: Sherman's March to the Sea*. New York: Harper, 2008.

Tucker, Spencer. *Andrew Foote: Civil War Admiral on Western Waters*. Annapolis, MD: Naval Institute Press, 2000.

Turner, Thomas Reed. *Beware the People Weeping: Public Opinion and the Assassination of Abraham Lincoln*. Baton Rouge: Louisiana State University Press, 1982.

Unger, Irwin. *The Greenback Era: A Social and Political History of American Finance, 1865–1879*. Princeton, NJ: Princeton University Press, 1968.

Urwin, Gregory J. W. *Black Flag over Dixie: Racial Atrocities and Reprisals in the Civil War*. Carbondale: Southern Illinois University Press, 2004.

Vandiver, Frank Everson. *Ploughshares into Swords: Josiah Gorgas and Confederate Ordinance*. College Station, TX: Texas A&M University Press, 1994.

Varon, Elizabeth R. *Appomattox: Victory, Defeat, and Freedom at the End of the Civil War*. New York: Oxford University Press, 2014.

——. *Disunion!: The Coming of the American Civil War, 1789–1859*. Chapel Hill: University of North Carolina Press, 2008.

Walker, Henry James. *Let Us Keep the Feast: The History of Christ Episcopal Church, Tuscaloosa, Alabama, 1828–1998*. Tallahassee, FL: Sentry Press, 2000.

Walther, Eric H. *William Lowndes Yancey and the Coming of the Civil War*. Chapel Hill: University of North Carolina Press, 2006.

Walvin, James. *England, Slaves and Freedom, 1776–1838*. Jackson: University Press of Mississippi, 1986.

Ward, Andrew. *River Run Red: The Fort Pillow Massacre in the American Civil War*. New York: Viking, 2005.

——. *Slaves' War: The Civil War in the Words of Former Slaves*. Boston: Mariner Books, 2008.

Warner, Ezra J., and W. Buck Yearns. *Biographical Register of the Confederate Congress*. Baton Rouge: Louisiana State University Press, 1975.

Warren, Robert Penn. *The Legacy of the Civil War*. Lincoln: University of Nebraska Press, 1998.

Webb, Sam L., and Margaret E. Armbrester. *Alabama Governors: A Political History of the State*. Tuscaloosa: University of Alabama Press, 2001.

Weitz, Mark A. *More Damning Than Slaughter: Desertion in the Confederate Army*. Lincoln: University of Nebraska Press, 2005.

Wells, Damon, *Stephen Douglas: The Last Years, 1857–1861*. Austin: University of Texas Press, 1971.

Welsh, Jack D. *Two Confederate Hospitals and Their Patients: Atlanta to Opelika.* Macon, GA: Mercer University Press, 2005.

Werlich, Robert. *"Beast": Butler: The Incredible Career of Major General Benjamin Franklin Butler.* Washington, DC: Quaker Press, 1962.

Wesley, Timothy L. *The Politics of Faith during the Civil War.* Baton Rouge: Louisiana State University Press, 2013.

White, Cheryl H. *Confederate General Leonidas Polk: Louisiana's Fighting Bishop.* Charleston, SC: History Press, 2013.

Wiggins, Sarah Woolfolk. *The Scalawag in Alabama Politics, 1865–1881.* Tuscaloosa: University of Alabama Press, 1977.

———. ed. *The Journals of Josiah Gorgas 1857–1878.* Tuscaloosa: University of Alabama Press, 1995.

Wiley, Bell I. *Life of Johnny Reb: The Common Soldier of the Confederacy.* Baton Rouge: Louisiana State University Press, 2000.

Willett, Robert L., Jr. *The Lightning Mule Brigade: Abel Streight's 1863 Raid into Alabama.* Carmel, IN: Guild Press, 1999.

Williams, David. *Bitterly Divided: The South's Inner Civil War.* New York: New Press, 2008.

———. *Rich Man's War: Class, Caste, and Confederate Defeat in the Lower Chattahoochee Valley.* Athens: University of Georgia Press, 1998.

Williams, David, Teresa Crisp Williams, and David Carlson. *Plain Folk in a Rich Man's War: Class and Dissent in Confederate Georgia.* Gainesville: University Press of Florida, 2002.

Williams, George Washington. *A History of the Negro Troops in the War of Rebellion 1861–1865.* New York: Bergman, 1968.

Williams, T. Harry. *P. G. T. Beauregard: Napoleon in Gray.* Baton Rouge: Louisiana State University Press, 1955.

Wills, Brian Steel. *A Battle from the Start: The Life of Nathan Bedford Forrest.* New York: Harper Perennial, 1993.

———. *The River Was Dyed with Blood: Nathan Bedford Forrest and Fort Pillow.* Norman: University of Oklahoma Press, 2014.

Wilson, Charles Reagan. *Baptized in Blood: The Religion of the Lost Cause, 1865–1920.* Athens: University of Georgia Press, 2009.

Wilson, James Harrison, *Recollections of Military Operations in the War For the Union, the Spanish War, the Boxer Rebellion, etc.* 2 vols. New York: D. Appleton and Company, 1912.

Wilson, Keith P. *Campfires of Freedom: The Camp Life of Black Soldiers during the Civil War.* Kent, OH: Kent State University Press, 2002.

Winkle, Kenneth. *Lincoln's Citadel: The Civil War in Washington, D.C.* New York: W. W. Norton, 2013.

Wittenberg, Eric J. *Like a Meteor Blazing Brightly: The Short But Controversial Life of Colonel Ulric Dahlgren.* Roseville, MN: Edinborough Press, 2009.

Wolfe, Suzanne Rau. *The University of Alabama, A Pictorial History*. Tuscaloosa: University of Alabama Press, 1983.

Wood, Forrest G. *Black Scare: The Racist Response to Emancipation and Reconstruction*. Berkeley: University of California Press, 1970.

Wood, W. J. *Civil War Generalship: The Art of Command*. Westport, CT: Praeger, 1997.

Woodward, Colin Edward. *Marching Masters: Slavery, Race, and the Confederate Army during the Civil War*. Charlottesville: University of Virginia Press, 2014.

Woodward, C. Vann. *The Burden of Southern History*. Baton Rouge: Louisiana State University Press, 2008.

Woodworth, Steven E. *Grant's Lieutenants: From Cairo to Vicksburg*. Lawrence: University Press of Kansas, 2001.

——. *Shiloh: Confederate High Tide in the Heartland*. Santa Barbara, CA: Greenwood Press, 2012).

——. *Six Armies in Tennessee: The Chickamauga and Chattanooga Campaign*. Lincoln: University of Nebraska Press, 1998.

Wright, Gavin. *Slavery and American Economic Development*. Baton Rouge: Louisiana State University Press, 2006.

Writers' Program. *Alabama: A Guide to the Deep South*. St. Clair Shores, MI: Somerset Publishers, 1973.

Wubben, Hubert H. *Civil War Iowa and the Copperhead Movement*. Ames: Iowa State University Press, 1980.

Wyeth, John Allan. *That Devil Forrest: Life of General Nathan Bedford Forrest*. Baton Rouge: Louisiana State University Press, 1989.

Zamoyski, Adam. *Moscow 1812: Napoleon's Fatal March*. London: Harper Collins, 2004.

Periodicals, Book Chapters, and Essays

Alexander, Thomas B. "The Basis of Alabama's Ante-Bellum Two-Party System." *Alabama Review* 19 (October 1966): 243–76.

Bailey, Fred Arthur. "The Textbooks of the Lost Cause: Censorship and the Creation of Southern State Histories." *Georgia Historical Quarterly* LXXV (Fall 1991), 507–33.

Bailey, Hugh C. "Disloyalty in Early Confederate Alabama." *Journal of Southern History* 23 (November 1957): 522–28.

Battles, Jason J. "Labor, Law, and the Freedmen's Bureau in Alabama, 1865–1867." In *The Yellowhammer War: The Civil War and Reconstruction in Alabama*, edited by Kenneth W. Noe, 240–57. Tuscaloosa: University of Alabama Press, 2013.

Beale, Mildred. "Charles Teed Pollard: Industrialist." *Alabama Historical Quarterly* 2 (Summer 1940): 494–505.

Bearss, Edwin C. "A Federal Raid up the Tennessee River." *Alabama Review* 17 (October 1964): 261–70.

——. "Rousseau's Raid on the Montgomery and West Point Railroad." *Alabama Historical Quarterly* 25 (Spring–Summer, 1963): 7–48.

Bergeron, Arthur W., Jr. "James Holt Clanton," in *The Confederate General*, ed. William C. Davis. New York: Free Press, 1991.

Boucher, Chauncey Samuel. "The Secession and Co-Operation Movements in South Carolina, 1848 to 1852," *Washington University Studies* V (April 1918): 67–138.

Burnett, Lonnie A. "Precipitating a Revolution: Alabama's Democracy in the Election of 1860." In *The Yellowhammer War: The Civil War and Reconstruction in Alabama*, edited by Kenneth W. Noe, 15–33. Tuscaloosa: University of Alabama Press, 2013.

Center, Clark E., Jr. "The Burning of the University of Alabama." *Alabama Heritage* 16 (Spring 1990): 30–45.

Culver, Emma Beall. "Thomas Hill Watts, A Statesman of the Old Regime." Montgomery, Alabama Historical Society, Reprint No. 19, 1904: 415–39.

Cunningham, O. Edward. "Captain Frank B. Gurley, Fourth Alabama Cavalry, C.S.A.: Murderer or Victim." *Alabama Review* 28 (January 1975): 83–103.

Currie, Daniel P. "Through the Looking Glass: The Confederate Constitution in Congress, 1861–1865." *Virginia Law Review* 90 (September 2004): 1257–1399.

Davidson, William H. "Brigadier General James Holt Clanton: Alabama's Rash Gallant." *Alabama Lawyer* 29 (1959): 285.

Davis, Hugh C. "Hilary A. Herbert: Bourbon Apologist," *Alabama Review* XX (July 1967): 216–25.

Dee, Christine. "Trying James Hickman: The Politics of Loyalty in a Civil War Community." *Alabama Review* 58 (April, 2005): 83–112.

Dodd, Donald B. "The Free State of Winston." *Alabama Heritage* 28 (Spring 1993: 8–19).

Doss, Harriet E. Amos. "Every Man Should Consider His Own Conscience: Black and White Alabamians' Reactions to the Assassination of Abraham Lincoln." In *The Yellowhammer War: The Civil War and Reconstruction in Alabama*, edited by Kenneth W. Noe, 165–77. Tuscaloosa: University of Alabama Press, 2013.

Eckinger, Helen. "The Militarization of the University of Alabama." *Alabama Review* 66 (July 2013): 163–85.

Eidsmoe, John A. "Warrior, Statesman, Jurist for the South: The Life, Legacy, and Law of Thomas Goode Jones." *Jones Law Review* 5, no. 1 (2001): 51.

English, Bertis. "Freedom's Church: Sociocultural Construction, Reconstruction, and Post-Reconstruction in Perry County, Alabama's African American Churches." In *The Yellowhammer War: The Civil War and Reconstruction in Alabama*, edited by Kenneth W. Noe, 258–80. Tuscaloosa: University of Alabama Press, 2013.

Fitzgerald, Michael W. "Another Kind of Glory: Black Participation and Its Consequences in the Campaign for Confederate Mobile." *Alabama Review* 54 (October 2001): 243–73.

———. "Extra Legal Violence and the Planter Class: The Ku Klux Klan in the Alabama Black Belt during Reconstruction." In *Local Matters: Race, Crime, and Justice in the Nineteenth-Century South*, edited by Christopher Waldrep and Donald G. Nieman 155–71. Athens: University of Georgia Press, 2001.

———. "From Unionists to Scalawags: Elite Dissent in Civil War Mobile." *Alabama Review* 55 (April 2002): 106–21.

———. "'He Was Always Preaching the Union:' the Wartime Origins of White Republicanism during Reconstruction," in *Yellowhammer War*, ed. Kenneth W. Noe, 235.

———. "Radical Republicanism and the White Yeomanry during Alabama Reconstruction, 1865–1868." *Journal of Southern History* 54 (November 1988): 565–96.

———. "Republican Factionalism and Black Empowerment: The Spencer-Warner Controversy and Alabama Reconstruction, 1868–1880." *Journal of Southern History* 64 (August 1998): 473.

Fleming, Walter L. "The Peace Movement in Alabama during the Civil War." *South Atlantic Quarterly* 2 (April and July 1903): 114–24, 246–60.

Folmar, John Kent. "Reaction to Reconstruction: John Forsyth and the Mobile Advertiser and Register, 1865–1867." *Alabama Historical Quarterly* XXXVII (Winter 1975): 245–64.

Granade, Ray. "Violence: An Instrument in Policy in Reconstruction Alabama." *Alabama Historical Quarterly* 30 (Fall–Winter, 1968): 181–202.

Gross, Jennifer Lynn. "Augusta Jane Evans: Alabama's Confederate *Macaria*." In *The Yellowhammer War: The Civil War and Reconstruction in Alabama*, ed. Kenneth W. Noe, 125–48. Tuscaloosa: University of Alabama Press, 2013.

Gunderson, Gerald. "The Origin of the American Civil War." *Journal of Economic History* 34 (December 1974): 915–50.

Hacker, J. David. "A Census-Based Count of the Civil War Dead." *Civil War History* 57 (December 2011): 307–48.

Hardy, John, *Selma: Her Institutions, and Her Men*. Selma, AL: Bert Neville and Clarence DeBray, 1957.

Hatch, Edwin I. "William McLin Brooks, 1815–1893." *Alabama Lawyer* 16 (July 1955): 324–335.

Hennessey, Melinda M. "Political Terrorism in the Black Belt: The Eutaw Riot," *Alabama Review* 33 (January 1980): 35–48.

Horton, Paul. "Lightning Rod Scalawag: The Unlikely Political Career of Thomas Minott Peters." *Alabama Review* 64 (April 2011): 116–42.

———. "Submitting to the Shadow of Slavery: The Secession Crisis and Civil War in Alabama's Lawrence County." *Civil War History* 44 (June 1988): 111–36.

Hubbs, G. Ward. "John B. Read's Okra Paper." *Alabama Review* 43 (October 1990): 289–96.

Jones, Allen W. "Unionism and Disaffection in South Alabama: The Case of Alfred Holley." *Alabama Review* 24 (April 1971): 114–32.

Kitchens, Joel D. "E. W. Peck: Alabama's First Scalawag Chief Justice." *Alabama Review* 54 (January 2001): 3–32.

Kyriakoudes, Louis M. "The Rise of Merchants and Market Towns in Reconstruction-Era Alabama." *Alabama Review* XLIX (April 1996): 83–107.

Lakweta, Angela. "The Eclectic Industrialism of Antebellum Baldwin County." *Alabama Review* 65 (January 2012): 3–39.

Lockett, James D. "The Last Ship That Brought Slaves From Africa to America: The Landing of the Clotilde at Mobile in the Autumn of 1859." *Western Journal of Black Studies* 22 (Fall 1998): 159–63.

Logue, Cal M. "Rhetorical Ridicule of Reconstruction Blacks." *Quarterly Journal of Speech* 62 (December 1976): 400–409.

Lynch, Jeanne Hall. "Thomas Hill Watts, Civil War Governor of Alabama, 1863–1865." Master's Thesis, Auburn University, 1957.

Mattoon, E. R. "The Lawyer as a Social Force." *Alabama Lawyer* 15 (January 1954): 55–65.

McConnell, Roland C. "From Preliminary to Final Emancipation Proclamation: The First Hundred Days." *Journal of Negro History* 48 (October 1963): 260–76.

McCorvey, Thomas C. "Southern Cadets in Action," *Century Magazine* XXXIX (November, 1889): 152–53.

McDonald, William L. "The Day They Set Fire to the Mills." *Journal of Muscle Shoals History* 7 (1979): 61.

McIlwain, Christopher Lyle, Sr. "United States District Judge Richard Busteed and the Alabama Klan Trials of 1872." *Alabama Review* 65 (October 2012): 263–89.

McKenzie, Robert H. "Reconstruction of the Alabama Iron Industry, 1865–1880." *Alabama Review* XXV (July 1972): 178–91.

McPherson, James M. "Long-Legged Yankee Lies: The Southern Textbook Crusade." In *Memory of the Civil War in American Culture*, edited by Alice Fahs, 64–78. Chapel Hill: University of North Carolina Press, 2004.

Mellown, Robert O. "Construction of the Alabama Insane Hospital 1852–1861." *Alabama Review* 38 (April 1985): 83–104.

Mellown, Robert O., and Gene Byrd. "F.A.P. Barnard and Alabama's First Observatory." *Journal of Alabama Academy of Science* 57 (January 1986): 39–44.

Miller, Randall M. "Daniel Pratt's Industrial Urbanism: The Cotton Mill Town in Ante-Bellum Alabama." *Alabama Historical Quarterly* XXXIV (Spring 1972), 5–35.

Murphy, James Leonidas. "Alabama and the Charleston Convention of 1860." *Studies in Southern and Alabama History,* ed., George Petrie, (Montgomery: Alabama Historical Society, 1905), 252–55.

Myers, John B. "The Alabama Freedmen and the Economic Adjustment during Presidential Reconstruction, 1865–1867." *Alabama Review* 26 (October 1973): 252–66.

Owens, Scott W. "The Federal Invasion of Pickens County, April, 1865: Croxton's Sipsey River Campaign." *Alabama Review* 62 (April 2009) 83–112.

Owsley, Frank L. "Defeatism in the Confederacy." *North Carolina Historical Review* 3 (July 1926): 446–56.

Panhorst, Michael. "Devotion, Deception, and the Ladies Memorial Association, 1865–1898: The Mystery of the Alabama Confederate Monument." *Alabama Review* 65 (July 2012): 182–200.

Partin, Robert. "The Use of History." *Alabama Review* 19 (April 1966): 109–24.

Pearce, George F., *Pensacola During the Civil War: A Thorn in the Side of the Confederacy*. Gainesville: University Press of Florida, 2000.

Pickens, Patton Keith. "A History of the Fifth Alabama Cavalry Regiment CSA." *Journal of Muscle Shoals History* 15 (1999): 93–125.

Potter, David M., *Lincoln and His Party in the Secession Crisis*. Baton Rouge: Louisiana State University Press, 1995.

Pruitt, Paul M, Jr. "Scalawag Dreams: Elisha Wolsey Peck's Career, and Two of His Speeches, 1867–1869." *Alabama Review* 66 (July 2013): 211–39.

Rable, George C. "Anatomy of a Unionist: Andrew Johnson in the Secession Crisis," *Tennessee Historical Quarterly* 32 (Winter 1973): 332–54.

———. "Despair, Hope, and Delusion: The Collapse of Confederate Morale Reexamined." In *The Collapse of the Confederacy*, edited by Mark Grimsley and Brooks D. Simpson, 129–67. Lincoln: University of Nebraska Press, 2001.

Ritchey, David. "Williamson R.W. Cobb: Rattler of Tinware and Crockery for Peace." *Alabama Historical Quarterly* 36 (Summer 1974): 112–20.

Robbins, John B. "The Confederacy and the Writ of Habeas Corpus." *Georgia Historical Quarterly* 55 (Summer 1971): 83–101.

Robinson, William Morrison, *Justice in Grey: A History of the Judicial System of the Confederate States of America* (New York: Russell & Russell, 1968),

Rogers, William Warren, Jr. "The Boyd Incident: Black Belt Violence during Reconstruction." *Civil War History* 21 (December 1975): 309–29.

———. "Safety Lies Only in Silence: Secrecy and Subversion in Montgomery's Unionist Community." In *Enemies of the Country: New Perspectives on Unionists in the Civil War South*, ed. John C. Inscoe and Robert C. Kenzer. Athens: University of Georgia Press, 2001: 172–87.

Scott, William C., Jr. "Philip Dale Roddey: Confederate General from Alabama." *Journal of Muscle Shoals History* 15 (1999): 37–49.

Seip, Terry L. "Of Ambition and Enterprise: The Making of Carpetbagger George E. Spencer." In *The Yellowhammer War: The Civil War and Reconstruction in Alabama*, edited by Kenneth W. Noe, 191–219. Tuscaloosa: University of Alabama Press, 2013.

Severance, Ben H. "Confederate Alabama's Finest Hour: The Battle of Salem Church, May 3, 1863." In *The Yellowhammer War: The Civil War and Reconstruction in Alabama*, ed. Kenneth W. Noe, 55–70. Tuscaloosa: University of Alabama Press, 2013.

Sewell, Alan. "Dissent: The Free State of Winston." *Civil War Times Illustrated* 20 (December 1981): 30–37.

Shaw, William L. "The Confederate Conscription and Exemption Acts." *American Journal of Legal History* 6 (October 1962): 368–405.

Sheridan, Richard C. "Civil War Manufacturing in the Tennessee Valley." *Journal of Muscle Shoals History* 15 (1999): 50–68.

Simpson, Brooks D. "Continuous Hammering and Mere Attrition: Lost Cause Critics and the Military Reputation of Ulysses S. Grant." In *The Myth of the Lost Cause and Civil War History*, ed. Gary W. Gallagher and Alan T. Nolan, 147–69. Bloomington: Indiana University Press, 2000.

Sloan, John Z. "The Ku Klux Klan and the Alabama Election of 1872." *Alabama Review* 18 (April 1965): 113–23.

Starnes, Greg. "Grey Troops at Blue Mountain." *Alabama Heritage* 111 (Winter 2014): 28–31.

Still, William W. "Selma and the Confederate States Navy." *Alabama Review* 15 (January 1962): 19–37.

Storey, Margaret M. "Civil War Unionists and the Political Culture of Loyalty in Alabama, 1860–1861," *Journal of Southern History* 69 (February 2003): 71–106.

———. "The Crucible of Reconstruction: Unionists and the Struggle for Alabama's Postwar Home Front." In *The Great Task Remaining Before Us: Reconstruction as America's Continuing Civil War*, ed. Paul A. Cimbala and Randall M. Miller, 69–87 (New York: Fordham University Press, 2010).

Summersell, Charles G. "Kolb and the Populist Revolt as Viewed by Newspapers." *Alabama Historical Quarterly* 19 (Fall and Winter 1957): 375–94.

Sword, Wiley, "'Our Fireside in Ruins': Consequences of the 1863 Chattanooga Campaign." In *Gateway to the Confederacy*, ed. Evan C. Jones and Wiley Sword, 241.

Symonds, Craig L. "War and Politics: Jefferson Davis Meets the Army of Tennessee." In *Gateway to the Confederacy: New Perspectives on the Chickamauga and Chattanooga Campaigns, 1862–1863*, ed. Evan C. Jones and Wiley Sword, 159–71. Baton Rouge: Louisana State University Press, 2014.

Teters, Kristopher A. "Fighting for the Cause? An Examination of the Motivations of Alabama's Confederate Soldiers from a Class Perspective." In *The Yellowhammer War and Reconstruction in Alabama*, ed. Kenneth W. Noe, 90–106. Tuscaloosa: University of Alabama, 2013.

Thornton, J. Mills. "Alabama's Presidential Reconstruction Legislature." In *A Political Nation: New Directions in Mid Nineteenth Century American Political History*, ed. Gary W. Gallagher and Rachel A. Sheldon, 167–87. Charlottesville: University of Virginia Press, 2012.

Treviño, Jennifer Ann Newman. "'The Aggressions of the North Can Be Borne No Longer': White Alabamian Women during the Secession Crisis and Outbreak of War." In *The Yellowhammer War: The Civil War and Reconstruction in Alabama*, ed. Kenneth W. Noe, 34–54. Tuscaloosa: University of Alabama Press, 2012.

Upchurch, Thomas Adams. "Senator John Tyler Morgan and the Genesis of Jim Crow Ideology, 1889–1891." *Alabama Review* 57 (April 2004): 110–31.

Van der Linden, Frank. *The Dark Intrigue: The True Story of a Civil War Conspiracy*. Golden, CO: Fulcrum Publishing, 2007.

Vandiver, Frank E. "General Hood as Logistician." *Military Affairs* 16 (Spring 1952): 1–11.

Waters, Zack C. "General Philip D. Roddey: 'Defender of North Alabama.'" *Alabama Heritage* 110 (Fall 2013): 24–33.

Watson, Elbert L. "The Story of Nickajack." *Alabama Review* 20 (January 1967): 17–26.

Wiggins, Sarah Woolfolk. "Alabama's Reconstruction after 150 Years." In *The Yellowhammer War: The Civil War and Reconstruction in Alabama*, ed. Kenneth W. Noe, 177–86. Tuscaloosa: University of Alabama Press, 2013.

Wills, Brian Steele. "The Confederate Sun Sets on Selma: Nathan Bedford Forrest and the Defense of Alabama in 1865." In *The Yellowhammer War: The Civil War and Reconstruction in Alabama*, ed. Kenneth W. Noe, 71–89. Tuscaloosa: University of Alabama Press, 2013.

Wilson, Harold. "Basil Manly, Apologist for Slavocracy." *Alabama Review* 15 (January 1962): 38–53.

Woolfolk, Sarah Van V. "George E. Spencer: A Carpetbagger in Alabama." *Alabama Review* 19 (January 1966): 41–52.

Zingg, Paul J. "John Archibald Campbell and the Hampton Roads Conference: Quixotic Diplomacy, 1865." *Alabama Historical Quarterly* XXXVI (Spring 1974): 21–34.

Index